A Constructive Christ
for the Pluralistic World

VOLUME 1

Christ and Reconciliation

VOLUME 2

Trinity and Revelation

TRINITY AND REVELATION

Veli-Matti Kärkkäinen

WILLIAM B. EERDMANS PUBLISHING COMPANY
GRAND RAPIDS, MICHIGAN / CAMBRIDGE, U.K.

Published 2014 by

Wm. B. Eerdmans Publishing Co.

2140 Oak Industrial Drive N.E., Grand Rapids, Michigan 49505 /
P.O. Box 163, Cambridge CB3 9PU U.K.

Library of Congress Cataloging-in-Publication Data

Kärkkäinen, Veli-Matti.
 Trinity and revelation / Veli-Matti Kärkkäinen.
  pages   cm. — (A constructive Christian theology for the pluralistic world; v. 2)
 Includes bibliographical references and index.
 ISBN 978-0-8028-6854-1 (pbk.)
 1. Trinity. 2. Revelation. 3. Christianity and other religions. I. Title.

  BT111.3K36 2014
  231′.044 — dc23

2013044664

www.eerdmans.com

Contents

Abbreviations

ANF	*The Ante-Nicene Fathers: Translations of the Writings of the Fathers down to A.D. 325.* Edited by Alexander Roberts and James Donaldson et al. 9 vols. Edinburgh, 1885-1897. Public domain; available at www.ccel.org
Aquinas, *ST*	*The Summa Theologica of St. Thomas Aquinas.* 2nd and rev. ed. 1920. Literally translated by Fathers of the English Dominican Province. Online Edition Copyright © 2008 by Kevin Knight; http://www.newadvent.org/summa/
Calvin, *Inst.*	*Institutes of the Christian Religion.* Translated by Henry Beveridge. Available at www.ccel.org
CD	Barth, *Church Dogmatics.* Edited by Geoffrey William Bromiley and Thomas Forsyth Torrance. Translated by G. W. Bromiley. 14 vols. Edinburgh: T. & T. Clark, 1956-1975. Online edition by Alexander Street Press, 1975
DEHF	*Divine Emptiness and Historical Fullness: A Buddhist-Jewish-Christian Conversation with Masao Abe.* Edited by Christopher Ives. Valley Forge, Pa.: Trinity, 1995
DV	*Dogmatic Constitution on Divine Revelation: Dei Verbum.* Pope Paul VI. November 18, 1965 (Vatican II). http://www .vatican.va/archive/hist_councils/ii_vatican_council/ documents/vat-ii_const_19651118_dei-verbum_en.html
GDT	*Global Dictionary of Theology.* Edited by Veli-Matti Kärk-käinen and William Dyrness. Assistant editors, Simon Chan and Juan Martinez. Downers Grove, Ill.: InterVarsity, 2008

HDT	Heidelberg Disputation. In *Luther's Works*, vol. 31. American ed. (Libronix Digital Library). Edited by Jaroslav Pelikan and Helmut T. Lehman. 55 vols. Minneapolis: Fortress, 2002
IWWLM	*In Whom We Live and Move and Have Our Being: Panentheistic Reflections on God's Presence in a Scientific World.* Edited by Philip Clayton and Arthur Peacocke. Grand Rapids: Eerdmans, 2004
LW	*Luther's Works.* American ed. (Libronix Digital Library). Edited by Jaroslav Pelikan and Helmut T. Lehman. 55 vols. Minneapolis: Fortress, 2002
NPNF¹	*A Select Library of the Nicene and Post-Nicene Fathers of the Christian Church.* Edited by Philip Schaff. 1st ser. 14 vols. Edinburgh, 1886. Public domain; available at www.ccel.org
NPNF²	*A Select Library of the Nicene and Post-Nicene Fathers of the Christian Church.* Edited by Philip Schaff and Henry Wace. 2nd ser. 14 vols. Edinburgh, 1890. Public domain; available at www.ccel.org
Pannenberg, ST	Wolfhart Pannenberg. *Systematic Theology.* Translated by Geoffrey W. Bromiley. 3 vols. Grand Rapids: Eerdmans, 1991, 1994, 1998
SBE	*Sacred Books of the East.* Translated by Max Müller. 50 vols. Oxford: Oxford University Press, 1879-1910. Also available at www.sacred-texts.com
Tillich, ST	Paul Tillich, *Systematic Theology.* Vol. 1. Chicago: University of Chicago Press, 1951
WA	Weimarer Ausgabe (the Weimar edition of Luther's works)

Unless otherwise indicated, all citations from patristic writers come from the standard series listed above.

Bible references are from the Revised Standard Version unless otherwise indicated.

The Qur'anic references are from The Holy Qur'ān: A New English Translation of Its Meanings © 2008 Royal Aal al-Bayt Institute for Islamic Thought, Amman, Jordan. This version of the Qur'ān is also available online at http://altafsir.com.

Hadith texts are from the collection at the Center for Muslim-Jewish Engagement of University of Southern California, http://www.usc.edu/schools/college/crcc/engagement/resources/texts/muslim/hadith/.

Buddhist texts, unless otherwise indicated, are from "Tipitaka: The Pali Canon." Edited by John T. Bullitt. *Access to Insight,* 10 May 2011 (http://www.accesstoinsight.org/tipitaka/index.html).

Hindu texts, unless otherwise indicated, are from *Sacred Books of the East,* mentioned above, available at: http://www.sacred-texts.com/hin/index.htm.

Preface

This book is one of the five volumes in the series titled CONSTRUCTIVE CHRISTIAN THEOLOGY FOR THE PLURALISTIC WORLD. The goal of this series is to present a dynamic constructive Christian theology for the pluralistic world shaped by cultural, ethnic, sociopolitical, economic, and religious diversity. While robustly Christian in its convictions, building on the deep and wide tradition of biblical, historical, philosophical, and contemporary systematic traditions, this project seeks to engage our present cultural and religious diversity in a way Christian theology has not done in the past. Although part of a larger series, each volume can still stand on its own feet, so to speak, and can be read as an individual work. The introductory chapter gives a brief orientation to the method chosen.

The volume *Christ and Reconciliation* has already been published; the remaining three volumes to follow the present volume are *Creation and Humanity, Spirit and Salvation,* and *Church and Hope.* The ultimate goal of the series is to provide a fresh and innovative vision of Christian doctrine and theology in a way that, roughly speaking, follows the outline, if not the order, of classical theology. Along with traditional topics, theological argumentation in this series also engages a number of topics, perspectives, and issues that systematic theologies are missing such as race, environment, ethnicity, inclusivity, violence, and colonialism. A consistent engagement with religious and interfaith studies is a distinctive feature of this series.

As with so many other books, I owe greater gratitude than I am able to express to my Fuller Theological Seminary editor Susan Carlson Wood, with whom I have had the opportunity to work on more than ten books. She has the unique capacity to help revise my second-language speaker's English into American prose. I also want to sincerely thank my research assistant and doctoral student at Fuller Dan Brockway, who checked the accuracy of each and every bibliographic reference. Joshua Muthalali compiled the index.

Introduction: A Hospitable and Inviting Methodological Vision

Constructive Theology as a Dialogue and "Conversation"

Just a few days before his death, Paul Tillich is reported to have confessed that if he had the opportunity to rewrite his three-volume *Systematic Theology*, he would do so engaging widely world religions. This was due to his brief exposure at the end of his life to the forms of Japanese Buddhism as well as the influence from his famed Romanian religious studies colleague Mircea Eliade.[1] While Karl Barth made occasional, scattered references to religions, he also dismissed any revelatory and *theological* role of religions. Even worse, he made the avoidance of dialogue with the natural sciences a theological theme — and thus could write a massive volume on creation without references to scientific understanding! So, here we have the two most important theological giants of the first part of the twentieth century seeking to offer comprehensive constructive *summae* of Christian vision by excluding both religious studies and natural sciences (although to Tillich's credit, he was more keen on seeking engagement with science). Even the two contemporary European giants of constructive theology, Pannenberg and Moltmann, while adopting sciences as integral dialogue partners, still miss religions. This is more deplorable in Pannenberg's case because he demands that systematic theology by its very definition must include all human knowledge, whether "secular" or theolog-

---

1. Tillich, *Future of Religions*, p. 91; see also Eliade's comment in his "Paul Tillich and the History of Religions," in Tillich, p. 31.

1

ical, in its domain.[2] On top of that, for all these theologians the theological *world* worth engaging includes merely European (and to some extent North American), almost exclusively male theologies (although Moltmann makes some effort to expand the dialogue partners, particularly in his methodological essay *Experiences in Theology*, written at the end of his career).

While deeply indebted to these theological heroes — as the frequent references to their works throughout the book testify — the current project is also critical of the grave limitations of their approaches and seeks to offer a new vision for systematic/constructive theology. That means a robust and consistent dialogue with not only the historical and contemporary theological disciplines — including the current diversity of gender, race, geographical, and social location, and agendas such as liberationism and postcolonialism — but also the beliefs and insights of living faiths (in this case, Judaism, Islam, Hinduism, and Buddhism) as well as the natural (and, at times, behavioral and social) sciences.

Rather than developing this new methodological vision in the form of an abstract and formal methodological discussion, which usually ends up being just that — *abstract* and *formal*, neither interesting nor useful — the current project unveils method with the help of material presentation. Whereas the more comprehensive and detailed methodological vision was laid out in the lengthy introduction to the first volume, *Christ and Reconciliation*, each subsequent volume continues and sharpens methodological orientations as it goes.

For orientation to the current volume, let it suffice to summarize in a brief outline the methodological vision presented and defended in the earlier volume.[3] The vision for doing constructive theology in a religiously pluralistic and culturally diverse "post-" world — namely, postmodern, postfoundationalist, poststructuralist, postcolonial, postmetaphysical, postpropositional, postliberal, postconservative, postsecular, post-Christian — can be sketched like this:

> Systematic/constructive theology is an integrative discipline that continuously searches for a coherent, balanced understanding of Christian truth and faith in light of Christian tradition (biblical and historical) and in the context of historical and contemporary thought, cultures, and living faiths. It aims at a coherent, inclusive, dialogical, and hospitable vision.

---

2. To his credit, though, Pannenberg acknowledges the lack of engagement of religious studies and "global" theologies (*ST* 1:xii).

3. Since that discussion contains detailed bibliographic references, I will not repeat them here unless there is a direct citation.

As the ultimate goal of constructive theology is not a "system," the nomenclature "systematic" is most unfortunate! Rather, it seeks for a coherent and balanced understanding. In terms of the theory of truth, it follows the suit of coherence theory. One current way of speaking of coherence is to compare it to a web or a net(work), which underwrites postfoundationalist rather than foundationalist epistemology. That metaphor is fitting as it speaks of the attempt to relate every statement to other relevant statements and ultimately to the "whole." The way this current project conceives coherence has to do with not only intratextual coherence but also the "fit" of theological statements with "reality." Hence, Christian theology whose "object" is God and everything else stemming from the creative work of God (Aquinas) operates with the widest possible notion of coherence.

Integrative discipline means that in order to practice constructive theology well, one has to utilize the results, insights, and materials of all other theological disciplines (in their contemporary diversity), cultural studies, religious studies, and natural (and other relevant) sciences. This means that the constructive theologian asks many questions — say, in relation to inclusivity, violence, care for the environment, and natural sciences — that the Bible and much of church history are silent about. At the end of the constructive task, however, the constructive theologian should make sure the proposal is in keeping with biblical revelation and, hopefully, with the best of tradition and contemporary theology.

If the principle of coherence in the search for the truth of Christian doctrinal claims is taken seriously, then by its very nature, constructive theology should seek to engage not only theological resources but also cultural, religious, sociopolitical, and other resources. Two tasks emerge out of this orientation: the challenge of cultural and social diversity, and the engagement of religions and their claims for meaning and truth. Constructive theology should make every effort to seek an inclusive vision in a "post-" world with preference for locality, particularity, and difference over "globality," universality, and sameness; and within a Christian church that has become a truly "world" church with the majority of believers in the Global South, consisting of a majority of young persons, women, and the poor. Inclusivity allows for diverse, at times even contradictory and opposing, voices and testimonies to be part of the dialogue. Inclusivity, then, is not another form of a modernist "universal story" that seeks to subsume everything under its power of explanation, but rather is a robust acknowledgment of the obvious fact that all opinions and insights are "views from somewhere."[4] The constructive theologian in search

4. Cf. Nagel, *The View from Nowhere.*

of inclusivity is not blind to her or his own limitations. As a middle-aged European white male — despite my long and varied global experience — I not only am "perspectival" in a particular way but also carry with me limitations and prejudices, as does a young African female theologian or a veteran Asian male theologian; the limitations in each case are just materially somewhat different! All our explanations are humble and modest and hence viable for dialogue and conversation.

Is this, then, an exercise in "contextual" theology? No, if this term means that some theologies are not contextual ("mainline" theologies done by Euro-American males) and others are, namely, those of women and other liberationists, postcolonialists, and theologians from the Global South. Another reason for rejecting the nomenclature "contextual" for this project is that the presentation of Christian doctrine done solely by traditional and contemporary Euro-American men would merely be "enriched" or "ornamented" — in the second movement — by insights from other theologians and theological agendas, such as those from liberation perspectives. While that would give some voice to nontraditional thinkers, those would still be made optional and "elective." In contrast to these common misconceptions, the current project is based on the conviction that all theologies are contextual since they emerge out of and are shaped by their contexts. They are just differently contextual. (The only justification for a cautionary use of the term "contextual" theology is *intention* and *awareness*: whereas theology until the twentieth century did not acknowledge its contextuality, some current theological movements not only do that but also make the mindfulness of context a theological theme.) Consequently, the discussion here includes the diversity of theological voices, whether by males or females, by those from the Global North or the Global South, and so forth. Of course, more space is devoted to theologies created by men than by women, by Euro-Americans than by Africans/Asians/Latin Americans, and by "mainliners" than by "contextual" theologians (as the terms are rightly understood) for the simple reason that these provide much of the literature and sources to be found. Furthermore, that the current project engages widely and deeply the whole Christian tradition (albeit its almost exclusive male-orientation and European origin) is not to be seen as working against inclusivity; rather, it is yet another way of affirming inclusivity in that all contemporary theological movements and agendas have their roots in the long and variegated Christian tradition. Irenaeus, Athanasius, Augustine, Aquinas, Teresa of Ávila, Luther, and Schleiermacher are the pedigree of not merely Euro-American but also of Asian/African/Latin American theologies, not only male but also female theologies, and so forth. As long as the "contextual" (read: non-European, nonmale) theologies are not invited into the center of theological discussion, they can be ignored, marginalized, and undermined. To that travesty, the current project seeks to offer a remedy.

The term "dialogical" in a more specific sense here means an intentional and intense engagement of other living faith traditions. As a result, systematic argumentation and discussion must be informed and challenged by theology of religions, which in a more general sense reflects on the relation of the Christian faith to other religions, and more importantly, with comparative theology,[5] whose purpose is to look at specific, focused issues among religions. (Heuristically speaking, the former is deductive, whereas the latter is inductive.) An important methodological guide in the comparative approach is to look for topics and themes pertinent to each tradition even when the comparison is done from a particular, in this case Christian, perspective.[6]

Theology that is robustly inclusivistic in its orientation, welcoming testimonies, insights, and interpretations from different traditions and contexts — hence, authentically inviting and dialogical — honors the otherness of the other. It calls for deep learning about the religious other.[7] It also makes space for an honest, genuine, authentic sharing of one's convictions. In pursuing the question of truth as revealed by the triune God, constructive theology also seeks to persuade and convince with the power of dialogical, humble, and respectful argumentation. Theology, then, becomes an act of hospitality, giving and receiving gifts. That some leading postmodern thinkers (Derrida, Levinas) are deeply suspicious of the possibility of "gift" is not a reason for not seeking for such giving. While only God gives perfect gifts, theologians in search of God's wisdom and love may also exchange gifts of inclusivity, belonging, mutual learning, and enrichment — in other words, be sharers of hospitality.

What the physicist-theologian John Polkinghorne calls "motivated beliefs" — by an analogy of how natural sciences advance, namely, on the one

---

5. Whereas comparative religion, whose contributions comparative theology widely utilizes, seeks to be "neutral" with regard to faith commitments and to look "objectively" at the features of religious traditions, comparative theology is a confessional enterprise — and if it is not, it is neither useful nor interesting.

6. That such an enterprise is based on sacred texts rather than everyday spiritual experiences, and mostly on classical texts rather than contemporary ones, should not be seen as invalidating the project. It is just to acknowledge that interfaith engagement itself may take various forms, most prominently in the encounter of committed men and women of various traditions, including prayer, worship, and the study of Scripture; academic theology facilitates comparative exercise in a different and complementary way.

7. See *Nostra Aetate* #1.

hand as a result of unexpected creative insights and, on the other hand, as a result of the painstaking accumulation and testing of the best hypotheses and theories — may be a good way to illustrate the current project's methodological vision (even though in theology the accumulation of knowledge hardly means, as it does in the sciences, that the knowledge of the past generations becomes obsolete). In other words, in science there is a dynamic balance between ever-new, at times daring insights and discoveries and a carefully tested and tried reservoir of theories and knowledge. This former Cambridge quantum physicist, now Anglican priest, articulates the implications for theological work:

> Christian theological discourse is not cut and dried, utterly prescriptive and allowing no room for subsequent intellectual manoeuvre. On the contrary, it encourages a diversity of contributions, while at the same time it sets limits to the range of possibilities that the Church can recognize as adequate to its experience. These limitations arise precisely from theology's quest for *motivated* belief rather than indulging in unbounded speculation; they are the theological equivalents of the requirements of empirical adequacy that set limits to the range of acceptable scientific theories.[8]

As a result — if I may put it somewhat daringly — should my approach to constructive theology be successful according to my own standards, the "traditionalists" would find my way of doing theology much too open to new voices, dialogue partners, and sets of issues, while "progressives" might lament that my proposal is still too much stuck with Christian tradition, both biblical and historical!

The present volume focuses on the doctrines of revelation and the Trinity, often considered the beginning topics in the presentation of Christian doctrine. The present volume does not follow the typical order, as Christology and reconciliation were discussed first. Whatever the order, the Trinity plays a special role as it relates to all other loci in Christian theology. Indeed, Christian theology is nothing but a discussion of the unfolding of the creative, providing, saving, and consummating work of the Father, Son, and Holy Spirit on the way to the eschatological consummation. Revelation, thus, is also cast in a trinitarian framework as it observes the way Father, Son, and Spirit reach out to humanity in gracious invitation. At the beginning of each part, a detailed note orients the reader to the order and topics to be discussed.

8. Polkinghorne, *Faith, Science, and Understanding*, pp. 42-43.

I. TRIUNE REVELATION

Any talk about the doctrine of revelation has to face two realities, in many ways antagonistic and contradictory. The first one is that among all world religions, sacred texts exist and those texts are taken as "divine revelation" of some sort. The second one is that in Christian theology since the Enlightenment, massive rebuttals have been mounted in rejection of the *doctrine* and often even any notion of divine revelation. The orientational discussion of that dynamic will occupy chapter 1.

The distinctively *Christian* theology of revelation, along with all other theological loci, is anchored in and shaped by the trinitarian vision. Chapter 2 seeks to outline such a coherent theological vision of the loving Father, in his desire to reach out to men and women, as well as the whole of creation, in sending his Son, the Word made flesh, in the power of the divine Spirit, to *be* the eternal divine revelation. If revelation is an event, divine embodiment, then it means that it is fully embedded in the life of this world and its history. It is best expressed with the biblical term "promise," both historical and eschatological in nature (chapter 3). This historical-eschatological word-act of the promise of God is not only about the final salvation awaited in the future, but also about liberation, inclusion, and hospitality in this life. In chapter 4, an attempt is made to develop and look at the implications of this liberative word in relation to sociopolitical, economic, and sexist problems as well as to the possibility of embracing the cultural and ethnic diversity of the current globalizing world and church.

As the divine revelation, Word made flesh, embedded in the unfolding of history as a word of promise, comes to us in Christian sacred Scripture, chapter 5 seeks to offer a contemporary account of the divine-human synergy in the coming-to-being of Christian Scripture and how to best understand its "inspiration." That divinely inspired yet genuinely human Word was received, canonized, and lived out in discipleship, liturgy, and preaching/teaching of Christian communities throughout centuries, as a result of which tradition emerged. The task of chapter 6 is to investigate the meaning and implications of this living tradition in the Christian community as it "used" Scripture as its ultimate norm of faith and practice.

Chapter 7, with a focus on natural theology and natural revelation, might appear to be out of sync with typical presentations of Christian doctrine. The distinction between "general" and "special" revelation established in later Christian tradition led dogmatic presentations to first talk about revelation based on human nature and nature (as in creation), and only then to speak of revelation in Christ. More recently that distinction led to an unfortunate and fatal separation, even putting in total opposition to each other "natural" and "special" knowledge of God (Barth). In contrast, the current project seeks to construct a robust *Christian* trinitarian natural theology. That task will be started in this context, developed further in part 2 in the doctrine of the triune God, and finally brought to a tentative conclusion in the doctrine of creation in the volume *Creation and Humanity*.

The last chapter of part 1 looks in some detail at the commonalities and dissimilarities among five living faiths — Hinduism, Buddhism, Islam, Judaism, and Christianity — with regard to their understanding of revelation and scriptures. While shorter interfaith engagements will be attempted throughout the discussion of the doctrine of revelation, for the sake of the integrity of systematic argumentation, it is justifiable to place the detailed mutual conversations at the end of part 1. Similarly, in part 2 the concentrated and detailed investigation of the Christian doctrine of God's relation to other living faiths will be reserved until the end, although occasional case studies will be given throughout.

1. On the Conditions of the Doctrine of Revelation

Is There a Revelation in Christian Religion?

The claim that "Revelation is neither a specifically Christian term nor a theological one"[1] may come as a surprise when the common assumption is that the idea "that Christianity needs — and, indeed, possesses — a divine revelation . . . [has] been regarded as a theological commonplace."[2] Theologians have found a number of problems with this evaluation. Foremost among them is the existence of widely differing notions of what revelation is and its meaning. Coupled with these is "the silence of the Bible in modern theology"[3] — and one may want to add, similarly, in postmodern theology: "the Bible no longer exercises anything like the authority it once did in many Christian communities. And in those communities where the Bible continues to exercise its traditional role there is little or no serious engagement with the problems of the twentieth century."[4] While perhaps an (intentional?) overstatement, the statement still makes a valid point. And it is a big shift in light of the fact that "Christianity came into the world as a religion of revelation, and as such claimed a supernatural origin for its message."[5]

1. Moltmann, *Experiences in Theology,* p. 61; this is a citation from Cloege, "Offenbarung," 4:1610.
2. Mitchell and Wiles, "Does Christianity Need a Revelation?" p. 103; Downing, *Has Christianity a Revelation?* See also J. Huxley, *Religion without Revelation.*
3. Heading in Grenz and Franke, *Beyond Foundationalism,* p. 58.
4. Stroup, *Promise of Narrative Theology,* p. 26.
5. Kelly, *Early Christian Doctrines,* p. 29.

In this context, it is theologically significant that while the Bible seldom plays a crucial role in the liberal Protestant Christianity of the late twentieth and early twenty-first century, in many "contextual" and "global" theologies, the opposite is the case. For example, several African American[6] and African[7] theologians have spoken to the central role of Scripture for all theology, systematic theology included.

Well known is the massive rebuttal of revelation on philosophical grounds in Karl Jaspers's *Philosophical Faith and Revelation* (1967), including the originally Kantian (and later Feuerbachian and Marxist) fear of the loss of human freedom.[8] The only version of revelation Jaspers could tolerate was of an elusive rather than direct nature and expressed in symbols rather than words.[9]

The rebuttal and objections to the doctrine of revelation are not limited to the twentieth century. They go back all the way to the time of emerging modernity as illustrated in the British Deist John Toland's *Christianity Not Mysterious* (1669), with the telling subtitle, *A Treatise Shewing, That There is Nothing in the Gospel Contrary to Reason, Nor Above it: And That No Christian Doctrine can be properly call'd A Mystery.* In deistic understanding, "revelation" does not bring about anything new, anything that the human mind could not grasp on its own. Even more devastating criticism against the traditional notion of revelation is launched by the Jewish philosopher Spinoza in his *Theological-Political Treatise,* written at the same time as Toland's work (1670).[10] Not only through reason but also by "reading" nature (which does not allow the traditional category of the miraculous), this Jewish philosopher thought the Divine could be discerned. The picture of the Divine that emerges out of philosophical reasoning differs vastly not only from the teaching of the church and its authorities but also from the one based in any traditional reading of the Bible. Equally challenging, though very different in many accounts, was David Hume's demand, in *An Enquiry concerning Human Understanding* (1748), to base true and reliable knowledge on experience and reasoning rather than naive beliefs. Hume did not, of course, debunk all notions of faith in God, nor deny categorically the possibility of miracles; but for the miracles to be validated, the conditions were such that next to nothing qualified as miraculous.[11]

---

6. Evans, *We Have Been Believers*, p. 33; Cone, *Black Theology of Liberation*, p. 31.

7. Bujo and Muya, eds., *African Theology*, pp. 105, 120.

8. Jaspers, *Philosophical Faith*, p. 10.

9. Jaspers, *Philosophical Faith*, p. 333.

10. Israel, ed., *Cambridge Texts in the Philosophy of History*. See also Levene, "Spinoza's Bible."

11. See Hume, *An Enquiry concerning Human Understanding*, book 10, part 1.

Famously, the leading Enlightenment philosopher Immanuel Kant blocked the way for revelation with his restriction of all human knowledge to the phenomenal order, leaving the transcendent unknown. The idealist philosophers (J. G. Fichte and G. W. F. Hegel), while not totally dismissing the concept of revelation, similarly objected to any notion of "supernatural" intervention of God, insisting that revelation "was a necessary phase in the immanent progress of the human spirit toward the fully rational truth of absolute philosophy."[12] Classical liberalism gleaned from these influences its immanentist view of revelation in which inspiration was nothing more than enhancement of "natural" human capacities for insights into religion. The early-twentieth-century history-of-religions approach, similarly, made the traditional notion of divine revelation a matter of experiencing the holy and numinous.[13] Even among those who continue to champion the necessity of the category of revelation, such as in the ambitious program of W. Pannenberg and his colleagues, discussed in a book he edited entitled *Revelation as History* (1961), the subtitle reveals a deep disavowal of any kind of authoritarian notion: *A Proposal for a More Open, Less Authoritarian View of an Important Theological Concept.*

Other objections to the *doctrine* of revelation abound in contemporary theology and philosophy, including the doubt whether it is possible for human language to capture the mystery of God and whether there really is a distinction between acquired and revealed knowledge, as well as the obvious similarities between most living faiths regarding "revelation." Perhaps the most fatal objection to the notion of revelation came through the rise of biblical criticism with its attempt to read the Scripture, all scriptures, in a way similar to any other human writing.[14]

While only a few feminists and other women theologians are willing to leave behind the *notion* of revelation, they are also deeply troubled about tradition's literalism, patriarchalism, and exclusivism.[15] Similarly, other liberationists seek to revise the traditional notion of revelation as abstract and theoretical into an engaged, critical reflection on praxis.[16] William J. Abraham

12. For a brief historical account, see Dulles, *Models of Revelation*, p. 21.

13. See further, Dulles, *Models of Revelation*, pp. 19-22; for a useful account of various philosophical objections to the notion of revelation, see also Penelhum, "Revelation and Philosophy," chap. 4.

14. For a useful listing of these and other contemporary objections to revelation, see Dulles, *Models of Revelation*, pp. 6-8.

15. See McKim, *Bible in Theology*, chap. 14.

16. Gutiérrez, *A Theology of Liberation*, chap. 1 and passim.

rightly observes: "the centre of gravity in theology has shifted from concern with the content of the recovery of the *kerygma* to concern with the social and political context in which the church must act and witness."[17]

In the matrix of contemporary religious plurality, the post-Enlightenment-driven "secular" claim that Christianity neither has revelation nor should have it sounds awkward and counterintuitive. Many if not all Hindu traditions regard Vedas to be transhuman — in other words, authored not by humans but by the deities. In Islam, the Qur'an is acknowledged as the highest authority, divine in origin. Taoism (in its religious side) can be considered fully a revealed religion, as "[i]ts scriptures are emanations from the beginning of creation, formed by the primordial breath *(yuanqi)* that existed at the first stirring of the Tao."[18] Even in Buddhism, huge amounts of sacred writings have emerged that are considered to have divine authority, particularly in various Mahayana traditions. In other words, as modern and contemporary *Christian* philosophy and theology have expressed serious doubts about all traditional notions of revelation and authority, in other living faiths by and large the conviction remains that, indeed, revelation is a given and the object of high regard, often even of worship. Hence, a careful look at the effects of modernity is needed.

The Doctrine of Revelation on Both Sides of Modernity

The *doctrine* of revelation cannot be found among either the biblical or the early theologians, notwithstanding the existence of a deep "revelational" intuition.[19] None of the creeds rule on the topic. The term "revelation," as used in a technical sense in contemporary theology, was not in place before the Reformation.

Only in the apologetic theology of the Middle Ages and particularly after the Enlightenment, in the aftermath of Protestant scholasticism, did the *doctrine* of revelation become a theological theme. Deism in particular called for a defined doctrine of revelation among those who wanted to stick with classical Christian tradition.[20] Whereas in older theology revelation denoted the supernatural communication of "heavenly teachings," in post-Enlightenment theology it had everything to do with the "self-revelation" of God. Idealist philosophy of modernity made God's self-revelation a matter of God being

---

17. Abraham, "Revelation Reaffirmed," p. 201; for postcolonial criticism, see Sugirtharajah, *The Bible and the Third World*.

18. Oldstone-Moore, "Taoism," p. 246.

19. See Dulles, *Models of Revelation*, pp. 3-4.

20. For a full-scale study, see Latourelle, *Theology of Revelation*.

both the "subject" and the "object" of revelation. In Barth's neo-orthodox rendering — *"God* reveals Himself. He reveals Himself *through Himself.* He reveals *Himself"*[21] — this program comes to full fruition. But is this the biblical view of revelation? In the Bible, God "always reveals 'something' or 'someone.' "[22]

In pre-Enlightenment tradition, "theology's constitutive correlation with revelation remained intact" and was based on the assumption that the "founding of theology on divine revelation is not a determination that is foreign to its nature."[23] In keeping with this assumption, for Reformation theology the basis of authority was Holy Scripture as "God's own word" rather than as a human word about God.[24] Roman Catholic theology, as late as the end of the nineteenth century, in Vatican Council I, agreed.[25] These premises came under critical rejection as a result of the Enlightenment and the collapse of the "Scripture principle."[26]

Importantly, at the same time, the key issue about the Word of God came to be the question of its divine inspiration. As God's Word was equated with the wording of the Bible because of its divine origin and authorship, the doctrine of verbal inspiration was officially formulated in Protestant orthodoxy and materially repeated at Vatican I. Guarding the verbal inspiration became a critical issue because it was feared that "[o]nce one concedes that anything in scripture is of human origin, its divine authority is lost." Opined J. A. Quenstedt in 1715: "If one admits that even a single verse was written without the direct influence of the Holy Spirit, then Satan will immediately claim the same for the whole chapter, the entire book, and finally the entire Bible, and in this way cancel all scripture's authority."[27] This focus on exact verbal inspiration was in keeping with and a result of Luther's insistence on Scripture as the theological principle from which theological statements are drawn.[28]

---

21. Barth, *CD* I/1, p. 296. For discussion and critique of revelation as divine "self-revelation" in Barth, see Pannenberg, introduction to *Revelation as History,* pp. 3-8 and passim.

22. Moltmann, *Experiences in Theology,* pp. 61-62, at 62.

23. Pannenberg, *ST* 1:2. For Aquinas as the model, see Aquinas, *ST* 1.1.2 and 6.

24. See further, Pannenberg, *ST* 1:31-32, at 31. For a fuller discussion with detailed documentation, see McKim, *Bible in Theology,* chap. 2.

25. *Dogmatic Constitution on the Catholic Faith,* session 3, chap. 3. For details, see McKim, *Bible in Theology,* chap. 1.

26. See the classic work by B. B. Warfield, *Revelation and Inspiration.* For a massive defense of the traditional position and rebuttal of notions of "liberalism," see Henry, *God, Revelation, and Authority.* See also Brunner, *Revelation and Reason,* p. 3.

27. As translated in Pannenberg, *ST* 1:32, from Quenstedt, *Theologi didactico-polemica,* I, p. 102.

28. Pannenberg, *ST* 1:33; also p. 36.

Coupled with this principle of "objective certainty" based on verbal inspiration and thus divine authority was the Reformation, particularly Reformed, insistence on the testimony of the Holy Spirit, as ably formulated by Calvin.[29] Spirit and Word are tightly linked with each other in his theology,[30] and it is from the Spirit that the Word receives its authentication.[31] But as a result of the gradual weakening of the doctrine of divine authority of Scripture "as something that precedes all human judgment, the doctrine of the internal testimony of the Spirit took on the sense of an *additional* principle of subjective experience and certainty which supplements the eternal Word and evaluates the truth claim and truth content of scripture."[32] The introduction of textual criticism and, after that, higher criticism gave impetus to this development. Although textual inaccuracies or mistakes did not go unnoticed by earlier interpreters, a systematic and intentional study of the textual transmission and accuracy of the text of Scripture led ultimately to the conflict between strict verbal inspiration and its human nature. Even the accommodation theory, which was already present in Calvin,[33] couldn't turn around this development.

In addition to these radical challenges brought about by the Enlightenment, an equally significant, more recent challenge has to do with ever widening and deepening diversity and plurality. It has to do with cultural-ethnic-geographical diversity within the Christian church, not to mention denominational plurality. Furthermore, the diversity also relates to religious plurality and forms of pluralism.

The Widening Horizon of the Discourse on Revelation and Scripture in a Pluralistic World

The problem with precritical Christian tradition was not the confidence it had about the truthfulness of the biblical revelation but the fact that it offered no resources in negotiating with other religious traditions that, each in its own way, made similar claims to ultimate truth. Common sense tells us that it is

29. Chap. 7 in book 1 of the *Institutes* is titled: "The Testimony of the Spirit Necessary to Give Full Authority of Scripture. . . ." See particularly 1.7.4.

30. See particularly 1.9.3.

31. 1.7.5. For a useful discussion, see Pelikan, *Reformation of Church and Dogma*, p. 187.

32. Pannenberg, *ST* 1:34.

33. The "accommodation theory" is found already among some Fathers. See Battles, "God Was Accommodating Himself," pp. 19-38. For Calvin, see also Torrance, "Knowledge of God," pp. 86-106.

not possible to assume that numerous such claims are equally correct — or incorrect! Hence, comparative theology is not saying that because there are a number of competing truth claims, none can be true. It rather looks for ways for a peaceful interaction of competing traditions, comparing notes, and giving distinctive testimony to what each tradition honestly believes. Consequently, in light of the religious and philosophical plurality of our times, "[i]t is useless to say that God makes his revelation self-authenticating."[34] Hence, such certainty cannot be a matter of simple self-evidence,[35] be it based on the notion of a "Christian" state — or Islamic or Buddhist or Hindu state — or consensus, or territorial occupancy, or something similar that is external in nature.[36]

It is now obvious to us even in the American context — and even more obvious in most European settings — that Christian faith can no longer be taken as the religion of the land.[37] True, most Americans still identify themselves with Christian tradition. However, as the polling by the Pew Forum on Religion and Public Life (2008) reports, "the United States is on the verge of becoming a minority Protestant country." The Roman Catholic Church has suffered even more dramatic losses. More than one-quarter of Americans have changed their faith allegiance or ended up confessing no faith.[38] Both religious diversity and pervasive secularism have transformed the American and European cultures in dramatic ways. In the Global South, religious diversity is taken for granted and is a matter of fact in many areas; secularism is doing much more poorly there. Consequently, "We do our theology from now on in the midst of many others 'who are not . . . of this fold.' Our own faith, if only we are aware of it, is a constantly renewed decision, taken in the knowledge that other faiths are readily available to us."[39]

While a rigid, fundamentalistic sticking with one's own scripture and its authority may lead to disastrous and violent consequences, what Martin E. Marty calls "lethal theology,"[40] one has to be mindful of the identity-forming

---

34. Ward, *Religion and Revelation*, p. 7.

35. Ward, *Religion and Revelation*, p. 7.

36. Even in contemporary science there is today the healthy admission that very few, if any, scientific results can be had with indubitable certainty (the dream and assumption of the Enlightenment), far less so in the humanities, in which the investigation proceeds in terms of argumentation, comparison of ideas, and similar nonobservational means.

37. Eck, *A New Religious America*, pp. 5-6, at 5, 61-65; see also Hutchinson, *Religious Pluralism in America*.

38. Pew Forum, "US Religious Landscape Survey," pp. 5-7, at 5, 7.

39. Hall, *Thinking the Faith*, pp. 208-9, at 209.

40. Marty, *When Faiths Collide*, pp. 30, 159-61.

agency of "canonical" scriptures in any religious tradition. So, how to negotiate the need to avoid religious conflicts and violence, on the one hand, and, on the other hand, to continue faithfully building on the received scriptural tradition?

Unfortunately, that question has not occupied the minds of most theologians so far. Sheer lack of knowledge of religions usually nurtures not only misguided remarks about them but also negative attitudes. Even such a careful theologian as Emil Brunner could say of other living faiths that they are "essentially eudaemonistic and anthropocentric"[41] and, even worse, "religions of self-redemption."[42] Rightly Timothy Tennent notes: "In the West, it is rare to find someone who has more than a cursory knowledge of the sacred texts of other religions. In contrast, because Christians in the Majority World are often in settings dominated by other religions, it is not uncommon to meet a Christian with a Muslim, Hindu, or Buddhist background who has an intimate knowledge of another sacred text."[43] Hence, a careful and well-informed tackling of religious diversity "here at home" and "out there" is an urgent task for any theology for the third millennium worth its salt.

These many objections and rebuttals to the whole notion of the *doctrine* of revelation should be acknowledged and carefully reflected upon if one is to make a serious attempt to construct a more satisfactory and adequate doctrinal account of the Christian theology of revelation. The Jesuit Avery Dulles makes the important but often neglected observation that the "theology of revelation offers peculiar methodological problems" in that it "is not a part of doctrinal theology (or dogmatics) as ordinarily understood, for doctrinal theology . . . customarily tests its assertions by their conformity with what is already recognized as revelation."[44] The current project seeks to develop a contemporary theology of revelation in the matrix of both contextual-global-intercultural diversity, including questions of inclusivity and power, and the diversity of living faiths and their claims to revelation and authority. Such an attempt is best described as "the polymorphous character of revelation."[45] Such a multifaceted and dynamic vision of revelation may offer resources for a new way of thinking of revelation in a diverse and pluralistic world. The ultimate goal is

41. Brunner, *Revelation and Reason*, p. 266.

42. Brunner, *Revelation and Reason*, p. 271.

43. Tennent, *Theology in the Context of World Christianity*, p. 55; see also Amaladoss, "Other Scriptures and the Christian," pp. 62-78.

44. Dulles, *Models of Revelation*, p. 14.

45. I borrow this heading from Abraham, "Revelation Reaffirmed," p. 206. See his important works: *The Divine Inspiration of Holy Scripture* and *Divine Revelation and the Limits of Historical Criticism*.

"to articulate a concept of revelation which will be true to the main orthodox Christian tradition, yet which will be open to a fruitful interaction with other traditions, and with the developing corpus of scientific knowledge."[46]

46. Ward, *Religion and Revelation*, p. 1.

2. Triune Revelation

If Christian theology as a whole is but the discernment of the works of the triune God — Father, Son, and Spirit — in the economy of salvation, then it is only natural that a Christian theology of *revelation* similarly is triune in its basic nature. Barth intuited this correctly when he considered the Trinity as the overarching context and goal of systematic argumentation, beginning in the prolegomena to his *Church Dogmatics,* in which he discussed revelation. He attempted to cast the doctrine of revelation in a trinitarian framework: "*God* reveals Himself. He reveals Himself *through Himself.* He reveals *Himself.*"[1] While Barth's intuitions were right and well directed, this way of formulating the meaning of revelation is hardly in keeping with the biblical narrative that ascends from the concrete history of salvation and God's overall creative, preserving, redeeming, and perfecting works, on to the knowledge of the Father, Son, and Spirit. Isn't Barth's approach rather an abstract exercise that bases itself on a *formal* principle taken from the Bible, and in doing so, represents a theological version of idealist philosophy of the past?

Barth could have avoided this road by being more attentive to his own statement elsewhere that the Bible points to "the life of God Himself turned to us, the Word of God coming to us by the Holy Spirit, Jesus Christ."[2] Here he is not expressing the idealist philosophy of an abstract, contentless *self-revelation* of God, but rather the economic language of the Bible. This outlook

---

1. Barth, *CD* I/1, p. 296. For discussion and critique of revelation as divine "self-revelation" in Barth, see Pannenberg, introduction to *Revelation as History,* pp. 3-8 and passim.

2. Barth, *CD* I/2, p. 483, see also pp. 512-13.

is finely expressed in the common ecumenical statement by Roman Catholics and Lutherans: "What God has done for the salvation of the world in Jesus Christ is transmitted in the gospel and made present in the Holy Spirit. The gospel as proclamation of God's saving action is therefore itself a salvation event."[3] This central Christian statement calls for further elucidation and amplification.[4]

Loving Father and the Cruciform Revelation

Vatican II's *Dei Verbum* represents a dramatic shift in theology of revelation as it turns to a personalist, relational, and dynamic notion of revelation (#2):

> In His goodness and wisdom God chose to reveal Himself and to make known to us the hidden purpose of His will (see Eph. 1:9) by which through Christ, the Word made flesh, man might in the Holy Spirit have access to the Father and come to share in the divine nature (see Eph. 2:18; 2 Peter 1:4). Through this revelation, therefore, the invisible God (see Col. 1:15; 1 Tim. 1:17) out of the abundance of His love speaks to men as friends (see Ex. 33:11; John 15:14-15) and lives among them (see Bar. 3:38), so that He may invite and take them into fellowship with Himself.

Fatherly love is the key here. Luther's theology of divine love, linked with his theology of the cross, makes a profound contribution in this respect to the trinitarian nature of God's revelation. In his Heidelberg Disputation (1518),[5] Luther makes an important distinction between two kinds of love: *amor Dei* and *amor hominis,* God's love and human love, respectively. Human love is always basically selfish and looks for its own good. Human love also fools men and women into seeking God with good works and through human wisdom.[6] Human love is oriented toward objects that are inherently good, where self-love defines the content and the object of the love. Men and

---

3. *Gospel and the Church — the Malta Report,* #16; also in Kasper, *Harvesting the Fruits,* p. 12.

4. See Faith and Order, "Scripture, Tradition and Traditions"; Metzger, "Relational Dynamic of Revelation," pp. 21-34.

5. Kärkkäinen, "Evil, Love and the Left Hand of God," pp. 215-34; McGrath, *Luther's Theology of the Cross.*

6. *LW* 31:57; HDT 28. See Bornkamm, "Die theologischen Thesen Luthers bei der Heidelberger Disputation 1518," pp. 130-46.

women love something they believe they can enjoy.[7] God loves in a way opposite to human love: "The love of God does not find, but creates, that which is pleasing to it. . . . Rather than seeking its own good, the love of God flows forth and bestows good."[8]

The God who acts like this is a hidden God. The theologian of the cross observes God in the shame and lowliness of the cross, whereas the theologian of glory looks for God in majesty and glory.[9] With reference to Exodus 33:18–34:9 (especially 33:23), in which Moses asks God to show God's face, God responds: "But . . . you cannot see my face; for man shall not see me and live" (33:20). Instead, God lets Moses see God's back. On the basis of this event, Luther differentiates between God's visible properties such as humanity, weakness, and folly, and God's invisible properties such as virtue, divinity, wisdom, justice, and goodness.[10] The theologian of glory goes astray in that she attempts to know God "through the creatures," in other words, by seeking God in the created order. In doing so, as Luther succinctly states, a theology of glory "calls evil good and good evil," whereas "a theology of the cross calls the thing what it actually is."[11]

The human mind naturally follows the logic of "knowledge is of like by the like."[12] "God is known in the analogies to him in the order of creation or in acts of history which point to him, or else he is known in his self-revelation, or only in the Holy Spirit of God."[13] There is of course no denying the granting of some knowledge of God to humanity in this analogous way. The problem is that if the "principle of likeness is applied strictly, God is only known by God."[14] Apart from this logical problem, the material problem with a one-sided application of the analogical principle is that according to the biblical testimonies, God has also chosen to reveal himself by means not only different from but totally opposed to the principle of analogy. This is the rule of opposites, so to speak. Hence, the analogical rule must be supplemented and at times corrected with the dialectical rule according to which "God is only revealed as 'God' in his opposite: godlessness and abandonment

7. Mannermaa, *Kaksi rakkautta*, pp. 14-15.

8. HDT 28; *LW* 31:57.

9. HDT 20; *LW* 31:52.

10. HDT 20; *LW* 31:52.

11. HDT 21; *LW* 31:53.

12. Aristotle, *Metaphysics* 3.4.10.

13. Moltmann, *The Crucified God*, p. 26; see also Moltmann, *Experiences in Theology*, pp. 151-55.

14. Moltmann, *The Crucified God*, p. 26.

by God."[15] Hence the Johannine Jesus' saying, "He who has seen me has seen the Father" (John 14:9), applies as much to the suffering and humiliated Jesus as to the victorious and glorious one. In the presence of the crucified God, one may hope to find room for what the Korean feminist theologian Chung Hyun Kung calls the "epistemology of the broken body."[16] Many lives of men and women, but certainly women, and particularly women in Asia and elsewhere in the majority world, are broken.

Indeed, according to Luther, God not only reveals himself but also works in the opposite way from human expectations: God conceals Godself in lowliness to reveal the greatness of God's love. Whereas the natural mind imagines the works of God to be beautiful, fine, and attractive, the opposite is the case. God's works "are always unattractive and appear evil, [but] they are nevertheless really eternal merits," insofar as they are in accordance with his true love.[17] He describes the works of God with biblical imagery, citing Isaiah 53:2, "He had no form or comeliness." "The LORD kills and brings to life; / he brings down to Sheol and raises up."[18] In other words, God makes us "nothing" *(nihil)* and "stupid" to reveal his real love to us.[19] To show the paradoxical nature of his theology of love and of the cross, Luther even goes so far as to say that God's works are not just veiled in their opposite but they also sometimes create bad results.[20] Furthermore, Luther argues that sometimes God uses even Satan for his *opus alienum* in order to work out his *opus proprium*.[21]

Several important lessons emerge out of Luther's theology in this respect; let me highlight two here. First, the divine revelation is a gift. It is God's hospitality, the loving God's desire to reach out and form a fellowship with men and women. Second, the revelation of God is as much an "unveiling" as it is a "veiling." It is paradoxical and surprising. It not only speaks of the incarnation of the Divine in human history, but more specifically as the suffering and humiliated one. The all-mighty and majestic God is to be "seen" as much in the deepest darkness of Golgotha as in the brightest light of the Mount of Transfiguration. The Korean-born theologian Andrew Sung Park looks at the meaning of the cross through the lens of the key cultural concept of his first culture, namely, *han.* That multifaceted concept denotes suffering and

15. Moltmann, *The Crucified God*, p. 27.
16. C. H. Kung, *The Struggle to Be the Sun Again*, p. 39.
17. HDT 17; *LW* 31:51; Kopperi, *Paradoksien teologia*, pp. 115-18 especially.
18. 1 Sam. 2:6 (Luther mistakenly refers to 1 Kings 2:6).
19. HDT 4; *LW* 31:43; see also *LW* 14:95; etc.; Mannermaa, *Kaksi rakkautta*, p. 43.
20. HDT 5, 6; *LW* 31:45.
21. HDT 6; *LW* 31:45.

pain, "a sense of unresolved resentment against injustices suffered, a sense of helplessness, . . . a feeling of acute pain and sorrow in one's guts and bowels."[22] Incarnation and crucifixion speak to the theme of *han:* "The all-powerful God was crucified. The cross is the symbol of God's han which makes known God's own vulnerability to human sin. . . . The cry of the wounded heart of God on the cross reverberates throughout the whole of history. God shamefully exposes the vulnerability of God on the cross, demanding the healing of the han of God. The cross is God's unshakable love for God's own creation. Like parents who give birth to and then love their children, God is wrapped up in a creational love with humanity."[23]

These reflections take us to the most profound manifestation of the Father's love in sending his Son to live and die for us, one among us — and so also offer a word of hope not only to men and women but also to the whole of creation.

Incarnated Son and Embodied Revelation

According to the formula of Irenaeus, "the Father is the invisible of the Son, but the Son the visible of the Father."[24] In *On the Incarnation of the Word of God,* Saint Athanasius offers the classic reasoning of the way the loving Father, "[w]ho by nature is invisible and not to be beheld," has made it possible for humans to know and see him by virtue of incarnation: "He, indeed, assumed humanity that we might become God. He manifested Himself by means of a body in order that we might perceive the Mind of the unseen Father." In a most remarkable statement, Athanasius summarizes the significance of incarnation: "For this purpose, then, the incorporeal and incorruptible and immaterial Word of God comes to our realm, howbeit he was not far from us before. For no part of Creation is left void of Him: He has filled all things everywhere, remaining present with His own Father" (8.1).

---

22. Joh, *Heart of the Cross,* p. xxi. (Joh attributes this definition to Han Wan Sang but gives a mistaken reference to another author; I was unable to trace the original source.) A careful discussion of the many meanings of *han* can be found in Park, *Wounded Heart of God,* chap. 1 particularly.

23. Park, *Wounded Heart of God,* p. 123. What I find problematic in Park's account of the cross and love of God manifested therein is that he speaks in this same context of the inability of God to "save Godself apart from salvation of humanity," in other words, apart from humanity's response to the salvific work of God (pp. 123-24).

24. Irenaeus, *Against Heresies* 4.6.6.

But what does it mean to call Jesus Christ the divine revelation? Richard Bauckham outlines three important paradigms for understanding.[25] One he describes as that in which "Jesus illustrates the moral character of God." In his person Jesus reveals to us the compassionate, loving, righteous, and holy nature of God. This paradigm seems to imply that while preciously valuable, revelation in Christ does not have to be unique — or can be unique only in degree. This is the view of both classical and contemporary liberalism, as illustrated in Hastings Rashdall's remark: "We cannot say intelligibly that God dwells in Christ, unless we have already recognized that in a sense God dwells in and reveals Himself in Humanity at large, and in each particular human soul."[26] The second paradigm is that "Jesus reveals the universal possibility of Divine-human union." This view goes beyond the mere possibility of knowing God to union with God. Jesus then, of course, represents the culmination of that union. The possibility of union calls for incarnation, the coming of the Divine in the human form. What kind of incarnation that is, is still negotiable, as is evident in the theology of John Macquarrie.[27] While he speaks of incarnation as "unique" in Jesus Christ, he is not thereby limiting incarnation totally to one human person.[28] In Bauckham's third paradigm, "Jesus reveals the unique presence and action of God which is Jesus' own history." In this view, "Jesus does not merely illustrate what God is like, nor is he merely the representatively fullest instantiation of humanity united with God. His unique human life, death, and resurrection are at the same time uniquely God's human history, in which God's unique act of self-giving love for all humanity took place."[29] This paradigm materially represents classical Christian tradition. This is where tradition's focus on Logos, the Word made flesh, comes to the fore as the uniquely Christian way of understanding salvation.

In contemporary theology probably no one has underlined the significance of incarnation as the means of God's self-identification with humanity as vocally as Karl Rahner. For him, "God has uttered himself to man victoriously and unsurpassably,"[30] as the human nature assumed by the Logos is not "a mask . . . assumed from without, from behind which the Logos hides to act things out in the world," but rather, it is "the constitutive, real symbol

---

25. Bauckham, "Jesus the Revelation of God," pp. 174-200.

26. Cited in Bauckham, "Jesus the Revelation of God," p. 177, without identifying the original source.

27. Macquarrie, *Jesus Christ in Modern Thought.*

28. Bauckham, "Jesus the Revelation of God," p. 179.

29. Bauckham, "Jesus the Revelation of God," p. 180.

30. Rahner, "Quest for Approaches," p. 200.

of the Logos himself."[31] "It is a fact of faith that when God desires to manifest himself, it is as a man that he does so," which appears only in the bodily form. Indeed, on the basis of this divine embodiment, we know not only the Divine but also the meaning of the human: "If we want to know what man is, or what flesh means, then we must, so to speak, choose this theological definition of the statement 'And the Word became flesh,' saying: flesh, man as a bodily, concrete, historical being is just what comes into being when the Logos, issuing from himself, utters himself. Man is therefore God's self-utterance, out of himself into the empty nothingness of the creature."[32] In this light Barth's linking revelation tightly with the Word incarnated is right on target even if, as mentioned, his formulation of the trinitarian nature of revelation reflects more idealist philosophy than the dynamic biblical narrative of God: "[R]evelation in fact does not differ from the person of Jesus Christ nor from the reconciliation accomplished in Him. To say revelation is to say 'the Word became flesh.'"[33]

The incarnated, embodied nature of Christian revelation is indeed its most distinctive feature among religions.[34] In Christian revelation, "God makes the Divine reality itself present in a particular historical form. The life of Jesus, for a fully incarnational form of Christian faith, is the self-expression of the Eternal in time."[35] Rightly then, it can be said:

> This is not, as in Islam, the revelation of a set of propositions, as though God were dictating laws or doctrines to be carefully written down. It is not, as in Hinduism, an inner experience of a supreme Self, as though someone had a particularly vivid or intense sense of the Supremely Real. It is not, as in Buddhism, an experience of release from sorrow, desire, and attachment. It is not, as in Judaism, Divine disclosure through the control of historical events, as though God were causing water, wind, or earth to act in extraordinary or miraculous ways. It is the unlimited Divine Life taking form in a particular human life. It is the realization of the Eternal in a particular historical individual.[36]

---

31. Rahner, *The Trinity*, pp. 32-33, at 33.
32. Rahner, "The Body in the Order of Salvation," p. 74.
33. Barth, *CD* I/1, p. 119. Vatican II's *Dei Verbum* #4 says materially the same.
34. Athanasius never tired of extolling the significance and virtues of the incarnation of the Logos in this regard. See *On the Incarnation of the Word of God*, 54, 55.
35. Ward, *Religion and Revelation*, p. 193.
36. Ward, *Religion and Revelation*, p. 193.

The divine embodiment is the distinctive principle that supports the idea of revelation — and salvation. This is a "postulate which sets human reality in the history and surrounding field of God's creation, reconciliation and redemption."[37]

Ward makes the theologically important historical observation that at the time of the coming in flesh of Jesus the Christ, as the fulfillment of the hopes of the Jewish religion to relate to God by faithfully following the Torah as the way of salvation, both "Greek and Indian ideas had touched the Galilean province which stood near to Alexander's route of conquest and communication between East and West." Not only were the Jews "looking for some sign of God's ancient promises to Israel, which seemed as far from fulfillment as ever," but also the peoples in the vast Roman Empire, India, and elsewhere in Asia were searching for the true knowledge of the Divine and the right way of life. "At that very particular and unrepeatable point of human history Jesus lived out his ministry."[38]

This observation may help Christian theology to make more sense of the obviously scandalous claim that the final and ultimate revelation has come in this one man, Jesus the Christ. This is not a claim about the superiority of Jesus, "considered in the abstract as a person of such-and-such intelligence, moral character, and temperament. . . . It is rather that God is manifesting the Divine Being decisively in this one historical life; so that this life becomes for ever the image of God, as a historically purposing and redemptive power and value."[39] Christian tradition has never claimed that the incarnation of the Word would express everything that there is to be known of the Divine — or else creation and history would be void of meaning. What Christian theology is saying "is that at a particular, limited point of time and space, the Divine Life transforms a particular human life by uniting it to itself. The particular is taken into God, as a foreshadowing of the destiny that awaits all finite things."[40]

The linking of Christian theology of revelation with the history and messianic expectations of Israel also poses a specific challenge to the relations between these two religions. Whereas Christian tradition claims the fulfillment in Jesus Christ of Israel's messianic expectations, for Israel the fulfillment is yet to come. Similarly, in Hinduism, embodiment as the way to the knowledge

37. Moltmann, *God in Creation*, pp. 244-45.

38. Ward, *Religion and Revelation*, p. 194.

39. Ward, *Religion and Revelation*, p. 195.

40. Ward, *Religion and Revelation*, p. 194. See also p. 196: "Christ does not narrow the Jewish vocation to just one person; he expands it until it spreads throughout the world, by internalizing and universalizing its teaching."

of the divine is not an absolutely foreign idea. The Jesuit expert on Hindu-Christian relations Francis X. Clooney speaks to this issue in his important discussion on "making sense of divine embodiment":[41]

> Many Christian and Hindu theologians agree that there is a God, maker of the world, and that there is only one such God, possessed of certain superlative qualities and likely to act in certain proper ways. Though God is mystery, God can be known well enough that he can be named. . . . Many of these same theologians . . . also hold that there are advantages and problems connected with asserting further that the God who makes the world could or should also have a body, as a necessary instrument for making things or for other kinds of activities in the world.[42]

Life-Giving Spirit and Living Revelation

In a healthy trinitarian grammar, the loving Father sends his Son, the Word made flesh, in the power and energies of the Holy Spirit.[43] 1 Corinthians 2:9-14 puts it succinctly:

> But, as it is written, "What no eye has seen, nor ear heard, nor the heart of man conceived, what God has prepared for those who love him," God has revealed to us through the Spirit. For the Spirit searches everything, even the depths of God. For what person knows a man's thoughts except the spirit of the man which is in him? So also no one comprehends the thoughts of God except the Spirit of God. Now we have received not the spirit of the world, but the Spirit which is from God, that we might understand the gifts bestowed on us by God. And we impart this in words not taught by human wisdom but taught by the Spirit, interpreting spiritual truths to those who possess the Spirit. The unspiritual man does not receive the gifts of the Spirit of God, for they are folly to him, and he is not able to understand them because they are spiritually discerned.

---

41. Title of chap. 4 in Clooney, *Hindu God, Christian God*, p. 94.

42. Clooney, *Hindu God, Christian God*, p. 94.

43. Rightly, revelation can be located under pneumatology as in Grenz, *Theology for the Community of God*, chap. 14.

Where tradition has usually failed is to jump directly from this biblical statement and similar passages to the consideration of the Spirit's role in inspiration and illumination without considering the wider horizon of the Spirit's ministry. Moltmann rightly remarks that to "see the Spirit at work only in the verbal inspiration of scripture is a reduction of the mighty efficacy of God the Spirit."[44] Without in any way diminishing this important ministry, there is a wider, more inclusive trinitarian linking of the Spirit with the process of revelation, not only its medium, the Scripture. Here again, Grenz gets it right: "The Spirit's mission is to complete the program of the triune God in the world. To this end, he is the Creator Spirit. Not only is he the source of life, the Spirit is the power of the eschatological renewal of life. He is the agent who brings into being the new creation (2 Cor. 5:17)."[45]

To set in a wider trinitarian framework the more specific ministry of the Spirit with regard to inspiration and illumination, we should remind ourselves of the foundational role of the Spirit in the world as the Spirit of Life. From the beginning of the biblical narrative, the Spirit's role in creation, as the principle of life, comes to the fore. The same Spirit of God that participated in creation over the chaotic primal waters (Gen. 1:2) is the principle of human life (Gen. 2:7) as well as life in the cosmos at large (Ps. 104:29-30). In this framework, Moltmann brilliantly argues, we can perceive

> the function of scripture *in the trinitarian history of God.* . . . In the perspective of the eschatological finality of the death and resurrection of Christ, scripture is *closed* and complete. Christ "died to sin once for all, but the life he lives he lives to God" (Rom 6.10). . . . But in the perspective of the Pentecostal beginning of the eschatological experiences of the Spirit, scripture is *open.* The eschatological experience of the Spirit is itself the *future* of scripture. . . . With this future "the fulfillment of scripture" in the kingdom of God begins. In this respect we have to understand "what is written" in the great framework of God's economy of the Spirit.[46]

If God is the "author" of Scripture in general, then "the Bible is the Spirit's book,"[47] both in its inspiration and its appropriation in daily life by the people of God. Of this part of the Spirit's ministry *Dei Verbum* says this:

44. Moltmann, *Experiences in Theology,* p. 136.
45. Grenz, *Theology for the Community of God,* p. 379.
46. Moltmann, *Experiences in Theology,* pp. 144-45.
47. Grenz, *Theology for the Community of God,* p. 379.

"The obedience of faith" (Rom. 16:26; see 1:5; 2 Cor. 10:5-6) "is to be given to God who reveals, an obedience by which man commits his whole self freely to God, offering the full submission of intellect and will to God who reveals," and freely assenting to the truth revealed by Him. To make this act of faith, the grace of God and the interior help of the Holy Spirit must precede and assist, moving the heart and turning it to God, opening the eyes of the mind and giving "joy and ease to everyone in assenting to the truth and believing it." To bring about an ever deeper understanding of revelation the same Holy Spirit constantly brings faith to completion by His gifts. (#5)

The Spirit's illuminating work in revelation and Scripture should never be made external to the truth the message carries, as has happened at times in the well-meant Pietistic turn to subjective certainty as a response to an alleged lack of certainty of truth. Nor can it be made a merely subjective, individual experience. Reacting against classical liberalism's conception of the inspiration of Scripture as the function of our faith, Barth rightly warned that it is not our faith but the power of God that underlies the inspiration of the Bible.[48] A remedy against this kind of danger is what has been called Barth's "objective pneumatology," his conviction that the Spirit in speaking to us cannot be collapsed into human subjectivity or experience.[49] As Barth wrote, "[t]he witness of Holy Scripture is therefore the witness of the Holy Spirit."[50] In this unified witness of Spirit and text, we are not just speaking of our *experience* of the divine Word, "but its actual presence."[51] Of course, our reception of the Spirit's witness is always colored by human subjectivity, and our interpretations of the Bible always threaten to take the Bible captive, but Barth is confident that the Spirit's speaking through the text "is objective enough to emerge victorious from all the inbreaks and outbreaks of man's subjectivity."[52]

The pneumatological framing of revelation in a healthy trinitarian framework helps us see the wideness of God's love toward all men and women, created in God's image, and indeed, toward the whole of creation. Rightly the late Canadian Baptist theologian Clark Pinnock remarks: "There is a cosmic range to the operations of the Spirit, the Lord and giver of life. . . . Spirit is the ecstasy that implements God's abundance and triggers the overflow of divine

---

48. Barth, *CD* I/2, p. 534.
49. See J. Thompson, *Holy Spirit in the Theology of Karl Barth.*
50. Barth, *CD* I/2, p. 538.
51. Barth, *CD* I/2, p. 533.
52. Barth, *CD* I/2, p. 534.

self-giving. . . . The universe in its entirety is the field of its operations."[53] Hence, we should not make "God's leading into the truth to be a matter of only parochial interest. It should be placed in a global setting, because God's interests are much wider than the church. God is self-revealed in creation and history as well as in the experiences of Israel and the story of Jesus. God does not leave himself without witness among the nations. . . . The Spirit is guiding, luring, wooing, influencing, drawing all humanity, not just the church. . . . Not everyone listens, but God speaks to all."[54]

Because revelation is a triune event, the Word made flesh, indeed, it is an *event* rather than an *idea;* it is linked to the history of this world. Revelation is made *historical;* this distinctively Christian view of divine revelation is a most unique feature among religions.

53. Pinnock, *Flame of Love,* pp. 49-50.
54. Pinnock, *Flame of Love,* p. 216.

3. Revelation as Historical-Eschatological Word of Promise

Theology of History

The incarnation and cross happen in the history of this world. Hence, the Christian doctrine of revelation cannot be constructed apart from a careful reflection on the meaning of history and its relation to God speaking to us. Here the expression "theology of history" merely denotes a reflection on the *theological* meaning and significance of historical events for Christian theology of revelation.

It is a commonplace to say — in my understanding rightly — that whereas Asiatic faiths are cosmic in orientation, the Semitic religions are historical. The difference between Christian and Hindu views of history illustrates this point. The meaningfulness and validity of Christian claims to the unique personhood and ministry of Jesus Christ require historical factuality for decisive events such as the crucifixion and resurrection. The Hindu belief in a number of divine embodiments, *avataras,* does not demand historical backing. Indeed, rightly understood, keeping deities divorced from the strictures of historical happenings makes them more "real," as they are not subject to the transience and "appearance-nature" of reality. "The Mahayanist believer is warned — precisely as the worshipper of Krishna is warned in the Vaishnavite scriptures that the Krishna Lila is not a history, but a process for ever unfolded in the heart of man — that matters of historical fact are without religious significance" (except, we should add, insofar as they point to or themselves constitute the means — whether remote or proximate, whether political, ethical, or spiritual — by which men may come to deliverance from selfness and the temporal order).[1] No wonder the Western mystic Aldous Huxley in his *Perennial Philosophy* (1945) endorses this statement in his attack on what he saw as Christian theology's "idolatrous preoccupation with events and things in time."[2] If historical events are merely an "appearance," as the Vedic teaching has it, then rootedness with history is a great delusion. "But what if history and time, particularity, creativity, and novelty, are fundamental features of the real world, and not just illusions of the limited ego? . . . What if human history is the arena wherein is played out the drama of the seeking of an active personal God for persons who have become alienated from God . . . ? Then events in time could hardly be overevaluated, since the temporal would be the place of a real and developing set of relationships between the Supreme and its creations."[3]

When history matters, it means that unlike the Hindu *avataras* who come to reestablish the eternal law *(sanatana dharma)*, Jesus announces and inaugurates in his person and ministry the kingdom of God, the righteous rule that has already appeared in his coming and is yet to come in its fullness in the eschaton. Jesus' meaning and significance are anchored in the particular history of the Jewish people and the widening out of this particular hope into the universal vision of salvation.

The Semitic faiths are not only anchored in history in a general sense, but more than that, they are anchored in a particular history of their forefather Abraham. Calling Judaism, Christianity, and Islam *Abrahamic* faiths is thus appropriate. They all invoke the "God of Abraham, Isaac, and Jacob" even in the midst of many debates and questions of this invocation's meaning. Whereas the cosmic religions see their gods manifested and evident in the laws and rhythms of the cosmos, the Semitic religions discern the existence and acts of God in history. Appeal to that particular history is at the same time the "experience of estrangement and hope, exile and future,"[4] as the Father of Faith is called to leave behind his home and begin the long journey toward the Promised Land (Gen. 12:1-3). Historical faith is a constant journey, a time of testing, an opportunity to trust in God's faithfulness over and over again. This brings to light the dramatic difference between the Semitic and Asiatic religions. Whereas the cosmic religions intend to bring people into harmony

---

1. Quoted in A. Huxley, *The Perennial Philosophy,* pp. 51-52 (without citing the original source, which I was not able to trace).

2. A. Huxley, *The Perennial Philosophy,* p. 52. I am indebted to Ward, *Religion and Revelation,* p. 197, for pointing me to this phrase in the book.

3. Ward, *Religion and Revelation,* pp. 197-98.

4. Moltmann, *Experiences in Theology,* p. 29.

with the eternal laws of nature, the historical religions encounter constantly "the lack of security and the vulnerability which are the consequence of departure from the shelter of natural and social environments."[5]

Historical religions take time seriously. For nomadic people, there is the past, what was left behind, and there is the future, what is hoped for. This is linear time: from beginning, to today, to telos, the hoped-for end goal. In Asiatic religions, time is cyclical. The future is not "new"; it is a repeat. For Abrahamic religions the "future brings something new and does not repeat what is past."[6] Remembering the past invokes divine acts of deliverance that still have bearing on today and anticipate the future, "a new thing" (Isa. 43:19).

Brilliantly Moltmann remarks that in the modern world and theology, the "end of history" has happened: through historical criticism the processes of historical "becoming" have been historicized "into hard facts and circumstances of the past"; through "unnumbered 'remembrance days' we transform unique events of history . . . into the eternal return of the same thing"; and "[i]n place of living remembrances and the traditions moulded by memories, today we have data-processing through the computerization of all the facts that we can lay hold of." The computer's memory, however, "does not remember . . . it merely 'stores.'"[7]

Revelation in History

Around the mid–twentieth century, Christian theology of revelation rediscovered the importance of the category of history.[8] First there emerged a movement appropriately called the "salvation history" school.[9] Without rejecting the traditional idea of God revealing himself or God speaking, the salvation historical approach conceived of revelation mainly in terms of divine historical acts and events. *Revelation as History*, by Pannenberg and his circle (1961), represents an even more radical turn to history. Rather than a particular "salvation history," universal history is the arena of God's revelation. In a sharp attack on all forms of neo-orthodox interpretations of revelation in terms of

---

5. Moltmann, *Experiences in Theology*, p. 30.

6. Moltmann, *Experiences in Theology*, p. 31.

7. Moltmann, *Experiences in Theology*, p. 42.

8. See Baillie, *Idea of Revelation in Recent Thought*, pp. 49-50; Barr, "Revelation through History," p. 62.

9. Temple, "Revelation and Its Mode," pp. 301-25; G. E. Wright, *God Who Acts*; Cullmann, *Christ and Time*.

God's *self*-revelation,[10] and especially on the Barthian severance of revelation from all historical connections, Pannenberg boldly announced:

> Revelation is no longer understood in terms of a supernatural disclosure or of a peculiarly religious experience and religious subjectivity, but in terms of the comprehensive whole of reality, which, however, is not simply given, but is a temporal process of a history that is not yet completed, but open to a future, which is anticipated in the teaching and personal history of Jesus. *To speak of revelation in this way does not involve any irreducible claims to authority, but is open to rational discussion and investigation.* . . . Instead of the authoritarian style of theological thought, the open rationality of the Enlightenment is preferred, but combined with a concern for the substance of the Christian tradition.[11]

This turn to history is diametrically opposed to not only Barth and other neo-orthodox but also to theologians such as Tillich (who of course was also highly influenced by neo-orthodoxy), who believed "Historical investigations should neither comfort nor worry theologians. . . . [Their] truth is to be judged by criteria which lie within the dimension of revelatory knowledge."[12]

The key claims in the revelation-as-history approach include the indirect nature of God's revelation in the forms of historical acts of God (thesis #1); its orientation to eschatology as it is only at the end that revelation can be completely comprehended (#2), although it has already provisionally happened in the resurrection of Jesus from the dead (#6); its openness to "anyone who has eyes to see" because "[i]t has a universal character" (#3); and its linkage in the person of Jesus with the history of Israel (##4, 5). What, then, is the role of Scripture? Rather than a "deposit of divine revelation," as in tradition, Scripture contains promise ("foretelling"); "forthtelling," indicating the will of God toward his people; and "kerygma," proclamation (which Pannenberg oddly calls "report"). Whereas the first two functions arise out of the history of Israel, the third one (proclamation) emerges for the first time in the NT (#7).[13] Even though in the first volume of *Systematic Theology* the mature Pannenberg specifies and amplifies the original approach by including a highly nuanced

---

10. As Pannenberg argues, in the introduction to *Revelation as History*, pp. 3-8.

11. Pannenberg, "Preface to the American Edition," in *Revelation as History*, p. ix, emphasis added.

12. Tillich, *ST* 1:130.

13. Pannenberg, "Dogmatic Theses on the Doctrine of Revelation," in *Revelation as History*, pp. 135, 153.

investigation of the idea of revelation in the biblical data[14] and both corrects and balances the downplaying of revelation as Word by titling the section "Revelation as History and as Word of God,"[15] as well as acknowledging the "brokenness of revelation,"[16] he still advocates the same basic orientation.

What is the value of the turn to history for a contemporary theology of revelation? Certainly, it is a healthy antidote to the positivism — and, hence, many would say "fideism" — of neo-orthodox theology. Christian faith as a historical religion, along with Judaism and Islam, cannot afford to ignore the deeply historical rootage of its "foundations." Saint Paul seems to argue the same in 1 Corinthians 15:12-15 concerning the factuality of Christ's resurrection.

That said, one has to specify carefully what kind of turn to history is theologically and epistemologically most appropriate. The salvation historical approach should not be dismissed in the way Pannenberg tends to do. Historical happenings are not "self-evident." Where one person sees the hand of God, someone else sees either chance or evil or nothing. Ironically, Pannenberg's claim that universal history is open to all eyes is no more "neutral" than the salvation historical claim because it takes an eye of faith to see God acting in history. Neither exodus nor the conquest of the land entails only a religious, let alone Christian, explanation. Many people can attribute to their deities similar kinds of historical events. The point John's Gospel makes is that not only most of the Gentiles but also nearly all of his own people, when they saw the one "full of grace and truth," completely failed to see "his glory, glory as of the only Son from the Father" (John 1:14). The historical event of Jesus' resurrection did not easily convince even the "insiders," the first believing women and disciples. True, these events took place in "secular" history, but the events of secular history can receive more than one interpretation. Interpretations are tradition-laden.

That said, I am not denying the historical rootage of Christian claims. Just consider Christ's resurrection. If it were merely an "inner experience" of the believing disciples without any historical validity, its theological value would be frustrated to the point of making it meaningless. On the other hand, it would be utterly naive to believe that by its own rational power resurrection could convince "everyone who has eyes to see." Hence, a radical middle way between Pannenberg and the salvation history school should be the goal. It

---

14. Pannenberg, *ST* 1:198-214, at 198.

15. The title of the last section of the discussion of the doctrine of revelation in *ST* 1 (pp. 230-58).

16. Pannenberg, *ST* 1:250; see also pp. 249-51.

seems to me that is indeed what Pannenberg is unconsciously, and against his intentions, expressing when, in *Revelation as History,* he says: "When these [events which reveal God] are taken seriously for what they are, and in the historical context to which they belong, then they speak their own language, the language of facts. God has proved his deity in this language of facts."[17] His expression, "taken seriously for what they are," is an admission that only from a certain perspective can the salvific events be discerned as such, namely, *salvific.* Then and only then, they "speak their own language"! (What still bothers me greatly about the rest of the statement is the claim that "God has proved his deity in this language of facts." There is hardly a way God will "prove" his deity.)

Behind Pannenberg's insistence on universal history as the main locus of divine revelation is a problematic epistemological naivete as expressed in the longer quotation above, namely, that "Instead of the authoritarian style of theological thought, the open rationality of the Enlightenment is preferred, but combined with a concern for substance of the Christian tradition."[18] One doesn't have to be a particular type of postmodernist to shy away from such a modernist-driven epistemological claim. There are a number of other highly problematic claims in this short statement (written a few years after *Revelation as History*), including the meaning and conditions of the terms "open rationality" and "authoritarian." Any claim to "open" rationality made with the terms "objective," "neutral," "unbiased," or "interest-free" is highly suspicious. Furthermore, the attempt to get rid of an authoritarian notion of revelation is hardly that; rather, it seems to me, it is an attempt to replace one type of authority — "divine" — with "scholarly historical" authority. While Pannenberg is well aware of the dangers of subjecting Christian revelation and faith to the pressure of the shifting results of scholarly disagreements — as Jesus research most dramatically has shown us during the past two hundred years — his approach is in danger of that.

Be that as it may, going back to my claim above that even the key biblical events are not "open to anyone who has eyes to see," it is not enough to speak of the "brokenness of revelation." That is a move in the right direction, but does not suffice. Other factors that Christian tradition considers as causing the "blindness" include the fallen nature of humanity, which, while not completely frustrating the discernment process, impedes it in a significant way. Furthermore, according to tradition, the finite, human mind needs to be

---

17. Pannenberg, "Dogmatic Theses," p. 137.
18. Pannenberg, preface to *Revelation as History,* p. ix.

enlightened and empowered by the Spirit of God. When speaking of the brokenness of revelation, Pannenberg mentions the important biblical insight that apostolic preaching of the gospel "imparts the life-giving Spirit of God" and "spreads abroad the radiance that shines from Christ's own glory" (see 2 Cor. 4:2-4). In other words, "the word of the apostolic message is Spirit-filled in virtue of its content, and for this reason can impart the Spirit."[19] Pannenberg's claim deserves full-hearted affirmation and important revision. The reason he has been so critical of any reference to the Spirit as a way of confirming the validity of divine revelation has to do with the legitimate, but one-sidedly expressed, fear stemming from neo-orthodoxy's dismissal of history and Pietism's replacement of historical "evidence" with "inner certainty." He fears that referring to the Spirit in this context is nothing but "supplement[ing] an event which is dumb and dull as such."[20] Of course, reference to the Spirit in terms of making true something that is not true, has to be rejected. But why cannot the reference to the Spirit as the condition of the "spiritual" discernment of the meaning of salvific events such as Israel's exodus or Christ's resurrection, rather than being an attempt to change the event to something that it truly is not, be a divine aid, helping the human person to discern its true meaning? I do not see why that would necessarily be, as Pannenberg fears, "a gnostic knowledge of secrets."[21]

Moltmann makes the important observation that the "universal history" school's strict insistence on *historical* validation of its claims such as that of Christ's resurrection raises the question of the meaning of "history." In other words, how far can one stretch the notion of "historical" happening without making its meaning equivocal in relation to ordinary history?

> The thesis that this event of the raising of Jesus must be "historically" verifiable in principle, would require us first of all so to alter the concept of the historical that it would allow of God's raising of the dead and would make it possible to see in this raising of the dead the prophesied end of history. To call the raising of Jesus historically verifiable is to presuppose a concept of history which is dominated by the expectation of a general resurrection of the dead as the end and consummation of history. Resurrection and the concept of history then contain a vicious circle for the understanding.[22]

19. Pannenberg, *ST* 1:249-50, at 250.
20. Pannenberg, *ST* 1:249.
21. Pannenberg, "Dogmatic Theses," p. 135.
22. Moltmann, *Theology of Hope*, p. 82.

Moltmann's in many ways useful criticism of Pannenberg's claim to historical verification must be affirmed but also qualified. Like Moltmann, the "universal history" school must pay much closer attention to the *meaning* of history. Unlike Moltmann, however, the Christian claim to Christ's resurrection can still be based on historical factuality, albeit not necessarily in a "self-evident" and "self-explanatory" way, as Pannenberg claims, and with much more epistemological modesty and humility. At its best, it can be accepted as a confident Christian claim that awaits final eschatological validation. If we interpret Christ's resurrection merely as a "suprahistorical" claim, as Moltmann seems to be doing, both its *historical* and its *theological* meaning are jeopardized, as I argue in my discussion of Christ's resurrection in the volume on Christology. In other words, Pannenberg's appeal to the historicity of key salvific events should not be dismissed; it just has to be qualified and put in a different epistemological and theological perspective, as I have attempted to do here.

The conclusion from the discussion so far is that, first, the historical nature of the trinitarian divine revelation is to be viewed through both the lens of "salvation" and the lens of "universal" history because there is indeed only one history, as there is one God, the Creator and Sustainer. Second, because history is an ambiguous concept, the finite, fallible, and fallen human mind needs the enlightening and clarifying aid of the Holy Spirit, which, however, does not mean that events that are not really true would be made to appear so only to the pious mind. Third, historical theology is always bound to the Word and vice versa. To clarifying that link we turn next.

Revelation as History and as Word[23]

Pannenberg's proposal suffers from a one-sided rejection of, or — as in his mature theology of revelation — a marginalizing role of, God's direct communication. It seems to me that no amount of hermeneutics helps us get around the fact that in a number of instances in the biblical narrative Yahweh/Father of Jesus Christ seems to be speaking directly to humanity, and that is to be considered revelation. Consider this familiar passage of Numbers 12:5-8: "And the LORD came down in a pillar of cloud, and stood at the door of the tent, and called Aaron and Miriam; and they both came forward. And he said, 'Hear my words: If there is a prophet among you, I the LORD make myself known to him

23. The title owes to Pannenberg, *ST* 1:230-58.

in a vision, I speak with him in a dream. Not so with my servant Moses; he is entrusted with all my house. With him I speak mouth to mouth, clearly, and not in dark speech; and he beholds the form of the LORD.' "[24] Pannenberg is of course right in insisting that even these kinds of sayings do not exhaustively "reveal" who Yahweh is. That observation certainly applies to Exodus 3:14-15, the pinnacle of divine self-revelation in the OT narrative. That said, however, the counterpoint is that Christian tradition has never meant by "revelation" the total unveiling of God. God remains as infinite mystery.

The divine Word, as a means of direct communication, may indeed amplify, clarify, and thus "add to" the revelation taking place in events and other modes. Pannenberg's fear that any "addition" or clarification by the Word to the meaning of the event would mean something external and foreign to the process of revelation is simply an unwarranted and highly suspect presupposition.

The way *Dei Verbum* links words and deeds seems to provide the needed balance between tradition's at times too-limited emphasis on the revelatory power of the Word and a Pannenbergian focus on historical events: "This plan of revelation is realized by deeds and words having an inner unity: the deeds wrought by God in the history of salvation manifest and confirm the teaching and realities signified by the words, while the words proclaim the deeds and clarify the mystery contained in them" (#2). Commenting on this passage, Avery Dulles rightly remarks that "neither word nor event is revelation apart from the other. . . . Any act of God, expressing a divine intention, possesses features of word and of deed alike."[25] The dual meaning of the Hebrew term *dabar* as "word" and "event" confirms the principle of mutual conditioning and inner unity of the revealing word and God's acts in history.[26]

In his turn to the dramatic (as in drama) imagination of the nature of theology, Kevin Vanhoozer rightly reminds us of the fallacy of positing acts and words — action and speech — as antagonistic to each other. "Theo-drama" is both "divine speech and action." From the beginning of the Bible, God "does" many things with speech. "And God said, 'Let there be light'; and there was light" (Gen. 1:3). The word of God is "living and active" (Heb. 4:12). Hence, theology needs to rediscover the nature of the word of God "as something God both says and does."[27] In other words, "The gospel is something *said* about

24. See further, Dulles, *Models of Revelation*, pp. 62-63.
25. Dulles, *Models of Revelation*, pp. 66-67.
26. Dulles, *Models of Revelation*, p. 67.
27. Vanhoozer, *Drama of Doctrine*, pp. 44-45. I have deleted the italics in the original.

something *done.* Yet just as God's word has been prised apart from Scripture, so has it been prised apart from his acts." The turn to history, either salvation history or universal history, need not be dismissive of words if it understands that *"Speaking is one of God's mighty acts."*[28]

An Eschatological-Historical Promise

God acts and speaks in history with a view to the future redeeming of divine promises. "Even linguistically the concept of revelation came to be associated with a future divine self-demonstration. 'The glory of the Lord shall be revealed, and all flesh shall see it together' (Isa. 40:5)."[29] This introduces the concepts of promise and hope — hopeful expectation of God's self-vindication and showing of his faithfulness in the future.

The publication of Moltmann's *Theology of Hope* in the mid-1960s launched a new movement called "theology of hope."[30] Taking its cue from the rediscovery of eschatology and the apocalyptic in NT theology initiated by Johannes Weiss and Albert Schweitzer, among others, at the turn of the twentieth century, as well as from Barth, to whom only theology that is thoroughly eschatological can be Christian theology, this Reformed German theologian moved eschatology from the margins to the center. Indeed, for him eschatology is not only the first chapter of theology but also its underlying motif. If so, the "turn to the future" would have bearing on all theological topics. Because God's future for us is "open," it is new, not merely an extension of the past. Reality is not predetermined but is historical in nature and under constant process and development, awaiting and hoping for the future. Future is ontologically prior to present and past. In this outlook, revelation has to do with hope, future. According to Moltmann, "the eschatological outlook is characteristic of all Christian proclamation, of every Christian existence and of the whole Church."[31]

Unlike Greek philosophy, "which sees in the *logos* the epiphany of the eternal present of being and finds the truth in that," in the Bible it was "in the hope-giving word of promise that Israel found God's truth. That is why history was here experienced in an entirely different and entirely open form."[32] In the biblical worldview, hope is expressed in terms of promise. Promise becomes

28. Vanhoozer, *Drama of Doctrine,* p. 46.
29. Pannenberg, *ST* 1:193.
30. For a brief discussion, see Kärkkäinen, "Hope, Theology of," pp. 404-5.
31. Moltmann, *Theology of Hope,* p. 16,
32. Moltmann, *Theology of Hope,* pp. 40-41.

the main revelatory category. In keeping with this refocus, Moltmann makes a distinction between the biblical "religion of promise" and the "epiphany religions of the revealed gods" of religions surrounding Israel.[33] The former is the religion of the nomadic people in search of the Land. What is remarkable about the Israelite faith is that even when Israel settled down and left behind the nomadic life of being constantly on the move, Israel did not leave behind the nomadic religion of promise![34]

Now, this promise, which looks into the future but is fully anchored in history and its unfolding, comes to us both as word and as act. Rightly then, we can say, "At the heart of the theo-drama, is a series of divine promises and fulfillments. The divine will-to-promise is not a gesture of oppression, a violent imposition of power, but a gesture of generosity, an initiative taken on behalf of another."[35] This promise is not an empty word. Rather, promise is rightly said to be a "speech-act."[36] As Luther put it, promise is *Tat-Wort* rather than *Deute-Wort*, something "done" rather than only "meaning."[37] God's promise has "backing" since God can deliver the promises; humans cannot. In this case, the divine promise can be rendered a *pro-missio*, a "sending-ahead of what is to come."[38] It is making future "present" in terms of anticipation.

The Reformers rightly intuited the close relationship between promise and faith as for them the gospel was a promise. In contrast, Protestant orthodoxy lost this connection and brought about the dualism between revelation and reason.[39] This divorced revelation from history and future hope, and made it an abstract theologico-philosophical concept.

The promissory nature of revelation makes it a dynamic, tension-filled category. "Hope's statements of promise . . . must stand in contradiction to the reality which can at present be experienced. They do not result from experiences, but are the condition for the possibility of new experiences."[40] The promise of Christ's resurrection,[41] the "anchor" of concrete hope, illustrates

33. Chap. 2 of Moltmann, *Theology of Hope,* is devoted to a detailed discussion of this theme under the heading "History and Promise."

34. See Moltmann, *Theology of Hope,* pp. 96-97 particularly.

35. Vanhoozer, *Drama of Doctrine,* p. 135.

36. Cf. Austin, *How to Do Things with Words.*

37. See further, Moltmann, *Experiences in Theology,* p. 94.

38. Moltmann, *Experiences in Theology,* p. 102.

39. See further, Moltmann, *Theology of Hope,* p. 44.

40. Moltmann, *Theology of Hope,* p. 18.

41. For a detailed discussion of the theme of "the resurrection and the future of Jesus Christ," see chap. 3 of Moltmann, *Theology of Hope.*

this best. It is against the reality of death and darkness that God's promissory word of hope is tested and lived out. Rising from the dead is not an event in keeping with our experiences but rather something that contradicts human experiences. "Present and future, experience and hope, stand in contradiction to each other in Christian eschatology, with the result that man is not brought into harmony and agreement with the given situation, but is drawn into the conflict between hope and experience."[42] Hence, we need to speak of "the believing hope."[43] Such a "[f]aith takes up this contradiction [between death and life] and thus becomes itself a contradiction to the world of death."[44] Living out this tension-filled life in faith is the only way to be convinced of God's faithfulness, a theme present everywhere in the biblical narrative. Hence "remembering" the salvific acts of Yahweh, as well as the salvific acts of God's Messiah of the new covenant, is a constant reminder to the people of God.[45]

Turning to the future, embracing the hope's promise, does not, however, lead to contempt for the present. It may but it shouldn't. "The hope that is staked on the *creator ex nihilo* becomes the happiness of the present when it loyally embraces all things in love, abandoning nothing to annihilation but bringing to light how open all things are to the possibilities in which they can live and shall live."[46] Moltmann reminds us that hope is not only, or merely, a "noble quality of the heart," but rather it is also a "thinking" hope. "Faith hopes in order to know what it believes."[47]

Moltmann's turn to promise as the framework for the Christian theology of revelation calls for both affirmation and correction. While certainly the biblical teaching makes a close connection between revelation and the promises of Yahweh (exodus, covenants, the conquest of the land, the return from exile), who is none other than the Father of Jesus Christ (resurrection, the pouring out of the Spirit, the coming of the kingdom), the "revelatory" aspect of revelation — in terms of unveiling something hitherto unknown — should not be rejected or set in opposition to promise. This liability of Moltmann's comes to the fore when one considers that even the resurrection of Christ, let alone other promissory events, would not have become such unless God had "revealed" its meaning and significance over the centuries. Nor would Christian faith "know" what to wait for in the future unless God had "unveiled" the

42. Moltmann, *Theology of Hope*, p. 18.
43. Subheading in Moltmann, *Theology of Hope*, p. 19.
44. Moltmann, *Theology of Hope*, p. 21.
45. See further, Moltmann, *Theology of Hope*, p. 109.
46. Moltmann, *Theology of Hope*, pp. 26-32, at 32.
47. Moltmann, *Theology of Hope*, pp. 32-33.

content of that expectation — granted that it is fragmentary, tentative, and finite because of human limitations. Even Moltmann's comment that "Promise announces the coming of a not yet existing reality from the future of the truth"[48] makes sense only if there is some kind of anticipation of what that "truth" is.

Similarly, as true as it is that the promise does not primarily "have the function of illuminating the existing reality of the world or of human nature . . . [but rather] contradicts existing reality,"[49] it is also true that this contradiction makes sense only if we anticipate the God of the promise as the God of life, rather than, say, as in theistic Hinduism, as the "Destroyer God" (Shiva). Theistic Hinduism claims to "know" one of its chief gods as the "Destroyer," whereas the Jewish and Christian traditions know God as "Savior" even in the midst of judgment. This is not to see the God of the Bible as the "timeless eternity" of Greek religions, but rather as one who "will be in his coming lordship."[50] Moltmann rightly reminds us that on the basis of God's faithfulness, the knowledge of God in the Bible is less a matter of abstract knowledge but has everything to do with re-cognizing him.[51] That said, re-cognition is hardly possible without a previous *cognition* on the basis of initial revelation. This claim can be sustained even though, as mentioned above, the "revelation" of God to men and women in the Bible already assumes some kind of knowledge of God, as Exodus 3 most strikingly illustrates.

That trinitarian revelation is historical means that it is always oriented toward the future; it is a promise. Because it is based on historical events, the promise is not utopian. This conviction supports and facilitates the act of holding on in faith and patience to the divine promises as recorded in the inspired text of Scripture. Like its dual nature as historical act and word, revelation as promise contains both hope and knowledge. In an attempt to construct a pluriform, integral notion of revelation, reductionist and one-sided accounts of revelation should be resisted.

To that effort belongs also the discussion in the following chapter. The trinitarian revelation that comes to us as act and word, as promise that contains hope and knowledge, is not meant only for the life to come, for the "salvation of the soul." It has everything to do with the realities of this earthly life. This state of affairs brings to light the difference in ethos between Judeo-

---

48. Moltmann, *Theology of Hope*, p. 85.
49. Moltmann, *Theology of Hope*, p. 86.
50. Moltmann, *Theology of Hope*, p. 87.
51. See Moltmann, *Theology of Hope*, pp. 116-17 particularly.

Christian faiths and other living faiths. The Scriptures of the former tradition support socioethical implications and speak of "obedience." Unlike in Islam, it is not merely — or even primarily — a matter of "submission" to the divine, but rather an embodying in one's own life, including the various levels of community, the core values advocated by the Scriptures and profoundly manifested in the Word made flesh.[52] The Jewish Torah, unlike the holy scriptures of Asian religions (particularly of Hinduism), calls for a loving, covenant-based, responsible obedience to God. It is not a matter of an imposed master-slave following of commands, but rather a parent-child picture of familial responsibility. To these ethical, social, political, and other "practical" implications of Christian Scriptures we turn next.

---

52. See further, Moltmann, *Theology of Hope*, pp. 129-34.

4. Liberating Word

"The Biblical Texts as Furthering Life"[1]

Moltmann rightly ridicules "theological systems which do not merely aim to be free of contradictions in themselves, but which aspire to remain uncontroverted from outside too. In these systems, theology becomes a strategy of self-immunization. Systems of this kind are like fortresses which cannot be broken into, but cannot be broken out of either, and which are therefore in the end starved out through public disinterest." While there is no error in the pursuit of coherence, there is in the exclusion of the outside world! Instead, we should pursue missionary and public theology "which participates in 'the sufferings of this present time,' and formulates its hopes for God at the places where contemporaries are and exist. Kingdom-of-God theology intervenes critically and prophetically in the public affairs of a given society, and draws public attention, not to the church's own interests," but to God's kingdom.[2]

Theology of revelation has tended to be abstract, overly intellectual, and "neutral." Whereas abstract theology leads to never-ending intellectual debates, says Moltmann with reference to the doctrine of Christ, "Christopraxis inevitably leads the community of Christ to the poor, the sick, to 'surplus people' and to the oppressed . . . to unimportant people, people 'of no account.'"[3] Liberation theologies and theologians from the Global South have been vocal

---

1. Heading in Moltmann, *Experiences in Theology*, p. 148.
2. Moltmann, *Experiences in Theology*, p. xx.
3. Moltmann, *Way of Jesus Christ*, p. 43.

critics of traditional theologies' exclusive attention to "theory" at the expense of praxis.

God's revelation, if it is *God's* word, is a liberating word, inclusive word, affirmative word — even when it is the word of judgment or it comes to us in the cruciform word. " 'God's Word is not bound.' It is not bound to a patriarchal culture and the disparagement of women, or to a slave-owning society."[4]

In this context, Moltmann speaks of "the biblical texts as furthering life," of hermeneutics of Scripture that attend to the affirming and strengthening of life and holism. Taking his cue from the biblical promise that the Spirit is the Spirit of life and that this Spirit is behind the revelation and Scripture, he lays out this ambitious vision: "What furthers life is whatever ministers to the *integrity of human life* in people and communities . . . whatever ministers to the *integration* of individual life into the life of the community, and the life of the human community into the warp and weft of all living things on earth . . . whatever spreads *reverence for life* and the *affirmation of life* through *love for life* . . . whatever *heals broken relationships and liberates life* that has been oppressed."[5]

Inclusive Word

Against common intuitions, the interpretation of texts is not an innocent act. The African American theologian James H. Evans reminds us that a "reactionary hermeneutic attempts to 'possess' the truth, ignore its own limitations, and protect its own privilege by masking reality rather than letting it come to light."[6] Susan Sontag's now classic *Against Interpretation* reminds us of the precarious nature of any hermeneutic, any reading of the text: "Thus interpretation is not (as most people assume) an absolute value, a gesture of mind situated in some timeless realm of capabilities. Interpretation must itself be evaluated, within a historical view of human consciousness. In some cultural contexts, interpretation is a liberating act. It is a means of revising, of transvaluing, of escaping the dead past. In other cultural contexts, it is reactionary, impertinent, cowardly, stifling."[7]

Hence, an essential task for a liberating and inclusive hermeneutics is to seek to expose the hidden — and, at times, not-so-hidden — motifs and

---

4. Moltmann, *Experiences in Theology*, p. xxii.
5. Moltmann, *Experiences in Theology*, pp. 149-50, at 149.
6. Evans, *We Have Been Believers*, p. 23.
7. Sontag, *Against Interpretation*, p. 7.

agendas behind the reading and interpretation. While human interpretation can never be completely cured of these symptoms, it can become, relatively speaking, an exercise in an inclusive, affirmative, and liberating reading of texts. An important part of that task is to unmask ways of speaking of God "that are exclusively, literally, and patriarchally male," and that have led to patriarchalism, exclusivity, and even oppression.[8] Too often, the Bible has been read through the lens of patriarchy. Christian revelation has been understood in terms of a "male" Divine addressing mostly male humans who then transmit the message to women.[9] Female images, metaphors, and symbols are needed to both challenge and correct the prevailing structures of patriarchalism.[10]

Inclusive talk about God is historically open-ended since the reality of God as mystery is beyond human imagination and can never be contained by any single symbol.[11] That divine discourse is mysterious is not to deny that it is historical and thus context-bound at the same time. Indeed, it is "always and only mediated through an experience that is specifically historical, the changing history of women's self-appraisal and self-naming."[12]

The feminist Elizabeth Johnson reminds us of the following: "Feminist interpretation makes piercingly clear that although egalitarian impulses are discernible in the Bible, the texts as such were written mostly by men and for men in a patriarchal cultural context and reflect this fact."[13] While there might be many reasons for the predominantly male-driven language in the Bible, the (then) contemporary sociopolitical and cultural background certainly plays a major role. That is exactly the reason why, for the sake of liberation and inclusivity, the traditional Christian ways of understanding revelation and doing theology must be subjected to a self-critical assessment in order to establish a more balanced approach. By acknowledging the metaphorical, symbolic, and mythical nature of revelation — in other words, its polyvalent meaning — without rejecting its proper propositional nature, one is given ample resources for the kind of liberative work this Catholic feminist is envisioning: "The healing, redeeming, liberating gestalt of the story of the God of Israel, the God of Jesus, in the midst of the disasters of history, guides the reading of texts, becoming the principle by which some recede

---

8. E. Johnson, *She Who Is*, p. 44.

9. E. Johnson, *She Who Is*, pp. 5, 36-37.

10. E. Johnson, *She Who Is*, 33; see also pp. 4-5.

11. E. Johnson, *She Who Is*, pp. 7, 44-45; for the importance of *image* and imagination in God-talk, see further, pp. 46-47.

12. E. Johnson, *She Who Is*, p. 75.

13. E. Johnson, *She Who Is*, p. 76.

and others, long neglected, advance in importance. In the midst of emerging emancipatory discourse about the mystery of God from the history of women's experience, biblical language about God in female metaphors becomes a precious discovery."[14]

An important aspect of the liberative and inclusive work of the Spirit that also has an integral relation to the Christian doctrine of revelation and Christian discourse deals with a main concern of women: the inclusion — or exclusion — of the body. Beginning her discussion of "revelation in feminist theology and philosophy," Esther Reed frames the topic with these words:

> Why all the fuss recently about God and bodies? Is it the familiar story of those early Christian fathers who supposedly found the body a burden, a prison, a source of temptation, and who longed for the freedom of death and heaven? Are women, brought up within a predominately male tradition, still having to break the taboos of childhood by talking about body parts and bodily functions, especially the messy ones? Are Christian feminists who write about the body capitalizing on a secular trend? Or, is [it] the subject of urgent importance if Christian feminists are to insist upon the indispensability of embodiment to an understanding of revelation?[15]

A related women's concern along with acknowledgment of the bodily nature of human beings is the importance of relationships. Human beings as holistic organisms relate to each other, depend on each other, draw from each other, contribute to each other. Rightly Mary Grey in *The Wisdom of Fools?* seeks to develop a theology of revelation in terms of connectedness, or as she puts it, in terms of making divine communication intelligible as "connected knowing." Grey envisions this connectedness in a most holistic sense, including gender and the relation of human beings to other creatures. "She investigates how embodiment is intrinsic to divine/human communication and articulates a Christian feminist understanding of revelation 'within a theology of mutual relation, as divine communication for our times, the "filter" through which we understand our culture, our identity.' "[16]

These two related concerns arising from feminist critique of traditional Christian theology in general and the doctrine of revelation in particular,

14. E. Johnson, *She Who Is*, pp. 77-78.

15. Reed, "Revelation in Feminist Theology and Philosophy," p. 156; see also Moltmann-Wendel, *I Am My Body*.

16. As paraphrased in Reed, "Revelation in Feminist Theology and Philosophy," p. 158; the citation is from Grey, *Wisdom of Fools?* p. 1.

namely, body/embodiment and relationality/connectedness, should be of great concern to any contemporary Christian vision of revelation. Rediscovering and reclaiming the body — and the physical, the earthly — is an important challenge to Christian theology in general, including particularly pneumatology (discussed in the volume on Spirit and salvation) and the doctrine of revelation. The turn to history, as discussed above, is the first important step in that direction as the foundational Christian claim of the coming in the flesh of the Divine. All notions of gnosticism, with its separation of the bodily, earthly, and "this-worldly" from the divine, godly, and "heavenly," must be uncovered and critiqued. Above, in the trinitarian framework, the theme of embodiment was developed as an essential aspect of the theology of revelation. And of course, trinitarian theology in itself is deeply and essentially relational. The triune God who reveals himself/herself to humanity is the model of eternal, equal, loving relationships. Hence, revelation — as discussed above — is in the first place the loving Father's reaching out to humanity in a number of ways, most prominently in the Word-become-flesh, in the power and energies of the Spirit, in light of the holistic view of the work of God in biblical tradition.[17]

Revelation as Liberation

The important ecumenical hermeneutical document of the Faith and Order Commission of the World Council of Churches, "A Treasure in Earthen Vessels," points to a significant aspect of biblical revelation and Bible reading that has not been minded in the past as it should have been. Under the heading "One Gospel in Many Contexts," the document speaks of Christian communities that live in various cultural, economic, political, and religious contexts. "These are the contexts in which their faith is lived and the Gospel is interpreted and proclaimed. The diversity of contexts in which the churches live calls for engagement with the diverse riches of Scripture." The document points to numerous examples in the biblical materials that support liberation and inclusion, such as that "in a context of social injustice, Mary's Magnificat (Luke 1:46-55; cf. 1 Sam. 2:1-10) and Jesus' inaugural sermon (Luke 4:18, quoting Isa. 42:7) may become a word of hope for the poor and the oppressed"; also, in "a context where Christians are a tiny minority among people of other faiths,

17. For a liberationist rebuttal of gnosticism, see J. K. Carter, *Race*, pp. 11-36, 229-51, and 343-69.

the affirmation of the common humanity of all women and men as created in God's image may turn attention to the presence of the Spirit outside the Christian churches."[18]

Against this background, a critical question asked by the pioneer black theologian James H. Cone gains new significance: "Why is it that the idea of *liberation* (inseparable from the biblical view of revelation) is conspicuously absent in theological discussions about the knowledge of God?"[19] Could one of the reasons be, Cone asks, that because the Nicene Fathers were not slaves themselves, their theology was removed from history and the realities of the world, and consequently, they saw salvation in spiritual terms alone?[20] Similarly, the Cuban-born Hispanic American Justo L. González laments that so few Christians, particularly those in the majority and in places of power, realize "the political agenda" in the Bible.[21] Even worse, these Bible readers assume not to be political themselves, as they do not stick with the liberationist or political agenda — without understanding that by default their Christianity is deeply embedded and engaged in politics, whether "left" or "right" wing!

As an alternative to this kind of allegedly universal, noncommitted, neutral, and objective approach, Cone is "determined to speak a liberating word for and to African American Christians, using the theological resources" at his disposal.[22] This is in keeping with his vision of Christian theology as "*a theology of liberation*. It is a rational study of the being of God in the world in light of the existential situation of an oppressed community, *relating* the forces of liberation to the essence of the gospel, which is Jesus Christ."[23] Any theology, including the theology of revelation, that is not mindful of the work for liberation has to be deemed racist, this passionate black advocate opines.[24] Apart from rhetorical excesses, his remarks make a valid point. Christian theology in general and theology of revelation in particular have been searching too eagerly for universal, neutral, and objective concepts and have neglected the suffering, oppression, and plight of men and women in particular situations. Again, rhetoric aside, Cone's remark is important: "[T]here can be no theology of the gospel which does not arise from an oppressed community. This is

18. Faith and Order, "A Treasure in Earthen Vessels," #38.
19. Cone, *Black Theology of Liberation*, p. 44.
20. Cone, *God of the Oppressed*, p. 181.
21. González, *Mañana*, pp. 83-85.
22. Cone, *Black Theology of Liberation*, p. xii.
23. Cone, *Black Theology of Liberation*, p. 1, emphasis in original.
24. Cone, *Black Theology of Liberation*, p. xiii.

because God is revealed in Jesus as a God whose righteousness is inseparable from the weak and helpless in human society."[25]

The Peruvian Gustavo Gutiérrez rightly remarks that the question of liberation is not a new one but rather a "classic question of the relation between faith and human existence, between faith and social reality, between faith and political action, or in other words, between the kingdom of God and the building up of the world."[26] In Gutiérrez's understanding, this calls us to shift from considering theology primarily as "wisdom," as in the early centuries, or as "rational knowledge," as from the twelfth century on, to considering theology "as critical reflection on praxis."[27] This kind of approach would foster "a greater sensitivity to the *anthropological aspects of revelation.*"[28] This turn to an anthropocentric valuing of divine revelation differs from classical liberalism's subject-driven, immanentist view in which revelation and Scripture are hardly anything more than human beings sharing their insights into religious experiences. The *theologically* grounded liberationist highlighting of the essential link between *theos* and *anthropos* makes the point that the transcendent divine revelation is not so transcendent as not to be rooted in historical process and humanity's experiences but rather something that helps illumine, shape, and critique the life of human being and communities. The French Dominican Yves Congar puts it well: "Seen as a whole, the direction of theological thinking has been characterized by a transference away from attention to the being *per se* of supernatural realities, and toward attention to their relationship with man, with the world, and with the problems and the affirmations of all those who for us represent the *Others.*"[29] Rightly, Gutiérrez notes that "[t]here is no *horizontalism* in this approach."[30]

Cone makes the important observation — easily confirmed by empirical observation — that there seems to be a correlation between a political and a religious/theological conservative mind-set. "Whites who insist on verbal infallibility are often the most violent racists."[31] Unfortunately, the same can be said of other races of Christians as well, and I wonder if the same applies to other religions as well. Fundamentalistic movements tend to be antagonistic

25. Cone, *Black Theology of Liberation*, p. 5.
26. Gutiérrez, *A Theology of Liberation*, p. 45.
27. Gutiérrez, *A Theology of Liberation*, pp. 4-6.
28. Gutiérrez, *A Theology of Liberation*, p. 7.
29. Congar, *Situation et Tâches Présentes de la Théologie*, p. 27, cited and translated in Gutiérrez, *A Theology of Liberation*, pp. 7-8.
30. Gutiérrez, *A Theology of Liberation*, p. 8.
31. Cone, *Black Theology of Liberation*, p. 32.

to sexual inclusivity, including ministry opportunities for women and other minorities. Such believers hold on to the absolute inerrancy of Scripture, as exegeted in their own communities, often with little critical engagement of other hermeneutical traditions; "[l]iteralism thirsts for the removal of doubt in religion, enabling believers to justify all kinds of political oppression in the name of God and country." Following that mind-set, during the years of American slavery, slaves were advised to be obedient to white masters on the basis of biblical statements to that effect.[32] In the name of Christian love, ethics, and the life-affirming, inclusive work of the Spirit, these kinds of attitudes must be judged and rejected. At the same time, not only those "outsiders" to liberation pursuits but also those "inside" should heed the wise word of advice from Gutiérrez, himself the pioneering Latin American liberationist. Speaking of engaging liberation theology, he says, "It is . . . to let ourselves be judged by the Word of the Lord, to think through our faith, to strengthen our love, and to give reason for our hope from within a commitment which seeks to become more radical, total, and efficacious."[33] True, the word of judgment against beliefs and acts that violate gospel values has to be said by the church that wishes to walk in the footsteps of her Lord. At the same time, as Christians we must be mindful that we stand under the same judgment ourselves. Liberation has to begin from the house of the Lord!

Speaking of "sources" of theology — an ancient topic in Christian tradition — Cone lists revelation and Scripture after black experience, black history, and black culture. While he acknowledges that "[s]ome religionists who have been influenced by the twentieth-century Protestant theologies of revelation will question" his ordering of sources, he adds that "the numerical order of the discussion is not necessarily in order of importance." All the sources, including tradition as the sixth one in Cone's template, are mutually conditioned and interdependent. Cone's important point here is that if "God's self-revelation to the human race [comes] through a historical act of human liberation," then the particular historical situation matters.[34] In this light, our discussion above concerning the historical rootedness of the divine revelation must be complemented with the insight that God's revelation may take place not only in "universal" history (revelation-as-history school) or even in "salvation history" in general, but also in particular contexts, as in the life of the Israelite people under the oppression of the Egyptians. "In the call of Moses God reveals no

---

32. Cone, *Black Theology of Liberation*, p. 32.
33. Gutiérrez, *A Theology of Liberation*, p. ix.
34. Cone, *Black Theology of Liberation*, p. 29.

new knowledge, engenders no new mysticism, but situates God's appearance in the context of and as a response to the enslavement of Israel."[35] That said, the "universal" scope of the divine revelation should not be limited. While it is true that God's revelation happens through the circumstances and experiences of oppression, there are also plenty of instances of revelation in the Bible that are not directly — perhaps not even indirectly — related to specific human oppression or some similar plight. Consider the claim by the Korean female theologian Chung Hyun Kung — famous, or infamous, for her opening address at the 1991 World Council of Churches' General Assembly in Canberra, Australia — "We are the text" and the " 'holy scriptures' are our changing 'context.' "[36] This is half-truth at its best. If any particular human situation, oppressive or not, were really the text, then revelation would be just that, *human*. A much more nuanced, dynamic, and mutually interdependent relationship between the locality and universality of revelation has to be attempted. Another leading black theologian, James H. Evans, formulates this tension succinctly and dynamically:

> The black theologian must relate the "canonical" story, in its prophetic mode, with the "folk" story of a people who hope against hope. To do this the theologian cannot be so immersed in the assurance, optimism, or myopia of the canonical story (the proclamation of the churches) that he or she is unable to see the challenge of the folk story. Conversely, the theologian cannot become so enchanted by the pathos of the folk story or so disillusioned by the tragic dimensions of African-American experience that the hope expressed in the canonical story is not seen. In sum, black theologians must tell a story that relates the hope of the biblical message with the realism of black experience.[37]

When practicing this kind of inclusive and comprehensive rooting of divine revelation in the historical experiences of men and women in their specific communities and circumstances, Cone's emphasis on revelation as *"a black event"*[38] can be put in perspective. Other groups such as Asian Americans — to be more precise, Korean Americans, Vietnamese Americans, Chinese Americans, Japanese Americans, and so forth — may embrace revelation in

---

35. Evans, *We Have Been Believers*, p. 11.
36. Cited in Moltmann, *Experiences in Theology*, p. 138.
37. Evans, *We Have Been Believers*, p. 7.
38. Cone, *Black Theology of Liberation*, p. 30.

a unique manner, even when it is "universal" divine revelation. The emphasis on the particularity and locality of revelation should not be seen as a pretense for replacing one type of exclusivism with another.[39] Instead of exclusivism and rejection of mutual dialogue and learning, an authentic inclusivity and mutually interdependent communion of various kinds of local experiences and contexts should be the aim. The biblical revelation itself, with its bewildering diversity in inclusive unity, is the paragon of this dynamic principle. "God's revelation is both dynamic and multidimensional. Its dynamism is evident in that it takes place in history. It is not an abstract, timeless event, but the manifestation of the will of a living God. The revelation of God is permanent, final, and ultimate in the sense that what we know of God is absolutely trustworthy. All of Christianity stands or falls with the promise of God to be faithful to God's word."[40]

An essential aspect of the dynamic and multidimensional character of revelation is that it is "also contingent, partial, and incomplete in the sense that human history is yet unfolding."[41] In other words, as discussed above, revelation is eschatological. Hence, the category of anticipation and hope: revelation is a promissory event, rooted in history and anchored in the faithfulness of God. For African Americans, for blacks in South Africa and the Caribbean, as well as for masses of oppressed groups in Latin American and Asian contexts, the faithfulness of God, based on the divine revelation in the Word-become-flesh, is a source of hope and strength. This is not an escapist turn. It is not a way to diminish the severity of current suffering and oppression. On the contrary, the continuing work for inclusivity, liberation, and giving opportunities for all receives its strength from the dynamic eschatological hope. The revelation "dynamism lies in the fact that at any given time the desire for liberation is a response to the concrete historical and existential concerns for the oppressed."[42] It also gives meaning to the setbacks and slow progress of this work in a world that itself awaits the final redemption. "There are both novelty and continuity, confirmation and surprise in every encounter between God and humanity."[43]

---

39. Contra Cone, *Black Theology of Liberation*, pp. 62-63.
40. Evans, *We Have Been Believers*, p. 13.
41. Evans, *We Have Been Believers*, p. 13.
42. Evans, *We Have Been Believers*, p. 15.
43. Evans, *We Have Been Believers*, p. 13.

The Liberating Power of Translation

From the polymorphous and multidimensional nature of Christian revelation, deeply embedded in history and cultures, follows its openness to "global"[44] diversity, which comes to us in many dimensions, from gender to culture to religion to nationality to ethnicity and so forth. The term "hybrid" has been taken up by postcolonial thinkers to speak of the bewildering diversity of societies and communities of the third millennium.[45] Similarly, the postcolonial theorist Homi K. Bhabha launched the terms "interstitial perspective," to denote in-between spaces and borderlands, and "interstitial subjectivity," to refer to complex and undefined ways of seeing identities.[46] The subway in a metropolitan area, "[l]ike a great subterranean serpent . . . in the maze beneath the city," full of people of mixed colors, races, dress, languages, dialects, and other characteristic features, may well serve as a fitting metaphor.[47]

Indeed, an essential question for Christian theology from the beginning has been how to "translate" the message in a way that would, on the one hand, come across in the most culturally authentic way, and on the other hand, help local Christians in their specific contexts to embody the gospel in liberating, life-affirming, and inclusive ways. While this challenge has always been with Christian theology — only think of the hybrid nature of earliest Christianity[48] — never before has it been more acute.

Much has been written on the failures of Christian missionaries as agents of colonialism, Western hegemony, and economic and political power plays. With the advent of the postcolonial paradigm, a more nuanced and more deeply exposing critique of forms of colonialism emerged. The term "cultural imperialism" came to be used in a wider and more inclusive sense referring to any cultural dominance, including academic and "high culture." Europe and the United States still hold the power in terms of access to and resources of education and publishing, and above all still possess linguistic hegemony — the use of English. The Christian church and its Scriptures have been closely linked with this colonialistic critique.

To put the missionary translation work of the past in perspective, the

44. For the ambiguity of the term "global," see Kärkkäinen and Dyrness, introduction to *GDT*, pp. vii-xiv.

45. Keller, Nausner, and Rivera, "Introduction," in *Postcolonial Theologies*, p. 1.

46. Bhabha, *The Location of Culture*.

47. "The Subway" is the first subheading in Keller, Nausner, and Rivera, "Introduction," in *Postcolonial Theologies*, p. 1.

48. Keller, Nausner, and Rivera, "Introduction," in *Postcolonial Theologies*, p. 4.

other side of the colonial story that has emerged in the newest missions history has to be highlighted. In this context, we are less concerned about "exonerating" Christian mission; rather, the purpose is to take a closer look at the relation of Scripture and translation work to culture and liberation. The current research has challenged the standard accusation against Christian mission according to which it constituted "colonization of the mind."[49] Similarly, the accusation that missionaries served as agents of "cultural imperialism" has been subjected to critique.[50] For example, the British missions historian Brian Stanley has demonstrated a lack of evidence for the claim that the British churches' support for mission and the peak of British imperialism were correlated.[51] In other words, missionaries did not support but were indeed critical of the way the British rulers were taking advantage of the resources of the colonized lands. Similarly, leading African historians Lamin Sanneh and the late Ogbu Kalu have revealed that at times well-meaning missionaries were used by local leaders as tools to further the local political or economic interests. These missionaries were at times, against their own will, used as instruments of local leaders.

Hence, the translation work, rather than being an agent of Western colonialism, power plays, and exclusivity, more often than not has been in the service of local empowerment, cultural development, ethnic affirmation, and other forms of inclusivity and liberation.[52] According to Sanneh, the translation of the Bible and the gospel story, which helped the vernacular, local languages become important factors in culture, played a crucial role not only in the spread of Christian mission in the non-Western world but also in the liberation of the indigenous people.

> Missionary translation was instrumental in the emergence of indigenous resistance to colonialism. Local Christians acquired from the vernacular translations confidence in the indigenous cause. While the colonial system represented a worldwide economic and military order, mission represented vindication for the vernacular. Local Christians apprehended the significance of world events, and as such the purposes of God, through the familiar medium of mother tongues, with subject peoples able to respond to colonial events in the light of vernacular self-understanding.[53]

49. Stanley, "Conversion to Christianity."
50. Porter, "Cultural Imperialism," p. 373.
51. Stanley, *Bible and the Flag.*
52. See further, Faith and Order, "A Treasure in Earthen Vessels," #41.
53. Sanneh, *Translating the Message,* p. 123. For another important work, see Walls, *Missionary Movement.*

Not only in Africa but also in Asia the same kind of improvement and development as a result of the renewal of the vernacular has been noted. In light of these observations, Sanneh questions the widely prevalent view that mission was little more than "imperialism at prayer." These observations clearly indicate that missionaries were not always, often not at all, acting in the interests of empire. Indeed, on the contrary, a number of recent scholars have suggested that missionary work was influential in raising national consciousness and encouraging independence from empire. Sanneh wonders, given the tremendous growth of Christianity in the postindependence Global South, whether colonialism could have been an *obstacle* to the spread of the Christian faith rather than its facilitator.[54]

The rootedness of Christian revelation in history, not only in salvation history but also in universal world history, including cultural, ethnic, and national diversity, makes translation not only possible but also inevitable and profitable. The Bible, and hence the Christian message and tradition at large, is made for diversity. Aptly the missiologist Andrew F. Walls calls the culture "the workplace of Christian theology."[55] Indeed, "It is a delightful paradox that the more Christ is translated into the various thought forms and life systems which form our various national identities, the richer all of us will be in our common Christian identity."[56] This happens, for example, when there is an "encounter between the life in Asia and the Word of God," as the Japanese Kosuke Koyama expresses it.[57]

The Christian openness to cultural and linguistic diversity goes further and deeper than does the mentality of other living faiths. It is well known that the "orthodox" language of the Qur'an is exclusively Arabic. Speaking of the Book, Q 12:2 states: "We have revealed it as an Arabic Qur'ān, so that you might understand." Hence, the principle of untranslatability is affirmed. This "produces a miss-match between Christians, who probably have no knowledge of biblical languages and who have no objection to Muslims using a translation of the Bible, and Muslims, who insist that an English, or a French 'rendering' of the Qur'an is *not* the Qur'an."[58] According to Muslim Rana Kabbani, the "screen of imperfect translation" of the Qur'an into other languages not only hinders the reader from apprehending the "linguistic triumph" of Arabic, but also makes it a "silent

---

54. Sanneh, *Whose Religion Is Christianity?* p. 18.
55. Walls, *Missionary Movement,* p. 146.
56. Walls, *Missionary Movement,* p. 54.
57. Koyama, "Foreword by an Asian Theologian," p. 13.
58. Bennett, *Understanding Christian-Muslim Relations,* p. 39.

text," and so, inaccessible in its content.[59] The veneration of the Arabic original emanates partly from the common Muslim belief that the Qur'anic scripture represents the purest and most beautiful form of that language.

What about Hindu scriptures? The Vedas are written in Sanskrit. There was a belief especially in the early years of Hinduism that Sanskrit was indeed the sacred language. However, with the spread of devotional compositions, that viewpoint came to be challenged and rejected. While most Hindus, apart from the Brahmins, of course, did not know Sanskrit, they were able to recite devotional verses in the vernacular.[60] This means that in practice Hinduism has a "two-story approach" to the question of translation. On the one hand, there is the deep conviction among many major Hindu traditions that the Vedas, which are considered to be transhuman in origin, "heard" by the *sriti* (the "seers"), have come in the sacred language that is being studied and commented on by the Brahmins. On the other hand, the growing devotional literature emerging among common folks is allowed in the vernacular.[61]

What might be the systematic implications of the Hindu position with regard to "revelation as translation" and the ramifications for facilitating and nurturing cultural differences and identities? Two points could be made. First, unlike the Muslim tradition, the openness of Hinduism to the use and translation of non-Sanskrit scriptures — recall that Hindu scriptures also include many materials apart from the Vedas — is an important step toward the democratization of religious access. Hence, for example, the existence of the Tamil scriptural tradition has nurtured the spiritual life of this significant Indian minority. Second, allowing the use of translation — perhaps somewhat reluctantly at least in the beginning — is just that, *an allowance;*[62] it does not help build local cultures and languages or facilitate liberation and "nation building" in the sense that biblical translations in the context of Christian missionary work have done.

Buddhist tradition, even the most conservative Theravada school, echoes the Christian openness to having scriptural teaching in one's own language. Departing from his Hindu background, Gautama Buddha was apparently open to having his teachings preserved in various local languages. The language of Pali in which the Buddhist "canon" of Tipitaka is written and which is honored by all schools of that religion, is considered no more sacred than is Sanskrit,

---

59. Kabbani, *A Letter to Christendom*, p. 34; I am indebted to Bennett, *Understanding Christian-Muslim Relations*, pp. 39-40.

60. Narayanan, "Hinduism," p. 49.

61. Narayanan, "Hinduism," p. 49.

62. For a useful discussion, see Clooney, *Hindu God, Christian God*, pp. 151-56.

the language for Mahayana traditions. As a result, huge and extensive treasures of sacred literature emerged quite early in Chinese, Japanese, and many other languages.

This comparison of Christian, Islamic, Hindu, and Buddhist traditions ought not to be misunderstood: it is not a contest between religions. The issue is a systematic and constructive analysis of how such a precious and valuable commodity as sacred scripture — very highly regarded in all religious traditions — plays a role in the inclusion, liberation, and embracing of the other. In Christian tradition, all Bible translations are equal in the sense that there is no preferred language, although their accuracy must be checked against the original Greek and Hebrew (as well as small portions of Aramaic) texts. Even the original texts are not considered sacred: indeed, even the beginning student of NT Greek, when studying, for example, the last book of the canon, easily observes how mundane and ordinary the original text is.

"Reading the Bible in Spanish"

This delightful heading comes from the Cuban American Justo González.[63] "Spanish" here does not of course mean merely the Spanish language but also Spanish culture and context. How would a Christian doctrine of revelation look when done in "Spanish" or "Chinese" or "Arabic"?[64] How would Bible hermeneutics function in different locations — and say, in light of postcolonial sensitivity?[65] What would an interpretation of Christian faith and revelation look like on African soil, one that would enable the African to feel at home in his new faith? asks Harry Sawyerr of Sierra Leone.[66] Responding to the biblical question concerning Jesus, "But who do you say that I am?" (Matt. 16:15), Koyama lays out the challenge: "This question comes to Asian Christians, who live in a world of great religious traditions, modernization impacts, ideologies of the left and right, international conflicts, hunger, poverty, militarism, and racism. Within these confusing and brutal realities of history the question comes to them. Here the depth of soul of the East is challenged to engage in a serious dialogue with the Word of God."[67]

63. Title for chap. 5 in González, *Mañana*.
64. An important discussion can be found in Sugirtharajah, ed., *Voices from the Margin*.
65. For such an effort, see Sugirtharajah, *Asian Biblical Hermeneutics*, chap. 1, under the telling title "From Orientalism to Post-Colonialism."
66. Sawyerr, *Creative Evangelism*, pp. 21, 23.
67. Koyama, "Foreword by an Asian Theologian," p. 14.

What about different ways of thinking and arguing? Asian theologians often remind us, the non-Asians, that narrative and (personal) story — along with poems, myths, and folklore — are preferred vehicles of communication of religion and theology in most contexts of that huge continent. As the Chinese David Ng puts it, "one's life story becomes a lifestory, a way of relating the events to providence."[68] Would the rise of narrative theology and biographical theology in the European and American academy help theologians from the Global South to connect more authentically with those aspects of theologies in Asia, Africa, and Latin America?[69]

What about expressing the content of divine revelation as presented in the Bible and Christian tradition in ways other than the propositional, argumentative, "scientific" ways of Western academia? Would discussions of categories like symbol, metaphor, myth, and similar modes help the global church to come into a more inclusive way of communication? Consider the Japanese Masao Takenaka's picture of doing theology in a mood so different from typical modern Western discursive analysis, compatible with ancient cultures of his own context: in his book *God Is Rice,* he calls this an "Ah-hah!" method, a dynamic way of doing theology much closer to the Bible, in which people do not come to know God by discussion or argument but by experiencing him. We "must awaken in ourselves the appreciation of the living reality who is God. In the Bible we have many surprising acknowledgements: 'Ah-hah! In this way, God is working in our world, in a way I did not know.'"[70]

With regard to the African continent, currently the most Christianized of all, the Ghanaian Presbyterian theologian Emmanuel Martey remarks that "[t]he African search for authentic and prophetic theology has at once been a rejection of the dominant Western theological paradigms and an acceptance of African realities and worldview in theological hermeneutics."[71] I would challenge Martey by saying that the search for an authentic African — or Asian or Caribbean — theology should not be seen in terms of rejection of the Western way of doing theology but rather as constructive criticism, reshaping, and revision.

These are all weighty and urgent questions and tasks. It takes a new generation of theologians to work them out, patiently and gradually. What is

68. Ng, "A Path of Concentric Circles," p. 82. For important methodological considerations from an Asian perspective, see also Min, "From Autobiography to Fellowship of Others."

69. The first major monograph on the topic of biographical theology was offered by the late Baptist James McClendon Jr., *Biography as Theology.*

70. Takenaka, *God Is Rice,* p. 9.

71. Martey, *African Theology,* p. xi.

hopeful about the state of contemporary Christian theology is that, while we have made only modest progress toward inclusivity, openness to diversity, and readiness for mutual learning and correction — and there are also opposing forces in the resistance to change of fundamentalism, the ethnocentrism of some church cultures, and the theological impasse regarding the question of ordination and some other ministry opportunities — to a growing degree we see an acknowledgment of the urgency to tackle the implications of globalization, diversity, and locality for Christian theology.

Having established the basis of the divine revelation in the trinitarian act of God — Father, Son, and Spirit — and having anchored it, therefore, in the real history of this earth, in the form of a promise that ultimately looks toward future fulfillment, we considered in some detail the liberative impulses. While the discussion, particularly in this last section, has often mentioned scriptures, we have not yet reflected on the theological meaning and significance of the "inscripturation" of the divine embodiment in Christ. That topic we take up in the next chapter, seeking to formulate an adequate understanding of the coming-to-being in the long history of the people of God of the "divine Word" written in "human words."

5. God's Word in Human Words

Inspiration of Scripture: Divine-Human Dynamic

In Christian tradition until the time of the Enlightenment, inspiration of Scripture had been understood in terms of more or less direct divine influence on human writers and, as in Islam, as a virtual dictation of finished revelation received by the prophet. Behind this traditional understanding of revelation is the assumption that revelation is a more or less timeless and changeless "product." Of course, many nuances have been introduced regarding the exact nature and "technics" of how the inspiration process took place. The spectrum ranges from "dictation theory" to inspiration of words to inspiration of thoughts (but not necessarily individual words), and beyond. Behind the traditional notion of inspiration (to use Christian tradition as an example) is the conviction that the reason why "the books of both the Old and New Testaments in their entirety, with all their parts, are sacred and canonical because written under the inspiration of the Holy Spirit . . . [is that] they have God as their author and have been handed on as such to the Church herself."[1]

The introductory chapter above discussed several developments stemming from the Enlightenment that brought a massive challenge to the traditional notion of the inspiration of Scripture. In response, classical liberalism took its advice from the epistemological and worldview changes and made inspiration virtually a matter of enhancement of human capacities to gain insight into matters of religion. The Bible, after all, in this outlook, is basically

1. *DV,* #11.

an important and unique collection of human testimonies to human religious experiences and human interpretations of those experiences, but it is not authority based on divine inspiration. While that view pays high regard to the Bible, it does not support the traditional idea of Scripture as God's "mouthpiece." Add to these challenges some *theological* changes in the understanding of revelation, discussed in chapter 3. Barth affirmed inspiration, but for him the Scripture functioned as (a fallible) witness to Christ. For Pannenberg, the question of the inspiration of the Bible is virtually circumvented as Scripture's main task is to be a record of historical events. And so forth. So, how would a contemporary Christian view of inspiration of Scripture be formulated in the post-Enlightenment world and in light of radical theological changes?

Modernity's aversion to all notions of divine intervention because of its reductionistic epistemology hardly calls for an extended response. There simply are no compelling reasons why, in light of the mysterious and utterly complicated nature of reality, one should close off one's mind from the possibility of intervention. (How to best understand divine intervention against the current understanding of reality is a topic discussed in detail in the context of the doctrine of creation and providence.) As long as biblical criticism naively followed the naturalist — in other words, atheistic — epistemology, it missed the *religious* and *theological* meaning of Scripture even though it added significantly to our understanding of the historical, cultural, political, anthropological, and similar aspects of sacred writings.

The way forward is not a return to the lost, idyllic pre-Enlightenment mind-set. The value of sober criticism in service of a more reliable knowledge is an undeniable achievement of modernity. Even fundamentalistic believers exercise a critical mind-set in politics, medicine, economics, and other non-theological fields. Rather, contemporary theology of inspiration should begin from the importance of incarnation as the guide to a proper understanding. Incarnation, embodiment, means that the triune God, in the project of divine revelation, is fully embedded in human realities. Finite, fallible human minds can only grasp so much of — and to only a certain degree — mysteries beyond the human mind. Rather than God dictating or mechanistically monitoring the choice of exact words in the communication of revelation, it is better to think of inspiration in terms of "concurrent causality" or "illumination." In this outlook, the humanity of the biblical writers is not set aside but is rather affirmed. On the other side, because we are speaking of *divine* intervention, it is a matter of "more" than just giving eloquence to *human* experiences of religion.

Vatican II's *Dei Verbum* puts this dynamic well and in a balanced way. First, it affirms the *divine* and hence "superhuman" nature of revelation:

"Through divine revelation, God chose to show forth and communicate Himself and the eternal decisions of His will regarding the salvation of men. That is to say, He chose to share with them those divine treasures which totally transcend the understanding of the human mind" (#6). In this process, the role of the Holy Spirit as the agent is properly acknowledged: "Those divinely revealed realities which are contained and presented in Sacred Scripture have been committed to writing under the inspiration of the Holy Spirit" (#11).[2] Looked at from the perspective of the Holy Spirit's energizing and guiding activity, there is no need to choose — as has been debated in theology — between the inspiration of the authors[3] and that of the writings themselves.[4] Both have support in the biblical canon.[5]

Having affirmed the divine dynamic in the inspiration of Scripture, *Dei Verbum* then speaks robustly of the *human* side in the process of Scripture's inspiration: "In composing the sacred books, God chose men and while employed by Him they made use of their powers and abilities, so that with Him acting in them and through them, they, as true authors, consigned to writing everything and only those things which He wanted" (#11).[6] Exactly because of this robust human element, the reader and interpreter of Scripture, rather than considering the text as the "fallen from heaven" unambiguous deposit of divine words, must approach it as a divine revelation given in human form: "However, since God speaks in Sacred Scripture through men in human fashion, the interpreter of Sacred Scripture, in order to see clearly what God wanted to communicate to us, should carefully investigate what meaning the sacred writers really intended, and what God wanted to manifest by means of their words" (#12).[7] Similarly, the ecumenical statement on hermeneutics by Faith and Order titled "A Treasure in Earthen Vessels" speaks of inspiration as a *human*-divine collaboration.[8]

The acknowledgment of the simultaneous divine and human form of Scripture makes it possible also to understand its breathtaking diversity. If

---

2. On the Protestant side, see "The Westminster Confession of Faith," 1.10, in *Creeds of the Churches*, p. 196; Ramm, *Pattern of Religious Authority*, p. 28.

3. Strong, *Systematic Theology*, 1:196.

4. Dodd, *Authority of the Bible*, p. 36. I am indebted to Grenz, *Theology for the Community of God*, p. 381, for this and the previous reference.

5. For the former: Jer. 36:1-2; Ezek. 11:5; Mic. 3:8; 2 Pet. 1:21; for the latter, the key passage is of course 2 Tim. 3:16.

6. For an important patristic discussion of the divine-human nature of Scripture, see Kondothra, "The Word — Human and Divine," pp. 385-88.

7. For a summary statement, see also #13 in *DV*.

8. Faith and Order, "A Treasure in Earthen Vessels," #2.

God had dropped the revelation from the skies, so to speak, one would expect something like a legal document with precise wording or a step-by-step manual brief enough to be grasped even by the feeble-minded. Not so the Bible — and interestingly enough, neither the Qur'an, which, however, even in current orthodox Muslim theology, is confessed to be directly given to the Prophet and faithfully recorded thereafter; the nature of the Qur'an as a book is difficult to understand; the book is even difficult to read, and hardly looks like a work in keeping with its confessed nature. The same of course can be said of, say, the Vedas, the most highly revered inspired scriptures of almost all forms of Hinduism. Both their style and content are highly elusive and virtually unknown to most Hindus!

The Bible contains all sorts of forms, from narrative to parables to poetry to wisdom sayings to histories to homilies to epistles to apocalypses to genealogies to legal documents to sacrificial manuals. The extensive Wisdom literature, while assuming God as the source of true(est) wisdom, rarely claims to be the "word of the Lord." It is rather shared and communal reflection over the course of generations. Historical books, as theological and "prophetic" as they are, while assuming the activity of Yahweh everywhere, often simply narrate the complex and surprising twists in the course of history and do not usually make explicit a lesson to the reader. The parables of Jesus are not only ambiguous in meaning but make the point that this is their main point! They are "mysteries" that seek to confuse as much as to clarify. Apocalyptic and eschatological sections of the Bible are cast in secretive and symbolic forms of expression. Even Paul's epistles and other similar writings of the NT are far from doctrinal treatises since they are occasional writings arising from missionary, pastoral, and other practical concerns.

The authentically mutual divine-human dynamic in inspiration and the preservation of Scripture — as uneven as the mutuality is in the sense that God is the "author" and source — also comes to light in the slow development process of the canon. The human acts of interpretation, memory, comparison between reliable and unreliable sources (as in Luke 1:1-4), weighing of opinions, and so on were an important, God-willed part of the process. Hence, "it becomes clear that the process of Divine inspiration must cover quite a long and complex series of human activities. . . . Compared with the compilation of the Koran, which was orally given by Muhammad and written down within a few years, this is an extremely complex and extended process. It suggests a very different view of scriptural inspiration from that of Divine dictation."[9]

9. Ward, *Religion and Revelation*, p. 220.

An important aspect of the revelatory process as narrated in the biblical canon is the continuous and daily wrestling with God, seeking for answers to new questions, expressing doubts, at times to the point that God is put on trial. Consider Job, Jeremiah, and other prophets desperately looking for answers to life's toughest questions. In this process,

> There may be heard words or perceived visions; or there may simply be the growth of a conviction that God wants one to do a certain thing, or holds out a promise of good. It is important that this conviction is not seen as solely the result of one's own pondering and reflection. Nor is it normally a sudden, clear message from God. It is a conviction arising out of a holding-up of one's concerns in the presence of God, so that God, in hidden ways, may shape and guide them until they reach a new, settled form. God is conceived to be an active partner in this process; but God's role is to shape, prompt, and respond rather than unilaterally to dictate.[10]

Although revelation rarely comes in those moments in an unambiguous, direct way, revelation is there, a deeper insight into divine mysteries in light of which human questions are illuminated. That classical liberalism made this virtually the only aspect of revelation should not make us dismiss its great significance in the gradual, slow process of "progressive" revelation in the canon. Holding on robustly to the principle of "God's word in human words" makes it possible to see the genuine and authentic humanity of the process of inspiration and hence the nature of the text: "To be sure, the biblical texts have a 'natural history'; they have human authors. Yet these human testimonies are caught up in the triune economy of word-acts and so ultimately become divine testimonies."[11]

The two classic NT texts 2 Timothy 3:16 and 2 Peter 1:21, while often interpreted in a way that supports the more "mechanistic," direct understanding of revelation, seem to be undergirding the kind of dynamic, "God's word in human words/human words as God's word" view sketched here. The reference in the former passage to *theopneustos* ("God-breathed"), in the analogy of Yahweh's breathing the breath of life into the first human being (Gen. 2:7), can be understood in terms "of the breathing-out of Scripture in a similar way [to what happened to Adam] as the giving of life and power to the formed

---

10. Ward, *Religion and Revelation,* p. 215; see also Wiles, "Revelation and Divine Action," pp. 105-7 particularly.

11. Vanhoozer, *Drama of Doctrine,* p. 177.

words of human writers."[12] As Adam became a "living soul" *(nephesh),* so the human writings, "dead" in themselves, become the living Word of God. The Greek expression *pheromenoi,* in the latter passage, referring to the influence ("moving") of human authors by the Holy Spirit, plays on the metaphor of being driven like a ship by the wind. Rather than the human agency being taken away, as in a contemporary airplane's autopilot mode, the ship sailing under the "wind of the Holy Spirit" reaches its destination gradually in the midst of many struggles. Ward summarizes well the contribution to our discussion of both of these passages: "one can think of God as motivating and empowering humans to create certain works, and as giving Divine life and power to these works, so that they can be fruitful for evoking worship and prayer, for instruction and guidance."[13] Indeed, that is what the text says, and the reference is to all the Old Testament, the Word of God of the early church: "From childhood you have been acquainted with the sacred writings which are able to instruct you for salvation through faith in Christ Jesus. All scripture is inspired by God and profitable for teaching, for reproof, for correction, and for training in righteousness, that the man of God may be complete, equipped for every good work" (2 Tim. 3:15-17).

Scripture as the Word of God and Human Testimony

According to the "Scripture principle" of pre-Enlightenment theology, particularly in Reformation orthodoxy, the "matter of Scripture" and the scriptural text were more or less identified with each other. When the Bible speaks, God speaks. The fundamentalist movement of the twentieth century materially affirmed the same. Barth came close to conflating the two but still maintained some kind of distinction. In the preface to the second edition of his *Epistle to the Romans* (1921), he sought to wrestle, like Calvin, with the text, "till the walls which separate the sixteenth century from the first become transparent . . . [until] Paul speaks, and the man of the sixteenth century hears."[14] In the first volume of his planned multivolume *Christliche Dogmatik im Entwurf* (1927),[15] titled *Prolegomena zur Christlichen Dogmatik,* Barth in a real sense wanted to go back to the Scripture principle as he stated that "the meaning

---

12. Ward, *Religion and Revelation,* p. 216.
13. Ward, *Religion and Revelation,* p. 216.
14. Barth, *The Epistle to the Romans,* preface to 2nd ed. (1921), pp. 7-8.
15. After the publication of the first volume, Barth discarded the whole project of this attempted multivolume dogmatics and soon set out to produce his *Church Dogmatics.*

and possibility, the object, of dogmatics is not the Christian faith but the Word of God. For Christian faith is grounded and contained in the Word of God, not vice versa."[16]

On the other side of the hermeneutical spectrum is a "hermeneutics from below," which looks at the Bible as merely *human* testimonies of faith: "Whereas in hermeneutics 'from above' it was the one divine determining subject which utters and 'reveals' itself, in hermeneutics 'from below' it is the one human subjectivity. . . . Whereas a text talks about the resurrection of Christ, for example, it is the author's faith in the resurrection expressed in this discourse which is investigated. . . . What the text is talking about is neglected in favour of the person or community which speaks in the text."[17] As the Catholic David Tracy puts it, Christian theology is but a "philosophical reflection upon the meanings present in common human experience and language and upon the meanings present in Christian fact."[18]

Barth was mentioned as someone who comes close to conflating the Scripture and the Word of God, but that statement calls for an important nuancing. The mature Barth is of course known as the advocate of the idea of Scripture as testimony or witness to Christ.[19] The reason Barth insisted on the testimonial nature of Scripture had to do with his overall concern to maintain the freedom of God. The Bible is not an object of our control, as though we could "freeze" the relationship between the scriptural words and the living God who self-reveals,[20] or as though the living God is "buried" within an ancient text as in a stone mausoleum.[21] Thereby Barth was not rejecting the nature of Scripture as the Word of God. He was rather defining its nature as the Word of God in terms of its work as witness: "Scripture as the original and legitimate witness of divine revelation is itself the Word of God."[22] The divine freedom is secured in that the Bible is God's Word "to the extent that God causes it to

---

16. Barth, *Die Christliche Dogmatik im Entwurf*, p. 87, as translated in Pannenberg, *ST* 1:45. That book has never been translated into English (and should not be confused in English rendering with the first volume of *CD*).

17. Moltmann, *Experiences in Theology*, p. 142.

18. Tracy, *Blessed Rage for Order*, p. 43.

19. Barth's logic is of course based on his template of the threefold form of the Word of God as the Word-made-flesh/Christ, Scripture, and proclamation. See *CD* I/1, pp. 88-124. The distinction between the three forms in Barth is not meant to imply three different "Words" but rather one (for that, see pp. 120-24, titled "The Unity of the Word of God").

20. *CD* I/1, p. 124.

21. *CD* I/1, p. 683.

22. *CD* I/1, p. 502.

be His Word, to the extent that He speaks through it."[23] It is in this light that Barth's saying, which apart from the proper perspective may sound like another affirmation of the fundamentalist view, has to be heard: "God Himself now says what the text says. The work of God is done through the text. The miracle of God takes place in this text formed of human words."[24] That is not to deny the human and, in Barth's view, limited and even fallible nature of the biblical witness. The Bible in this witness is thus "a chorus of very different and independent but harmonious voices. An organism which in its many and varied texts is full of vitality in the community."[25]

As a witness, therefore, Scripture is also thoroughly human and fallible for Barth: "we call the Bible the Word of God only when we recognize its human imperfection in the face of its divine perfection, and its divine perfection in spite of its human imperfection."[26] The fallibility or weakness of the Bible covers the entirety of Scripture as a finite medium, for the authors "can be at fault in any word, and have been at fault in every word."[27] Thus, we may take offense at the Bible, even at its theological assumptions.[28]

To balance Barth, it has to be noted that an authentic encounter between the Divine and human includes also the propositional element, even though it goes beyond the propositional. How else could we identify the one we are to encounter — particularly in the religiously pluralistic world? Here the neo-orthodox fear of any notion of revelation as the way to convey information and knowledge fails badly.[29] How do we recognize the One we encounter unless there is some conveying of information? How can we trust the Bible even as a witness, let alone as a religious authority? Why can't the Muslims say exactly the same of the Qur'an? Historical processes are far from self-referential in nature. Where one sees the "hand of God," another sees the "hand of Allah," yet another the "hand of Chance," and yet another, nothing or no one! Ward puts it well:

> Of course such an encounter will entail some true propositions, but it is not itself the relating of such propositions, and it will not by any means an-

23. *CD* I/2, p. 109. For this section, I am indebted to Macchia, "God Says What the Text Says."

24. *CD* I/2, p. 532.

25. *CD* I/2, p. 674.

26. *CD* I/2, p. 508.

27. *CD* I/2, p. 530.

28. *CD* I/2, p. 507.

29. Brunner, *Revelation and Reason*, p. 8; Tillich, *ST* 1:124.

swer all the theoretical questions I may have. It may be extremely difficult
to put a personal experience of encounter into precise propositions at all. I
think it is quite intelligible to suppose that I may become acquainted with
something so overpowering and immense that I have no words to describe
it. Only on later reflection will I come to work out what is involved in
such an encounter, and develop theories such as those of incarnation or
atonement which seek to articulate, and then always in a very inadequate
fashion, the propositional truths which are implied by the encounter to
which Scripture witnesses and which the Church seeks to renew.[30]

If "the fatal equation of revelation with the inspiration of Scripture"[31]
was the main concern in traditional theology until the first part of the twentieth century, the pendulum has since swung in the opposite direction: currently, many postmodern and other theologies suffer from a fatal separation
of divine revelation from the sacred writings. The roots go back to classical
liberalism, even though several turns have been taken since, particularly with
the advent of postmodernism. Schleiermacher's response to his own question: "What is revelation?" is illustrative: "Every original and new intuition of
the universe is one."[32] That kind of totally immanentist view, however, raises
the obvious objection: How would we ever be content and satisfied with the
revelatory aid merely from human fellows, as genuine and authentic as their
religious sensibilities may be? More importantly, how do we know — without
any revelation — that indeed in Jesus of Nazareth this religious consciousness
came to fulfillment? Furthermore, in light of the current epistemological cli-
mate, we have a much harder time in separating "feelings" from "facts," or to
be more precise: Is it ever possible to speak of feelings, even religious ones,
without any facts or propositions?[33]

While not without its problems, as noted above, Barth's mature view
of the relationship between Scripture and revelation is an ingenious negotiation between the traditional identification of the two and liberal separation
of them, and is thus a useful and important asset. For Barth, the Scripture is
the witness.[34] Barth's concern to make a distinction between the unlimited,
infinite revelation/Word of God and the limited/finite Scripture, the function
of human-divine dynamics, is to be welcomed. What raises concerns here is

---

30. Ward, *Religion and Revelation*, p. 221.
31. Brunner, *Revelation and Reason*, p. 7.
32. Schleiermacher, *On Religion*, Second Speech, p. 49.
33. See further, Ward, *Religion and Revelation*, pp. 228-29.
34. So also Bloesch, *Essentials of Evangelical Theology*, 1:62-63.

the virtual separation between Scripture and revelation/Word of God, or to be more precise, the (unintentional, I suppose) tendency to make divine revelation a matter of subjective reception by human beings. Again, this is not to deny the importance of Spirit-aided reception of — opening of eyes to — the "spiritual" meaning of the Bible. My concern is to resist the idea that the Bible *becomes* the Word of God only at the moment of human reception. "On the contrary, the Bible's status as scripture is not dependent on whether or not we *individually* acknowledge the Spirit's voice speaking through scripture. Rather, the Bible remains objectively scripture because it is the book of the church. From its inception, the community of Christ . . . has been a people who gather around the text to hear the Spirit's voice speaking through it."[35]

That said, to balance the discussion, it is also important to speak of the Spirit's role in the process of Christians "growing as hearers." As Pinnock puts it: "Not [only] as isolated individuals but as members of the community, God calls us to listen to other interpretations and experience a deepening of insight. Through the Word of God, the Spirit continues to transform our lives and lead us into a stronger love for God and neighbor. Just as Spirit gradually sanctifies individuals, so he leads the church into a deeper apprehension over time."[36]

As mentioned, with all its problems and need for balancing, Barth's desire to avoid the liberal collapsing of Scripture's inspiration into a human act and his insistence on Scripture as witness to an encounter with the Divine together provide an important asset in the work of constructing a contemporary doctrine of inspiration. A promising way to fine-tune and correct Barth's intuition is to speak of an encounter between God and humanity that requires and is based on truthful communication.

A Truthful Encounter

Of old, Christian tradition held that whatever other forms of communication God uses in conveying the divine revelation to us, it has some real "content." When revealing himself in Christ, God is thereby telling us "some things." In contemporary parlance we can speak of that aspect of revelation as propositional. An extreme modern form of emphasizing propositional revelation is the fundamentalist idea of revelation primarily as doctrine, as mentioned above. The fundamentalist view, however, says too much — and, ironically,

---

35. Grenz and Franke, *Beyond Foundationalism*, p. 68.
36. Pinnock, *Flame of Love*, p. 218.

too little. "Too much," in the sense that it elevates the propositional-cognitive content to a place that undermines other facets of Scripture; hence, it also says "too little," as it fails to account for the nonpropositional nature of revelation. Tillich's judgment is spot-on: traditional and fundamentalistic "kerygmatic theology's" conception of revelation as the "unchangeable truth of the message" irrespective of changing situations and its identification with the Bible as such, should be subject to critique.[37]

Common sense tells us that one can hardly speak of revelation of any sort, divine or human, without some "content." In that sense, we have to be critical of the extremes of classical liberalism and newer forms of that orientation represented in the "revelation as new awareness" model (in Dulles's typology,[38] a view he does not endorse) in which revelation hardly conveys any "whatness" and is merely either a facilitation of human capacities to gain a deeper insight into religiosity or a human sharing of human experiences of religion.[39] Nor is it right to dichotomize God's self-communication either as "informational about the divine" or as "salvational truth."[40] They of course presuppose each other.

Common sense also tells us that, as necessary as the propositional aspect is, it can hardly encompass all — in many cases, hardly even most of — true personal revelation, as in the biblical belief in revelation of the personal God in the divine-human person of Jesus Christ. To reveal my "heart" to my spouse, she has to know quite a bit about me for such an unveiling to happen and make sense; however, that "quite a bit" comes to her in many ways, from spoken words to emotional and physical touching to imagination to intuition to learning about the family history, and so forth. The insight developed above that God's speaking is also a form of God's acting may help us transcend the failing dichotomy between propositional and personal. "Language is not simply a tool for information processing but a rich medium of communicative action and personal interaction. That God can use human language as a medium for his communicative action is no stranger than his employing the humanity of Jesus as a medium for revelation and reconciliation."[41]

37. Tillich, *ST* 1:4.

38. Chap. 2 in Dulles, *Models of Revelation*, presents briefly this and other "models" of revelation.

39. A telling example of the total denial of any "real" communication can be found in Baum, *Faith and Doctrine*, p. 27.

40. Baum, foreword to *The New Agenda*, p. 16.

41. Vanhoozer, *Drama of Doctrine*, pp. 47-48. I have deleted the italics that appeared in the original.

Propositional and personal, however, are not to be taken as antagonistic. Surprisingly to many, Barth himself saw this accurately. God speaks through the particulars of the biblical text, for "God does reveal Himself in statements, through the medium of speech, and indeed human speech. His Word is always this or that word spoken by the prophets and apostles and proclaimed in the Church. The personal character of God's Word is not, then, to be played off against its verbal or spiritual character."[42]

The presence of promises in the biblical canon calls for a more inclusive understanding of the nature of language. Even though for promises to have any meaning they must have propositional content, promises are also much more than propositions. They are invitations to trust, to take a risk. They call for commitment. Hence, "Promising is a form of *doing* something in *saying* something." There is also the personal element here because "[to] promise is to use words in such a way as to bring about a particular kind of interpersonal relationship."[43]

The obvious problem with a one-sided focus on propositional knowledge is its ignorance of experience. To be more precise: it is not right to say that propositional knowledge denies the role of experience but rather that it is often blind to it. It simply is the case that no human knowing is possible apart from experience. Every form of knowledge is being filtered through human experience.[44] Related is Vanhoozer's remark: "Propositional theology at its worst is guilty of *dedramatizing* Scripture."[45] The task ahead of us then is to reflect carefully on the role of propositional, cognitive, content-driven aspects in the revelatory process of the triune God to humanity and on what other forms are needed to complement that. In the words of Vanhoozer: "The aim is to rehabilitate the cognitive-propositional approach to theology by expanding what we mean by 'cognitive' and by dramatizing what we mean by 'proposition.'"[46] That is a necessary task, but it is not yet sufficient; indeed, what we must do is not only inquire into the "supplemental" role of nonpropositional knowledge but also ask whether much of the "cognitive" or "content-driven" (i.e., propo-

---

42. Barth, *CD* I/1, pp. 137-38. For these Barth passages, I am indebted to Macchia, "God Says What the Text Says," p. 6.

43. Vanhoozer, *Drama of Doctrine*, p. 64.

44. In this respect, Paul Tillich's remark — in a discussion of the Wesleyan Quadrilateral — that experience cannot be counted as one of the four "sources" (along with Bible, tradition, and reason) because everything else is conveyed to us and filtered through experience, makes a valid point (*ST* 1:42).

45. Vanhoozer, *Drama of Doctrine*, p. 87.

46. Vanhoozer, *Drama of Doctrine*, p. 88.

sitional) knowledge can only be accessed through means such as metaphors and symbols. The discussion of the role and nature of metaphors and symbols can only be started here. We have to come back to it in various systematic loci, first in the context of God-talk, then in Christology, eschatology, and so forth.

The biblical record can hardly be reduced to merely propositional form. The divine revelation in the biblical narrative comes in many and variegated forms along with historical events and words, including prophetic and other inspired utterances, dreams, and visions, including apocalyptic ones.[47] The propositional form is only one of many different types. It is also becoming clear to contemporary hermeneutists that ancient and medieval exegetes, for the most part, did not "hold to the narrowly literalistic views espoused by twentieth-century conservatives. The church Fathers and their medieval followers, by and large, were open to a great variety of allegorical and spiritual interpretations that went well beyond the literal meaning of isolated propositions, and sometimes even bypassed the literal sense."[48] Epistemologically one-sided, the "propositional model rests on an objectifying theory of knowledge," widely critiqued in various types of modern philosophies. While propositions play a role in meaningful communication, communication consists of so much more. And certainly the biblical narrative utilizes all kinds of communication forms — from testimonies to symbols, to stories, historical narratives, declarations, prophetic utterances, allusions, dreams, visions, and other "supernatural" phenomena.

The scientist-turned-philosopher Michael Polanyi has reminded us of the importance of *tacit* knowledge, the kind of knowing that is emerging, tentative, nondiscursive, nonpropositional.[49] The saying "There are things that we know but cannot tell" captures an important dimension of tacit knowledge and its relation to communication. This kind of knowledge is no less genuine than, say, an analytic statement; it is just a different type! Doesn't religion embrace much of this kind of knowing and communication? The acknowledgment of that does not have to lead to the denial of the content of many religious and theological statements but rather helps us gain a more proper and inclusive view of the function of language in religion. Hence, there is the continuing need for "[g]rowing as hearers . . . because the truth of profound matters is not easily grasped and the implications not quickly apparent. In matters of

47. Dunn, "Biblical Concepts of Revelation"; Pannenberg, *ST* 1:198-214, titled "The Multiplicity of Biblical Ideas of Revelation."

48. Dulles, *Models of Revelation*, p. 48.

49. See Polanyi, *Personal Knowledge*. See also his *Tacit Dimension*.

ultimacy, one discovers treasures without completely possessing them. Improvement in understanding is always possible — and also desirable, because of our limitations and shortcomings."[50]

While the biblical revelation cannot be captured without propositions, it is also essential to reflect on the special nature of propositions in Scripture. In the Bible, propositions are not merely a means of transmitting information, but they are also "historically situated." They speak to specific historic events and their meanings. Hence, they are "concerned with the transcendent dimension of and future possibilities in a particular historical situation," as is evident for example in Jeremiah 32:27-35, in the word of God received by the prophet concerning the divine intention behind the destruction of Jerusalem. Furthermore, this kind of transcendent, divine word calls for a personal response. In sum: "Revealed propositions in the biblical tradition are typically historical (not timeless truths), existential (not neutral descriptions), morally demanding (not factually informative), and covenantal (not universal)."[51]

To communicate these many dimensions of the polymorphous revelation, human language has to be expanded to categories such as metaphor and symbol. They convey "content" but do so differently than does discursive, analytic language. The meaning of metaphors and symbols, hence, has to be reflected on more carefully.

The Revelatory Power of Metaphors and Symbols

A major trend in the twentieth-century understanding of revelation is what Dulles names "the idea of revelation as symbolic disclosure," and several feminist theologians call metaphorical theology. In this outlook, "revelation never occurs in a purely interior experience," as in various classical liberal traditions and the "new awareness" model (Dulles), or as "an unmediated encounter with God," as in much of traditional theology of revelation. Rather, revelation "is always mediated through symbol — that is to say, through an externally perceived sign that works mysteriously on the human consciousness so as to suggest more than it can clearly describe or define. Revelatory symbols are those which express and mediate God's self-communication."[52] This description of the meaning and role of symbolic mediation helps us avoid the

50. Pinnock, *Flame of Love*, p. 219.
51. Ward, *Religion and Revelation*, p. 226.
52. Dulles, *Models of Revelation*, p. 131.

trap of merely "experience"- or "awareness"-laden approaches to revelation in which God's self-communication is made void of all content; it also reminds the content-driven, propositionally laden approaches of the need to consider the necessary role of mediation in all human knowledge and communication, particularly when it comes to *divine* self-communication.

Symbols are more than "indicators." Whereas indicators such as road signs function in a purely subsidiary manner, symbols draw attention to themselves. Consider the reactions of a patriot in the presence of the national flag. In this instance, "the subsidiary clues [such as the flag] . . . are of intrinsic interest to us, and they enter into meanings in such a way that we are *carried away* by these meanings."[53] What makes these symbols so powerful and significant — again, using a national flag as an illustration — "is the integration of our whole existence as lived in our country," indeed, that "we have put our whole existence into. We have surrendered ourselves into that 'piece of cloth.' "[54]

The Roman Catholic Roger Haight's *Jesus Symbol of God* suggests a theory of language that is applicable to other theological loci as well. In a careful and balanced way this Jesuit theologian seeks to transcend a "naive revelational positivism"[55] with the help of the category of symbol as a concrete historical medium. Any created reality, such as a person, an object, or an event, that makes known and present another reality, such as the transcendent reality of God, not only is represented by the symbol but also is distinguished from it. The symbol points, in this case, to the transcendent reality of God (pp. 196-98). Symbolic language, which is structurally poetic, imaginative, and figurative (pp. 177, 256), expresses a certain experience of God (p. 11). Herein the strength of symbolic language as something that transcends but does not eliminate propositional and other forms of communication comes to the fore. Where Haight's proposal warrants criticism is his claim that the symbolic mediation does not provide any (or at least, not much) objective information about God himself (pp. 9, 210, 282, 471). As argued above: Why should a symbolic — or metaphorical — way of communication be seen as an alternative to the propositional way? Rather, following the feminist Sallie McFague, we could say in a more balanced manner that "metaphor [read also: symbol] and concept are . . . inextricably and symbiotically related in theology."[56] An "imaginative picture,"

---

53. Polanyi and Prosch, *Meaning*, pp. 69-75, at 71. The national flag as well as a hero's tombstone are used as illustrations in the text (p. 72).

54. Polanyi and Prosch, *Meaning*, p. 72.

55. Haight, *Jesus Symbol of God*, p. 173 n. 65. The page numbers in parentheses in this paragraph refer to this book.

56. McFague, *Models of God*, p. xi.

what McFague calls "the metaphors and models," underlies the conceptual types of communication in theology.[57]

The discussion of symbols and metaphors is not a new phenomenon in theology. Aquinas raised the question in the very beginning of his *Summa Theologiae*, "Whether Holy Scripture should use metaphors" (1.1.10). He considered carefully several objections, including that using them in the "lower sciences" might make them inappropriate for theology, considered at the time the queen of sciences, and that metaphors might not be the right tools for conveying the truth of the gospel. However, Thomas concluded that indeed it is proper to use metaphors when interpreting Scripture's meaning and speaking of God. "For God provides for everything according to the capacity of its nature." A great benefit of the use of metaphors, opines the Angelic Doctor, is that "spiritual truths be expounded by means of figures taken from corporeal things, in order that thereby even the simple who are unable by themselves to grasp intellectual things may be able to understand them." Much earlier, Aristotle had provided the classic formulation: "Metaphor consists in giving the thing a name that belongs to something else."[58] "Metaphorical language is the language of images and comparisons. A metaphor is an abbreviated parable, which takes the form of 'just as — so.'"[59] Sometimes God is compared to a compassionate father (Ps. 103:13) or a comforting mother (Isa. 66:13). Behind the metaphorical and symbolic use of language in religion and theology is simply the desire "to make the unexperienceable divine reality comprehensible with the help of metaphors taken from the world which human beings experience."[60] Metaphors are not only useful in that they have a surplus of meaning — they evoke imagination — they are also necessary.[61]

The clue to the power of metaphor — which, technically, is nothing other than "misnaming"[62] — is that "a good metaphor implies an intuitive perception of the similarity of the dissimilars."[63] Whereas concepts have to be unequivocal and hence have the same meaning at all times, metaphors, by their very nature, are equivocal. Whereas concepts "limit and demarcate . . . [metaphors] *de*-restrict and can throw open the realm of possibilities." In that sense,

---

57. McFague, *Models of God*, p. xi.

58. Aristotle, *Poetics* 21.

59. Moltmann, *Experiences in Theology*, p. 161.

60. Moltmann, *Experiences in Theology*, p. 161.

61. Argued forcefully and in a nuanced way in J. K. A. Smith, *Fall of Interpretation*, pp. 25-27.

62. See Polanyi and Prosch, *Meaning*, p. 75.

63. Aristotle, *Poetics* 22.

metaphors may assume the form of play.[64] That does not mean metaphors are "thinner" in content or mean "less." On the contrary, metaphors attempt to say "more" as they seek to express something that transcends the limits of human concepts. Metaphors that have "staying power" can be called "models."[65]

Between symbols and metaphors there is of course an integral relationship. Just consider a familiar biblical example: "I am the way" (John 14:6). It is metaphor as it names something other than what it is, and it is symbolic of Jesus' role as the mediator of the knowledge of God. Many such statements can be expressed propositionally — at least to some extent — but not all can be, or at least not as powerfully and deeply. One can keep symbols and metaphors closely connected without having to say categorically that any symbol-sentence is a metaphor because it "transfers to one subject what is proper to another."[66] Much of biblical narrative of course comes in the form of "symbolic ingredients," from theophanies at Sinai to prophetic visions and ecstatic experiences of the apocalyptic seers, to the descent of the dove at the moment of Jesus' baptism, and so forth. Or consider the symbol of light and darkness, or the cross of Jesus. Indeed, even Jesus' teaching of the kingdom of God not only uses the pedagogical form of parables but is also highly symbolic and metaphoric in nature.[67] Even more, as Rahner importantly remarks: "The theology of the Logos is strictly a theology of the symbol, and indeed the supreme form of it."[68]

Symbolic and metaphoric communication is participatory in nature as it invites the inhabiting of the environment in order to have its intended effect. Usually one has to inhabit the community or "indwell" the tradition to grasp the symbol. Significantly, Polanyi remarks that it is in religious worship and religious activities that the indwelling takes place most profoundly.[69] This is "participatory knowledge of God."[70] There is often a connection between history and symbols, as illustrated in the history of Israel. People standing in that history and tradition are touched by the symbols. They are not merely rhetorical devices, because they have the capacity to transform, shape, and

---

64. Moltmann, *Experiences in Theology*, p. 162.

65. McFague, *Models of God*, p. 34; McFague, *Metaphorical Theology*, p. 23. For the defining work, see Barbour, *Myths, Models, and Paradigms*.

66. Dulles, *Models of Revelation*, p. 133 (Dulles himself does not necessarily affirm that statement).

67. See further, Dulles, *Models of Revelation*, p. 135.

68. Rahner, "A Fragmentary Aspect," p. 235.

69. Polanyi, *Personal Knowledge*, p. 198.

70. Wood, "Participatory Knowledge of God in Liturgy," pp. 93-116.

heal as well as to express and invite commitment, as with a national flag. The flag incites patriotism, heroism, self-sacrifice. Furthermore, symbols give us access to realities not always grasped by other kinds of communication such as propositions. Yet this is not to deny their close connection with thinking; Ricoeur's famous phrase puts it succinctly, symbols "give rise to thought."[71]

The reason traditional and contemporary fundamentalist theologies of revelation have not been keen on symbols and metaphors is their alleged dismissal of cognitive content. That symbols evoke imagination and can play with several meanings does not make them meaningless in communicating content; indeed, the polysemy (or multivalence) may help convey dimensions and features that otherwise would be inaccessible. "If our world is richer than statistics and bloodless abstractions, we need a language with power of suggestion."[72]

To affirm the need for the metaphoric and symbolic is not to dismiss the propositional, the "concept." The critique by Levinas, Derrida, and others of "metaphysics of presence," namely, that the "concept" always represents power, the abuse of power, is simply mistaken and unnuanced. According to Levinas, the Western philosophical tradition, with its preoccupation with ontological categories demanding understanding and mastery of the world outside of us, has violence and power built into its very structure. This means suppressing the otherness of the other.[73] Hence, the turn to metaphors as an alternative. The reason this is useful is that beyond the metaphor there is nothing![74] That view fosters the shift to the "metaphysics of absence." The great problem with this deconstructionist understanding of metaphor is that not only is it inherently contradictory (raising the question of whether "metaphor" itself in this deconstructive meaning is "metaphor" — or something "beyond"!), but it is also inaccurate, as neither classical nor contemporary theology claims any full or "totalitarian" divine presence in the Bible, or even in Christ. Even worse, the turn to deconstruction "does not . . . offer any assistance on the question of *which* constructions are better than others."[75] If beyond the language — both concepts and metaphors — there is nothing, then how could deconstructionists know that?

71. Ricoeur, *Symbolism of Evil*, p. 348.

72. Dulles, *Models of Revelation*, p. 142.

73. Levinas, *Basic Philosophical Writings*, p. 11.

74. This statement is of course in keeping with Derrida's often-quoted statement that "there is nothing outside the text." A fine introduction to Derrida's view of deconstruction and metaphor is his "White Mythology: Metaphor in the Text of Philosophy." See further, Norris, *Deconstruction*, and Lentricchia, *After the New Criticism*, chap. 5.

75. McFague, *Models of God*, p. 26.

Instead, when metaphors and symbols are not taken as an alternative to concept, to the propositional — indeed, when seen as a form of conveying "information," though differently than does the concept — then it is possible, and necessary, to assess which way of speaking is more true and more appropriate in a given situation or for a given purpose.

So far the inspiration of Scripture as propositional, metaphorical, and symbolic — in keeping with the goal of constructing a pluriform theology of revelation — has been established. What about myth and the mystical element? Do they play any role? Many religions claim they do.

The Category of Myth and Mysticism

In a seminal essay titled "Performing the Scriptures," Nicholas Lash makes the self-evident but surprisingly often ignored point that "for different kinds of texts, different kinds of activity count as the fundamental form of their interpretation."[76] Rightly Vanhoozer notes in relation to this remark: "One thinks of Shakespeare plays, or Beethoven sonatas, or even instructions for assembling bookshelves. Each of these texts is intended as a guide for specific human activities."[77] If so, would myth belong to the repertoire of Scripture performance? Or the mystical?

According to Reformed thinker Paul K. Jewett, "Of the several terms used to describe contemporary theological discourse, none is given greater prominence in present-day literature than *myth*."[78] While the statement may reflect more the times of the writing, it still makes the valid point that the category of myth plays an important role in contemporary religious and theological discourse.[79] The notion of myth has served various agendas in Christian theology. Well known is R. Bultmann's turn to myth as a way to evade the question of the historical basis of biblical and Christian claims to events such as resurrection: myth means "the use of imagery to express the

76. Lash, *Theology of the Way to Emmaus*, p. 40.

77. Vanhoozer, *Drama of Doctrine*, p. 101.

78. Jewett, *God, Creation, and Revelation*, p. 28.

79. In theology, the term goes back to the beginnings of the Quest of the Historical Jesus. Whereas for H. Reimarus the presence of mythical elements such as the miraculous indicated that the early disciples could be considered fraudulent (in their effort to support their theological interpretation of Jesus with claims to miracles that by default were impossible for the modernist mind-set), D. F. Strauss took them as necessary (albeit, of course, mistaken in light of the modernist worldview) ways of communication of "primitive" people.

other worldly in terms of this world and the divine in terms of human life, the other side in terms of this side."[80] To understand the contemporary use of the category of myth in theology, we may look at how the NT juxtaposes it with narratives that speak of events that have really happened (2 Tim. 4:4). That is, of course, the way myth is understood in works such as John Hick's *Myth of God Incarnate* (1977). There are also instances of other uses of "myth," such as Pannenberg's argument that in Christian faith, in continuity with the OT traditions, "myth is not eliminated . . . but integrated and transcended" as the typical distinction of sacred and profane is being eliminated in terms of the eschatological consummation, and thus what happens is "the turning away from the mythical orientation to primal time" toward God's future. The Christ event not only supersedes and replaces the primal myths but also helps reconfigure and reshape them.[81] Thus, Pannenberg and Bultmann employ the category of myth in radically different ways. But since myth by and large is used not only in religious studies but also in biblical studies and theology mainly as a way to attempt to evade the question of truth and historicity, it might be advisable to refer to categories of symbol and metaphor when speaking of nonpropositional dimensions of revelation and divine communication.

Arguing that the cognitive content of revelation and Scripture cannot be sacrificed for the spiritual experience or "new awareness" is not to deny the importance of the nondiscursive, mystical, and mysterious dimensions of revelation, however. It is just to avoid the reductionism of theologies that make revelation and Scripture void of any knowledge. In the model Dulles labels "revelation as new awareness," "revelation is a transcendent fulfillment of the inner drive of the human spirit toward fuller consciousness. . . . Rather than going beyond experience, revelation is itself an experience of participation in divine life."[82] Clearly, there is a connection here with the typical religious mystical and ecstatic experiences, including those of biblical authors and mystics in the Christian tradition. It may be labeled differently, such as seeing the light (Saint Symeon the New Theologian), but in my understanding it speaks of a similar kind of experience. Although one may imagine such an experience devoid of any revelatory content, it doesn't have to be so; it can also be seen as yet another way of divine revelation in the inner depths of one's being. The English poet Samuel Taylor Coleridge's pointed observation serves as a

80. Bultmann, "New Testament and Mythology," p. 10 n. 2.
81. Pannenberg, *ST* 1:186-87.
82. Dulles, *Models of Revelation*, p. 98.

wonderful rule here: "It is by Symbols alone that we can acquire intellectual knowledge of the Divine."[83]

Karl Rahner's turn to the transcendental dimension of communication and experience comes into play here in a significant way. Against the misunderstanding of some of his Protestant critics, Rahner allowed both for transcendental and for "categorical" (historical) revelation. Of the former he says: "revelation is not possible in the original bearer of revelation without the occurrence of what may be called 'mysticism as the experience of grace.'"[84] The revelation of God, whether directly as in spoken word and historical events or indirectly as in other forms of communication, is an act of grace, a graceful and loving reaching out of the Father toward his children.[85]

In these kinds of statements Rahner was gleaning from several Catholic sources, including Pierre Teilhard de Chardin, who, like Rahner, did not reduce revelation only to mysticism even though he also argued that revelation "is an act no longer of *cognition* but of *recognition*: the whole complex interaction of two beings who freely open themselves to one another and give themselves — the emergence, under the influence of grace, of theological faith."[86] In light of humanity having been created in the image of God and the presence of the triune God in the world, one should expect some reciprocity between the Giver and receiver of revelation. This is not to reduce Christian revelation to the category of immanentist mysticism or to compromise its divine newness, but rather to put it in the perspective of God's continuing work in the world. God's revelation, while new and while encountering resistance because of fallen humanity's turning away from the Creator, is still a "homecoming" (John 1:11). This principle applies not only to the perfected form of revelation, God's embodiment in Jesus of Nazareth, but also to forms of revelation that have their source in the Word made flesh.

Where Teilhard de Chardin's view has to be challenged is in his claim that "God never reveals himself from outside, by intrusion, but *from within*, by stimulation and enrichment of the human psychic current,"[87] even when he ultimately relates revelation to Christ, in the ascending movement toward

---

83. Cited in Dulles, *Models of Revelation*, p. 131 (without the original source).

84. Rahner, "Mysticism," p. 1010; see also *Foundations*, p. 116.

85. *DV*, #2.

86. Teilhard de Chardin, "Outline of a Dialectic of Spirit," p. 148. For a monographic presentation, see Kropf, *Teilhard, Scripture, and Revelation*.

87. Teilhard de Chardin, *Christianity and Evolution*, p. 143, cited in Dulles, *Models of Revelation*, p. 99.

the Omega point.[88] The biblical narrative tells us that Yahweh, the Father of Jesus Christ, revealed himself in numerous ways, both "from inside" and "from outside," including ways that might appear to be intrusive! There is no denying the absolute freedom of God in the process of revelation or the willful turning away of men and women from God who is seeking them.

It is important that Christian faith not miss the mystical and symbolic mediation of revelation if it wants to communicate with Asiatic faiths, Islamic Sufism, folk religions, and the new religiosity of the West. Those religions often come to the task of "revelation" through mysticism, symbols, heightened awareness, and similar means. While the category of revelation in Christian tradition — as well as in Judaism and Islam — goes beyond the level of mysticism and symbols, it still very much also includes that.

This chapter has sought to formulate the coming-to-existence of Christian Scripture as a genuine divine-human synergy in which the divine is the primary and determinative counterpart. Based in history and its unfolding, hence existing in the form of promise looking toward the eschatological fulfillment (chapter 3), the triune revelation is most fully communicated to us in the Word made flesh (chapter 2) and "inscripturated" in the canonical Scripture (chapter 4). Our next task looks at the formation of the *canon,* which in itself represents the growth of tradition. How was it that the First Testament of the Jewish people and the emerging Second Testament of the Christian church became the ultimate norm of faith and practice? How is the way that Scripture is used in the church related to its authoritative status? What is the role of tradition? What about the community of Christ, which is the guardian of tradition? To these questions we turn next.

---

88. For details, see Kropf, *Teilhard, Scripture, and Revelation,* pp. 273-79 particularly.

6. Scripture, Community, and Tradition

Which Use of the Bible? Whose "Authorship"?

An important ecumenical statement by the Faith and Order Commission of the World Council of Churches titled "The Authority of the Bible" prefers not to deduce the authority of the Bible from its inspiration, as was done in the dogmatic tradition. Rather, it establishes the authority of the Bible on the ground of its religious value for the church, and then proceeds to postulate inspiration as the source of that authority.[1] This view might usefully be called "functional," and it belongs to the same diverse family as David Kelsey's view of Scripture as normative because it shapes identities and transforms individuals and communities,[2] as well as David Tracy's notion of "classic."[3]

George Lindbeck has formulated most ably the turn to the Bible's unique significance as the function of the way the current church understands and appropriates it. Hence, he replaces the "cognitive-propositionalist" model that takes biblical and theological statements as truth claims about objective realities and the "experiential-expressivist" model, which "interprets doctrines as noninformative and nondiscursive symbols of inner feelings, attitudes, or existential orientations," with a "cultural-linguistic"

1. Faith and Order, Louvain 1971.
2. Kelsey, "The Bible and the Christian Theology," pp. 385-402.
3. For Tracy, "classic" is a technical term that refers to texts (religious, but not only those) that possess a surplus of permanent meaning and thus become authoritative; at the same time, the classic always resists definitive interpretation. See further, Tracy, *Analogical Imagination*, especially pp. 101-7.

model.[4] Taking a cue from the later Wittgenstein's turn to language, this model regards church doctrines not "as expressive symbols or as truth claims, but as communally authoritative rules of discourse, attitude and action." Hence, this approach can be called a "regulative" or "rule" theory.[5] Biblical statements, then, receive their authority from ecclesiastical usage. The biblical scholar Hans Frei's main contribution to the project is his refusal to seek the meaning and significance of biblical teachings "behind" the text as in the historical-critical method's endless probing into the sociocultural and historical background that has led to "the eclipse of biblical narrative."[6] Rather than letting the world take over the biblical narrative, these Yale theologians "desire to renew in a post-traditional and post-liberal mode the ancient practice of absorbing the universe into the biblical world."[7] That said, "the literal meaning of the text is precisely that meaning which finds the greatest degree of agreement in the use of the text in the religious community. If there is agreement in that use, then take that to be the literal sense."[8] If the ecclesiastical usage determines the "sense" and "authority" of Scripture, then there is no need — and in Lindbeck's case, not even the possibility — for any kind of thick extratextual reference. The doctrinal "rules" aim merely — or at least predominantly — at the inner coherence of Christian thought. They are not interested in extratextual references.[9]

The obvious question to the postliberal approach is whether there is any way to negotiate between different traditions and their narratives. Is there any way to negotiate between the Vedas of Hindus, the Qur'an of Muslims, the Book of Mormon, and the Bible? Furthermore, if the ecclesiastical usage is the norming norm, what or who is to norm the ecclesiastical usage? There are both good and bad ways of using the Bible. And what about the Scripture's role as the critic of the people of God?[10] To put it another way, it is only a half-truth to say, following Wittgenstein, that "Practice gives the words their sense";[11] it is as much true that words not only make sense but also "regulate" practices. Otherwise, any practice would go. The

---

4. Lindbeck, *Nature of Doctrine*, p. 16.
5. Lindbeck, *Nature of Doctrine*, p. 17.
6. Frei, *The Eclipse of Biblical Narrative*.
7. Lindbeck, *Nature of Doctrine*, p. 135.
8. Frei, *Types of Christian Theology*, p. 15.
9. See further, Lindbeck, *Nature of Doctrine*, pp. 63-69 especially.
10. Vanhoozer, *Drama of Doctrine*, p. 44.
11. Wittgenstein, *Culture and Value*, p. 85; I am indebted to Vanhoozer, *Drama of Doctrine*, p. 96.

biblical text or doctrinal statement is not a self-contained, self-referential phenomenon.[12]

An innovative version of Scripture-as-used-by-the-church is the "turn" to canon, for which the OT scholar Brevard Childs is best known. Rather than looking at how the *contemporary* church uses the Bible — and thus makes it authoritative — this approach looks at how the church of the *past*, in the process of canonization and the coming into existence of what came to be the canonical Scriptures, discerned and established Scripture's authority. In *Introduction to the Old Testament as Scripture* (1979), he critiques harshly the then-prevailing historical-critical methodology that, on top of other mistakes, virtually tears asunder the canon and only looks at various layers and sections of writings without any unity, or even without many leading themes. Childs insists that Scripture's meaning can only be determined in its canonized form, as Scripture, and in relation to the ancient community of faith.[13] The way canon emerged was that the ancient church "bore witness to the effect that certain writings had on its faith and life."[14] Walter Brueggemann, a leading contemporary OT scholar, follows the direction of Childs but in a distinctive way. Rather than speaking of the canonical process as Childs does, he places the "authority" of Scripture in the way the ancient community (Israel) functioned as an interpretive community. Brueggemann does this by his turn to rhetoric. Israel's testimonies to Yahweh and his works are rhetorical "tools" to affect and create a new world.[15] Hence, Brueggemann's approach can be labeled "canonical-linguistic-*cum*-rhetorical."[16]

The benefit of the functional and canonical approaches is that they highlight the role of community in the process of inspiration. If the Bible is the book of the church, then its coming to existence — unlike the Qur'an, which comes without any mediation — has to do with the way the believing community came to discern its unique significance and thus authority. It also helps us balance the one-sided focus of tradition on the inspired nature of the writings themselves.[17]

---

12. For the problematic notion of the "essence" of culture, see Tanner, *Theories of Culture*, pp. 153-55.

13. Childs, *Introduction to the Old Testament as Scripture*, p. 60.

14. Childs, *Biblical Theology in Crisis*, p. 105.

15. Brueggemann, *Theology of the Old Testament*, pp. 65, 118-19; *Texts under Negotiation*.

16. For his debt to the Yale School, see Brueggemann, *Theology of the Old Testament*, p. 86.

17. For an unwillingness to extend the idea of inspiration to all parts of the canon, see P. Achtemeier, *Inspiration of Scripture*, pp. 99-104.

Another and related lasting value of the functional and especially the canonical approach is that "[t]he Bible is seen . . . not as a finished and static fact or collection of facts to be analyzed by increasingly sophisticated methods, but as a potentiality of meaning which is actualized by succeeding generations in light of their needs and by means of approaches supplied and authenticated by their world views."[18] In functional and canonical approaches, "inspiration" and "illumination," understood with the standard theological distinction between them, are not only connected but virtually conflated.

The problem with the canonical approach is that it shares the liability of the Scripture-as-used-by-the-church approach, and then some. The problem is, "whose testimony and rhetoric counts: the text's or the interpretative community's?"[19] Whereas this question is common to both of these functional orientations, the burden of proof of the Childs-Brueggemann approach has to do with why we privilege the ancient community rather than our contemporary community. I fear that choosing either community — that of the past or that of the present — as the ultimate locus of religious authority moves theology closer to being little more than ethnography.[20] While it may be interesting to map out how communities of different ages use Scripture for their own purposes, in this case for creating the world, in terms of religious authority, that is neither useful nor of lasting value. Communities come and go.

An important attempt to address that liability and also build bridges between what used to be called "liberal" and "conservative" orientations, is Vanhoozer's "canonical-linguistic" proposal. *The Drama of Doctrine* seeks to defend the principle of *sola Scriptura* in a way that would fully affirm the linguistic turn and — as the title expresses — envision Christian doctrine as a dramatic event. His leading thesis is that "the canonical-linguistic approach maintains that the normative use is ultimately not that of ecclesial *culture* but of the biblical *canon*."[21] Vanhoozer charts his epistemological course in the waters of postmodern rejection of foundationalism, critique of propositionalism, and celebration of plurality of meanings — and at the same time, he does everything in his power not to steer away from the primacy of canon and *sola Scriptura* as well as the existence of "objective" realities "out there" to which metaphors ultimately refer. He argues that metaphors are essential as they say "more" than rather than "less" than propositions. This is to say that metaphors

18. McKnight, "Errantry and Inerrancy," p. 146; I am indebted to Grenz, *Theology for the Community of God*, pp. 384-85.

19. Vanhoozer, *Drama of Doctrine*, pp. 96-97.

20. For a similar kind of criticism, see Vanhoozer, *Drama of Doctrine*, p. 98 and passim.

21. Vanhoozer, *Drama of Doctrine*, p. 16.

convey some information but not only that — or that they convey information in a way propositions cannot. The use of metaphors fosters the possibility of "polyphonic truth," multiple meanings, and imagination. It actively seeks to be contextual. Unlike many postmodernist and cultural-linguistic models, however, metaphors do not lose cognitive content. Furthermore, the meaning of the text is first of all the meaning intended by the author. In sum: there is an "extratextual" reference to realities outside, such as the resurrection of Christ, in the midst of many meanings and many metaphors.[22]

In addition to correcting the liabilities of the functional and canonical approaches to the Bible's meaning and authority, Vanhoozer's canonical-linguistic turn also reminds us of the need to tend to the importance of the "original authorship" of the Bible. Until the Enlightenment and even some time thereafter, it was taken for granted that what the text means is what the original author meant it to mean. This commonsense assumption was not taken naively, however, as seen from the ancient distinction between the four senses of Scripture: the historical (or literal), the allegorical, the tropological (or moral), and the anagogical.[23]

An important development came with the rise of modern hermeneutics as pioneered by Schleiermacher.[24] Schleiermacher understood well that we are liable to misunderstand texts written at a different time or in a different culture from our own. When reading the texts, we tend to import our own personal and cultural prejudices or presuppositions, and thereby miss or distort the meaning of the text. A proper cure for that missed interpretation is for the reader to seek to discover, by a process of reconstruction from textual clues, what was in the mind of the author. Ideally, the hermeneutist could "experience" what the original author's intentions were. This is the ultimate goal of hermeneutics, and it goes beyond the mere "grammatical" interpretation (the value of which should not be undermined per se) to "psychological" interpretation, which seeks to uncover the "mind" of the writer. With the turn to the original author's "inner psychology," Schleiermacher also did away with the traditional idea of right biblical interpretation in need of a special aid such as divine inspiration (of either the author or the interpreter). With all its strengths, including the dismantling of a naive, precritical belief in the capacity of the reader to "read correctly" ancient texts, this modern hermeneutics

22. See Vanhoozer, *Drama of Doctrine*, particularly chap. 9.

23. The definitive discussion can be found in Aquinas, *ST* 1.1.11, taking its point of departure in Augustine's classic formulation.

24. Still the definitive work is Schleiermacher, *Hermeneutics*. A useful brief discussion of Schleiermacher's hermeneutics can be found in Gadamer, *Truth and Method*, pp. 166-67.

of course suffers from the danger of making the hermeneutics of the *text* at hand a guesswork of its author's changing psychological states. There simply is no way for us to become "mind readers" of ancient authors, and even if we could, the classical Christian belief in the use of human authors, whatever their mental states, as "instruments" of the divine Spirit — of course, not mechanically understood but in the context of the genuine divine-human dynamic explained above — would be thereby dismissed.

The emphasis on the authorial meaning as the clue to understanding writings of the past, however, has remained with contemporary postmodern hermeneutics. The *Postmodern Bible* states that our understanding of the text is "inseparable from what we *want* it to mean, from how we *will* it to mean."[25] While not everybody, even after the advent of postmodernity, is willing to go as far Derrida's "death of the author,"[26] a determinate shift has happened. The meaning of the text is less a matter of what the author meant and more about how the contemporary reader takes its meaning or about how the church uses the Bible. "It is up to *us* to re-imagine Christianity, to re-invent faith for our time."[27] The reader-response hermeneutics basically shifts the accent from the discernment of the original author's intended meaning to the meaning the text has here and now for the contemporary reader.[28] Whereas the historical-critical paradigm as well as the various and diverse "message behind the text" approaches look for the meaning of the text behind the text, the eyes of the reader-response paradigm advocate focus, so to speak, on what is happening in front of the text, namely, on their own encounter with the text in the act of reading.[29]

So, we are now faced with several different proposals about what makes

25. *Postmodern Bible*, p. 14.

26. For insightful comments, see Vanhoozer, "The Bible," p. 10. For a full-scale discussion, see Vanhoozer, *Is There Meaning in This Text?*

27. Cupitt, *Long-Legged Fly*, p. 2. A much more balanced and informed approach can be found in Aichele, Miscall, and Walsh, "An Elephant in the Room."

28. The formative text is Fish, *Is There a Text in This Class?* An important work in terms of application of the reader-response paradigm to a specific biblical text is Fowler, *Let the Reader Understand.* Two other contemporary hermeneutical turns in biblical studies and theology basically echo this mind-set, namely, shifting the emphasis from author to the reader: "reception theory" and "impact history." The now-classic introduction to the former is Jauss, *Towards an Aesthetic of Reception.* The latter approach gleans from ancient and modern studies of rhetoric and its persuasive influence on the audience. Defining texts (also in some ways critical of other reader-response approaches) are Booth, *The Rhetoric of Fiction* and *The Rhetoric of Irony.*

29. See further, Haynes and McKenzie, eds., *To Each Its Own Meaning;* for a specific

canonical Scripture "authoritative" and norming, and what is its meaning. Pre-Enlightenment theology did not have to deal with the question, as Scripture's divine inspiration was taken for granted along with its "plain meaning" in terms of the original authorial meaning, but now we have various postmodern rebuttals of the primacy of the original authorial meaning in favor of the contemporary reader's meaning. The Yale School and Childs determine the meaning and hence authority in terms of its use by the community, current or ancient, respectively. What would be a constructive proposal beyond — but also learning from — these impasses? Is there a way to reformulate the ancient church's conviction of the Scripture as the ultimate norm?

Scripture as the Ultimate Norm of Theology

The main Christian traditions affirm that Scripture is the *norma normans non normata* (the ultimate norm above which there is no other norm), the highest authority of faith and practice. Only classical liberalism, many forms of postmodernism, and religious pluralism either deny this affirmation or revise it to the point it is hard to recognize. However, to say that the biblical message is the ultimate norm does not yet define in what sense that is meant. This takes us to the complicated question of the relationship between the "message" and the text (of Scripture).

A number of approaches in one way or another posit the "message" behind the text. For classical liberalism the message can be found in the abiding religious experiences of which the Bible is a valuable and unique record. For fundamentalists, the message is the doctrinal content of the Bible; hence, in the fundamentalist outlook, systematic theology is basically an attempt to collect and organize, as best one can, the doctrinal statements gleaned from the biblical narrative.[30] Of course, the latter tradition considers Scripture the Word of God and intends to grasp its message by focusing on the doctrine. Yet another form of the message-behind-the-text orientation is neo-orthodoxy; in this approach the Bible is the witness to revelation (the "message") behind the fallible human words of Scripture. Still another form of positing the message behind the text is the turn to the "mighty acts" of God in sacred history as the locus

---

example of the application of this method to interpretation of a biblical text, see Lodge, *Romans 9–11*.

30. For the Princeton orthodoxy, see, e.g., Hodge, *Systematic Theology*, 1:609-10. For contemporary fundamentalism, see Grudem, *Systematic Theology*, p. 21.

of revelation[31] or, as discussed above, revelation-as-history's turn to universal history as the locus. One may also list in this category the turn to the "sense" of the biblical text as the key to determining its meaning and significance. This approach, as embodied by Hans Frei of the Yale School, is the most sophisticated arbiter between the message and text as it explicitly resists the typical historical-critical paradigm's reluctance to tend to the meaning of the text in its endless search for historical, cultural, sociopolitical, and other "meanings." However, the reason why even Frei's approach materially follows the message-behind-the-text orientation is that it is the biblical *narrative* (rather than an event in ancient history) that gives the "sense" of the text.[32] Furthermore, it neglects extratextual references (as noted in the discussion of Lindbeck's model). Hence, the question of the normativeness of the text — vis-à-vis, say, the Qur'anic text — beyond the Christian "ghetto" is left out of the discussion.

Grenz rightly observes that "[t]he perspective that brings these seemingly diverse approaches together is the assumption that the Bible discloses an underlying divine revelation that constitutes the authoritative biblical message,"[33] but that this revelation is neither identical nor integrally bound with the canonical text as we now have it.[34] Mentioned above are modern hermeneutics' turn to the psychological analysis of the author's intention as well as the current postmodern turn to the meaning of Scripture to the current reader as the key to determining its meaning. Although neither of these is looking for the authoritative biblical message behind the text, both share with the other approaches mentioned the desire to look for something "behind" or "in front of" the text as the criterion for determining its meaning.

Contemporary theology should listen carefully to these attempts to dissolve the naive equation of Scripture and its authoritative message.[35] These

---

31. Bloesch, *Theology of Word and Spirit*, p. 187.

32. In important ways, even the highly nuanced postmodern hermeneutics of Adam, *Faithful Interpretation*, represents the "meaning behind the text" approach, in this case locating it in contemporary community (or communities).

33. Grenz and Franke, *Beyond Foundationalism*, p. 69.

34. I wonder if even Nicholas Wolterstorff (*Divine Discourse*, pp. 42-54 and passim), who clearly wants to affirm "authorial-discourse" hermeneutics, finally falls prey to some kind of message-behind-the-text ideology. At the least, he both clarifies and confuses the role of the Spirit's speaking through the message of the Bible as he speaks of it as "double agency discourse." According to that scheme, the Spirit speaks at times through deputized speech and at other times through appropriating the discourse of the biblical authors, hence in some sense circumventing the canonical text's primacy with a robust focus on the original authors. For similar critique, see also Grenz and Franke, *Beyond Foundationalism*, pp. 73-74.

35. One of the theologically most sophisticated such efforts, in a fine and balanced way

approaches stand as "a warning against positing a simple, one-to-one correspondence between the revelation of God and the Bible, that is, between the Word of God and the words of scripture."[36] Furthermore, they rightly remind us of the wider scope, so to speak, of the revelation of God/Word of God in relation to written Scripture. The revelation of God, of course, precedes the Bible, since the latter presupposes the reality of revelation.[37] That said, the message behind/in-front-of the text suffers from too wide a wedge between the text and the message that ultimately, as is most radically seen in the postmodern approaches, leads to subjectivism, be it personal or collective, and the loss of the ultimate authority of Scripture altogether. Furthermore, methodologically these approaches, when pressed, have to acknowledge that indeed there is no absolutely reliable access to the message "behind." Hence, Christian theology is left without the biblical message wrought by the Holy Spirit as the ultimate norm.

A more balanced view of the integral — even though not identical — relation of the message to the text begins with the historical note that

> the relationship between revelation and text is actually somewhat fluid. Revelation arose not only prior to but also together with the process of canonical scripture. In part, God's revelatory work came in and through the formation of scripture, as under the guiding hand of the Spirit the community of faith sought to understand the ongoing work of God in the world in the light of God's earlier activity as described in the oral and written traditions of the community. The faith community sought as well to determine what God's covenant with their forebears meant for them as they sought to be God's covenant partners in the present. The canonical texts reflect this ongoing conversation within the ancient Hebrew community and the early church.[38]

Hence, the separation between the authoritative message and the scriptural text will not do; they have to be kept tightly together. This is not to limit the sovereignty of the Spirit in speaking to the church, but rather to tend obediently to the Spirit's voice through the message of Scripture.

Indeed, linking the authority of Scripture to the meaning intended by

---

(although not without some problems, indicated in the discussion below), is Abraham, *Divine Inspiration of Holy Scripture.*

36. Grenz and Franke, *Beyond Foundationalism,* pp. 70-71.

37. See further, Barr, *Scope and Authority of the Bible,* p. 16.

38. Grenz and Franke, *Beyond Foundationalism,* p. 72.

the original author(s) — ultimately the function of the dynamic human-divine joint work — and keeping the text and message closely knit together (without complete equation) make it possible to affirm the continuing and lasting value of Scripture as the ultimate authority. To be more precise: this is to affirm the Spirit's ongoing speaking through Scripture as the ultimate authority. In this continuing work of the Spirit through the Scripture, rooted in the historical salvific acts of God, displayed in the history of this world, in the fulfillment of eschatological-historical promises culminating in the divine embodiment, the Word made flesh, the triune God is at work until the end of time.

To say the Spirit is at work in helping the readers of the Bible to gain fresh, living insights into the meaning of the text does not undervalue what the text means. Rather, it affirms it. "The Spirit leads the church not away from but deeper into the biblical world. Indeed, the Spirit-led church is 'the creature of the Word.'" And "Neither the church nor the Spirit can improve upon what God accomplished in Jesus Christ"![39]

Several contemporary theologians have found in speech-act theory, as pioneered by J. L. Austin,[40] a fitting terminological and material apparatus to describe this process.[41] Austin distinguishes three types of speech-acts: "locutionary," the simple enunciation of sentence; "illocutionary," expressing the speaker's intention; and "perlocutionary," which refers to what was achieved by the speaker. The surplus of speech-act theory is that it speaks of *speaking*, communication as an act. Hence, it also helps transcend the failing dualism of either words or acts that characterizes many debates in the doctrine of revelation. When applied to the work of the Spirit in and through Scripture, speech-act theory reminds us of the Word of God as creative, livening, and transforming "power." The Spirit's speaking through the Scripture's text is an illocutionary act as the biblical text is appropriating the biblical text, that is, "by appropriating the discourse of the biblical author."[42] The goal of that (perlocution) is not only the human appropriation of the Word of God at a personal and communal level, but even more, the living out of the precepts, inspiration, promises, and corrections of the "mind of Christ."

That the message of the Bible, which the Spirit appropriates, is integrally

---

39. Vanhoozer, *Drama of Doctrine*, p. 201; the citation is from Schwöbel, "Creature of the Word."

40. Austin, *How to Do Things with Words*.

41. A major philosophical-theological and hermeneutical investigation utilizing the speech-act theory is Wolterstorff, *Divine Discourse*.

42. Grenz and Franke, *Beyond Foundationalism*, pp. 73-74. I am indebted in this paragraph to their proposition.

related to the canonical text is not to say that the Spirit is "tied" to the original meaning of the text. Both hermeneutically and theologically, that kind of limitation would fail. Paul Ricoeur has reminded us that once the text is out there, in a real sense of the word, it gains a life of its own. However, this "life" of the text does not have to be so distanced from or unrelated to the original text that it cuts off the relationship; indeed, the Bible maintains an important relation between what the text "originally" said and what it continues saying in new contexts and new life situations. Hence, proper exegesis and hermeneutics serve theology well. Theologically, the Spirit "blows where it wills" (John 3:8), and hence the Spirit's continuing speaking to churches and outside the churches cannot be reined in. But again, according to the Johannine Jesus' promises, the Paraclete "bring[s] to your remembrance all that I have said to you" (John 14:26).

That the Spirit speaks to the church with a specific purpose in mind is well attested in the Bible. According to 2 Timothy 3:16, the perlocutionary speech-act of the Spirit aims at teaching, reproving, correcting, and instructing. We can add promising, shaping, guiding, sanctifying, and other similar goals. A fitting way of speaking in a most comprehensive way of this Spirit's manifold work through the message of the Bible is to draw from both postmodern literary criticism and sociology of religion under the category of the "creating of the world":

> A major role of literature in general is to enable readers (and readership) to create a world or worlds for themselves, cognitively, affectively, behaviourally — in all the ways that individuals and groups are related to their world. At implicit and explicit levels, readers create their own worlds in the process of reading. . . . Biblical texts share in this role in a particular way; they provide resources for the creation of a comprehensive universe, which has space for the human and for the divine and which sees the human in the light of the divine and the divine in the light of the human.[43]

Behind this idea lies the groundbreaking insight named the "social construction of reality."[44] The main thesis here is that the "reality" of the world, including its social order and meaning, is not given to humanity from nowhere, but rather is the function of human construction. This is not to deny the externality (and "objectivity") of the world, but to insist on the collective human

---

43. McKnight, *Postmodern Use of the Bible*, pp. 261-62. For this citation, I am indebted to Grenz and Franke, *Beyond Foundationalism*, p. 78.

44. The defining work here is Berger and Luckmann, *Social Construction of Reality*.

imagination — in the very thick sense of the term — as the source of "creating the world." Peter L. Berger, one of the architects of this paradigm, is a sociologist of religion who emphasizes the central role religion plays in this social world-building.[45] Indeed, religion helps construct "a sacred cosmos" with its stability.[46]

The above-quoted statement about literature's role in the creation of reality requires an important clarification. It is not through human beings who read the text that the creation of the world happens; it is rather the Spirit's agency as the Spirit speaks to the listening and obedient Christians through the message (text) of Scripture. "Just as God created the world 'in the beginning' through the act of speaking the Word, so also God creates a world in the present by the Spirit speaking through scripture. . . . Through appropriating the Word written — that is, by means of the biblical text — the Spirit creates a world centered on Jesus Christ, who is the Word disclosed."[47] Here there is an integral relationship between Jesus and the Spirit. As in the rest of God's creation, men and women are invited to be cocreators. Through the energies of the Spirit, Christians continue constructing their reality in keeping with the mind of Christ. In this framework, the lasting value of the Yale School's yearning for "absorbing the universe into the biblical world"[48] can be affirmed. However, unlike Lindbeck's proposal, this process of absorbing the world into the biblical world is not merely a human enterprise but rather a work of the Spirit, and it does not exclude but rather entails extratextual reference in order to make us confident about whose text? which author?

We noted above that for Scripture to function as the ultimate norm, the current canonical form has to be the (main) locus of the meaning of the text. While this does not have to mean a total identification of revelation/"meaning" with the text, there has to be an integral connection. This means that one cannot (only) speak of *a* meaning of the text among (many) others, even though, rightly, contemporary theology speaks for the importance of the diversity of voices in the canon. But this diversity is diversity-in-unity/unity-in-diversity. There is a shared common core, the gospel. Here the importance of the turn to narrative comes to the fore. While for some, narrative theology means yet another escape from the "factuality" (the propositional nature) of the Bible, it does not have to. It is the category of narrative that makes talk about the unity of Scripture possible and important. "Despite the variety of literary material

---

45. See Berger, *The Sacred Canopy*, p. 3.
46. Berger, *The Sacred Canopy*, p. 25.
47. Grenz and Franke, *Beyond Foundationalism*, p. 78.
48. Lindbeck, *Nature of Doctrine*, p. 135.

in the Bible — psalms, law, parables, prophecies, and so on — the Bible tells one overarching story from creation to consummation." Were revelation a "communication of timeless truths otherwise inaccessible,"[49] then narrative, story, would not be an appropriate vehicle. But revelation is not that. Revelation is a narrative — a true and reliable one — about what God has done for our salvation. "Revelation is an act of interpersonal communication. By acting in history to save humanity, God has drawn back the veil of mystery and disclosed a portion of who he is. The knowledge of God arises from his identity as embodied in the narrative of salvation."[50] True narrative appropriately articulates the theme of a person's — divine and human — identity, including that on the communal level.[51]

To say that the canonical text — to be more precise, the meaning of the text of the canonical writings — is the ultimate norm of theology and practice is to say much in a pluralistic world. It is an important and normative statement. However, it does not say everything that must be said. "While the canon is (more or less) fixed, its interpretation is not"![52] In other words, who is to tell us how to best interpret and appropriate the message of the canonical text? Here the role of tradition and church comes to play in a significant way.

Scripture and Church

For patristic writers, the ultimate authority — read: divine authority — was located in Scripture, simple and pure.[53] No lesser witness than Saint Augustine can be mentioned as a main representative.[54] This view remained more or less intact until the high Middle Ages — but not all the way up to the Reformation, as is often assumed. It became an important issue a couple of centuries before the Reformation and a topic of fierce debate among theologians. The reason had to do with the new acknowledgment of the significance of exegesis in determining the meaning of biblical statements. The idea arose that biblical exegesis was to be granted higher status than the authority of the church

49. Pinnock, *Flame of Love*, p. 225.
50. Pinnock, *Flame of Love*, p. 224.
51. Vanhoozer, *Drama of Doctrine*, pp. 93-94, at 93; see also Hart, *Faith Thinking*, p. 107.
52. Vanhoozer, *Drama of Doctrine*, p. 123.
53. See Kelly, *Early Christian Doctrines*, p. 36; for a detailed discussion in early theology of the relationship between tradition and Scripture, see pp. 29-51.
54. Augustine, *City of God* 11.3. Similarly also, *Letter* 147.4. For a useful discussion, see Eno, "Authority," pp. 80-82.

(magisterium) in interpreting Scripture.[55] Only at the Council of Trent did the "Counter-Reformation" agenda help consolidate the supreme authority of the church magisterium as the highest level of arbitration of interpretation. That was, of course, a reaction to the Protestant insistence on *sola Scriptura*.

"The question as to what came first, the Word or the church, is meaningless, because the Word as inspired by the Spirit exists only when men hear it, or that the church makes the Word just as the Word makes the church into the church."[56] It is not only the Word and the church that stand in mutually conditioning relationship.[57] Indeed, there are the Holy Spirit, the apostolic tradition, the church, and the canonical text working together.[58] Hence, the saying, "Church, Gospel, and tradition always stand and fall together."[59]

Early theology, as mentioned, took for granted that Christ, as the Word and Truth of God, was the ultimate source of doctrine and faith, and that deposit of revelation was available in written Scripture. Even apostolic tradition — so highly revered especially in the earliest period of history — the preaching and belief of the church, as well as the liturgical experience of the church, were taken as subsets of and subordinate to Scripture (even when there was the gradual addition of what now is the NT to the OT, the original Scripture of the early church). That said, there hardly was any intuition of an opposition between Scripture and tradition, so evident in later history of theology. Hence, we can speak of the coinherence of Scripture and tradition in early theology.

Eventually, however, the question emerged concerning the status of extrascriptural tradition. Basil the Great in the East and Augustine in the West helped formulate this issue. According to the Cappadocian theologian, "Of the beliefs and practices whether generally accepted or publicly enjoined which are preserved in the Church some we possess derived from written teaching; others we have received delivered to us 'in a mystery' by the tradition of the apostles; and both of these in relation to true religion have the same force."[60] While this may sound like diminishing the value of Scripture, it is not; it is

---

55. See further, Pannenberg, "Crisis of the Scripture Principle," pp. 4-5.

56. Bonhoeffer, *Communion of Saints*, p. 161; for an important discussion, see Weber, *Foundations of Dogmatics*, 1:248-86.

57. See Moltmann, *Experiences in Theology*, p. 135.

58. See further, Vanhoozer, *Drama of Doctrine*, pp. 116-19.

59. The saying is attributed to J. A. Möhler as reported by Geiselmann, *The Meaning of Tradition*, p. 23; cited in Vanhoozer, *Drama of Doctrine*, p. 121.

60. Basil, *On The Holy Spirit* 27.66. Oberman (*Harvest of Medieval Theology*, p. 369) rightly observes the importance of this statement to later Roman Catholic understanding of the significance of tradition.

rather the elevation of growing tradition to a higher status.[61] Similarly, Saint Augustine, without in any way downplaying the supreme importance of Scripture, affirms the "*authoritative* extrascriptural oral tradition," in other words, tradition, which goes back to the apostles but cannot be found in sacred writings per se.[62]

A couple of centuries before the Reformation, the issue raised by Basil and Augustine was picked up in the fierce debates between those who advocated *sola Scriptura* and those of the "Scripture and tradition" camp. On the one hand, this issue concerned canon lawyers who sought to find legitimization for the canon laws alongside Scriptures.[63] The issue also emerged among the exegetes who were getting more and more concerned about the correct hermeneutical "foundation," and tradition's role therein. Ultimately, three positions were in place by the time of the Reformation: the view that every truth necessary for salvation can be found in Scripture, and only therein; the standpoint according to which the divine truth is found both in Scripture and the tradition of the church going back to the apostles; and the opinion that, since the Holy Spirit abides permanently in the church, the church not only controls the interpretation of Scripture but may also add to revelation.[64]

To this situation spoke the Protestant Reformation's insistence on *sola Scriptura*.[65] That principle, however, was not meant to deny the role of tradition but rather to define the ultimate norm of revelation and faith: written Scripture. The placement of ancient symbols of faith (the Apostles', Nicene, and Athanasian Creeds) at the beginning of *The Book of Concord*, the Lutheran Confessions, speaks volumes of the Reformers' desire to continue affirming the significance of tradition.[66] As a response to Reformation, the Council of Trent saw it necessary to even further highlight the importance of tradition.[67] However, Vatican II came to affirm that "there exists a close connection and communication between sacred tradition and Sacred Scripture. For both of them, flowing from the same divine wellspring, in a certain way merge into a unity and tend toward

---

61. In the same paragraph (*On the Holy Spirit* 27.66), Basil says: "For were we to attempt to reject such customs as have no written authority, on the ground that the importance they possess is small, we should unintentionally injure the Gospel in its very vitals."

62. Oberman, *Harvest of Medieval Theology*, p. 370; I am indebted to Grenz and Franke, *Beyond Foundationalism*, p. 96.

63. See Oberman, *Harvest of Medieval Theology*, p. 372.

64. See Tavard, *Holy Writ or Holy Church*, pp. 47-66.

65. For an important discussion, see Davies, *Problem of Authority*.

66. See also Lane, "Calvin's Use of the Fathers and Medievals," pp. 149-205.

67. Council of Trent, "Decree concerning the Canonical Scriptures," p. 17.

the same end."[68] Hence, in contemporary Roman Catholic understanding, "Sacred tradition and Sacred Scripture form one sacred deposit of the word of God, committed to the Church."[69]

The "Protestant principle" (Tillich) does not, then, mean neglecting tradition, but rather, as argued above, it means setting the text of Scripture as the highest norm of faith and theology that is currently the ecumenical consensus. Neither is the Protestant view an attempt to downplay the role of the church in relation to community and tradition. It is a principle of setting the Christian community under the authority and life-giving power of the Word of God. But this has to be done in a nuanced way. In Barth's theology, the church is tightly linked with Scripture. Apart from the Bible, "the Church is not addressed; it is engaged in dialogue with itself."[70] Thus, "the Church cannot evade Scripture. It cannot try to appeal past it directly to God, to Christ or to the Holy Spirit. It cannot assess and adjudge Scripture from a view of revelation gained apart from Scripture and not related to it."[71] The Bible as a written text thus has authority over all subsequent witnesses, even as it stands in essential unity with proclamation in the event of God's Word.[72] This is a needed reminder of the primacy of Scripture as the *theological* authority over the church.

Where Barth's view needs balancing is his claim that Scripture is autonomous and independent of all exegesis in its authority over the church.[73] According to him, it is thus Christ as the chief subject matter of the Bible and not human experience that provides the hermeneutical key and source of authority when it comes to the Bible: "To say that Jesus Christ rules the Church is equivalent to saying that Holy Scripture rules the Church. The one explains the other, the one can be understood only through the other."[74] Of course, as an abstract principle there is nothing wrong with insisting on the highest authority of Scripture, and hence Christ, as the ultimate authority. What is problematic is that Barth seems to ignore the robustly mutual nature of Scripture and church. My critique of the postliberal insistence on Scripture's authority as the function of its ecclesiastical usage is not to be interpreted as undermining the importance of Christian community to Bible reading. The role of the community just has to be put in a proper theological perspective.

68. *DV,* #9.
69. *DV,* #10.
70. *CD* I/1, p. 105.
71. *CD* I/2, p. 544.
72. *CD* I/1, p. 102.
73. *CD* I/2, p. 583.
74. *CD* I/2, p. 693.

Instead of regarding the ecclesial practice of reading the Scripture as not only creating the world but also determining the doctrine, we hold that the canonical text, as received and affirmed by the church, guides and "regulates" all practices of the church.

The turn to "practices"[75] in itself is a needed corrective to abstract, "theoretical," and often distanced-from-real-life reading of the Bible. Practice, however, is just that, *practice*. For us to make a distinction between good and bad practices, we need a criterion. That is the gospel message as presented in the canonical texts.

The church's important role in relation to Scripture comes to the fore in the brilliant distinction of Vanhoozer between *sola Scriptura* and *solo Scriptura*.[76] In the latter, "one Christian measures the scriptural interpretations of other Christians against the standard of his [or her] own scriptural interpretation."[77] The Protestant principle of the clarity of Scripture coupled with the priesthood of all believers — understood more as the priesthood of each and every individual believer rather than the communal and mutually conditioning priesthood of many together — caters to the highly individualistic "solo" Scripture mentality. That orientation is strengthened with post-Enlightenment hyperindividuality. If we are not careful, "the loss of tradition in Protestant theology" may follow.[78] Ironically, even the Protestant principle of the clarity of Scripture, when understood primarily in individualistic terms, may weaken the appreciation of tradition.[79] Orthodox theologian John Zizioulas's untiring insistence on the primacy of communion as the way to understanding both the divine (trinitarian) "personhood" and human personhood is a needed corrective.[80]

In response to the common individualistic misunderstanding, we have to say, "To locate divine authority in the canon is not to imply that individual readers may presume that they have immediate and unproblematic access to God's word."[81] Fruitful reading always happens in the Christian community,

---

75. Volf and Bass, eds., *Practicing Theology.*

76. Vanhoozer, *Drama of Doctrine*, p. 154.

77. Mathison, *Shape of Sola Scriptura*, p. 240; cited in Vanhoozer, *Drama of Doctrine*, p. 154.

78. Heading in Grenz and Franke, *Beyond Foundationalism*, p. 102.

79. See further, Pannenberg, *ST* 1:28-32.

80. Zizioulas, *Being as Communion*, pp. 100-101 particularly. Where Zizioulas's idea of communion as truth/truth as communion is liable has to do with the undermining of the cognitive nature of truth. That is rightly noted and critiqued by Volf, *After Our Likeness*, pp. 91-97.

81. Vanhoozer, *Drama of Doctrine*, p. 151.

and it is guided — and if need be, corrected — by living tradition. In other words, "*Sola scriptura* does not mean *nulla traditio* ('no tradition'), nor does it entail ignoring the Rule of Faith: 'It is clear that the *sola scriptura* did not mean scripture without tradition, but scripture as prior norm, potentially set in judgment over the tradition.'"[82]

Consequently, the Protestant principle of *sola Scriptura* should not be understood as a way of rejecting or undermining the role of tradition, but rather, as linking the two together. This is what Vanhoozer means when he says that the canonical-linguistic model "affirms both the necessity of *sola scriptura* and the necessity, even the inevitability, of tradition." The holding together of Scripture and tradition helps avoid what can be called "'biblical positivism' ('there is only script') and 'ecclesiastical positivism' ('there is only [ecclesiastical] performance')."[83] Whereas the former rejects tradition and creative understanding, the latter denies the authority of Scripture as canon. Vatican II's *Dei Verbum* (#2) formulates correctly the principle of mutuality: "Hence there exists a close connection and communication between sacred tradition and Sacred Scripture." Similarly, it has to be said that "Church and tradition are inseparable. By tradition we do not mean traditionalism. The Tradition of the Church is not an object which we possess, but a reality by which we are possessed."[84]

The importance of tradition is closely tied to the notion of the catholicity of the church.[85] The "catholic" teaching is to be found in Scripture, the highest authority, and the church's continuing proclamation, liturgy, and the sense of the faithful. Vincent of Lérins's classical formulation speaks of the authority of tradition as that which has been believed "everywhere, always and by all."[86] From around the same time in the fifth century, the rule found in *On the Catholic Faith*, attributed to Boethius, first states that "the Christian Faith is proclaimed by the authority of the New Testament and of the Old," making Scripture the highest authority, and then amplifies that statement in an important way: "This catholic church, then, spread throughout the world, is known by three particular marks: whatever is believed and taught in it has the authority of the Scriptures, or of universal tradition, or at least of its own

82. Vanhoozer, *Drama of Doctrine*, p. 233; citation in the text from Muller, "Scripture," 4:37.

83. Vanhoozer, *Drama of Doctrine*, p. 153.

84. Faith and Order, "Scripture, Tradition and Traditions," #56.

85. This was noted in Faith and Order, "Scripture, Tradition and Traditions," #70; see Cyril of Jerusalem, *Catechetical Lecture* 18, 23.

86. Vincent of Lérins, *Commonitorium*, chap. 4, #3.

and proper usage. And this authority is binding on the whole Church as is also the universal tradition of the Fathers."[87]

The binding nature of the authority of tradition is linked with the criterion of truth as consensus. Ecclesiastical consensus also has to be acknowledged as the common way for doctrine to develop. Consensus theory alone, however, hardly suffices, as the fierce debates around the time of the Reformation testify.[88]

Living Tradition and "Closed Canon"

"Tradition" in theological meaning refers both to the process of communication and to the content.[89] "Thus tradition means the handing down of Christian teaching during the course of the history of the church, but it also means that which was handed down."[90] At first it might seem that the very notion of tradition suggests something frozen, unchanging, fixed.[91] That, however, is not the case with the Spirit-led tradition among the people of God. In biblical and theological understanding, tradition is not a dead phenomenon. It is, as both Eastern Orthodox[92] and Roman Catholic theology insist, a living, dynamic, and hence, evolving process:

> This tradition which comes from the Apostles develop [*sic*] in the Church with the help of the Holy Spirit. For there is a growth in the understanding of the realities and the words which have been handed down. This happens through the contemplation and study made by believers, who treasure these things in their hearts (see Luke 2:19, 51) through a penetrating understanding of the spiritual realities which they experience, and through

87. Boethius, *On the Catholic Faith,* p. 71; for useful discussion, see Pelikan, *Emergence of the Catholic Tradition,* pp. 333-34 particularly.

88. See further, Pannenberg, *ST* 1:24-26.

89. Famously, the statement "Scripture, Tradition and Traditions," #39, makes a distinction between "Tradition" (capital *T*), "tradition" (lowercase *t*), and "traditions." The first refers to the gospel itself, "transmitted from generation to generation in and by the Church, Christ himself present in the life of the Church." The second term means the traditional process, and the third term refers to different Christian traditions (as in Lutheran and Roman Catholic).

90. Pelikan, *Emergence of the Catholic Tradition,* p. 7.

91. Pelikan, *Emergence of the Catholic Tradition;* Pelikan himself does not of course endorse this view.

92. Nissiotis, "Unity of Scripture and Tradition," pp. 183-208; Stamoolis, "Scripture and Tradition in the Orthodox Church," pp. 131-43.

the preaching of those who have received through Episcopal succession the sure gift of truth. For as the centuries succeed one another, the Church constantly moves forward toward the fullness of divine truth until the words of God reach their complete fulfillment in her.[93]

History, historical process over time, rather than being foreign to tradition is indeed its condition. From the *historical* nature of Christian faith follows necessarily the importance of tradition. Any religion based on historical acts and the preserving of that in the community of faith cannot resist the notion of tradition, nor should it.

That tradition is a living, dynamic process does not mean that therefore it is not regulated by the canon. It is so regulated even while we of course acknowledge that "[c]learly tradition — the oral transmission of the gospel — preceded the actual formation of the New Testament. . . . [H]owever, the apostolic tradition goes back to Jesus' own practice of interpreting his life and ministry in terms of the Old Testament Scriptures. The event of Jesus Christ is ultimately unintelligible apart from the Old Testament Scriptures. In this sense, then, Scripture — namely, the books of the Old Testament — precedes the apostolic tradition."[94] That tradition is regulated by canon does not mean that therefore tradition is only the "recipient" of authority. It is in light of shared ecclesiastical and theological tradition that Bible interpretation happens in the church. Even the Protestant *sola Scriptura* principle, as discussed above, is not a statement against tradition. Vanhoozer makes the obvious yet often neglected remark that "Church history is replete with examples of heretics who attempt to support their views biblically."[95] Rightly Polanyi argues that "[a] society which wants to preserve a fund of personal knowledge, must submit to tradition."[96] Hence, there is a mutual conditioning of tradition — combined with the living *sensus fidei* of God's people — and canon, yet the biblical text found in canonical Scriptures is the ultimate authority.

The whole concept of tradition — whether in epistemology or religion — has been difficult for the Enlightenment mind-set.[97] Only recently has the

93. *DV*, #8; similarly the Montreal 1963 Faith and Order statement "Scripture, Tradition and Traditions" (#46); see Grenz and Franke, *Beyond Foundationalism*, p. 94.

94. Vanhoozer, *Drama of Doctrine*, p. 139.

95. Vanhoozer, *Drama of Doctrine*, p. 113. Already Irenaeus in his *Against Heresies* 1.3 discussed "texts of Holy Scripture used by these heretics to support their opinions."

96. Polanyi, *Personal Knowledge*, p. 53.

97. For useful brief remarks on "the assault on tradition" coming from modernity and other sources, see Hart, *Faith Thinking*, pp. 167-68.

notion of tradition been rediscovered and its legitimate, indispensable role reaffirmed. Although for the Enlightenment mind-set, as embodied particularly in Kant, tradition represented deviation from true knowledge, which relies on universal reason — allegedly untainted by personal history, communal tradition, and so forth — contemporary philosophy has rediscovered the category of tradition in epistemology. Famously, the ethicist-philosopher Alasdair MacIntyre considers tradition not only inevitable but also a form of rationality. Human knowing is tradition-based.[98] In the same vein, the philosopher of science Polanyi insists that, not only in the humanities, but even in the natural sciences, knowledge happens through "indwelling the tradition."[99]

That said, one also has to raise the question: Which tradition? Whose church? When speaking of tradition, do we mean the ancient church or the current one; "our" church or the universal church? In other words, what kinds of developments are right and useful? Tradition is not infallible even though it is immensely valuable — and inevitable![100] The important book by the French Dominican Yves Congar, *True and False Reform of the Church,* reminds us that even reform efforts can go right or wrong. On the other side of the ecumenical spectrum are those liberal Protestants to whom tradition is but continuing revelation and hence can surpass and correct Scripture.[101] With these and other "uses" of tradition in view, Vanhoozer offers three important points to consider when assessing the value and role of tradition as the interpretive framework for interpreting Scripture:

> First, some of what passes for tradition is more akin to invention than discovery. . . . [T]heology needs to do more than repeat the past; the imagination does have a role to play. . . . Yet some imaginings are indeed "vain." Second, traditions are susceptible, like individuals, to prideful self-glorification. Belonging to a particular tradition, then, is no more guarantee of the truth of one's interpretations than were the "dreams of Cartesian orphans" who thought they could attain objectivity as individuals. Third, it is not clear how tradition can be criticized given the presumption of coincidence, that is, the notion that tradition is Scripture rightly interpreted.[102]

98. MacIntyre, *Whose Justice? Which Rationality?*

99. Polanyi, *Tacit Dimension.*

100. Contra Congar, *I Believe in the Holy Spirit,* p. 151.

101. Vanhoozer (*Drama of Doctrine,* p. 161) cites David Brown *(Tradition and Imagination)* as an example of this kind of view of tradition.

102. Vanhoozer, *Drama of Doctrine,* p. 162.

Hence, while acknowledging both the inevitability and value of tradition, theology and ecclesiastical culture should also allow for a healthy criticism and continuous assessment of the state of tradition. True, the Holy Spirit is given to the church and the same Spirit guides the disciples of Jesus into all truth; however, as the bewildering diversity of the notions of what is true in the midst of the divisions of the Christian churches indicates, not all traditions have heard the Spirit's whispering at the same level of accuracy! Rather than making human tradition an absolute norm, theology does better to be humble and recognize that tradition is *human* tradition. As in personal life, in tradition there are imperfect developments, sinful attitudes, power plays, instances of egoism and self-glorification — and just plain human imperfection![103] Yet another liability of the "uncritical use of tradition," the Methodist Thomas C. Oden reminds us, is that it "may leave the unwanted implication that Christian teaching is essentially an archaic or dogmatic traditionalism that is determined simply by rigid formulas and ingroup prejudices." On the contrary, tradition in both Christian and Jewish understanding "is a vital social reality that receives and transmits the history of revelation. Tradition wants to be danced, sung, feasted upon, and celebrated."[104]

Tradition, Identity, and Context

Tradition is integrally linked with the question of identity. "'Tradition' names the way in which Christian identity is sustained across differences of time and place. The mission of tradition is the 'mediation of the past.'"[105] It is highly significant that the earliest form of the received Christian tradition, *regula fidei* ("rule of faith"), was a baptismal symbol whose only — or even primary — function was to express not the content of faith but rather the form of commitment. "In Christ," an important NT expression, the baptismal candidate gained a new identity.[106]

Faithfulness to tradition does not mean mere repetition of received formulae. Indeed, that may lead exactly to the opposite not only because in a changing situation something said earlier may mean something else, but also

---

103. For an insightful discussion of "the fallibility of tradition" and "the naivete of tradition," see Vanhoozer, *Drama of Doctrine*, pp. 163-65.

104. Oden, *Systematic Theology*, 1:338.

105. Vanhoozer, *Drama of Doctrine*, p. 125; the quotation at the end is from Gunton, *Brief Theology of Revelation*, p. 102.

106. See further, Vanhoozer, *Drama of Doctrine*, pp. 203-4.

because, as mentioned above, texts, once written, tend to gain a life of their own.[107] Hence, the relationship between "identity" and "sameness"/"difference" calls for careful and deep reflection. Not for nothing should we therefore speak of various "senses of tradition"[108] as we do "senses" of Scripture. On the one hand, one has to secure close enough identity to speak of continuity. On the other hand, "some differences are expressions of faithfulness and may be productive of greater understanding."[109] Paul Ricoeur's distinction between the two Latin words *idem* and *ipse*, "sameness," as in "what," and "identity," as in "who,"[110] well illustrates the dynamic between the need to secure continuity and make room for continuing reinterpretation of the received tradition. The *ipse* kind of identity is less about "numerical" identity and more about narrative, "personal" (including communal) continuity, which is creative, responsive to new challenges, and dynamic. The *ipse* identity not only allows for but also entails improvisation in new and complicated life situations and, say, new cultural contexts,[111] known in missiological literature as contextualization[112] or "translation."[113] The title of the recent landmark missiological monograph by two leading Roman Catholic scholars captures this dynamic aptly: *Constants in Context*.[114] Holding on to this dynamic best secures what can be called "faithful improvisation."[115] Pinnock rightly reminds us that when speaking of doctrinal fidelity, we should also be mindful of "the imperative of timeliness." This means that while "[t]heology must be faithful to revelation . . . [it] also speak[s] about things that matter in present situations." That is because "[d]octrines are to be timely witnesses, not timeless abstractions."[116]

The role of tradition in contemporary culture and philosophy is a tension-filled issue. The epistemological critic of Western culture Lesslie

107. See the important and now classic discussion in Ricoeur, "Hermeneutical Function of Distanciation."

108. Thiel, *Senses of Tradition*.

109. Vanhoozer, *Drama of Doctrine*, p. 126.

110. Ricoeur, *Oneself as Another*, pp. 116-22; I am indebted to Vanhoozer, *Drama of Doctrine*, p. 127.

111. Importantly, the Faith and Order (Montreal, 1963) "Scripture, Tradition and Traditions" devoted a whole section ("III. The Christian Tradition and Cultural Diversity") to the topic of cultural diversity.

112. See further, Bevans, *Models of Contextual Theology*.

113. Sanneh, *Translating the Message*.

114. Bevans and Schroeder, *Constants in Context*.

115. Vanhoozer, *Drama of Doctrine*, pp. 335-44 (under the telling heading "faithful improvisation"); see Castelo, "Improvisational Quality of Ecclesial Holiness," pp. 87-104.

116. Pinnock, *Flame of Love*, p. 215.

Newbigin has brought this dilemma into sharp focus. According to him, modernity, on the one hand, denies the whole concept of tradition in its alleged "neutral" standpoint. The Cartesian method mistakenly believes itself to be tradition-free. Postmodernism enthusiastically affirms traditions, "regimes of truth," happily existing side by side. No one tradition is better or worse, and no one tradition has the right to impose its own rationality upon the others.[117]

The necessity of acknowledging the tradition-laden nature of all human knowledge is based on the postmodern conviction, nurtured by contemporary sociology of knowledge, that all knowledge is socially and thus "contextually" shaped. "There is no rationality except a socially embodied rationality."[118] Any knowledge is rooted in and emerges out of a particular context, location, situation. Newbigin boldly accepts that all truth is socially and historically embodied.[119] This "situational" nature of human knowledge means that knowing can only happen from within tradition; however, this does not mean that therefore no one can claim to speak truth. Indeed, to "pretend to *possess* the truth in its fullness is arrogance," whereas the "claim to have been given the decisive clue for the human search after truth is not arrogant; it is the exercise of our responsibility as part of the human family."[120] This seeking after the truth happens first and foremost in the Christian community. Whereas modernity focuses on the individual person's knowledge, Christian rationality believes in a communally received knowledge. For the Christian church this tradition is the narrative, the story of the gospel confessed by all Christians:

> The Christian community, the universal Church, embracing more and more fully all the cultural traditions of humankind, is called to be that community in which tradition of rational discourse is developed which leads to a true understanding of reality, because it takes as its starting point and as its permanent criterion of truth the self-revelation of God in Jesus Christ. It is necessarily a particular community among all the human communities. . . . But it has a universal mission, for it is the community chosen and sent by God for this purpose. This particularity, however scandalous it may seem to a certain kind of cosmopolitan mind, is inescapable.[121]

117. Newbigin, *A Word in Season*, p. 187.
118. Newbigin, *Gospel in a Pluralist Society*, p. 87.
119. Newbigin, "Religious Pluralism," p. 50.
120. Newbigin, "Religious Pluralism," p. 54.
121. Newbigin, *Gospel in a Pluralist Society*, pp. 87-88.

There is always the danger of domestication of the tradition or, as in postmodernism, its reduction into *a* story among other equal stories — that, in Newbigin's mind, would lead to pluralism and denial of the particularity of the gospel. The gospel can be protected from this kind of domestication, he believes: "The truth is that the gospel escapes domestication, retains its proper strangeness, its power to question us, only when we are faithful to its universal, supranational, supracultural nature."[122] By making universal truth claims, Christian faith coexists with other traditions and their claims to truth.[123] Out of the framework of the gospel narrative, Christian tradition, the church seeks to understand reality — rather than vice versa.[124]

As mentioned in the orientation to part 1, it would be natural to move from this chapter to considering the meaning of Scripture and revelation in other living faiths. Before that is attempted (in chapter 8), however, the topic of natural theology and natural revelation will be taken up. It may seem out of place since the theme of "general revelation" is usually discussed at the beginning of the doctrine of revelation as a preamble to "revelation proper." Why that is not the order followed here will become evident in the discussion of the next chapter.

---

122. Newbigin, "Enduring Validity of Cross-Cultural Mission," p. 50.
123. Newbigin, *Gospel in a Pluralist Society,* p. 64.
124. Newbigin, *Gospel in a Pluralist Society,* p. 53.

7. Natural Theology as Christian Theology

Natural Knowledge of God Is "Natural"

Both common sense and Christian tradition[1] have always believed that the "traces" of God are to be found in the world God created.[2] This intuition can even be placed in a wider framework in the history of religions and of cultures: "The idea that a transcendent reality can be known or at least intimated through the mundane has a long history and is not a specifically religious idea."[3] To say that common sense and Christian intuition have posited the existence of God on the basis of the created order is not to say that the expressed doctrine of natural theology has always been a pedigree of Christian theology. Indeed, "natural theology — as this notion would now be understood — is a recent invention."[4]

When compared to typical systematic presentations, it may seem odd for talk about natural revelation and natural theology to come so late, almost at the end of the discussion of the doctrine of revelation. Isn't it the norm to divide the doctrine of revelation into two parts — general and special revelation — and then to speak of the former first? While that approach is possible and in many ways useful, the reason for the current choice of order has to do with the marginalized — almost exclusively preparatory — role assigned to

---

1. For early Christian fathers, see Pelikan, *Christianity and Classical Culture.*
2. For an important statement, see Tillich, *ST* 1:118.
3. McGrath, *Fine-Tuned Universe,* p. 11.
4. McGrath, *Scientific Theology,* 1:242.

natural theology in modern theology. Indeed, there are theological traditions such as neo-orthodoxy in which natural theology has a hard time getting a word into the dogmatic discussion, apart from when it's critiqued. The thesis of this discussion argues for both the possibility and the need for a robust *Christian* natural theology and that, whatever preparatory role (in relation to special revelation) it may play, natural theology is an essential part of the polymorphous doctrine of revelation. Indeed, it will be argued that natural theology is not "natural" in the sense that it wouldn't be part of the divine revelation. Similar to the doctrine of revelation in general, which is thoroughly and robustly trinitarian, the discussion of natural theology in this project concerns itself with "the dynamics of a *trinitarian* natural theology."[5]

Important here is how one understands the category of "nature." Whereas for common sense "nature" seems to be a self-evident concept, it is not necessarily so when subjected to scrutiny. It is socially constructed. However, this does not make impossible the theological evaluation of nature — not at all. The acknowledgment of the socially constructed idea of "nature" rather opens the door for a robustly Christian understanding of nature. For Christian theology, nature is "creation."[6] All Christian talk about natural theology rejects the idea of the autonomy of nature, either as in creation or as in human nature. For Christian theology, all nature is contingent and derives from God. Hence also, all natural knowledge and natural theology are based on God, and God alone.

Until the beginning of the twentieth century, the "natural" knowledge of God by human beings created in the image of God was not contested. Biblical passages such as Psalm 19, Romans 1:19-21, and Acts 17:16-34, among others, seemed to affirm it unequivocally.[7] Said Athanasius: "For by means of the creation itself, the Word reveals God the Creator; and by means of the world [does he declare] the Lord the Maker of the world; and by means of the formation [of man] the Artificer who formed him."[8] In Aquinas's theology, natural knowledge of God was of course an important theme,[9] as it was in Calvin's.[10] Even Luther, who was also critical of perversions of natural knowledge of God prior to revelation in Christ, took the natural knowledge of God for granted,

---

5. Title of chap. 6 in McGrath, *Fine-Tuned Universe.*

6. For details, see McGrath, *Scientific Theology,* vol. 1, chap. 3.

7. Tradition named this capacity *cognitio* or *notitia naturalis.* In Aquinas, *cognitio naturalis* is distinguished but not separated from *cognitio supernaturalis,* which is mediated by God's revelation in Christ (*ST* 2.2.2 a 3 ad 1).

8. Irenaeus, *Against Heresies* 4.6.6.

9. The classic statement of Thomas is in *ST* 1.1.12.

10. Calvin, *Inst.* 1.3; see Muller, "Duplex cognitio Dei."

even among the idolaters.[11] The Swedish botanist Carl von Linné of the eighteenth century saw clearly the vestiges of God. English natural theology came to its zenith in William Paley's *Natural Theology; or, Evidences of the Existence and Attributes of the Deity* in the beginning of the nineteenth century (1802), which utilized the famous — or infamous[12] — metaphor of a clock or watch.

In contemporary theology, *Dei Verbum's* formulation expresses well this confidence in wider Christian tradition: "God, who through the Word creates all things (see John 1:3) and keeps them in existence, gives men an enduring witness to Himself in created realities (see Rom. 1:19-20)" (#3). Whereas criticism of the idea of natural theology began from the time of Schleiermacher, before Barth the natural knowledge of God was not contested.[13] Even Barth, of course, did not categorically contest the notion of some kind of natural knowledge of God;[14] he just did not take it for a revelation and, rather than making it an asset, considered it a major obstacle to the saving knowledge of God.[15]

How Natural Theology Became "Unnatural"

Moltmann makes the important statement: "Inasmuch as natural theology has to do with the universality of God, we might also view it as one dimension of revealed theology, for the universality of the one God is also part of God's revelation."[16] This observation of Moltmann is in keeping with the original meaning of natural theology both in its pre-Christian meaning and in its adopted Christian meaning. Among the Stoics, the term meant something that is true by nature, in other words, of itself, as opposed to a claim whose validation needs human positing, whether on account of tradition, or custom, or political theology. "Natural theology, then, is the talk about God that corresponds to the nature of the divine itself, unfalsified by the political interests related to the state cults or by the literary imaginings, or lies, of the poets."[17] This meaning is illustrated in Cicero's *De natura deorum (On the Nature of the Deities)*. In

11. WA 56:176; *LW* 25:157 (on Rom. 1:20).

12. The contemporary English atheist Richard Dawkins's *Blind Watchmaker* mocks Paley's natural theology.

13. See Pannenberg, *ST* 1:74.

14. On Barth's remarks on Rom. 1:20-21, see *CD* I/2, pp. 306-7.

15. The classic discussion is of course in *CD* I/2, §17: "The Revelation of God as the Abolition of Religion."

16. Moltmann, *Experiences in Theology,* p. 73.

17. Pannenberg, *ST* 1:76-77.

other words, even in philosophy, "natural" did not mean natural as in coming from human nature, but rather, it meant something in keeping with the true nature of the deity.

Consequently, early Christian theology did not use natural theology to develop proofs for the existence of God. God's existence was taken for granted. Rather, early theologians saw natural theology as an aid in the investigation into the nature of God. This task was urgent to early theology — beyond the need to establish a pedagogical contact with philosophers — because "[a]t stake was the truth of the Christian God as not just the national God of the Jews but the God of all peoples. The natural theology of the philosophers had formulated a criterion for judging whether any God could be seriously considered as the author of the whole cosmos, and Christian theology had to meet this criterion if its claim could be taken seriously that the God who redeems us in Jesus Christ is the Creator of heaven and earth and thus the one true God of all peoples."[18] This adoption of philosophers' natural theology did not pass without criticism. In light of biblical revelation, *Christian* natural theology also had to critique and revise the received tradition.[19] The main point for the sake of this discussion is that the adoption of natural theology in its original meaning offered a tremendous aid to the mission of the church as it sought to convince the contemporary people that the God of the Bible is the only true God. This orientation can perhaps already be seen in the Pauline statement to the Galatians (4:8) about the gods of religions, which "by nature are no gods."[20]

Hence, for patristic writers natural theology was not a preparatory stage on the way to revealed theology after later Christian distinctions. "It is plain that for Augustine the Christian doctrine of God did not differ in principle from the natural theology of the philosophers in its platonic form. . . . As Augustine saw it, the Christian doctrine of God was identical with a purified form of true natural theology, i.e., theology commensurate with the nature of God. He believed that this theology had found its clearest expression in the biblical testimony."[21]

Only in medieval Latin theology did the understanding of the nature and role of natural theology change drastically; that change forms the background for — and has caused the suspicion against — any discussion of natural theol-

18. Pannenberg, *ST* 1:79.
19. Pannenberg, *ST* 1:79.
20. See Pannenberg, *ST* 1:79.
21. Pannenberg, *ST* 1:80-81.

ogy in modern and contemporary theology. As soon as Aristotle rather than Plato became the normative philosopher, leading Christian theologians came to limit significantly and revise the meaning of natural theology. In Aquinas, what can be known on account of rational knowledge is clearly distinguished from the proper articles of faith. The former becomes the preamble to the latter (the *preambula ad articulos fidei*).[22] In later Thomism and scholasticism in general, the typical "two-story" distinction of theology between "natural" and "revealed" became a norm. Here, therefore, the meaning of "natural" undergoes a dramatic shift: rather than denoting something that is in keeping with the (true) nature of God, "natural" means knowledge of God in keeping with *human* nature and human rational knowledge.[23]

Until the time of the Enlightenment, medieval theology as well as Reformation tradition, even with the changed meaning of natural theology, still maintained their close connection with divine revelation. What happened with the rise of the "Age of Reason" was the use of natural theology as a way to prove the existence of God apart from biblical revelation or even any religious commitments; this is illustrated even in the contemporary definition of natural theology by William P. Alston: "the enterprise of providing support for religious beliefs by starting from the premises that neither are nor presuppose any religious beliefs."[24] Behind that project is the Enlightenment's desire for the autonomy and sovereignty of human reason.[25] Furthermore, there is also the idea — unfounded, of course — of the "objectivity" and universality of the notion of "nature." In other words, Enlightenment epistemology mistakenly assumed that notions such as *natural* religion and *natural* knowledge were not interest-laden.[26] On this assumption, the Enlightenment shared the ancient tradition of classical Greek writers.[27] As mentioned above — and as will be discussed in detail in the volume on creation and theological anthropology — far from being an innocent concept, "nature" is a social construction.

This drastically changed meaning of the nature and role in theology of "natural theology" is clearly behind Barth's highly polemical attitude toward natural theology, as for him it comes from (human) nature, and hence means

22. Aquinas, *ST* 1.2.1.

23. Pannenberg, *ST* 1:81; see also pp. 73-82.

24. Alston, *Perceiving God*, p. 289.

25. See further, McGrath, *Open Secret*, pp. 3-8.

26. For details, see these standard discussions: Raven, *Natural Religion and Christian Theology*; Byrne, *Natural Religion and the Nature of Religion*.

27. See further, Lloyd, "Greek Antiquity," pp. 1-24; I am indebted to McGrath, *Open Secret*, p. 143 n. 8.

nothing less than an effort of "domesticating the Gospel."[28] Indeed, for him, natural theology thus conceived expresses our "self-preservation and self-affirmation" against God and hence is essentially a matter of "self-justification."[29]

Of course, there are instances in which natural theology has been abused in a way that is non-Christian. That is where Barth's *Nein!* (no) to Brunner makes the valid point: as long as appeal to the knowledge of God — and the true "nature" of things — is used as a pretext for either ignoring the divine revelation in Christ or as a way of human self-affirmation against God, it is to be rejected. That was also Luther's motif in the Heidelberg Disputation (1518); he labeled that kind of "natural" theology a "theology of glory." However, the abuse of the category of natural theology should not become the theological guide, as it happens in Barth.

The assessment and correction of Barth's view have to begin with the important observation that it has no relation to the original Christian meaning (nor to the pre-Christian philosophical view). Indeed, Barth's view is not only different from, but ironically, is also absolutely opposite to, tradition.[30] I have a hard time imagining a Christian theologian who wouldn't agree with Barth's criticism of what he calls "natural theology" but should have named "*perverted* natural theology." Against Barth, ironically, we have to say, following Pannenberg, that "[t]o show that Christianity is in agreement with natural religion is thus to strengthen the authority of the Christian revelation."[31]

In this light another kind of criticism coming from the tradition of Reformed theology similarly appears to be without foundation. I have in mind the American Reformed epistemology tradition, as represented by such contemporary luminaries as Alvin Plantinga, Nicholas Wolterstorff, and William P. Alston. Where Plantinga goes wrong in the first place is that for him natural theology is an attempt to *prove* the existence of God. In other words, for him, natural theology seeks to find evidential basis for belief in God, and doing so, it ends up assuming another "foundation" below or beyond the ground belief that simply posits the existence of God. Not surprisingly then, for Plantinga, Aquinas is the prime example of a natural theologian.[32] Reformed epistemology's rejection of natural theology has a number of problems, the first of which is historical. Natural theology originally did not mean anything like

28. Barth, *CD* II/1, p. 142.
29. Barth, *CD* II/1, p. 136.
30. See further, Pannenberg, *ST* 1:103.
31. Pannenberg, *ST* 1:103.
32. See Plantinga, "Reason and Belief in God," pp. 16-93. For a balanced critique and assessment of Plantinga and his colleagues, see also McGrath, *Scientific Theology*, 1:264-67.

what Plantinga and others are assuming, that is, a *human* attempt to build an evidentialist case.[33] The second problem is theological and derives from the historical. Even when natural theology's meaning changed (from keeping with the nature of God to human nature), it was not utilized for evidentialist purposes, not even in Aquinas.

In sum, the Barthian opposition to all notions of natural theology is not only problematic in terms of biblical teaching of natural theology, as will be detailed below, but is also historically misleading as it ignores the original meaning of the term. Related to the historical liability is the fact that Barth's view has to be deemed a deviation from the wider Reformed tradition beginning with Calvin and running all the way to such contemporary luminaries as T. F. Torrance.[34] Two other problems face Barth's project: his opposition to natural theology is integrally linked to his indifference toward dialogue with the sciences,[35] discussed in the volume on creation and anthropology; and his highly dubious view of the nature of religion and religiosity. This latter observation calls for some elucidation.

Keith Ward observes correctly that Barth's claim that "Religion is unbelief"[36] and his characterization of "religion as idolatry and self-righteousness"[37] are not based on a careful study of religions (which Barth never attempted) but rather are an a priori negative stance against all forms of human religiosity, expressed dramatically in his statement that "the entelechy of man's I-ness is not divine in nature but, on the contrary, is in contradiction to the divine nature."[38] The problem here is not so much the critical attitude toward religions and human religiosity that, as we can tell on the basis of empirical observations, comes to us with mixed, at times perverted, motifs, but that even Barth's judgment, *qua* human judgment, is just that, *human*. What if this one is erroneous as much as — or even more than — other *human* judgments of religions? Barth's resolution that, rather than human religiosity, divine revelation as expressed in the Bible is the answer, is of course another *human* judgment! How can this one not be as sinful and erroneous as other human claims? What if this claim (Barth's) is based on pride and self-affirmation — or some other, less than valid motif?[39]

---

33. Plantinga, "Reformed Objection to Natural Theology," pp. 49-62.

34. For an important dialogue with Barth, see Torrance, "Problem of Natural Theology," pp. 121-35. For Torrance's natural theology, see McGrath, *Scientific Theology*, 1:279-86.

35. See further, Anderson, "Barth and a New Direction," pp. 241-66.

36. Barth, *CD* I/2, p. 299; see also p. 301.

37. Barth, *CD* I/2, p. 314.

38. Barth, *CD* I/2, p. 7.

39. Ward, *Religion and Revelation*, p. 17.

Brunner, Barth's alleged opponent, is not materially doing anything much different. The true test of whether the revelation is true is simply that it comes "from God himself."[40] So, how is this different from Barth's appeal to be the mouthpiece of God vis-à-vis the alleged human interlocutors? The Muslims are of course saying the same in reference to the Qur'an, as are adherents of other religions. Brunner is making things even worse as he claims that only "[t]hat which can be based on rational grounds" is revelation![41] If this is not *human* (self-)affirmation, then what is? The deepest irony in the assessment of religions and revelation in the theologies of these two neo-orthodox theologians is that whereas they "insist that reason cannot judge revelation . . . they themselves judge all revelations" as unworthy.[42]

This is where we stand at the beginning of the third millennium: on the one hand, we have serious objections to and rebuttals of any program of natural theology; indeed, the whole project is "hindered both by a definitional miasma, and the lingering memories of past controversies."[43] On the other hand, we have luminaries both in the "Barthian" camp, such as the later T. F. Torrance, who found a way to establish a natural theology, and outside that camp, such as the theologian-scientist Alister McGrath, who has issued a passionate call for the renewal of natural theology. Among other leading systematicians, towering figures such as Moltmann and Pannenberg simply take it as axiomatic — after a careful dialogue with tradition — that to establish an integral connection between theology and the rest of the culture, including science, natural theology is needed. What would a renewed Christian natural theology look like?

Natural Theology as Trinitarian Christian Theology

Barth's view that natural theology undermines the authority of the Bible[44] is misleading. McGrath echoes a "widespread consensus within the scholarly community that the Old Testament includes a significant number of appeals

---

40. Brunner, *Revelation and Reason*, p. 207.

41. Brunner, *Revelation and Reason*; I am indebted to the careful discussion in Ward, *Religion and Revelation*, p. 17.

42. Ward, *Religion and Revelation*, p. 21; For a fuller discussion, see my "Karl Barth and the Theology of Religions," pp. 236-57.

43. McGrath, *Open Secret*, p. 2.

44. See Barth's comments in Barth and Brunner, *Natural Theology*, pp. 82, 87, 107; I am indebted to McGrath, *Scientific Theology*, 1:257.

to both what we might call 'natural theology' and 'natural law.' "[45] Not surprisingly, the OT Wisdom literature contains a number of relevant references to this topic — as will be discussed below. The classic formulation appears in Proverbs 3:19-20:

> The LORD by wisdom founded the earth;
>> by understanding he established the heavens;
> by his knowledge the deeps broke forth,
>> and the clouds drop down the dew.

It is only "natural" to believe that this created order, from the smallest to the largest creatures, indeed radiates the wisdom and rationality of God. This is not to say that it is self-evident or fully open to all; rather, it is to establish the possibility for discernment. Although with the psalmist we gladly observe how

> The heavens are telling the glory of God;
>> and the firmament proclaims his handiwork (Ps. 19:1),

and indeed even more:

> Day to day pours forth speech,
>> and night to night declares knowledge (v. 2),

it is still a matter of human discernment. Where one sees the handiwork of God, another does not. Rightly, McGrath notes, when commenting on this psalm and other familiar OT passages (Ps. 8:3-4; Isa. 55:9), these passages affirm natural theology's "possibility, while pointing to the fundamental contradictions and tensions that this possibility creates."[46] In other words, the speech of nature, in order to "disclose the transcendent . . . must be 'seen' or 'read' in certain specific ways — ways that are not themselves necessarily mandated by nature itself."[47] While "nature is patient of . . . multiple readings . . . [n]ature does not provide its own authorized interpretation."[48] What David Kelsey, in his theological anthropology, says of the quotidian, also applies to nature, cre-

---

45. McGrath, *Scientific Theology,* 1:257-58. For a standard discussion, see Barr, *Biblical Faith and Natural Theology.* The topic of natural law is discussed in the context of creation and anthropology.

46. McGrath, *Open Secret,* p. 1.

47. McGrath, *Open Secret,* p. 3; see also chap. 6.

48. McGrath, *Open Secret,* p. 148.

ation: the "quotidian is inherently ambiguous experientially. This ambiguity is rooted ontologically — that is, in the creatureliness of the quotidian."[49] Nature, like texts, needs to be first translated and then interpreted!

Set in the larger interreligious matrix, nature is open to readings through the lens of Jewish-Christian, Islamic, Hindu, Confucian — or, say, agnostic, atheistic, or pantheistic — traditions.[50] In Islamic traditions, one can hardly speak of natural theology. For Muslim intuitions, the acknowledgment of natural theology would lead to the undermining of the absolute authority of the Qur'an. Even the highly regarded *kalam* tradition of Islam — the closest parallel to Christian scholasticism — hardly qualifies as a proper candidate for natural theology known in Christian tradition.[51] While the *kalam* cosmological argumentation had significant advocates in Islamic tradition, it has fallen from grace among most contemporary thinkers. Indeed, there is a marked and significant difference between Jewish-Christian and Islamic traditions: whereas in the former, Jewish-Christian Scriptures mandate an engagement with the natural order, in the latter, such engagement is at best tolerated, and often completely eschewed.[52]

Another important aspect of the biblical natural theology is that the speech of creation about the Creator is not made autonomous. Rather, it is tightly linked to its source, the God of the Bible. Psalm 19 makes this clear. Having sung the praises of the knowledge of God in the created order (vv. 1-6), the poem seamlessly continues to speak of the "law of the LORD [which] is perfect" (v. 7) and the "fear of the LORD" (v. 9). In other words, the OT "does not endorse any notion of nature as an autonomous source of knowledge of God."[53] Nor does the NT.[54] In Romans 1:20, Paul makes it clear that it is by virtue of God's doing that humanity can know God on the basis of the created order. Commenting on this passage and on John 1:11 ("He came to his own home, and his own people received him not"), Pannenberg rightly concludes: "Of course we are also told that his own did not receive him, but the painful sharpness of this fact is this: The ones who did not receive him were not strangers but from the very first they were his own people. If this is so, then it

---

49. Kelsey, *Eccentric Existence*, 1:202.

50. For an important statement on the religious ambivalence of nature, see Hick, *An Interpretation of Religion*, p. 73.

51. See Craig and Sinclair, "*Kalam* Cosmological Argument."

52. McGrath, *Open Secret*, p. 183; see also pp. 181-82.

53. McGrath, *Scientific Theology*, 1:259.

54. For a useful discussion, see McGrath, *Scientific Theology*, 1:260-64. For the classic passage in Acts 17, see the still-standard study, Gärtner, *Areopagus Speech*.

cannot have been totally alien to their being or their knowledge, for the being of creatures, even of sinners, is constituted by the creative presence of God, his Logos, and his Spirit among them."[55]

In principle, Barth was not of course wrong in linking all true knowledge of God to Christ; in his doing so, however, he failed to see that exactly because all true knowledge of God is grounded in Christ, it may be found everywhere in God's creation, of which Christ is the agent. Human beings, having been created in the image of God, can only know God to the extent God allows himself to be known in nature, including nature as in creation or nature as in human nature. Again Pannenberg rightly concludes: "By nature, i.e., from creation, God, the God of the apostolic gospel (Rom. 1:19-20), is known to all people. This is not a statement of natural theology. It is a statement that is made about us in the light of the revelation of God in Jesus Christ."[56] The expression "by nature" in this statement should not be limited to nature as in creation; it also refers to *human* nature and has everything to do with what tradition calls innate *(insitia)* knowledge of God.[57]

One important aspect here is what might be called "the persistence of the transcendent,"[58] that is, the fact that it seems to belong to human nature to be open to and inquire into the realities beyond the visible world. Not for nothing does Princeton philosopher-theologian Wentzel J. van Huyssteen speak of the image of God in terms of the emergence of a natural human tendency to believe in God.[59]

The notion of "innate" knowledge of God must be affirmed on the basis of the doctrine of the *imago Dei,* but differently from tradition, the distinction between innate and acquired knowledge of God must be handled with care. Is there any "knowledge" that comes so much "from outside" that it is not "acquired"? In other words: In light of current brain science about how human knowledge works, isn't all knowing in one sense acquired in terms of having been incorporated into the whole of the human person's knowledge and, thus, embodied? That said, we have to pay tribute to tradition's distinction (if not separation) between these two ways of knowledge of God.

---

55. Pannenberg, *ST* 1:75.

56. Pannenberg, *ST* 1:107-8.

57. See Athanasius, *On the Incarnation of the Word* 3; for Augustine, see McGrath, *Scientific Theology,* 1:253-54. Pannenberg also helpfully relates the innate knowledge of God to *syneidēsis,* "conscience" (*ST* 1:108-13); see also the preamble to John Paul II's encyclical *Veritatis Splendor* (1993).

58. Title of chap. 2 in McGrath, *Open Secret.*

59. Van Huyssteen, *Alone in the World?*

Moltmann makes the brilliant observation that, rightly understood, natural theology is not only consonant with true Christian theology, but "Christian theology *itself* is the true natural theology" if Christian theology seeks to transcend the limitations of "a church doctrine confined to its own closed circle" and wishes to be public theology.[60] Such theology, I argue, is in keeping with the "nature" of the created order *qua* created (rather than as a self-contained system) and God as the true God of the Bible (rather than the human-made gods of religions). If God is the "all-determining reality" (Pannenberg), then the truth claims of theology necessarily are also public in nature. Christian natural theology has great potential to help the bridge-building effort of the Christian church and theology as we seek to relate to public life, environmental concerns, various aspects of human cultures, and similar issues.

Moltmann reminds us that even for Aquinas, Christian theology presupposes natural theology as the (supernatural) "grace" that fulfills and sanctifies rather than destroys "nature," even if natural theology belongs to the *preambula ad articulos fidei*,[61] the preliminaries for the articles of faith. That said, it should also be emphasized that Christian theology is the presupposition of natural theology.[62] The "book of nature" does not yield an unambiguous testimony to God. To some it may appear to be that; for many, nature's witness is not there.[63] Hence, there is a mutual, integral relationship between Christian natural theology and Christian revealed theology. Indeed, there is only one Christian doctrine of revelation, polymorphous in nature.[64] The lesson is that — similarly to geometry, which can, but should not, be seen as an independent discipline from physics — natural theology shares with revealed theology an "indissoluble unity."

Consequently, rightly understood natural theology is part of the trinitarian polymorphous divine revelation. The Father creates through the Son in the power of the Spirit. As a result, all of reality, having been created in the divine wisdom, gives access through the life-giving Spirit to the knowledge of the God of the Bible in Jesus Christ. Human nature, even in its fallen state[65] but still maintaining its status as the *imago Dei*, is most appropriately an echo of

---

60. Moltmann, *Experiences in Theology,* p. 65.

61. Aquinas, *ST* 1.2.

62. Similarly, Torrance, "Problem of Natural Theology," pp. 128-29 particularly.

63. Moltmann, *Experiences in Theology,* p. 67.

64. For a delightful analogy in relation to physical sciences, see Torrance, "Problem of Natural Theology," p. 129.

65. For the discussion on "the implications of sin for a natural theology," see McGrath, *Scientific Theology,* 1:286-94.

the trinitarian God, not on its own account but only on account of its contingency in Father, Son, and Holy Spirit.[66] "A Christian natural theology is about seeing nature in a specific manner, which allows the observers to discern in what is seen the truth, beauty, and goodness of a trinitarian God who is already known; and which allows nature to function as a pathway towards this same God for secular culture as a whole. The meaning of 'nature' is not something that is self-evident, but something that requires to be discerned."[67]

An important theological resource for a robustly Christian trinitarian natural theology has to do with incarnation. Among other things, incarnation blurs any categorical distinction between "natural" and "supernatural." "Nature and supernature are not to be thought of as two separate worlds, but as different expressions of the same reality."[68] Hence a created order may truly, albeit not fully, give access to the existence and nature of the Creator, the God of the Bible.

If there is a symbiotic relationship between "special" revelation and natural theology, then it means that the whole of creation, reflecting the Creator, may yield knowledge of God. In addition to nature (as in natural environment), human nature, history (of Israel particularly), and wisdom traditions that can be found among human cultures, both in written and oral forms, could be expected to participate in the process of natural revelation.

Wisdom as Revelation

When turning our attention to the category of wisdom, we are — intentionally! — about to cross the boundary line between what in tradition is called general and special revelation. On the one hand, we can speak of wisdom in general terms, denoting all kinds of wise and rightful thoughts and acts within and outside the religious realm. On the other hand, in theological parlance, Wisdom may also relate to one part of the Jewish-Christian canon, the Wisdom literature — as well as to one of the semipersonified manifestations of the God of the Bible (*hokmah* in the Hebrew Bible). Wisdom and natural theology are related because, according to the biblical testimonies, the world was created

66. For an important discussion of the trinitarian nature of natural theology, see Torrance, *Transformation and Convergence*, p. 293.

67. McGrath, *Open Secret*, pp. 147-48.

68. See the important discussion of this theme in Hauerwas, *With the Grain of the Universe*, pp. 15-16; for a short statement, see McGrath, *Open Secret*, pp. 4-5, 14-15 (quotation from McGrath, pp. 14-15).

in wisdom. "Wisdom thinks resolutely within the framework of a theology of creation."[69] In the Jewish religion, the category of wisdom is so important that one part of the Torah is Wisdom literature.[70] Not only in the Bible, but also more widely in ancient Near Eastern religions, wisdom literature is vast and varied. Israel borrowed widely from the treasure house of their neighbors even when, as with creation myths, that plunder required a lot of revision in order to be incorporated into Yahwistic monotheism.[71]

What is significant about the Wisdom tradition of the OT is that rather than being a form of direct revelation from God, as it were, it is "the fruit of long experience of human character and society — the wisdom of the ages."[72] The biblical scholar J. D. G. Dunn makes the important observation that "As something of God may be 'read off' creation, so valuable lessons about right living and good practice can be drawn by those who have long experience of human foibles, ambition, social policy, manipulation, and so on. That is why ancient societies usually linked wisdom with age."[73] Wisdom was a matter of maturation, cultivation of habits, acquiring the right skills, learning how to control one's tongue, and so forth. That said, while human wisdom *qua* human is highly regarded in Wisdom literature, there is also the belief in a "higher" form of wisdom on which true human wisdom is founded, the divine wisdom. "Humans sense this and search for it. But it is beyond their reach. It can only be given from without, from God,"[74] as illustrated in a profound way in Job 28. Although according to this poem humans are able to uncover even the depths of nature (vv. 1-11), they continue to wonder, "But where shall wisdom be found? / And where is the place of understanding?" (v. 12):

> Man does not know the way to it,
> and it is not found in the land of the living.

69. Zimmerli, "Place and Limit of the Wisdom Literature," p. 316; see also Perdue, *Wisdom and Creation*.

70. For standard discussions, see Rad, *Wisdom in Israel*; Day, *Wisdom in Ancient Israel*.

71. Well-known parallels that demonstrate borrowing from non-Israelite sources include Proverbs and *The Instruction of Amenemopet* (Egyptian, around 1200 B.C.E.), Ecclesiastes and *The Epic of Gilgamesh* (Akkadian, around 2000-1600 B.C.E.), and Job and *I Will Praise the Lord of Wisdom* (Akkadian, between 2000 and 1500 B.C.E.). For an exciting theological discussion, including Christianity's relation to other living faiths, see Wiebe, *Christian Theology in a Pluralistic Context*, chap. 4, "How the Christian Tradition Has Used Material from Other Religions," and chap. 5, "A Model from Old Testament Wisdom Literature."

72. Dunn, "Biblical Concepts," p. 7.

73. Dunn, "Biblical Concepts," p. 7.

74. Dunn, "Biblical Concepts," p. 8.

The deep says, "It is not in me,"
    and the sea says, "It is not with me." . . .
It is hid from the eyes of all living. (vv. 13-14, 21a)

The response to this human incapacity is simply that "God understands the way to it, and he knows its place" (v. 23); the way for humans to have access to it is "the fear of the LORD, that is wisdom; / and to depart from evil is understanding" (v. 28). The source of wisdom is divine, and it is linked with trust and commitment to Yahweh. Jesus affirms this same principle in Matthew 11:25-26. New Testament authors likewise confirm this principle (1 Cor. 1:17–2:16; James 1:5).[75]

The study of the rich wisdom heritage in other living faiths would yield an invaluable collection of insights, lessons, and guidelines for good and right living. Often various traditions overlap a great deal, which is of course to be expected if ultimately all wisdom is to be found in Christ — even when that is not known to all people who embrace that wisdom. Similarly, Christian theology embraces wisdom and knowledge gained from scientific study and similar academic pursuits. What the British atheistic naturalist evolutionary biologist Richard Dawkins, or the devout Muslim astronomer and physicist Nidhal Guessoum from the United Arab Emirates, or the French-Nepalese practicing-Buddhist cell geneticist Matthieu Ricard discovers in his academic research is no less valuable to Christians than the work of most committed Christian scientists such as the British mathematical physicist-turned-Anglican-priest John Polkinghorne. Again, because neither nature nor results from their studies are self-evident, each of these faith practitioners would supply a different interpretation. From the point of view of Christian tradition, however, they all study the same reality, creation. This discussion leads us to the last chapter in part 1, which considers the understanding of sacred scriptures and revelation among four living faiths.

---

75. See further, Dunn, "Biblical Concepts," pp. 8-10.

8. Revelation and Scripture among Religions

The Challenge and Complexity of Interfaith Engagement of Scriptures

Putting Christian Scripture and doctrine of revelation in a mutual dialogue with other living faiths is an enormous challenge. To begin with, the reservoir of sacred scriptures is amazingly huge among religions — illustrated by Max Müller's classic, *Sacred Books of the East*, in fifty hefty volumes; yet even that "library" misses noteworthy portions of scriptures from various parts of Asia!

Whereas until recent decades religious studies as an academic discipline used to undermine the importance of *written* scriptures for the study of religions, giving preference to nontextual elements such as ritual, myth, and symbols,[1] more recently a new appreciation of the importance of written scriptures to the study and knowledge of religions has emerged. That is not to undermine the importance of other elements such as folk religiosity, arts, and ritual, but rather to acknowledge that basically all living faiths are either based on or have been shaped in the presence of authoritative scriptures.[2] "In all religions the scriptural word is seen as a means of revealing or realizing the Divine."[3]

While most religions have either the canonical or otherwise determined

---

1. A prime example of that approach is van der Leeuw, *Religion in Essence and Manifestation* (1933). In this massive work, only one short chapter (64) discusses scriptures, and even that is mostly Western scriptures.

2. For a highly useful and accessible introductory discussion, see Voorst, *Anthology of World Scriptures*, pp. 2-4, with ample bibliographic references for further study.

3. Coward, "Introduction," p. 1.

"primary" scripture (Torah, Qur'an, Bible, Vedas, Tipitaka), they also have a huge secondary literature that typically is believed to be based on and derive its (relative) authority from the primary revelation. Hence the Jews have the extensive Talmud, the "Oral Torah"; the Muslims have the huge collection of Hadiths; the main way to study the Vedas is the growing commentary literature in Vedic Hinduism and the whole *smrti* tradition for the rest of the Hindus. The Christian church has accumulated a massive secondary literature of creedal and other definitive traditions. An important theological task not only for Christians but also for Jews, Hindus, and Muslims is to discern the relationship between the "canonical" and "extracanonical" texts, to use the Christian parlance.

So far we have spoken of "scriptures" as if the term were self-evident. It is not. A number of aspects vary among religions regarding what is called scripture. First of all, religions such as Judaism, Islam, and Christianity have a clearly defined and closed canon. In many others, most profoundly in Buddhism, especially in Mahayana traditions, there is hardly any notion of a "closed canon." Hinduism lies somewhere in between, as it has the twofold structure of primary, most authoritative scriptures, the Vedas *(shruti)*, and the secondary *smrti* collections of various types of materials, from epics to songs to folklore and so forth. Even the collection of Vedas, let alone the rest of the Hindu scriptures, is immense. Hence, in a typical household in India, a small part of an important epic in the *smrti* collection, the Bhagavad-Gita, may be the only scripture available. Or consider Taoism, which embraces more than 1,000 scriptural texts!

Scriptures also play different roles in various religions. Whereas Judaism, Christianity, and Islam — as well as most profoundly Zoroastrianism — can be rightly called "religions of the book" because of the necessary and authoritative role played by the written canonical scripture, in Hinduism the spoken word is primary. The Vedas, even though found in written form in Sanskrit, are considered divine speech, and hence the written form is inferior to the "oral text."[4] Hence, Julius Lipner rightly and importantly speaks of "[t]he voice of scripture as Veda" when speaking of "scripture" in Hinduism. He also reminds us that the term "scripture," from Latin, "to write," poorly describes Hindu intuition; hence, the Sanskrit term *sabda*, from "to make a sound" and "to call," is more appropriate.[5] Furthermore, whereas almost all religions of the world regard their scriptures as inspired and of divine origin, that is not the case with all traditions. Buddhism has no concept of divine inspiration. Even more

---

4. This delightful expression is in Voorst, *Anthology of World Scriptures*, p. 6.
5. Lipner, *Hindus*, p. 25.

profoundly, Confucianism regards its scripture as a human product, although hugely important for religion. One could also, perhaps somewhat ironically, point to liberal Protestantism in Christianity, according to which the Bible is merely an invaluable human sharing of responses to religious experiences.

Finally, the nature and function of scripture among various traditions vary greatly. For the typical Muslim the Qur'anic revelation is truly verbatim and relates to all aspects of life. Typical contemporary Jews and Christians consider Scripture the ultimate authority, even though, apart from fundamentalists, they consider its principles and thoughts to be the inspired guide to faith and practice. For most Buddhists, scripture's main role and authority lie in its capacity to convey Buddha's enlightenment and precepts. It is the scripture's "object" rather than the scripture as such that is highly venerated and authoritative. In Hinduism, Brahmins study Vedas as the divinely originated religious (and in many traditions, philosophical) authority, whereas for most Hindus, scriptural content comes in the form of folklore, rituals, artistic forms, and the general cultural environment in India.

With these diversities in mind, we should be mindful of the danger of generalizations and assumptions. The Christian theologian sees the interfaith exchange between scriptures and notions of revelation among other living faiths through the lens of his or her own tradition. The Muslim scholar would do the same, and so forth. The Christian student does well to remember what has been called the "Protestant bias" in the study of religions' scriptures.[6] This simply means the following:

> Certain mainstream Protestant ideas about the nature of scripture colored the study of the scriptures of other religions and only today are being identified and corrected. They can be listed serially: a preoccupation with textuality to the exclusion of orality, from the Protestant emphasis on the scripture as *written*; an individualistic orientation that assumes that scriptures are to be read mainly by the individual, from Protestant ideas of the "priesthood of all believers" and universal literacy; the notion that scriptures are widely authoritative over every aspect of religious life, from the Protestant assertion that the scriptures are the sole authority in the Christian faith; and the assumption that scriptures are best understood by academically recognized methods of study, from mainstream Protestant attachment to sound academic procedures.[7]

6. See further, Levering, "Introduction," pp. 3-5.
7. Voorst, *Anthology of World Scriptures*, p. 17.

One bias calls for more comment: the at times almost exclusive preference for written rather than oral scriptures, which is the hallmark of not only the current Protestant world but also of the whole of Christian tradition. Indeed, the prioritization of the written over the oral is a larger cultural development going back to the invention of the printing press on the eve of the Protestant Reformation.[8] The Protestant Reformation took full advantage of the new printing capacities in its desire to put the Bible into the hands of every Christian. Industrialization and more recently globalization with the expansion of information production have contributed to the hegemony of the written over the spoken. Even the current virtual world relies on written texts as much as it includes other forms of communication. The French philosopher Jacques Ellul rightly saw "the humiliation of the word," particularly the spoken word, in our current culture, no longer limited to the Global North but also, with the rise of Western-type of schooling, taking place in the Global South.

For Ellul, the printed and spoken word are not merely two complementary and convenient ways of communication; they differ in nature from each other. Since spoken words function as symbols and evoke emotions, they cannot be reduced to mere facts (even though they also contain cognitive content). The modern and contemporary fixation with the printed text treats printed words as signs that have a fixed reference and by and large convey information.[9] Ellul is of course too smart to naively dismiss the importance of printed text — as prolific a writer as he is; his point is that we should work hard in holding on to the complementary and necessarily mutually dependent roles of writing and speaking, seeing and hearing, symbolic and informative. That is an essential observation for our discussion. The pluriform nature of Christian revelation calls for an inclusive, multifaceted, and multilayered concept of communication, including the oral.

The eclipse of the oral Scripture in Christian tradition is an odd development when looked at historically. The First Testament of the Bible, shared by the Jewish tradition, builds essentially on the role of oral transmission of scriptural content and emphasizes the importance of remembering and reciting the Lord's commands and blessings. Consider only Deuteronomy 6, the great pedagogical mandate for all Israelite parents to instill in their children's minds the precepts of the Lord. Much better than Christianity, Judaism has maintained the habit of learning and reciting scriptural words even after bib-

---

8. See the seminal study by Ong, *Orality and Literacy.*

9. Ellul, *Humiliation of the Word,* pp. 1-4 particularly (a short introduction that states succinctly the basic thesis by comparing seeing and hearing).

lical times. Jesus and the apostles, as Jews, memorized and recited Scriptures daily. The early church also did that as the Gospels were not yet written and were circulating in oral form. In the Islamic tradition, oral memorization and recital of scripture took on even greater importance. "Indeed, spiritual merit in Islam is said to be measured by the thoroughness of one's oral knowledge of the scripture. According to the tradition, on the day of resurrection everyone will be called upon to rise up and recite the Qur'an."[10] Examples from other living faith traditions could be easily accumulated to make the case for the significance of the oral form of scripture, an intuition basically lost in contemporary Christian faith and theology.[11]

Coupled with the eclipse of the oral "scriptures," Western religious studies and theological studies have also bracketed out the importance of noncognitive, "spiritual" forms of appreciating, appropriating, and living out scriptures. The post-Enlightenment academic paradigm has one-sidedly sought to merely analyze, using the best critical tools, religious texts with little consideration of their pluriform meaning and use in all living traditions. This is, of course, related to the Enlightenment-based replacement of the concept of God with religion.[12] The theologian Keith Ward's observation is right on target: "The language of religion is like the language of poetry; and it is a major heresy of post-Enlightenment rationalism to try to turn poetry into pseudo-science, to turn the images of religion, whose function is to evoke eternity, into mundane descriptions of improbable facts."[13] In the same spirit, Harold Coward, himself a leading scholar of world religions, gives this correction: "But discursive academic study is always of secondary importance, since knowledge of the Transcendent can never be fully captured and communicated in words. Spiritual transformation takes place more through the continuous action of the memorized words, which have become a part of the very structure of consciousness, than through intellectual study. The poetic power of the words to point beyond themselves and resonate strongly with the Transcendent is a major force in the religious transformation of consciousness."[14]

In religions, scriptures — at least the "canonical ones" — play a "foundational" role, not only in guiding belief and practice but also in forming the way the world is viewed. In his investigation into five religious traditions, Ward

---

10. Coward, "Introduction," p. 5.

11. For a highly useful discussion, see Coward, "Introduction," pp. 1-14.

12. The implications are discussed in the introductory methodological chapter to the volume *Christ and Reconciliation*.

13. Ward, *Images of Eternity*, p. 3.

14. Coward, "Introduction," p. 3.

seeks to discern what he calls "a revelatory matrix." "A revelatory matrix is a paradigm metaphor which encapsulates a particular vision of the world." An example is the famous idea mentioned in the Isa Upanishad: "Those who see all beings in the Self and the Self in all things, will never doubt It."[15] A matrix is not there only for explanation. "It seeks to evoke a way of life which is regulated, in its most general forms of apprehension and action, by a controlling metaphor. . . . The term 'matrix' seems appropriate for it, because it is a basic mould or pattern which forms our most general perception of things and our reactions to them."[16]

A revelatory matrix at work in major living faiths has three interrelated functions: "It is regulative for human understanding, providing a paradigm by which an explanation can be given of how things are and of how they came to be as they are."[17] Just think of how well this definition applies to Christian theology of revelation, particularly as it is built on the self-revelation of the triune God in the embodiment of the eternal Logos in one historical person. "The source of the matrix is revelation; either the claim to omniscience, as traditionally with Sakyamuni [Gautama Buddha] and Jesus, or a claim to inspired knowledge given by a suprahuman source to a chosen person, as with the authors of the Veda, Torah, and Koran." Rather than merely seeking to describe the Divine, revelation proposes a way of liberation from sin as in Christianity or *dukkha* as in Buddhism or "ignorance" as in Hinduism.[18]

Some recent approaches in systematic and constructive theology may turn out to be helpful in capturing a more holistic view of scriptures not only in Christian but also in other faith traditions. These include approaches such as discussed in Vanhoozer's *Drama of Doctrine*, engaged widely in the discussion above, and in William A. Dyrness's *Poetic Theology*, which builds on the intuition that since religion — and knowledge of God — comes to us in so many forms, the category of the "poetic" in the most inclusive sense, going back to the Aristotelian notion of "making," is needed along with the more traditional discursive approach.

In a systematic/constructive theology project such as the current one in which the category of revelation and the notions of scripture are approached mainly from the perspective of textual analysis and with a focus on "official" authoritative texts such as Vedas or Torah or Qur'an, we need the constant

15. Ward, *Images of Eternity*, p. 42; citation from Isa Upanishad 6 (also called Vagasaneyi-Samhita Upanishad); *SBE* 1:312.

16. Ward, *Images of Eternity*, p. 42.

17. Ward, *Images of Eternity*, p. 42.

18. Ward, *Images of Eternity*, p. 43.

reminder of the primacy in many religions of oral rather than written, poetic rather than discursive,[19] communal rather than individual orientations. In addition to its help in academic constructive work, this wider framework may help the Christian church and theologians be more inclusive and "relevant."

Hindu Scriptures and Authority in a Christian Perspective

The Matrix of Hindu Scriptures

The notion of scripture in Hinduism is pluriform and inclusive in nature. "No other living tradition can claim scriptures as numerous or as ancient as Hinduism."[20] Hindu scriptures are commonly divided into two categories. First, there are the Vedas, which are called the *sruti* ("what is heard"), received directly by the *rishis*, "seers." This is the foundational, primary scripture, honored by all Hindu traditions. Second, there are the secondary scriptures, the *smrti* ("what is remembered"), which are considered to be humanly authored and come in the forms of epics, narratives, and folklore. Basically all forms of Hinduism consider the ancient Vedas as the scripture par excellence. Indeed, it can be said that what keeps together and allows meaningful discussion of Hinduism as a unified — albeit extremely diversified — tradition is the common belief in the Vedas as foundational, authoritative, divine revelation.

The Vedic literature is by and large unknown to most Hindus apart from the higher castes (especially Brahmins). Instead, most Hindus get their scriptural teaching from various epics, religious folklore called the Puranas, among which the two most important and widely used are *Ramayana*, a story of Rama, depicted as an incarnation of Vishnu in later tradition, and *Mahabharata* ("Great Epic"), part of which is the Bhagavad-Gita, the most important single writing of scripture among all Hindus. Furthermore, unlike in contemporary Christianity, religious and religiously inspired art such as music, dance, and paintings is often taken as revelatory in nature. To this list one should add an important caveat that has to do with the most foundational Hindu concept of *dharma*. Variously translated as "righteousness," "duty," and

19. A supreme example of the need to turn to the poetic rather than discursive is Jodo Shinshu Buddhism, in which ritual chanting is the main spiritual practice. Its founder, Shinran, found the rational study of Buddhism disappointing and came up with the chant of *nembutsu*, which touches first and foremost emotional, existential, and other deep areas in our lives.

20. Klostermaier, *Survey of Hinduism*, p. 65. Taoism comes close, if not even ranking ahead of Hinduism, in the number and diversity of scriptures.

"ethics/morality," it denotes common human virtues such as generosity, compassion, and abstaining from violence. In addition to this *dharma,* which is common to all humanity, there is every human person's own *dharma* that leads to liberation. Now, where is this *dharma* to be found? It is found in the Vedas and epics, but also in the practices and behavior of good people and in promptings and insights of one's mind and conscience.[21]

The Vedas originated beginning around 1500 B.C.E. Each of the four collections (Rig Veda, Sama Veda, Yajur Veda, and Atharva Veda) has four parts: Samhitas, hymns to various deities;[22] Brahmanas, rules for Vedic rituals; Aranyakas, "forest" discussions, symbolic and philosophical reflections on the rituals; and, for the purposes of theological discourse, the most important, the Upanishads. By far the most important and most often cited Veda is the first one, the Rig Veda. The last collection's name comes from "sitting near [the teacher]" and contains the developing philosophic-theological reflection on the divine and the world. The Upanishads were composed around 600 B.C.E. or later.[23]

The theologies based on the Upanishads, called Vedanta, embody much of Hinduism to the West.[24] A few qualifications, however, will assist those not well versed in Indian traditions. First, Vedanta is merely one of the six main schools or traditions of Hinduism, even though it is by far the best known. Second, philosophical in nature, based on the Vedas, it is not necessarily the Hindu religion of common folks. It is the philosophically oriented and often abstract account of the faith of India known to Hindu "theologians." In that sense, it is much closer to the theology of Augustine, Aquinas, and Schleiermacher than to, say, the folk Catholicism of many Latin American countries or the Pentecostalism of various African locations. Third, very importantly, even the Vedanta school has several quite widely different subtraditions. For the purposes of this conversation — to be amplified in part 2 with regard to

21. For a lucid exposition, see Narayanan, "Hinduism," pp. 41-49, 62-63.

22. The deities *(devatas)* to whom hymns are addressed in the Samhita of each Veda include Agni, god of fire; Indra, god of heavens; Yama, god of death; and Varuna, god of waters. These collections of hymns are enormous; the Samhita of Rig Veda alone contains 1,028 hymns with over 10,000 verses.

23. While tradition numbers 108 Upanishads, about 10 have become prominent because of extensive commentary literature written by *advaita* (nondualist) interpreters of various subschools.

24. Vedanta is also known as "Later" (Uttara) Mimamsa, related to the important text its representatives comment on extensively, the Uttara Mimamsa Sutras, better known in the West as Brahma Sutras, by Badarayana of the fifth century C.E.

the doctrine of God — the most important is the divide between the advaitic, nondualistic (literally: "not-two"), monistic tradition and the moderately dualistic tradition.

As said, other scriptures, apart from the Vedas, belong to the realm of *smrti*, "remembered" literature. Like the epics, these have human authors. But even then, their inspired nature is not being denied although their authority is lower than that of the Vedas. Ironically, this "second-class" form of inspired scriptures has played a far more significant role in the actual lives of Hindu communities and individuals than the Vedas, for the reasons mentioned, including the common person's very limited access to the most authoritative sources. The *smrti* part of inspired scriptures includes a huge number of epics, among which the two epics *Ramayana* and, especially, *Mahabharata* (part of which is the Bhagavad-Gita) are the most well known; if anything does, they form the scripture of the common folks. While *Mahabharata* is huge — more than 100,000 verses, making it the world's longest poem — one short part of it, Bhagavad-Gita ("Sacred Song"), is the "Bible" of most Hindus. This is the scripture that almost all Hindu households possess. As epics, both of these narrative collections portray an exciting story with many turns, in *Mahabharata* of the war between two families (the Kauravas and Pandavas) and in Bhagavad-Gita, of Arjuna of the Pandava family, who consults his cousin Krishna about the wisdom of fighting against the family. Krishna is a major Hindu figure who in later tradition, like Rama but more importantly than Rama, is depicted as one of the main *avataras* of the deity Vishnu. The Hindu devotional literature *(bhakti)* is immense, and it appears in many languages.

Even though scripture comes first and foremost in oral form for Hindus, whether in daily recitation or in the ritual or repetition of mantras or *japa*, a single word or a brief verse from scripture, either audibly or silently, and its main goal is liberation rather than accumulation of information, this does not undermine careful study, analysis, and debate about the meaning. The well-known verse from *Laws of Manu* (12:103) is often invoked as an example of the need to ascertain as carefully as possible the exact meaning of the scriptural text: "(Even forgetful) students of the (sacred) books are more distinguished than the ignorant, those who remember them surpass the (forgetful) students, those who possess a knowledge (of the meaning) are more distinguished than those who (only) remember (the words), men who follow (the teaching of the texts) surpass those who (merely) know (their meaning)."[25]

---

25. "The Laws of Manu," ca. 1500 B.C.E., trans. G. Buhler, in *Indian History Sourcebook*, at http://hinduism.about.com/library/weekly/extra/bl-lawsofmanu12.htm.

We can see the profound importance of the Vedas even in contemporary Hinduism from the continuing inquiry into their meaning, including the renewed interest in modern times, beginning from the Hindu renewals of the nineteenth century, which were, ironically, prompted by the modern Christian missionary movement. In response to the common Christian charge of unqualified polytheism, some leading Hindu intellectuals such as Ram Mohan Roy (d. 1833) argued for the uncompromising monotheism of the Upanishads, as opposed to what he saw as the degenerate form of modern Hinduism based on Puranas and Tantras, which of course seem to be advocating a plurality of deities without much discussion of their possible unity in a concept of one god. Roy's translation of the Upanishads into Bengali and English in the early nineteenth century was an effort similar in many ways to the Protestant Reformers' desire to get the Bible into the hands of the common folk. According to Julius Lipner, Roy is to be credited with "restoring the Vedas to public consciousness in modern India, both as an object of study and as a source of religious inspiration."[26]

Competing Hermeneutics

While all six Hindu traditions consider study and knowledge of scripture the necessary source of theology,[27] two traditions excel in Vedic exegesis: the ritualistic, nontheistic Purva Mimamsa and all Vedanta schools (which, as mentioned, focus on the study of the Upanishads).[28] Profound hermeneutical differences exist between the two main traditions devoted to the study of the Vedas; this observation is useful for Christian students who are often bewildered by the internal divisions of their own tradition. Since Purva Mimamsa is oriented toward ritual and is nontheistic, it regards the Vedas' main purpose as guiding in the right ritual. Hence, the Vedas in this hermeneutic are not looked upon as guides for how to live in the world or, perhaps surprisingly to outsiders, even as information about the deities or immortality. That is not to say that this tradition is antitheistic after Western logic, but rather that it is

26. Lipner, *Hindus*, p. 66.

27. The six orthodox traditions are Nyaya, Vaisesika, Samkhya, Yoga, Purva Mimamsa, and Vedanta. Buddhism and Jainism, as well as the Hindu tradition of Caravakas, reject the Vedas and hence are not considered orthodox. For a basic discussion of the revelatory meaning of the Vedas, see Chemparathy, "Veda as Revelation," pp. 253-74.

28. Much of Vedantic theologians' focus is devoted to commenting on the fifth century C.E. work Brahma Sutras (originally Uttara Mimamsa Sutras) attributed to Badarayana.

something similar to Theravada Buddhism, which grants the existence of the deities but considers their existence more or less irrelevant for pursuing the goal of liberation. Purva Mimamsa acknowledges gods as legitimate recipients of worship and invocation but eschews the inquiry into their nature.[29] Not surprisingly then, this school gives precedence to the first three parts of each Veda (Samhitas, Brahmanas, and Aranyakas), all of which are ritually oriented and contain hymns for the deities.

The Vedanta schools, also known as the "Later" (Uttara) Mimamsa, in contrast, engage extensively and painstakingly the task of commenting on the Upanishads, in which they see the revelation of the Ultimate or Absolute, Brahman, as the main theme. Usually Vedanta theologians begin with and concentrate on attentive commentary of Brahma Sutra, including the careful consideration of the nature and works of the deities. But even within this tradition, there are significant divisions between those who are strictly monistic, the nondualist *advaita* school represented most famously by Samkara of the eighth century, and the qualified nondualist *(Visistadvaita)* school of Ramanuja of the eleventh century. For Samkara, Brahman is totally void of all limitations and is identical with *atman* (the soul or the self). Because of ignorance, the human soul is encumbered with body and mind and thus subject to *dukkha* (sorrow) and continuous *samsara,* endless cycles of birth and death, unless through knowledge one attains liberation when the identity between Brahman and *atman* is realized. Attaining this realization is the ultimate goal of the Upanishads and hence their study. In addition to the Upanishads, Samkara's followers consult diligently the above-mentioned Brahma Sutra and Bhagavad-Gita,[30] the last of which presents the threefold path of *jnana yoga* (knowledge/insight), *bhakti yoga* (devotion), and *karma yoga* (ritual action). To be more precise, Bhagavad-Gita's focus on yoga goes beyond and integrates into a single vision of unity any of these three main yoga schools.[31] This united vision is about the "Path by which man unites his finite self with Infinite Being. It is the inner Path of which all these separate yogas are so many one-sided aspects."[32]

One of the fiercest critics of Samkara's strict nondualistic hermeneutics was Ramanuja. Unlike Samkara, he places more equal weight on all four sec-

29. See further, Clooney, *Hindu God, Christian God,* pp. 18-19.

30. These three primary texts are often referred to as *prasthana trayi,* the triple foundation of the Vedanta.

31. There are, of course, more than three yoga traditions in India, such as the eightfold yoga of Patanjali.

32. Prem, "From *The Yoga of the Bhagavat Gita,*" p. 42; see also Rambachan, "Hinduism," p. 105.

tions of the Vedas as opposed to focusing only on the last section, the Upanishads. His qualified nondualist tradition refutes Samkara's identity between Brahman and *atman*. Rather than identity, Ramanuja argues that the Vedas teach the principle of inseparability *(aprthak siddhi)*. Of course, Ramanuja believed that Brahman was nondual *(advaita)*, but for him that belief did not negate but rather affirmed the internal diversity and complexity of the divine. This is an important topic to be discussed further in the doctrine of God.[33]

Enough said of the vastly different hermeneutics among Hindu schools regarding the proper understanding of the Vedas. And of course, these three traditions — Mimamsa and the two *advaita* traditions — do not encompass all Hindu traditions! In the discussion of the doctrine of God and creation, careful attention must be paid to the internal divisions of the various Vedanta schools as well as among all the main Hindu philosophical traditions.

Hindu and Christian Views of Scripture: Parallels and Differences

An important indication of the depth of scholarship and the use of reason's best resources in India is the millennia-long investigation into the nature and functions of language, a topic dear also to past and recent Christian theologians. Linguistic speculations among Hindu scholars go back to before recorded human history. In many ways the Indian reflection on the nature of language was more inclusive than that in Christian tradition,[34] as it studied topics such as language's relation to consciousness, including nonhuman consciousness, and all aspects of the world and human experience.[35] Indeed, the Vedas themselves speak of the nature of language and words used in these texts. An entire hymn in Rig Veda (71 of book 10) is devoted to the discussion of the origin of language. Very importantly, in the Vedas, language is not only closely connected with the divine but also directly identified with Brahman, as Brihadaranyaka Upanishad puts it (4.1.2): "Ganaka Vaideha replied: 'Gitvan Sailini told me that speech (vâk) is Brahman.'" According to Rig Veda, there are as many words as there are manifestations of the divine.[36]

While the nature of the language of scripture in this outlook differs from

33. For a highly useful and accessible nontechnical discussion, see Rambachan, "Hinduism," pp. 104-5.

34. See the important discussion in D'Sa, "Christian Scriptures and Other Scriptures," pp. 236-42.

35. See further, Coward, *Sacred Word*, pp. 111-16.

36. In *SBE* 15; see 5.10.2 and 10.114.8. I am indebted to Coward, *Sacred Word*, p. 113.

the Christian view, it is not without parallels. The Christian reader of the Upanishadic passage above is of course reminded of the first verse of John's Gospel: "In the beginning was the Word, and the Word was with God, and the Word was God." The difference between the two traditions is that in Vedic teaching words (plural) are manifestations of the manifestations of Brahman, while in the Christian view the Word, which became embodied in one particular human person, Jesus of Nazareth (John 1:14), is to be equated with God. That said, Hindu theologians have gained insights into the nature of the language of scripture that are valuable to the Christian tradition as well. An important lesson for Christian theologians is that Hindu thinkers were able to avoid two reductionist mistakes typical of the modern Western view of language: "they did not reduce language to the status of a merely human convention having only scientific or factual referents; nor did they fall into the error of metaphysical reductionism, which so devalues the meanings of human words that language ends up as obscure mysticism."[37] Both of these extremes are not unknown in Christian philosophy and theology, and both are detrimental to the kind of pluriform nature of revelation developed in this project.

Christian theology could also reflect on the potential promise of the close link between ritual and language. "The meaningfulness of *mantras* is not of the merely intellectual kind, it is meaning which has power *(śakti)*. *Mantras* have the power to remove ignorance *(avidyā)*, reveal truth *(dharma)*, and realize release *(mokṣa)*."[38] While Christian theology hardly wishes to go as far as to use mantras in a semimagical way, which often happens particularly in folk piety, there certainly are some parallels between the Hindu view and the best of Christian sacramental understanding of the words in liturgy and sacraments. According to a Christian sacramental understanding, words uttered by human beings in such settings bring about what they promise. The history of Christian theology reminds us of various ways of trying to explain how that happens, and that has led to deep divisions among Christians. However, beyond and beneath those debates there is an intuition — shared with Hindus — that certain words are creative, powerful, and "sacramental" since they are linked with the divine and divine actions.

Both Hinduism and Christianity build on scriptural authority. According to the noted Hindu scholar and statesman Sarvepalli Radhakrishnan, an

---

37. Coward, *Sacred Word*, p. 111.

38. Coward, *Sacred Word*, p. 115. Even mightier than any single mantra is the chanting of *Om*. While different Hindu schools debate whether *Om* is Brahman itself or a near verbal expression of Brahman, in all Hindu traditions it is the most sacred sound, and in it are contained all other mantras. The description of *Om* in Chandogya Upanishad 1.1.1-3, 7, 9 (*SBE* 1) is classic.

important characteristic of Indian philosophy is "its so-called acceptance of authority." He goes on to explain: "Although the systems of Indian philosophy vary in the degree to which they are specifically related to the ancient *śruti,* not one of the systems — orthodox or unorthodox, except the Cārvāka[39] — openly stands in violation of the accepted intuitive insights of its ancient seers, whether it be the Hindu seers of the Upaniṣads, the intuitive experience of the Buddha, or the similarly intuitive wisdom of Mahāvīra, the founder of Jainism, as we have it today." Always keen on contemporary developments of Hindu traditions in modern society, Radhakrishnan adds that "[r]everence for authority does not militate against progress, but it does lend a unity of spirit by providing a continuity of thought which has rendered philosophy especially significant in Indian life."[40] A contemporary Christian may mistakenly assume that with the rise of highly rational, philosophical views of the divine developed among Vedanta traditions, the authority of the (last part of) the Vedas is replaced with a typical post-Enlightenment historical-critical attitude. Nothing could be more off the mark. With all their rational powers, even the philosophically oriented Vedanta scholars build solidly on the divine revelation.[41] The affirmation of Vedic authority is so central to Hinduism as a religious tradition — at least in principle — that those who did not subscribe to it, such as adherents of Buddhism and Jainism, early deviations from Hinduism, were named *nastikas,* those who said "there is no such thing" (as Vedic authority). Hence, they were considered "heretics" and under destructive influences.[42] The post-Enlightenment Christian theological rejection of all notions of authority not only in the Christian religion but also, by implication, among other faiths, is yet to engage in a critical and constructive reflection on the significance of authority in most living faiths of the contemporary world. This is a task for both intra-Christian and interfaith investigation.

As explained above, because of their divine origin and eternal nature, the Vedas are taken to be infallible, free from all error. Says Sankara: "Brahman is the source, i.e. the cause of the great body of Scripture."[43] Hence, Scripture is

---

39. Also known as Lokayata, Carvaka is a Hindu tradition that embraces skepticism and some sort of epistemological indifference, and hence does not consider the Vedas or any other similar work as authoritative.

40. Radhakrishnan, "Nature of Hinduism," p. 13. For a highly nuanced discussion of the ways the Vedic authority and especially its "saving knowledge" have been appropriated and defined in various Hindu traditions, see Lipner, *Hindus,* chap. 2.

41. See further, Ward, *Images of Eternity,* p. 5.

42. Lipner, *Hindus,* p. 27.

43. Sankara, *Vedanta-Sutras* 1.1.3; *SBE* 34:20.

both a necessary and a sufficient source of the knowledge of Brahman.[44] It is highly significant that not only among the Vedanta theologians and others who are theistic, but also among the ritualistically oriented nontheistic Mimamsa tradition, the infallibility of the Vedas is defended and taken for granted.[45] One can also say with full justification that all orthodox Hindu traditions stick with a strong doctrine of verbal revelation.[46] Materially, they affirm a similar kind of doctrine of the infallibility of sacred scripture as affirmed by classical Christianity and Judaism, as well as Islam. "So one common theme of these traditions is the existence of a revealed, propositional text which communicates truths unknowable by the human mind or reason alone. Orthodox Vedanta is just as dogmatic in making this claim as any orthodox Jew or Muslim"[47] or, I would like to add, any conservative Christian. Rightly, therefore, Ward concludes, "In that sense, Vedanta is not really quite as tolerant or as capable of adapting itself to include other religious traditions as is sometimes thought."[48] Here again, there are a challenge and continuing task for post-Enlightenment Christian theology, which tends to eschew any notions of "authority."

Above, it was argued that in most living faiths, the ultimate frame of reference for thinking of revelation is "a revelatory matrix." Behind the idea of the revelatory matrix is the observation that, to use the Hindu Mimamsa tradition as a showcase, "the quest for religious truth begins with submission to the privileged linguistic communication that is the Veda, the canon of Sanskrit sacred texts for ritual practice, recitation, and meditation."[49] Perhaps the Yale School's insistence that the Christian side see the world through the scriptural lens rather than vice versa may serve as a parallel. These two traditions share a similar concern to link scripture to ritual and practice. Indeed, there seems to be such a link because, for the Mimamsa tradition, notwithstanding its relentless affirmation of the eternal and inerrant nature of the Veda,

> it is not a special message from a particular personal speaker. It is not the voice of God nor God's self-communication. . . . It is effective simply by its linguistic power as it shapes personal and social values. . . . [I]t is fun-

44. Sankara, *Vedanta-Sutras* 1.1.4; *SBE* 34:22-23.
45. For comments, see Clooney, *Hindu God, Christian God,* pp. 18-19.
46. Only in revisionist forms of Hinduism is verbal inspiration replaced with some kind of personal experience of enlightenment. For a highly useful and nuanced discussion, see Lipner, *Face of Truth,* chaps. 1 and 2.
47. Ward, *Images of Eternity,* p. 6.
48. Ward, *Images of Eternity,* p. 6.
49. Clooney, *Hindu God, Christian God,* pp. 138-39.

damentally a privileged linguistic event that shapes the cognitive context in which everything else is to be understood. To hear or recite the Veda is to become subject to the revelatory influence of its language and educated by it. . . . [I]t confronts one from the start and molds how one perceives the world and reasons about it.[50]

Of course, placing the Yale School and Mimamsa side by side does not dismiss the great differences between them: whereas the former is deeply theistic, the latter is not, a viewpoint sharply critiqued also by other Hindu schools, particularly by the Vedantas. That said, "when the Mimamsa theologians ruled out linking its [Veda's] significance to the value of any referent mentioned in it" and "[i]nstead . . . focused on its performative power," they strongly echoed the postliberal idea of revelation. Above I have critiqued Lindbeck and others for their epistemology and will not repeat it here. But the enduring value of the Yale School and Mimamsa should be acknowledged, namely, that Scripture provides the faithful not only the principles and practices needed for the ritual but also the lens through which to look at everything else in the world.[51] It is highly interesting for Christian theology that the Mimamsa tradition is in this respect critiqued severely by the Vedantic tradition that, instead of focusing on the ritual and performance, turns attention to the "cognitive" and informational nature of the Vedas. Vedantas are not of course rejecting scripture's importance for ritual and performance, but they place the teaching about Brahma and self, including the way of release from ignorance, at the heart of the scriptures. "Since [for the Vedantic tradition] Brahman exists outside the Veda, one cannot stipulate that it is knowable only through texts in the way rituals are known through texts."[52] At work here in the Vedanta critique of Mimamsa is the desire to correct the one-sided view of scripture merely in terms of its "ecclesial usage," to use the Christian parlance. The current project, hence, sides with the Vedantas in this respect.[53]

That said, we also need to look more carefully at what kind of knowledge is in view in the Hindu understanding of scripture. The word *veda* derives from

50. Clooney, *Hindu God, Christian God*, p. 139.

51. Interestingly, Clooney, whose discussion of Mimamsa I have engaged in this context, does not make any reference to the Yale School but rather claims that "[t]his strict Mimamsa position, a reading of the world focused entirely on the commitment to right performance by the right people, exemplifies a severe commitment to an a priori revelation. In effect, it is positively Barthian" (*Hindu God, Christian God*, p. 141).

52. Clooney, *Hindu God, Christian God*, p. 147.

53. See further, Clooney, *Hindu God, Christian God*, pp. 148-50.

the Sanskrit root *vid*, "to know." The knowledge in mind, however, is neither the Western Enlightenment-based "objective" knowledge nor even necessarily the biblical (OT) *hokhma*, which has as the ultimate goal the "fear of the Lord" and, related to that, guidance to right(eous) living in this life. Even when Indian philosophers highly value the use of reason, as demonstrated by the complicated and complex debates among Vedanta scholars, "intuition is accepted as the only method through which the ultimate can be known."[54] The Vedic knowledge has everything to do with the ultimate goal of the "salvific" vision of *moksa*, liberation. Behind the need for liberation as *moksa* is *avidya*, ignorance, lack of true knowledge. This ignorance has to do with the true nature of the self *(atmana)*, the Absolute (Brahman), and the world *(jagat)*. Even the Upanishads, the most philosophically oriented part of each Veda, do not seek detached abstract knowledge but rather have as their main goal liberation from ignorance. Etymologically, the Sanskrit term derives from "to remove" or "to destroy," thus implying the removal of ignorance through right knowledge.[55] For this kind of goal, mere intellectual knowledge is not enough. In the words of Radhakrishnan: "Reason is not useless or fallacious, but it is insufficient. To know reality one must have an actual experience of it. One does not merely *know* the truth in Indian philosophy; one *realizes* it. The word which most aptly describes philosophy in India is *darśana* . . . meaning 'to see.' "[56]

In Christian understanding, Scripture's ultimate goal is to lead men and women into salvific knowledge of and personal fellowship with the personal triune God who has revealed himself in the Word become flesh, in the power of the Holy Spirit. Rather than an insight into the way of liberation from false attachment or ignorance — even though both of these goals have meaning for Christians as well — faith as trust and assent is the main goal. Subsequently, scriptural teaching is necessary for continuing cultivation of Christian values, mind-set, and virtues.

The term "liberation" has been used a number of times in this discussion. A closer look at the many meanings of this crucial term highlights a significant and noteworthy difference between Judeo-Christian religion and other religions. Whereas for Hinduism and other Asiatic traditions, liberation denotes release from ignorance and *dukkha*, and it entails detachment from this world, in Judeo-Christian understanding, liberation, despite its eschatological goal

54. Radhakrishnan, "Nature of Hinduism," p. 12.

55. See further, Rambachan, "Hinduism," pp. 86-89. Two famous examples of dialogues between the teacher and student illustrate well the ultimate goal of attaining knowledge: *Chandogya Upanisad*, chap. 7 of Sama Veda, and *Brhadaranyaka Upanisad*, chap. 2 of Yajur Veda.

56. Radhakrishnan, "Nature of Hinduism," pp. 12-13.

(in the Christian tradition), integrally embraces sociopolitical and ethical dimensions. "In the Semitic tradition a succession of prophets was possessed by the Word of God, who was experienced as absolute moral demand, judge of all human conduct. Their visions were of a personal God who demanded justice and mercy."[57] Not so in either Greek traditions or the traditions of India. Ward rightly observes: "The Greek speculative tradition of a Supreme Reason and Good . . . was never able to combine coherently with the cults of the Greek gods, who passed into oblivion."[58] Detachment from the world rather than a robust, embodied engagement of the divine with earthly realities is the vision of many Hellenistic cults and mystery religions. Similarly in India, to begin with, there is no prophetic tradition of preaching justice and judgment; there are only seers and hearers of the eternal voice of the divine. Nor is there a historical purpose or goal that — as in the Christian expectation of the righteous rule of God — summons men and women to "seek first his kingdom."[59]

An essential Christian — as well as Jewish — theme of Scripture focuses on godlike lifestyle and behavior at all levels of human life, whether in the family, society, or the world. A significant part of this prophetic tradition of Scripture, hence, has to do with values of equality, fairness, reconciliation, and liberation among human beings as individuals and as groups. In other words, Christian theology of revelation includes as essential a concept of liberation that has sociopolitical and ethical ramifications, as discussed in some detail above in chapter 4. Whereas the Hebrew prophets and the Christian church that adopted the First Testament into its canon were driven by moral passion, there is very little if any moral or prophetic-ethical teaching or pursuit in the whole of the Vedic tradition. The divine and morality are not linked as they are integrally in Hebrew-Christian tradition. In this respect, Christian tradition owes much to Judaism.[60]

This dramatic difference of orientation between the Semitic and Asiatic traditions has to do with both historical and theological considerations. In terms of historical context, the Judeo-Christian view of revelation derives the category of historical promise pointing to eschatological consummation from its originally nomadic lifestyle, an experience of life as the way to "home." In the birthplaces of the Vedas, the historical situation was much different: the Vedic religion was born among the "noble" ones, the Aryans, who were indeed

57. Ward, *Religion and Revelation*, p. 134.
58. Ward, *Religion and Revelation*, p. 134.
59. Ward, *Religion and Revelation*, p. 135.
60. "The distinctive contribution of Hebrew thought to religion was the establishing of a central connection between moral conduct and religious practice." Ward, *Religion and Revelation*, p. 113; see also pp. 106-7.

conquerors, rather than herdsmen or slaves.[61] Christian theology of history can imagine that the nomadic origins of the people of God were divinely willed and sanctioned for the coming into existence of the biblical history–oriented, eschatologically loaded, promise theology, as constructed above.

Regarding theological considerations, the turn to themes of ethical justice and liberation also has to do with the distinction between the Creator and creation evident in Semitic traditions but not in Asiatic ones. "Whereas the Hebrew objectivization of God as a transcendent creator led to seeing history as the arena of the activity of one moral Spirit, Indian thought tended to see history as the arena of the working-out of the consequences of human actions, through a series of rebirths."[62] As long as the unfolding of history is a matter of eternal repetition, the function of good and bad causes *(karma)*, the linking of ethical consciousness with the divine does not emerge. This of course is not to say that, therefore, the idea — and more importantly: *ideal* — of morality is lacking in Indian philosophy. It is not. But its nature and function differ vastly as perceived as *sanatana dharma,* the eternal cosmic order. The Torah or the Sermon on the Mount is geared toward how things should be on this earth when God's will is done "on earth as it is in heaven."[63]

As mentioned, many, if not all, Hindu traditions regard the Vedas as transhuman, that is, authored not by humans but by the deities.[64] In the famous words of the sixteenth-century poet Tulasidasa: "Infinite is God and infinite are his stories, told and heard in diverse ways by the virtuous."[65] The texts are echoes of divine speech. Vedas are widely regarded by Hindus as eternal and revealed in each new cycle of time. The human recipients (*rishis,* "seers") did not invent them but rather "heard" them; hence, Vedas are called *shruti* ("what is heard").[66] Like the universe, which Hindus believe to be without origin, the Vedas are without beginning and are revealed at the start of each cycle of the universe. While revealed more than once, they are always

---

61. See further, Ward, *Religion and Revelation,* pp. 135-36.

62. Ward, *Religion and Revelation,* p. 136; see also p. 135.

63. See further, Ward, *Religion and Revelation,* p. 137.

64. Even for those Hindu traditions, such as the ritually oriented Mimamsa movements, that do not anchor Vedas in the concept of the god/deity, the authority of revelation is uncompromised because of scripture's capacity to give the right guidelines for ritual performance.

65. Quoted in Rambachan, "Hinduism," p. 85.

66. Ramanuja, the eleventh-century qualified nondualist Vedanta scholar, in his commentary on the Vedanta Sutras, explains carefully that the Vedas are eternal in nature and origin, and their reception by the "seers" does not compromise their eternal nature (*Vedanta Sutras* 1.3.28; p. 333).

revealed in the same way. "The order of the sacred words must remain fixed, and committing them to memory is a disciplined process."[67] Furthermore, coming directly as divine revelation, Vedas are considered to have no human authors. Hence they are also flawless and without limitations.[68] One can see here two central theological differences between the dynamic, historically based Christian notion of revelation as developed above and the Hindu view of revelation as the "record" of the order sanctioned by the divine. First of all, Christian revelation is historical, based on historical events, and is "on the way" to eschatological fulfillment in the coming of God's kingdom. Second, Christian Scripture is confessed to be humanly authored, as discussed above, and therefore bears the kinds of limitations stemming from fine human work. It is God's word in human words.

Yet another important difference between the Jewish-Christian and Hindu notions of scripture has to do with the belief that the Vedas are uncreated, beginningless echoes of the divine. There are no beginnings in the Vedas, whereas the First Testament begins with accounts and lists of the "beginnings," as even the common name for the first book, Genesis, indicates.[69] That said, in some sense a parallel might be made between the eternal Veda and the biblical statement in John's Gospel of the Logos, particularly in that the Vedic word *(vac)* is believed to have creative power "through which the entire creation is brought forth in each cycle."[70] The Johannine statement of course comes to the Christian's mind: "In the beginning was the Word, and the Word was with God, and the Word was God. He was in the beginning with God; all things were made through him, and without him was not anything made that was made. In him was life, and the life was the light of men" (John 1:1-4). In this Christian understanding of the Word, the term "beginning" is not a historical moment such as the beginning of our cosmos but rather a reference to the eternality, as the divine counterpart to God, of the Logos.[71] The leading advaitic commentator from the eighth century, Sankara, writes:

67. Narayanan, "Hinduism," p. 42.

68. As Hinduism is everywhere characterized by diversity, even with regard to the "authorship" of the Vedas, there are internal differences of opinion even though the main outline presented above applies well to nearly all traditions. The ritually oriented, nontheistic Purva Mimamsa tradition does not even consider god as the author for the obvious reason that, like the universe, it is self-existent. The point made for our discussion is still valid, namely, that, unlike the Christian view, human authorship of scriptures is denied.

69. See further, Coward, *Sacred Word,* p. 105.

70. Rambachan, "Hinduism," p. 92.

71. See also Coward, *Sacred Word,* p. 105.

Thus Scripture declares in different places that the word precedes the creation. — *Smrti* also delivers itself as follows, "In the beginning a divine voice, eternal, without beginning or end, formed of the Vedas was uttered by Svayambhû, from which all activities proceeded . . ." — Again, we read, "In the beginning Maheśvara shaped from the words of the Veda the names and forms of all beings and the procedure of all actions." And again, "The several names, actions, and conditions of all things he shaped in the beginning from the words of the Veda" (Manu I, 21). Moreover, we all know from observation that any one when setting about some thing which he wishes to accomplish first remembers the word denoting the thing, and after that sets to work. We therefore conclude that before the creation the Vedic words became manifest in the mind of Pragâpati the creator, and that after that he created the things corresponding to those words.[72]

Parallels appear here between the Christian idea of the Logos as creative Word and the Vedic understanding, although the former also is linked integrally (hypostatically) to the one person of Jesus the Christ.

Also different are the Christian and Hindu understandings of "inspiration," to use the Christian vocabulary. Whereas in Christian understanding the divine inspiration of Scripture, even as the genuinely "human" word, is miraculous, that is not the Hindu view of the coming into existence of the Vedas. The reception by the "seers" of the Vedic revelation as oral speech originating in eternity was a matter of "the progressive purifying of consciousness through the disciplines of yoga, [which] had simply removed the mental obstructions to the revelation of the Divine Word." Hence, "[i]n this Vedic idea of revelation there is no suggestion of the miraculous or supernatural."[73] On the other hand, there is nothing like the long struggle of the prophets and other biblical authors with God in real historical events or the notion of progressive revelation, developing and clarifying incrementally over the course of history. Differently from the Vedas, the sense of the "noncanonical" Bhagavad-Gita idea of revelation comes much closer to the Christian idea of incarnation, as it contains the story of the incarnation of Vishnu, Krishna. Coupled with a strong *bhakti*-devotional orientation and a personalized God, popular Hindu piety based on that celebrated narrative shares similarities with Christian tradition.

72. The long discussion in Sankara, *Vedanta-Sutras* 1.3.28; *SBE* 34:203-4 (the whole of this section, pp. 201-11), is devoted to this topic.

73. Coward, *Sacred Word*, p. 106.

Related to the distinctive idea of revelation as Vedas, the words and sentences "function only as the 'ladder' to raise one to the direct, intuitive experience of the complete Divine Word. Once the full enlightenment experience is achieved, the 'ladder of scripture' is no longer needed." Rightly Coward notes here a profound difference between Hinduism and the three traditions of the book: "The very idea that scripture can be transcended is heresy to Jews, Christians, and Muslims. For them the obstructions of human limitations are such that even the most saintly person would get only part-way up the ladder; Scripture (Torah, Bible, or Qur'an) could never be transcended in the sense that most Hindus accept."[74]

What about Hinduism's relation to other religious traditions and their holy scriptures? Is Hinduism all-inclusive? Does it embrace all other traditions in its belief that beyond all notions of the divine there is one Brahman and that "[t]he various religions and their scriptures are simply different secondary revelations of the one Divine Reality — *Brahman*"?[75] Not really — or, to be more precise, the seemingly inclusive attitude toward other traditions among the Hindus must be greatly qualified and put in perspective. There are deep — and in many ways, irreconcilable — internal differences among the main Hindu schools and traditions.[76] Fierce and animated intra-Hindu debates about the proper interpretation of the Vedas remind one of the continuing ecumenical divisions of the Christian church — and among other religious communities as well! Furthermore, the adoption of the authority of the Vedas anathematized the early significant dissenters: Buddhists and Jainists. At its best, to use a Christian lens, it seems to me that the "inclusivism" present in post–Vatican II Catholicism might be the closest parallel to the Hindu view of other religions. Coward summarizes well (without reference to Catholicism):

> Because it [Hinduism] asserts that the Vedas are the most perfect revelation of *Brahman,* Hinduism sees its scripture as providing the criterion against which all other scriptures must be tested. Thus the Hindu tolerance of other religions is directly proportionate to their congruence with

74. Coward, *Sacred Word*, p. 106. See also Sharma, *Classical Hindu Thought*, p. 33.

75. Coward, *Sacred Word*, p. 129. Coward himself does not support this statement but rather, as the discussion indicates, puts it in perspective. For his fine and nuanced discussion, see Coward, *Pluralism*, chap. 4.

76. Ward (*Images of Eternity*, p. 6) lists examples of mutual condemnations between Sankara and Ramanuja, and then in relation to Buddhists; similarly, Clooney (*Hindu God, Christian God*, pp. 143-46) accumulates a list of textual examples from Kumarila Bhatta, an eighth-century Mimamsa theologian, against Buddhists and in support of their exclusion.

the Vedas. There is no doubt that for the Hindu there is only one Divine, as revealed by the Hindu scriptures, and that any other revelation (e.g., Torah, New Testament, or Qur'an) is seen as a secondary manifestation to be verified against the Hindu Veda.[77]

The possibility and nature of a Hindu "theology of religions" will be discussed in the volume *Church and Hope*. Here it suffices to say that in orthodox Hinduism by and large the "canonical" scriptural tradition serves the same function it does in most living faiths, that is, the building of boundaries between "us" and "others." This is the identity-forming function of tradition, in this case, scriptural tradition.

Is There Revelation in Buddhist Traditions?

The Dhamma and Its Proliferation

While it is true that "Buddhism is, in one sense, a religion without revelation . . . [as] there is no active communication from a God in most forms of Buddhism," it is also true that "there is certainly an authoritative teaching in Buddhism, derived from the enlightened insight of Gautama."[78] Ironically, among all religions, Buddhism, with its multiple denominations, has produced the largest mass of sacred texts in various languages.[79] It makes sense to speak of scripture in Buddhism as long as one keeps in mind some distinctive features that mark it off from other, more "typical" religious traditions. The Buddhist scripture is focused on the founder, the Gautama who became Buddha as a result of enlightenment. While there is some similarity in this respect with the Christian New Testament focus, although not solely, on the founder, Jesus of Nazareth, Jesus confessed as Christ, the salvific meaning of the founder is different in Buddhism. The Buddha presented in the defining scriptures is not a savior after the Christian interpretation, but rather the embodiment and grand example of the goal attained, namely, the enlightenment that leads to release (nirvana).[80] Salvation in Buddhism is ultimately a matter of one's own pursuit:

77. Coward, *Sacred Word*, p. 129.

78. Ward, *Religion and Revelation*, p. 58; Coward, *Sacred Word*, p. 138.

79. For example, the Chinese Buddhist canon would require more than 500,000 pages if translated into Western languages! See Coward, *Sacred Word*, p. 138.

80. "If the Buddha is to be called a 'saviour' at all, it is only in the sense that he dis-

"One is one's own refuge, who else could be the refuge?"[81] The Buddhist schools also debate whether the content of Buddha's enlightenment can ever be put into words, since Gautama experienced it in silence under the Boddhi Tree. Be that as it may, it "has not prevented the development of a complex and elaborate scriptural tradition to transmit his words to subsequent generations."[82]

Since Buddhism at large is not a theistic religion in the sense of the three Semitic religions and Hinduism, the focus of its scripture is geared toward helping the human in the pursuit of enlightenment. That said, a number of qualifications are in order. The nontheistic nature of Buddhism does not mean that it is therefore atheistic. All forms of Buddhism, even the most traditional Theravada tradition, acknowledge deities and divine beings. However, somewhat like the Hindu Mimamsa tradition, the deities are not the focus of either revelation or spiritual pursuit. Second, in some Buddhist traditions, particularly among those related to the Mahayana family of traditions, the divine beings play a more profound role. In the Lotus Sutra, the "Bible" of many Mahayana faithful, one is struck with its way of speaking of Buddha in divine terms, of the authority of his sayings, and his "salvific" works.[83] And one subfamily of the Mahayana movement, Pure Land Buddhism, not only acknowledges god but also looks upon god as "savior."[84] All in all, the Buddhist tradition does not speak with one voice. Yet, as a whole and in light of its original (Theravada) vision, any talk about divinely revealed, inspired holy scripture — after Hindu or Semitic religions — is foreign to Buddhism.

In his first sermon, after the enlightenment, "First Turning of the Wheel of *Dhamma*,"[85] Gautama (also called Shakyamuni), or noble origins, crystal-

---

covered and showed the Path to Liberation, Nirvana. But we must tread the Path ourselves." Rahula, *What the Buddha Taught*, pp. 1-2.

81. Dhammapada 12.4; *SBE* 10 (in some other versions, 12.160, when verses are numbered from the beginning of the work, rather than from the beginning of each chapter). The English translation of this passage varies; I have followed here the one adopted by Rahula, *What the Buddha Taught*, p. 1. Similarly, Dhammapada 20.4 (20.276) puts it: "You yourselves must strive; the Buddhas only point the way."

82. Eckel, "Buddhism," p. 143.

83. Read only, for example, *Saddharmapundarika* (Lotus Sutra), chap. 24 (a few pages in English), which strongly echoes not only the Vedic teaching but also teachings of many theistic religions concerning the divinely given revelation, as authoritative message, which leads to salvation. Here the savior Buddha is named Avalokitesvara, known as Amitabha in the Japanese (and some Chinese) Pure Land traditions.

84. The role of Amitabha Buddha as "savior" is discussed in the volumes *Christ and Reconciliation* and *Spirit and Salvation*.

85. Also known as "Setting the Wheel of *Dhamma* in Motion."

lized his theology under the four Noble Truths: "The Noble Truth of *dukkha*, monks, is this: Birth is *dukkha*, aging is *dukkha*, sickness is *dukkha*, death is *dukkha*, association with the unpleasant is *dukkha*, dissociation from the pleasant is *dukkha*, not to receive what one desires is *dukkha* — in brief the five aggregates subject to grasping are *dukkha*."[86] With all their differences, all Buddhist schools consider *dukkha* (suffering) and the rest of the Noble Truths (the origin and way of extinction) as the *summa* of everything in Buddhism and its scriptures.[87] Hence, extinction of *dukkha* is the main goal of this religious path. Suffering is inescapable as long as one is in the circle of life and death (samsara). To be more precise, it is the craving (the second Noble Truth) that is the real root and cause.[88] Behind the (misplaced) craving, according to the Buddha, is ignorance.[89] The logic of the emergence and continuation of suffering rooted in craving due to ignorance is indebted to the law of *kamma*.[90]

Dhamma (Pali; *Dharma* in Sanskrit), which is variously translated as "law," "teaching," or "principle(s)," contains, in addition to the Noble Truths, the Eightfold Path, the summary of the means toward the goal of release from samsara, and key principles related to reality, such as "dependent origination"

86. *Dhammacakkappavattana Sutta* 11 of Samyutta Nikaya 56.11. I have replaced the English translation "suffering" (in other renderings "pain" or "stress" or similar) with *dukkha* for the simple reason that the term is notoriously difficult to translate, as even a quick look at different English renderings of the Pali original reveals: terms such as "suffering," "pain," "stress," and "unsatisfactoriness" are used. None of them, however, can capture the ambiguity of the original term — and most of them, taken in isolation from the Buddhist worldview, can easily lead us astray. Some Buddhist experts such as Valpola Rahula simply do not translate it into contemporary languages and stick with the Pali original.

87. Chandngarm, *Arriyasatsee*, pp. 9-14.

88. Similarly to the notion of *dukkha*, the term *tanha* ("craving" or "desire") used by Buddha is a multifaceted concept. It is customary to divide it into three meanings: craving for sensual pleasures, craving for existence, and craving for nonexistence (which means the longing to avoid unpleasant conditions or situations such as when an old person does not want to grow old).

89. See *Paticca-samuppada-vibhanga Sutta: Analysis of Dependent Co-arising* of Samuyttanikaya Nikaya 12.2, for the famous analysis of Gautama concerning the idea of "dependent origination," which names ignorance as the genesis of the cycle of actions and dispositions that ultimately lead to suffering, and identifies "complete abandoning of ignorance" as the way out of it.

90. *Kamma* ("the law of reaping and sowing") has two sides in the Buddhist analysis: on the one hand the "bad" *kamma*, which consists of "unskillful" actions and attitudes such as greed or hatred, and on the other hand the "good" *kamma*, which consists of "skillful" actions and attitudes such as nongreed, nonhatred, and nondelusion. Good *kamma* produces good while bad *kamma* has bad effects. Dammapitaka, *Dictionary of Buddhism*, p. 60.

and "no-self."[91] To be a Buddhist means taking "refuge" in Buddha, *Dhamma,* and *sangha* (community, particularly monastic community in Theravada schools). In what ways can we speak of taking "refuge" in Buddha? Buddhists often refer to the core teachings of Buddha as "Dhamma Body." This concept arose early as, following the *parinirvana* (final nirvana) of Gautama, a group of his disciples began to venerate his cremated remains, which led to the formation of Buddhist worship patterns at large. These worship patterns are called "Form Body," in contrast to the teachings. Despite hermeneutical disputes among the Buddhist schools about this dual concept, all agree that as Dhamma Body — and Form Body — Buddha continues to be present among his followers. Later Mahayana tradition, as will be discussed below, underwent a significant elaboration and reconfiguration of the manifestation and continuing presence of Buddha.

Following the approximately forty-five-year teaching career of Buddha, each of the early schools developed rich scriptural collections; unfortunately, only the Pali-language Tipitaka ("Three Baskets") was preserved, and that is the "canonical" scripture of the oldest and most traditional Theravada school.[92] According to written Buddhist history, after Buddha's death the First Buddhist Council (486 B.C.E.) was invoked to recite the teachings of the Enlightened One. The council established criteria and procedures for the memorization of Buddha's words. Only after about five hundred years was the canonical collection now known as Tipitaka put into writing. As in Hinduism, oral tradition is highly appreciated in Buddhism even though most schools also highly revere the canonical writings.

According to tradition, Tipitaka was written down in 29 B.C.E. in Sri Lanka under King Vattagamani. Sutta Pitaka contains mainly doctrinal discourses, which appear in shorter poems and longer narratives. Some of those narratives related to earlier lives of Buddha. A separate, huge collection of former incarnations of Buddha, often numbered around five hundred, is called Jataka, and in English is published in no fewer than six volumes! While non-canonical, this is a highly popular collection, and samples of it circulate widely among Buddhist laypeople. The second "basket" of Tipitaka is the Vinaya Pi-

91. These two themes are discussed in some detail in the doctrine of creation and theological anthropology of the volume *Creation and Humanity.*

92. Of the rapid divisions and proliferation of Buddhism from its beginnings onward, a profound example is the rise of about eighteen different schools *(nikaya)* during the first century after the death of Gautama. Of those, the only surviving is Theravada. Hence, its scriptural canon is defining for all later developments. Theravada tradition is concentrated in Cambodia, Laos, Myanmar, Sri Lanka, and Thailand.

taka, which is mainly about (monastic) rules of conduct and discipline. Many of the Buddhist moral principles can be found here, often illustrated with narratives and stories. Abhidhamma Pitaka is the most systematic form of Buddhist thought and beliefs. An important early Buddhist teacher of the fifth century C.E., Buddhaghosa collected and translated important commentaries on canonical texts. His own most important contribution is Visuddhimagga, "The Path to Purification," a highly significant guide particularly to religious practices among the Theravadans. Like the Hindu Vedas, it is inaccessible to most faithful adherents, and very few have the luxury to study widely the extensive canonical collection of more than forty volumes. Instead, a small portion from the canonical text, called Dhammapada, is close to what we may call the "Buddhist Bible." It is drawn from Sutta Pitaka's Khuddaka Nikaya ("Minor Collection"). Basically it is a slim anthology of verses, which for the Jewish-Christian writer brings to mind the OT Proverbs, that crystallizes much of the core teaching of the Buddha and Buddhism.[93] Buddhaghosa's celebrated commentary on Dhammapada is an important source of Buddhist theology.

Around the beginning of the common era, the most significant split occurred, giving birth to the Mahayana school.[94] This branch developed a rich and variegated treasure of scriptures as well as a competing hermeneutics alongside the older tradition. Significantly, the Mahayana tradition claimed to build on Buddha's own teaching — thus representing the mentality of some Christian "back to the Bible" restorationist movements — with the alleged "Second Turning of the Wheel of *Dhamma*." This sermon was believed to be hidden for a while and then rediscovered by this renewal movement — again, a development not unknown in other religious traditions. Mahayana advocates a much more open access to the pursuit of nirvana for all men and women, not only to a few religious.[95] It also developed the theological interpretation of Buddha into the significant notion of *trikaya*, "three bodies," three interrelated ways to access the manifestation and knowledge of Buddha. The *nirmaoa-kaya* is the "historical body" of Buddha in this life, particularly as Gautama, who

93. A little more than 400 verses, in English translation it takes only about 150 pages and hence — similarly to catechisms in Christian tradition — serves well the purposes of lay education and teaching.

94. Mahayana is currently present in India, Vietnam, Tibet (mainly in the form of Tantric Buddhism or Vajrayana), China, Taiwan, Korea, and Japan, among other locations. That tradition is also the most familiar form of Buddhism in the Global North.

95. Whereas in Theravada, the *arhat*, enlightened one, wishes to "cross the river" and extinguish in nirvana all desires, thus reaching personal salvation, in Mahayana, the enlightened Boddhisattvas postpone their own final bliss for the sake of helping others.

was enlightened. The *sambhoga-kaya*, "heavenly body," also called "blissful body," refers to some kinds of transcendent Buddhas who guide the Boddhi-sattvas, men and women who have been enlightened but for the sake of others wish to postpone entering nirvana. These heavenly bodies may also appear in historical forms, if need be. The *dharma-kaya* is the most ultimate form of the "three bodies," that is, doctrine, and could be translated in various ways, such as "essential body" or "cosmic body." As a type of ultimate cosmic principle, the essence of reality, it also is beyond dualistic pairs such as immanence and transcendence.[96]

The development and dissemination of Mahayana tradition through-out various Asian locations are closely connected with the proliferation of sacred literature. As early as the second century c.e., the earliest texts were translated into Chinese. During the second half of the first millennium c.e., the Chinese Tripitaka (Sanskrit translation of the Pali name Tipitaka) was codified into Chinese writing, and the Tibetan collection of sacred writings a couple of hundred years after. In both of these locations, the monastic con-nection is evident. While no canonization is in place here, a "canon within the canon," to use Christian parlance, evolved quite early. Both the Chinese and Tibetan collections of sutras include a section called "Perfection of Wisdom" (Prajnaparamita), an essential Mahayana teaching about Bodhisattvas (the Enlightened Ones) and the principle of "emptiness" (sunyata). Once this core text expanded to become huge — over 100,000 lines — it was condensed into short texts such as the Diamond Sutra and the Heart Sutra, the best-known parts of the Sanskrit "canon." Alongside these two collections of sutras, the Lotus Sutra functions in much of East Asia as an accessible, limited collec-tion of key Mahayana teachings. Quite distinct from the Mahayana tradition, the Tibetan Tantric or Vajranaya school produced large collections of sacred writings as well, including Mahavairochana Tantra, "The Tantra of the Great Vairochana."

While Mahayana and all other Buddhist schools consider Tipitaka to be founding scriptures, Mahayana has produced a number of significant sutras that are rejected by most Theravadans. While the production of rich sacred lit-erature is the hallmark of Mahayana, no canon has been formulated.[97] Hence, when speaking of the Buddhist "canon," one must keep in mind that there is no fixed pan-Buddhist canon even though Tipitaka is greatly appreciated by

96. That said, the concept of Dharmakaya is understood and appropriated in a number of ways among various Mahayana traditions.

97. See Robinson and Johnson, *The Buddhist Religion,* p. 84.

all, and that only in the Theravada school can the written Tipitaka be said to function as canonical writing.[98]

The Function and Authority of Scripture

Perhaps against expectations, Buddhist traditions as a whole have produced more sacred literature than any single religious tradition, even more than Hinduism. I think there is a significant theological reason for this occurrence: "Perhaps Buddhists have more scripture than others because, in their view, scriptural words do not have a special status such as the *qur'ans* of Islam or the *vāk* of Hinduism. For the Buddhist, words, even most scriptural words, are not divine but merely conventional — created by humans for the purpose of solving practical problems in everyday life."[99] Consider the well-known fact that, unlike, say, most Vedanta theologians to whom metaphysical and "abstract" philosophical questions are important, Buddha himself on various occasions sought to avoid speculation and just focus on the "practical" issues.[100] Reflected here is a main cause of the path chosen by Gautama, namely, his complete dissatisfaction with the Hindu orientation to Vedas in his homeland India. Coming from the high caste (*ksatriya*, soldier), he must have spent some of his youth studying the Vedas.

What bothered the young nobleman was not only the sometimes-speculative approach to the scriptures among the Brahmins, but particularly the fact that, lacking direct experience of Brahman, the students of the Vedas had to rely solely on the authority of the "seers," the human recipients of the eternal divine voices. That is why in Gautama's reasoning, the Vedas could not be accepted as revelation.[101] Gautama sought to escape the necessity

---

98. For a highly useful and accessible presentation of the sacred writings in various Buddhist schools, see Eckel, "Buddhism," pp. 143-52.

99. Coward, *Sacred Word*, p. 138.

100. In this context, one is reminded of Buddha's parable of the house on fire (*Aggi-Vacchagotta Sutta:* To Vacchagotta on Fire, #72 of Majjhima Nikaya) as a way of shifting interest in metaphysical speculations about the infinite/fine nature of reality to practical matters of rescue. His famous parable of a man wounded by a poisoned arrow makes the same point (*Cula-Malunkyovada Sutta:* The Shorter Instructions to Malunkya, #63 of Majjhima Nikaya). Furthermore, Buddha's comparison between teaching and a raft to cross over the river not only makes the point evident among many Hindu theologians that scripture only has an intermediary agency (having reached its goal, it can be left behind) but also radicalizes it (*Alagaddupama Sutta:* The Snake Simile, #22 of Majjhima Nikaya).

101. See further, Coward, *Sacred Word*, pp. 139-40.

of taking the Vedic teaching on faith by seeking and allegedly reaching the defining personal experience. Unlike gnosticism or similar movements that consider the experience of the few "enlightened" unattainable by the masses, in Gautama's vision and in the understanding of most of his followers, that is not the case, particularly in the Mahayana school. Rightly, Lewis Lancaster observes:

> While the followers of the Buddha considered that his words possessed special power, the idea that the teaching arose from insights achieved in a special state of yogic development, a state open and available to all who have the ability and the desire to exert the tremendous effort needed to achieve it, meant that the words based on the experience need not be considered as unique or limited to one person in one time. Indeed, the Buddhists held that Sākayamuni was but one of a line of Buddhas who have appeared in this world system to expound the Dharma, and that there will be others to follow.[102]

Now, some observations and critical questions emerge from the perspective of Christian tradition and in light of the long discussion of the role of "authority" in revelation and faith. First of all, a sympathetic Christian critic would remind Buddha's followers that in the absence of the experience of the enlightenment — even among those who still earnestly pursue it — the only way to get guidance is to trust the authority, namely, the report of Buddha. It seems to me that all religious — as well as philosophical and metaphysical — explanations always build to some extent on authority and tradition, even the post-Enlightenment, Christian, allegedly "contra-authority" viewpoints. A contingent, finite, and fallible human person or even humanity as a whole "is not an island." Second, the Buddhist belief that even Gautama represented continuity of religious insights, albeit in a dramatically "new" way, seems to suggest that even his experience of enlightenment is not so novel that it would not be building on tradition and authority. Coward rightly remarks:

> For Buddhism, as was the case for Hinduism, the truth taught by the scriptures is beginningless, eternal. Like the ṛṣis (as they are understood within Hinduism), Gautama acts to clear away the obstructions that obscure the eternal truth. Other Buddhists have done this before him, and will do it again after him. But always it is the same truth that is revealed.

102. Lancaster, "Buddhist Literature," p. 215, quoted in Coward, *Sacred Word,* p. 140.

Revelation in this Buddhist sense is *parivartina* — turning something over, explaining it, making plain the hidden. This is the role of the Buddhas: to make visible the timeless truth to the unenlightened; to point out the path to *Nirvāṇa* and guide the way.[103]

A sympathetic observer of the Buddhist approach to scripture may note yet another irony or dynamic tension.[104] Reginald A. Ray puts it well:

> Throughout its history, Buddhist tradition has maintained a paradoxical attitude towards its sacred texts. On the one hand, those texts have themselves been the objects of the utmost veneration: and life, limb, and more have been sacrificed to ensure their unaltered preservation and correct understanding. At the same time, Buddhism avers that the sacred text has, in and of itself, no particular value. Its worth depends entirely on what is done with it, and at best, the sacred text is never more than an aid that must be abandoned by each individual at a certain point on his journey toward the Buddhist goal of enlightenment. Thus in Buddhism, the sacred text is an answer to spiritual longing, and also no answer at all, or rather an "answer" in the way it points beyond and, in fact, away from itself.[105]

This twofold, dynamic attitude toward the scripture is best illustrated in the famous "Discourse on the Great Decease," which recounts the death of Gautama. On the one hand, it urges the disciple Ananda to be the "lamp" and "refuge" unto himself, and on the other hand, it tells him that the *Dhamma* is the lamp and refuge![106]

In Buddhist texts one never hears the saying "Thus said Buddha" — as is customary in the Christian canon, "Thus said the Lord." Buddhist texts, on the contrary, at times begin with an epithet, "Thus I have heard," and it is most often Gautama himself who is the hearer! And even when the Theravada tradition claims to preserve the "words" of Gautama, always there is the theological assumption that "the *dharma* transcends all words and the capability

---

103. Coward, *Sacred Word,* p. 141.

104. Fittingly, Eva K. Neumaier titles her essay "The Dilemma of Authoritative Utterance in Buddhism."

105. Ray, "Buddhism," p. 148.

106. *Mahaparinibbana Sutta* 1.33. For a highly useful and dynamic reflection on the question of the authority and function of scripture in Buddhism, see Ray, "Buddhism," pp. 148-88; that essay also deals with questions about the authenticity of sacred texts as well as the role of tradition.

of language."[107] As Eva K. Neumaier correctly observes: "On the one hand, Buddhists have compiled hundreds of volumes of 'canonical' Buddha words while, on the other hand, maintaining that all words are, at best, only approximations of the truth, and at worst, altogether useless."[108]

So, what do Buddhists believe are the "authority" and defining function of scripture? While there certainly are doctrines in Buddhism, rather than "believing the doctrines" as described in the tightly formulated canons of Semitic religions and Vedic Hinduism, the main function and authority of scripture in all Buddhist schools is to serve as an aid to accessing Buddha's experience of the Awakening, and hence, as an opportunity for each Buddhist to tread that path. True, Buddha's teaching speaks of doubt as one of the five hindrances[109] to an understanding of the truth and to spiritual progress. But the "doubt" spoken of by the Buddha is not a sinful attitude as often understood in Semitic traditions in terms of being unwilling to submit to and embrace divinely revealed truth. As Walpola Rahula brilliantly puts it:

> Doubt . . . is not a "sin," because there are no articles of faith in Buddhism. In fact there is no "sin" in Buddhism, as sin is understood in some religions. The root of all evil is ignorance . . . and false views. . . . It is an undeniable fact that as long as there is doubt, perplexity, wavering, no progress is possible. It is also equally undeniable that there must be doubt as long as one does not understand or see clearly. But in order to progress further it is also absolutely necessary to get rid of doubt. To get rid of doubt one has to see clearly.[110]

Hence, Buddha also always encouraged his disciples to test every teaching, even his own, in order to attain full conviction.[111] Considering ignorance as the root of evil is of course a shared conviction with Hinduism, even though the role of scripture differs vastly between the two traditions: Vedas are be-

---

107. Neumaier, "Dilemma of Authoritative Utterance," p. 138.

108. Neumaier, "Dilemma of Authoritative Utterance," pp. 138-39.

109. The other four hindrances are usually listed as sensuous lust, ill-will, physical and mental languor, and restlessness and worry. See Rahula, *What the Buddha Taught*, p. 3.

110. Rahula, *What the Buddha Taught*, p. 3.

111. See *Vimamsaka Sutta* ("The Examination"), #47 of Majjhima Nikaya. It can be found in English at http://www.dhammaweb.net/Tipitaka/read.php?id=81 (8/18/2011). *Ukkacita-Sutta* ("Bombast"), Anguttara Nikaya 2.46, similarly makes a distinction between two kinds of people: those who listen attentively and critically to the *dhamma*, and those who listen uncritically to other teachings.

lieved to be eternal divine voices whereas Tipitaka is an authoritative access to Buddha's experience and teachings.

The key to Buddhist pursuit of removing ignorance — based on the attachment to *dukkha* — is insight, or perhaps, what Rahula calls "seeing":

> Almost all religions are built on faith — rather "blind" faith it would seem. But in Buddhism emphasis is laid on "seeing," knowing, understanding, and not on faith, or belief. In Buddhist texts there is a word *saddhā* (Skt. *Āraddhā*) which is usually translated as "faith" or "belief." But *saddhā* is not "faith," as such, but rather "confidence" born out of conviction. In popular Buddhism and also in ordinary usage in the texts the word *saddhā*, it must be admitted, has an element of "faith" in the sense that it signifies devotion to the Buddha, the *Dhamma* (Teaching) and the *Sangha* (The Order).[112]

The valid point in Rahula's explanation is the shift away from a "blind" or merely intellectual belief, a concept foreign to Buddhist pursuit of enlightenment. However, in Christian tradition, "faith" has little to do with "blind" or merely intellectual grasping either!

To highlight the importance of "seeing" and insight helps put the role of Buddhist scripture in proper perspective. We do this not to circumvent the cognitive or even doctrinal nature of the sacred literature as much as to point to the specifically human-centered orientation of all Buddhist schools, particularly Theravada. Yun-Hua Jan's placement of scripture into the wider matrix of human pursuit in the Buddhist path is most instructive: "Through a regulated life in accordance with *Vinaya* rules, to study doctrinal statements attributed to the Buddha as presented in the *sūtras*, to practise the teaching and to reflect on some of the points in the light of the commentaries are the consistent directives in Buddhist tradition. It is only through this threefold effort, the religious goal of Buddhahood, or *Nirvāṇa* might be attainable."[113]

Gospel and Dhamma

A certain parallelism was noted above between the Hindu understanding of the Vedas as eternal, creative words and the Christian idea of the Word/

---

112. Rahula, *What the Buddha Taught*, p. 8.
113. Jan, "Dimensions of Indian Buddhism," p. 162, as cited in Coward, *Sacred Word*, p. 138.

Logos. Samyutta Nikaya says: "Enough, Vakkali! What is there to see in this vile body? He who sees Dhamma, Vakkali, sees me; he who sees me sees Dhamma. Truly seeing Dhamma, one sees me; seeing me one sees Dhamma."[114] A Christian observer is tempted to see some parallels here with the idea of the living Word of God (and of course, the ministry of the Paraclete of the Johannine Gospel). Although the partial yet important parallelism between Hinduism and Christian tradition appears more pointed in that for both traditions the "Word" is eternal and divine, establishing the parallelism between Buddhism and Christian theologies seems to me a stretch of the imagination. The differences are too dramatic, not only because of Buddhism's ambivalence about theistic notions, but also because of its approach to scripture and "revelation" as expounded above. Instead, a valid conclusion might be that in all these three traditions — and of course, Islam and Judaism should be included — the power of the sacred word and its relation to sacred text are important either as "revelation" or as revelation and effective power on the way to "salvation."

While contemporary theology of religions and comparative theology, as mentioned, tend, somewhat one-sidedly, to highlight similarities between faith traditions, it is also important, for the sake of clarification of issues and fruitful dialogue, to point to real and essential differences. Keith Ward's conclusion could hardly be better expressed and is worth this longer citation:

> If one asks what the viewpoint of enlightenment can be, one may say that it is an experience of supreme transcendence of all selfish attachment, of supreme compassion for all beings, of supreme tranquility and bliss, and of supreme insight into human motivation and duplicity. The theist, however, will not be able to say that it is an experience of supreme insight into the true conditions of human being — since precisely the most important theistic assumption, the existence of a personal being on whom all things depend, is entirely lacking. But the theist has to face a difficult question: how could the most important thing be lacking, after such a determined quest for truth and liberation was taken to be successful?[115]

Other significant differences exist between Christian faith and Buddhism when it comes to revelation. Since these have been noted above, including some relevant comments in the discussion of Hinduism, let it suffice to

---

114. Vakkali Sutta in Samyutta Nikaya, pp. 22, 87.
115. Ward, *Religion and Revelation*, p. 160.

list them briefly here: the detachment of revelation from the historical process; the lack of any notion of inspiration of the sacred text; and a very different linking of the sacred words/scripture to the "founder" of the faith than in Christian tradition — Jesus not only speaks authoritatively but *is* the *eternal* Word made *flesh*. And so forth.

This is not to say that Christian tradition couldn't learn from Buddhism. With the Jewish faith, Christian theology is reminded of the danger of "an objectivization of God as a supreme person who is judge and savior" with the robust linking of revelation to moral demands of God; this may lead to "a belittling of human life and responsibility, to an ethic of blind obedience to authoritative commands and to a spirituality of guilt and flattery."[116] Islam should be placed here alongside Judaism and Christianity. Buddhism's strength, which ironically is also its weakness in Christian estimation, is the focus on "human responsibility . . . and a practice leading to personal fulfillment while shedding all the myths of authoritative obedience which existed in the Brahmanical tradition." That said, Ward also helpfully reminds us that "it would be a terrible misunderstanding to take Buddhism simply as a humanist protest against religious authoritarianism, against a moralism which subjugates human freedom in the name of God."[117] Totally unlike atheistic or other forms of "secular" ethics, for Buddhism — as a *religious* tradition — the fulfillment points to transcendence, *ultimate* release.

The complicated and complex nature and role of authority in Buddhism were looked at in some detail above. And earlier in the volume, the Christian insistence on the divinely inspired yet genuinely human nature of Scripture, including its relation to community and tradition, was investigated quite carefully. How do Christian and Buddhist notions of authority relate to each other? Two points are in order. First of all, both traditions build on authority. Second, they do this so differently that their views conflict dramatically. The Buddhist conviction about its view's correctness is based on the teachings of the Buddhas, in whose lives, most profoundly in the life of the Gautama Buddha, the insight gained led to fulfillment. But since no Buddhas are living physically with us now, the account of these Buddhas' enlightenment must be taken by faith. The same goes for Christians, who build on the words of Jesus Christ that are available only through the writings of the early witnesses.

When investigated more thoroughly, however, the basis of these two

116. Ward, *Religion and Revelation*, p. 160.
117. Ward, *Religion and Revelation*, pp. 160-61.

materially different — albeit formally quite similar — claims to truth goes back to dramatic metaphysical/philosophical/theological differences. In Buddhism, there is no enduring self, indeed no enduring reality at all. In theistic religion, not only is there an enduring self, having been created in the image of God, but more importantly, there is the Ultimate Reality, God, and enduring reality (creation). The comparison must stop there because neither "self" nor God is an observable entity or experience. The nonendurance of self and reality makes full sense in the matrix of Buddhist philosophy as it seeks to expose and release us from what it sees as a false attachment to falsely imagined realities. For the Christian believer, and other Semitic theists, the direction is the complete opposite: everything in the final analysis depends on God. Where "the whole Buddhist world-view and discipline leads away from theism,"[118] everything in Christian faith leads toward God, the source of revelation as Father, Son, and Holy Spirit, and its consummator in the coming of the kingdom.

How does Tipitaka take other religious traditions and their scriptures? Estimates vary. The noted Buddhist expert Walpola Rahula — in my understanding — somewhat naively praises the absolute open-mindedness of Buddhist tradition in relation to all other living faiths. He goes so far as to say that at no point in Buddhist history has any blood been shed because of religious strife or the desire to convert.[119] I fear that a study of the history of Buddhist lands from India to Sri Lanka to Thailand to China and beyond may not yield as rosy a picture. Be that as it may, others take a more moderate stance. Like Hinduism, concerning which there is the widespread — mistaken! — assumption that tolerance and openness are the leading themes, Buddhism is firmly anchored in the conviction that through Buddha was given the final and fullest revelation and that this is the criterion for the value of other claims to revelation.

It seems to me Coward is right when, specifically comparing the Tipitaka to other living faiths' scriptures, he names the Buddhist attitude "critical tolerance":

> Critical in the sense that any removal of moral freedom and responsibility in these [other] scriptures will be rejected. Tolerant in that so long as moral responsibility is safeguarded, other teachings contained in these

118. Ward, *Religion and Revelation,* p. 166; this paragraph is heavily indebted to pp. 165-66.

119. Rahula, *What the Buddha Taught,* p. 5 particularly.

[other] scriptures such as, for example, belief in God — teachings that the *Tripiṭaka* rejects — will be put up with. The approach of the Buddha to other scriptures is to superimpose his teaching over the other scripture. So long as the main points of the Buddhist teaching, or *Dharma,* can be found (i.e., belief in survival after death, moral values, freedom, responsibility, and the noninevitability of salvation or release) then other unacceptable aspects such as free grace from God can be tolerated.[120]

Similar to that of orthodox Hinduism, this view is very different from the contemporary Roman Catholic theology of religions, often named "inclusivism." Different from traditional Christian and even contemporary mainline Muslim "exclusivism,"[121] postconciliar Catholic theology is open to the salvation of many in other religions, but it determines the conditions for salvation, as well as the value of those traditions, on the basis of its own tradition. In Catholicism, "fulfillment" can be found without a need to undermine the relative value of truth and beauty in other religions that are inferior to it.

These kinds of investigations hinder a careful common investigation into the possibility of a truly interfaith theology when too often and too naively the real differences are pushed away and similarities are highlighted at any cost. The Oxford systematician Keith Ward is a delightful exception to this tendency. Writing from a highly irenic and tolerant perspective, he sees time after time the importance of observing how the claims of various religious traditions are not only different but also in many ways irreconcilable. It simply does not make any sense to claim that the human-centered (rightly understood), "nontheistic" approach adopted in the Tipitaka is speaking the same truth as the fully theistic Qur'anic and Christian accounts of "salvation." "The teachings of the *Tripiṭaka* are clearly different from the Christianity of St. Paul, the devotional Hinduism of the *Bhagavad-Gītā,* or the Qur'an. The scriptures of these last three teach that it is God's grace that makes possible religious attainment, whereas, for the Buddhist *Tripiṭaka* it is human effort, not supernatural intervention, that is effective."[122]

120. Coward, *Sacred Word,* p. 157.

121. This nomenclature, widely used in discourse on Christian theology of religions, has recently come under severe criticism and needs to be replaced by more appropriate terms. That, however, is a topic for another context. It will be most fully dealt with in the introductory chapter to the volume *Church and Hope,* in the investigation of the place of Christian community among other religious communities.

122. Coward, *Sacred Word,* p. 157.

The Qur'an and the Bible

Islamic Canon and Sacred Texts

Unlike Hinduism and Buddhism, in which the canon is either vast or hardly defined, but similar to Judeo-Christian traditions, Islam has a clearly defined canon, the Qur'an. Linked to later exposition and expansion of the Qur'anic materials, there is also a huge and vast Hadith tradition that consists of the sayings of the Prophet and other sages. The sayings and actions of Muhammad narrated in the Hadith are not believed to be revealed, although they are inspired.[123] By the ninth century, as many as 600,000 Hadiths had been recorded, which were then condensed into about 25,000. By far the most important is the Hadith of Bukkhari; significant also are the Hadiths of Muslim, of Sunan Abu-Dawud, and of Malik's Muwatta. Understandably Islamic tradition has brought about commentary literature, similar to that of other living faiths. Especially the Sunni exegesis during the first Islamic centuries became famous for its meticulous and tedious work. Along with the mainline Sunni and Shiite schools, the mystical Sufi schools have produced an amazingly diverse devotional and mystical literary and poetic treasury.

The discussion so far has established the central role of scripture not only in Christianity (and by implication in Judaism) but also in two major world religions from Asia. Not only is scripture central in Islam, but also probably in all living faiths. Yet it is in Islam that scripture plays the most profound role. "Out of the Qur'an arises the Islamic community, its law, literature, art, and religion. Perhaps more than any other religious community, Muslims are a 'people of the Book.'"[124]

The Qur'an does not do away with earlier revelations, the Jewish First Testament and the Christian Second Testament, but rather considers itself their fulfillment and correction. Similar to how Hindus view the Vedas, most Muslims consider the Qur'an the eternal speech of God.[125] Again, like Hinduism, the oral scripture is the primary mode. What is interesting is that the

---

123. For a succinct comment on key Islamic distinctions between "inspiration" *(ilham)*, "sending down" *(tanzil)*, and "prophetic rapture" *(wahy)*, see Ward, *Religion and Revelation,* pp. 174-75.

124. Coward, *Sacred Word,* p. 81. Still an important succinct source to basic issues is Welch, "Al-Kur'ān." A massive contemporary source is the *Blackwell Companion to the Qur'ān* (2006).

125. This is the official standpoint of the major tradition of Islam, the Sunni theology. The minority Shiite school teaches that the Qur'an was created in time (that statement, how-

term *Qur'an* in Arabic means both "recitation" and "reading," thus embracing both oral and written aspects.

Unlike in Hinduism, whose *rishis* (seers) merely "hear" the eternal speech in the Vedas, passively, by virtue of having been cultivated spiritually to tap into the divine, the recipient in Islam, the prophet Muhammad, is more than just a passive recipient. Hence, the usual nomenclature of the "messenger" probably says too little of the role of the prophet.[126] "The Qur'an as Scripture comes only to him [Muhammad]: it has penmen other than himself but does not come from their pens, nor is it *about* him. 'Herald,' 'emissary,' even 'commissioner,' would all possibly serve, were they not encumbered by associations that are too sentimental or too vulgar."[127] Coward puts it well: "God is the speaker of the revelation, the angel Gabriel is the intermediary agent, and Muhammad is the recipient. Not a passive recipient, however, for God's word acts by its own energy and makes Muhammad the instrument, the 'sent-doer,' by which all people are warned by God and called to respond."[128] A mediator — the angel Gabriel, or at times, the Holy Spirit (Q 16:102), or the Trustworthy Spirit (26:193) — is needed because of the categorical separation between the transcendence of God and the immanence of humanity.[129]

Unlike in the Bible of the Judeo-Christian tradition, in which most of the divine speech comes in human forms, often embedded in the struggles of human life and in the events of history, and which often contains substantial narratives about key figures such as prophets and apostles, in the Islamic Qur'an "there is no notion of an inspiration from God that is then clothed and uttered in the best words a human mind can create. In the Qur'an, Muhammad receives a direct, fully composed revelation from God, which he then recites to others."[130] While progressive contemporary scholars, mainly based in the

---

ever, does not make the Qur'anic word less authoritative). See Momen, *Introduction to Shi'i Islam*, p. 176; I am indebted to Cornell, "Listening to God through the Qur'an," n. 51.

126. Cragg notes that the term *rasul* used in Islamic creedal traditions of Muhammad as the mediator of the Qur'an cannot be satisfactorily translated in English. The term conveys the meaning "doing/doer" in the root of "sentness." Cragg, *House of Islam*, p. 19; I am indebted to Coward, *Sacred Word*, p. 82.

127. Cragg, *House of Islam*, p. 19, cited in Coward, *Sacred Word*, p. 82.

128. Coward, *Sacred Word*, p. 82.

129. See further, Cornell, "Listening to God through the Qur'an," pp. 40-42.

130. Coward, *Sacred Word*, p. 82. An important Qur'anic explanation of the "sending down" of the divine revelation on the "Night of Destiny" is in 53:5-11. For more on the divine origin and authority of scripture, see 16:102; 26:192-5; 42:7. For its inimitability, see 2:23; 10:38. Whether Muhammad was illiterate or not is a debated question because of the ambiguity of interpretation of 7:158 ("uninstructed," in other renderings "unlettered" or similar).

West, acknowledge the personal, religious, sociohistorical, and similar contextual factors in the formation of the canon,[131] orthodox Islam regards the Arabic Qur'an as the direct, authoritative speech of God conveyed through the Prophet. In that sense, Muhammad's role is critical and unique.[132] Unlike the Christian understanding of the formation of the canon as a centuries-long divine-human synergy, orthodox Islam rests on the firm conviction that the formation and closing of the Qur'anic canon were a divine act through Muhammad. Indeed, there is an old tradition according to which the Qur'an is but a copy of a "Guarded Tablet" in heaven (85:22).[133]

The belief that the revelation of the Qur'an came to Muhammad directly from God does not mean that it all came at one time and in the form of dictation, as it were. According to Q 17:106, "We have revealed it by [successive] revelation." Hadith traditions give vivid accounts of various ways the reception of revelation took place, including through dramatic emotional states.[134] However, theologically, unlike the experiences of the OT prophets or the NT apostle Paul, these emotional and personal struggles were not part of the revelation and revelatory process in Islamic understanding.

Although the sacred texts of the living faiths were conveyed originally in particular languages — Vedas in Sanskrit, Tipitaka in Pali, Torah in Hebrew, the New Testament in Greek — the Qur'an insists that its original language, Arabic, is also its only "revelatory" language.[135] The Qur'an can only exist in Arabic; all translations fall short of full revelation.[136] The form of Arabic used in the Qur'an is of the tribe of Quraysh, that of Muhammad. Interestingly, stylistically it is identical with none of the known bodies of Arabic. Even the Arabic of the Hadith is different from that of the Qur'an. "The uniqueness of the language of the Qur'an has become a dominant element in Muslim orthodoxy."[137]

As with the Vedas and Tipitaka, the oral form of (the Arabic) Qur'an is the most foundational and most authentic revelation. Beginning from Muhammad, who was commanded by the Angel to commit revelation to memory

131. So Sachedina, *Islamic Roots of Democratic Pluralism*, pp. 45-46.

132. Q 42:7, 17, 52.

133. Kassis, "The Qur'an," pp. 72-73.

134. See Hadith of Bukhari 1.1.2 and 3.

135. Q 42:7: "And thus have We revealed to you an Arabic Qur'ān." So also 12:2; 13:37; 16:103; 20:113; 26:195; 39:28.

136. Hence Kabbani (*A Letter to Christendom*, p. 34) bluntly says that a translated text is a different text!

137. Kassis, "The Qur'an," p. 70.

and who then recited it to the first disciples, there has been an unbroken line of reciters *(iurra)* of the Qur'an. As mentioned above, Islam holds a firm belief that great blessings come from this recital, not only in this life but also in the life to come. "The Qur'an is uttered to call others to it, to expiate sins, to protect against punishment, and to ensure blessings in paradise."[138]

Like the NT, the Qur'an defines its main and ultimate goal as the salvation of humankind. It also often refers to itself as the guide (14:1; 2:185; among others). An extreme view of the infallibility of the Qur'anic revelation and words is affirmed by all orthodox Muslim traditions. Sura 11, which speaks of Muhammad's task as prophet, opens with this affirmation: "(This is) a Scripture the revelations whereof are perfected and then expounded. (It cometh) from One Wise, Informed" (11:1, Marmaduke Pickthall trans.). According to 2:2, "That Book, in it there is no doubt" (see also 5:15-16; 5:48).

The Qur'anic view of scripture is understandably strongly propositional. That said, part of the Islamic doctrine of scripture has to do with its "sacramental" nature, to use the Christian vocabulary. The Arabic term *ayat,* which also means "verse" (of the sura), carries the meaning of "sign," to be more precise, a divine or divinely sanctioned sign.[139] Consider Jesus' miracles as "signs" (named as such in the Gospel of John, and understood as such in the Synoptics) as a material parallel.[140]

Not surprisingly, the Islamic tradition has paid close attention to careful and authoritative exegesis *(tafsir)* of the Qur'an. Indeed, because the Qur'an lays the foundation for and regulates all aspects of life and society, more is at stake in the hermeneutics of scripture in Islam than with most other traditions.[141] As mentioned, in early times the Sunni school excelled in a most detailed exegesis. The tenth-century Abū Ja'far Muhammad aṭ-Ṭabarī and the

---

138. Coward, *Sacred Word,* pp. 85-86.

139. A masterful — albeit not so easy to understand for the contemporary reader — classic study on the meaning of symbols and signs in the scriptural canon is offered by the most important Sunni theologian, the celebrated eleventh-century Al-Ghazzali, in his little work *The Niche for Lights* (also known as *Mishkat al-Anwarâ*), which is basically a commentary on Qur'an 24:34 (the so-called "Light" passage). See part II, titled "The Science of Symbolism" (available at sacred-texts.com).

140. There is a belief that the "verses" and "chapters" were placed in a certain order by Muhammad himself. The "verses" can be identified auditively by rhyme and rhythm. See Kassis, "The Qur'an," pp. 70-71.

141. Denffer, *Loading Options Ulu m al-Qur'an,* p. 123. An important part of the exegesis negotiates the universal and limited applicability of passages (say, polygamy) in light of the "occasions of revelation" principle; for succinct comments, see Bennett, *Understanding Christian-Muslim Relations,* pp. 41-42.

twelfth-century Fakhr ad-Dīin ar-Rāzī are often lifted up as most brilliant commentators. While the former established the procedure of citing all relevant Hadith comments with regard to the Qur'anic passage under exegesis, the latter also helped move exegesis in a philosophical and rationalistic direction. The main difference between the Sunni and Shiite schools is that the latter regards the imams as also inspired (and perhaps even infallible), a claim strongly rejected by the Sunni. Indeed, the Shiite school has a strictly regulated theology of succession, which maintains that while all Muslims may understand the scripture at the basic level, the authoritative interpretation comes only from the imams who are considered to be standing in the line of Ali, the legitimate successor of the Prophet. Hence, this line of "apostolic succession" goes all the way to Muhammad via Ali. It does not take much imagination for a Christian to see parallels with Christian tradition's deeply divisive debates about the episcopal succession and its relation to a rightful magisterium, the church's teaching office. Indeed, there is the notion not only of continuing inspiration but also (at least in some sense) of infallibility attached to the office of the imam, as Ali and his successors have received the "inner knowledge" of Muhammad. Again, reflecting some aspects of Christian tradition, it is not the differing exegetical techniques that make the difference but rather the deeply differing notion of succession and authority. The way of doing exegesis varies only in the Sufi traditions with their immersion in mystical materials and their use of Greek philosophical materials.[142]

Because of the nature of the Qur'an's divine origin — void of historical contextual factors and absolutely infallible — it is understandable that orthodox Muslim traditions reject the kind of historical-critical study that has been the hallmark of the Christian — and more recently Jewish — study of Scriptures for a long time now. This is not to say that no such inquiry into the Qur'an exists; rather, it means that it is marginal and rejected by the "curia" and the masses of the faithful.

Qur'an as the Fulfillment of Revelation

What is the relationship of the Qur'an to other scriptures? This is a dynamic and complex question that calls for a nuanced reflection. Well known is the statement in Q 42:15 that clearly bespeaks universality: "I believe in whatever

---

142. For a useful account of Islamic exegesis, see Coward, *Sacred Word*, pp. 94-101.

Book God has revealed."[143] The Holy Qur'an makes it clear that the divine revelation as guide is available to all nations (Q 35:24). The one source of revelation is based on the conviction that all humankind is of the same origin (Q 2:213; so also 5:48). Hence, the current "A Common Word"[144] project between Muslims and Christians took its inspiration from Q 3:64: "Say: 'O People of the Scripture! Come now to a word agreed upon between us and you, that we worship none but God.'"

To balance and complicate this openness and universality, there is an equally important principle of sufficiency and completeness in the Qur'an. The passage from Q 43:3-4 puts this dynamic in perspective: "Lo! We have made it an Arabic Qur'ān that perhaps you may understand. And it is indeed in the Mother Book, [which is] with Us [and it is] indeed exalted." Whereas the former verse states that the Arabic Qur'an, this particular book, is the vehicle for understanding divine revelation, the latter verse seems to be referring to a "Mother Book" (also mentioned in 13:39) — a universal treasure of divine revelation of which even the Qur'an is a part.[145] If so, this means that all the sacred books of the religions derive from the same divine origin. That would again bespeak universality.

On the other hand, Islamic theology of revelation also includes the determined insistence on the supremacy and finality of the Qur'anic revelation, something similar to the Roman Catholic fulfillment theology of religions. Sura 5:44-48 makes this clear by presenting the Jewish Torah and the Christian NT as stepping-stones to the final revelation given in the Qur'an. Not only does the Qur'an provide fulfillment; it also provides correction and criteria. It is in light of the Qur'an that the value of other revelations is assessed. The obvious problem posed by this interpretation is that whereas it seems to fit well Judeo-Christian Scriptures, it has a hard time negotiating other faith traditions' revelations. I am not aware of any satisfactory solutions to this problem.[146]

A major challenge to a common reading of Christian and Muslim scriptures is the common Muslim charge of *tahrif,* usually translated as "alteration."

---

143. Even the context of this passage speaks for a unity of divine revelation (42:13-14).

144. For the project, see "The Official Website of A Common Word" at http://www.acommonword.com/.

145. Often the passage in 56:78-80 is invoked in this discussion even though its exegesis — as illustrated in different renderings in English — is debated: "That (this) is indeed a noble Qur'an. In a Book kept hidden Which none toucheth save the purified, A revelation from the Lord of the Worlds" (Marmaduke Pickthall's translation).

146. For thoughtful and important reflections, see Koshul, "Affirming the Self," pp. 111-19; also, Coward, *Pluralism,* pp. 55-59.

The eleventh-century Ibn Hazm is routinely named as one of the earliest Islamic thinkers who definitely established the importance of *tahrif* as a counter-Christian tool.[147] The term *tahrif* is used in more than one sense. At its most basic level, it refers to problems of textual variants and, hence, the lack of the authentic original. It may also denote deliberate altering of the text — the most typical charge being that Ezra altered the OT text. But it can also simply mean a misguided interpretation of the texts.[148] A brilliant form of *tahrif* accusation, going back all the way to the important fourteenth-century Muslim apologetic, Ibn Taymiyyah's massive rebuttal of Christianity in response to the Christian writings of Paul of Antioch, is that perhaps the NT is like Hadith rather than scripture.[149] In light of Islamic tradition, this makes sense as the NT contains not only sayings of Jesus but also his activities, not unlike the Hadith of Islam. The current *tahrif* criticism of the Bible uses skillfully — and selectively — the insights of (Christian) historical-critical study in rebutting the truthfulness and reliability of the text.[150]

The dilemma of Muslim-Christian views of revelation does not have to do with the strangeness but rather with the deep affinity between these two traditions. Both claim a strictly defined canon and both appeal to one God as its source and provider. Yet they differ dramatically concerning which one of the books is the ultimate revelation. Adding to the complexity of this question are the dramatic differences in understanding of the category of revelation

147. Ibn Hazm's *Kitab-al-Fasl, The Book of Distinctions* is an important early study of other religions and their claims to revelation from an Islamic perspective. The work is not very available in English, but an important section thereof, titled "On the Inconsistencies of the Four Gospels," can be found in Constable, ed., *Medieval Iberia*.

148. Christian apologetics and polemics began to deal with the charge of *tahrif* as early as the ninth Christian century. The Christian Arabic writing *Risalah* by Al-Kindy (of whom we know little) takes up the challenge and seeks to combat it. The book (Sir William Muir's 1887 translation) can be found at http://www.answering-islam.org/Books/Al-Kindi/. The nineteenth-century apologist Karl Gottlieb Pfander used *Risalah* extensively in the continuing defense of the Bible against *tahrif* charges. The 1910 English translation of his *Balance of Truth* (orig. German 1823) is available at http://www.answering-islam.org/Books/Pfander/Balance/index.htm; pp. 27-30 summarize succinctly Pfander's criteria for a true revelation as opposed to the failings of truths in the Qur'an.

149. For discussion, see Bennett, *Understanding Christian-Muslim Relations*, pp. 124-26 particularly.

150. This trend began as early as the nineteenth century, pioneered by one of the most important modern apologeticists, whose writings are still consulted in Islamic polemics (Ramhatullah Ibn Khalil al-'Uthmany), al-Kairawani, who offered a massive rebuttal of Pfander's *Balance of Truth*. For discussion, see Bennett, *Understanding Christian-Muslim Relations*, pp. 131-37 particularly.

in general and of the other party's revelation in particular. Clinton Bennett succinctly lays out this complexity — which, of course, is an urgent invitation to continuing careful dialogue:

> In many respects, the conservative Christian view of the Bible as infallible and as inspired word for word is closer to how Muslims view the Qur'an than to the liberal Christian view of the Bible as a potentially fallible, human response to experience of the divine. On the Muslim right, the Bible is regarded as so corrupt that it no longer has any value. On the Christian left, an attempt is made to understand how the Qur'an can be accepted as "revelation." One difficulty is that Christians who deconstruct the Bible are likely to transfer this approach to the Qur'an as well, which is unacceptable, even to more liberal Muslims. Yet despite each side's view of the Other's scripture, Christians and Muslims from both the "right" and "left" cite from the Other's scripture to support their views. Christians have their favourite Qur'anic passages while Muslims have favourite Bible passages. More often than not, when Christians and Muslims use each other's scriptures, they do so in a manner that ignores or refutes how Christians and Muslims understand the passages concerned.[151]

Qur'an and Christ as Living Word

Muslim-Christian relations are plagued with great ironies. On the one hand, Islam is the only non-Christian tradition that requires the faithful to acknowledge and believe in Jesus Christ! There is a plethora of references to him in the Qur'an (about one hundred).[152] On top of that, the Qur'an contains references to and narratives about many key figures of the OT. On the other hand, because of the principle of "self-sufficiency" and vastly different hermeneutics from the beginning of Islam, the presence of common materials between the Qur'an and the Bible has generated deep and irreconcilable conflicts.

As is routinely — and correctly — remarked, it is not the prophet but rather the book that is the closest parallel to Christ, the center of Christianity. Unlike Christian faith, which is determined by belief in Christ, Islam is not

---

151. Bennett, *Understanding Christian-Muslim Relations*, p. 16.

152. See Barker and Gregg, "Muslim Perceptions of Jesus," p. 83. There are about 100 references to Jesus in the Qur'an and many more in the Hadith traditions; those are discussed in some detail in the volume *Christ and Reconciliation*.

based on Muhammad but rather on the Qur'an and Allah. Neither Christ nor Muhammad in Islamic interpretation is divine; only God is.[153] Hence, it is in Christ's role as the living Word of God in relation to the divine revelation of the Qur'an that the deepest commonalities are to be investigated.[154] Rightly it has been noted that whereas Jesus in Christian tradition is the "Word made flesh," the Qur'an in Islam is the divine word "inlibrate."[155]

There are surprisingly deep similarities among the accounts in the Qur'an of the power of its word and OT claims about the word of the Lord and NT statements about Christ as the creative word. Consider Q 59:21: "Had We sent down this Qur'ān upon a mountain, you would have surely seen it humbled, rent asunder by the fear of God. And such similitudes do We strike for mankind, that perhaps they may reflect." Again, just as the Word of the Lord has many functions in the Bible, whether for encouragement or healing or miraculous acts, the Islamic tradition speaks of the living words of the Qur'an:

> In addition to its destructive power, the words of the Qur'an are also a positive source for healing and tranquility. According to tradition when the Qur'an is recited divine tranquility (sakīnah) descends, mercy covers the reciters, angels draw near to them, and God remembers them. Tradition also tells how one of the companions of Muhammad came to him and reported seeing something like lamps between heaven and earth as he recited while riding horseback during the night. Muhammad is reported to have said that the lights were angels descended to hear the recitation of the Qur'an. For the pious Muslim, then, the chanted words of the Qur'an have the numinous power to cause destruction, to bring mercy, to provide protection, to give knowledge, and to evoke miraculous signs.[156]

The noted Muslim scholar Mahmoud Ayoub makes the startling claim that the Islamic notion to "live in the Qur'an" as it is faithfully and piously

---

153. In some strands of Islam, particularly in the esoteric Sufism, the veneration of Muhammad goes way beyond the established tradition, making him not only an embodiment of "Perfect Man" but also a carrier of divine light and expression of divine attributes. In the popular cult of this tradition, no less than 201 names of Muhammad play a central part (cf. 99 beautiful names of Allah). See further, Leirvik, *Images of Jesus Christ in Islam*, p. 47.

154. Hence, the heading "The 'Christ of Islam' Is the Koran," in Imbach, *Three Faces of Jesus*, p. 87. See further, Balíc, "Image of Jesus in Contemporary Islamic Theology," p. 1; see pp. 1-8.

155. Cornell, "Listening to God through the Qur'an," p. 37.

156. Coward, *Sacred Word*, p. 86, based on Ayoub, *The Qur'an*, pp. 8-9 particularly.

recited is a very close parallel to the NT idea of being "in Christ."[157] There is, however, also a significant difference here, aptly noticed by Ayoub, that whereas in the beginning of the Gospel of John the Word is not only with God but *is* God, "no one has asserted that the Qur'an is God."[158] In terms of the dialogue among Islam, Christianity, and Judaism, one topic well worth careful consideration is whether not only the Qur'an and the Word but also the Jewish Torah would function as parallels, a topic to which we turn below.[159]

The First and the Second Testaments

Salient Features of Torah as Revelation

It might strike one as odd to discuss the Jewish view of Scripture last, after the more foreign traditions from Asia and even Islam. There are two reasons for this choice. First, unlike some other topics, such as Christology and the Trinity, that are plagued with deep and irreconcilable conflicts, as discussed in those loci, Christian and Jewish traditions hold more in common when it comes to Scripture. Second, because the Christian Bible is partly Jewish, a number of common convictions, as well as differences from other traditions, have already been treated.

The origins and reception of both Hindu and Islamic religions are non-historical.[160] Whereas the origin of the Vedas is the eternal divine speech and that of the Qur'an the divine dictation via the angel to the Prophet, according to "the first book of the Hebrew Bible, Judaism has its historical origins in the act of obedience."[161] The origins of the Hebrew people lie in the response of faith of the forefather Abram (later named Abraham), who obediently set out on a journey to the Promised Land (Gen. 12:1-3). As the later history of the First Testament narrates it, this "missionary call" was meant to bring blessing not only to the family of Israel but also to the whole world. Hence, the universal scope of this particular and local revelation.

As a result, several interrelated aspects shape and make distinctive the Jewish revelation and its Scriptures. First, it is deeply embedded in the histor-

---

157. Ayoub, *The Qur'an*, p. 11; I am indebted to Coward, *Sacred Word*, p. 86.

158. Ayoub, "Word of God in Islam," p. 73.

159. "Torah and Christ are both seen, respectively, as Word of God." Kogan, *Opening the Covenant*, p. 31.

160. For a careful comparison between Jewish and Islamic views of history, see Ward, *Religion and Revelation*, pp. 175-76.

161. Corrigan et al., *Jews, Christians, Muslims*, p. 3.

ical process. While divine in its origin, the revelation is given and received in the matrix of human life at personal, tribal, national, and international levels. Second, its focus is on ethical and moral obedience. This is not to deny the importance of moral precepts in other living faiths — only consider Buddhism. It is to say that in other living faiths the connection between moral conduct and religious practice, belief in God and righteous walks of life as expression thereof, is not established in the integral way it is in Judaism[162] — and of course, by implication, in Christianity. Third, because revelation comes in the unfolding of history, it looks into history, to the future, for fulfillment. But being oriented to Yahweh's final intervention, the most significant sign and manifestation of which is the arrival of the Messiah, does not mean that therefore Jewish faith is otherworldly. It is not. Indeed, one of the most significant differences between the Jewish and Christian views of revelation is that the latter is deeply eschatologically oriented and hence its revelational category of promise is also eschatological, as discussed above. Judaism focuses on the implications of revelation for this world. Ward succinctly notes: "For Judaism, revelation comes in the form of Teaching; not a teaching about the nature of the universe, but a set of practical principles for communal life, enjoining wholeness, a loving and obedient relationship to God, and social justice."[163]

The focus on this-worldly needs and concerns, however, has nothing to do with the ethos of Christian classical liberalism, which made Jesus merely a convenient ethical teacher. Judaism's this-worldly orientation is fully and absolutely based in Yahweh, the creator, almighty ruler, and personal Father of all. Israel is to submit in love and covenant faithfulness to the One who loves and is faithful. Part of the revelation is also the readiness — albeit at times, quite reluctant — to become the object of Yahweh's fatherly rebuke when ethical standards and covenant faithfulness are lacking. Rightly it can be noted that the First Testament is "surely the most self-critical body of literature any people has ever produced . . . [and] has ultimately only one hero: God."[164]

For the Jewish faith, revelation is propositional in nature. Two important considerations help highlight the importance of the propositional nature of revelation. On the one hand, according to ancient tradition — although not supported by recent Jewish historical academic study — Moses basically

---

162. For a detailed theological discussion, see Ward, *Religion and Revelation*, pp. 113-33. He summarizes (p. 128): "The Jewish claim is that Torah enshrines a deeper insight into the demands of morality than unaided human speculation can provide, arising from the inspiration provided by God."

163. Ward, *Religion and Revelation*, p. 153.

164. Kogan, *Opening the Covenant*, p. 7.

received the Law by way of divine "dictation." On the other hand, what he received — whether, in light of contemporary understanding of the formation of canon, it happened as "dictation" or not — the detailed lists of commands, exhortations, laws, and practices conveyed by Yahweh, can only be appreciated as cognitive, propositional statements. How different is the content of the Hebrew Bible's law code from the style and content of, say, the Rig Veda of Hinduism? And yet, Vedanta and other Hindu theologians take Vedas as propositional statements as well, whatever else they are.

The center and most sacred part of the Jewish canon, Tanakh,[165] is Torah ("teaching," "instruction"). In written form it is the "Five Books of Moses." An important counterpart is the Oral Torah, which came to full flourishing with the emergence of rabbinic Judaism beginning around the start of the common era, but which was believed to have been revealed to Moses along with the written Torah as well. The two other parts of the canon, albeit not as sacred, are Nevi'im (prophetic books) and Ketuvim ("Writings").[166] A significant portion of the second part, the prophetic books, is composed of writings that could be better labeled "historical books" (Joshua, Judges, 1-2 Samuel, 1-2 Kings). In the Jewish theological outlook, however, they are rightly located since Yahweh is the Lord of history and hence, the post-Enlightenment separation of "secular" and "sacred" history is a foreign idea. Similarly, the last book of the Hebrew Bible (which, incidentally, in the Christian OT is placed after 1-2 Kings), the two-volume Chronicles, is placed at the end of the canon because it ends on a hopeful note of the release from the exodus. It is a book of promise, pointing toward future fulfillment. It is fittingly placed in the collection that is mainly about wisdom and religious poetry and parable.

If "prophetic Judaism" (the Judaism until the beginning of the common era) brought about the Hebrew Bible as we have it now, rabbinic Judaism produced the huge and varied collections of the so-called Oral Torah; the nomenclature "oral," of course, has to be taken in a qualified sense here. While put into written form in Mishnahs (and commented on in Talmuds), the first transmission of it from Yahweh to Moses is believed to have been oral. While not canonical in the sense of Torah (and the rest of the Hebrew Bible), it is irreplaceable in that it helps make the written Torah living and applicable to ever-new situations. Hence the importance of midrash, the meticulous examination of the written text to find its right and true meaning.

---

165. Tanakh is an acronym formed from the first letters of the three sections of Scripture: Torah, Nevi'im, and Ketuvim.

166. See the important remarks in Rosenbaum, "Judaism," pp. 12-17.

Rabbinic Judaism became the dominant form of the religion following the devastation caused by the destruction of the Second Temple in 70 C.E., which of course meant yet another loss of the land and more importantly the temple, the earthly locus and guarantee of God's presence. Not surprisingly, rabbinic Judaism was not a uniform movement; it consisted of several factions, such as the Pharisees and Sadducees, both of which held Torah as the canonical Scripture but had opposite views concerning the value of extrascriptural tradition. The Sadducees took only the received text of the written Scripture as authoritative, as it had been entrusted to the priesthood, and consequently they regarded any tradition whose source was not in the written Scripture as human invention.

The Pharisees, who became the mainstream of rabbinic Judaism after 70 C.E., did not think the canonical status of the written Scripture excluded the later developing tradition. Through painstaking study of the Law (Torah) and the rest of the canon, they uncovered meanings not apparent at a cursory reading. For the Pharisees — and indeed, for rabbinic Judaism at large — revelation is thus "progressive," unlike traditional prophetic Judaism, which believes in the reception by Moses of Yahweh's revelation; if the term "progressive revelation" is too much, then we should speak at least of "progressive interpretation of revelation" in rabbinicism.[167] This huge Oral Torah is classified under the general categories of halakah, ritual and legal practices and traditions, and haggadah, with its focus on homiletics, ethics, exegesis, and theology. The first major such work that also became foundational to the Oral Torah is the Mishnah, compiled in the second century C.E. Huge collections of Talmudic tractates — the most important of which are the Babylonian and Palestinian — emerged as commentaries on the Mishnah over several centuries. The Babylonian Talmud, completed in the sixth century C.E., is the most important of these works and an indispensable resource for everything Jewish.[168]

In medieval times revisionist movements arose, such as Karaism, which questioned and basically rejected the rabbinic notion of Jewish tradition, and kabbalism, which, unlike Karaism, did not reject either rabbinic tradition or the Oral Torah, but rather filled it with new meanings, often highly speculative and imaginative.

As important as prophetic and rabbinic Judaism is to that religion, in the contemporary world there are a number of nonorthodox movements, from the

---

167. See Coward, *Sacred Word*, p. 13.
168. For a highly accessible discussion, see Segal, "Judaism," pp. 15-33.

Reform movements of the mid–nineteenth century to various liberal schools of our era. While all these movements, in some sense or another, consider Torah the canonical Scripture, they disagree widely about how to deal with the rules *(mitzvoth)* of Torah in the contemporary world. Should they be taken "literally," as the unchanging will of God for all ages? Are they supposed to be considered principles with different applications? Or are they such that many of them cannot be taken as an expression of the will of God at all? Consider just the many dietary and other rules of Leviticus or the passages in Psalms and elsewhere that seem to ordain violence.

Scripture and the Covenants

To locate the Jewish tradition in the multifaith matrix, it is helpful to follow Ward's characterization. He identifies Judaism as seminal and intermediate. It is seminal in its functioning as the basis for two other faiths, Christianity and Islam, and it is intermediate because it is a local or tribal tradition. However — and this is significant for Christian considerations — its view of revelation is universal in that it speaks of Yahweh as the creator and God of all men and women and the whole of creation. Hinduism shares materially the same three characteristics: it provides many Asian faiths the foundational ideas of karma, rebirth, its view of reality as "appearance" and release as "salvation"; yet it is intermediate with its focus on and rootage in India; and its view of revelation is universal because it seeks to offer all men and women the right view of reality and path of release.[169]

When it comes to the relation of the two peoples of God who share the same Torah as their Scripture, we have to begin with the sad and long track record of Christian anti-Semitism. As early as the second century C.E., Marcion wanted the Christian church to reject the OT as canonical Scripture. The history of anti-Semitism runs from the Church Fathers (John Chrysostom, Jerome, Augustine) to Reformers (Luther) to twentieth-century theologians (Karl Adam) to popes, too numerous to list.[170]

At the center of the tension between the two sibling faiths lies the obvious but important fact that "historically Christianity has been theologically

---

169. Ward, *Religion and Revelation,* pp. 111-12.

170. According to Lapide (*Israelis, Jews, and Jesus,* p. 81), "In the period from the fourth to the sixteenth century no fewer than 106 popes and 92 Church councils issued anti-Jewish laws and regulations."

exclusive and humanistically universal, while Judaism has been theologically universal and humanistically exclusive." Christian theological exclusivism, however, is qualified by the equally important conviction that Christ died for all and that, therefore, all people from all nations can be beneficiaries of this salvific work.[171] As long as the Christian church wishes to stay faithful to its canonical Scriptures, which include not only the First but also the Second Testament, she is faced with this continuing challenge, so eloquently and ironically described by the contemporary Jewish scholar Michael S. Kogan: "how to be faithful to the New Testament command to witness for Christ to all peoples and to convert all nations, while, at the same time, affirming the ongoing validity of the covenant between God and Israel via Abraham and Moses. Can the church have it both ways?"[172]

The Jewish conviction of being the elected people is based on Torah, which speaks of the covenant struck between Yahweh and Israel. However, if the people of God do not adhere to the covenant, its benefits may be lost. On the other hand, from as early as the third century C.E., rabbinic Judaism has appealed to the Noachic covenant as a means for offering the "way of salvation" to non-Jews.[173] This admission is not a matter of compromising Israel's covenant status; it is rather to act in light of the universally oriented revelation. The Christian side faces the challenge of, without compromising the new covenant "struck" in Jesus Christ — because that is the message of the NT — not invalidating God's covenant with the OT people. Kogan poses the challenge to his Jewish counterparts: "Are Jews really ready and willing to affirm that God, the God of Israel and of all humanity, was involved in the life of Jesus, in the founding of the Christian faith, in its growth and spread across much of the world, and in its central place in the hearts of hundreds of millions of their fellow beings?" Kogan's conviction is that the response of yes is inevitable from the perspective of the universal nature of revelation in his faith.[174] This kind of acknowledgment of the place of the Christian church in

---

171. Kogan, *Opening the Covenant*, pp. xii-xiii.

172. Kogan, *Opening the Covenant*, p. xii.

173. According to the Noachic covenant, Gentiles, provided they keep the seven laws described in the Oral Torah (which are claimed to be based on the teaching of Genesis even though there is no direct reference to it), may be saved. The seven laws are described in the Tosefta (tractate *Avodah Zarah* 9.4).

174. Kogan, *Opening the Covenant*, p. xiii; see also p. 13; on p. 32 Kogan makes the striking statement that the existence of "many billions [who] worship Israel's God, only some 15 millions of them being Jews," means that "[t]his is either some gigantic accident or the partial fulfillment of God's commission to Abraham."

God's economy of salvation is not something totally novel in Jewish history. Just consider the greatest medieval Jewish theologian, Moses Maimonides — routinely compared to Saint Thomas Aquinas in Christian tradition — who surmised that not only Christianity but also Islam is part of the divine plan to prepare the world for the reception of the message of the biblical God.[175]

When mutual trust is being established, mutual dialogue and common Scripture may begin with issues related to the discussion of current themes such as the implications of the divine Word as incarnate and the Christian "deviation" from the teachings of the First Testament. Is the whole idea of divine embodiment totally unacceptable to Jewish Scriptures? Kogan scrutinizes texts such as Yahweh walking in the garden (Gen. 3:8) or appearing to Abraham (18:1) and concludes: "For Jewish believers, then, the thought may come to mind that, if God can take human form in a series of accounts put forward in one's own sacred texts, one would be unjustified in dismissing out of hand the possibility that the same God might act in a similar fashion in accounts put forward in another text revered as sacred by a closely related tradition."[176] What about the implications of the shared *material* conviction that whereas in Judaism the Word of God is Torah, in Christianity it is Christ/ Logos?[177] And so forth.

Common Scripture Reading as a Form of Interfaith Theologizing

This brief consideration of the views of scripture and revelation in other living faiths from the viewpoint of Christian theology has highlighted both continuities and discontinuities. Not only between religions but also within each tradition there are significant differences that must be noticed if one seeks a serious interfaith engagement. Keith Ward illustrates both of these aspects by placing side by side the Buddhist and Islamic views of scripture and revelation. While these two traditions display significant differences from each other, there is also significant diversity within each of them.

> Orthodox Muslim accounts speak of a direct verbal transmission by God; while Buddhists rely on very old traditions recalling the teaching of the

---

175. This paragraph is based on Heschel, "Jewish Views of Jesus," pp. 149-51.

176. Kogan, *Opening the Covenant*, p. 115. For a highly promising and constructive essay on Jewish views of incarnation, see E. R. Wolfson, "Judaism and Incarnation," pp. 239-54.

177. See Kogan, *Opening the Covenant*, p. 31.

enlightened one, whose own experience is the guarantor of truth. Within each tradition there is the logical possibility of a continuous range of positions between the two poles of propositional dictation and enlightened experience. While the orthodox tend to make claims for infallibility as strong as possible, other believers allow for the possibility of such an element and degree of personal experience and developing historical context that a degree of partiality and fallibility is introduced. It may be argued that this allows revelation to be considered as much more a personal interaction between human and divine, whereas infallibilist accounts treat revelation in a rather mechanical way, as the passive reception of information. Moreover, a stress on factors of personal temperament and cultural context may help one to appreciate the rich diversity of different traditions, and make possible a more tolerant and appreciative attitude to other traditions than one's own.[178]

Significant differences between Christian tradition and other faith traditions highlighted in the discussion above include these: Whereas Christian — and Jewish — views of revelation are fully embedded in and in a genuine way emerge out of the historical process, in Asiatic and Islamic traditions history plays no role. A related, significant difference has to do with the lack of ethical-moral emphasis in Asiatic faiths whereas that is a key aspect of Judeo-Christian Scripture. The Islamic tradition is somewhat unique in that a significant part of "submission" to Allah has to do with obedience to Qur'anic ethics. However, because of neglect of historical and contextual factors in the reception of revelation — as some leading revisionist Muslim critics are pointing out[179] — scripture's relevance to sociopolitical and ethical pursuit is vague. Other significant differences include "fundamentalistic" insistence on the infallibility of scripture not only in Islam but also in Vedic Hinduism. This is related to the reluctance to engage critical studies of scripture. Differing from all other traditions, the Christian doctrine of revelation is focused on and derives from the divine embodiment, the Word made flesh; hence, it is trinitarian through and through.

The understanding of revelation as historical in Christian tradition calls for more remarks. It not only distinguishes it from other traditions; it also poses a challenge and opportunity for Christian theology and the church, as explained by Lewis E. Winkler:

178. Ward, *Religion and Revelation*, p. 55.
179. Most vocally Sachedina, *Islamic Roots of Democratic Pluralism*.

if one affirms that God reveals himself through history not only in Christianity but also other religions, much more needs to be done by Christians to answer questions surrounding the recognition, discernment, and significance of these outside revelatory resources. How can we differentiate the cultural, anthropological, and even demonic when dialoging with other faith traditions? In addition, how can we look more closely at history and see more clearly how it reveals important truths about God, his creation, and ourselves as human beings?[180]

Such discernment and recognition must attend to both similarities and dissimilarities — at times, even to the deep conflicts. An important theological question asks, Why do we have these irreconcilable conflicts in the understanding of revelation among the religions? and What do we do with them? Consider only Muslim and Christian differences between their understandings of revelation. The difference from Buddhism is easier to understand because of its nontheistic — or "differently theistic" — nature, which naturally leads to a human-centered pursuit of release, and even with Hinduism, Christian tradition has less of a hard time. The difference is because these two theistic religions (even apart from whether Hinduism is mono- or polytheistic) understand the divine so very differently. Islam presents Christian faith with a profound challenge as both build not only on a clearly defined authoritative canon but also, more importantly, on a personal notion of God who is the source and giver of revelation.

Unless one is satisfied with the naive pluralistic denial of differences that hardly does justice to any tradition, even to one's own, a careful consideration of the theological implications of real conflicts is called for. It seems to me that Keith Ward's response to this dilemma is as good as any: "Apparently, God has not given an unambiguous revelation and preserved it unequivocally from error. God has permitted many alleged competing revelations to have currency in the modern world."[181] Isn't that a reason to maintain modesty and humility, without rejecting proper confidence, about the truth of revelation in Christ? Isn't that a reason to continue careful reflection on how to best understand the complicated relationship between the divine and human elements in the inspiration of Scripture and formation of the canon? Isn't that a reason to continue investigating the relationship between the propositional and symbolic in Scripture? And so forth.

180. Winkler, *Contemporary Muslim and Christian Responses to Religious Plurality,* p. 309.

181. Ward, *Religion and Revelation,* p. 174.

It seems to me the Christian doctrine of revelation, pluriform in nature, which seeks to negotiate the dynamics of historical and eternal, inerrant and fallible, infinite and finite, propositional and symbolic, "spiritual" and sociopolitical, may offer the best resources for such a continuing enterprise.

As Christian theology continues constructing an adequate theology of revelation and Scripture, gleaning from rich sources of tradition and from the wide diversity of contemporary global theology, it also is well served by inviting scholars and practitioners from other faith traditions into a common reading of scriptures — every tradition's own scriptures. This is an act of hospitality: "we" are opening our Scriptures for others to read and "they" are opening theirs. We are not only talking about how similar or different our theologies of revelation are; we are learning from and contributing to each other by reading together.

One of the theologically most promising initiatives in this respect is called "Scriptural Reasoning." It is actually a loose network of various types of international and interfaith enterprises that aims at helping scholars and clergy study sacred scriptures together.[182] It was started at the turn of the millennium among Jewish, Christian, and Islamic representatives and has so far concentrated heavily on monotheistic faiths for the simple reason that they share much in common.[183] It is likely that soon Scriptural Reasoning will be tried among other religions as well. The strength and promise of these kinds of interfaith enterprises are that they not only study *about* scriptures, they also study *scriptures* together.

Having considered in some detail key aspects of a contemporary doctrine of revelation — in light of Christian tradition, contemporary global and contextual diversity, as well as in relation to four living faiths — we move in part 2 to the heart to which revelation points in each tradition (with the exception of Theravada Buddhism), namely, the concept of God or the Divine. While revelation in each living tradition has much to say about life "here and now," they all have as their ultimate goal "release" or "salvation," which, as much as it may have implications for this life, as is the case particularly in Judeo-Christian traditions, points to transcendence, something "final."

182. For basics, see Ford and Pecknold, eds., *Promise of Scriptural Reasoning.* A highly useful, continuously updated database is the Web site of *Journal of Scriptural Reasoning* at http://etext.lib.virginia.edu/journals/ssr/. Other noteworthy current works include Cheetham et al., eds., *Interreligious Hermeneutics in Pluralistic Europe*; Kepnes and Koshul, eds., *Scripture, Reason, and the Contemporary Islam-West Encounter.*

183. For basic guidelines, see Kepnes, "Handbook for Scriptural Reasoning"; Ford, "Interfaith Wisdom."

II. TRIUNE GOD

The first chapter of part 2 (chap. 9) seeks to establish the conditions for speaking of God in a contemporary culture plagued with secularism and speaking of theology that is challenged by forms of atheism, old and new, as well as objections to the possibility or meaningfulness of speaking of God. Another "foundational" task of clarifying the possibility and form of Christian theology of God in contemporary culture has to do with whether the Christian doctrine of God, based on biblical revelation, could — and even more importantly, *should* — engage and draw from philosophical resources, particularly metaphysics and natural theology's "proofs" of God. This project argues that against all its rebuttals, metaphysics is not only necessary for any meaningful talk about God but that it should also be mindful of the changed epistemological and philosophical context of late modernity. Part of that discussion, the chapter continues the argument presented in chapter 7 for natural theology as trinitarian Christian theology.

In chapter 10 the material presentation of a contemporary doctrine of God for a pluralistic world is attempted under the novel nomenclature "Classical Panentheism." Critiquing and reinterpreting both classical theism and contemporary forms of panentheism, the project seeks to offer a new vision of Christian theology of God. That vision is further clarified, expanded, and amplified in chapter 11, which will focus on the doctrine of the Trinity. Of course, trinitarian theology has been present in the discussion from the beginning of the volume. Recall that in chapter 2 a trinitarian vision of revelation was offered and that chapter 7 defended natural theology as *trinitarian* Christian theology. An important part of the trinitarian presentation of the doctrine of

God is discussion of God's works in the world, classically named the "divine attributes," the theme of chapter 12.

The last three chapters discuss carefully the implications and meaning of the trinitarian theology of God in relation to cultural, sociopolitical, and religious plurality. With the title "Divine Hospitality," chapter 13 seeks to argue for the (inclusively understood) liberationist impulse in the biblical trinitarian doctrine of God. It speaks for and leads those who put their trust in God to seek liberation, inclusivism, equality, justice, and human flourishing. Doing so, it resists violence, another important topic of discussion for the third millennium in that context. Before relating the Christian confession of the trinitarian God to other living faiths, a critical and sympathetic discussion of *Christian* pluralistic attempts to negotiate the plurality of religions is in order in chapter 14. Similarly to the end of part 1, in part 2 the longest chapter (15) is devoted to continuing the investigation of comparative theology, in this context focusing on the relation of the Christian view of God to conceptions of the Divine/ Ultimate Reality in three living faiths, Islam, Buddhism, and Hinduism. This volume ends with a brief epilogue, relating again the doctrine of the Trinity, as the discernment of the unfolding of the economy of salvation of the one God, Father, Son, and Spirit, to the wider systematic/constructive theological vision in a religiously pluralistic world.

9. On the Conditions and Contours of God-Talk

The Doctrine of God in a New Environment

Several important recent "turns" have both challenged and offered new resources for the constructive theology of God. In the aftermath of modernity, a secular age has pervaded most of the cultures of the Global North. New atheism has emerged to challenge the belief in God. Related to the marginalization of religion has been the heralding of the "end of metaphysics." Constructive theology also faces the question of the role of natural theology, if any, in the doctrine of God.

At the same time, constructive theology looks toward new kinds of opportunities. One has to do with important changes in worldview and understanding of reality. Due to the move away from a substance ontology and (semi)mechanistic Newtonian worldview with rigid notions of causality and determinism toward a relational ontology and a dynamic and emerging worldview with quantum theory's probabilistic and in some sense "chaotic" views of causality, we may now present the doctrine of God in a way more appropriate to both the dynamic narrative of the Bible and the complex contemporary world of ours. An important related factor here is the interface between science and theology, which Polkinghorne names a new form of "contextual" theology.[1] It means that the construction of the doctrine of God cannot neglect anything in the cosmos.

Both a challenge and an opportunity, diversity and plurality are with us

---

1. See Polkinghorne, *Theology in the Context of Science*, chap. 1.

in a new and pervasive way, not only because of the advent of postmodernisms with a focus on differences but also because of massive philosophical, cultural, sociopolitical, and religious reasons. With the shrinking of the global village, religious plurality as well as forms of religious pluralism, *ideologies,* are putting talk about God in a new perspective. Within the Christian church and theology, another kind of diversity is emerging, namely, the coming of age of the "global church." Furthermore, questions of diversity, equality, inclusion, liberation, and justice are being considered an integral part of the theological task. Hence, new ways of conceiving God are to be attempted.

God in a Secular Age

According to Pannenberg, "[i]n earlier cultures the words 'God' and 'gods' had a more or less clearly defined place in the cultural world and human vocabulary." Not so anymore: "In modern secular cultures the word 'God' has increasingly lost this function, at any rate in the public mind."[2] Hence God has become a "problem" rather than a solution.[3] This means the "reality denoted by the term [God] has thus become uncertain. In the context of a public consciousness that is emancipated from religion, statements about God that presuppose his reality no longer count as factual statements. . . . [T]he truth claims of statements about God are not even worth discussing publicly."[4] Not only Christian but also some Muslim theologians have observed how "[t]he secular culture tends toward a negative characterization of anything religious as soon as it crosses the boundary from the private to the public sphere."[5] Some Buddhist thinkers have made the same point.[6]

The questioning of God is not merely a recent phenomenon. Writing in 1799, the thirty-one-year-old Friedrich Schleiermacher lamented how "unexpected" it must be to his modern audience to hear talk about religion, "so completely neglected by them." Apart from the sad observation that "only a few

---

2. Pannenberg, *ST* 1:63. The title for this section is taken from C. Taylor, *A Secular Age.*
3. P. Clayton, *Problem of God,* p. 3.
4. Pannenberg, *ST* 1:63-64.
5. Sachedina, *Islamic Roots of Democratic Pluralism,* p. 3; see also his *Role of Islam in the Public Square.*
6. For sharp Buddhist critique and rejection of "scientism," which confuses the *methodology* of natural sciences as empirical induction with the *ideology* of secularism and atheism, see Abe, "Kenotic God and Dynamic Sunyata," pp. 26-29; Abe then speaks of another current form of atheism, stemming from Nietzschean nihilism (pp. 29-31).

have understood something of religion while millions have variously played with its trappings," the father of liberal Protestantism rightly observed that for "cultivated persons" of his time, "there are no other household gods than the maxims of the sages and the songs of the poets," so much so that "no room is left over for the eternal and holy being…beyond the world."[7]

Indeed, since the Enlightenment, it has been assumed and expected that religion will disappear altogether as science and "civilization" march onward.[8] This is known as the "secularization thesis." It was first presented by thinkers such as sociologists Auguste Comte and Émile Durkheim, economist-philosophers Karl Marx and Friedrich Engels, psychoanalyst Sigmund Freud, ethicist Herbert Spencer, and sociologist of religion Ernst Troeltsch. Particularly beginning from the "secular decade" of the 1960s, a number of leading contemporary sociologists of religion[9] and even some theologians[10] have enthusiastically embraced the thesis.[11]

Is the secularization thesis true? The answer is *no* — and *yes!* When it comes to the loss of power of religions over secular institutions such as, say, universities[12] — with the exception of some Islamic contexts — the thesis has appeared to be quite accurate. Furthermore, when it comes to religion in the Global North, the thesis is not far off the target.[13] But where the secularization thesis has embarrassingly failed is the prophecy of the disappearance of religions globally considered.[14] Says Peter L. Berger, once a spokesman for the death of religions in modern society: "[T]he assumption that we live in a secularized world is false. The world today, with some exceptions . . . , is as furiously religious as it ever was, and in some places more so than ever."[15]

Furthermore, against all odds, fundamentalist[16] and other traditional

7. Schleiermacher, *On Religion*, p. 3.

8. Schultz, "Secularization," p. 171.

9. Berger, *The Sacred Canopy*; Luckmann, *Invisible Religion*; Martin, *A General Theory of Secularization*.

10. Cox, *Secular City*.

11. For a thoughtful and well-documented discussion, see Runia, "The Challenge of the Modern World to the Church."

12. See Marsden, *The Soul of the University*.

13. See further, S. Carter, *Culture of Disbelief*; Chadwick, *The Secularization of the European Mind*; Jacoby, *Freethinkers*.

14. See Schultz, "Secularization," p. 174.

15. Berger, "Desecularization of the World," p. 2.

16. See the massive five-volume series edited by Marty and Appleby, *The Fundamentalism Project*.

forms of religion, within both Christian and other faith traditions, seem to be growing.[17] In Christianity this is an undisputed fact shown by "statisticians,"[18] as Christianity is moving from the Global North to the Global South, as a result of which particularly evangelical and Pentecostal/charismatic movements are rapidly growing. Similar observations are now coming from Jewish, Muslim, Hindu, and Buddhist communities around the globe. Whereas the "assimilationist" or "liberal" expressions of religions are losing momentum, the traditional ones are strengthening. One rule-conforming exception is Europe, particularly western Europe. Another exception has to do with the tiny number of scholars of religions trained in the best universities of the Global North who echo the secularist mind-set of their Western teachers.[19]

The Canadian philosopher Charles Taylor offers a more nuanced analysis of secularism as he traces carefully the history of the European-American cultural shift away from a culture in which it was virtually impossible not to believe in God to an era in which belief in God is but one option — and to many a marginal one.[20] Public spaces "have been allegedly emptied of God, or of any reference to ultimate reality." On the other hand, alleged tolerance is the new norm.[21] Taylor distinguishes three different notions of secularism: the retreat of religion from the public space (type 1), the decline in belief and practice (type 2), and the change in the conditions of belief (type 3).[22] Secularism even in the Global North does not necessarily mean leaving behind all notions of God or transcendence, although that also takes place in many persons' lives. What makes the difference with regard to the context for God-talk in the Global North is that belief in God is made a matter of personal choice. This change of conditions of belief (type 3), while of course related to and influenced by the changed role of religion in the public sphere (type 1) and the diminishing degree to which people practice religion (type 2), is what the original advocates of the secularization theory missed and what really makes the difference. In the secular society everyone must be a "heretic"![23] Whereas in premodern societies heretical views were discouraged at the expense of communal and cultural uniformity, in contemporary Western culture there is no "plausibility structure," acceptance of which is taken for granted without

17. Berger, "Desecularization of the World," p. 6.
18. For an important earlier work, see Jenkins, *The Next Christendom*.
19. See further, Berger, "Desecularization of the World," pp. 9-11.
20. For an important discussion see C. Smith, ed., *The Secular Revolution*.
21. C. Taylor, *A Secular Age*, pp. 1-3, quotation on p. 2.
22. See also chap. 15 in *A Secular Age*.
23. Berger, *The Heretical Imperative*.

argument, and dissent from which is considered heresy. Understandably, the number of those in premodern society who wanted to be labeled heretics was small, whereas in the contemporary culture, formulating one's own views has become an imperative. Consequently, all are heretics!

Considered in a longer historical perspective, there are clearly distinguishable shifts in the public relation to God/gods. In ancient cultures, including the biblical ones, the "problem" of God had to do with the simple question "Which God?" because in polytheistic environments deities were local. There was the rivalry of the gods, well known from the history of the OT as well. Not seldom did it lead to a "power encounter"[24] in which the strongest God appeared to be the true God. Beginning in modernity, the question shifted to "Does God exist?," as atheistic challenges were leveled against belief in God.[25] In contemporary postmodern times, the question is, Does God matter? At the same time, as the Italian philosopher Gianni Vattimo's *After Christianity* notes, religion has not necessarily been left behind in Europe (and the USA), as what he calls "secular transcendence" is gaining momentum.[26]

While (classical) liberals sought to encounter the secular age with the strategy of accommodation or "correlation," other kinds of responses have also been put in place. On the one hand, on the American scene we have the "Constantinian" project of the Religious Right, which seeks to reestablish a "Christian nation" in alignment with political powers.[27] On the other hand, there is the Radical Orthodoxy movement, which rejects any project of correlation and apologetic. It not only opposes but also denies secularism. For this British theological program, there is no "neutral" secularism. Instead, academic, political, and other spaces are but "temples of other gods"[28] of modernity.[29] Rather than correlation, a robustly and distinctively Christian theological vision is put in place. Understandably, the current project cannot follow that — in itself admirable — tactic as it cuts off bridges with nontheological disciplines and can hardly avoid the impression of dogmatism. Here Radical Orthodoxy shares the weakness of the Yale School and a Hauerwasian effort to make the

---

24. While the secular-minded religious — and even theological — academia of the Global North has basically missed the topic of "power encounter," Christians, including Christian missionaries, in the Global South know it as a daily reality.

25. See further, Grenz, *Theology for the Community of God*, pp. 30-33 particularly.

26. Vattimo, *After Christianity*.

27. For a discussion and critique, see Hauerwas and Willimon, *Resident Aliens*, pp. 17-24.

28. See J. K. A. Smith, *Introducing Radical Orthodoxy*, p. 42.

29. Milbank, *Theology and Social Theory*.

church the "Christian colony."[30] Rightly, Radical Orthodoxy's approach has been described as "reason within the bounds of religion."[31]

While the short-lived death-of-God movement's response in the 1960s to secularism was neither interesting nor sustainable — since it was an immanentist, human-made project even when it did not literally deny the "existence" of God[32] — the Harvard theologian Harvey Cox in a more nuanced way advocated "secularization" as "an authentic outcome of the impact of biblical faith on Western history."[33] In contrast to "secularism," which denotes an ideology or closed worldview that functions like a new religion, *secularization* takes the biblical faith's turn to the "word" seriously and seeks to avoid secularism in its normal sense.[34] The problems with Cox's suggestion are twofold. First, empirically, secularization did not happen. Second, even if it had happened, theologically it is not viable to make such a radical turn to accommodation. On the contrary, theistic religions, including Christianity, should expose a naive Enlightenment-based omission of God, while at the same time establishing a robust contact with culture at large.[35]

In light of the dramatically changing context for God-talk as well as doubts about the possibility of even speaking of God, for the purposes of constructive contemporary theology of God, next in order is a careful look at the objections and alternative proposals.

Objections against God-Talk

Whether God-Talk Is Meaningless

In 1929, the (then) analytic philosopher Ludwig Wittgenstein argued that both the ethical and religious use of language was linguistic abuse since it lacked a

---

30. The family resemblance with Yale theologians and Hauerwas is explicitly acknowledged by Pickstock, "Reply to David Ford and Guy Collins," p. 406.

31. Hedley, "Should Divinity Overcome Metaphysics?" p. 274.

32. The leading idea of Altizer (*Gospel of Christian Atheism*, p. 22) is the absolute immanence of God in humanity, which results in "dissolving even the memory or the shadow of transcendence" of God.

33. Cox, *Secular City*, p. 18.

34. Cox, *Secular City*, pp. 16-32 especially. A materially similar kind of analysis of the forces of secularization as something akin to religion, in this case Judaism, is offered by Erich Fromm in his *Art of Loving* (1956).

35. See Cox, *Secular City*, p. 130.

proper reference. Hence, these sentences are "nonsense."[36] While later Wittgenstein changed his position and made the use of language a matter of "language games" — that is, words and sentence make sense in the framework for which they are designed — logical positivists continued the early Wittgenstein's intuitions. Thus Rudolf Carnap argued that the only way one could be certain of a statement's truth or falsity was by verifying the statement through perceptions, observations, or experience; metaphysical assertions, however, do not lend themselves to such verification.[37] A. J. Ayer similarly concluded that statements about God are meaningless.[38] The idea of the cognitive meaninglessness of theological statements died hard; it received support from some leading theologians as well.[39] Langdon Gilkey issued the warning against the meaningfulness of theological statements as truth claims and concluded that it was very difficult to continue speaking intelligently of God in the contemporary situation.[40]

Analytic philosophy's insistence on the empirical verification of religious and metaphysical statements is problematic on more than one count. The statement itself — that a sentence to be meaningful must have empirical verification — is nonsensical according to analytic philosophy's criterion of truth; this very statement cannot be subject to empirical verification! Furthermore, on this side of the advent of postmodernity, one is much less confident about the unambiguity of what qualifies as "empirical evidence." As Richard Swinburne rightly reminds us, we are able to understand a lot of sentences not based on empirical observation but rather because they otherwise make sense.[41]

The later Wittgenstein's insistence on "language games" as the frame of reference for determining the meaningfulness of religious sentences took a turn in the right direction.[42] The contemporary philosopher D. Z. Phillips has carefully argued that religious and theological language is not only a unique language game but also a tradition and *way of life*, into which one is born and which is learned over the years.[43] The truth value of religious statements can

---

36. Wittgenstein, "Lecture on Ethics," pp. 139-42. In this section, I am indebted to Amnell, *Uskonto ilman uskontoa*, pp. 16-20.

37. Carnap, "The Rejection of Metaphysics," pp. 208, 210.

38. Ayer, *Language, Truth, and Logic*, p. 144.

39. Kauffmann, *God the Problem*, p. 7.

40. Gilkey, *Naming the Whirlwind*, p. 16.

41. Swinburne, "God-Talk Is Not Evidently Nonsense," p. 151.

42. Wittgenstein, *Philosophical Investigations*, §90: "Our investigation is therefore a grammatical one."

43. Phillips, *Faith and Philosophical Enquiry*, pp. 78, 59, 230.

be determined not from outside but rather from inside tradition.[44] Hence, terms such as "love" and "belief" do not have the same meaning in theology as they have elsewhere. God is not an object among other objects whose existence or truthfulness can be placed under human scrutiny.[45] That proposal, however, also is liable to serious problems. First, the claim that theological sentences such as that "God exists" have only intertextual validity says too little; it shares the serious weakness of the Yale School's linguistic-regulative theory of truth. The second major problem has to do with the claim that key theologico-metaphysical statements such as "love" are totally equivocal, different from usual language use.[46] If true, it would block dialogue with non-theological fields. However, acknowledging the fallacy of equivocality is no reason to affirm the opposite view, namely, univocality, which believes that terms applied to God would have an identical meaning with terms related to created reality.[47] Christian tradition rather speaks of an *analogical* relation between human and divine language.[48]

Whether God-Talk Is Impossible

Granting that talk about God is considered meaningful does not yet guarantee its possibility for finite human beings. While a whole dose of humility is required of anyone who wishes to say something of God, speak we must since "so much has been said about God and the gods in human history . . . , that we can see what a loss and impoverishment it would mean were the term 'God' to vanish from our daily speech."[49] Indeed, "[a]ny intelligent attempt to talk about God — talk that is critically aware of its conditions and limitations — must begin and end with confession of the inconceivable majesty of God which transcends all our concepts."[50] Ironically, this is not the case only because God

44. Phillips, *Faith and Philosophical Enquiry,* pp. 4-5, 11-12.

45. Phillips, *Faith and Philosophical Enquiry,* pp. 17-18, 60, 87.

46. A classic example is offered by the Spanish Jewish scholar of the twelfth century, Moses Maimonides, *Guide to the Perplexed.*

47. An exception to this rule is the attempt of William Alston to defend partial univocity: "Functionalism and Theological Language," pp. 65-67.

48. Aquinas, *ST* 1a.13 is the key passage. While Aquinas is routinely mentioned as the key developer of analogical meaning, in all his extensive writings he doesn't really speak widely about the issue! See McInerny, *Aquinas and Analogy.*

49. Pannenberg, *ST* 1:338.

50. Pannenberg, *ST* 1:337.

is transcendent and infinite but also because "the lofty mystery we call God is always close to the speaker and to all creatures, and prior to all our concepts it encloses and sustains all being, so that it is always the supreme condition of all reflection upon it and of all the resultant conceptualization."[51]

While there have been some exceptions,[52] Christian theology has always acknowledged the finite, partial, and fallible nature of human knowledge of God. Augustine never wearied of reminding us of the limits of our knowledge of the nature of God. "If you understand, it is not God."[53] "We can more easily say what he is not than what he is."[54]

The limitations of human knowledge of God became a theological theme in the apophatic, mystical orientation of the Eastern tradition. With all their intellectual efforts, the Cappadocians acknowledged that theology could never venture far from personal experience because no words could adequately talk about God. Gregory of Nyssa maintained that the true knowledge of God was "the seeing that consists in not seeing, because that which is sought transcends all knowledge, being separated on all sides by incomprehensibility."[55] This has been appropriately called the tradition of "learned ignorance."[56] Apophaticism is not of course a refusal to talk about God. Even to say what God is not, assumes some kind of knowledge of God. The apophatic approach rather fully acknowledges the grave limitations of human speech of God. It is a humble approach and thus corresponds to the huge gap between the divine and the human.[57]

In contemporary theology, metaphors acknowledge the partial nature of human knowing, somewhat similarly to tradition's use of analogy. Metaphor "is seeing one thing *as* something else,"[58] and as such, has a limiting character to it, since metaphor contains the dual message of "it is *and it is not.*"[59] Metaphors are not only useful in that they have a surplus of meaning — they evoke imagination — but they are also necessary.[60] There is no

---

51. Pannenberg, *ST* 1:337.

52. Duns Scotus is a rule-confirming exception, and the most ardent contemporary critic of his univocal predication of being is Milbank, *The Word Made Strange*, pp. 36-53.

53. Augustine, *Sermones* 117.3.5.

54. Augustine, *Enarrationes in Psalmos* 85.12.

55. Gregory of Nyssa, *The Life of Moses* 2.163.

56. Clendenin, *Eastern Orthodox Christianity*, pp. 55-56, at 56.

57. See Placher, *History of Christian Theology*, pp. 94-96.

58. McFague, *Metaphorical Theology*, p. 15.

59. McFague, *Metaphorical Theology*, p. 13.

60. Argued forcefully and in a nuanced way in J. K. A. Smith, *Fall of Interpretation*, pp. 25-27.

choosing between "literal" and "metaphorical" meaning, but rather, between what kind of metaphor is being used. "[M]etaphor *is* ordinary language."[61] To be more precise, there is a choosing of the relation of the metaphor to what it describes. N. T. Wright puts it succinctly: "Recognition of god-language as fundamentally metaphorical does not mean that it does not have a referent, and that some at least of the metaphors may not actually possess a particular appropriateness to this referent."[62] John Hick's attempt to get rid of all historical and "factual" constraints with the help of metaphors is a route not followed in this discussion. Metaphors, while they carry meaning from one semantic field to another (as the etymology, *meta-pherein*, literally translated implies), are not meant therefore to say "less," but — as often happens — "more."

In the final analysis talk about God is an act of doxology.[63] Therein the "speakers rise above the limits of their own finitude to the thought of the infinite God."[64] LaCugna rightly reminds us of the ancient conviction that personhood is both ineffable and incomprehensible.[65] Hence, human talk about God can never exhaust God, nor can the "mystery of God who is alive and whose ongoing relationship with creation and persons . . . be frozen or fixed in time." God remains "the incomprehensible Origin of everything that is."[66] That said, in this "process the conceptual contours do not have to lose their sharpness. Doxology can also have the form of systematic reflection."[67] In other words, reference to doxology is not an attempt to undermine the importance of rational talk but is rather an attempt to seek a balance between apophatic (negative) and kataphatic (positive) approaches.[68]

Whether God-Talk Should Be Replaced by Talk about Religion

Rather than speaking of God, most contemporary scholars of religion and a number of theologians speak of *religion*. All agree that religion is integrally

---

61. McFague, *Metaphorical Theology*, p. 16.

62. N. T. Wright, *New Testament and the People of God*, 1:129.

63. So, e.g., Moltmann, *Trinity and the Kingdom*, pp. 152, 161; Pannenberg, *ST* 1:55-56; see also his earlier essay, "Analogy and Doxology."

64. Pannenberg, *ST* 1:55.

65. LaCugna, *God for Us*, pp. 325, 323.

66. LaCugna, *God for Us*, p. 321.

67. Pannenberg, *ST* 1:55.

68. LaCugna, *God for Us*, p. 333.

linked with belief in God/gods.[69] But opinions vary drastically as to whether monotheism or something else was the beginning. Briefly put: while the animistic (and preanimistic) theories of the origins of religion regard monotheism as the evolved, later development, the original monotheism theory suggests the opposite: that belief in the "high God," one god, was the beginning of religion and only later did polytheism evolve.[70] While a majority of the scholars of religion today reject the idea of original monotheism, they are not thereby denying the importance of belief in the "supreme being," "high god," one deity, even among preliterate tribes, let alone in more "developed" cultures. An innovative version of the original monotheism theory is Ruether's claim that "the most ancient human image of the divine was female." Regardless of references to some archaeological evidence, religious scholarship has dismissed this speculative theory. It simply lacks historical evidence.[71]

With the rise of the idea of "natural religion" at the time of the Enlightenment, as illustrated in John Locke's *Reasonableness of Christianity* (1695) and John Toland's *Christianity Not Mysterious* (1696), it was widely assumed that what lay in the beginning was "natural religion," out of which subsequently positive religions developed and diversified. David Hume, in his *Natural History of Religion* (1757), turned this belief upside down and argued that, on the contrary, in the beginning was polytheism, out of which painfully and slowly emerged the belief in a purified theistic idea of God. Indeed, "[h]uman passions, not reason, supposedly generated religion," he averred.[72] In that light, later Schleiermacher's devastating critique of "natural religion" in his fifth speech of *On Religion* is understandable.[73] On this basis, Schleiermacher was also able to consider all positive religions of the time as valuable expressions of religiosity and, hence, to affirm religious plurality.[74]

---

69. Probably the most sensational theory of origin — not surprisingly rejected by most contemporary scholars — is John Allegro's reference to the use of drugs, linked with a fertility cult. See Allegro, *The Sacred Mushroom and the Cross*.

70. Original monotheism was the main thesis of the massive twelve-volume work of the early-twentieth-century Christian scholar of religion Wilhelm Schmidt (*Der Ursprung der Gottesidee* [*The Origin of the Idea of God*], 1912-55).

71. Ruether, *Sexism and God-Talk*, p. 47.

72. Pannenberg, *ST* 1:97.

73. Schleiermacher, *On Religion*, fifth speech, pp. 95-124, particularly pp. 98-100, 109-111, 122.

74. See further, Pannenberg, *ST* 1:97-98.

In the pre-Christian usage of Cicero, *relegere* (literally "to read again," then "to choose"), in contrast to *negligere* ("to neglect"), implied that we human beings should be careful to tend to gods and the obligation placed on us by them. Importantly, "religion" was distinguished from "superstition."[75] Early Christian theology took over this usage, the understanding of religion as duty to worship and obey God.[76] What was essential for early theology, in contrast to the pre-Christian usage, was the tight linking of religion to the one God of the Bible instead of the gods of religions.[77] At the same time, alongside the worship of God, the *knowledge* and doctrine of God became integrally intertwined.[78] What radically changed as the result of the Enlightenment was that religion was divorced (in the Global North) from the concept of God and, as a result, belief in God became the function of religion rather than, as prior to modernity, religion emerging as a result of faith in God. This is a momentous shift and calls for a careful theological analysis.

Hence, in contemporary religious studies, religion is defined apart from the concept of God. Typical is this definition: "Religion is the organization of life around the depth dimensions of experience — varied in form, completeness, and clarity in accordance with the environing culture."[79] Not only in religious studies but also in systematic theology, there have been definite moves away from the integral link between God and religion. Of course, this was suggested by the atheistic critique.[80] For Schleiermacher, religion was a thoroughly anthropological phenomenon.[81] Tillich's definition of religion as "a matter of ultimate concern for us" materially echoes the anthropological orientation.[82] An important contribution to the question of the "essence" of religion is Rudolf Otto's *Idea of the Holy*, in which the category of the "numinous" replaces Schleiermacher's thin account of the feeling of dependence. Other attempts to remove the concept of God from the center of religion have

---

75. Cicero, *On the Nature of God* 2.28 (p. 282).

76. See especially Lactantius, *The Divine Institutes,* which is a major study on what differentiates true religion from "false religion" and "superstition."

77. Hence, Augustine (*City of God* 19.17) makes the categorical distinction between "true" and "false" religion based on whether it referred only to the one God of the Bible or to many deities.

78. Augustine, *On True Religion* 5.

79. King, "Religion," p. 286. I am indebted to Schwarz, *The God Who Is*, p. 67.

80. "GOD as God — the infinite, universal, non-anthropomorphic being of the understanding, has no more significance for religion than a fundamental general principle has for a special science." Feuerbach, *Essence of Christianity*, p. 43.

81. Just consider *On Religion*, pp. 36, 101.

82. Tillich, *ST* 1:12.

been presented.[83] Religious "experience" seems to be to many such a natural resort, as God can only be had through spiritual experience.[84] The problem with "experience," however, is that the religious experience does not seek to interpret the concept of God, but rather, the opposite is the case: the concept of God interprets experience.[85]

The attempt to find a substitute for God as the center must be deemed theologically bankrupt, as it would make theology basically an ethnography or sociology of religions. More importantly, it would violate the self-understanding of religions themselves. Religion without God would make the study of religions merely an observation of interesting beliefs, rites, and rituals behind which there really is "nothing."[86] It would totally circumvent the question of the truth of religious statements and make them merely personal opinions. At the same time, theology in any classical sense would turn into the archaic study of history of theological ideas without any attempt to construct any meaningful *theological* vision. Furthermore, detaching the concept of God from that of religion for the sake of supporting interfaith engagement is a counterproductive exercise. It hampers genuine dialogue, since one of the dialogue partners, in this case Christian faith, would not be authentically presenting its own views.

So far we have talked about the (im)possibility of talking about God in any meaningful and constructive way. Some critics of theisms in general and Christian theism in particular, however, go deeper in their rejection of God-talk and deny the whole existence of what is named "God" or "gods," or at least shift its meaning to the point that one wonders if classical talk about God at large is left behind. Various types of atheistic challenges therefore have to be scrutinized before we can suggest a proposal for the possibility and meaningfulness of constructive Christian theology of God.

---

83. W. C. Smith, *Meaning and End of Religion,* recommended the category of "faith" instead of religion as it stresses the importance of personal relation to deity.

84. For such an attempt, see Dalferth, *Religiöse Rede von Gott. Beiträge zur evangelischen Theologie* (Munich: Kaiser, 1981), pp. 393-494. A broader view of religious experience as the center of religion is posited by Lewis, *Our Experience of God.* Another classic work is Ramsey, *Religious Language.*

85. See further, Pannenberg, *ST* 1:65-67 and chap. 3.

86. Most ironically, the celebrated scholar of religions G. van der Leeuw (*Religion in Essence and Manifestation,* 1:23) laments that the removal of God brings the study of religion into conflict with religions themselves because in them God is the main agent; however, this Dutch scholar says, this state of affairs is unavoidable in the academic study of religions!

The Atheistic Rebuttals of Faith in God

On the "Theology of Atheists"

While atheism is a phenomenon predating the Enlightenment, the form and role of atheism in ancient societies were vastly different from those of the post-Enlightenment world. Biblical writers simply dismiss as "fools" those who deny God (Ps. 14:1), or mock those who trust in gods made by human hands (Isa. 37:19; 40:18-26). Those few dissenting thinkers in antiquity such as Anaxagoras or Socrates, often identified as atheists, were not denying the existence of god(s) after modern atheism, but rather wished to shift the focus from the cult of gods to independent thinking or to encourage independent persons to select gods other than those sanctioned by the state.[87] Indeed, early Christians were charged with "atheism," having left behind the Jewish faith and not worshiping the gods of the Roman Empire.[88]

Not all "atheists" are God-deniers. In the contemporary world Derrida has had a most ambivalent relation to any notion of religion. The reasons are many; in the case of the Christian tradition, its wide use of Greek concepts such as substance, reason, *logos* matter to him. At the same time, particularly toward the end of his life, he saw the inevitability of religion. Even when religion is resisted, it is not going away. Speaking of the massive project of secularization in the West (but not in Islamic lands, which he knew from his childhood), he concludes that "secularization is always ambiguous in that it frees itself from the religious, all the while being marked in its very concept by it, by the theological indeed, the ontotheological."[89] Hence, his ambiguous position: "Nevertheless, although I confirm that it is right to say that I am an atheist, I can't say, myself, 'I am an atheist.' It's not a *position*."[90] Not surprisingly, he concludes in the same context that for him the believer and atheist are not necessarily different things.[91]

Brilliantly Moltmann suggests that — in light of Christian theology — we should speak of "the theology of atheists." Rather than limiting "theology to believing Christians," he is prompted to ask, "is not every unbeliever who has a reason for his atheism and his decision not to believe a theologian

---

87. See Plato, *Works* 10.910a, b, for condemnation of those who choose their own gods and set up shrines for worship that is against the law of the land.

88. See Frend, *The Rise of Christianity*, p. 148.

89. Derrida, *Rogues*, p. 28.

90. Caputo, Hart, and Sherwood, "Epoché and Faith," p. 47.

91. Caputo, Hart, and Sherwood, "Epoché and Faith," pp. 37-38.

too?"[92] Indeed, in attacking belief in God, atheists teach the rest of us valuable lessons about God and belief. Particularly protest atheism, "which wrestles with God as Job did, and for the sake of the suffering of created beings which cries out to high heaven denies that there is a just God who rules the world in love . . . is profoundly theological" as it tackles the question of theodicy.[93] Then there are those like the great Russian writer Dostoyevsky, who was really both a believer and an unbeliever at the same time, theist and atheist. No one can be left untouched by Dostoyevsky's passion and insight into the question and problem of God.

For the purposes of this systematic discussion, various forms of atheism can be distinguished in the following way: "modern atheisms," "atheism of materialist naturalism," and "postmodern 'theological' atheism."

Modern Atheisms

Not all modern atheists were materialists or antagonistic to "spiritual" or idealistic views. Indeed, it is ironic that, on philosophical grounds, severe criticism of the concept of the personal God came from the idealist J. G. Fichte, a pupil of Hegel. Fichte simply could not reconcile the ideas of "personal" and "infinite" with the notion of God as a being. If a being, then God must be "substance," but then infinity is in danger as entities in space-time can hardly be infinite. If God were a "person," then God would be an "I" in contrast to other "I's." Again, infinity would be compromised.[94] Fichte's critique holds as long as one thinks in terms of substance ontology, but falters when turning to relational ontology.

A very different atheistic agenda comes from "the last real atheist,"[95] Nietzsche, the son of a Lutheran pastor who was influenced by cultural figures such as Arthur Schopenhauer who tackled the problem of apparent meaninglessness and strife in the world. From Darwin he learned that the human mind is hardly anything beyond nature, and hence ethics, arts, and similar human enterprises are "natural" rather than religious in origin.[96] Known for an am-

92. Moltmann, *Experiences in Theology*, p. 15.

93. Moltmann, *Experiences in Theology*, p. 16.

94. Fichte, "Über den Grund unseres Glaubens an eine göttliche Weltregierung," 5:187-88.

95. Markham, *Against Atheism*, title of chap. 2.

96. This is most vocally argued in his originally three-volume work, consisting of aphorisms and maxims: *Human, All Too Human* (1878).

biguous style,[97] "his opaque prose is itself part of the message: knowledge is difficult; truth is fiction; and morality now must be invented."[98] Unlike typical atheists, Nietzsche is not content with merely denying the existence of God. His project is to "kill" God as he dramatically describes the act of the "madman" in his *Gay Science (The Joyful Wisdom)*. "God is dead! God remains dead! And we have killed him!" cries the Madman, and he wonders, "Shall we not ourselves have to become Gods . . . ?"[99] Nietzsche's atheism is robust and offers an alternative, in the form of a Superman,[100] a new human person — perhaps collective personhood — who is able to construct a new basis for humanity, morality, arts, and other human endeavors now that the transcendent, metaphysical basis of Christianity and other religions has been once and for all left behind.

The most vocal modern advocate of the charge that religion is a matter of human projection was Ludwig Feuerbach, philosopher Hegel's pupil-turned-atheist. Whereas his teacher distinguished between the human spirit and the Absolute Spirit ("divine spirit"), Feuerbach not only collapsed the two but also made all talk about "spirit," and thus religion, "a matter of human projection and imagination." Therefore, "the true sense of Theology is Anthropology."[101] "The beginning, middle and end of Religion is MAN."[102] Hence, humanity should get rid of this counterproductive and unhealthy projection. Unless "anthropology is made theology," that is, unless religious statements about God are allowed to be descriptions of humanity rather than of some illusionary, human-made God, religion will turn out to be not only absurd but also oppressive and suppressive. Religion makes men and women dependent on this projected God-concept. Feuerbach's aim was "to affirm the true nature of man."[103]

Feuerbach's ideas were picked up by Karl Marx, another student of Hegel who wished to offer a new materialist vision.[104] In that project, the

97. For his comments on his own style, see Nietzsche, *Ecce Homo* (1888), pp. 62-63. Although this book was written in only a few weeks and was his last work before a severe mental collapse, it still is representative.

98. Markham, *Against Atheism*, p. 31.

99. Nietzsche, *Gay Science* (1882/1887), #125, pp. 79-80.

100. The German term *Übermensch* means literally "overhuman," i.e., something that goes beyond and above the ordinary human person. The main work for the introduction of Superman is *Thus Spake Zarathustra* [1883-1885].

101. Feuerbach, *Essence of Christianity*, p. ix (preface to the 2nd ed.).

102. Feuerbach, *Essence of Christianity*, p. 183.

103. Feuerbach, *Lectures on the Essence of Religion*, p. 23, cited in Schwarz, *The God Who Is*, p. 6.

104. "Philosophers have only *interpreted* the world, in various ways; the point is to *change* it." Marx, *Critique of Feuerbach*, #11, p. 155.

Feuerbachian eschewal of religion as a function of inducing dependence was radicalized as Marx considered religion "the opium of the people." Hence, "The abolition of religion as the illusory happiness of the people is a demand for their true happiness."[105] To sum up: "The critique of religion ends in the doctrine that man is the supreme being for man."[106]

Whereas Feuerbach and Marx agreed on the illusory and imaginary nature of faith in God, Sigmund Freud regarded psychoanalysis as the final contribution in the project of criticism of religion.[107] Indeed, for him religion was not only a matter of mistaken dependence but also a matter of sickness of mind.[108] In his *Totem and Taboo*, with the telling subtitle *Resemblance between the Psychic Lives of Savages and Neurotics* (1912-13), Freud offered a highly speculative account of the rise of religion throughout the evolution of humanity from primitive to modern times, as a function of the Oedipus complex: having killed their father because of their jealousy for their mother, the sons felt deep guilt and projected their repentance to a totem as representation of the dead father, as well as abstained from touching any females, believing that not only the mother but all females had belonged to the father in the past. From totemism, humanity transitions to animism as notions of spirits and spiritual beings develop, then to Judaism, which focuses on Moses' central role and his killing of the scapegoat.[109] Finally comes Christianity, whose main architect Freud considers to be Paul rather than Jesus. In comparison to Judaism, Christianity was able to deal with the guilt feelings due to the murder of the primeval father by having Jesus be killed instead. While one can hardly find a religious scholar who gives much credit to this illusionary theory of the origin of religion, Freud's project of "curing" our minds from the sickness of religion is alive and well. In contemporary times the project of treating religion as a figment of the human mind[110] has been taken up by some leading natural-scientist-atheists, most prominently the Oxford University ethologist Richard Dawkins, the chemist Peter Atkins,

---

105. The context of this widely quoted statement is this: "Religion is the sigh of the oppressed creature, the heart of the heartless world and soul of the soulless conditions. It is the opium of the people." Marx, *Critique of Hegel's Philosophy of Right*, p. 131.

106. Marx, *Critique of Hegel's Philosophy of Right*, p. 137 (in the section, "A Contribution to the Critique of Hegel's Philosophy of Right").

107. Freud, *New Introductory Lectures*, p. 207.

108. See Schwarz, *The God Who Is*, p. 14.

109. The Jewish Freud paid attention to the religion of his forefathers. See his *Moses and Monotheism*.

110. I am indebted to the title of chap. 1 in Schwarz, *The God Who Is*.

also from Oxford, as well as the British-American popular science writer Christopher Hitchens.

Negatively put: all the forms of modern atheism are based on speculation rather than on serious study of either the history of religions or specific religious texts. Hence, by and large, they are academically worthless. Furthermore, their take on religion is hopelessly one-sided and lacks nuance. Against every misuse of religion can be found numerous historical examples of religious people who lived most noble and selfless lives. At the same time, when critiquing religion for many of the ills among men and women, these atheists do not bother looking at the meaning of similar kinds of ills produced by secularism. A related weakness is that the atheistic utopia of the disappearance of religion has not happened. Hence, their reading of the "signs of the times" has been utterly failing.

Positively put: ironically, we have to grant that the turn to anthropology in itself is a necessary and useful theological idea. It is only through an anthropological (and more widely, creaturely) lens that the ultimate "object" of Christian theology, the triune God, can be approached. There is no "god's point of view" for considering God that is available apart from humanity and humanity's place in creation.

Contemporary "New Atheism" and Scientific Naturalism

The roots of new atheism — "fundamentalist atheism"[111] — go back all the way to the post-Reformation emergence of the modern worldview, scientific enterprise, and Newtonian mechanistic worldview. Although a number of the leading early pioneers of modern sciences, such as Isaac Newton, were believers, their ideas could easily be transformed for antitheistic use. With regard to the "first cause" argument, which served so conveniently in the older model of physics, already William of Ockham had remarked that both the initial originator and subsequent sustainer were needed to guarantee continuous motion. But once motion was in place, it was not necessary to assume an eternally existing cause — any more than a human baby entails an eternal begetter.[112] More importantly, Newton's invention of inertia, which seemed to apply to both terrestrial and extraterrestrial spheres, could be taken as a reason to ignore God as the mover. Pierre Laplace's often-cited response to Napoleon's question of

---

111. Title of chap. 1 in Markham, *Against Atheism.*
112. See further, Pannenberg, "Anthropology and the Question of God," pp. 82-83.

where God was in the system, "I have no need of that hypothesis,"[113] with all its simplicity conveys the ethos of the new mechanistic thinking.

A number of leading contemporary natural scientists are self-pronounced atheists, such as the two Americans Frank J. Tipler, mathematical physicist and cosmologist, and Steven Weinberg, theoretical physicist. The most vocal advocate of atheism based on the "scientific worldview" at the international level has been Dawkins. He is best known for the highly popular books *The Selfish Gene* (1976), *The Blind Watchmaker* (1986) — the title mocking William Paley's famous metaphor of a divine watchmaker — and *The God Delusion* (2006). Dawkins advances forcefully atheism and removal of religion from the public square, supported by staunch naturalist materialism. Two other well-known atheists are Hitchens, best known for *God Is Not Great: How Religion Poisons Everything*, and author and speaker Sam Harris, whose most famous title is *The End of Faith: Religion, Terror ,and the Future of Reason*.

These atheists' claims can be summarized as follows.[114] First, the concept of God is incoherent. The problems listed under this category are well known in theological conversation, including the difficulty of the notion of the "personal God," its relation to the notions of omnipotence and omniscience, as well as the problem of evil. Second, faith means the opposite of reason: "religious faith is simply *unjustified* belief in matters of ultimate concern,"[115] "a state of mind that leads people to believe something — it does not matter what — in the total absence of supporting evidence."[116] Third, whereas theism is without any rational grounds, atheism can be shown to be "true." For Dawkins, the intellectual basis of atheism is simply the theory of evolution,[117] from which he proceeds to "a confident atheistic worldview, which he preaches with what often seems to be messianic zeal and unassailable certainty."[118] Hitchens dismisses any notion of faith simply as a prescientific mentality and by implication seems to believe that any intelligent, contemporary person must regard atheism as valid. Fourth, because it is true, Harris says, atheism is able to provide a healthy worldview whereas theism fails to do that.[119] Part of the contribution of atheism in the minds of these three advocates is its tolerance vis-à-vis intolerance of other faiths. Fifth, atheism helps avoid religious educa-

---

113. Hahn, "Laplace and the Mechanistic Universe," p. 256.
114. See Markham, *Against Atheism*, chap. 1.
115. S. Harris, *End of Faith*, p. 65.
116. Dawkins, *Selfish Gene*, p. 330.
117. See, e.g., *God Delusion*, p. 52.
118. McGrath, *Order of Things*, p. 23.
119. See S. Harris, *End of Faith*, p. 48.

tion that is simply child abuse.[120] Finally, all these writers highlight the integral link between violence and faith in God.[121]

In response, McGrath notes that, first, "for Dawkins, the natural sciences possess the capacity to explain the world," eliminating the need for collaborating with other academic disciplines, least of all theology and religious studies.[122] This "science explains everything" approach, however, has encountered devastating critique.[123] Not only is there no such thing as "explaining the world" — as science *qua* science only seeks to explain phenomena and stays away from metaphysical explanations such as purpose — there are also a number of important issues that clearly go beyond the borders of science, such as what was "before" and what "caused" the big bang.[124] Second, according to Dawkins, after the advent of Darwinianism no legitimate place is left for God, and derivatively, for theology — unless one speaks of "God delusion." This argument, however, grossly ignores the simple fact that contemporary Christian theology — apart from "creationists" — takes for granted Darwinist evolutionist theory.[125] Furthermore, Dawkins's seemingly naive belief in the power of the gradual evolvement of more complex things out of simple ones, still begs for some kind of explanation. Merely positing "the mount improbable"[126] hardly satisfies the minds of either scientists or theologians. If God is removed as the explanation for the incredibly fine-tuned complexity that brought about and sustains life, some other explanation is still called for.

Third, for Dawkins, as mentioned above, faith is an attitude without any rational basis.[127] The problem with this statement is that very few, if any, Christian theologians — of the past or of recent times — would ever own this kind of definition of faith.[128] For Christian tradition, faith is closely related

---

120. Dawkins, *God Delusion*, p. 347.

121. For recent Christian theological rebuttals of the new atheism, see Haught, *God and the New Atheism*; Craig and Meister, eds., *God Is Great, God Is Good*; Markham, *Against Atheism*; McGrath, *Dawkins' God*.

122. McGrath, *Order of Things*, p. 24.

123. For a careful theological critique, see Ward, *God, Chance, and Necessity*, chap. 4 and passim.

124. See further, Bennett and Hacker, *Philosophical Foundations of Neuroscience*, pp. 372-76 particularly.

125. McGrath, *Order of Things*, p. 27, rightly exposes the historically absurd claim, quite common in literature, that Darwin's theory would entail the end of faith in God, as presented naively and uncritically, e.g., in Mayr, *What Evolution Is*, p. 9.

126. Dawkins, *Climbing Mount Improbable*.

127. See, e.g., *Selfish Gene*, p. 198.

128. For correction of Dawkins's (*A Devil's Chaplain*, p. 139) uninformed use of Ter-

with reason even though it goes beyond and transcends it.[129] Fourth, Dawkins argues that theology is a virus of the mind, a "meme," a "pathological infection."[130] The problem here is that there is absolutely no scientific evidence for the existence and function of "memes," let alone any idea of how that could transfer from one person to another. Finally, Dawkins claims that theology and theism impoverish our view of the universe. In other words, religion and belief are aesthetically deficient.[131] This is as unfounded and absurd a claim as any. The investigation of Christian tradition shows overwhelming evidence that Christian theologians have admired the beauty, design, and splendor of nature in most robust ways.[132]

The main methodological fallacy in Dawkins's atheistic rhetoric has to do with his seemingly unnuanced confusion of methodological naturalism and metaphysical naturalism. The former is the stated approach in all natural sciences, which requires that natural phenomena be explained and investigated within the sphere of the known and observed natural events. The divine or mystical or something similar cannot be invoked in a scientific explanation. But methodological naturalism ends here; it "abstains from making assertions about the nature of reality and instead lays down rules for discovering reliable knowledge about the universe."[133] Whatever goes beyond this methodological choice has to do with metaphysics — and that is where Dawkins unabashedly and naively goes all the time.

What is embarrassing about Dawkins's writing is its seeming dogmatism in its belief in Darwinism as a way of "explaining everything"[134] and its intolerance, even hostility, toward those who disagree with him. Indeed, it is self-contradictory to hear this trio speaking against lack of tolerance as they themselves mince no words in passing negative judgment on believers!

Any theological assessment of and response to atheism stemming from the scientific worldview should remember the well-known fact that it is the Judeo-Christian worldview, in close alliance with the Hellenistic worldview, that made possible and facilitated the study of nature as we know it in modern

---

tullian's often-quoted statement, "It is certain because it is impossible," see McGrath's *Order of Things*, pp. 31-33.

129. McGrath, *Order of Things*, pp. 31-41.

130. Dawkins, *Selfish Gene*, p. 192, cited in McGrath, *Order of Things*, p. 41.

131. McGrath, *Order of Things*, p. 49, from Dawkins, "A Survival Machine," pp. 75-95.

132. See McGrath, *Order of Things*, pp. 49-53.

133. McCalla, *Creationist Debate*, p. 193, cited in Schwarz, *The God Who Is*, p. 27.

134. For a careful theological critique, see Ward, *God, Chance, and Necessity*, chap. 4 and passim.

and contemporary science.[135] The new atheism writers seem not to be aware of this important historical link between science and Judeo-Christian faith, nor do they appreciate its huge significance for all Western culture and now for the rest of the globalized world.[136]

Postmodern "Theological Atheists"

Neither Nietzsche's nor Feuerbach's legacy died out at the closing of the nineteenth century. Nietzsche prepared the way for the emergence of various types of postmodernism, particularly those focused on the meaning of texts in relation to other texts (rather than in relation to "reality"). In his essay "On Truth and Lies in a Nonmoral Sense," he responds to his own question, "What then is truth?" in a way that is deceitfully postmodern in ethos: "A movable host of metaphors, metonymies, and anthropomorphisms. . . . Truths are illusions which we have forgotten are illusions; they are metaphors that have become worn out and have been drained of sensuous force, coins which have lost their embossing and are now considered as metal and no longer coins."[137] Not surprisingly, a number of postmodern writers of various stripes have revisited Nietzsche's storehouses and found much there they agree with.

Along with the leading American poststructuralist theologian Mark C. Taylor, the well-known contemporary atheist-turned-Anglican-priest Don Cupitt embodies the latest forms of "theological atheism," in a radical post-metaphysical, antirealist, and "immanentist" orientation.[138] The impetus for Cupitt to drift away from Christian theism has to do with a deep desire to redeem full human freedom and autonomy, emancipated from all notions of authority and limits.[139] Hence, he was drawn to write *Taking Leave of God* (1980). In epistemology, Cupitt moved from realism to antirealism, as argued forcefully in *Is Nothing Sacred?* with a telling subtitle, *The Non-Realist Philosophy of Religion* (2002).[140]

135. Schwarz, *The God Who Is*, p. 20.

136. An excellent study is Nebelsick, *Circles of God*.

137. "On Truth and Lies," p. 79. I am indebted to Markham, *Against Atheism*, pp. 38-39.

138. In the discussion of Cupitt and Taylor, including some of their critics, I am deeply indebted to the careful and detailed discussion in Amnell, *Uskonto ilman uskontoa*. My debt includes finding a number of references.

139. Cupitt, *Sea of Faith*, pp. 1-4; Cupitt, *Taking Leave of God*, p. ix.

140. Cupitt, *Is Nothing Sacred?* p. xi. For a detailed listing of influences that prompted the antirealist epistemology, see pp. ix-xviii.

Cupitt's 1987 work *The Long-Legged Fly* is postmodernism writ large.[141] Owing to Derrida, truth claims concern only intratextual validity.[142] In this new vision of faith, not only do antirealism and pluralism reign but also monism: there is only "one world," in which old categories such as immanent and transcendent must be radically reframed.[143] Similarly, divinity and humanity are to be radically revised. Radicalizing the nineteenth-century Hegelian-Straussian notions of incarnation as myth (without any reference to them), Cupitt locates the incarnation in the human person.[144] Finally, his post-Christian vision is articulated in the 1997 work *After God: The Future of Religion:* "Today, however, the whole cosmological or grand narrative side of religion has totally collapsed. We know, if we know anything, that there is no rationally ordered scheme of things out there, no grand-narrative meaning-of-life already laid on for our lives to be fitted into. We know, if we know anything, that there isn't literally any supernatural order, and there is not literally any life after death. This is all there is, and, as everyone knows, when you're dead you're dead."[145]

When looking for substitutes for the concept of God at the center of religion, Cupitt is drawn to a number of proposals such as "death, otherness, the void, difference, Christ, the Good, love." These concepts tell less about "God" and more about the transient and finite nature of us as human beings.[146] In other words, these metaphors speak of "emptiness," in the Buddhist parlance, sunyata.[147]

Enter M. C. Taylor. "I thought I was done with God — or that God was done with me. But I suppose I am not, at least not yet."[148] Taylor locates himself between two deep tensions: between Hegel *versus* Kierkegaard and Barth *versus* Altizer (the death-of-God theologian). For Hegel, "God is not only completely and absolutely knowable, but is nothing other than the Concept itself . . . the category of categories itself which is the condition of the possibility of all thought and being," in other words, the ground of epistemology and ontology. This for Taylor means nothing less than the "death" of God as it negates God's transcendence. God can be fully known, and hence, humanity becomes the measure of divinity. This is onto-theology at its best. Kierkegaard's

---

141. Cupitt, *Long-Legged Fly;* see also *Only Human,* p. xii.
142. Cupitt, *Radicals and the Future of the Church,* p. 55.
143. Cupitt, *Philosophy's Own Religion,* p. 134.
144. See Cupitt, "Unsystematic Ethics and Politics," pp. 149-55.
145. Cupitt, *After God,* p. 103.
146. Cupitt, *Radicals and the Future of the Church,* pp. 110-11.
147. Cupitt, *Philosophy's Own Religion,* p. 151.
148. M. Taylor, *About Religion,* p. 29.

approach is diametrically opposite as God is so absolutely different that no human rational concept can reach him.[149] A later version with a materially similar dynamic can be found in the juxtaposition of Barth and Altizer. Against the immanentism of his classical liberal teachers, Barth's God was "wholly other," so much so that there is no connecting point between humanity and God. On the other hand, in Altizer's *Gospel of Christian Atheism,* not only is God no longer transcendent, but he also undergoes the *kenosis,* self-emptying, so thoroughly that he disappears! He is dead. Ironically, while diametrically opposed to each other, both Barth and Altizer affirm the category of presence, though differently. Whereas for Barth, God's kingdom is present somewhere else than "here," for Altizer the kingdom is present "here" and now.[150] Add Hegel and Kierkegaard into the equation: the former says "both-and" and the latter, "either-or." Taylor's choice is "neither-nor": "In my oscillation I have begun to suspect that the neither-nor between both-and and either-or involves a different difference and an other other."[151] That is a postmodern, "nondialectical a/theology."[152]

Hence, Taylor presents yet another removal of God from the center of religion. "While I no longer believe in God, I can no longer avoid in believing in the sacred." For him, the "sacred" now is the denegation of God and vice versa.[153] By saying that he no longer believes in God, Taylor is not pronouncing himself an atheist in the normal sense of the word. Indeed, he goes so far as to say that it is only through the negation, the replacement of God by the sacred, that God is allowed to be God, everything different from what is not God.[154] Indeed, a/theology, he claims, is beyond dualistic options such as "atheism" and "theism"; it is "after God" (he published a book of this title in 2007). It is not clear what is the role of God in that "theology," as "religion is a complex adaptive network of symbols, myths, and rituals that both give life meaning and purpose and disrupt, dislocate, and disfigure every stabilizing structure."[155] This much, however, is clear: "A/theology is, in large measure, a critique of the notion of transcendent God, who is 'self-clos'd, all-repelling.'"[156]

Taylor's "theological atheism" is a vehement rejection of classical meta-

---

149. See M. Taylor, *About Religion,* pp. 33-37.

150. M. Taylor, *About Religion,* p. 39.

151. M. Taylor, *Altarity,* p. xxx; see also *About Religion,* pp. 39-41.

152. M. Taylor, *About Religion,* p. 39.

153. M. Taylor, *About Religion,* p. 31, italics omitted.

154. M. Taylor, *About Religion,* p. 32.

155. M. Taylor, *After God,* p. 137.

156. M. Taylor, *Erring,* p. 104.

physics and onto-theology based on the — absolutely correct! — observation that in classical theology God, not only the "word" God,[157] but God's "real existence," is the ultimate ground for being and knowing. That is where the ways between classical theology, including the current project, and postmodern theological atheism part. This project argues that, first, no theistic God, let alone the God of the Bible, can be had without some form of metaphysics; second, that metaphysics of "presence" is neither oppressive nor violent but a gracious and hospitable invitation to communion; and third, that while only so much can be said of God, God really *is,* not only as a word but also as the foundation and source of everything in the cosmos. Should that be called onto-theology, then let it be. If Derrida calls his view "religion without religion,"[158] then I guess Taylor might go with "religion without God." The English philosopher of religion Brian Hebblethwaite rightly argues that the postmodern, antirealist, and postmetaphysical, deeply immanentist response to modernity is neither necessary nor useful. It makes all the difference whether one speaks of the "reality of God in an unqualified, objective sense" as in Christian theism or merely in terms of "expressivist reinterpretation" used by Cupitt and the like.[159]

In the final analysis, the dividing line between postmodern theological atheism and classical Christian tradition has to do with the radically differing understanding of truth. For Taylor, Derrida, and the like, outside the text — "signification" — there is no reality or truth in the sense of classical Christian and philosophical traditions' meaning.[160] While this project rejects foundationalism, where disagreement emerges with Taylor is the — in my opinion — mistaken conclusion that, therefore, "Within the boundless field of signification, truth itself appears to be an optical illusion."[161] Contrary to Taylor, this project argues that a robust acknowledgment of the historical, *post*foundationalist, and hence, partial and perspectival, nature of human knowledge does not lead to rejecting the whole pursuit of knowledge. This project also critiques those whom Taylor calls "literalists" (read: naive foundationalists).[162] There is a "radical middle" between the two extreme options. We also have to subject to criticism

---

157. M. Taylor (*Erring*, p. 104) clearly follows Derrida in making "word," language, the only referent (signifier) to "God": "God is what word means, and word is what 'God' means." In classical theology, the "word" God refers to the ultimate reality named "God," who also exists apart from naming!

158. Derrida, *Gift of Death*, p. 49.

159. Hebblethwaite, *The Ocean of Truth*, p. 3.

160. Cupitt (*Long-Legged Fly*, p. 7) agrees.

161. M. Taylor, *Erring*, p. 176.

162. M. Taylor, *Erring*, pp. 172-74.

the postmodern rejection of "logocentrism," the classical (Christian) vision in which truth, anchored as it is in God, while only partially and "analogically" accessible to the finite human mind, is "really there," apart from human imagination or "writing." That critical-realist standpoint must be maintained or else no constructive and systematic coherent vision of Christian theology is possible at all. Ironically, Mark Taylor comes to the right conclusion: "If God, self, and history are so closely bound, then the death of God and the disappearance of the self would seem to spell the end of history."[163] That is, indeed, the case if the postmodern atheistic logic were followed to its conclusions!

Having looked in some detail at the objections to the possibility of God-talk in contemporary culture and rebuttals of belief in God, we will continue clarifying the conditions of theology by raising the questions of whether metaphysics is possible and desirable and whether natural theology with regard to what used to be called "proofs for the existence of God" — better named now "traces of God" in the created reality — can and should be affirmed. The latter topic thus continues the discussion begun in chapter 7.

The Re-turn of Metaphysics

Philosophical Theology and the Universality of Christian Faith

In classical understanding, theology was understood as the *logos* about *theos*.[164] While we have established that because of human incapacity to access God directly an anthropological turn is necessary, that methodological choice does not therefore entail sidetracking God as the "object" of theology. When speaking of "God," Christian theology on the one hand has to preserve the uniqueness of the biblical view of God, Yahweh, the Father of Jesus Christ, and on the other hand establish a critical link between that and the concepts of god among religions and in philosophy. "The God of Abraham, Isaac and Jacob and the God of the philosophers is the same God."[165] This is the claim the early church made in relation to Greco-Roman culture to avoid cutting off the necessary bridges with the secular culture and other religions. "If Christian theology now rejects the concept of God in philosophical theology that views God as one, arguing that theology deals only with the Christian God and not

---

163. M. Taylor, *Erring*, pp. 53-61, at 54.
164. Aquinas, *ST* 1.1.7.
165. Tillich, *Biblical Religion*, p. 85.

another, then it is involuntarily regressing to a situation of a plurality of gods in which Christian talk about God has reference to the specific biblical God as one God among others."[166]

In the ancient philosophies of Plato, Aristotle, and others, metaphysics served the important function of the transcendental basis for justice, goodness, and values, as well as for the order of society in general. To speak of God, Christian theology has always relied, alongside biblical materials, on what is called "metaphysics" (and ontology).[167] However, beginning from the latter part of the nineteenth century, both in philosophy and (Protestant) theology, the "end of metaphysics" was pronounced. After the advent of postmodernism, the final death blow to all notions of metaphysics was believed to have taken place; we live now in a "postmetaphysical age."[168]

What is metaphysics?[169] A highly debated concept in contemporary philosophy, it usually refers to the study of the "ultimate reality,"[170] regardless of whether a specific work such as Aristotle's *Metaphysike* is the origin or, in this case, the etymology is a correct guide ("beyond physical"). Now we know that even science is not innocent metaphysically; for natural science to execute its investigation of nature, a number of metaphysical assumptions must be in place, beginning from the orderliness of the world, human capacity to gain knowledge of the world, and so forth.[171] That is not to say that there is therefore no clear boundary line between natural science and theology; yes, there is, but that boundary line does not consist of one discipline (natural sciences) not being related to metaphysics, while the other is. They are just differently metaphysical.

Modern Rebuttals

Among the nineteenth- and twentieth-century philosophers, the most vocal opponents to any notion of metaphysics were Nietzsche and Heidegger.[172]

---

166. Pannenberg, *ST* 1:69.

167. Pannenberg, *Metaphysics and the Idea of God*, pp. 11-12 particularly; Grenz, *Named God*, p. 1.

168. Pannenberg, *Metaphysics and the Idea of God*, p. 3.

169. A useful discussion for the purposes of theology can be found in McGrath, *Scientific Theology*, vol. 3, chap. 15; see also Grenz, *Named God*, pp. 2-7 particularly.

170. So Inwagen, *Metaphysics*, pp. 4-5.

171. See Trigg, *Rationality and Science*, p. 225.

172. For a useful discussion, see Horner, *Jean-Luc Marion*, chap. 4. Martin Heidegger's

The theological roots of antimetaphysical attitudes go back to the nineteenth-century neo-Kantian distinction between God's "essence" and God's "effects," which means that we do not have any means of knowing anything about God; we only can know the effects of God in our lives.[173] Schleiermacher had already established that orientation.[174] Another liberal, Albrecht Ritschl, famously criticized the mixing of metaphysics and theology in his short book *Theologie und Metaphysik* (1881). The reason for rejecting metaphysics was that it was supposed to be an illegitimate blending of philosophy and religion based on revelation.[175] What Ritschl started as a rebuttal of metaphysics, the historian of dogma A. von Harnack made a full-scale program as he famously declared the evolving of Christian theology — intertwined with Hellenistic and other "pagan" philosophies — a "deterioration of dogma."[176] Behind this rebuttal was also a vehement attack upon "natural theology."[177] At the same time, these liberal critics of earlier Christian theologians were totally blind to the deep metaphysical-philosophical (modernist, Protestant, neo-Kantian) presuppositions of their own!

In the twentieth century, the rejection of metaphysics was related of course to the rise of logical positivism and analytic philosophy. From a different perspective, a rather conservative movement, called open theism or free will theism, also has issued a call for rejecting metaphysics in favor of a more biblically based understanding. However, it seems to me, behind this judgment lies a hopelessly unnuanced understanding of "metaphysics": what these critics are saying is that certain features of the uses of Hellenistic categories, such as the immutability and impassibility of God in classical theism, may not be appropriate.[178] Most recently, postmodern approaches, particularly of deconstructionist orientations, have heralded the final end of metaphysics.[179]

---

somewhat ambiguous relation to metaphysics was laid out briefly in his inaugural lecture at the University of Freiburg in 1929, "What Is Metaphysics?"

173. For study of this "transcendental effect," see Saarinen, *Gottes Wirken auf uns*.

174. Schleiermacher, *On Religion*, second speech (pp. 18-54).

175. See further, Pannenberg, *ST* 1:98.

176. As brilliantly presented and argued in his multivolume *History of Dogma*. The most famous statement of Harnack, often quoted and often misinterpreted, is, "The Gospel, as Jesus proclaimed it, has to do with the Father only and not with the Son." Harnack, *What Is Christianity?* p. 154.

177. For a succinct discussion, see Pannenberg, *ST* 1:98-100.

178. See Pinnock, *Most Moved Mover*; chap. 2 deals with critique of metaphysics under the telling title "Overcoming a Pagan Inheritance"!

179. For a brief commentary, see Lowe, "Metaphysics, Opposition to," p. 559.

The Postmodern "End of Metaphysics"

Behind much of late modern rejection of metaphysics is Heidegger's sharp criticism of the Cartesian metaphysics' link with substance ontology.[180] While that concern was valid at the turn of the twentieth century, it is no longer warranted after the advent of relational ontology.

Many have wondered if a return to metaphysics would entail foundationalist epistemology. That is not the case, however. The feminist Rebecca S. Chopp rightly notes that "The refusal to continue foundationalism does not let us beg off the metaphysical question." Indeed, she says, on the contrary, "Precisely as we attempt to move away from foundationalism to theology, we need to employ some kind of revised metaphysical inquiry."[181]

An important link in the postmodern avoidance of metaphysics is its antirealistic epistemology. "Anti-realism . . . serves the agenda of postmodernity well, in that all can be accounted for as a human construction which may immediately be deconstructed by those with the necessary skills to yield a more pleasing intellectual artifice in due course."[182] Once antirealism is replaced by critical realism, as in this project, metaphysical reflection appears in a more positive light.

In a postmodern outlook, the modernist ethos is unidirectional in its understanding of history, which is seen in terms of a development into something better, higher, brighter. Some postmodern critics have noted that this modernist optimism is but a secularized version of the Judeo-Christian idea of the meaningfulness of history. "Grand narratives" of never-ending development and success do not sit well at all with the postmodern eschewal of metaphysics.[183]

For many postmodernists, there are no external referents for language, hence there is no "reality" apart from the interpreter. Consequently, the modernist use of "universal reason" is rejected as that would make reason a tool for discovering "truth" somewhere out there. The point for the current discussion is obvious: with this understanding of history, language, and reason, metaphysics — as the study of something behind *(meta)* the "world" *(physike)* — is blocked.[184] To that list can be added "subject" or "self"; for the postmodernist

180. Heidegger, *Being and Time*, p. 126.

181. Chopp, "Feminist Queries and Metaphysical Musings," pp. 47-48; I am indebted to Grenz, *Named God*, p. 6.

182. McGrath, *Scientific Theology*, 2:178.

183. White, *Political Theory and Postmodernism*, pp. 5, 9, 11, 16, 19, 21, 39, 72-73, 116.

184. I am indebted to Amnell, *Uskonto ilman uskontoa*, pp. 20-23.

mind-set there is no enduring, lasting self,[185] because that, again, would entail metaphysics.

Derrida has other problems with metaphysics. Well known are his attacks — highly idiosyncratic and usually exaggerated — against Plato's metaphysics as a "poison" as expressed in his *Phaedrus*[186] (as *pharmakon* means both "medicine" and "poison"), and more generally, metaphysics as "white mythology,"[187] as white men's (from Plato to Heidegger) way of exercising power. Metaphysics is associated with sexism and violence — and more generally with the exercise of power and subjugation.[188]

Too bad that Derrida's reading list seems not to have included any female philosophers who wrote metaphysical texts! Similarly, Derrida seems to be forgetting that violence has been practiced with persons of all metaphysical persuasions as well as those who — mistakenly, though! — allege to have none. This is but one example of a highly suspect and unnuanced global statement coming from this late French deconstructionist.

A key concern among a number of postmodern opponents of metaphysics, particularly of the Continental traditions, has to do with the idea of "metaphysics of presence" because, in this outlook, the "concept" always represents power, the abuse of power.[189] According to the Jewish philosopher Levinas, the Western philosophical tradition, with its preoccupation with ontological categories grasping for understanding and for mastery of the world outside of us, has violence and power built into its very structure. This means suppressing the otherness of the other.[190] Now, in this critique of the concept and of propositional, cognitive communication, turning to the metaphor is a useful tactic, as beyond the metaphor there is nothing![191] Instead of the "metaphysics of presence," these thinkers suggest the "metaphysics of absence." For these opponents of metaphysics, metaphor suggests absence whereas concept yields presence. Even worse, for these postmodern deconstructionists, Judeo-Christian tradition represents "desire for completeness and totality,

---

185. See further, Martin and Barresi, *Rise and Fall of Soul and Self*; C. Taylor, *Sources of the Self*.

186. For the English translation of the originally French essay, see Derrida, "Plato's Pharmacy," pp. 63-171.

187. Derrida, "White Mythology."

188. For a penetrating analysis, see Vattimo, *The End of Modernity*, pp. 4, 7-8, 12, 101.

189. Similarly, Westphal, *Overcoming Onto-Theology*, p. 4.

190. Levinas, *Basic Philosophical Writings*, pp. 11-12 particularly.

191. See Derrida, "White Mythology"; see also Norris, *Deconstruction*; Lentricchia, *After the New Criticism*, chap. 5.

full presence." The Chalcedonian Christology, then, represents the worst type of all-embracing, totalitarian presence in its assertion that in Christ "God is present, fully and completely, in one human being." Similarly, with regard to the doctrine of revelation, these critics see theology asserting claims to "have assurance of this Presence in the Book, the Text of texts, in which human words truly refer to the Word itself."[192]

This deconstructionist understanding of metaphor is only half-truth at its best. Not only is it inherently contradictory (raising the question whether "metaphor" itself in this deconstructive meaning is "metaphor" — or something "beyond"!), but it is also inaccurate, as neither classical nor contemporary theology claims any full or "totalitarian" divine presence in either Christ or the Bible. Even worse, the turn to deconstruction "does not . . . offer any assistance on the question of *which* constructions are better than others. It deals eloquently with the 'is not' of metaphor, but it refuses to deal with the 'is.'"[193] If beyond the language — both concepts and metaphors — there is nothing, then how could deconstructionists "know" that? Rightly McFague insists that "there is a reality to which our constructions refer, even though the only way we have of reaching it is by creating versions of it."[194] Those versions we call symbols, metaphors, models.

While the British Radical Orthodoxy movement has been critical of some aspects of classical metaphysics, Milbank and others have also issued a robust call for a specific type of metaphysics, against its postmodern critics.[195] What Radical Orthodoxy rejects is the totalizing forces of "onto-theology," so named by Heidegger.[196] "Onto-theology" simply means an attempt to establish the category of B/being in reference to God. While postmodern criticism harshly critiques any such attempt, Radical Orthodoxy is not really rejecting the ultimate aim of "onto-theology," namely, making God the basis for being; what it is rejecting is any notion of *independence* of being. It is the flattening of the world to a sheer immanence — "and thus unhooked from its dependence on a transcendent Creator . . . as an autonomous system." Instead, it proposes an "ontology of participation."[197] Based on the Augustinian idea that in itself all being is nothing — and critiquing Duns Scotus's making of being independent

192. As helpfully paraphrased by McFague, *Models of God*, p. 24.
193. McFague, *Models of God*, p. 26.
194. McFague, *Models of God*, p. 26.
195. J. K. A. Smith, *Introducing Radical Orthodoxy*, p. 43 and passim.
196. Milbank, *The Word Made Strange*, pp. 44-45; Milbank, *Theology and Social Theory*.
197. For a short statement, see J. K. A. Smith, *Introducing Radical Orthodoxy*, pp. 74-75, 193-95, at 193.

from God[198] — Radical Orthodoxy wishes to unmask and leave behind any notion of the autonomy of metaphysics and ontology. Hence, "only theology overcomes metaphysics."[199] This "overcoming" is not rejection but rather an important reorientation: only such ontology/metaphysics that is based on and derived from God suffices. Hence, the nomenclature "postsecular" is appropriate for this movement as it seeks to overcome the independence of ontology and metaphysics most dramatically claimed by modernity — which led to secularism,[200] and according to Radical Orthodox theologians, not only secularism and "immanentization" result, but also nihilism.[201]

A subtle and important critique of classical metaphysics comes from the French Roman Catholic philosopher-theologian Jean-Luc Marion. The notion of "God without being"[202] has given rise to obvious misunderstanding — not much different from that related to Tillich's theology of God, the "death" of God. Nothing like that is meant by Marion. He simply wants to get rid of classical metaphysics as the framework for speaking of the "being" of God. Classical metaphysics is based on the Cartesian dualism between object and subject. When God is made a "being" among other beings, then "God" is read off from other beings (whom God has created) and thus, ultimately, becomes thinkable on the formal conditions established by the thinker. Hence, God becomes "idol."[203] On the contrary, the God of the Bible — "foolishness to the Greeks"[204] and their philosophical wisdom — is beyond human positing and control. "God can give himself to be thought without idolatry only starting from himself alone: to give himself to be thought as love, hence as gift; to give himself to be thought as a thought of the gift."[205]

Rightly David Tracy, in the foreword to *God without Being,* says that whereas liberal and other theologies responding to modernism wanted to do theo-*logy,* seeking to correlate biblical faith with current (modern) philosophy, Marion wished to do *theo*-logy, based on revelation.[206] In other words, what

---

198. For a brief statement, see Milbank, *The Word Made Strange,* p. 44. See further, Pickstock, *After Writing,* pp. 121-34.

199. Title of chap. 2 in Milbank, *The Word Made Strange.*

200. See further, Pickstock, *After Writing.*

201. As correctly observed by Hyman, *Predicament of Postmodern Theology,* p. 29. For a useful discussion, see J. K. A. Smith, *Introducing Radical Orthodoxy,* pp. 100-103.

202. Marion, *God without Being.*

203. Marion, *The Idol and Distance.*

204. Marion, *God without Being,* p. 89.

205. Marion, *God without Being,* p. 49.

206. David Tracy, foreword to Marion, *God without Being,* pp. ix-xv, at xii.

we encounter when we think of God, according to this French thinker, is not an object but rather "givenness," indeed overflowing, saturated givenness,[207] supreme givenness.[208] His starting point is in the phenomenology of Martin Heidegger and Edmund Husserl. The basic claim of Husserl is that each phenomenon should be accepted and received just as it gives itself; phenomena are "self-giving." Our speech and experience of objects are only partial. There is a surplus, an excess. For Marion, in God — whom we know on the basis of the revelation of God — there is an excess of givenness that resists any objectification.[209] God is Gift (against Derrida). The gift is "the final trait of every phenomenon revealing itself."[210] Clearly, Marion has not rejected either metaphysics or God; he has just mounted a massive critique against certain foundational fallacies of Western metaphysics.

The "Re-turn" of Metaphysics

Getting rid of metaphysics might "prove to be more problematic than might at first seem to be the case. Metaphysical assumptions are actually implicit within the ideologies of those who oppose the notion."[211] Metaphysics is not something one may either choose or not choose. Every rational argumentation and worldview is based on metaphysical premises, on assumptions that go beyond the physical, observable world. Keith Ward illustrates this by taking up three most common assumptions of atheists and materialists: "Materialism says that the only things that exist are material things in space. There is no purpose or meaning in the universe. Scientific principles are the only proper forms of explanation."[212] Now, are these claims "empirical," "scientific," in need of no philosophical-metaphysical assumptions? No, they are not. These claims "do not belong to physics or chemistry or psychology or biology. They are certainly statements of faith."[213]

Metaphysics is unavoidable. This is to what history also testifies: "the

---

207. For an important discussion, see Marion, "The Saturated Phenomenon," pp. 185-89.

208. Marion, *Being Given.*

209. A highly useful and nuanced discussion can be found in Robinette, "A Gift to Theology?"

210. Marion, "Sketch of a Phenomenological Concept of Gift," p. 123.

211. McGrath, *Scientific Theology,* 3:266.

212. Ward, *God, Chance, and Necessity,* p. 99.

213. Ward, *God, Chance, and Necessity,* p. 99; see also Polkinghorne, "God and Physics," p. 65.

conventional doctrine of God [of classical theism] has a double origin, in the Bible and in Greek thinking."[214] It is just a historical fact that the legacy of Platonic and (later) Aristotelian philosophy towered over the intellectual landscape of early theology. Had it been another form of philosophical orientation and location, say advaitic Hinduism or, later, philosophical Islamic tradition(s), those would have been critically adopted as resources, one would assume. Hence, the heading to this subsection should be taken literally: "return" denotes both return (as in "coming back") and a new turn. In other words, it is not enough only to reassert metaphysics; it is also a matter of responding to the question, "What kind of metaphysics?"

The most influential reaffirmation of metaphysics in twentieth-century philosophy and theology owes to the founder of process theology, Alfred North Whitehead, whose *Process and Reality* has been hailed as the twentieth century's "most important book of speculative metaphysics."[215] According to Whitehead, "Christianity . . . has always been a religion seeking a metaphysic."[216] Not only religion and philosophy, but also science, so Whitehead believed, necessarily base themselves on metaphysics.[217] While the current project does not materially follow process philosophy's direction,[218] its rejection of substance ontology, mechanistic explanation, and materialism, as well as its rediscovery of consciousness, emerging worldview, and dynamic ontology, provide any theology of God with great resources. Its added value is the necessary link with sciences and interest in other religions. The Catholic systematician Walter Kasper rightly notes that the "Christian is so to speak compelled to become a metaphysician on account of his faith."[219] In Catholic theology, indeed, metaphysics per se was never abandoned, not even in the twentieth century, although it underwent important revisions.[220] In twentieth-century Protestant theology, both Tillich and Barth, albeit differently, assumed metaphysics as part of theological construction. The last decades of that century brought to the theological arena a number of

214. O'Hanlon, *Immutability of God*, p. 1.

215. Neville, "Foreword," p. xv.

216. Whitehead, *Religion in the Making*, p. 50.

217. Whitehead, *Adventures of Ideas,* p. 223. For the rejection of "brute matter, or material, spread through space," as the basis for "scientific materialism," see his *Science and the Modern World*, p. 17.

218. For a sympathetic critique with which the current project in the main agrees, see Pannenberg, *Metaphysics and the Idea of God*, chap. 6.

219. Kasper, *Jesus*, p. 21.

220. For a short comment, see Pannenberg, *Metaphysics and the Idea of God*, p. 5.

"mainline" Protestant theological programs that did the same, led by Pannenberg[221] and others.

To avoid falling into the trap of mastery or the danger of "totalitarianism," which Kierkegaard saw embodied in Hegel's world-embracing system, the constructive theologian must be constantly mindful of the finitude and historical limitations of any human thought when speaking of God.[222] And not only speaking but also *writing!* Well known is Derrida's alleged opposition to "writing" — even though he himself seemed to have a lot of things to write! Rather than an effort to "master reality" as Derrida feared, constructive theology seeks to rediscover the truth of God, which is "there" and precedes the investigator.[223] As long as the theologian's "[m]etaphysical reflection . . . [seeks to] take on the form of a *conjectural reconstruction* in relation to its object, one which distinguishes itself from its intended truth while at the same time construing itself as a preliminary form of this truth,"[224] it avoids the trap of mastery and is instead a humble approach.

An aspect of this metaphysical "humility" is acknowledging the limitations of the "god" of metaphysics. Metaphysics can only help set conditions and contours for speaking of God. It is true, as Heidegger famously said, that we "can neither pray nor sacrifice to this god [of metaphysics and philosophy]. Before the *causa sui,* man can neither fall to his knees in awe nor can he play music and dance before this god."[225] But the god of metaphysical reflection is not supposed to be the "personal" God — Father, Son, and Spirit in Christian tradition — to whom honor, loyalty, and love are given. Metaphysical reflection helps establish the rationality of speaking of such a "personal" God.

Part of the necessity of seasoned metaphysical reflection is the inquiry into the "traces" of God in the created reality, classically named natural theology, to which we turn next.

The "Traces" of God in the Created Reality

Common sense and Christian intuition have posited the existence of God on the basis of the created order, including the human person. The attempts to

---

221. See the important statements in Pannenberg, *ST* 1:69.

222. For similar comments, see Pannenberg, *Metaphysics and the Idea of God,* chap. 5, especially p. 93.

223. So also Pannenberg, *Metaphysics and the Idea of God,* p. 11.

224. Pannenberg, *Metaphysics and the Idea of God,* pp. 93-94.

225. Heidegger, *Identity and Difference,* p. 72.

"prove" the existence of God/gods go back to antiquity. Plato's *Laws* make an attempt at "producing adequate proofs, that gods exist" (10.885c, d), although it is also noted that this belief is universal among the Greeks and others (886a). Theologically, it is significant that for Plato God is "the measure of all things" (4.716c) and, according to *Sophist* (265e),[226] God is also the maker of the world. Plato's pupil Aristotle, speaking in *Metaphysics* of different domains of science, both natural and practical, points to the unique object of "theology": that "which exists separately and is immovable . . . [which] surely must be the Divine, and this must be the first and most fundamental principle."[227] Both in *Metaphysics* and in *Physics,* Aristotle considers carefully the value of the proofs of the "first mover" and order of things, which were later picked up — as cosmological and teleological arguments — in medieval theology.

In Jewish thought, Moses Maimonides' *Guide of the Perplexed* similarly uses cosmological and teleological arguments. Well known are the Qur'anic verses (30:16-27) that argue for the rationality and inevitability of belief in God on the basis of the created order, including human life.[228] Important Islamic theologians who influenced Christian tradition, Averroes and, earlier, Avicenna, knew well these Aristotelian proofs. Even as early as the ninth century (C.E.), for Muslim theologian Al-Farabi, the proofs from motion, efficient cause, and contingency played the major role.[229] While Saint Thomas also utilized these resources in his own work,[230] even more "foundational" than philosophical reasoning were the biblical perspectives, which he took as *preambula fidei.*[231] Going beyond Semitic faiths, "[b]oth the argument from design and the cosmological argument are common within Hinduism, and Anselm's approximate contemporary, Udayana . . . puts forward aspects of the ontological argument in his debates with the Buddhists and propounds in total over twenty different arguments for the existence of the deity."[232]

226. *Plato in Twelve Volumes,* vol. 12.

227. *Metaphysics* 11.1064a, in *Aristotle in 23 Volumes,* vols. 17, 18.

228. See also 67:1-4, 19. Speaking of the Muslims' knowledge of God, Brockopp ("Islam," p. 85) notes that "Muslims believe that God is the creator and sustainer of the universe, so signs of his glory can be found everywhere in the natural world — a person can know God merely by smelling a rose and remembering where that rose came from." For important comments, see Rahman, *Major Themes of the Qur'an,* p. 68.

229. Hammond, *Philosophy of Alfarabi,* pp. 19-21.

230. For example, Thomas wrote an extensive *Commentary on the Metaphysics of Aristotle.*

231. Aquinas, *ST* 1.2.2 ad 1.

232. Brockington, *Hinduism and Christianity,* p. 20; for detailed discussion, see Clooney, *Hindu God, Christian God.*

Hence, it makes sense and would be important to argue "the existence of God as an interreligious theological project," as the famed comparativist Francis Clooney puts it. It is important because "[s]ome Christian and some Hindu theologians have argued that it is reasonable to investigate the causes of the world and on that basis to postulate that there is a God who is the world's cause." While this is not to elevate reason to the top position — since all theistic faiths, whether Semitic or Asian, ultimately build on revelation — it is to "agree implicitly that a sound and well-expressed induction should be compelling for all thoughtful persons, regardless of specific cultural, philosophical, and religious peculiarities." And although the following statement can be grossly misunderstood by some postmodernists, it seems to many, on the basis of careful study of the scriptures and writings of theistic faiths, that "[r]eason survives cultural and religious differences, and in a comparative and dialogical context reasoning leads plausibly toward the conclusion that there is a God."[233] To that dialogical and comparative task in the contemporary world we must also add the natural sciences. The rest of this chapter delves in some detail into the arguments for God's existence in the Christian philosophical and theological heritage, to be complemented and challenged in chapter 15 in dialogue with four living faiths. The scientific engagement happens most fully in the volume *Creation and Humanity.*

"Greater Than That Which Can Be Conceived"

Before Anselm of Canterbury presented his famous ontological argument in his *Proslogium* (chap. 2), in the earlier work *Monologium* he had attempted to show the rationality — and in that sense, the "necessary"[234] nature — of the being of God as the most "supreme" and highest culmination of attributes such as "being," "life," "reason," and "safety."[235] If that kind of Being existed, it must be "greater" than anything else. Hence, his argument in the *Proslogium:* "Even the fool is convinced that there is something, at any rate in the understanding, than which nothing greater can be conceived, for when he hears this, he understands it, and whatever is understood is in the understanding. And certainly that than which a greater cannot be conceived cannot exist in the understanding alone. For

---

233. Clooney, *Hindu God, Christian God,* p. 58.
234. For important comments, see Brecher, *Anselm's Argument,* pp. 114-15.
235. Anselm, *Monologium,* chap. 16, p. 66.

if it be in the understanding alone, it is possible to conceive it as existing in reality, which is greater."[236]

It is easy to imagine what kind of criticism this reasoning elicits. Even if we suppose its basic validity, we have to ask what kind of God is "proved" by the ontological argument. This God is absolutely simple; the divine attributes are not accidents, but are rather the very essence of God. God is present in every place and time, and is not in any place or time, for all times and places are in God.[237] Even worse for Anselm, there are many — most importantly Immanuel Kant — who think the whole reasoning fails. Kant raised the obvious question of whether it is really necessary to posit an existence on the basis of an *idea* of an existence. Existence has to be "added" to the thought if real existence is in view. "A hundred real dollars contain no more than a hundred possible dollars."[238] Human imagination seems able to posit entities, events, and beings that do not necessarily have to exist — unless one goes with some contemporary cosmologists and theoretical physicists whose "multiverse" hypothesis suggests that everything imagined exists, albeit in other "universes" than ours. It has also been noted — correctly — that perhaps Anselm makes existence in reality a property similar to other properties or attributes of God.[239] Those objections to Anselm granted, it might be the case that the standard reading of his ontological argument is faulty and misses the point. Hans Schwarz offers a noteworthy correction of the standard interpretation: "Anselm was well aware that God's existence in reality is different from the existence in reality of excellent islands or of a hundred thalers [a coin]. God's existence is not of a possible but of a necessary kind. Anselm argued that there are things that can be conceived of as either existing or not existing. But these things cannot be God. If God could be conceived of as not existing, existing things would be of higher quality than God and he would not be that, than which nothing greater can be thought."[240]

Rather than attempting to mount indubitable evidence of the existence of God, Anselm rather — in the true spirit of the whole project of the proofs — claims that any reasonable person would be convinced of God's existence if God were conceived of as greater than that which can be conceived. Only "fools" would deny that. Obviously, he counted himself in the company of the intelligent.[241]

236. Anselm, *Proslogium*, chap. 2, p. 66.
237. Anselm, *Monologium*, chaps. 16, 17, 20, 21-24; *Proslogium*, chap. 12.
238. Kant, *Critique of Pure Reason*, p. 348.
239. See the classic essay by Hartshorne, "What Did Anselm Discover?" pp. 321-33.
240. Schwarz, *The God Who Is*, p. 40.
241. Anselm, *Proslogium*, chap. 4, p. 10. For all his resistance to proofs in general, Barth

René Descartes took the ontological argument (though never mentioning Anselm) and made a significant contribution by linking it with his idea of infinity. According to the *Third Meditation,* unlike "ideas of corporeal things that are clear and distinct," ideas concerning "substance, duration, number, and the like," which he assumed had originated in his own mind, the idea of God seemed to be such that it did not originate with him. "A substance infinite, eternal, immutable, independent, all-knowing, all-powerful, and by which I myself, and every other thing . . . exists," does not owe its origin to the human mind. Hence, "it is absolutely necessary to conclude . . . that God exists."[242] Although the human mind is able to grasp the idea of a finite mind, it cannot understand an infinite mind (23), except by way of "negation of the finite." Hence, this important final conclusion: "I clearly perceive that there is more reality in the infinite substance than in the finite, and therefore . . . in some way I possess the perception (notion) of the infinite before that of the finite, that is, the perception of God before that of myself" (24).[243] Descartes is of course well aware that this reasoning might be faulty, for example, in terms of the idea of infinity being nothing other than a description of infinite attributes of human beings — perhaps in the far future (26, 27).[244] His main point, however, is valid, namely, that it is not the Infinite that can be grasped in light of the finite but rather the opposite: it is only in light of the Infinite that the finite can be grasped, as something different from the Infinite. Hence, the idea of Infinity, God, is more "foundational" and primary.

Of course, what this intuition of the infinite is, is just that, an *intuition,* a tentative awareness that "[o]ver against the open horizon of the infinite our own existence, all reality, and the divine basis of everything finite are present to us," but that is not yet a direct awareness or knowledge of God.[245] It takes revelation to name the object of the intuition God, the God of the Bible. Yet it is "all the same a real thing"; it is more than just "a disposition or aptitude"; it is even more than a "question," since no one can live continuously with a

---

saw clearly that the main point for Anselm was that "God gave himself as the object of his knowledge and God illumined him that he might know him as object." Barth, *Anselm,* p. 78; I am indebted to Schwarz, *The God Who Is,* p. 41.

242. Descartes, *Meditations on the First Philosophy,* meditation III, ##21, 22. Numbers in parentheses in the rest of this section refer to paragraphs in this meditation.

243. Hegel later picked up the same idea that the finite cannot be thought of without conceiving of the Infinite, thus making the Infinite primary. See his *Phenomenology of Mind,* pp. 207-13.

244. That idea Descartes rejects on the basis that whereas in the human being, in principle, there might be potential for endless growth in knowledge, it is just that, *potential,* whereas in God infinity is "actual."

245. Pannenberg, *ST* 1:113-14.

question. We seek answers, albeit provisional and tentative.[246] Descartes's *Fifth Meditation* builds on and deepens the logic of this reasoning. If God is the "first thought," and God cannot be thought of except as something existing, then God must exist necessarily.[247] Descartes was not presuming that this seemingly tight logic of reasoning would "prove" the existence of God beyond doubt. Like Anselm, he took God's existence as the basis for all knowledge, not only knowledge of the divine.[248]

This theo-centric approach to reality was of course to be shattered soon, first with the coming of a mechanistic worldview, which did not require God as a hypothesis, as it were, and later by post-Enlightenment atheistic critique. As mentioned above, classical theology did not regard the proofs of God as "proofs" in the later apologetic sense, in terms of attempting to show that by the force of logic God's existence must be acknowledged. Rather, the classical proofs were a means of making God-talk reasonable. The proofs were presented by those who already presupposed God's existence. Anselm himself serves as a telling example: "For I do not seek to understand that I may believe, but I believe in order to understand."[249] That Anselm and other similar presenters of proofs relied heavily on rational powers did not thereby mean that they would not have based their theology on the acceptance of biblical revelation and catholic tenets of faith.

Knowledge of God from the World

Along with the ontological, the cosmological argumentation has also occupied the minds of Christian theologians. While the Angelic Doctor presented no fewer than eleven different proofs and rejected thirteen proposals,[250] five of the proofs, presented in the first part of *Summa Theologiae,* are best known:[251] the

---

246. Pannenberg, *ST* 1:115-16.

247. Descartes, *Meditations on the First Philosophy,* meditation V, #10.

248. See particularly meditation V, #16, the last paragraph of that meditation.

249. Anselm, *Proslogium,* chap. 1, p. 7. Importantly, this sentence is preceded by this humble acknowledgment: "I do not endeavor, O Lord, to penetrate thy sublimity, for in no wise do I compare my understanding with that; but I long to understand in some degree thy truth, which my heart believes and loves" (pp. 6-7).

250. J. Clayton, "Gottesbeweise II. Mittelalter," p. 732; I am indebted to Schwarz, *The God Who Is,* p. 38.

251. *Summa contra Gentiles* 1.13 contains another kind of classification that gives preeminence to the first way, that is, the idea of the prime mover.

proofs from motion, causality, contingency, grades of perfection, and purpose (telos).[252] Behind the use of cosmological proofs is the intuition that "we attain to knowledge and recognition of God, to an idea of God, only by experience of the world . . . by way of knowledge of the material world, by experience of things that we know through the senses."[253] The "proofs" all boil down to the conclusion that nothing finite can exist and support itself; in other words, it is contingent. Even Kant, who was very skeptical about the whole project of the proofs, granted that the cosmological proof has little against speculative reason and, hence, is a strong argument.[254] Of course, it is true, as Kant rightly observed, that the principle of causality only applies to the observed world.[255] What Kant missed — similarly to the logical positivist Bertrand Russell[256] — is that the ultimate question for Christian theology with regard to the existence of God is not to be able to explain the causes and effects in this observed world but rather to look for a metaphysical answer to the question of the ultimate origins. If God is the creator, then what happened "before" about 13.7 billion years ago when the big bang is assumed to have taken place, is the focus of theistic explanation. (Of course, in this context, speaking of "before," a reference to time, is highly problematic since time — and space — came into being as the result of the big bang.) The main point for this discussion is simple: the Kantian critique of classical metaphysics' and theology's understanding of causality hardly is a death blow against the continuing value of the cosmological proof[257] — with a focus on the contingency and final nature of the created reality — as a way of making talk about God meaningful and reasonable.

Hence, contemporary theological argumentation is moving "from the first cause to the infinite"[258] when it comes to God as the "explanation" of the possibility of the world. Merely looking for the first cause would keep us in the

---

252. The teleological argument was already suggested by the pagan philosopher Marcus Tullius Cicero, *On the Nature of God* 3.9 (p. 326). Even Darwin acknowledged the intuition of purpose in nature but could not make up his mind about what to think of it. Charles Darwin in a letter to Asa Gray, November 26, 1860, in *Correspondence of Charles Darwin*, p. 496.

253. Pannenberg, *ST* 1:82-83.

254. Kant, *Critique of Pure Reason*, p. 353.

255. Kant, *Critique of Pure Reason*, p. 367.

256. The logical positivist Bertrand Russell (*Why I Am Not a Christian*, pp. 6-7) missed the point by looking only at the (im)possibility of determining the first "cause."

257. The same can be said of Hume's critique, which Kant also engages in his own discussion of cosmological arguments. For Hume's rejection of sense experience (which he otherwise highly regarded) as the avenue for direct knowledge of causation in the world, see his *Dialogues concerning Natural Religion*, pp. 15-25, 47-56.

258. Title for chap. 2 in Grenz, *Named God*.

confines of time and space and be subject to Kantian criticism of discerning the cause. In the aftermath of the demise of the Newtonian mechanistic worldview, a dynamic worldview and ontology have emerged, as well as a "fine-tuned" way of looking at causality, an indication of which is the famed "anthropic principle." In all of this, the cooperation of the ontological and cosmological argumentation comes to play an important role. Already the fifteenth-century theologian Nicholas of Cusa came to see the importance of the concept of the infinite. He saw in mathematics a pathway to truth, as that science demonstrated what he called the "coincidences of opposites": "the concept of the 'infinite' presents to the mind a series of illuminating paradoxes, for when extended to infinity conceptions that have been rejected as impossible suddenly become possible and plausible."[259] According to Nicholas, the universe is infinite in a "contracted" manner, and "reflects the 'absolute maximum' that is God, who is the *complicatio* or enfolding as well as the *explicatio* or unfolding of all things."[260] Descartes, Kant,[261] Fichte, Hegel,[262] and Schleiermacher, who took up the task of reflecting on the infinite in relation to God, rightly stressed that for the infinite to be *infinite,* it cannot be limited by the finite; hence, the infinite both distinguishes itself from the finite and embraces it.[263]

While the more detailed investigation of the concept of the infinite in relation to the doctrine of God will be taken up below, let it suffice to mention here that in contemporary theology the ontological and cosmological argumentation together serve the function of making talk about the idea of God — to be supplemented by the real "naming" of God on the basis of revelation — intelligible and reasonable. Ideas such as "highest perfection" can hardly get us in themselves to the idea of God. The reason is simply this: "The idea of God, however construed, has a considerably higher specificity than is inherent in the general picture of a being with maximal perfection. For the idea of God cannot be separated from the elements of personality (however

259. As paraphrased by Grenz, *Named God,* p. 66.

260. Grenz, *Named God,* p. 67, on the basis of Nicholas of Cusa, *On Learned Ignorance* 2.11.150 (in *Selected Spiritual Writings,* pp. 154-55) and 2.1.91–2.4.116 (pp. 128-40).

261. Kant, of course, later developed the concept of "all-sufficiency" *(ens a se)* and found it more fitting for rational theology. Despite that, in his developing musings on (absolute) space, it seems to me that he continued affirming the term "infinity" as well.

262. Hegel saw rightly that in thinking of a border one thinks of what is beyond the border. *Hegel's Science of Logic,* pp. 127-29. Differently from Kant, who approached the concept of infinity from the perspective of mathematics, Hegel rightly conceived the notion only against the conception of the finite (pp. 116-17, 137-38).

263. See Edwards, "Of Being," 6:203, as quoted in Grenz, *Named God,* p. 74; for a useful discussion of Edwards, see pp. 72-78.

we are to understand it) and of a will (whatever form it takes)."[264] Hence, with their benefits, the philosophical concepts only get us so far. Along with the ontological and cosmological argument, there is the anthropological argument, whose importance has ascended in recent years.

The Incurable Religiosity and Morality of Humanity

One important aspect in the anthropological argument is what might be called "the persistence of the transcendent,"[265] the fact that it seems to belong to human nature to be open to and inquire into the realities beyond the visible world. Rightly, the Lutheran American theologian Ted Peters notes that "[b]ehind, underneath, or above what we see and hear is a transcendent yet present reality that is suprasensory, supranatural, spiritual, divine, or all of these."[266] This is what the sociologist of religion Berger names "a rumor of angels."[267] Not for nothing does the Princeton philosopher-theologian Wentzel J. van Huyssteen speak of the image of God in terms of the emergence of a natural human tendency to believe in God.[268] One way of expressing the religious nature of humanity and the universality of religion among all human cultures is to speak of "ec-centricity" or "self-transcendence" or "openness to the world."[269] That said, the purpose of the anthropological argument is not to try to "prove" the existence of God, nor could it ever, since "from the religious disposition there does not follow the truth of religious statements about the reality and operations of God or the gods."[270]

The anthropological argument is important for this simple reason: "Dogmatics, although it treats all other themes from the standpoint of God and thus discusses them in exposition of the concept of God, cannot begin directly with

---

264. Pannenberg, *Metaphysics and the Idea of God*, p. 28.

265. Title of chap. 2 in McGrath, *Open Secret*.

266. Peters, *God — the World's Future*, p. 83.

267. The title of one of his books. Berger points to everyday occurrences such as a child waking up in the night who, when comforted by the parent, feels safe. According to Peters, something "beyond" is going on here. For a discussion of many such examples in science and arts, see Polkinghorne, *God of Hope*, pp. 30-36. This physicist-priest names these experiences "intuitions of reality" (heading to the section).

268. Van Huyssteen, *Alone in the World?* I am indebted to McGrath, *Open Secret*, p. 195.

269. For classic contemporary discussions, see Pannenberg, *Anthropology in Theological Perspective*, chap. 2; Rahner, *Hearers of the Word*, pp. 92-93; Küng, *Does God Exist?* pp. 438-39 particularly.

270. Pannenberg, *ST* 1:155-57, at 156.

the reality of God. More precisely, the reality of God is initially present only as a human notion, word, or concept."[271] Of course, the turn to the anthropological argument can become an asset for the atheistic critique of the concept of God as merely projection. That danger, however, should not be a reason to undermine the necessity and usefulness of the anthropological argument in the contemporary world. In opposition to atheistic projection theories, however, Christian theology refuses to make the reality of God merely a human idea. Rather, "the function of anthropological proofs [is] to show that the concept of God is an essential part of a proper human self-understanding, whether in relation to human reason or to other basic fulfillments of human existence."[272] In other words, the anthropological argument is based on the existence and force of a religious disposition as part of human structure, so much so that we speak of "incurable religiosity,"[273] as the failed atheistic-totalitarian experiments in China, the former Soviet Union, and elsewhere have shown.

Closely linked with the anthropological is what is traditionally called the "moral argument," which of course was most profoundly developed by Kant in his *Critique of Practical Reason*. While Kant was not the first to posit such an argument,[274] he made the moral argument a theological-philosophical theme as he was impressed by "the moral law within" as much as he was by "the starry heavens."[275] This moral law pushes us toward the highest level of morality, even though it can hardly be attained in this life alone. Hence, the immortality of the soul and the existence of God to secure such a possibility. True, Kant's faith is "pure rational faith," but God is presupposed.[276] Later idealist philosophers such as Fichte put emphasis on the moral order of the world.[277]

Yet another facet of the anthropological argument is what is sometimes called "the argument of common consent," or more appropriately, the universality of religion among virtually all peoples and people groups at all

---

271. Pannenberg, *ST* 1:61. For an important statement about the need of anthropology for a robust doctrine of God, see Pannenberg, *Anthropology in Theological Perspective*, pp. 11-23.

272. Pannenberg, *ST* 1:92-93.

273. Pannenberg, *ST* 1:157.

274. The Spanish physician, philosopher, and theologian Raimund of Sabund of the fifteenth century had already presented an important treatise titled *Theologia Naturalis Sive Liber Creaturarum (Theology of Nature or the Book of Creation)*. Raimund's reasoning focused on the need to have a superhuman Being who can execute rewards and punishment in order for morality to be meaningful. For a short statement, see Schwarz, *The God Who Is*, p. 56.

275. Kant, *Critique of Practical Reason*, p. 164.

276. Kant, *Critique of Practical Reason*, p. 130.

277. For details, see Schwarz, *The God Who Is*, p. 58.

times throughout history.[278] Again, in itself, the universality of religion hardly qualifies for a proof of God; in the hands of Feuerbachians — and Dawkins! — it may rather indicate the deplorable deception that plagues the whole of humanity! On the other hand, the persistence of religions in diverse cultures and under all kinds of circumstances from "primitive" to industrialized-urban-modern to totalitarian-atheist to postmodern, begs for an explanation. That in contemporary times a growing number of people are turning away from traditional belief in the existence of God is seen by some as a weakening of the universality of religion argument.[279] But the move away from belief in God, at least to date, has been predominantly a phenomenon of the Global North, and even there, quite selectively, as discussed above. In addition, even in the Global North, religiosity is not necessarily disappearing. Rather, a return of religion is taking place. In other words, the "common consent" argument is alive and well even in the beginning of the third millennium.

The anthropological argument has taken various forms and paid attention to various aspects of the relation of humanity to God.[280] Establishing the possibility and necessity of metaphysics — and more widely, philosophical theology — as well as natural theology as resources for constructive theology, is not yet determining the material presentation of the doctrine of God. That task will be attempted in light of biblical testimonies, historical contextualizations, and current systematic proposals (chap. 10). Chapter 11 continues the constructive proposal by discussing the most distinctive feature of Christian theism, the confession of faith in one God as Father, Son, and Spirit. It is only on the basis of a robust trinitarian theology that God's relation to the world (chap. 12) can be developed. An important part of the discussion is highlighting the liberative, reconciliatory, and inclusivistic features of the doctrine of God. That is best presented under the theme of the hospitality of God (chap. 13). Whereas Saint Augustine — and Christian tradition — took it for granted that God, the source of flourishing, must be the God of the Bible, not every Christian theologian of the twentieth century agrees; *theo*-logical purists have challenged that claim, and will be discussed in chapter 14. The final, long chapter picks up the discussion from the end of the doctrine of revelation (chap. 8) and continues the engagement of Christian theology with four living faiths. It places the triune God of the Bible in dialogue with the concepts of the divine in other faith traditions (chap. 15).

278. See further, O'Brien, *Truths Men Live By*, pp. 141-42.
279. See Schwarz, *The God Who Is*, p. 59.
280. For a summative statement, see Pannenberg, *ST* 1:93.

10. "Classical Panentheism"

For Orientation: Classical Theism, Panentheism, or "Classical Panentheism"?

"Much of the reinterpretation of the doctrine of God" in contemporary theology "can be traced to a rising reaction against classical theism — the legacy of Hellenism that has left an indelible imprint on Christian theology."[1] While everybody agrees that such a reinterpretation of the doctrine of God is badly needed, not everybody agrees on how to best attempt it. Some even seem to believe that the God of classical theism is so hopelessly misguided that it is best left behind. Not only the most radical death-of-God theologies — short-lived as they were in the 1960s and 1970s[2] — but also (American) process theologies, like some women's and postcolonial interpretations, have by and large sought to begin from a new "foundation." Then there are important constructive attempts to cast the doctrine of God in a new framework, which, while not leaving behind some key convictions of classical Christian traditions, seek to offer radically revised interpretations. An interesting development in American theology lately has been open theism (or free will theism). This "evangelical" interpretation learns from process theology and other revisionist views and, while critical of classical theism, seeks to be fairly orthodox. Several leading women's theologians have tested the borders of classical theology and

---

1. Bloesch, *God the Almighty,* p. 21.
2. For a highly useful discussion, see D. Peterson, "Speaking of God after the Death of God."

attempted a revision. The same can be said of other liberationists and many theologians from the Global South.

Because of the uneasy and often deeply critical relation of contemporary theologies to classical traditions, it has become commonplace to preface constructive theologies with not only a lament of the "sins" of classical theism but also a vision of either panentheism or in some extreme cases pantheism. On the other hand, fundamentalist and conservative theologies usually contain a harsh criticism of, or at least a serious warning against, "going too far" toward making God dependent on the world. In an important monograph titled *Panentheism: The Other God of the Philosophers,* the conservative American Reformed philosopher-theologian John W. Cooper laments the turn to "panentheism" in much of contemporary doctrine of God. On the basis of a rigorous cartography spanning the whole history of Christian thought, Cooper discerns that this turn to panentheism has its roots in Platonic and other pagan philosophies.

This chapter will take up Cooper's claim (albeit, I fear, against his intentions) and propose a new and fresh solution to the question of how to frame the doctrine of God. The proposal is best named "classical panentheism"! It is based on a twofold argument. First, classical theism in itself was a more or less justified development in the intellectual context in which it operated, and therefore many of the criticisms against it are ill placed. It was essential for the emerging patristic theology of God to be able to present the dynamic biblical narrative of God in Greek-Hellenistic thought forms, not only to "contextualize" the Christian message, but first and foremost to release it from the confines of Jewish faith. Similar justification can be given for later forms of classical theism in tradition. The fact that, for the purposes of contemporary worldview and theological sensibilities, some key orientations of classical theism are in dire need of revision is no reason for that tradition's blank dismissal and unfair criticism.

Second, panentheism has been with Christian tradition from the beginning; indeed, ironically, the main claim of Cooper's detailed historical study is that the contemporary theologians espousing panentheism are standing on the broad shoulders of predecessors throughout history! Related is the observation that classical theism as a scholarly construct never was a coherent phenomenon, not only because of deep diversity among various conceptions of God throughout Christian history but also because, even in its more typical form, theology of God always was mindful of the need to maintain the dynamic of God's transcendence and immanence. Hence, what I call here "classical panentheism" might be the best way to construct a contemporary doctrine of

God, building on tradition sympathetically and critically. In its revised and "modernized" form — in the context of current intellectual, cultural, religious, and scientific impulses — classical panentheism has the potential of providing the most coherent "radical middle." Consequently, "the God of the philosophers," if with that is meant classical panentheism, might as well be "the God of Abraham, Isaac, and Jacob."[3]

Classical Theism: A Generous Assessment

It has become customary to speak of "classical theism" as a generic term designating the approaches of traditional postbiblical developments of early Christian theology that sought to express its faith in the biblical God with the help of Greco-Roman philosophical categories and later found its highest sophistication in medieval scholasticism, post-Reformation Protestant orthodoxy, and early modern theology. Classical theism is not limited to Christianity; in many ways similar kinds of doctrines of God can be found in Judaism (Moses Maimonides), including Hellenistic Judaism (Philo), and in Islam (Abu Hamid al-Ghazali).

The picture of God that emerged out of that philosophical and speculative gristmill has come under devastating criticism. Complaints have been many: the God of classical theism, as an "Unmoved Mover," while enjoying his own perfect fullness of being, is distanced from the world, unaffected by the happenings of history, unrelated to Christian life (let alone social and political struggles), and so on. Furthermore, say critics from a wide variety of traditions, that kind of God is also far removed from the dynamic, narrative, life-related discourse of the Bible, especially that of the Old Testament. The process theologian David Ray Griffin's textbook caricature lists the following elements: "pure actuality," "immutability and impassibility," "timelessness," "simplicity," "necessity," "omnipotence and omniscience."[4]

How do these developments relate to the biblical narrative and testimonies? While no theologian would argue that in the NT there is anything like the tradition outlined above, some occasional passages may reflect and point in the direction of classical theism, such as Paul's affirmation in 1 Corinthians 8:4-5 that "there is no God but one" and that "so-called gods in heaven or on earth" do not exist. "Paul seems to be echoing the convictions of some

---

3. This is of course a response to the doubts by Pascal, "The Memorial," p. 178.
4. Griffin, God, Power, and Evil.

influential Greek thinkers and is using (in verses that follow, as also in Rom. 11:36) a typical philosophical structure of argument to make his point."[5] Other examples cited include Acts 14 and 17, where Paul finds parallels with existing philosophical and religious thought forms. A passage from the Pastoral Epistles (1 Tim. 1:17) talks about God in terms that bear obvious similarities to philosophical approaches: "To the King of ages, immortal, invisible, the only God." Terms such as "immortal" and "invisible" clearly ring philosophical tones of the times, as does the passage in Galatians that contrasts God with those gods that "by nature are no gods" (4:8), utilizing contemporary philosophical distinctions.

Beginning from early patristic theologies, with the alignment of the biblical narrative of God with the philosophy and metaphysics of Hellenistic traditions, the trend toward classical theistic notions emerged and became more common. Commenting on such early writers as Aristides,[6] Theophilus, and Clement of Alexandria,[7] Robert M. Grant rightly observes: "These early Christian writers, then, while in every instance maintaining the primacy of faith in response to the self-revelation of God, do not hesitate to make use of the points of contact between God's revelation and the modes of expression prevalent in Hellenistic Judaism and in Graeco-Roman philosophy generally."[8] This development was necessary and useful for the purposes of the church's mission in its then-contemporary world. The apologists of the second century and beyond majored in this enterprise.[9] The important point is that not only in the apostolic fathers but even in such an early document as the apocryphal *Preaching of Peter*[10] an ingenious combining of biblical and philosophical discussions of God can be found.

To put classical theism in perspective and assess its meaning for contemporary constructive theology, it is instructive to see how in Protestant orthodoxy, on the other end of the historical span, in a changed cultural milieu of emerging modernity, including the rise of science and (modern) materialism, theology was drawn to new contextualizations of the doctrine

---

5. Grant, *Early Christian Doctrine of God*, p. 6.

6. For Aristides, God is the Aristotelian "unmoved Mover and Ruler of the universe," for "everything that moves is more powerful than what is moved, and that which rules is more powerful than what is ruled." Quoted in Grant, *Early Christian Doctrine of God*, p. 17.

7. Clement of Alexandria, *The Miscellanies* 1.5: "Philosophy was given to Greeks . . . [as] a schoolmaster to bring the Hellenic mind . . . to Christ."

8. Grant, *Early Christian Doctrine of God*, p. 11.

9. See, e.g., Justin Martyr, *First Apology* 44.8-9; *Second Apology* 10.1-3.

10. These sayings are quoted by Clement of Alexandria, *Stromata* 6.39.2-3.

of God.[11] So, how did these descriptions come to be and what did they mean in that particular context of emerging modernity?

Take the description of God as "immaterial substance." What in the eighth-century John of Damascus's *Orthodox Faith* (1.4) is "incorporeal" as the designation of the Deity, in the seventeenth- and eighteenth-century Reformed scholastic manuals is called "utterly incorporeal essence," wholly uncontaminated by "materiality."[12] What is behind this move? Whereas in the Damascene "incorporeal" meant that God was "above all existing things, nay even above existence itself . . . infinite and incomprehensible" (1.4), in the post-Reformation theologies "immaterial substance" was an attack against relating God to "matter" and materialism. Behind the struggle is the complicated history of how to negotiate the relation of the divinity to the material, going all the way back to Plato and Aristotle. Descartes, of course, in his highly dualistic philosophy, sundered matter and the spirit/divine.[13] In all these constellations, "the divine . . . is as far as possible from matter, but somehow at the same time functions as its ultimate formative principle."[14] Along with dualism, modern scientific materialism aligned itself with atomistic materialism. Against that background, the theological notion of "immaterial substance" becomes understandable although in hindsight highly misleading. It blinds theology to the simple fact that in the Bible — including biblical pneumatology — the divine or the Spirit of God or the presence of God is not detached from and antagonistic to earthly, bodily, and material realities. Incarnation alone would oppose that tendency.[15]

Consider next the early modern theological view of God as "single subject" and the related concept of the "simplicity" of God. Behind that conception is the early Christian understanding of God — and particularly the biblical idea of God as Spirit — in terms of reason: again, an idea established by ancient Greek philosophy. Alongside reason, will came to play a significant role, as in Aquinas, who explains the procession of the Word, the Son, in terms of intellect and that of the Spirit as divine will.[16] While it is understandable in

---

11. For a detailed historical and theological discussion, see Shults, *Reforming the Doctrine of God,* chaps. 2, 3, and 4. My discussion of these themes is deeply indebted to him. Because he provides detailed original documentation, it suffices to turn the reader to that source.

12. For references and sources, see Muller, *Post-Reformation Reformed Dogmatics,* 3:271-77, 298-300.

13. See further, Shults, *Reforming the Doctrine of God,* pp. 18-22.

14. Shults, *Reforming the Doctrine of God,* p. 17.

15. Shults, *Reforming the Doctrine of God,* p. 35.

16. Aquinas, *ST* 1.34.1 (Word); 1.27.3 (Spirit); see further, Shults, *Reforming the Doctrine of God,* pp. 44-48.

light of these philosophical and theological developments to think of God as a single subject, it also sounds odd in light of the biblical narrative and early creedal affirmations of the Father, Son, and Spirit as a living, dynamic, and mutual communion of love whose presence reaches out to the world. In contemporary theology, luckily, there are several key resources that help us correct and reorient the notion of God as "single subject." The turn to relationality has led to the reconception of the category of "person." Rather than an isolated "individual," "person" is essentially a relational and communal concept. In contemporary trinitarian thinking the theological fruit have been harvested.

Finally, consider the idea of God as "first cause," which we tentatively discussed in the context of the "proofs" of God's existence. Based on long tradition, "Some of the Protestant Scholastics relied heavily on the idea of God as *causa-prima* . . . [the] effective first cause of all things."[17] Particularly in early modern theology, the "cause" is understood in the context of the (semi)mechanistic Newtonian causality. The notion of the first cause in that framework may easily lead to Deism, and often did. Even when it doesn't, the notion of God as first cause too easily makes God a distanced, "unmoved" Mover.[18] Of course, God is conceived as the "cause" — source, origin — of everything in the biblical and early Christian tradition. However, the "early church was not obsessed with proving God's existence as the first cause of the world: its concern was pointing all people to the One who is the source of the future (eternal) life and whose presence *(parousia)* offers a share in that life."[19] Suffice it to say here that again the turn to relationality and communion theology helps us put in perspective the idea of God as the "cause." The loving, caring God — Father, Son, and Spirit — is with his creation from "beginning" to "end," providing not only for existence but also the goal and fulfillment.

While there is no denying the weaknesses and limitations of classical theistic traditions in light of our current worldview and knowledge, as well as theological developments, mere harsh criticism and dismissal,[20] so prevalent in contemporary literature, are neither justified nor necessarily helpful in the process of reshaping the traditions of God. Even when theological tradition

17. Shults, *Reforming the Doctrine of God*, p. 66, with references to original sources.

18. For the Newtonian connection, see Shults, *Reforming the Doctrine of God*, pp. 69-73; for the understanding of causality in contemporary science and its relation to theology of God, see pp. 83-87.

19. Shults, *Reforming the Doctrine of God*, p. 93.

20. An example of that kind of extreme, unjustified criticism is that classical theism "gave unto God the attributes which belonged exclusively to Caesar." Whitehead, *Process and Reality*, p. 342.

resolved the questions in ways inappropriate for our times, as they spoke of the biblical God in terms of "immaterial substance, single subject, and first cause," some important intuitions guided their work:

> The biblical God is neither reducible to nor determined by the categories of the material world, and so if our only options were that God is either a material or an immaterial substance, we would embrace the latter. The biblical God is not less than personal but intensely personal, and so if we felt forced to choose between describing God as impersonal or as a single (personal) subject, we would select the latter. The biblical God is not dependent on creatures for power or being, and so if we were caught in a dilemma between depicting God either as an immanent part of a cause-effect nexus or as a transcendent first cause, we would gladly impale ourselves on the latter horn of this dilemma. In each case the Protestant Scholastics attempted to maintain deep Christian intuitions about the relation of God to the world within the constraints of the categories of early modern cosmology, which forced these choices.[21]

These intuitions can be and should be contextualized in a new and fresh way in the constructive theology appropriate for the third millennium. The next step in that endeavor has to do with assessment of the turn to panentheism in contemporary theology against and in light of long tradition. To that we now turn.

Panentheism: A Seasoned Embrace

Panentheism in Christian Tradition

This section takes up a twofold task. First, on the basis of specific historical examples and testimonies it seeks to confirm the presence of panentheism in Christian tradition, deriving from both the dynamic biblical narrative of God and critical interaction with and contextualization of insights from surrounding cultures. The argument here is that panentheistically oriented and flavored conceptions of God are not foreign to tradition and are not another example of semiheretical, suspect invasion. Second, building on that result, we argue that the turn to panentheism in our current cultural, intellectual, and

---

21. Shults, *Reforming the Doctrine of God,* p. 11.

religious environment is but the continuation of theology's contextualization efforts. This, as everything in Christian constructive theology, is a matter of discerning "Whose Panentheism? Which God?" rather than either classical theism or panentheism. The key criteria of discernment here are those classical tradition has always used, namely, biblical and traditional contours, communal discernment, as well as contextual fit. Speaking of "contextual fit" is not to advise theology to accommodate uncritically ever-new "secular" or even religious fads, but rather to understand that every theological assessment of the "fit" already comes from a particular perspective.

As an appropriate launching pad for this discussion, take the bold global statement by Bishop Kallistos of Diokleia: "There are . . . good grounds for asserting that Judaism, Christianity, and Islam are all fundamentally 'panentheist,' if by 'panentheism' is meant the belief that god, while *above* the world, is at the same time *within* the world, everywhere present as the heart of its heart, the core of its core."[22] The Orthodox bishop supports this statement with reference to both biblical and theological tradition. The long panentheistic orientation — "the delicate equilibrium between transcendence and immanence" — however, was impaired, beginning from the seventeenth century, as the otherness and distance of God from the world, mainly among the Western but also among some Eastern theologians, took the upper hand. The end result was Deism.[23] In light of these considerations, the Eastern Orthodox bishop says this about the God-world relationship: "Our primary image should be that of indwelling. Above and beyond creation, God is also its true inwardness, its 'within.'"[24]

The Hebrew Scripture teaches a dynamic panentheistic vision. On the one hand, Elohim/Yahweh is spoken of as the absolutely majestic, transcendent, "incomprehensible," "hidden" Divine (Job 38:4; Isa. 45:15; 55); on the other hand, this same God asks rhetorically, "Am I a God at hand . . . and not a God afar off?" (Jer. 23:23), whose presence men and women cannot avoid wherever they go (Ps. 139:7-8). Similarly the NT speaks of God in dynamic terms. Paul's speech in Acts 17 makes every effort — in one and the same passage! — to paint the picture of God's transcendence as well as God's immanence as robustly as possible. On the one hand, "The God who made the world and everything in it, being Lord of heaven and earth, does not live in

22. Ware, "God Immanent Yet Transcendent," pp. 157-68.
23. Ware, "God Immanent Yet Transcendent," p. 159. For a useful tracing of panentheism in patristic theology and in Orthodox iconography and literature, see also Mousalimas, "The Divine in Nature."
24. Ware, "God Immanent Yet Transcendent," p. 159.

shrines made by man, nor is he served by human hands, as though he needed anything, since he himself gives to all men life and breath and everything. And he made from one every nation of men to live on all the face of the earth, having determined allotted periods and the boundaries of their habitation" (vv. 24-26). Could one describe God's majesty, otherness, and transcendence in more stark terms? However, in the same context, there is the remarkable statement, a biblical "definition" of panentheism: "Yet he is not far from each one of us, for 'In him we live and move and have our being'; as even some of your poets have said, 'For we are indeed his offspring'" (vv. 27b-28).[25]

Consider approaches to God in Christian history that represent classical panentheism. On the one hand, Eastern Christian tradition makes every effort to ascertain the total "incomprehensibility" and hence transcendence of God, lest the majestic God be made a function of human handling.[26] On the other hand, it elevates spiritual experience, vision, "ascent" to God as the main way of knowing God. That "knowledge" can only be had of God who is "near" us. A major conceptual device in the East to preserve the freedom of God in his transcendence, yet affirm God's "withinness" in the world, is the Palamite distinction between the "essence" and "energies" of God.[27] "In his essence God is infinitely transcendent, utterly beyond all created being, beyond all understanding and all participation from the human side. But in his energies — which are nothing else than God himself in action — God is inexhaustibly immanent, maintaining all things in being, animating them, making each of them a sacrament of his dynamic presence."[28] While Palamas established the energy/essence distinction, it was already assumed by the Fathers.[29]

Such mystical, experience-based, spirituality-driven conceptions of God appear also in the West in theologians such as John Scotus Eriugena and Nicholas of Cusa, as well as in the mystical tradition of the fourteenth and fifteenth centuries, including Meister Eckhart and Thomas à Kempis, let alone a number of medieval female mystics such as Hildegard of Bingen and

25. For a brief consideration of many of these passages, see Ware, "God Immanent Yet Transcendent," pp. 157-58. For a highly useful discussion, see Mousalimas, "Immanence and Transcendence," pp. 375-80.

26. See Gregory of Nyssa, *The Life of Moses* 2.163.

27. See further, Meyendorff, "Introduction" to Palamas, *The Triads*, pp. 20-22; for Palamas's own exposition, see pp. 93-111.

28. Ware, "God Immanent Yet Transcendent," p. 160; for the details of "Palamite Panentheism," as Ware calls it (p. 165), see this essay by Ware.

29. See further, Louth, "Cosmic Vision of Saint Maximos the Confessor," pp. 184-96; Nesteruk, "Universe as Hypostatic Inherence," pp. 169-85.

Catherine of Siena.[30] John Scotus Eriugena concentrated so much on the divine immanence that some have called him not only a panentheist but also a pantheist;[31] the latter designation, however, is misleading. A robust panentheist he was in many regards as he emphasized that the divine nature embraces everything; apart from God or outside of God there is nothing. "God is Being unlimited and undifferentiated; the Word is Being circumscribed and divided."[32] "And not only is God in everything, he is identical with all that is, for God and the creature are not two but one and the same."[33] Perhaps not surprisingly, with his dynamic view of the pantheistic immanence of God, Scotus envisioned a type of evolution. The universe is not static or at rest; it is continually developing.[34] Coming from a different perspective and agenda and time, the great American preacher Jonathan Edwards seems to have affirmed a type of panentheism as he remarked: "God is the sum of all being, and there is no being without his being; all things are in him, and he in all."[35]

The liberal Schleiermacher represented an extreme form of panentheism as he surmised, "There is no God without the world, just as there is no world without God."[36] Behind Schleiermacher's panentheism is of course his radically immanentist view of God as the expression of the feeling of "absolute dependence."[37] What Schleiermacher did in theology, the idealists, Schelling, Fichte, and Hegel,[38] and the Jewish monist Spinoza,[39] did in philosophy, leading up to panentheism that has lost touch with "a personal God." Both Schleiermacher's and the philosophers' approaches differ so radically from the balanced Christian panentheism that they cannot be taken as guides.

Cooper claims that with some qualifications "the history of panentheism is largely the history of Neoplatonism."[40] This statement calls for two comments. First, by the same token it can be said that the history of classical theism

---

30. For some aspects of these theologies, see Cooper, *Panentheism*, chap. 3. For easy access to selected original texts of these theologians, see Madges, *God and the World*.

31. Fortman, ed., *Theology of God*, p. 154.

32. John Scotus Eriugena, *De divisione naturae* 1.12; 3.17.

33. Fortman, ed., *Theology of God*, p. 154, with reference to John Scotus Eriugena, *De divisione naturae* 3.17.

34. Fortman, ed., *Theology of God*, pp. 154-55.

35. Edwards, "Entry 880.1," as cited in Cooper, *Panentheism*, p. 74.

36. As quoted in Cooper, *Panentheism*, p. 84.

37. For the classic statement, see Schleiermacher, *Christian Faith*, §50, especially p. 194.

38. See Cooper, *Panentheism*, chap. 4.

39. For a careful discussion, see P. Clayton, *Problem of God*, chap. 7.

40. Cooper, *Panentheism*, p. 19; for the investigation of Platonic and other ancient philosophical background, see chap. 2.

is to a large extent a function of dialogue with and influence from Platonic philosophy, including Neoplatonism as in Augustine, and, later, Aristotelian philosophy. Stating that is not an assessment of the legitimacy of — or lack thereof — either tradition. Second, while Hellenistic philosophy certainly left its mark on panentheism, the resurgence and shaping of panentheism, especially in its more current forms, are a function of more recent worldview changes.

The Panentheistic Turn in Contemporary Theology

Among twentieth-century theologians, the turn to panentheism has come to full fruition. The most radical form is that of American process theology.[41] A more classical approach is that of the Roman Catholic priest-paleontologist Teilhard de Chardin, whose cosmic evolutionary spirituality made every effort to harmonize with twentieth-century natural sciences. Mindful of charges of pantheism, he made every effort to affirm the transcendence of God.[42]

The most widely debated panentheistic *theological* turn is Moltmann's "trinitarian panentheism."[43] A key motif is the resistance to the classical notion of God's impassibility. Instead, he proposes a robust view of "the crucified God" who is deeply involved in the pains and joys of his people and the world.[44] Not surprisingly, the doctrine of creation follows from and supports Moltmann's panentheism. For him creation is the fruit of the loving God's longing for his other and for that other's free response to the divine love. That is why the idea of the world is inherent in the nature of God himself from eternity.[45] Hence, there is a reciprocal relationship between the world and God,[46] which will culminate in the eschaton in the mutual indwelling of God and creation.[47]

41. One groundbreaking theological presentation, based on Whitehead's process philosophy, was Hartshorne, *Divine Relativity*; for an accessible survey, see Cooper, *Panentheism*, chap. 7.

42. Teilhard de Chardin, "Outline of a Dialectic of Spirit" (1946), pp. 143-51; p. 143 has the heading "The Phenomenon of Man and the Existence of a Transcendent God."

43. So called by Bauckham, *Theology of Jürgen Moltmann*, p. 17. On the comparison of classical theism and pantheism, see Moltmann, *Trinity and the Kingdom*, pp. 105-8.

44. Moltmann, *The Crucified God*.

45. Moltmann, *Trinity and the Kingdom*, p. 138.

46. Moltmann, *Trinity and the Kingdom*, p. 98, among others.

47. Moltmann, *Coming of God*.

Understandably, panentheism "strikes a chord with many feminist thinkers, who regard traditional models that emphasize God's distance and absolute power as being overtly patriarchal. Panentheism, by contrast, emphasizes God's connectedness and responsiveness to the world."[48] Elizabeth Johnson's theological vision — based on values of "mutual relations," "radical equality," and "community in diversity" — builds on God as loving communion, as relational, while utterly transcendent, also intimately related to everything that exists. The triune God constantly sustains life and resists destructive powers of nonbeing and violence.[49] This vision of the mutual indwelling of God also links with the metaphor of friendship, which has a close affinity with women's experience of closeness and sharing.[50] Similarly, panentheism has great appeal to eco-feminists.[51] Moreover, a number of other liberation theologians deeply concerned about suffering, injustice, and inequality in the world have turned to panentheism. Cone reinterprets God's immanence in terms of divine presence in the midst of the struggle for liberation, and transcendence as God's unlimited capacity to bring about changes rather than God's being " 'above' or 'beyond.' "[52] Similarly, Gutiérrez builds on a robust panentheistic theology by speaking of the divine presence not only in the world and among human beings in general, but particularly among the poor, marginalized, and exploited ones.[53]

While conservative-evangelical theology by and large has been quite suspicious of the panentheistic turn, one strand, named "open theism" or "free will theism,"[54] has harshly critiqued classical theism's "pagan legacy"[55] that ignores relationality,[56] responsiveness, and communion in the doctrine of God and instead presents a view of God as "a solitary narcissistic being, who suffers from his own completeness."[57] As an alternative, open theists introduce God as loving parent, responsive, open to the future, and in constant dialogue with

---

48. G. Peterson, "Whither Panentheism?" p. 396. For a useful discussion, see Frankenberry, "Classical Theism, Panentheism, and Pantheism," pp. 29-46.

49. E. Johnson, *She Who Is*, pp. 228-30; see also Baker-Fletcher, *Dancing with God*.

50. E. Johnson, *She Who Is*, pp. 233-36.

51. E. Johnson, *Women, Earth, and Creator Spirit*; Ruether, *Gaia and God*; McFague, *Body of God*. Among male theologians, an important panentheistic-ecological proposal comes from Fox, *Coming of the Cosmic Christ*.

52. Cone, *Black Theology of Liberation*, pp. 76-78, at 77.

53. Gutiérrez, *A Theology of Liberation*, pp. 156-57.

54. See Pinnock, *Openness of God*; Pinnock, *Most Moved Mover*.

55. Pinnock, *Most Moved Mover*, p. 68.

56. See Woodruff, "Examining Problems and Assumptions."

57. Pinnock, *Most Moved Mover*, p. 6, quoting Kasper, *The God of Jesus Christ*, p. ?

creatures and creation.[58] Rightly open theism has been deemed to seek a middle way between classical theism and process theism's extreme panentheism.[59]

Particularly deep interest in panentheism is shown by a growing number of theologians who dialogue with natural sciences.[60] The biochemist-priest Arthur Peacocke reminds us of the importance for the doctrine of God of the radically changed "scientific perspective of the world, especially the living world, [which] inexorably impresses upon us a *dynamic* picture of the world of entities, structures, and processes involved in continuous and incessant change and in process without ceasing."[61] In other words, the current scientific account of the natural world, "both cosmological and terrestrial . . . [yields] the seamless character of the web that has been spun on the loom of time: at no point do modern natural scientists have to invoke any nonnatural causes to explain their observations and inferences about the past." This outlook seems "to require a much more intimate involvement of God in the actual processes of the world as described by science than has hitherto been commonly proposed."[62] Natural sciences have "provoked a renewed emphasis on the immanence of God as creator 'in, with, and under' creative, natural processes of the world unveiled by the sciences."[63]

What Kind of Panentheism?

The claim that "We are all panentheists now"[64] is neither interesting nor useful unless one specifies what is meant by that nomenclature.[65] Routinely the definition in *Oxford Dictionary of the Christian Church* is taken as the point of departure: "The belief that the Being of God includes and penetrates the whole universe, so that every part of it exists in Him, but (as against panthe-

---

58. For details, see Pinnock, *Most Moved Mover*, pp. 79-104.
59. P. Clayton, "Kenotic Trinitarian Panentheism," p. 251.
60. For an early contribution, see K. Heim, *Christian Faith and Natural Science* (1949).
61. Peacocke, "Introduction," p. xx.
62. Peacocke, "Introduction," p. xx.
63. Peacocke, "Introduction," p. xx.
64. G. Peterson, "Whither Panentheism?" p. 395.
65. The term "panentheism," as is routinely noted, was coined in the beginning of the nineteenth century by Karl C. H. Krause, a contemporary of Hegel, another idealist philosopher. When parsed, the term of course comes from *pan* (all) + *en* (in) + *theos* (God), i.e., "all in God." A massive, richly documented analysis is provided by Brierley, "Naming a Quiet Revolution," pp. 1-15. Another useful and constructive entry from the same compendium is Gregersen, "Three Varieties of Panentheism," pp. 19-35.

ism) that His Being is more than, and is not exhausted by, the universe."[66] This definition adds the helpful note that what exists in God is not only the "world" as in our globe, but the whole universe. It is necessary in the beginning of the third millennium to remind theology of the need to include in the concept of "creation" and "world" the whole vast universe. As is frequently noted, much hinges upon how to understand the *en* (in) in the term "pan-en-theism." To take up an obvious example: Does *en* mean that God literally "contains" creation in a space-like manner? Christian tradition of course says *no,* since that would frustrate God's transcendence by defining God according to the same spatial dimensions as our world.[67]

The term "classical" in this project means to say that the panentheism advocated here is not a new phenomenon in Christian theology but rather is based on biblical and theological tradition. While the world in some sense exists in God and God is intimately and thoroughly present to creation, God is not contained by the creation. God is "more," much more. Hence, the dipolar panentheism of (American) process theology is rejected as it tends to subsume God within the world process even if God is bigger and mightier than other "actual entities."[68] Furthermore, I agree with Pannenberg, contrary to Moltmann,[69] that creation is not necessary. God does not "need" the world; creation is not necessary to the Deity because inner-trinitarian relations can be understood as actions; because he created the world out of his absolute freedom, the loving God cannot not be related to creation.[70] In other words, while creation cannot exist without the Creator, God can exist without creation.[71]

A common way of understanding the mutual relationship between the Creator and creature today intuits the world as "God's body."[72] As widely as that idea is currently affirmed, it was not common at all in tradition. While the present volumes robustly speak of the "divine embodiment" in relation to

---

66. *Oxford Dictionary of the Christian Church,* ed. F. L. Cross and E. A. Livingstone, 3rd ed. (Oxford: Oxford University Press, 1997), p. 1027.

67. John of Damascus, *On the Orthodox Faith* 13.11.

68. Birch and Cobb, *Liberation of Life,* p. 196.

69. Moltmann, *Trinity and the Kingdom,* p. 138.

70. Pannenberg, *ST* 2:1.

71. Cf. Ward, *Divine Action,* chap. 1.

72. Process theologians at large support the idea of the world as God's body. For informed, useful, brief statements, see P. Clayton's "The Case for Christian Panentheism," pp. 201-8, and "The Panentheistic Turn in Christian Theology," pp. 289-93. Among the eco-feminists, the most vocal has been Sallie McFague; see her *Body of God.* For liberationists, see Boff, *Trinity and Society,* pp. 118-22. Ward ("The World as the Body of God," pp. 62-72) looks at the topic from the perspective of Hinduism, particularly the Vedanta theology of Ramanuja.

incarnation,[73] the idea of creation as God's body strikes one as problematic for obvious reasons: "[T]here are things beyond human bodies, but it is not clear what, if anything, can be said to be 'beyond' the cosmos. Another weak point is that the parts of human bodies do not have conscious relations with the person who is their whole, unlike parts of the cosmos and God. Again, whereas it is held that God has perfect knowledge of the cosmos, human beings do not have perfect knowledge of their bodies."[74] Yet another problem with the idea of the universe as God's body is the implication that the world belongs to the same ontological order with God.[75]

Philip Clayton, who supports the idea of the world as God's body, is able to avoid the danger of placing God in the same ontological order — in other words, he can secure the transcendence of God — with the help of the finite/infinite distinction. Even if, for example, it be shown that the "space" of the universe is infinite or that the "number" of entities, say, atoms, is infinite, the "difference in nature or being" (between finite and infinite) makes it possible to think of God as "containing" the infinite space and number without being equated with them. Rather than either/or logic, panentheism pushes theology to think in terms of both/and: "To think of the world as within God and at the same time as different from God is to think in terms of a both/and: there is *both* identification or inclusion *and* distinction of God and world." Even physical matter cannot be said to exist on its own; it is dependent on God, not to mention living beings.[76]

Peacocke, who oscillates between embracing and rejecting the mind-body metaphor as a way of speaking about the God-world relation, also offers three important qualifications whose value materially goes beyond the use of this metaphor. Having stated that "God is *internally* present to all the world's entities, structures, and processes in a way analogous to the way we as persons are present and act in our bodies," he argues that whereas God creates the world, we humans do not, and that whereas God is omniscient, we humans know only so much of what happens in our bodies. Finally, "in using human personal agency as analogous to the way God interacts with the world, we are not implying the 'world is God's body' nor that God is 'a person' — rather that God is more coherently thought of as 'at least personal,' indeed as 'more than personal' . . . for there are many essential aspects of

---

73. See further, *Christ and Reconciliation*, vol. 1 of the present series.
74. Brierley, "Naming a Quiet Revolution," pp. 6-7.
75. Peacocke, *Paths from Science towards God*, p. 109.
76. P. Clayton, *God and Contemporary Science*, pp. 90-91, at 91.

God's nature which cannot be subsumed under the categories applicable to human persons."[77]

In sum: whether one is fond of the mind-body analogy (as Clayton is and Peacock seems not to be), the qualifications and clarifications provided by the two theologians help preserve the legitimate intuitions of classical theology, namely, the freedom and "beyondness" of the transcendent, majestic God.

Here the constructive side of Tillich's often-misunderstood opposition to the talk about God's "existence" should be registered as an aid to classical panentheism. He rejects both "supranaturalism" — which "separates God as a being, the highest being, from all other beings, alongside and above which he has his existence," but by doing so confines God to the space-time continuum and substance ontology — and "naturalism," which "identifies God with the universe, with its essence or with special powers within it," and which, despite being much closer to Tillich's own intuitions, fails in that "it denies the infinite distance between the whole of finite things and their infinite ground, with the consequence that the term 'God' becomes interchangeable with the term 'universe.'" Instead theology should seek a third way, which indeed is no stranger to the best of tradition from Augustine to Aquinas to the Reformers, as in it God "is the infinite and unconditional power of being or, in the most radical abstraction, he is being-itself. In this respect God is neither alongside things nor even 'above' them; he is nearer to them than they are to themselves. He is their creative ground, here and now, always and everywhere." This is what Tillich called the "self-transcendent" and "ecstatic" notion of God.[78]

John Polkinghorne has argued that while he is not comfortable with the term "panentheism," he envisions that kind of mutual indwelling in eschatology. The main reason for his reluctance to use the term — apart from great conceptual and linguistic problems — has to do with its potential mixing of the divine (uncreated) and created existence ontologically, even though he also readily acknowledges the need to revise classical theism's undue emphasis on transcendence.[79] I have two comments on Polkinghorne's proposal. First, while I fully share his concerns, I also think that the panentheism advocated in this project can avoid them. Second, the more I read his writings, the less I see a difference between his theology and classical panentheism.

What about the transcendence of God? Despite all the assertions to

---

77. Peacocke, "Articulating God's Presence," pp. 150-51, at 151.

78. Tillich, *ST* 2:5-10, at 6, 7.

79. Polkinghorne, *Science and the Trinity*, pp. 94-98; *Faith, Science, and Understanding*, pp. 90-94; *God of Hope*, pp. 114-15.

the contrary, many may wonder if panentheism in any form leads to the virtual dismissal of the divine transcendence. An important recent study by the postcolonial feminist Mayra Rivera titled *The Touch of Transcendence*, which inspired the heading for this subsection, attempts a careful discussion of the various meanings of the notion of transcendence for the doctrine of God. Even though the current project does not fully espouse the kind of panentheism she advocates,[80] it is also indebted to and learns from this analysis. Along with many postcolonialists, feminists, and other liberationists, Rivera reminds us that "[t]ranscendence is often associated with hierarchical distance," God's distance from the world. "'Divine transcendence' thus indicates God's aloofness, separation, independence, and immateriality — in short, his super/iority." Behind these misconceptions may lie the general Western tendency to prefer sameness over alterity and thus conceive otherness as separation. This way of conceiving transcendence may easily orient religious life away from the pursuit of social transformation, instead promoting the individualistic aspiration to attain a positive otherworldly existence.[81]

Yet another way of conceiving the transcendence-immanence distinction considers the matrix of human relationships. Famously the Jewish philosopher Levinas has defined "immanence" in relation to the way human beings encounter the different as that which is "self-sufficient, self-same, solipsistic; it tolerates no Other. . . . Immanence means sameness," whereas transcendence "is the opening of sameness to its Other. Transcendence breaks the totality of any system — conceptual or political, earthly or heavenly — appearing concretely 'in the face of the Other.'"[82] Incorporating human relations into the fabric of the transcendence-immanence distinction is not a cheap way to reduce the divine otherness to human "immanence"; it is rather to acknowledge the obvious, that "[t]he metaphors and images used in discourses of interhuman transcendence and in those of divine transcendence converge and intertwine."

Liberationists of various stripes have protested against allegedly politically, socially, and economically innocent and "neutral" notions of divine transcendence that "would identify God with the status quo." Rather than "reducing faith to political action, thereby eliminating the transcendence of God,"[83] "Latin American liberation theology, which is based on the search

80. Rivera, *Touch of Transcendence*, p. 3.

81. Rivera, *Touch of Transcendence*, pp. ix, 1. For a similar important critique, see Ellacuria, "The Historicity of Christian Salvation," p. 254.

82. As paraphrased by Rivera, *Touch of Transcendence*, p. 59, on the basis of Levinas, *Totality and Infinity*, p. 24.

83. Goizueta, "Locating the Absolutely Absolute Other," p. 183. Milbank has argued that

for the materiality of transcendence, knows how God is to be found in the presence of the untouchables. . . . [Transcendence] is God touching its own limits in the untouchables."[84] For liberationists, the transcendence of God is not only an affirmation of the otherness of God but also the capacity of God to interrupt and shake the status quo — which, even in the name of religion, continues to support unjust structures — and to bring about liberation for those who are dismissed, ignored, and undermined.

Thus, a relational and more inclusive understanding of God's transcendence is not an effort to water down the otherness of God. Barth's intuition of the "wholly other" nature of the divine[85] was correct to the point that he tried "to express what cannot be represented: the ineffability of God. This paradox is inescapable."[86] However, the way he constructed transcendence not only followed tradition but also unduly radicalized the absence of God from the world and even their opposition to each other. This is materially similar to how the British Radical Orthodox theologians juxtapose transcendence with "immanentism" understood solely as secularism or "void."[87] Milbank is right of course in his persistent contention that when in modernity — and in his understanding, even in postmodernity — the world was "accorded full reality, meaning and value in itself," resulting in the emergence of a spatial "plane of immanence," the end result was the loss of purpose and teleology as divinely sanctioned.[88] The problem with Radical Orthodoxy's "refusal of secularism," however, is its insistence on the absence of God from the world (the "secular").[89]

Part of the tradition's misguided way of imagining transcendence involves the linking of it with "immateriality," thus making embodiment, physicality, and the "earthly" less valuable than or even opposed to the higher realm of "spirituality."[90] Incarnation alone, the divine embodiment, would interrupt such conceptions. Nevertheless, even the conception of God as "spirit" is not a statement against physicality. Rather than using spatial concepts, the proper

---

liberation theology replaces transcendence with social processes and has advocated "immanent principles of secularization and politics." "Founding the Supernatural," pp. 42-43.

84. Althaus-Reid, "El Tocado (Le Toucher)," p. 394; I am indebted to Rivera, *Touch of Transcendence*, p. 135.

85. For classic statements, see Barth, *The Epistle to the Romans*, pp. 10, 31; *CD* II/1, p. 541; for the "Word" as wholly other, see *CD* I/1, p. 164.

86. Rivera, *Touch of Transcendence*, p. 17.

87. For the programmatic statement, see introduction to Milbank, Pickstock, and Ward, *Radical Orthodoxy*, p. 3.

88. Milbank, *Being Reconciled*, p. 194.

89. Similarly Rivera, *Touch of Transcendence*, p. 35 and passim.

90. Rivera, *Touch of Transcendence*, p. 7.

way to conceive of transcendence is relational.[91] In other words, grounding creation in God is not to subsume the divine life in the immanent but rather to give meaning and "ground" to creation itself.[92]

Before focusing on a detailed investigation of the trinitarian contours of the Christian doctrine of God that helps us sharpen and clarify the meaning and implications of classical panentheism — as well as the investigation of God's activity in the world, known in classical theology under the rubric "the attributes of God" — this chapter concludes by considering resources that contemporary philosophy, science, and theology offer to the doctrine of God. These include the rediscovery of the biblical narrative of God, the replacement of substance ontology with relationality, and the turn to the ontology of future. These all support classical panentheism and also help balance and correct classical theism.

Contemporary Resources for a Reconceived Doctrine of God

The Dynamic Narrative of God

The book title *A Pilgrim God for a Pilgrim People*[93] illustrates the dynamic way the Bible presents the narrative of God. The Bible does provide us with a narrative, a story of God that consists of testimonies, parables, metaphors, disputes, and so forth, which are diverse, which sometimes stand in dynamic continuity with us, and which are authentically human. Systematic theologians should be mindful of the warnings of OT theologians not to oversystematize the dynamic biblical narrative.[94] The American Walter Brueggemann describes the "doctrine" of God through the lens of "Israel's core testimony" in terms of testimonies of God's mighty deeds, in metaphors of what God is like, and in names of God; the British American John Goldingay lays out the main movements of the story of Yahweh in the OT from "God began" to "God promised" to "God delivered" to "God preserved."[95] Rather than attempting an abstract, formal presentation of God, the biblical narrative pushes constructive theology to envision God in personal, dynamic, elusive, and emerging terms. Hence,

---

91. For a detailed discussion of "relational transcendence," see chap. 5 in Rivera, *Touch of Transcendence*.

92. Cf. Rivera, *Touch of Transcendence*, p. 2.

93. Carroll, *Pilgrim God*.

94. Goldingay, *Israel's Gospel*, p. 32; Brueggemann, *Theology of the Old Testament*, p. 117.

95. Goldingay, *Israel's Gospel*, p. 32.

the God of the Bible comes to be known "economically," in the context of his dealings with the world and life experiences of humanity. Even when seemingly more tightly formulated descriptions appear, these are set in the context of the economy of salvation and personal dealings with God: "The LORD, the LORD, a God merciful and gracious, slow to anger, and abounding in steadfast love and faithfulness, keeping steadfast love for thousands, forgiving iniquity and transgression and sin, but who will by no means clear the guilty, visiting the iniquity of the fathers upon the children and the children's children, to the third and the fourth generation" (Exod. 34:6-7). Similarly to the OT, the way men and women get to know the Father,[96] through and in Jesus' ministry, is related to the very experiences and concerns of everyday life:

> God shows himself to be Father by caring for his creatures (Matt. 6:26; cf. Luke 12:30). He causes his sun to shine and his rain to fall on the bad as well as the good (Matt. 5:45). He is a model of the love for enemies which Jesus taught (5:44-45). He is ready to forgive those who turn to him (Luke 15:7, 10, 11ff.), ask for his forgiveness (11:4), and forgive others (Matt. 11:25; cf. 6:14-15; 18:23-35). He lets himself be invoked as Father, and like earthly fathers, and even more than they, he grants good things to his children when they ask (Matt. 7:11).[97]

In sum, the biblical narrative of God — dynamic, experience-based, open-ended, developing, contextual — is a theology "from below," economic, rather than one "from above," based on abstract speculations and formulae. It is relational and communal as the God of the Bible is an inviting God. The narrative and responsive theology of God in Scripture thus supports the project of classical panentheism.

Relationality

In the twentieth century, the relational view has replaced substance ontology.[98] But in Christian theology, relationality is no new phenomenon. Only consider Trinity and incarnation.[99]

---

96. See further, M. Thompson, *Promise of the Father.*
97. Pannenberg, *ST* 1:259.
98. See Polkinghorne, ed., *The Trinity and the Entangled World.*
99. Shults, *Reforming Theological Anthropology,* p. 11; chap. 1 contains the history from

Greek philosophy was more interested in oneness, sameness, and substance than in diversity, alterity, and relationality. While there were different opinions about what lies "behind" the substance, the focus was on the unchanging substance as opposed to "accidents," which change (such as the color of the table). Aristotle's *Categories* lists the category of "relative," among the ten categories, headed by "substance" (1b25).[100] Whereas substance is "primary," relationality is not only "secondary" but also accidental and less real.[101] While Aristotle's scheme was not universally followed — both Plato's and Plotinus's lists of categories were a bit more appreciative of relationality and difference[102] — it is also true that substance ontology soon became the norm for Christian theology. Only with the rise of modern thinkers did substance ontology come under criticism and slowly give way to a more relational understanding. The problem for John Locke was that, regarding "substance, we have no idea of what it is, but only a confused, obscure one of what it does" (it "supports accidents").[103] Similarly David Hume, in his 1748 *Enquiry concerning Human Understanding*, could only speak of "substance" in terms of convention and habit. The decisive move happened when Kant, in his detailed list of categories, included "of relation" along with quantity, quality, and modality. Under relationality are "subsistence," "causality," and "community."[104] In other words, here substance is made a subcategory of relation. Hegel agreed with Kant, speaking of "absolute relation" as the primary, as well as doing away with the whole substance/accident distinction.[105] The American philosopher Charles Sanders Peirce further highlighted the importance of relationality and continuous process rather than substance and atomism.[106] Whitehead and other process theologians, of course, made relationality a key resource. In contemporary systematic theology, relationality has been adopted as the standard, as evident, for example, in Pannenberg and Moltmann.

Relationality helps conceive of the nature and activity of God in a dy-

---

Aristotle to contemporary times. His *Reforming the Doctrine of God*, pp. 5-9, includes a concise discussion. My brief discussion here is deeply indebted to Shults.

100. *Complete Works of Aristotle*; I follow the standard form of referencing.

101. Aristotle, *Metaphysics*, in *Works*, 1088a21-25.

102. Plotinus, *Sixth Ennead*, tractate 2, #16.

103. Locke, *Essay concerning Human Understanding* (1689), bk. 2, chap. 13, #19.

104. Kant, *Critique of Pure Reason*, p. 64.

105. For details and references, see Shults, *Reforming Theological Anthropology*, pp. 22-25.

106. See further, Peirce, "On a New List of Categories."

namic way, going back to the testimonies in Scriptures.[107] Among contemporary constructive theologians, consider LaCugna: drawing from various sources such as the personalist philosophy of John MacMurray, Eastern Orthodox communion theology, Latin American liberationists, and feminist theologies,[108] she develops a thoroughgoing trinitarian "theology of relationship" in which "the 'essence' of God is relational."[109] Hers is "an ontology of relation" based on the idea of personhood as communion, in-relation-to the other(s).[110] While the Cappadocians were the trailblazers for communion theology with their idea of *"relation* or *person (hypostasis)* as the mode of God's *ousia,"*[111] LaCugna rightly reminds us that not only the Christian East but also the West has affirmed communion as the nature of ultimate reality.[112]

The Category of Infinity

While the modern philosophers helped rediscover the significance of the concept of infinity, "[t]he concept of the actual Infinite has had a firm place in the Christian doctrine of God since Gregory of Nyssa."[113] The discussion of God's "attributes" will utilize the category of infinity as the major conceptual tool, as it best expresses the unlimited majesty and immensity of the divine essence and being. When speaking of God's infinity, however, one has to be mindful of the obvious fallacy, that of understanding infinity as something that is merely "more" than the being and capacities of created beings. Augustine was trapped in this dilemma for a while, until finally he "awoke" to the insight that God is "infinite . . . in another way."[114] This "another way" of divine infinity "moves beyond the idea of God as a being that is simply extensively greater than creatures."[115]

For early Christian theology to come to the right intuition of infinity, it

---

107. Shults, *Reforming the Doctrine of God,* p. 10.

108. All these approaches are discussed in LaCugna, *God for Us,* pp. 255-88.

109. So also Pannenberg, *ST* 1:334; see also pp. 335, 366-67.

110. LaCugna, *God for Us,* p. 243; so also p. 383; and LaCugna, "Philosophers and Theologians on the Trinity," p. 177.

111. LaCugna, *God for Us,* p. 243.

112. LaCugna, *God for Us,* pp. 244-46.

113. Pannenberg, *Metaphysics and the Idea of God,* p. 34.

114. *Confessions* 7.14. I am indebted to Shults, *Reforming the Doctrine of God,* p. 98.

115. Shults, *Reforming the Doctrine of God,* p. 98; in this context Shults quotes another saying of Augustine from his *On the Trinity* 5.2: God is "great without quantity."

had to separate its conception from that of Greek philosophers.[116] "Through reflection on the biblical ideas of creation, incarnation, and regeneration, a 'positive' view of the infinite emerged: a 'perfect' Infinity that is qualitatively distinct from the finite, yet encompasses, permeates and draws the finite into existence."[117] The urgent reason patristic theology had to conceive of infinity in this way was to avoid placing the divine essence under finitude and temporality. Hence, the concepts of "simplicity" and "immutability." Saint Irenaeus, when speaking of the divine *Plērōma*, said that God "should contain all things in His immensity, and should be contained by no one. . . . But if there is anything beyond Him He is not then the Plērōma of all."[118] Rightly, "[h]ere limitlessness (in-finity) is understood not simply as a lack of limit, or indefinite extension, but as a metaphysical reality whose 'immensity' embraces all things."[119]

The Eastern Fathers' emphasis on apophatic theology is indebted to the right notion of infinity, as expressed by Gregory of Nyssa: "it is not possible that that which is by nature infinite should be comprehended in any conception expressed by words";[120] indeed, "[t]he divine by its very nature is infinite, enclosed by no boundary."[121] Brilliantly, then, the contemporary Orthodox theologian Lossky concludes that this is nothing less than recognizing that God "transcends the opposition between the transcendent and the immanent."[122] The feminist Kathryn Tanner has added an interesting caveat to a contemporary understanding of infinity. She speaks of "contrastive" and "noncontrastive" accounts of divine transcendence. Whereas the former inversely contrasts transcendence and immanence, meaning that the more focus placed on one, the less on the other, the latter "suggests an extreme of divine involvement with the world — a divine involvement in the form of a productive agency extending to everything that is in equally direct manner."[123] In other words, the "noncontrastive" approach saves God from becoming one

---

116. For Plato and Aristotle, infinity was defined as that which is "without form or limit," which in their thinking could not be linked with God, who was taken to be "pure form" over against "matter." See Shults, *Reforming the Doctrine of God*, p. 99.

117. Shults, *Reforming the Doctrine of God*, p. 99.

118. *Against Heresies* 2.1, cited in Shults, *Reforming the Doctrine of God*, p. 100.

119. Shults, *Reforming the Doctrine of God*, p. 100.

120. *Against Eunomius* 3.5.

121. *Life of Moses*, cited in Shults, *Reforming the Doctrine of God*, p. 102. A further reference is given in Brighman, "Apophatic Theology and Divine Infinity," pp. 97-114.

122. Lossky, *In the Image and Likeness of God*, p. 29, cited in Shults, *Reforming the Doctrine of God*, p. 102.

123. Tanner, *God and Creation*, p. 46.

being among others and instead supports divine transcendence simultaneously with robust presence and activity everywhere — values dear to classical panentheism.

The category of infinity — what Shults names "intensive infinity" — combined with relationality, offers contemporary theology superb resources: on the one hand, safeguarding the "limitless" (infinite) "otherness," "beyondness," transcendence of God, including God's "attributes," without being trapped in "extensive" or "numerical" terms, and, on the other hand, "relating" — literally! — God to everything in the universe that God has created, including the lives of the creatures. Dualism and the "either/or" logic of substance ontology can be avoided. For example, God is both transcendent and immanent. God is both distinct and related. Likewise, these resources also help theology to think carefully and more promisingly than in the past about God's relation to time and space (discussed in the doctrine of creation). Furthermore, it is clear that these resources greatly aid the science-theology dialogue.

11. One God as Communion of Persons

The Role of the Trinity in Christian Theology and Doctrine of God

Why Did the Trinity Get Sidetracked in Tradition?

"When I say God, I mean Father, Son, and Holy Spirit" — is the classic saying of one of the Cappadocians, Saint Gregory of Nazianzus.[1] Commenting on it, Orthodox Bishop Kallistos rightly says that "the doctrine of the Trinity is not just one possible way of thinking about God. It is the only way. The one God of the Christian church cannot be conceived except as Trinity."[2] But if so, "[w]hy are most Christians in the West . . . really only 'monotheists' where the experience and practice of their faith is concerned?"[3]

Indeed, what happened in the history of the Christian *doctrine* of the Trinity contributed to its marginalization and its becoming both abstract and removed from liturgy, spirituality, and life in general. The way the doctrine of the Trinity evolved in the post-Augustinian tradition in the West, influenced by Neoplatonism, *implied* that the oneness of God was the defining issue while the Trinity may or may not be integral to the doctrine.[4] This implication meant that the presentation of Christian theology began from the one God and then

---

1. *Oration* 45.4, cited in Ware, "The Holy Trinity," p. 107.
2. Ware, "The Holy Trinity," p. 107.
3. Moltmann, *Trinity and the Kingdom*, p. 1; see also Rahner, *The Trinity*, pp. 10-11.
4. Pannenberg (*ST* 1:282) notes that Peter Lombard of the early Middle Ages is an exception. In his *Sentences*, book 1, Lombard started with the Trinity and then moved to consider Trinity and unity (1:282).

went on to the God triune both in medieval[5] and Reformation[6] theology and beyond. While some Protestant theologians such as A. Calov argued that the Trinity is indispensable for the presentation of the Christian doctrine of God, "[t]here was a feeling, nevertheless, that the OT justifies a prior presentation of God as the Supreme Being (Ex. 3:14) and also of his attributes. . . . The doctrine of the Trinity was then added to the existing idea of the one God as the specifically Christian revelation. It could thus act as an appendix to the general doctrine of God."[7] In modern Western theology the marginalization of the doctrine reached its zenith in Schleiermacher, as routinely noted.[8] Often cited as well is Kant's chiding remark that the doctrine has "no practical relevance at all, even if we think we understand it," and we do not, since "it transcends all our concepts."[9]

One important reason for the marginalization had to do with the theological method that began to change over time. Unlike earlier theology, which discerned the Trinity in salvation history as unfolding in the biblical testimonies, later theology became more interested in the "inner" life of God instead of the "economy" of salvation, making the Trinity an abstract speculation rather than reading it from the works of God. Hegel's philosophical, idealistic approach to the Trinity is the hallmark of this tradition.[10]

The Trinity's place in theology and faith also has to do with a widely debated question in tradition, namely, whether the Trinity is a matter of faith and revelation alone or whether it can be inferred with the help of human reason. A number of important voices (Augustine, Aquinas, Gilbert de La Porrée) regarded the Trinity as a matter of faith even if the existence of God could be partially known by reason and there are vestiges of the Trinity in the "human soul."[11] However, tradition was not always consistent with a denial of the rational basis of the Trinity. Aquinas derives the trinitarian statements from the concept of one God. How can this be explained? He puts this question to himself and responds that indeed revelation is needed but that human reason can argue from

---

5. While Aquinas discusses the Trinity first in his *Summa contra Gentiles* 4.1-26 (pp. 35-146), the main discussion is in *ST* 1.27-43 (following unity in 1-16).

6. Pannenberg, *ST* 1:281, with examples from Melanchthon and Calvin.

7. Pannenberg, *ST* 1:281-82.

8. Schleiermacher, *Christian Faith*, pp. 738-51; for a different judgment, see Grenz, *Rediscovering the Triune God*, pp. 17-24.

9. Kant, *Conflict of the Faculties*, pp. 65, 67.

10. For informed discussion, see Grenz, *Rediscovering the Triune God*, pp. 24-32; Pannenberg, *ST* 1:292-98.

11. Pannenberg, *ST* 1:282, with references to original works.

and elaborate on the basis of what it already presupposes from revelation.[12] Only Reformation theology consistently followed the rule that the Trinity is accessible only by faith, on the basis of scriptural revelation — even though a generic concept of God, one God, may be known by "general revelation."[13]

However, the insistence on the Trinity as a datum of revelation, ironically, led to the counterthesis by antitrinitarians at the time of the Reformation: they argued that the only thing we can say of the Trinity has to do with economy; there is no getting back to the inner life of God.[14] (This is basically the same claim made by contemporary economic trinitarians, such as Oneness Pentecostals: while freely speaking of Father, Son, and Spirit, they refuse to speculate beyond the economic language, as they see it, of the New Testament.)[15] While anchoring the doctrine of the Trinity firmly in Scripture in Reformation theology might seem to be a great advancement, ironically, after the advent of critical biblical scholarship with its rejection of the noncritical exegetical tradition (including that of older Protestant theology)[16] and reluctance to find the *doctrine* of the Trinity in the Bible, the doctrine of the Trinity was left without "foundations."[17]

Yet another distinctive way the post-Augustinian tradition came to conceive of God has a bearing on the role of the Trinity, albeit indirectly. Whereas Augustine focused much of his attention on love as the proper biblical category for developing the idea of the triune God, for Aquinas intellect and will were the key actions in the spiritual world.[18] While the idea of perceiving the divine nature in terms of intellect (and will) is not totally foreign to the Bible, it is hardly the best approach. The Augustinian emphasis on love with corollary relational and communal implications does much more justice to biblical material.[19] That

12. Aquinas, *ST* 1.32.1. ad 2. For Anselm's highly rationalistic attempt to "prove" the Trinity, see Olson and Hall, *The Trinity*, pp. 55-57.

13. Pannenberg, *ST* 1:289-90.

14. Pannenberg, *ST* 1:290-91. For Faustus Socinus, see further, Olson and Hall, *The Trinity*, pp. 77-79.

15. See further, "Oneness Pentecostalism," pp. 936-44.

16. In tradition, it was customary to refer not only to the underdeveloped nature of Old Testament faith before the coming of the Messiah, but also to try to find clues to the alleged plurality in the Israelite concept of God in passages such as Gen. 1:26; Isa. 6:1, or in the interpretation of the theophanies of the "Angel of Yahweh" (e.g., Gen. 18) as preincarnation appearances of the second person of the Trinity.

17. See further, Pannenberg, *ST* 1:301-2.

18. See further, O'Collins, *The Tripersonal God*, pp. 144-45.

19. However, Thomas developed the idea of an intellectual nature toward relationality, combining it with love and will. Olson and Hall, *The Trinity*, p. 64.

statement holds even though, regrettably, neither Augustine nor his followers fully grasped the potential of love as an intimate, relational, and communal way of speaking about God.

Yet another highly disputed, and complicated, question, which had everything to do with the place and role of the Trinity in theology, dealt with the relation between unity and trinity. Can unity be derived from trinity, or vice versa? The usual way of resolving the issue in Christian tradition was to insist on the unity of the divine substance prior to trinitarian distinctions. This not only was the approach of Augustine and his legacy but also in a sense of the Cappadocians in their insistence on the unity of the trinitarian persons in their outward works.[20] The end result of the medieval and Reformation developments regarding the Trinity and its place in Christian theology was this: "By thus distinguishing and arranging the presentation of the one God and that of the Trinity Thomas gave the structure of the doctrine of God its classical form for the age that followed. Basic to this structure is the derivation of the trinity of persons from the concept of the unity of substance."[21] Curiously enough, even later Eastern theology was not immune to this tendency, even though its practice of it was more nuanced. The eighth-century John of Damascus's *Orthodox Faith* first briefly discusses the topic of one God and his incomprehensible nature, and only then launches into the Trinity. Yet the difference from Aquinas is noteworthy in that, unlike the Angelic Doctor, the Damascene names the Trinity as the overall topic of the first two chapters and his treatment of one God is minimally brief when compared to his Western counterpart.

While it is fair to say that contemporary theology by and large is seeing a trinitarian renaissance, there is hesitation among some theologians. An example is African American theology, which, while having labored extensively in the area of the general doctrine of God, has either by and large ignored discussion of the Trinity (James Cone) or felt that it is another exercise in Greek-Hellenistic metaphysical reflection with meager practical relevance to liberation.[22] This is of course very different from the majority of liberationists, including female and Latin American theologians, to whom the Trinity has appeared to be a liberative resource, both critically and constructively.

20. For details, see Kärkkäinen, *The Trinity,* pp. 19-56 particularly.
21. Pannenberg, *ST* 1:288; so also Rahner, *The Trinity,* pp. 16-17, and LaCugna, *God for Us,* p. 145. In defense of Aquinas, see Cunningham, *These Three Are One,* pp. 32-33.
22. Hood, *Must God Remain Greek?* pp. 109-10, 124.

Trinity, the Distinctively Christian View of God

So, what is the role of the Trinity in the presentation of the doctrine of the Christian God? And, consequently, what is the Trinity's place in that presentation? Should trinity follow unity, or the other way around?[23] The question boils down to this simple formulation: "If it can be shown that the Christian Doctrine of God is best expressed in the form of one God, then Trinity is a secondary addition, at best a helpful appendix to the doctrine but not necessary for presenting the God of the Bible."[24] And, consequently: in case the Trinity is an indispensable part of the doctrine of God, then it cannot be omitted without breaking the logic of Christian theology. Barth made a programmatic statement that is supported by contemporary theologians, namely, that the "doctrine of the Trinity is what basically distinguishes the Christian doctrine of God as Christian, and therefore what already distinguishes the Christian concept of revelation as Christian, in contrast to all other possible doctrines of God or concepts of revelation." Hence, Barth argued that God's self-revelation — that "God reveals Himself as the Lord" — can be called "the root of the doctrine of the Trinity."[25] Trinitarian doctrine is nothing more and nothing less than an analysis of this statement, based on the biblical revelation.

Barth's "revelational trinitarianism"[26] set forth the bold claim that it is not unity but rather trinity that is at the heart of the revelation of God. This is widely affirmed in contemporary theology, including by some leading intercultural theologians such as the Korean American Jung Young Lee, who seeks to develop the Trinity in Asian perspective, and the Indian-American-European Raimundo Panikkar, who has argued that not only for Christian theology but, more widely, for the understanding of the world(view) at large, the notion of the Trinity is indispensable. Lee comes to this conclusion by establishing the link between Christian tradition and the (ancient) Confucian-Chinese teaching in *I Ching* concerning the primacy of "change"[27] — a dynamic conception of God that, after panentheism, supports responsiveness, relationality, and engagement[28] — and the widely affirmed Asian notion of yin-yang.[29] He suggests that the Creator (Father) is correlated with change, the Word (Son) with

23. See Pannenberg, *ST* 1:280-99.
24. Kärkkäinen, *The Trinity*, p. 53; Pannenberg, *ST* 1:291.
25. *CD* I/1, pp. 301 and 377.
26. Grenz, *Social God*, p. 34.
27. As discussed in Lee, *Theology of Change*.
28. For details, see Lee, *God Suffers for Us*; Lee, *Embracing Change*.
29. See Lee, *Trinity in Asian Perspective*, p. 25.

yang, and the Spirit with yin. He wonders if this correlation "explains the heart of Christian paradoxes: 'the threeness in one and oneness in three.'"[30] Unlike many comparative theologians who tend to see the Trinity as "baggage" in an interfaith encounter, Panikkar takes it as a major resource, as will be discussed below in chapter 15.

Some of the key resources for the "universal" rediscovery of the Trinity have to do with the turn away from abstract, speculative, and "theoretical" investigations into God's immanent life and toward economic, "from below," concrete, and "practical" accounts. As is routinely noted, this turn was most brilliantly heralded by Rahner with his widely affirmed "rule": *"The 'economic' Trinity is the 'immanent' Trinity and the 'immanent' Trinity is the 'economic' Trinity."*[31] This simply means that access to any knowledge of God moves up, so to speak, from the observation of God's work in creation, providence, reconciliation, and consummation. Whatever can be known of God by the limited, finite human mind is based on the economy of salvation rather than on God's inner life. Yet we can trust that this knowledge of God, however limited and occasional, is reliable because God, as faithful Creator and Savior, is the same in God's own life (immanent Trinity) as in God's works in the world (economic Trinity). This "rule" may help theology go beyond the understanding of the Trinity as logical mystery and see it as saving mystery. At the heart of this theological account lies not a metaphysical speculation but rather an experience — and reflection thereon — of God's creative, providential, salvific, and consummative work in the history of the world. What makes possible the economic approach to the knowledge of the triune God is the gracious embodiment of the divine in the incarnation of the Logos. This indeed makes the Christian belief in the Trinity unique: "unlike the adherents of other faiths, Christians believe that God has entered fully and directly into the created order, and has become *concretely embodied* in the world."[32]

The American Lutheran Robert W. Jenson represents wonderfully this economic, Scripture-based approach by firmly anchoring the account of the Trinity on the revelatory narrative of the Bible. The unfolding of the trinitarian narrative in the biblical revelation is a "drama of God." Like any genuine drama, it has elements of surprise, yet — as Jenson helpfully reminds us — this real drama, being the drama of God, is not likely to be frustrated in its final result. While the final manifestation of the identity of the biblical God will not

---

30. Lee, *Trinity in Asian Perspective*, p. 55.
31. Rahner, *The Trinity*, p. 22, emphasis in original.
32. Cunningham, "The Trinity," p. 186.

be seen until the eschaton, we know enough to trust that this God is in control of twists and turns of the dramatic story.[33]

Trinity at the Center — but How?

To establish the indispensability of the Trinity for the presentation of the Christian God does not yet require a decision on whether trinity should precede unity or, as in tradition, unity should precede trinity. A related question for constructive theology, especially if trinity is being discussed first, is, what is the relation of the trinitarian confession to the OT and Jewish faith?

Barth placed the discussion of the Trinity not only in the beginning of his *Church Dogmatics* but even in the prolegomenon, in the opening part of the discussion of revelation.[34] The reason was that he saw the Trinity revealed in the formula *"God* reveals Himself. He reveals Himself *through Himself.* He reveals *Himself."*[35] Pannenberg both affirms and corrects Barth's move. He does so by reversing the order of traditional systematic treatment and beginning with the doctrine of the Trinity, and then moving to the question of the unity and attributes of God.[36] There are two reasons for that decision. First, for him, all systematic theology is but exposition of the doctrine of the triune God, and therefore, it is only with the consummation of the world from creation to redemption to eschatological coming of the kingdom that the doctrine of God finally reaches its ultimate goal.[37] Hence, instead of Barth's formal approach to the Trinity, which can easily be understood after idealist philosophy's *self*-revelation rather than the biblical notion of God who "always reveals 'something' or 'someone,' "[38] Pannenberg is able to follow the "method from below" and link the Trinity to (salvation) history. Second, Pannenberg sees the order and content of his trinitarian doctrine built on the narrative of NT revelation.[39]

---

33. See Jenson, *The Triune Identity*; Jenson, *Systematic Theology,* vol. 1, *The Triune God.*

34. CD I/1, §§8-9, for basic discussion of trinity and unity; §§10-12 for Father, Son, and Spirit.

35. CD I/1, p. 296. For discussion and critique of revelation as divine "self-revelation" in Barth, see Pannenberg, introduction to Pannenberg, ed., *Revelation as History,* pp. 3-8 and passim.

36. Chap. 5 in *ST* 1 is titled "The Trinitarian God," and chap. 6, "The Unity and Attributes of the Divine Essence."

37. Pannenberg, *ST* 1:447-48; see also pp. 59-61, 335.

38. Moltmann, *Experiences in Theology,* pp. 61-62, at 62.

39. Pannenberg, *ST* 1:299; see also p. 304, among others.

But rather than following the formal principle of Barth, he wishes to anchor the Trinity in the actual NT narrative of the coming of Jesus as the Son of the Father.[40] As Son, Jesus both distinguished himself from the Father in submitting himself to his Father and to the service of the coming of the kingdom,[41] and "also realized that he was very closely linked to the Father in his work."[42]

Moltmann similarly turns to Christology as the gateway to the Trinity.[43] But even more: he wishes to anchor the doctrine of the Trinity specifically on one event in the history of Jesus, namely, the crucifixion; "the cross of the Son stands from eternity in the centre of the Trinity."[44] This is in keeping with Moltmann's deep and wide critique of tradition's doctrine of divine impassibility, the "apathy axiom"[45] that he wants to replace with *theopathy*.[46] For him, the event of the cross — particularly the cry of dereliction — represents "a deep division in God himself, in so far as God abandoned God and contradicted himself, and at the same time a unity in God, in so far as God was at one with God and corresponded to himself."[47] Thus, the cross belongs to the inner life of God; it is not only — and not even primarily — about the relation of God to estranged humanity.[48]

Pannenberg is correct in that the Trinity is not based on a formal, logical inference (Barth) but rather on the unfolding of the biblical narrative at the center of which stands the coming of the Son to inaugurate the kingdom of the Father in the power of the Spirit. Yet at the same time, one needs to remind Pannenberg of the obvious fact that if we follow the unfolding of the biblical narrative, the one God is introduced first and only then is the threeness. Even when Pannenberg's counterargument about the primacy of the future, based on the proleptic confirmatory significance of Jesus' resurrection, is acknowledged, there is nothing wrong in Christian theology's making the one God the first chapter and then moving to the consideration of the three. The only potential danger in that order is that it may push the doctrine of the Trinity to the margin — as it has done beginning from the Middle Ages. However

40. On criticism of Barth in this respect, see Pannenberg, *ST* 1:296, 303.

41. Pannenberg, *ST* 1:263; so also p. 309, among others.

42. Pannenberg, *ST* 1:263-64, at 263.

43. As acknowledged by Pannenberg, *ST* 1:304.

44. Moltmann, *Trinity and the Kingdom*, p. xvi; so also, e.g., p. 78.

45. Moltmann, *Trinity and the Kingdom*, p. 22.

46. Moltmann, *Trinity and the Kingdom*, p. 25. A helpful discussion can be found in Bauckham, *Theology of Jürgen Moltmann*, chap. 3.

47. Moltmann, *The Crucified God*, p. 244.

48. Moltmann, *The Crucified God*, p. 249.

one orders the discussion of God, the biblical narrative of the coming of the Son of the Father in the power of the Spirit is the proper economic way of approaching the knowledge of God. It seems to me that the whole history of Jesus (Pannenberg) is the preferred way to focus on one instance in that history, whether it be the cross (Moltmann) or another event.

That the current project follows the traditional order of discussion, first unity and then trinity, is not to be seen as marginalizing the Trinity but rather as the way of first winning the "rational" starting point for talk about God as well as tentatively clarifying the nature of our approach to God (classical panentheism), which also underwrites — and is supported by — the dynamic communion theology of the Trinity. The previous chapters were written with a view of the trinitarian confession, as the discussion of revelation (especially chap. 4) clearly indicated. On the other hand, the rest of the volume is but a continuation of the exposition of the works of the triune God in the world.

One God as Father, Son, and Spirit

The Emerging Trinitarian Consciousness

Establishing the necessity and centrality of the Trinity in the distinctively Christian understanding of God does not yet define the ways to relate the plurality to the unity and vice versa. At the expense of oversimplifying a complex history of developments, we can say that while in the tradition the unity was taken for granted and the challenge was to establish authentically the trinity, in much of contemporary theology, the trinity has been taken for granted and the unity has been a challenge.

Whence, then, the emergence of the plurality, the trinity in the one God in the emerging of Christianity from its strictly monotheistic Jewish roots? "The initial impetus . . . was spawned by the theological puzzle posed by the early church's confession of the lordship of Jesus and the experience of the indwelling Holy Spirit, both of which developments emerged within the context of the nonnegotiable commitment to the one God of the Old Testament that the early believers inherited from Israel."[49] Clearly, the way the New Testament introduces its incipient trinitarianism is through the coming of Jesus Christ, who was believed to share in the divinity of the Father God. There is,

---

49. Grenz, *Rediscovering the Triune God*, p. 7.

indeed, a "trinitarian face" to the history of Jesus,[50] not only a binitarian face, although the Father-Son relationship was at the forefront both in the NT and in evolving creedal tradition. By virtue of the resurrection, which confirmed Jesus' claim of having been sent by his Father, the divinity of the Son who was raised by the Father through the power of the Spirit was established (Rom. 1:3-4).[51] Resurrection from the dead was seen by early Christian theology as suggesting that "the Son of God was also at the side of God from all eternity."[52] Hence, the application of the highest divine title, *Kyrios*, to the risen and exalted Son. The confession of Jesus Christ as the one and only *Kyrios* in no way weakens the confession of the one God. "The former confession is so related to the latter that all things proceed from the one God, the Father, but all are mediated through the one Kyrios (1 Cor. 8:6)."[53]

The critical stage in moving from a binitarian to a trinitarian understanding of God had to do with the growing insistence on the Spirit as the "medium of the communion of Jesus with the Father and the mediator of the participation of believers in Christ."[54] The God who raised the Son from the dead by the power of the Spirit (Rom. 1:4) will raise believers from the dead as well (8:11). In the "Spirit Christologies" of the Synoptic Gospels, Jesus is anointed by the Spirit at his baptism and receives a confirmation from the Father, "Thou art my beloved Son" (Mark 1:11 par.). Pannenberg makes here the important statement that "[t]he involvement of the Spirit in God's presence in the work of Jesus and in the fellowship of the Son with the Father is the basis of the fact that the Christian understanding of God found its developed and definitive form in the doctrine of the Trinity and not in a biunity of the Father and the Son." That said, however, "The NT statements do not clarify the interrelations of the three but they clearly emphasize the fact that they are interrelated."[55]

The Difficulty of Establishing Genuine Plurality in One God

According to conventional theological wisdom, "in general, Greek theology [of the Christian East] emphasizes the divine hypostases (persons), whereas

---

50. O'Collins, *The Tripersonal God*, p. 35.
51. See the important article by Bauckham, "Sonship of the Historical Jesus."
52. See further, Pannenberg, *ST* 1:264-65.
53. Pannenberg, *ST* 1:266.
54. Pannenberg, *ST* 1:266.
55. Pannenberg, *ST* 1:268-69.

Latin theology [of the Christian West] emphasizes the divine nature."[56] In other words, it is claimed that the East begins with the threeness of the Trinity, the West with the oneness or unity.[57] While not without grounds, this description is also a caricature[58] and will be qualified in the course of discussion.

Origen sought to differentiate the three members of the Godhead based on their distinctive operations; while the Father works in all things, the Son only in rational creatures, and the Spirit only in the church.[59] This approach, however, is highly problematic. First, its view of the Son and particularly the Spirit is highly reductionistic, as if the Spirit, to take up an obvious example, is not also the Spirit of life. More importantly for this discussion, the mere functioning in distinct spheres would hardly establish distinct "persons." Finally, in light of later theology, Origen's suggestion also violates the common rule according to which the works of the Trinity *ad extra* are united rather than strictly separated.

Even the Eastern theologians often had a hard time establishing the distinctions, although, as is routinely claimed, "it was natural that they should make the three hypostases, rather than the one divine substance, their starting point."[60] It seems that in general the Cappadocians could only resort to church tradition, Scripture, and the baptismal formula as the basis of distinction.[61]

A more promising way to establish distinction in the one God looks at the inner relations of the Son, Father, and Spirit. On the basis of the Paraclete passages in John 14, Tertullian suggested that the Son distinguished both the Father and the Spirit from himself.[62] Origen similarly had affirmed that Jesus' referring to the Father and the Paraclete as distinct from himself implies the existence of three persons and one shared substance or entity.[63] This suggests that the "self-differentiation of the Son from the Father on the one side and

---

56. LaCugna, "The Trinitarian Mystery of God," p. 170.

57. The classic work contrasting Eastern and Western views is Régnon, *Études de théologie positive sur la sainte Trinité*; see also Congar, *I Believe in the Holy Spirit*, 3:xv-xxi.

58. O'Collins, *The Tripersonal God*, p. 140.

59. Origen, *On First Principles* 1.3.5-8. Rightly the Cappadocians and Athanasius highlighted the common participation of all trinitarian members in the works in the world. The unity of works is both a condition and a consequence of the unity of essence. See further, Wiles, "Some Reflections on the Origins," pp. 11-13 particularly.

60. Kelly, *Early Christian Doctrines*, p. 264.

61. Wiles, "Some Reflections on the Origins," p. 14; Pannenberg, *ST* 1:278.

62. Tertullian, *Against Praxeas*, sec. 9, quoting John 14:28 and 14:16.

63. Origen, *Homilies on Numbers* 12.1, referenced in Pannenberg, *ST* 1:272 n. 48.

the Spirit on the other forms a basis for the thesis that there is a threefold distinction in the deity."[64] While obviously liable in some ways, the simple yet profound idea of Athanasius according to which the Father would not be Father without the Son and that therefore the Father never was without the Son, points in the same direction.[65] The abiding contribution of this rule is the implication of relationality and mutuality as the way to define the distinction as well as the unity.[66]

The general conclusion is that, notwithstanding the establishment of the full deity of the Son first and later the Spirit in patristic theology and the creeds, early tradition was unable to satisfactorily resolve the question of the basis for establishing the identities of Son and Spirit, including their mutual distinction and their unity. Rightly, tradition sought to negotiate between two extremes: tritheism,[67] on the one hand, and modalism, the idea of lack of personal distinctions in the one Godhead, on the other hand. The subordinationist tendency was strong and deep, the subjecting of the Son and Spirit to the Father,[68] whether as "two hands" of the Father in the Christian West[69] or making the Father the "source" *(archē)* of the Deity in the East.

Even though suffering from subordinationism (because of considering the Father the unilateral "source"), the Cappadocians were moving in the right direction and made a lasting contribution. Basil the Great made this important statement: "For all things that are the Father's are beheld in the Son, and all things that are the Son's are the Father's; because the whole Son is in the Father and has all the Father in Himself. Thus the hypostasis of the Son becomes as it were form and face of the knowledge of the Father, and the

---

64. Pannenberg, *ST* 1:272; see also pp. 278, 279.

65. Athanasius, *Four Discourses against the Arians* 1.29. Athanasius was not the first to express this idea. Origen had already taught it earlier in his *First Principles* 1.2.9-10.

66. In his letters to Serapion, Athanasius made efforts to transfer the argument from the Father-Son relation to considering the Spirit-Father-Son web of relations; those attempts hardly are convincing since it is very difficult to discern the compelling logic behind it. See further, Pannenberg, *ST* 1:279.

67. A charge leveled against the Cappadocians who were more keen on the distinctions. Aware of these suspicions, Gregory of Nyssa wrote a study titled *On "Not Three Gods" to Ablabius.*

68. Justin Martyr's idea of the Son being "second" and the Spirit being "in the third place" in the Godhead is a classic example of a subordinationist view. *First Apology,* sec. 13.

69. See Irenaeus, *Against Heresies* 4.20.1, for the famous idea of Spirit and Son as "two hands" the Father uses in creation. That said, it has to be noted to Irenaeus's credit that for him the Son (as Word) has always been with the Father (2.30.9; 4.20.3) and the Son is the one who makes the Father known (4.20.6; 4.6.7).

hypostasis of the Father is known in the form of the Son, while the proper quality which is contemplated therein remains for the plain distinction of the hypostases."[70]

It seems justified to also link this perichoretic principle, by derivation, to the Spirit. LaCugna is on to something when she suggests that in the Cappadocian theology each person "*is* the divine *ousia;* the divine *ousia* exists hypostatically, and there is no *ousia* apart from the *hypostases.* To exist as God is to be the Father who begets the Son and breathes forth the Spirit."[71] Therefore, trinitarian persons cannot be thought of as disconnected from each other; in other words, "*it is impossible to think of the divine essence in itself or by itself.*"[72] This constitutes a major achievement in the development of trinitarian theology regarding the question of how to relate the unity to the distinctions. Unlike some Western views in which the unity of the Godhead almost appears to be understood in terms of something "separate behind" the threeness, here the "persons" *(hypostases)* and "being/essence" *(ousia)* are related to each other in a mutual, perichoretic way. Out of this grows the contemporary emphasis on communion theology in which the only way to think of one God is to think of one God as existing as Father, Son, and Spirit.[73] O'Collins's observation is important: "At the heart of God, the Cappadocians saw an interpersonal communion or *koinonia,* with communion as the function of all three divine persons and not simply of the Holy Spirit. For this interpersonal model of the Trinity, God's inner being is relational, with each of the three persons totally related to the other two in 'reciprocal delight' — to borrow an Athanasian expression."[74] This contribution of Athanasius and the Cappadocians is significant beyond the Christian East and has lasting value for our times as well. As Pannenberg, who otherwise is somewhat critical of the Augustinian legacy, has shown convincingly, "Augustine took over the relational definition of the trinitarian distinctions which the Cappadocians, following Athanasius, had developed. He made the point that the distinctions of the persons are conditioned by their mutual relations."[75] For Augustine the

---

70. Basil of Caesarea, *Letters* 38.8 (*NPNF*[2] 8:141). (It is not certain if Basil or Gregory of Nyssa is the author; in any case, this quotation nicely reflects the view of the Cappadocians.)

71. LaCugna, *God for Us,* p. 69.

72. LaCugna, *God for Us,* p. 70.

73. See Gregory of Nazianzus, *Orations* 31.14.

74. O'Collins, *The Tripersonal God,* pp. 131-32.

75. Pannenberg (*ST* 1:284) here refers to Augustine, *On the Trinity* 8.1. In his *Sermon on Matthew* 3:13, Augustine speaks of a distinction of persons and an inseparableness of operation. Augustine, *Sermon on New Testament Lessons: Matthew* 3:13 2.1-23, especially 2.15, in *NPNF*[2]

relations are eternal.[76] The Eastern idea of *perichoresis,* mutual interpenetration, hence is not foreign to him.[77]

True, in post-Augustinian tradition the unity took the upper hand and made the entire Western tradition up until Barth subject to the liability of employing mostly mental or psychological analogies of the Trinity, which usually led to the primacy of a divine single mind, named by Pannenberg a "pre-trinitarian, theistic idea of God."[78] The same has to be said of the two related ways tradition has tried to establish the Trinity, that is, from the concept of God as supreme substance and as absolute subject, both of which build on a nontrinitarian conception of God. Nor does the notion of Spirit, favored by Hegel and other idealists, in itself take us to authentic "personal" distinctions of Father, Son, and Spirit. Even the Augustinian starting point with the concept of love, refined by Richard of St. Victor, although biblically based and conducive to personalistic and communion theology, could not rise to its full potential in this regard. As Pannenberg concludes, these kinds of attempts to derive plurality from the unity end up with an idea of the "one divine subjectivity" that does not leave room for a genuine plurality of persons in the one God.[79]

Even in contemporary theology there are theological orientations whose attempts to establish an authentic threeness in the Deity raise a number of questions. (American) process theology is an important example here. Quite surprisingly in light of its relational, dynamic, and emerging ethos,[80] that tradition has not paid much attention to the Trinity until quite recently, and even when it has, many rightly wonder if a binitarian account of the divinity can ever be transformed into a tripersonal one.[81] A similar judgment seems

---

6:259-66, at 262. See also Augustine, *On the Trinity* 5.11.12 for an important statement about relationality in the Trinity.

76. Pannenberg, *ST* 1:284.

77. In *On the Trinity* (6.10.12 [*NPNF*[1] 3:103]), Augustine says it strongly: "in that highest Trinity one is as much as the three together, nor are two anything more than one. And They are infinite in themselves. So both each are in each, and all in each, and each in all, and all in all, and all are one."

78. Pannenberg, "Father, Son, Spirit," p. 251.

79. Pannenberg, *ST* 1:296, 298.

80. Suchocki, "Introduction," p. x; see also Peters, *God as Trinity,* pp. 114-15.

81. Already in 1977 Norman Pittenger published *The Divine Triunity.* So far the most important attempt is Bracken and Suchocki, eds., *Trinity in Process;* also important is Bracken, *The Triune Symbol.* However, as Peters (*God as Trinity,* p. 114) somewhat pejoratively notes, in process thought "two makes three," meaning that the distinction between the "primordial" and "contingent" does not easily translate into an authentic *trinitarian* doctrine. No wonder

in order with regard to the experimentation by some Asian and Asian American theologians regarding the use of the ancient binitarian yin-yang template as the resource for constructing a Christian doctrine of creation, mentioned above. While Lee's claim that trinity is a "foundational" structure of the Trinity can be affirmed from the Christian perspective, the way he seeks to construct the trinitarian account based on the concepts of change and yin-yang sounds artificial and less than convincing.[82]

Threeness, Relationality, and Mutuality

Contemporary constructive theology begins with threeness, Father, Son, and Spirit as they appear in NT narrative.[83] In that sense, Luther's approach, unlike the mainstream Reformation and particularly post-Reformation tradition, points in the same direction. As Eberhard Jüngel importantly has noted, for Luther the God revealed in Jesus Christ is indeed the trinitarian God. In that sense, the "hiddenness" of God does not have to do with the trinity but rather the unity, the "essence" of God. Luther based this also on the Johannine statement "He who has seen me has seen the Father."[84]

Moltmann begins with the trinity of the persons and goes on to ask about the unity. "What then emerges is a concept of the divine unity as the union of tri-unity, a concept which is differentiated and is therefore capable of being thought first of all." Rather than on one divine substance, it focuses on "relationships and communities."[85] Moltmann sees this point of departure being supported by the relationality and panentheistic notion of mutuality of God and world.[86] At the same time, he critiques both Barth and Rahner for modalistic tendencies and the priority given to the unity at the expense of the trinity.[87] In the same way, Pannenberg not only discusses trinity before unity in his *Systematic Theology* (vol. 1) but also takes the coming of Jesus as the

---

some process theologians have outright admitted that "process theology is not interested in formulating distinctions within God for the sake of conforming with traditional Trinitarian notions." Cobb and Griffin, *Process Theology*, p. 110.

82. See Kärkkäinen, *The Trinity*, chap. 22.

83. See Moltmann, *Trinity and the Kingdom*, p. 64.

84. Jüngel, *Entsprechungen*, pp. 227, 237-38, 246-47; LW 5:42; WA 43:459.30-33.

85. Moltmann, *Trinity and the Kingdom*, p. 19.

86. Moltmann, *Trinity and the Kingdom*, p. 19.

87. For his dialogue with Barth and Rahner, see Moltmann, *Trinity and the Kingdom*, pp. 139-48. See also J. H. Davis, "Opening Dialogue."

obedient Son as the starting point. Both Moltmann and Pannenberg also see relational ontology and relational understanding of personhood supporting the primacy of the threeness of God. "The three divine Persons exist in their particular, unique natures as Father, Son and Spirit in their relationships to one another, and are determined through these relationships. . . . Being a person in this respect means existing-in-relationship."[88] This is of course a tribute to Hegel's idea of the person giving one's self to the counterpart and thus receiving one's personhood from the other.[89]

Once the threeness of the Christian God is established, two major tasks then face constructive theology: the mutuality of the three persons and the problem of unity. Moltmann and Pannenberg attempt the first task somewhat similarly. Building on the Pauline teaching (1 Cor. 15:27-28; Phil. 2:9-11), they refer to the eschatological consummation when Christ — to whom has been given the authority (Matt. 28:18) and under whom the Father has subjected everything — hands over the kingdom to the Father to glorify God. Even the lifting up of the name of Jesus Christ above all names serves the glorification of the Father.[90] The Spirit represents the unity of Father and Son and distinguishes himself/herself from the two by, for example, raising the Son from the dead as the "agent" of the Father. In the Spirit's work of glorifying both the Son and through the Son the Father, the Spirit also shows himself/herself to be a "subject," distinct from but not separated from Father and Son: "[T]he glorifying of the Son and the Father by the Spirit is the personal act which most decisively expresses the subjectivity of the Spirit over against the other two persons, and above all that we must regard this doxological activity of the Spirit as an intratrinitarian relation because it is not directed outward but to the Son and the Father."[91] There is thus no unilateral "source" of the Deity, nor any subordination.[92] Instead, there is authentic mutuality and "dependency."[93] Trinity is not derived from the unity, or vice versa.

88. Moltmann, *Trinity and the Kingdom,* p. 172, among others.

89. Moltmann, *Trinity and the Kingdom,* p. 174.

90. Moltmann, *Trinity and the Kingdom,* pp. 92-93 and passim; see also Pannenberg, *ST* 1:313 and passim.

91. Pannenberg, *ST* 1:330; this is similar to Moltmann, *Trinity and the Kingdom,* pp. 126-27, 143.

92. For Pannenberg's revision of traditional terminology, see *ST* 1:305-7, at 305.

93. Fittingly, that section on trinitarian discussion is titled "The Reciprocal Self-Distinction of Father, Son, and Spirit as the Concrete Form of Trinitarian Relations." Pannenberg, *ST* 1:308.

God's Life as Communion

To say that one God exists as Father, Son, and Spirit is to speak of communion, personal communion of the three. The turn to a relational understanding of personhood at large has helped rediscover communion theology.[94] The Orthodox theologian John Zizioulas's important collection of essays with a telling title, *Being as Communion* (1985),[95] has become a clarion call for contemporary theologians. The main thesis of Zizioulas's theology is simple and profound: God is not first "one substance" and only then exists as "trinity"; rather the "Holy Trinity is a *primordial* ontological concept and not a notion which is added to the divine substance."[96] In other words, "the substance of God, 'God,' has no ontological content, no true being, apart from communion," mutual relationships of love.[97] God's being coincides with God's personhood, which cannot be construed apart from communion.[98] Biblically that is expressed by the idea of God as "love," which is "*constitutive* of His substance, i.e., it is that which makes God what He is, the one God."[99] Hence, God is the person as the community of three persons. God's being coincides with God's *communal* personhood.

The notion of communion is not a new idea; indeed, it is an ancient one, going back to the NT witness and patristic theology. While communion theology has been embraced universally in contemporary theology, not all appropriate it similarly. Whereas Zizioulas as an Orthodox theologian conceives it hierarchically, making the Father the source *(aitia)* of the Trinity,[100] Moltmann and a number of contemporary female theologians have passionately argued for an equalitarian notion of communion. These theologians have made the Trinity a "social program," a guide to form equalitarian communities. Several leading women theologians have reminded us that to the notion of communion belong the principles of mutuality and relationality: "God, too, lives from and for another: God the Father gives birth to the Son, breathes forth the

94. See Grenz, *Social God*, pp. 3-14.

95. Zizioulas, *Being as Communion*. See also his "Human Capacity."

96. Cf. "In the Beginning Is Communion." Chapter title in Boff, *Trinity and Society*, p. 9.

97. Zizioulas, *Being as Communion*, p. 17.

98. Zizioulas, "Teaching of the 2nd Ecumenical Council on the Holy Spirit," p. 37.

99. Zizioulas, *Being as Communion*, p. 46, emphasis in original; see also Zizioulas, "Human Capacity," p. 410.

100. Zizioulas, *Being as Communion*, p. 41; see also Zizioulas, "On Being a Person," p. 41.

Spirit, elects the creature from before all time. . . . God's rule is accomplished by saving and healing love."[101]

No wonder, then, that communion theology may also underwrite cautious panentheism. Behind the appreciation of the communion nature of God is the intuition that while distinct, God and the world do not represent two totally different realities; they are intertwined. An older, static conception of reality is giving way to a more dynamic one in which "categories such as history, process, freedom, and so on, then dynamism, interplay of relationships, and dialectics of mutual inclusiveness make their appearance." In that kind of worldview, the world presents itself as the "receptacle of God's self-communication" and "begins to belong to the history of the triune God."[102]

The Unity of the Tripersonal God

What about the unity of the tripersonal God? As mentioned, in contemporary theology unity rather than trinity is the challenge. Discerning the different approaches taken by Moltmann and Pannenberg is useful. Moltmann is willing to refer to unity "neither as homogenous substance nor as identical subject." Rather, he considers unity in light of the trinitarian history and develops it in trinitarian terms,[103] in terms of "the union of the tri-unity" (p. 19). He turns to the eschatological consummation as the key to the unity of the Trinity and the way to reconcile the relationship between the economic and immanent Trinity. Rather than a static conception, unity is a process: "The unity of the Father, the Son and the Spirit is then the eschatological question about the consummation of the trinitarian history of God" (p. 149). Since the trinitarian members as "three divine subjects are co-active in this history," there is no way to define the unity in terms of "monadic unity," but rather as "the *union* of the Father, the Son and the Spirit," as "their *fellowship*" (p. 95). From tradition Moltmann takes the ancient concept of *perichoresis,* the mutual indwelling of trinitarian persons in each other, "the unitedness, the at-oneness of the three Persons with one another, or: the unitedness, at-oneness of the triune God." This unity "must be perceived in the *perichoresis* of the divine Persons" (p. 150).

In the social notion of "personhood" Moltmann sees the way to affirm

---

101. LaCugna, *God for Us,* pp. 383; see also Baker-Fletcher, *Dancing with God.*

102. Boff, *Trinity and Society,* pp. 112-13, at 113.

103. Moltmann, *Trinity and the Kingdom,* p. 19. Parenthetical references in these paragraphs refer to pages in this text.

both the distinction and the unity of Father, Son, and Spirit, "since personal character and social character are only two aspects of the same thing. The concept of person must therefore in itself contain the concept of unitedness or at-oneness" (p. 150). The *perichoresis* spoken of here, notes Moltmann, must not be understood as the second movement, in which "three different individuals . . . only subsequently enter into relationship with another," which, of course, would raise the danger of tritheism. Nor is the *perichoresis* to be understood in terms of modalism in which (like Barth in Moltmann's estimation) Father, Son, and Spirit are only "three repetitions of the One God." There is no reducing the threeness to the unity, nor dissolving the unity in the threeness. Moltmann contends: "The unity of the triunity lies in the eternal perichoresis of the trinitarian persons. Interpreted perichoretically, the trinitarian persons form their own unity by themselves in the circulation of the divine life" (p. 175). This *perichoresis* will be consummated in the eschaton in the coming union of God and the world. This again goes back to the trinitarian history of Son, Spirit, and Father. Because of the fact that "glorifying by the Spirit effects the union of the Son with the Father as well as our own union with and in God (John 17:21)," Moltmann can "link the consummation of salvation history in eschatology with the consummation of the Trinitarian life of God in itself."[104]

Pannenberg's tactics for securing the unity differ significantly from those of the Tübingen theologian. Unlike Moltmann and many other social trinitarians, the Munich theologian's trinitarian doctrine also bears similarity with traditional approaches in that he affirms a single divine essence. While threeness is the starting point for considering the Christian God, that does not compromise unity but rather helps establish it: "For beyond the unity of God no more can be said about God. . . . Thus, the doctrine of the Trinity is in fact concrete monotheism in contrast to notions of an abstract transcendence of the one God and abstract notions of a divine unity that leave no place for plurality" (pp. 335-36). While Pannenberg is sympathetic to the effort to base unity on *perichoresis* rather than the traditional way of beginning with unity (whether it be substance or Spirit or love or Father as source), he also observes correctly that in tradition *perichoresis* was used not to establish but rather to illustrate the unity that was already assumed on another basis. In other words, *perichoresis* might be a necessary but not sufficient way to secure unity.

Agreeing with tradition that the concept of "essence" is needed to affirm the unity of three persons, Pannenberg also revises this concept radically in

---

104. Pannenberg, *ST* 1:330, with reference to Moltmann, *Trinity and the Kingdom*, p. 126 especially. Numbers in parentheses in the ensuing text refer to Pannenberg, *ST* 1.

order to move beyond the now-disputed substance ontology. He conceives "the divine essence as the epitome of the personal relations among Father, Son, and Spirit" (p. 334). The reason is simply that "[w]e cannot connect with this any attempt to derive the trinitarian threeness from the unity of the divine essence. The task is simply to envision as such the unity of the divine life and work that is manifest in the mutual relations of Father, Son and Spirit. This requires a concept of essence that is not external to the category of relations" (pp. 334-35; see also 366-67). Relationality also ties the discussion of the unity to the economy of salvation, including the coming of the kingdom.

The discussion of unity, then, is also the basis for talking about the "attributes" of God, which bear upon God's relations to the world. Now what could this "relational essence" be? Looking for biblical materials, Pannenberg finds two "definitions" of God that may serve as descriptions of the essence: "God is love" (1 John 4:8) and "God is spirit" (John 4:24). Philosophically speaking, both of these notions speak of infinity (p. 383). The Spirit, theologically speaking, denotes the third person of the Trinity as well as the persons' shared divine life-field. "The idea of the divine life as a dynamic field sees the divine Spirit who unites the three persons as proceeding from the Father, received by the Son, and common to both" (p. 383). Similarly, love, which unites the Father, Son, and Spirit, as well as the creatures with their Creator, is limitless (infinite). "As the one and only essence of God it has its existence in the Father, Son, and Holy Spirit . . . and . . . constitutes the unity of the one God in the communion of these three persons" (p. 428). In keeping with the notion of love, each of the three persons achieves selfhood ec-statically, in relation to the other two, in the I-Thou relationship (p. 430).

Defining the divine essence in terms of relations allows, on the one hand, the reciprocal, mutually dependent understanding of relations between Father, Son, and Spirit and, on the other hand, helps affirm God's relations with the world, which is the key to the principle of the unity of the immanent and economic Trinity (p. 367). In this understanding, "constitutive for each person of the Trinity are the other two persons and the relation to them. The world, in turn, arises not as a self-unfolding of the divine subject who makes the world but as God's free bringing forth of a world that differs from God out of the overflow of God's love. It is the product of the mutual activity of the Father, Son, and Spirit."[105]

Moltmann's social doctrine of the Trinity suffers from the weakness that it "may unnecessarily take him too far toward sacrificing divine unity. His

---

105. Grenz, *Reason for Hope*, p. 60.

emphasis on the three separate subjects of centers of action risks a final plurality."[106] While he is of course not a tritheist in any sense of the word,[107] his continued emphasis on three discrete subjects or centers of activity makes it difficult to conceive of a principle of unity that is comparable to that of the plurality. Contra Moltmann and following Pannenberg, this project will suppose the *relational* understanding of the divine essence. In biblical-theological terminology, the essence can be conceived of as spirit or love, and philosophically speaking as infinity. That kind of account of essence is living and dynamic, and follows communion theology.

Some African theologians, most prominently the Roman Catholic Charles Nyamiti, who have sought to establish the Trinity based on ancestral relationships drawn from local cultures,[108] have faced the challenge of affirming unity. Like process thought, those cultural traditions possess key features that in principle might be conducive to an authentic trinitarian account such as relatedness, communion, and the central role of intermediaries, both ancestors and spiritual beings.[109] To Nyamiti's credit, while utilizing robustly local cultural-religious ancestral resources, he also builds intentionally on key Christian resources with the intent to remain with creedal tradition.[110] He makes the bold claim that the ancestral way of constructing the classical doctrine is superior to the classical ways, and this for several reasons, such as, the ancestral way of viewing the Trinity highlights the importance of communion and participation unlike any other view; the Holy Spirit is seen as integral or internal rather than "external" to the Trinity; the holiness of the Father is an integral part of his being; the ancestors being the models of exemplary conduct illustrates perfectly the Son's role as the perfect image of his Father, in obedience and humility.[111] Having mentioned these resources, Nyamiti notes, however, that mediation does not fit trinitarian doctrine, and his critics have also eliminated or radically questioned the consanguineous type of kinship and the sacred status of the ancestor, gained through death. That, however, would leave only two of the five key elements intact, namely, exemplary con-

---

106. Peters, *God as Trinity*, p. 109.

107. Contra Molnar, *Divine Freedom*, pp. 201-2. While not charging him with tritheism, Torrance shows serious concern: *Christian Doctrine of God*, p. 247 n. 39.

108. Nyamiti, *African Tradition*; see also his *Christ as Our Ancestor*.

109. See Stinton, "Africa, East and West," pp. 125-28, for "theologies of mediation" in which the role of ancestors and other intermediaries in Africa is discussed from a Christian perspective.

110. See Vähäkangas, "Trinitarian Processions."

111. See further, Nyamiti, "The Trinity," pp. 51-52.

duct and right to sacred communication, which are hardly sufficient resources for constructing an authentic trinitarian account.[112]

Whatever the judgment concerning the appropriateness of the trinitarian account achieved by Nyamiti, the more important question is to what extent this particular social analogy can secure the unity of God. His effort builds on the centrality of the idea of communion and participation — a route taken by many Western theologians as well. Indeed, Nyamiti regards the *African* approach to communion superior in defending the unity when compared to typical Western notions: "In the Trinity, participation implies the communication of the one single divine life and power among the three Persons. This in no way implies having a *part* of the divine life or power: the Father shares his *entire being* with the Son and the Spirit. Here the African sense of participation is closer to the truth than is the Western 'pars capere,' to have a part." As a result, the divine persons are "one and identical in life, nature and power."[113] Nyamiti's approach to unity shares the strengths and weaknesses of typical contemporary social analogies, which — unlike Pannenberg's approach — do not refer to any kind of notion of divine essence. While I appreciate the desire to acknowledge and resist the danger of tritheism, I am also left wondering why mere *sharing* (in this case of life and power) necessarily entails absolute unity. Communion implies *com*-union, but not necessarily *union*. Nyamiti's proposal, to be convincing, requires much clarification.

Having established the threeness of one God and reflected on their mutual relations, we embark upon the last major task of this discussion: to reflect on the triune God's relation to the world and its consummation. That discussion will of course continue in the rest of the volume — and beyond, until the end of systematic argumentation.

God and World: Economic and Immanent Trinity

Is Rahner's "rule" about the identity of the economic and immanent Trinity epistemological or (also) ontological? If the former, it relates to "the order of theological knowledge [that] must adhere to the historical form of God's self-communication in Christ and the Spirit."[114] In other words, it is simply

---

112. See further, Vähäkangas, "Trinitarian Processions," p. 67; for a wider critical engagement of Nyamiti's proposal, see Kärkkäinen, *The Trinity,* chap. 25.

113. Nyamiti, *African Tradition,* p. 62, emphases in original.

114. LaCugna, "Introduction," p. xv.

saying that there is no gap between the way God exists in himself and the way God relates to the world and to us. If the latter, then — as many successors of Rahner, both Roman Catholics (LaCugna) and Protestants (Moltmann), have argued — there is claimed to be an ontological identity between the economic and immanent Trinity. The danger with this is that the finite, fallible human mind claims to know too much of the infinite and mysterious God.

However one negotiates the epistemological or ontological distinction, one has to be cautious about too strict an identity between the economic and immanent Trinity. That could potentially lead to the compromising of the divine freedom.[115] The immanent-economic distinction protects the freedom of God and the graciousness of salvation.[116] It is a legitimate concern whether "the total collapse of the immanent Trinity into the economic Trinity result[s] in a finite God who is dependent for divine definition upon the world."[117] Hence, Rahner's rule must be qualified to make room for the kind of asymmetry between the economic and immanent Trinity that preserves God's freedom. The French Dominican Yves Congar rightly says that while there is only one Trinity, "'this [self-communication] takes place in a mode that is not connatural with the being of the divine Persons.' The mode of the economy is condescension, *kenosis*. Thus there remains a certain degree of disparity between what God is *in se*, and what God is able to be *ad extra*."[118] The revised formulation of the rule expresses this: "The incomprehensible and ineffable mystery of God is not diminished by God's self-expression in the history of salvation. Nonetheless, because of the unity of *theologia* and *oikonomia*, the specific details of God's self-revelation in Christ and the Spirit reveal God's nature."[119]

The other challenge to the principle of the identity between the economic and immanent Trinity is the question of the "newness" of the revelation of God, or better, the lack thereof. What I mean is this: If God's self-revelation in Christ in terms of God becoming human does not introduce anything "new" to the world and the divine life, wouldn't that strip the incarnation of its profound meaning, particularly in light of tradition's insistence on the "permanence of incarnation"? However one speaks of the "change" in God,

---

115. That is the concern of J. Thompson, *Modern Trinitarian Perspectives*, p. 28.

116. Olson and Hall, *The Trinity*, p. 98.

117. Peters, *God — the World's Future*, p. 108.

118. As paraphrased by LaCugna, *God for Us*, p. 219, quotation within the quotation from Congar, *I Believe in the Holy Spirit*, 3:15.

119. LaCugna, *God for Us*, p. 221.

one has to agree that after the incarnation, the cross, and resurrection, in one way or another God "exists in a different way."[120]

On the other side, insisting on the *distinction* between the immanent and economic Trinity too strongly raises the problem of "subordinationism," the idea of the economic Trinity being merely "a temporal image of a much more real and hence much more important eternal and unrelated Trinity."[121] In other words, what happens in the world is a kind of superficial act as in a play, more or less distinct from the absolutely unmoved deity of eternity.[122] Rahner's rule is of course presented to combat this error, which is not foreign to older theology in its insistence on the immutability of the Deity.

Not surprisingly, contemporary theologians have appropriated Rahner's rule in widely differing ways. Rahner's pupil LaCugna has presented the most radical interpretation of the identity. She virtually refuses to make any distinction at all as she "argue[s] that an ontological distinction between God *in se* and God *pro nobis* is, finally, inconsistent with biblical revelation, with early Christian creeds, and with Christian prayer and worship."[123] Her main critique against tradition is that, with the disjoining of *oikonomia* and *theologia,* the focus changed to the inquiry into the "mystery of God" understood as *theologia* (pp. 22-24), the end result being marginalization and finally defeat of the doctrine of the Trinity.[124] Hence, to correct this perceived lacuna, LaCugna virtually makes *theologia oikonomia;* the economy of salvation is not only the beginning but also the *end* of our knowledge of God (p. 321). Therefore, if there is any distinction allowed between the economic and the immanent, it is "strictly conceptual" (p. 212). The only other way this late Catholic theologian softens the strict identity of the economic/immanent distinction has to do with doxology. In the doxological mode, the doctrine of the Trinity is more like a signpost or an icon than a fixed doctrine (pp. 321-22). It seems to me the end result of LaCugna's program is the collapse of the immanent Trinity into the economic, which leads not only to compromising divine freedom but also to diminishing the absolute mystery of God.[125] Yet another problem is that "[w]ithout a notion

120. See Rahner, *Foundations,* pp. 220-21.

121. Peters, *God — the World's Future,* p. 107.

122. See further, Peters, *God as Trinity,* p. 102, with reference to Kasper, *The God of Jesus Christ,* pp. 275-76.

123. LaCugna, *God for Us,* p. 6. Page numbers in parentheses in this paragraph refer to this text.

124. See further, the important article by LaCugna, "Philosophers and Theologians on the Trinity."

125. See, e.g., Weinandy, "The Immanent and Economic Trinity," p. 661. Even critics

of the immanent Trinity, the claim that in the *oikonomia* we encounter God as God really is lacks sufficient ground."[126]

Moltmann is more careful in applying the rule even though it seems to me that ultimately even he ends up collapsing the immanent in the economic Trinity.[127] His anchoring of the Trinity on the cross leads him in that direction: "In order to grasp the death of the Son in its significance for God himself, I found myself bound to surrender the traditional distinction between the immanent and the economic Trinity, according to which the cross comes to stand only in the economy of salvation, but not within the immanent Trinity."[128] Furthermore, Moltmann argues that the economic Trinity not only reveals the immanent Trinity but also has a retroactive effect on it. "The pain of the cross determines the inner life of the triune God from eternity to eternity," similarly to the responsive love in glorification through the Spirit.[129] Coupled with eschatological reference, the coming together of the immanent and economic Trinity finally takes us to the culmination of Moltmann's theological vision and is the way he reconciles the economic-immanent Trinity distinction: "The economic Trinity completes and perfects itself to immanent Trinity when the history and experience of salvation are completed and perfected. When everything is 'in God' and 'God is all in all,' then the economic Trinity is raised into and transcended in the immanent Trinity."[130] Rightly Pannenberg concludes that Moltmann thus "link[s] the consummation of salvation history in eschatology with the consummation of the trinitarian life of God in itself."[131]

Fully aware of why Christian theology has held the distinction, Moltmann, however, is also critical of it. For the concept of God as love that resists the speculative and artificial distinction between freedom and necessity — as if God could exist alone without the Other with whom to share love — the distinction seems to be both arbitrary and self-contradictory. Therefore, for

---

as careful and nuanced as Stanley Grenz (*Social God,* p. 55) and Ted Peters (*God as Trinity,* p. 143) have come to this conclusion. Not all agree with this judgment; see Medley, *Imago Trinitatis,* p. 146.

126. Leslie, "Does God Have a Life?" pp. 377-98.

127. Even the most sympathetic and moderate critics have expressed this opinion, such as Powell, *The Trinity in German Thought,* pp. 201-2.

128. Moltmann, *Trinity and the Kingdom,* p. 160.

129. Moltmann, *Trinity and the Kingdom,* pp. 160-61, at 161.

130. Moltmann, *Trinity and the Kingdom,* p. 161.

131. Pannenberg, *ST* 1:330, with reference to Moltmann, *Trinity and the Kingdom,* p. 126 especially.

Moltmann, the immanent and economic Trinities rather "form a continuity and merge into one another."[132] The only legitimate way of continuing the distinction, somewhat similarly to LaCugna, is to relegate it to doxology, the human response to the experience of salvation and anticipation of the coming kingdom.[133] Doxological response means participation in and transformation into God rather than an attempt to know God *in se*.[134] Rightly Pannenberg discerns that "the equation of the two means the absorption of the immanent Trinity in the economic Trinity. This steals from the Trinity of the salvation history all sense and significance. For this Trinity has sense and significance only if God is the same in salvation history as he is from eternity."[135]

I find Pannenberg's approach, in contrast to those of LaCugna and Moltmann, commendable and also the one that best underwrites this project's classical panentheistic approach. Well aware of the need to correct tradition's tendency to make the relationship between history and the divine life more or less independent,[136] Pannenberg is also critical of those contemporary revisions that for him result in the danger of the "absorption of the immanent Trinity in the economic Trinity."[137] He rejects process theology's idea of a divine becoming in history if that means that the triune God achieves reality only by virtue of eschatological consummation. While more sympathetic to Moltmann's view, Pannenberg finds problematic the absorption of the immanent Trinity in the economic.[138] Pannenberg's idea of the dependency of God on the world does not make God prisoner to history, but rather means "the dependence of the trinitarian persons upon one another as the kingdom is handed over and handed back in connection with the economy of salvation."[139] Having created the world (out of freedom rather than necessity), God cannot be God without his kingdom and thus the consummation of salvation history, but it is not that the consummation "brings about" the reality of God but rather that it "is only the locus of the decision that the trinitarian God is always the true God from eternity to eternity." The lordship and deity of God will be manifested at the end of history as God shows himself to be the one God he promised to

132. Moltmann, *Trinity and the Kingdom*, p. 152.
133. Moltmann, *Trinity and the Kingdom*, pp. 152, 161.
134. Moltmann, *Trinity and the Kingdom*, p. 152.
135. Pannenberg, *ST* 1:331.
136. Pannenberg, *ST* 1:332-33.
137. Pannenberg, *ST* 1:331.
138. See Pannenberg, *ST* 1:330-31.
139. Pannenberg, *ST* 1:329; see also 331.

be.[140] "The unity of God in the trinity of persons must also be the basis of the distinction and unity of the immanent Trinity and the economic Trinity."[141]

Obviously, Pannenberg takes Rahner's rule as the basis but expands and reformulates it in a significant way. For him, the rule "means that the doctrine of the Trinity does not merely begin with the revelation of God in Jesus Christ and then work back to a trinity in the eternal essence of God, but that it must constantly link the trinity in the eternal essence of God to his historical revelation, since revelation cannot be viewed as extraneous to his deity."[142] This means that the unity — albeit not equation, because of disparity — of the economic and immanent Trinity happens in relation to history and finds its culmination in the eschaton. What happens in salvation history — including the incarnation, cross, and resurrection — is not so external to the divine life that it would be meaningless. On the other hand, in his own transcendent, majestic life, God is God and neither evolves nor becomes. That formulation is supported in this project.

So far we have considered the economic-immanent distinction in a somewhat formal way. The contemporary turn to narrative reminds us that "[s]ince the biblical God can truly be identified by narrative, his hypostatic being, his self-identity, is constituted in *dramatic coherence*." The narrative of God in the biblical canon contains unexpected events that cannot all be predicted. But even then we can see "afterwards . . . it was just what had to happen."[143] In biblical revelation there are times when the Lord "explicitly puts his self-identity at narrative risk," as in Isaiah 40–45 where Yahweh's role as the ruler of history is at stake, or most importantly at the crucifixion, in which "the one called 'Father' here hands the one called 'Son' over to oppositional and deadly creatures."[144]

In interpreting the meaning of these ambiguities and challenges to the task of discerning God's self-identity, Robert Jenson walks a thin line of wanting to avoid, on the one hand, the danger of considering them as mere theatrical acts,[145] and on the other hand, leaving the self-identity question unanswered.[146] This brings the importance of the future into the picture: "Since the Lord's self-identity is constituted in dramatic coherence, it is established

140. Pannenberg, *ST* 1:331-32, at 331.
141. Pannenberg, *ST* 1:333.
142. Pannenberg, *ST* 1:328.
143. Jenson, *Systematic Theology*, 1:64, emphasis in original.
144. Jenson, *Systematic Theology*, 1:65.
145. Jenson, *The Triune Identity*, p. 4.
146. Jenson, *Systematic Theology*, 1:64, 65.

not from the beginning but from the end, not at birth but at death, not in *persistence* but in *anticipation*."[147] Anticipation means that the "future that moves a story must somehow be available within it if we are to live the story while it is still in progress."[148] To avoid the danger of divine becoming in history (process theology) or absorption of the immanent into the economic Trinity,[149] it is worth repeating that the determination of the trinitarian identity at the "end" of the (historical) narrative is not its *determination* by the events of history but rather its *manifestation*. Neither God's power nor the divine (fore) knowledge has to be superfluous or unrelated to the events of history. As in all created, contingent, dependent life, a fair amount of freedom is given, yet not to the point that the eternal divine life is the function of historical happenings (even if the life of the whole universe is included, not only that of our planet). Using his somewhat idiosyncratic terminology, Jenson notes rightly that if God's "eternity" means "'Faithfulness' to the last future,"[150] then it means "the certainty of his [God's] triumph."[151]

Before we investigate the works of God in the history of the world in light of the trinitarian panentheism developed in this project, we visit a long-standing debate about the relationship between the Christian East's and the Christian West's understanding of the Trinity.

Do the Christian East and West Confess the Same Trinitarian Faith?

The ongoing and unresolved ecumenical and theological question is simply this: What are the ramifications of the *filioque* clause, according to which the Spirit proceeds from the Father *and* the Son, as in the official creedal tradition under the leadership of the Christian West,[152] in contrast to procession only from the Father, as the Christian East still insists? Are there any prospects for rapprochement? The investigation proceeds here in two stages. First, instead of

147. Jenson, *Systematic Theology*, 1:66, emphasis in original.

148. Jenson, *Systematic Theology*, 1:67.

149. In his earlier work *The Triune Identity* — notwithstanding some words of caution (p. 139) — the immanent Trinity virtually comes to be absorbed into the economic eschatologically; see p. 140.

150. Jenson, *The Triune Identity*, p. 141; *Systematic Theology*, 1:46-50, 94-101.

151. Jenson, *The Triune Identity*, p. 141; *Systematic Theology*, 1:157.

152. The standard view is that this addition was first accepted by the Council of Toledo in 589 and ratified by the 809 Aachen Synod. It was incorporated in later creeds such as that of the Fourth Lateran Council in 1215 and the Council of Lyons in 1274.

a generic historical study, the chief features of the Christian West's trinitarian formulations as formulated by Augustine will be scrutinized in light of current scholarship, which has offered a more nuanced picture with greater potential for convergence with the East. Thereafter, the current ecumenical proposals of rapprochement and their assessment will be in order.

The Augustinian Legacy

The older consensus is that because of his Neoplatonic leanings, Augustine one-sidedly put stress on the unity of the divine essence and had a hard time accounting for distinctions. That would of course mean that his approach would be diametrically opposed to the Eastern view.[153] All this has even caused some to speak of the "theological crisis of the West"![154] Not all are convinced that this is a fair reading of Augustine.[155] On the one hand, we know now that an unnuanced attribution to the Cappadocians — as a counterpart to the West — of either a social doctrine of the Trinity or a consistent and authentic establishment of the threeness is an unfounded assumption. On the other hand, it is also widely debated whether, rather than starting with the unity of the divine essence, Augustine built on the Cappadocians' view rather than serving as a counterexample.[156]

Augustine of course affirms the tradition concerning consubstantiality as well as distinctions of the Son and Spirit.[157] Furthermore, somewhat like Eastern theologians, Augustine depicts the Father as the *principium*, the primary or beginning of the Deity.[158] He conceives the Spirit as communion (of the Father and the Son), their shared love, and a gift.[159] In book 8 of *De Trinitate*, he develops the Trinity with the help of the idea of interpersonal love in terms

153. E.g., Prestige, *God in Patristic Thought*, p. 237; and Margerie, *Christian Trinity*, pp. 110-21.

154. Gunton, "Augustine, the Trinity," pp. 33-58.

155. The most vocal critic of the alleged Neoplatonic influence on Augustine is Barnes, "Rereading Augustine's Theology of the Trinity," pp. 145-76. A careful, cautious interpretation, quite critical of the old consensus, is offered by Studer, *Trinity and Incarnation*, pp. 167-85.

156. Cary, "Historical Perspectives on Trinitarian Doctrine," p. 9.

157. E.g., Augustine, *Letters* 169.540: "The Son is not the Father, the Father is not the Son, and neither the Father nor the Son is the Holy Spirit. . . . [T]hese are equal and co-eternal, and absolutely of one nature . . . an inseparable trinity."

158. Augustine, *On the Trinity* 4.20.28-29. See further, Studer, *Grace of Christ*, pp. 104-5.

159. Augustine, *On the Trinity* 5.11.12; 15.27.50 (communion); 15.17.27 (love); 5.12.13; 5.15.16 (gift).

of filiation and paternity. The Father is Lover, the Son the Beloved, and the Spirit the mutual Love that connects the two. Furthermore, for Augustine, incarnation is a major trinitarian event,[160] which in turn makes his theology less abstract and "psychological" and more authentically anchored in the economy of salvation, a trademark of the East as well.[161]

There is no doubt that with all his stress on the unity, for Augustine the relations are eternal.[162] The Eastern idea of *perichoresis*, mutual interpenetration, is no stranger to him.[163] At the same time, Augustine was also building on the Cappadocians' idea mentioned above of the unity of the three persons in their outward works, the consequence of which is that from the creaturely works we may know the divine unity. His use of psychological analogies, hence, should not be given undue attention nor taken out of the context of his wider trinitarian framework. For him they are just that, *analogies,* and — importantly — they follow (in chaps. 8–15 of *De Trinitate*)[164] the careful biblical exposition (chaps. 1–7). It is somewhat ironic that particularly in later Western tradition analogies based on the notions of self-presence, self-knowledge, and self-love lean toward a "monopersonal, modalist view of God"[165] even though they grow out of an interpersonal, thus communal and relational, context, especially when it comes to love. Significantly, Richard of St. Victor in the medieval era picks up the relational aspect of Augustine's emphasis on love and develops it into a communion theology.

What about the Spirit's procession? The Spirit proceeds "originally" from the Father and also in common from both the Father and the Son, as something given by the Father.[166] In other words, Augustine is careful in safeguarding the Father as the primary source of the Spirit.[167] And even when the Son is included in the act of procession of the Spirit, it is not from two sources but rather from a single source in order to protect the divine unity.[168] Again Augustine's legacy is somewhat ambiguous. On the one hand, there is no denying

---

160. See further, Barnes, "Rereading Augustine's Theology of the Trinity," pp. 154-68; Studer, *Trinity and Incarnation,* pp. 168-85 especially.

161. See, e.g., Augustine, *Letters* 169.2.5-9.

162. Pannenberg, *ST* 1:284.

163. See particularly Augustine, *On the Trinity* 6.10.12.

164. Analogies are also discussed in *[Homilies] Tractates on the Gospel of St. John* 23, as well as in *Letters* 11 and 169, among others.

165. O'Collins, *The Tripersonal God,* p. 137.

166. Augustine, *On the Trinity* 15.26.47.

167. See Augustine, *On the Trinity* 4.20.29.

168. Augustine, *On the Trinity* 5.14.

that Augustine's idea of the Spirit as the shared love between Father and Son and his teaching about the double procession of the Spirit helped the Christian West to ratify the *filioque* clause. On the other hand, had the West been more sensitive to the shared tradition and to the sensibilities of the East, Augustine's idea of the procession of the Spirit from the Father through the Son could have helped avoid the conflict between East and West. Eastern theologians are not necessarily against the idea of the Spirit proceeding from the Father (who is the source, after all) through the Son. And for Augustine, unlike so much of later Western tradition, the Spirit's derivation also from the Son does not necessarily mean inferiority in status any more than does the Son's generation from the Father (this was of course the affirmation against the Arians).[169]

All this said, there is no denying that while Augustine himself was keener on distinctions between Father, Son, and Spirit; understood relations as eternal; and forged a strong link with salvation history (incarnation), in post-Augustinian tradition the unity took the upper hand. Furthermore, the link with salvation history was severely weakened and (psychological) analogies became abstract and speculative. These moves went in a different direction than did Eastern theologians' stress on the significance of the *hypostatic* distinctions among Father, Son, and Spirit, in other words, the "concrete particularity of Father, Son, and Spirit."[170]

Is the Origin of the Spirit Still a Theological Impasse?

The NT does not clarify the interrelations of Father, Son, and Spirit. On the one hand, Jesus says that he himself will send the Spirit (John 16:7), or that he will send the Spirit *(Parakletos)* who proceeds from the Father (15:26). On the other hand, Jesus prays to the Father for him to send the Spirit (14:16), and the Father will send the Spirit in Jesus' name (14:26). Because of the lack of clarity in the biblical record, it is understandable that the Christian West added the Spirit's dual procession, *filioque*.

The Christian East objected vigorously to this addition, claiming that it was a one-sided addition made without ecumenical consultation,[171] that it compromised the monarchy of the Father as the source of divinity,[172] and that

169. See further, O'Collins, *The Tripersonal God*, p. 139.

170. Grenz, *Rediscovering the Triune God*, p. 8. See also Gunton, *Promise of Trinitarian Theology*, p. 39.

171. See Stylianopoulos and Heim, eds., *Spirit of Truth*, p. 32.

172. Ware, *The Orthodox Church*, pp. 210-14.

it subordinated the Spirit to Jesus with theological corollaries in ecclesiology, the doctrine of salvation, and so on.[173] With all its exaggerations and passionate rhetoric, the Eastern critique of the *filioque* is important both ecumenically and theologically and should not be dismissed.[174] The West did not have the right to unilaterally add *filioque*.[175] That said, in my judgment, *filioque* is not heretical even though ecumenically and theologically it is unacceptable and therefore should be removed.[176] It would be important for the East to be able to acknowledge the nonheretical nature of the addition. Furthermore, the Christian East should keep in mind that with all its problems, at first *filioque* was used in the West in support of consubstantiality, an idea shared by both traditions.

While there are those who for some reason or another support the *filioque* clause,[177] there is a growing consensus among Western theologians about the need to delete the addition and thus return to the original form of the creed.[178] Moltmann for years has appealed for the removal of the addition and has suggested a more conciliar way of putting it, namely, that the Spirit proceeds "from the Father of the Son." He wants to emphasize the biblical idea of reciprocity of Spirit and Son.[179] An alternative to *filioque*, "from the Father through the Son," would also be acceptable to the Christian East. It would defend the monarchy of the Father (and in that sense, some kind of subordination of the Son to the Father, an idea not foreign to the East) and still be ambiguous enough.[180]

I agree with Pannenberg that beyond *filioque* there is a weakness that

173. The main objections were first articulated by the ninth-century patriarch of Constantinople Photios in his *On the Mystagogy of the Holy Spirit*, pp. 51-52, 71-72 especially. See also Lossky, "The Procession of the Holy Spirit in Orthodox Trinitarian Doctrine," chap. 4 of *In the Image and Likeness of God*; Nissiotis, "Main Ecclesiological Problem of the Second Vatican Council," pp. 31-62.

174. For an important Orthodox statement, see Needham, "Filioque Clause."

175. Peters, *God as Trinity*, p. 65.

176. Pannenberg, *ST* 1:319 concurs. Peters makes the brilliant point that in principle there is nothing against adding to the creeds as long as it is done in concert. Peters, *God as Trinity*, p. 66.

177. Most famously, Barth *CD* I/1, p. 480. See also Bray, "The *Filioque* Clause."

178. For a helpful discussion, see Vischer, *Spirit of God, Spirit of Christ*. For Roman Catholic support of the removal of the *filioque* clause, see Congar, *I Believe in the Holy Spirit*, 3:72ff. Regarding an important effort for rapprochement between East and West, see Torrance, *Theological Dialogue between Orthodox and Reformed Churches*, 2:219-32.

179. Moltmann, *Trinity and the Kingdom*, pp. 178-79, 185-87.

180. Bobrinskoy, *Mystery of the Trinity*, pp. 302-3.

plagues both traditions, that is, the understanding of relations mainly in terms of origins. Both East and West share that view in their own distinctive ways: the East by insisting on the role of the Father as the source and the West by making Son and Spirit derive their deity from the Father.[181] This blurs the key idea of Athanasius that relations are based on mutuality rather than origin. Another Lutheran, Ted Peters, who supports the removal of the *filioque* clause, however, remarks that the idea of the Spirit proceeding both from the Son and from the Father also points to something valuable. It highlights relationality and communality, the Spirit being the shared love between Father and Son (and by extension, between the triune God and the world). Furthermore, on this side of Pentecost, it reminds us of the importance of resurrection and ascension: the risen Christ in the Spirit is the presence of Christ. "In this work of transcending and applying the historical event of Jesus Christ to our personal lives, we must think of the Spirit as proceeding from Jesus Christ."[182] Finally, Peters notes, within the divine life the Spirit indeed is the principle of relationship and unity. "The separation that takes place between Father and Son — the separation that defines the Father as Father and the Son as Son — is healed by the Spirit. It is the Spirit that maintains unity in difference."[183]

181. Pannenberg, *ST* 1:319.
182. Peters, *God as Trinity,* p. 66.
183. Peters, *God as Trinity,* p. 66.

12. The Relational God and the Divine Attributes

How to Speak of God's Attributes — or Whether to Speak of Them

"From Below"

"Many theologians appeal to the concept of divine attributes in an attempt to pierce through the veil of mystery to the one, eternal divine essence. However," notes Stanley Grenz, "because God is triune . . . our quest to speak of the being and attributes of God actually constitutes an attempt to characterize the relational nature of God — God in relationship."[1] Hence, the consideration of the divine attributes ought to begin with and proceed on the basis of the works of the triune God, Father, Son, and Spirit, in the world. Unlike tradition, the contemporary theological conviction is that whereas the unity of God is hidden as it conclusively emerges only out of the "contradictions of historical experience" as the God of the Bible shows himself to be who he promised to be, "[t]he trinitarian distinctions of Father, Son, and Spirit are not hidden."[2] That intuition anchors any talk about the nature and features of God in Trinity and thereby to the biblical narrative.

According to the late Reformed British theologian Colin Gunton, the basic problem in much of classical discussion of the attributes is that the theologian begins with a "commonsense" (of course, philosophically grounded)[3]

---

1. Grenz, *Theology for the Community of God,* p. 77.
2. Pannenberg, *ST* 1:340.
3. For critique of substance ontology in this context, see Macquarrie, *Principles of Sys-*

listing of attributes and then believes that is what makes God! It is not that those lists are necessarily so wrong as that the starting point is abstract, "from above," and human-made, rather than based on and deriving from the economy of salvation.[4] A related problem here is that "[i]f God is the very *instantiation* of what the human being considers to be appropriate to the divine, then talk of God's attributes is very easily domesticated such that the attributes function as glosses upon human ways of knowing or of conceiving the divine."[5] This, of course, is not to reject the deep Christian intuition that "[b]y his revelation in the Son the essence of the otherwise incomprehensible God is disclosed,"[6] although for the finite, fallible human mind only so much can be claimed of that knowledge.

Early on in Christian theology, God's essence was defined as a/the "being, the absolute being, being in its fullness and perfection," as in Augustine: "being above which, beyond which, and without which nothing at all exists."[7] When the concept of "being" was linked with the I AM saying of Exodus 3:14,[8] particularly in the context of the Aristotelian idea of God-as-the-first-cause, it resulted in the "elevation of timeless, metaphysical causality over the temporally and economically structured biblical characterizations of God's action in the world."[9] While he was deeply aware of the incapacity of the human mind to fathom the divine essence, the Angelic Doctor's description of God follows that approach. Having discussed the existence of God in the beginning of *Summa Theologiae* (1.1.2) under the rubric the "Essence of God" (1.1.3-11), Aquinas seeks to describe God in terms of "simplicity," "perfection," "infinity," "immutability," "eternity," and "unity," among others.[10] A number of examples from later times, particularly post-Reformation Scholastic writers, both Lutheran and Reformed,[11] could be added.[12] Lest it be misunderstood

---

tematic Theology, pp. 74-75; Whitehead, *Process and Reality*, p. xiii. For comments, see Alston, "Substance and the Trinity," p. 201.

4. So also Gunton, *Act and Being*, pp. 1, 8; Holmes, "Theological Function," p. 206.

5. Holmes, "Theological Function," p. 207.

6. Pannenberg, *ST* 1:340.

7. Cited in Fortman, ed., *Theology of God*, p. 120.

8. As in Pseudo-Dionysius, *De Fide Orthodoxa* 1.9.

9. Gunton, *Act and Being*, p. 16.

10. That said, the Angelic Doctor also acknowledges in the beginning of the discussion that "we do not know the essence of God" (1.2.1).

11. See Muller, *Post-Reformation Reformed Dogmatics*.

12. Important similar kinds of statements can be easily found in the Fourth Lateran Council of 1215, repeated in Vatican I, 1870, or, say, the Westminster Shorter Catechism. For details and documentation, see Kärkkäinen, *Doctrine of God*, pp. 58-59.

that these kinds of sophisticated "definitions" of God belong only to the tradition of the Christian West, we should recall the classic description of God in the eighth-century Eastern Orthodox John of Damascus's *Exposition of the Orthodox Faith* (1.8), which enumerates a whole litany of "attributes" of God, such as "having no beginning, uncreated, unbegotten, imperishable and immortal, everlasting, infinite, uncircumscribed, boundless, of infinite power, simple, uncompound, incorporeal, without flux, passionless, unchangeable, unalterable, unseen," and so forth.

Contemporary theology now includes not only significant reorientations and revisions in the discussion of the divine attributes but also a growing number of voices that either question the whole enterprise or undermine it. This is not because these theological movements are not interested in who and what kind of God the God of the Bible is, but rather because they have lost confidence in the possibility and usefulness of tradition's way of pursuing the question. Hence, the discussion of God by postcolonialists[13] or American black theologians[14] lacks the traditional treatments of attributes. In the latter, they are replaced by reflections on characteristics of the triune God that can be seen as supporting liberation.[15] Female theologians typically eschew listings of attributes and instead describe God in creative, narrative-dynamic categories.[16] Cultural differences among Christian traditions also have much to bear on the topic. Theologians from the various contexts of the African continent, for example, have developed creative, locally driven characterizations of God.[17]

Leaving behind abstract, "from above" listings of divine attributes, however, one may still attempt to describe the divine attributes, as long as one follows the contemporary intuitions: beginning from the biblical narrative and reading them off from the works of Father, Son, and Spirit in the world. Taken from the biblical narrative rather than from abstract reasoning, the attributes[18] appear in

---

13. Pui-lan's *Postcolonial Imagination* ignores the topic altogether while it speaks of God quite a bit.

14. Cone's *Black Theology of Liberation* addresses the topic only insofar as it has to do with liberation and mainly in the context of discussion of God's immanence.

15. Cone, *Black Theology of Liberation*, p. 64.

16. For important examples, see McFague, *Models of God*, part 2; E. Johnson, *She Who Is*, part 3.

17. For descriptions of God and the divine attributes in African cultures, see W. A. Brown, "Concepts of God in Africa," pp. 5-16, and among African Christians, Harries, "Perceived Nature of God," pp. 395-409.

18. Barth preferred the term (divine) "perfection" (*CD* II/1, p. 322).

a new light, indeed, in a way that makes them not only dynamic but also concrete.[19] Then the discussions are informed by the narrative of how God exercises, for example, God's power, also in "weakness, ignominy and lowliness," rather than as "God in general or a supreme being."[20] In the biblical canon, as the OT scholar Brueggemann helpfully outlines, rather than fixed nouns or definitions, the OT ways of describing Yahweh are more like metaphors, specifically, metaphors of "governance" — Yahweh as judge, king, warrior, and father — and of "sustenance," related to nurturing, caring, and enhancing life.[21]

Another important biblical way of speaking of the nature of God has to do with the *name* of God. Unlike in our current culture — but similar to many cultures of the Global South — in the ancient world one's name "gives power over the one who bears it."[22] Indeed, in the biblical narrative, the "name" of Yahweh, like the "word" and "spirit," becomes a semipersonified agent of God, God's representation. Important in this regard is the revealing of the name Yahweh in Exodus 3:14. Notwithstanding wide exegetical disputes[23] about the meaning of the I AM self-designation, three theological implications seem to be present: first, that the naming of God can only be had by God rather than by other deities or humans; second, if the reference is (also) to the future, it refers to what systematicians have come to call "eschatological ontology," the primacy of the future, and hence the open-ended nature of the future (at least in a qualified sense); third, while naming himself, God also hides himself, as the "content" of the name is left open. The feminist Johnson adds a highly interesting caveat. In her search for complementary, corrective, and balanced ways of naming God, she suggests SHE WHO IS. When used not as exclusive of the traditional naming, in light of the fact that "YHWH is a limit expression, not a defining name but an unnamable one . . . [and therefore] [t]here is no name that we can comprehend that would satisfactorily designate the Holy One," Johnson's proposal carries a lot of weight and significance.[24]

Reading the attributes of God from the narrative of God in the canon and the economy of salvation in the world tells us that they are *"short-hand descriptions* of the God whose immanent essence is set forth in the story of

---

19. Unknown among the English-speaking theological guild is the massive contemporary work of Krötke, *Gottes Klarheiten*. It aims at "clarity," and hence the concrete nature of the attributes, in order to help contemporary people link with the concept of God.

20. Holmes, "Theological Function," pp. 206-7.

21. Brueggemann, *Theology of the Old Testament*, chap. 6.

22. Pannenberg, *ST* 1:359-60, at 359.

23. See Grenz, *Named God*, pp. 135-51.

24. E. Johnson, *She Who Is*, pp. 241-43, at 241.

Israel and Jesus" and a way of "confession."[25] Indeed, at their core, the attributes are doxological in nature. Just consider this one representative biblical testimony in Psalm 136: every "description" of Yahweh and his mighty acts is accompanied by the congregation's response, "his steadfast love endures for ever"! The picture of God that emerges "from below" is distinctively different from some of the classical abstract descriptions in which God's action (attributes) is severed from his being, as if what God is doing does not touch the divine life.[26] In other words, the economic and immanent Trinity were not only distinguished but altogether separated.[27] The distinction between "absolute" and "relative" attributes may, ironically, strengthen this fallacy: as if, for example, God's holiness did not characterize both his being and action.[28] The God of the Bible is passionate, responsive, and deeply relational.

The Living God

If theological tradition has tended to detach the attributes of God from salvation history and make them somewhat external to the divine life — which, unfortunately, often removed them from soteriology[29] and liturgy — in contemporary theology the opposite is the case. A number of theologians have not only wished to read God's attributes off from the economy of salvation but also — some of them — tended to virtually deny anything "beyond" the attributes. In other words, the immanent Trinity is in danger of being subsumed under the economic. That approach was duly critiqued above in the negotiation of the relationship between economic and immanent Trinity.

While it is true that "[i]n the Scriptures of the Old and New Testaments, God is identified neither as the world's nameless ground of interconnectedness, nor as a fundamental principle of unrestricted choice, whether characterized as the basis of all human possibility or, alternatively, as the basic threat to human existence," it is also the case that the attributes "are at each and every moment and in the most proper sense descriptions of *the living God*. For the

25. Holmes, "Theological Function," p. 207; the latter citations in Holmes come from Webster, *Holiness*, without specific page number.

26. The classic statement is of course Anselm, *Proslogium* 8, who says, when speaking of God's compassion, "thou dost not feel emotion . . . [and] art not affected by any share in our wretchedness."

27. So also Gunton, *Act and Being*, p. 23.

28. See further, Gunton, *Act and Being*, pp. 24-25.

29. Charry, "Soteriological Importance of the Divine Perfections," p. 132.

canon of the Old and New Testament Scriptures, it is the living and active God who lies at the heart of its narrated history." That is, God who "has life in himself" (John 5:26) is "livingness" in the inner-trinitarian divine life, not only in relation to creation.[30] As argued above, while there is an integral connection between the economic and immanent Trinity, it is essential to maintain that in "the doctrine of God the immanent Trinity must not only be regarded as always preceding the economic, but that also an asymmetrical relationship be posited between the two,"[31] lest the "reality" of God's own life be subsumed under the works of God in the world. Pannenberg makes the brilliant observation that while we must think of God's existence "as an active presence in the reality of the world . . . [we] must think of it as an existence transcending the world and worldly things only when the essence of God is recognized to be eternal and thus high above the perishability of created things."[32]

As long as substance ontology was the dominant paradigm, theological tradition routinely started the discussion of attributes with the careful consideration of their relation to the divine essence. While generally it was agreed that attributes cannot be separate from the essence, opinions varied as to how to establish the necessary connection.[33] Following the strict rule of the "simplicity" of God — rejecting the absurd idea that God is made of "parts"[34] — it seemed almost impossible to negotiate the relationship between God's essence and God's attributes. If simplicity rules out any distinction, then how can we distinguish essence and attributes and distinguish among the attributes themselves? While those debates are not completely irrelevant to current theology, they have lost urgency in the context of a dynamic epistemology in which even the essence of God is conceived relationally.[35] The investigation proceeds from the dynamic biblical narrative, and attributes have to do with doxology and salvation history. In other words, the attributes tell us of God in relation to the world. At the same time, rooted in the undivided, common essence of God, the notion of the infinity of God (while it does not allow us to ultimately define the essence of God) helps us link the attributes in a way that categorical

30. Wynne, "The Livingness of God," p. 192.

31. Holmes, "God's Attributes as God's Clarities," p. 66; so also Molnar, *Divine Freedom*, p. 63.

32. Pannenberg, *ST* 1:357.

33. This was the debate between nominalists and realists.

34. For the classic understanding, see Augustine, *City of God* 11.10; Anselm, *Proslogium* 18. For a useful definition of "simplicity," see Morris, *Our Idea of God*, p. 113. For a contemporary discussion, see Erickson, *God the Father Almighty*, chap. 10.

35. See Jenson, *The Triune Identity*, p. 107; *Systematic Theology*, 1:105-7.

substance ontology does not.[36] In an authentic trinitarian, relational context the relating of attributes to the divine essence, through the lens of the immanence-transcendence distinction, is possible in a comprehensive way: "The relational structure of the concept [of the divine essence] also includes God's relations with the world. In trinitarian theology the principle of the unity of immanent and economic Trinity in the doctrine of God embraces these relations."[37]

Another important shift in contemporary theology relevant to consideration of God's nature and works in the world has to do with the turn to the future. Beginning from the 1960s, Moltmann, Pannenberg, and others (R. Jenson, for example),[38] sensitive to the secular and atheistic critique of the potential loss of human freedom in the traditional theology of God (particularly as long as God was conceived of as a "being" among other beings),[39] sought to "locate" God in the future, as the "power of the future"[40] who comes to "meet" us from the future. Hence, the primacy of eschatology in theology. While detailed discussion of this "eschatological ontology" belongs to eschatology — including questions such as, how can something that is not "yet existent and yet . . . already determines present experience"[41] make sense? — suffice it to say that the turn to the future is useful as a theological template since "we no longer seek to answer theological questions from the perspective of the past — from the decisions God made before the creation of the world. Rather we engage in the theological enterprise by viewing reality from the perspective of the future — from God's ultimate goal for creation."[42] To take up an obvious example: although the basic intuition behind the idea of God as the "first cause" — that God is the creator of all reality — is not left behind, current theology is also not beginning from that idea. All in all, following the biblical dynamic narrative culminating in the coming of the kingdom and new creation, the future is open for the loving and majestic works of God as God shows himself to be faithful to promises of salvation, liberation, and hope.

When divine attributes are considered in the context of classical panentheism along with a robust communion theology, they make sense and help

---

36. For the earliest developed notion of infinity in patristic theology applied to the doctrine of God, see Gregory of Nyssa, *Against Eunomius* 3.5, among others; see further, Pannenberg, *ST* 1:342-43.

37. Pannenberg, *ST* 1:367.

38. See further, Kärkkäinen, "Hope, Theology of," in *GDT*.

39. See Pannenberg, "Speaking about God," p. 109.

40. Moltmann, *The Experiment Hope*, p. 51.

41. Pannenberg, "Speaking about God," p. 110.

42. Grenz, *Theology for the Community of God*, p. 80.

us gain some significant insights into the nature and characteristics of Father, Son, and Spirit, the Ineffable One who has embodied itself "for us and for our salvation." The attributes tell more about how God engages the world God has created than about his ineffable divine being.

God as Spirit and "Person"

Following the "from below," biblically based route when considering the nature of God builds on the intuition that it is in God's action and "in the working of his power" that the essence and attributes of God are known.[43] While the difficult and complex question of how to best understand the "divine action" in light of a contemporary scientific worldview is discussed in the doctrine of creation, let it suffice here to conclude that "action is a mode of being of the one who acts, and it is so in the sense of a being which is outside the self as something else is brought forth by the action, and it is shown and decided who the one who acts is and what he or she can do."[44] Since we know action as a purposeful activity, we can discern the "evidence of qualities of will and ability which are also qualities of essence."[45] Behind the actions of the triune God of the Bible is the love of God, the "epitome of his essence" out of which all his qualities and attributes flow.[46] Probably the most inclusive and comprehensive description of the acting, loving God — indeed based on the biblical "definition" — is God as "spirit" (John 4:24).[47] This description has gained the primary place in approaching the nature and attributes of God in current theology for two important reasons. First, it can be linked with the philosophical-theological notion of infinity. Second, in the trinitarian framework, it speaks not only of the divine essence uniting Father, Son, and Spirit as one God, but also of the Holy Spirit as the third "person" of the Trinity.[48]

What does it mean to describe God as spirit? Early theology, listening carefully to Hellenistic philosophy, was led to conceive the divine spirit as

---

43. Pannenberg, *ST* 1:359.

44. Pannenberg, *ST* 1:367.

45. Pannenberg, *ST* 1:368, with regard to a small but important work on the attributes by Cremer, *Die christliche Lehre von den Eigenschaften Gotte* (1897).

46. Pannenberg, *ST* 1:369.

47. The other "definition" of God is "God is love" (1 John 4:8).

48. Tillich's now-classic discussion of "God as living" (*ST* 1:241-52) follows roughly the same logic as the discussion here: from the affirmation of "God as living" he moves to the consideration of "God as spirit and the trinitarian principles."

"will" or "reason" in order to avoid the absurd idea of associating God with anything material — with the corollary notions of divisibility, composition, extensions, and locality — because of the mistaken interpretation of the incomparability of God as incorporeal; in light of the Stoic understanding according to which even the divine *pneuma* was a very fine substance, stuff, "incorporeality" seemed inevitable in defending the divine nature.[49] Thus, defining "spirit" in terms of reason and will followed, to the point that in subsequent Christian thinking, when Descartes's writings were translated from French to English, spirit was taken as "mind" *(nous)*.

Only the return to the biblical account of the *ruach Yahweh* as the life-principle, not detached from but rather energizing and supporting all life of the cosmos, including the physical/material, could help theology correct this reductionism.[50] The biblical understanding of the Spirit of God as the active and energetic life-principle differs from the limited notion of reason and volition. From the beginning of the biblical narrative, the Spirit's role in creation, as the principle of life, comes to the fore. The same Spirit of God that participated in creation over the chaotic primal waters (Gen. 1:2) is the principle of human life as well (Gen. 2:7). This very same divine energy also sustains all life in the cosmos (Ps. 104:29-30). While theologically not fully satisfactory in all accounts, Hegel's concept of the Spirit comes closer to the biblical understanding as the "term *(Geist)* combines the concept of rationality reflected in the English word 'mind' with the dimension of the supermaterial bound up with our term 'spirit' . . . , an active subject, an activity, or a process."[51] In light of the biblical teaching, contemporary theology has the capacity to embrace an inclusive, holistic view of spirit — and thus of God.

> The authors of Scripture did not rely on the categorical distinction between material and immaterial substance to express their experience of the biblical God. They did not spend their energy trying to hold together divine transcendence and immanence. . . . Their experience of the redemptive activity of the biblical God was a being — encountered by a powerful presence that was wholly beyond their finite control. The absolute reality of this intensive presence bore down on them in a way that opened up the possibility of new life.[52]

---

49. Pannenberg, *ST* 1:372-73.
50. See the important discussion in Moltmann, *Spirit of Life*, p. 40.
51. Grenz, *Theology for the Community of God*, p. 82.
52. Shults, *Reforming the Doctrine of God*, p. 35.

The biblical way to conceive of God in relation to the world speaks of an "incomparable divine *presence*."[53]

This concept of presence can make an important connection with contemporary natural sciences. As different from the theistic worldview of biblical Christianity as the contemporary, basically "naturalist" (atheistic) worldview of contemporary sciences (biology, physics, cosmology) may be, it is also necessary and useful to seek connections. Pannenberg has famously argued that the biblical notion of "God as spirit" might be consonant with the current scientific view of life as the function of "spirit/energy/movement," expressed with the concept of (force-)field.[54] The biblical account sees the divine Spirit as the power/energy that brings about and supports life.

Recently a number of theologians have suggested that the philosophical concept of infinity may best correspond to the biblical-theological concept of "spirit." It is clear that the term "infinite" is not a biblical term. However, the *idea* is widely attested in the biblical testimonies as the faithful speak of God in terms of his incomparability with other creatures in the created reality. We should not think of these biblical testimonies as an exercise in failing mathematical, metaphysical conceptions that think of "infinity" as an unending set of numbers; rather, they are noncritical, authentic metaphorical and doxological ways of highlighting the immense "greatness" of God above anything that can be thought of. Consider biblical testimonies to God such as these: "Behold, heaven and the highest heaven cannot contain thee" (1 Kings 8:27; see also Jer. 23:23-24); "His greatness is unsearchable" (Ps. 145:3); "Can you find out the limit of the Almighty?" (Job 11:7). Probably no other biblical testimony comes as close to the heart of infinity as Psalm 139:7-10. In the NT, the many Pauline expressions speaking of *plērōma*, "fullness," express the same idea (Eph. 1:17-23; 3:16-21; 4:6, 10). Three biblical metaphors and concepts of God — "name," "reign," and "face" — similarly speak of the infinite nature of God, which cannot be compared to anything created but which also embraces it.[55]

While speaking of God as spirit — and philosophically as infinite — is essential in our contemporary cultural context and worldview, that is not all that must be said of the biblical God. Two important caveats must be added. First, the biblical teaching of God-as-Spirit has to do with the fact that "[l]ying

53. Shults, *Reforming the Doctrine of God,* p. 36.
54. Pannenberg, "God as Spirit — and Natural Science," pp. 783-94; Pannenberg, *ST* 1:382-83. The well-known critique by the physicist-priest Polkinghorne of some aspects of Pannenberg's use of "field" from M. Faraday does not materially invalidate his theological approach. "Wolfhart Pannenberg's Engagement with the Natural Sciences," pp. 151-58.
55. Shults, *Reforming the Doctrine of God,* pp. 37-39.

behind God's relationship to the world as the giver of life is a prior internal divine relationship, an eternal relationship within the triune God," namely, that "as the Father has life in himself, so he has granted the Son to have life in himself" (John 5:26).[56] There are both a trinitarian note here and the reminder of the importance of the immanent Trinity as the basis of all our reflections on the works and actions of God in the world. Second, from the trinitarian perspective,

> it must be added that God is not *only pneuma*. He is also a personal reality, more precisely a threefold personal reality. The divine spirit exists in personal centers, in the Father, the Son, and the hypostasis of the Holy Spirit. Perhaps we may say that the field of the divine spirit has three singularities, Father, Son, and Holy Spirit, and it exists only in these three singularities, though radiating through all the world of nature, their creation. In all of his creation, God the Father is working through his Word and through his life-giving Spirit.[57]

In other words, the Spirit of God is not only the life force of God making possible all life, the undivided divine essence, but also the third "person" of the Trinity.

The personal nature of God is in keeping with the way Jesus addressed his God as Father, *abba*.[58] We cannot of course take the undivided essence of the Deity as personal;[59] rather, the "essence has its existence in the person just as the self is manifested in the I."[60] Hence, the "subject" of God is not the undivided divine essence — as if something "beyond" Father, Son, and Spirit — but rather, "in the Father, Son, and Spirit the divine essence has the specific form of its existence."[61] Conceiving of God as "person" carries with it several important implications. First, it speaks of God's incomprehensibility. "We are all persons, because none of us is totally at the disposal of the knowing eye of

---

56. Grenz, *Theology for the Community of God*, p. 83.

57. See Berkson, *Fields of Force*; Wolfhart Pannenberg, *Historicity of Nature: Essays on Science and Theology*, ed. Niels Henrik Gregersen (West Conshohocken, Pa.: Templeton Foundation Press, 2008), p. 72.

58. For an important discussion of the fatherhood of God in the Bible, see Witherington and Ice, *The Shadow of the Almighty*. For the classic study, see Jeremias, *Prayers of Jesus*.

59. That is the correct intuition in the Christian East's turn to the Father, as person, as the "source" of the Trinity instead of the nonpersonal divine essence, even if, as the current project seeks to argue, there are more satisfactory ways of securing the personal nature of the Deity without resorting to a hierarchical view of the Trinity.

60. Pannenberg, *ST* 1:358-59, at 359.

61. Pannenberg, *ST* 1:359.

another." Second, the talk about God as person also implies the divine "will," as, at least in human experience, it takes the exercise of will and intentions to make a person. Third, personhood implies freedom. Whereas "nature" denotes determinism, although not absolutely in light of contemporary scientific (quantum theory's) understanding, a "person" is supposed to be able to exercise freedom (with regard to human persons, of course, in a limited sense).[62]

Eternal God

How should we classify the divine attributes? Tradition built on the important intuition that there should be a difference, or at least a distinction, between the "incommunicable" and "communicable" ones; the former are unique to God's nature, whereas the latter, while perfect in God, can, to a lesser degree, also be human attributes.[63] While that distinction is not without merit (particularly with regard to attributes beginning with the prefix "omni-," unique to God), it may also blur the complexity of many attributes such as holiness, which, as an expression of God's infinity, represents both the "*omni*-holiness" (of God) and the partial-developmental holiness of humans. Here I follow the classification that builds on and continues the argumentation above, based on the concept of infinity, which can be seen as corresponding to the two biblical "definitions" of God, namely, as spirit and love. Infinity also encompasses the theological term "eternity," which is often used as an overarching category denoting the divine attributes of omnipotence, omnipresence, and omniscience (along with eternity, of course).[64] When it comes to the notion of love, that can be seen as an inclusive and comprehensive category of speaking of characteristics such as passionate ("suffering") love, mercy, and so on. Briefly put, we can outline the current elusive, emerging categories of attributes as follows:[65]

I. Eternal God as
   a. Holy
   b. Faithful
   c. All-Wise, -Powerful, and -Present

62. Grenz, *Theology for the Community of God,* pp. 84-85.
63. See, e.g., Hodge, *Systematic Theology,* vol. 1, chap. 5.
64. Barth's (*CD* II/1, p. 464) objections to grouping omnipresence under infinity are misplaced as he fails to see the "negation of the finite" in the concept.
65. I am indebted to Pannenberg, *ST* 1, §6.

II. Loving God as
   a. Compassionate
   b. Good
   c. Merciful
   d. Just and Righteous

The Holy One

Through the lens of the concept of infinity the biblical conviction of holiness can be defined as both a characteristic that separates God from everything else and a characteristic that makes it possible to embrace everything, as infinity can be not only a matter of distinction from the finite but also of its inclusion. In discussions of this attribute, theological tradition up until our times has so heavily focused on the first part of the meaning, separation — which in biblical usage comes through as moral uprightness, divine transcendence, and God's uniqueness[66] — that the equally essential meaning of the fact that it not only "opposes the profane world . . . [but also] embraces it, bringing it into fellowship with the holy God,"[67] has not been duly noted. In other words, the holiness of God "enters the profane world, penetrates it, and makes it holy."[68]

In an important essay, the Scottish Reformed theologian John Webster makes this all-important link between God's infinite holiness, on the one hand, in terms of "the majestic incomparability, difference and purity which he is in himself as Father, Son and Holy Spirit, and [on the other hand] which is manifest and operative in the economy of his works in the love with which he elects, reconciles and perfects human partners for fellowship with himself."[69] It is important, particularly in our times, to stress that "God's holiness is his *majestic incomparability*"[70] not only in his uniqueness but also for our protection, as the "holy threatens the profane world because God does not remain a totally otherworldly God but manifests his deity in the human world."[71] At the same

---

66. Grenz, *Theology for the Community of God*, p. 93.

67. Pannenberg, *ST* 1:399. Hegel put it classically: "The infinite, however, is held to be absolute without qualification for it is determined expressly as negation of the finite." *Hegel's Science of Logic*, I, section 1, chap. 2 (c): §270 (available at http://www.marxists.org/reference/archive/hegel/works/hl/hlbeing.htm).

68. Pannenberg, *ST* 1:400.

69. Webster, "Holiness and Love of God," p. 256.

70. Webster, "Holiness and Love of God," p. 256.

71. Pannenberg, *ST* 1:398.

time, it is equally important to say that this holy God is "[i]ncomparable and different in his being and act[s] as the three-in-one,"[72] lest God's holiness be made only a matter of moral excellence (as true as the divine moral excellence is per se) and, even more importantly, lest holiness be opposed to the divine love.[73] We must avoid the latter because "[t]hinking of God's holiness in isolation from God's identity means that a contradiction is inscribed deep into the doctrine of God: the contradiction between God's holiness and his love," which of course carries over to the doctrine of atonement "where divine holiness can be presented as an ethical righteousness which is at variance with God's attitude of merciful love towards sinners." The implications of this fallacy for the trinitarian view are well known, as it "often takes the form of an estrangement of Father and Son in the work of atonement: the Father is the source of holy wrath against sin, the Son its victim in the place of sinners."[74] An equally failing tactic, common in much of modern and contemporary theology, is to lessen the contradiction by undermining holiness in favor of love.[75]

These kinds of theological contradictions, with deep practical implications, can only be healed when, as argued here, the holiness of God is seen as both separation from and healing inclusion of everything unholy. God's holiness is to be seen as his essential limitless characteristic to which "corresponds a further act of holiness in which God extends himself to maintain the being of his creature." Then and only then can we see that the divine "[h]oliness is manifest and operative in God's loving works of relating to the creature, taking up its cause and sanctifying it for life with himself."[76]

Faithful and Everlasting

The commonsense intuition of "eternal" denoting everlasting time that never comes to an end[77] and the Greek conception of eternal as the timelessness of

---

72. Webster, "Holiness and Love of God," p. 257.

73. As Webster ("Holiness and Love of God," p. 257) rightly notes in this context, Kant's mistake was that he ended up defining God's holiness merely in terms of morality, and even worse, God as "holy legislator." Kant, *Lectures on the Philosophical Doctrine of Religion*, pp. 408-9.

74. Webster, "Holiness and Love of God," p. 258.

75. See further, Webster, "Holiness and Love of God," p. 258.

76. Webster, "Holiness and Love of God," p. 259.

77. Significantly Pannenberg (*ST* 1:401) notes that, indeed, the OT does not know any other meaning for the term "eternal." However, this is not to argue that therefore the biblical *idea* of Yahweh's eternality is merely unending time.

God as the one who exists absolutely "outside" or "beyond" time (and its cor-ollary: change) are not so much wrong as they are limited and miss the deeper meaning of the biblical-theological term. Biblically speaking, the Greek con-ception sounds both odd and misleading. "The biblical God sees, knows, cares, and responds to the plight of his creatures. The biblical community, therefore, did not claim to know a God who is impassible. Rather, they spoke of the one who is faithfully present through time." The all-important implication thus is that "we ought not to conceive of God's eternality as timeless impassibility but as omnipresence with respect to time. God is present in all time, and therefore all time is present to God."[78] For this discussion of the divine eternality, the essential point is the reference to the faithfulness and dependability of the bib-lical God. This is famously and vigorously argued by Jenson, who after careful biblical scrutiny concludes that God's "eternity" means " '[f]aithfulness' to the last future"[79] that hence assures us of "the certainty of his [God's] triumph."[80] Yahweh's eternity means faithfulness through time (as in Ps. 119:89-90). The Hebrew term *emunah* (faithfulness) is the "reliability of a promise" of Yahweh. Unlike other gods, Yahweh is not immune to time; rather, Yahweh shows his faithfulness over the course of time. This is not a statement about ontological immutability as in classical theism but about continuity, faithfulness.[81] As discussed in part I (chap. 3), God's faithfulness in the Bible is being tested and validated when his promises are being redeemed throughout historical events, culminating in exodus, return from exile, and particularly resurrection of the Messiah. God reveals himself in promises that are anchored in history and point to the final eschatological coming of the righteous rule of God.

As long as (the Aristotelian) substance ontology and (Newtonian) mech-anistic worldview constituted the dominant paradigm, the conception of eter-nity in Christian theology was stuck with the notions of aseity, immutability, and hence impassibility. If God is related to time, and hence to the history of the world, change is inevitable, and possibility lurking behind. Here again, the turn to relationality and the robust trinitarian account of God — both in his immanent life and in relation to the world — offer a way out of this dilemma. A significant part of the classical approach also had to do with the understanding of God's eternity as opposed to (earthly) time. The idea of the timeless God seemed to protect God from all dealings with earthly history.

78. Grenz, *Theology for the Community of God*, p. 91.
79. Jenson, *The Triune Identity*, p. 141; *Systematic Theology*, 1:46-50, 94-101.
80. Jenson, *The Triune Identity*, p. 141; *Systematic Theology*, 1:157.
81. Jenson, *The Triune Identity*, pp. 39-40, and *Systematic Theology*, 1:46-50, 94-101. For a helpful brief explanation, see also Peters, *God as Trinity*, p. 129.

The concept of time is notoriously difficult and complicated both in philosophy and in theology.[82] While a detailed discussion of time, along with space, belongs to the doctrine of creation, any consideration of eternality calls for some preliminary reflections on time. Speaking of eternity in relation to God, the beginning point is the idea developed above, namely, God's living-ness, that God has life in himself. "The Spirit of God is opposed to the frailty of all things earthly, of all 'flesh' (Isa. 31:3), for he is the source of all life and thus has unrestricted life in himself."[83] Hence, the right intuition among early theologians of the "incorruptibility" of God, based on the biblical affirmations of God's "immortality" (Rom. 1:23; the term "eternal" seems to carry the same meaning in 16:26).[84] God is not subject to the process of decay that humans and the rest of creation, including the cosmos, are subject to. In that light, early theology's alignment with the Platonic teaching concerning the eternity of the Deity is highly problematic.[85] Early tradition should have been critical of Platonism's opposing of the divine eternity to all change[86] and thus to history. While that notion of eternity secures the biblical idea that while creation "will perish . . . thou dost endure . . . [as] thou art the same, and thy years have no end" (Ps. 102:26-27), it is not in keeping with "the thought that God as always the same embraces all time and has all temporal things present to him." That difference is because "Platonic eternity bears no relation to time."[87]

Christian theology would have been much better served with another pagan philosophical approach to time: that of Plotinus. He "defined eternity as the presence of the totality of life. Life for him as the enduring self which al-ways has the whole present to it, not one thing at one time, another at another, but the whole simultaneously as undivided perfection."[88] So understood, eter-

---

82. See further, Craig, *Time and Eternity*, p. 11: "apart from the idea of God, I know of no concept so profound and so baffling as that of time."

83. Pannenberg, *ST* 1:401; for a detailed philosophical discussion, see Pannenberg, *Metaphysics and the Idea of God*, chap. 4 and passim.

84. Also important are the biblical statements about God such as Isa. 44:6, "I am the first and I am the last," expressed similarly in a number of other places: 41:4; 48:12; Rev. 2:8; 21:6; 22:13.

85. Plato, *Phaedrus* 247d; *Timaeus* 37d-e. For Augustine's (general) note on the affinity of Plato to Christian tradition, see *City of God* 8.5-6.

86. Plato, *Phaedo* 80 (the whole section).

87. Pannenberg, *ST* 1:403.

88. Pannenberg, *ST* 1:403, with reference to Plotinus, *Enneads* 3.7.3. His definition reads thus: "the Life — instantaneously entire, complete, at no point broken into period or part — which belongs to the Authentic Existent by its very existence, this is the thing we were probing for — this is Eternity."

nity is not opposed to time but rather a presupposition for its understanding. Plotinus, with his in many ways promising reflection on time, nevertheless erred in the appeal to the "soul," which, in the mediation of time to the totality of life ("eternity"), experiences time and thus introduces succession into infinity.[89] Only the Christian thinker Boethius could redeem the idea of eternity properly as "the simultaneous and complete possession of infinite life."[90]

The idea of eternity as the totality of life, when combined with trinitarian theology and its claim for the identity (if not equation) of the economic and immanent Trinity, gives theology the needed resources to relate the divine eternity to the historical time of creation without making God a finite being, or making God prisoner to creation. Against the suspicions of the advocates of the "timeless" God's incapacity to relate to any specific event in history, it must be said that "[i]f God is, then his whole life and all things created by him must be present to him at one and the same time. This is not to set aside the distinction of what is temporally different. On the contrary, differing precisely as regards its temporal position, it is present to the eternal God." But that can of course only be said if "the reality of God is not understood as undifferentiated identity but as intrinsically differentiated unity,"[91] in other words, God as three-in-one. While we have to be careful not to speak of "order and succession" or a "before and an after"[92] with regard to the immanent Trinity, that can be said derivatively of the economic Trinity as "[i]t corresponds to the realization that the immanent Trinity is identical with the economic Trinity." Consequently, "[i]n virtue of trinitarian differentiation God's eternity includes the time of creatures in its full range, from the beginning of creation to its eschatological consummation."[93]

In sum: the God of the Bible is seen to be faithful to his creation as the ever-present Creator and Provider God cares for the creatures and creation without ceasing and as the heavenly Father is mindful of the joys and suffering of his children. The classical attributes of omnipotence, omnipresence, and omniscience hence belong under the category of the eternality of God. Similarly, the discussion of God's love, which comes to the fore in his infinite

---

89. Plotinus, *Enneads* 3.7.11.

90. Boethius, *The Consolation of Philosophy,* bk. 5, p. 160. Barth, as is well known, took up this idea and made it a key theme to his deliberations on eternity (*CD* II/1, p. 610).

91. Pannenberg, *ST* 1:405.

92. As Barth inaccurately and without needed nuancing (but probably aiming at the materially correct result!) says in *CD* II/1, p. 615.

93. Pannenberg, *ST* 1:405-6. Augustine's idea of time as a created entity is in the main correct, although he inaccurately continued the Platonic separation of time from eternity.

compassion, in his capacity to share the sufferings of the world he has created, and in his goodness, mercy, and saving righteousness, is an expression of Fatherly love. To the brief consideration of those themes we turn next, and leave the more detailed discussion of time to the doctrine of creation and its relation to the coming eschatological "taking up" of time by eternity to eschatology.

All-Wise, All-Present, and All-Powerful God

The biblical conviction of God's ever-presence in his creation (Jer. 23:24) as well as his absolute transcending of all that is made, even the "heaven and the highest heaven" (1 Kings 8:27), is another way of saying theologically "eternity" and philosophically "infinity." "[W]hereas God's eternity means that all things are always present to *him,* the stress in his omnipresence is that he is present *to all things at the place of their existence.*"[94]

Traditional theology made a distinction between God's "immensity," as one of God's intrinsic or incommunicable attributes, and his "omnipresence," which had to do with God's relation to the world. That distinction, however, must be corrected as the two are best seen in conjunction. "Precisely as the one who incommensurably transcends his creation, God is still present to even the least of his creatures. As in the case of his eternity, then, there are combined in his omnipresence elements of both immanence and transcendence in keeping with the criterion of the true Infinite."[95] Whereas tradition tackled issues such as that between God's "essential" presence and the presence of his power and creative force (Protestant scholasticism), and that regarding how to avoid the notions of the divine essence extended across the whole world (as Spinoza thought),[96] the issues in contemporary theology, with its keen interest in the natural sciences, relate to questions such as how to best speak of omnipresence without making God spatial, which of course would make God a finite being. While Newton's idea of absolute space[97] has been replaced by Einstein's relativity theory in which space-time forms one integral process, Newton's basic intuition of God using space as a means for the creation of creatures each in its own

94. Pannenberg, *ST* 1:410.
95. Pannenberg, *ST* 1:412.
96. For a brief discussion with sources, see Pannenberg, *ST* 1:411.
97. Cf. Isaac Newton, *Opticks,* bk. 3, qu. 28, p. 345: "does it not appear from phaenomena that there is a Being incorporeal, living, intelligent, omnipresent, who in infinite space, as it were in his Sensory, sees the things themselves intimately, and thoroughly perceives them, and comprehends them wholly by their immediate presence to himself?"

place, thus God constituting space by his eternity and immensity, has not been superseded by the new theory. Where Newton is weak theologically is in his incapacity to "explain the union of transcendence and presence in God's relation to his creature because he did not develop his thought in terms of trinitarian theology."[98] In theological perspective, the presence of God is explained in terms of the divine Spirit that not only brings about all creatures but also upholds them everywhere. This is deep immanence. At the same time, the trinitarian doctrine helps explain the transcendence of God since God in his immanent life, as integrally related as that is to the economic life, can never be contained by creation.

God's knowledge (omniscience), widely attested in Scripture,[99] is related to God's presence in creation in that all things are present to God at all times[100] (rather than that God must be "present" everywhere to "know" the things, even though God's omnipresence is not thereby denied either). "When we speak of God's knowledge we mean that nothing in all his creation escapes him. All things are present to him and are kept by him in his presence,"[101] as classically affirmed in Psalm 139. Of course, in a narrow sense, the presence of things with us is the condition of human knowing as well, but unlike God's *infinite* knowledge, human knowledge is bound by time and space locations, along with other limitations of finitude.

God's knowledge and wisdom come to the fore in the act of creation, for which Scriptures often praise him, as discussed in the doctrine of revelation. The discussion of providence and theodicy deals with the related questions of divine foreknowledge, and the doctrine of election takes up the topic of predestination, which of course, however understood, hinges upon the knowledge of God.

Similarly related to God's eternality and infinity is the attribute of omnipotence, another characteristic widely attested in Scripture (Job 42:2; Isa. 45:7; Jer. 32:17; Rom. 1:20; etc.), particularly in the context of creation, to the point that it is said that this God "gives life to the dead and calls into existence the things that do not exist" (Rom. 4:17). Omnipotence can of course only be attributed to God, who is both omnipresent and omniscient. "As all things are present to God in his eternity, and he is present to them, so he has power over all things. His omnipresence for its part is full of the dynamic of his Spirit."[102]

---

98. Pannenberg, *ST* 1:414.

99. God not only knows our needs (Matt. 6:32) but even knows the things hidden (Prov. 24:12).

100. As wonderfully combined in Sirach (Ecclesiasticus) 42:18-19.

101. Pannenberg, *ST* 1:379-80.

102. Pannenberg, *ST* 1:415.

Classical theologians' abstract reflections on distinctions of God's power as "passive, which exists not at all in God; and active, which we must assign to Him in the highest degree,"[103] or on whether he acts only within the strict order of occurrences set by him in creation, seem not to be useful and can be harmful in restricting talk about God's power to that only in relation to creation and, even worse, to a certain type of created order. In light of biblical teaching and current theological intuitions, it is far better to think of God's action as free and open-ended in terms of future possibilities — say, with regard to the cosmic evolutionary process and its "end" — and, if the divine will so wishes, not determined by the observed regularity of either intentional or physical processes. Yes, "[t]he freedom of the God who acts in history finds expression in the contingency of historical events. But this freedom is always the freedom of the Creator, whose action in ways that are above all human provision aim at the consummation of his creation."[104]

Whereas in traditional theology the attribute of omnipotence played a central role, in the beginning of the third millennium any reference to the divine power — or any kind of conception of power, for that matter — raises eyebrows and subjects the speaker to the charge of the abuse of power. It is also integrally related to the suspicion of religion's link with violence. Against those valid suspicions, the Cuban American González rightly notes that the biblical God does not "rule the world with an iron fist, as Pharaoh ruled over Egypt or Pinochet ruled Chile. God does not destroy all opposition with a bolt from heaven, nor is opposition something God has created — like the military dictator who sets up an opposition party in order to claim that his rule is democratic." Does this view compromise the power of God? No, says González. "The Crucified is also the Risen One, who shall come again in glory to judge the quick and the dead. What it denies is an easy jump from creation to resurrection, with no cross." The cross is indispensable; it is "the supreme instance of the manner in which God's power operates." Yet some may claim that this view denies God's omnipotence. González responds that Scripture nowhere claims God to be omnipotent in the sense of being able to do "whatever strikes the divine fancy."[105]

For any constructive theology, the question of God's power and its relation to the questions of inclusivity, equality, belonging, and human flourishing is vital. Those themes will be taken up in some detail in the next chapter, "Divine Hospitality."

103. Aquinas, *ST* 1.25.1.
104. Pannenberg, *ST* 1:418.
105. González, *Mañana*, pp. 93-94.

The God of Love

The biblical statement "God is love" (1 John 4:8, 16)[106] finds its theological basis in the trinitarian doctrine: Father, Son, and Spirit love each other eternally, as was manifested in the love between Jesus and the Father (John 3:35). Love is not only a quality, a characteristic; it is also, as discussed above, the "essence" of God. Hence, we can speak of the divine love as infinite, as we can speak of God's "essence" as spirit. Like the spirit who finds its manifestation in Father, Son, and Spirit, love "has its existence in the Father, Son, and Holy Spirit."[107] Utilizing a major cultural concept, deeply relational and communal, the Japanese thinker Nozomu Miyahira calls this inner-trinitarian love "concord" or "betweenness," among the Father, Son, and Spirit, expressing itself in mutual knowing, entrusting, and glorifying.[108]

The sending of the Son to the world and its salvation manifested the Fatherly love in a profound way (John 3:16), and Jesus opened this shared loving relationship also to those who loved him (John 14:21; 15:9; 17:23), to the extent that the divine love has been poured out into the hearts of his followers through the Holy Spirit (Rom. 5:5). Nothing can separate them from God's love (Rom. 8:31-39). The main point of Jesus' teaching, conveyed primarily in parables, was to announce the coming of God's righteous rule and to identify "the mission and work of Jesus as the event of God's merciful love."[109] While in the coming of Jesus the divine love came to its fullest expression, Yahweh's electing covenant love is already manifested in the Jewish Bible (Hos. 11; 14:8; Jer. 31:3; Deut. 7:8; 10:15).

The theme of divine love plays a significant role in many other religions besides Judaism and Christianity. According to the Muslim theologian al-Ghazali:

> The love of God is the highest of all topics, and is the final aim to which we have been tending hitherto. We have spoken of spiritual dangers as they hinder the love of God in a man's heart, and we have spoken of various

106. For a profound statement of God as the "subject" of love, see Barth, *CD* II/1, p. 275. See Jüngel, *God as the Mystery*, for an important rebuttal of Feuerbach's (*Essence of Christianity*, p. 52) claim of God's love being merely a "predicate" but not a "subject." Anchored in God, love is also integrally related with truth, as Benedict XVI's encyclical *Caritas in Veritate* (2009) importantly argues.

107. Pannenberg, *ST* 1:428.

108. Miyahira, *Towards a Theology of the Concord of God*, p. 182 and passim.

109. Pannenberg, *ST* 1:423.

good qualities as being the necessary preliminaries to it. Human perfection resides in this, that the love of God should conquer a man's heart and possess it wholly, and even if it does not possess it wholly it should predominate in the heart over the love of all other things. Nevertheless, rightly to understand the love of God is so difficult a matter that one sect of theologians have altogether denied that man can love a Being who is not of his own species, and they have defined the love of God as consisting merely in obedience. Those who hold such views do not know what real religion is. All Moslems are agreed that the love of God is a duty.[110]

An essential feature of the divine love[111] is self-giving, gift, as will be discussed in the beginning of the next chapter in relation to the divine hospitality. God gives himself to the creatures in numerous ways, which we could call the "attributes of the divine love": compassion, goodness, grace, righteousness, and patience.[112]

The Compassion of the Suffering God

At the heart of contemporary criticism of tradition's way of speaking of God stand two related terms: immutability and impassibility. Only the replacement of the abstract, somewhat rigid substance ontology by the dynamic relational account of God helped current theology recast the question of divine involvement in the life of the creatures. As argued above, the God of faithfulness is not an "Unmoved Mover"[113] but a loving, *com*-passionate, "cosuffering" Father. The feminist Elizabeth Johnson pointedly expresses it: "the crucified God of compassion."[114]

In the coming of Jesus, God's compassionate heart is opened to us in the most profound way: "Once the personal history of Jesus, including his death, is made central to the theology of God, then we must conclude that God suffers

110. al-Ghazali, *Alchemy of Happiness,* chap. 8, p. 100.
111. Lindberg, *Love;* Jeanrond, *Theology of Love;* Oord, *Defining Love.* Also important is Nygren, *Agape and Eros.*
112. Cf. Pannenberg, *ST* 1:432-42.
113. God's perfection for Thomas involves his complete immutability. Neither his knowledge nor his will changes (*ST* 1.14.5). In line with Aristotelian metaphysics, Thomas maintains that the divine being must be "pure action without the admixture of any potentiality, because potentiality itself is later than action. Now everything which in any way is changed is in some way in a state of potentiality, whence it is obvious that God cannot be changed" (2a.22.1).
114. E. Johnson, *Quest for the Living God,* chap. 3.

in Christ."[115] In light of the suffering Messiah on the cross, theology speaks of the *theopathy* rather than the *apathy* of God. God's compassionate suffering for us is not passive suffering, but rather "active passion," as it defends and advocates for the rights of the weak and marginalized. It is voluntary identification with the suffering of the world and is based on love.[116] As Moltmann famously has put it, suffering at the cross is not only salvific to us but also a deeply trinitarian event. Jesus' cry of dereliction is not only the cry of the innocent victim,[117] but also a cry of the Father who deserts his Son: "The grief of the Father here is just as important as the death of the Son."[118] In other words, the Son suffers the pain of being cut off from the life of the Father and the Father suffers the pain of giving up his Son. By doing so, God "also accepts and adopts [suffering] in himself, making it part of his own eternal life."[119] "God's being is in suffering and the suffering is in God's being itself," because God is love.[120] Therefore, in his pointed style, Moltmann says: "A God who cannot suffer is poorer than any man. For a God who is incapable of suffering is a being who cannot be involved. Suffering and injustice do not affect him. . . . But the one who cannot suffer cannot love either. So he is also a loveless being."[121]

Korean theologians express the essence of divine love and compassion with the term *han*, "a feeling of acute pain and sorrow in one's guts and bowels."[122] Not only Jesus' death on the cross but also his whole life "bespeaks of the han of God for the children of the poor. . . . Jesus' suffering for three hours on the cross was one thing; his many years' suffering . . . was a profound source of Jesus' han."[123] Traditionally, theology has been shy about speaking of the suffering of God — although Luther's theology of the cross and similar notions belong to tradition — not only to safeguard the notions of immutability and impassibility but also in fear of diminishing or compromising God's power. That is a valid intuition, as some interpretations seem to end up doing just that.[124] According to the biblical narrative, at times God's "power is made

---

115. LaCugna, *God for Us*, pp. 300-301, at 301.
116. Moltmann, *Trinity and the Kingdom*, p. 23.
117. Moltmann, *The Crucified God*, pp. 146-47.
118. Moltmann, *The Crucified God*, p. 243.
119. Moltmann, *Trinity and the Kingdom*, p. 119.
120. Moltmann, *The Crucified God*, p. 227.
121. Moltmann, *The Crucified God*, p. 222.
122. Joh, *Heart of the Cross*, p. xxi.
123. Park, *Wounded Heart of God*, p. 125.
124. Park, *Wounded Heart of God*, pp. 123-40, speaks of the incapacity of God to "save Godself apart from salvation of humanity," in other words, apart from humanity's response to the salvific work of God (p. 123).

perfect in weakness" (2 Cor. 12:9). God's power is not that of a merciless and passionless tyrant, but rather the limitless capacity of the loving, compassionate Father to rescue, support, and deliver whatever the situation.

Importantly, the African American Robert E. Hood, speaking of the divine attributes both from an African and an African American perspective, names, along with divine ubiquity and divine creator, "divine pastoral care" as one of the key attributes, which "is intimate to God's nature and is revealed in God's relationship with the animal and plant kingdom as well as with humankind."[125] Here the breadth of the divine love and compassion is also related to the whole of creation. Sometimes this pastoral care of God is expressed by addressing God as Mother, "the great mother" or, as among the Fon, "Mawu, the generic name for Mawu-Lisa, Mawu being the female element in the deity and Lisa the male."[126]

Good and Gracious God

Goodness as one of the essential features of the love of the covenant-faithful God is a reason for constant praise and thankfulness in the First Testament:

> Praise the LORD!
> O give thanks to the LORD, for he is good;
>   for his steadfast love endures for ever!
>
> (Ps. 106:1; so also 107:1; 118:1; 1 Chron. 16:34)

No wonder the people of God are summoned to "taste and see that the LORD is good" (Ps. 34:8). "In the message of Jesus the God whom he proclaims as Father is characterized supremely, and elevated above all other beings, by his goodness."[127] As the fountain of goodness, the heavenly Father responds to his children not only when they ask him (Matt. 7:11), but also regardless of merit (20:15), whether they are bad or good (5:45).

As love also does, tradition maintains that God is good "necessarily," in other words, God cannot but be good.[128] According to Aquinas, the main

---

125. Hood, *Must God Remain Greek?* pp. 128-40, at 136.

126. Hood, *Must God Remain Greek?* pp. 137-38; for a more detailed discussion, see Mbiti, *Concepts of God in Africa*, pp. 92-93.

127. Pannenberg, *ST* 1:432.

128. Although behind this insistence is the "perfect being" notion that we cannot hold in every sense (most importantly, in the way tradition linked it to immutability and impassibility), the basic intuition is right on target.

reason why "God cannot will evil" is that "since the object of the will is the apprehended good, the will cannot aim at evil unless in some way it is proposed to it as a good; and this cannot take place without error. But in the divine knowledge there cannot be error." On the contrary, "God is the highest good," unable to "bear any mingling with evil."[129] The goodness of God, of course, has come under questioning because of the existence of evil in the world that God has created good. That most complicated theological question will be discussed in the doctrine of providence.

In biblical teaching, God's goodness and "his saving and forgiving activity as an expression of his mercy (Matt. 18:33; cf. Luke 10:37)" go together. In its more inclusive sense, behind the term "mercy" is the Hebrew concept *hesed*, covenant-based loving-kindness, grace, and favor. "God's merciful turning to the needy, the suffering, and the helpless must thus be seen as a specific expression of his goodness."[130]

As an expression of God's goodness that is liberally shown to people without merit (Exod. 33:19; Dan. 9:18; Rom. 9:15-16, 18) and regardless of the quality of their lives, God shows mercy even to those who rebel against him (Dan. 9:9). Perhaps the most profound show of mercy is the loving embrace of the prodigal son (Luke 15:20). In the NT the sending of God's Son is similarly seen as the expression of love (John 3:16) and mercy (Titus 3:5; Eph. 2:4-5). While God's moral integrity is never in question, the NT says, "Mercy triumphs over judgment" (James 2:13).

God of Righteousness and Patience

In what ways could righteousness be linked with the love of God? Common sense would make the other connection: that righteousness is rather a subcategory of or at least linked with judgment of God. The integral relation of righteousness to the love of God is established in its biblical link with covenant righteousness. In that context, "[i]ts content is not a norm but an action, the

---

129. *Summa contra Gentiles* 1.95.3-4. Swinburne has expanded Thomas's defense by adding "impulse" to ignorance as the source of evil deeds; in God, however, there is no irrational impulse, and on that basis God can be held necessarily good (*Coherence of Theism*, p. 202). While materially affirming the goodness of God, Stephen Davis argues contrary to Aquinas that God is not thereby necessarily good because in principle it is possible for God to do evil although he never does it (*Logic and the Nature of God*, pp. 94-95 particularly). A useful discussion can be found in Erickson, *God the Father Almighty*, chap. 11.

130. Pannenberg, *ST* 1:432-33.

demonstration of salvation."[131] This is exactly what lies behind the Pauline statement: "This was to show God's righteousness, because in his divine forbearance he had passed over former sins; it was to prove at the present time that he himself is righteous and that he justifies him who has faith in Jesus" (Rom. 3:25-26). Contrary to the legalistic-forensic mind-set that would take the condemnation of the lawbreaker as the means of showing the righteousness of the judge, in the biblical covenant framework, it is the forgiveness of sins and pronouncing freedom from the debt of wrongdoing, on the basis of the divine act of mercy in Jesus Christ, that demonstrate God's righteousness. A similar type of logic is at work in 2 Corinthians 5:21 — "For our sake he made him to be sin who knew no sin, so that in him we might become the righteousness of God" — in which the saving reconciliation to God of sinners by God is seen as the way of establishing God's righteousness.

From early on, Christian theology was in danger of losing the biblical covenant-based notion of God's righteousness as first, in the controversy with Gnostics, it was led to define righteousness in penal terms and then do everything to relate it to God's mercy, and later, as in Aquinas — when God's goodness was seen as the source of the existence of all things while righteousness was the principle of order and proportionality (ST 1.21.4) — righteousness was linked with the punishment of the reprobate (as opposed to goodness, which helped saved the elect, 1.23.5). Even though Luther's groundbreaking insight was that, rather than penal justice, God's righteousness is salvific righteousness that makes believers righteous, theological tradition still by and large continued to link righteousness with penalty. Barth came again to link mercy and righteousness in a way much closer to biblical theology.[132] Only in contemporary theology, thanks to the new perspective on Paul and the ecumenical advances in the reinterpretation of justification by faith, has the biblical covenant understanding of the righteousness of God been recovered. Furthermore, the rediscovery of the biblical concept of God's faithfulness, which similarly to righteousness speaks of "the identity and consistency of the eternal God in his turning in love to his creatures"[133] and creation, has strengthened this understanding.

At the same time, in order to fully rediscover the biblical notion of the righteousness of God as part of God's love, its "practical" implications in relation to liberation and justice must be affirmed in a more robust way. According

---

131. Pannenberg, ST 1:433.
132. For details, see Pannenberg, ST 1:434-36. For Barth, CD II/1, p. 383.
133. Pannenberg, ST 1:436.

to the black theologian James Cone, "It is important to note . . . that the righteousness of God is not an abstract quality in the being of God, as with Greek philosophy. It is rather God's active involvement in history, making right what human beings have made wrong. The consistent theme in Israelite prophecy is Yahweh's concern for the lack of social, economic, and political justice for those who are poor and unwanted in society. Yahweh, according to Hebrew prophecy, will not tolerate injustice against the poor; God will vindicate the poor."[134] And indeed, in light of Jesus' resurrection, it becomes evident that "God's liberating work is not only for the house of Israel, but for all who are enslaved."[135] The next chapter, "Divine Hospitality," will develop that theme.

The God of faithfulness and justice — God of love and goodness — is infinitely patient toward the creatures. That is their hope, their only hope, for rescue. The link to faithfulness is particularly strong here in that both of these features "have to do with persistence in time, with the identity of God in the flux of time."[136] To appreciate the divine patience, we must remind ourselves of the relative freedom and independence granted to creatures by the Creator. Rather than forcing the creatures to live in union with their Creator, he makes space for their independence — and then, notwithstanding their continued rebellion, pursues them for their salvation. Patience is an expression of love that both affirms the independence of the creatures and makes every effort to establish communion. It is therefore not an accident that in several important OT passages where we find the emerging listing of Yahweh's attributes, patience is mentioned along with righteousness, mercy, and grace (Exod. 34:6; Pss. 86:15; 103:8; 145:8). Being not an "Unmoved Mover" but rather a Covenant-Keeper and heavenly Father, he is moved by human response, such as intercession, and is willing to reconsider plans, as in the story of Abraham's plea for Sodom (Gen. 18:26-33; see also Isa. 54:8). No other theologian has probed as deeply into the significance and nature of the divine patience as Tertullian in his *Letter on Patience:* "He endures ungrateful peoples who worship the trifles fashioned by their skill and the works of their hands, who persecute His name and His children, and who, in their lewdness, their greed, their godlessness and depravity, grow worse from day to day; by His patience He hopes to draw them to Himself. There are many, you see, who do not believe in the Lord because for so long a time they have no experience of His wrath (directed) against the world" (chap. 2).

---

134. Cone, *Black Theology of Liberation,* p. 2.
135. Cone, *Black Theology of Liberation,* p. 3.
136. Pannenberg, *ST* 1:438.

13. Divine Hospitality

God the Giver and Gift

To speak of God is to speak of giving, gift, and hospitality, in the words of Letty M. Russell, "reframing the idea of hospitality through identifying characteristics of God's gift of welcome."[1] No one else in the history of theology has spoken of this theme as powerfully as Martin Luther. "Rather than seeking its own good, the love of God flows forth and bestows good."[2] God's love seeks that which is worthless in itself and donates not only gifts but oneself.[3] At the cross, God's self-giving, the most profound act of hospitality, came to expression.[4] The divinity of the triune God consists in that "God gives" himself. The essence of God, then, is identical with the essential divine properties in which he gives himself, called the "names" of God: Word, justice, truth, wisdom, love, goodness, eternal life, and so forth. God is, as Luther put it, the "whole beatitude of his saints"; the name of God donates God's goodness, God himself; the spiritual goods are God's gifts in the Christian.[5] In sum: hospitality is a Christian virtue, derived from God, who is giver and gift. That said, it is also true that "[h]ospitality does not begin and end with

1. L. Russell, *Just Hospitality,* p. 77; for "reframing," see Lakoff, *Don't Think of the Elephant!* p. 15.
2. *HDT* 28; *LW* 31:57.
3. Mannermaa, *Kaksi rakkautta,* pp. 9-11.
4. An important discussion of the theme can be found in Newlands and Smith, *Hospitable God.*
5. WA 3:454.4-10; 158.18-19; 303.20-26.

Christianity."[6] It can be found in secular cultures and among all religions. It is also present in everyday life apart from religion.

Talk about hospitality, however, raises the question whether it "sound[s] dangerously like a particularly comfortable religious title, a coffee table Christianity to soothe away the cares of the actual world in which we live."[7] True, *hospitality* can be easily abused — as *love* and *mercy* can be — yet in light of biblical revelation, the opposite is the case: "hospitality carries risks," it includes sacrifice, self-giving, discipleship, turning to others.[8] Indeed, in Christian tradition, "it is the hospitality of cross and resurrection. It acts often in spite of unpalatable reality. It arises as a protest against rights violations, a hope against hope. . . . The hospitality of God is dynamic. It invites active human commitment in reciprocal, specific, sensibly executed hospitable action."[9] Letty Russell aptly characterizes some key features of the divine hospitality: "In the Bible, God's welcome — hospitality — has at least four overlapping central components: (1) unexpected divine presence; (2) advocacy for the marginalized; (3) mutual welcome; and (4) creation of community."[10] The radical nature of hospitality is intensified because we live in a world that often is not hospitable. Even more, our religions are not always hospitable![11]

While it is a universal phenomenon, not everyone is convinced that hospitality — anymore than gift — is possible. Most famously this doubt has been expressed by Derrida, whose *Given Time*[12] is a current massive attempt to deconstruct the whole notion of the possibility of gift. The reason is simply this: in our world, there is no way of giving a gift without the expectation of some kind of reciprocity. Derrida goes so far in his insistence on "unconditional hospitality" as to say that we should "say yes to who or what turns up, before any determination, before any anticipation, before any identification,"[13] even if the guest "may be the devil"![14] Derrida is of course right that in our

---

6. Newlands and Smith, *Hospitable God,* p. 27; for an exciting and useful account of hospitality outside of Christianity, including in other faiths, see chap. 2 in Newlands and Smith, *Hospitable God.*

7. Newlands and Smith, *Hospitable God,* pp. 3-4.

8. See further, Newlands and Smith, *Hospitable God,* p. 4.

9. Newlands and Smith, *Hospitable God,* p. 9.

10. L. Russell, *Just Hospitality,* p. 82.

11. Newlands and Smith, *Hospitable God,* p. 13. For an important discussion, see Caputo and Scanlon, eds., *God, the Gift, and Postmodernism.*

12. Derrida, *Given Time;* another key source is Dufourmantelle and Derrida, *Of Hospitality.*

13. Dufourmantelle and Derrida, *Of Hospitality,* p. 77.

14. Derrida, "Hospitality, Justice, and Responsibility," p. 70.

kind of world — finite and sinful — absolutely unconditional hospitality is impossible for men and women. Derrida's skepticism, however, must be qualified and put in perspective. First, there is a difference between human and divine hospitality and gift giving. While the former is limited and imperfect, the latter is absolute and possible. Only the divine gift can be a "pure gift."[15] Second, when it comes to human hospitality, only with the coming of the eschatological kingdom is it possible for men and women to participate in hospitality without the limits of the fallen world. Third, in the meantime we have to be content with less than absolute standards for gift and hospitality. It is still far better to give a gift and show hospitality even in an imperfect form than to take away from others, be complacent, or just ignore the other. The same "already"–"not yet" dynamic characterizes all Christian existence.

In an important study, *Hospitable God,* George Newlands and Allen Smith note: "Though we may not find the word 'hospitable' on every page of the doctrinal tradition about God, we suggest that hospitality provides a summative term which may express eloquently affirmations and concerns which lie at the heart of the Christian gospel. Hospitality reflects the understanding of God, and of the shape of service to God and to our fellow human beings, that is central to other major world faiths."[16] Consequently, "Hospitality is not optional for Christians, nor is it limited to those who are specially gifted for it. It is, instead, a necessary practice in the community of faith."[17]

Hospitality as Inclusion

The Challenge and Conditions of Overcoming the Hegemony of Male-Dominated God-Talk

Violence can appear in many forms, including omission and neglect of the other. The question "Who can sit at the Lord's table?"[18] is hence an essential *theological* question. Whatever else theology is, it is talking, writing, language. Rightly the Jewish philosopher Emmanuel Levinas said, "The essence of language is friendship and hospitality."[19]

15. See the important discussion in Tanner, *Economy of Grace,* pp. 58, 63.
16. Newlands and Smith, *Hospitable God,* p. 22.
17. Pohl, *Making Room,* p. 31.
18. Maxey, "Who Can Sit at the Lord's Table?" pp. 51-63.
19. Levinas, *Totality and Infinity,* p. 305. Also famous is the call for "linguistic hospitality" of Ricoeur; see *On Translation,* his little book with three important essays.

The traditional way of speaking of the divinity has been dominated and shaped by men. It has taken up issues and perspectives arising out of male experience. One of the main concerns then of the feminist Grace Jantzen is that the traditional male-dominated way of speaking of faith tends to concentrate on beliefs. She suggests relativizing the central place given to beliefs and turning rather to the importance of desire and feeling. Learning from the Belgian-born feminist theorist and multidisciplinary scholar Luce Irigaray, she also recommends the use of categories such as the unconscious in considering our way of speaking of religion. Of course, those categories seem to be destabilizing to predominantly propositionally based argumentative logic.[20] Moving away from beliefs based on rational argumentation that leads to either/or dualism, Jantzen seeks to transcend hierarchical juxtapositions typical in religious philosophy and theology such as sacred/secular, transcendent/immanent, and theistic/atheistic. This postmodern strategy she calls "double reading."[21] Along with the turn to "feeling," Jantzen, like some other women theologians, commends the turn to pantheistically driven, nature-based emerging interpretations of the Divine.[22] Now, why this turn? According to Jantzen, it supports women's self-knowledge, self-valuation, and growth in goodness. Valuable and "true" conceptions of the Divine are those that help women reach their best potential.[23] What kind of divinity is Jantzen speaking of? This kind of pantheistic divinity, which is potentially found in every person, does not build on the idea of unity, as in typical male-dominated theology, but facilitates difference.[24] Second, while it may not be totally immanentist, it is so much this-worldly that the earthly and bodily belong to the nature of divinity in a way very different from what Jantzen believes is the case with the male-dominated tradition of mainstream theology.[25]

While Jantzen and those like-minded make the essential and critical point of inviting all constructive theologians to overcome the hegemony of exclusive, patriarchal, and reductionist ways of speaking of God, her vision of inclusivity also reflects serious theological problems. First, the attempt to replace doctrines and beliefs with feelings and desires misses the important

20. This theme is discussed throughout Jantzen, *Becoming Divine;* for introductory remarks, see pp. 24-25.

21. Jantzen, *Becoming Divine,* p. 8.

22. A key expression here is "becoming divine." Jantzen also acknowledges the resistance to the project among many feminists as well (*Becoming Divine,* p. 7).

23. Jantzen, *Becoming Divine,* p. 90.

24. Jantzen, *Becoming Divine,* p. 265.

25. Jantzen, *Becoming Divine,* pp. 274-75.

point that feelings and desires are no more innocent than beliefs. Desires may exclude, exercise violence, as well as oppose growth and flourishing. Furthermore, beliefs and feelings are inevitably bound together. A female theologian in search of a holistic, inclusive vision should know better; all that human beings do and experience includes "everything" — body, intellect, emotions, values, dreams, and so forth. Second, the turn to nature-based pantheistic interpretations distances itself so radically from the monotheistic Christian tradition that it can hardly be said to speak of Yahweh, the Father of Jesus Christ. At the same time, the pantheistic identification of God not only makes the transcendent God too much a matter of this world but also is an act of worshiping the physical reality.[26]

Christian theology at large and talk about God are not necessarily and inherently dualistic in terms of body-soul, spirit-soul, or earth-heaven couplets. Christian tradition has the capacity to facilitate an inclusive, nondualistic, and life-affirming way of speaking of God without tapping into predominantly feeling-and-desire-based pantheism and nature worship.

How to Name the Christian God

Women theologians have repeatedly reminded us that the way we name the divine shapes not only our theology but also our view of reality at large.[27] Metaphors used for God are not neutral; there is an agenda behind each metaphor employed.[28] Words "function" and "act."[29]

Counterintuitively, however, the effort to make God-talk inclusive has also elicited opposition among some theologians. The late evangelical Reformed theologian Donald G. Bloesch, highly suspicious of the dangers of inclusive language for God, named the attempt to make God-talk more inclusive a project of "resymbolization,"[30] which for him meant the opposite of "real knowledge" of the eternal God.[31] Bloesch believed that instead of

26. Trigg, *Rationality and Religion*, pp. 199-200 particularly.

27. Famously expressed by McFague (*Models of God*, p. 3) in response to the old saying "sticks and stones may break my bones, but names can never hurt me": "It is the 'names' that hurt, one would prefer the sticks and stones." See also Bacon, *What's Right with the Trinity?*

28. Soskice, *Metaphor and Religious Language*, pp. 62-63.

29. "Language change is an essential part of action." Wren, *What Language Shall I Borrow?* p. 82, cited in Bacon, *What's Right with the Trinity?* p. 4.

30. Bloesch, *Battle for the Trinity*, p. 1.

31. Bloesch, *Battle for the Trinity*, pp. 11-12.

metaphorical language, which in his view regards language as opaque to revelation, we should stick with traditional language that, however, does not endorse sexism.[32] Ultimately, Bloesch argued, "the debate over sexist language is ultimately a debate concerning the nature of God."[33] Setting aside in this context the many problems present in Bloesch's understanding of theological language (a topic discussed in part I of this volume), the point for this discussion is simply this: the consideration of which way we address God has much to do with how we understand the nature of God. That is simply because, to use Janet Martin Soskice's phrase, "the implications of one metaphor are very different from those of another . . . metaphor is not a neutral or ornamental aspect of speech."[34] Indeed, metaphors and symbols used of the divine are not innocent.

On the other end of the spectrum is the desire to replace all traditional talk of God based on predominantly masculine metaphors.[35] Between the two extremes — namely, a fundamentalistically driven insistence on sticking with traditional naming of God to the exclusion of any attempt at transformation of language and a desire to replace all traditional names of God with exclusively female-based metaphors — there are important nuances.[36] Let us name the opinion that calls for an immediate moratorium of traditional naming the "substitution argument." Being metaphors, "Father" and "Son" can be exchanged for more appropriate ones at the theologian's wish. Let us name the other extreme, critical of the appeal to the metaphorical nature of God-talk, the "nonsubstitution argument": for those theologians, trinitarian names are proper names and can never be replaced. In the middle there is the "mediating position," which, while accepting the metaphorical nature of God-language, is not ready to leave behind traditional naming but desires rather to qualify and correct it, as well as find alternative metaphors.

The substitution position considers traditional trinitarian language not only sexist but also supportive of oppressive structures.[37] To heal this problem we must take seriously the metaphorical nature of God-talk. If God is a

32. Of course, Bloesch is not alone in that project, nor is that kind of opinion limited to male theologians. See E. Achtemeier, "Exchanging God for 'No Gods,'" pp. 1-16; Frame, "Men and Women in the Image of God," pp. 229-30; Eller, *Language of Canaan*.

33. Bloesch, *Is the Bible Sexist?* p. 66.

34. Soskice, *Metaphor and Religious Language*, pp. 62-63.

35. Goldenberg, *Changing of the Gods*. See also Plaskow and Christ, eds., *Weaving the Visions*; Hampson, *Theology and Feminism*.

36. For the heart of the debate, see LaCugna, "God in Communion with Us," p. 99.

37. See Chopp, *Power to Speak*, p. 21.

mysterious unknown, as even classical theology maintains, it is very hard to point to a specific "name" for God, at least in the sense of a fixed "proper" name.[38] At best, names for God are analogical and thus only approximate their object.[39] A whole new repertoire of descriptions of God is then available, such as Source, Word, and Spirit; Creator, Liberator, and Comforter; Creator, Redeemer, and Sanctifier; God, Christ, and Spirit; Parent, Child, and Paraclete; Mother, Daughter, and Spirit; Mother, Lover, and Friend; Father, Child, and Mother.[40] The goddess language has also been employed by some theologians.[41] The point is that a gender-free way of addressing the triune God would avoid the problems related to traditional discourse.[42]

The mediating position wishes to redeem the sexist and patriarchal nature of Christian trinitarian discourse without replacing Father, Son, and Spirit with other names, but at the same time arguing that other complementary names should be utilized as well. Having acknowledged the oppressive nature of the language, this approach takes comfort in the leading principle of relationality in ancient and contemporary trinitarian theology. Rightly understood, "Trinity is more supportive of feminist values than is a strict monotheism" since it is about persons in communion and relationships.[43] Also, Christian tradition does not ascribe maleness to the divine and thus does not necessarily contribute to oppression.

The nonsubstitutionist position rejects any attempt to replace "Father," "Son," and "Spirit" with other terms. The American Lutheran theologian Robert W. Jenson argues that traditional trinitarian names form the proper name of God.[44] Proper names are irreplaceable. Another Lutheran, the German Pannenberg, similarly argues against the possibility of exchanging "Father" and "Son" for other metaphors, even for the sake of inclusion. According to him, while undoubtedly related to the patriarchal constitution of the Israelite family, the term "Father" has absolutely nothing to do with sexuality; one indication of that is that at times, though not often, the OT can refer to God with mother imagery. God transcends all sexual differences. The sociological starting point of Father language in the Bible, time-bound as it is, "does not

38. See Denny, "Names and Naming," pp. 300-307.

39. Peters, *God as Trinity*, p. 47.

40. See further, O'Collins, *The Tripersonal God*, p. 184.

41. Ruether, *Sexism and God-Talk*; Christ, "Why Women Need the Goddess," pp. 273-87.

42. See Bondi, "Some Issues Relevant to a Modern Interpretation," pp. 21-30. A rebuttal is offered by Belonick, "Revelation and Metaphors," pp. 31-42.

43. Wilson-Kastner, *Faith, Feminism, and the Christ*, p. 122.

44. Jenson, *The Triune Identity*, p. xii.

justify the demand for a revision of the concept of God as Father because there have now been changes in the family structure and the social order." The reason is that "[o]n the lips of Jesus, 'Father' became a proper name for God."[45] The conclusion is that we cannot eliminate God as the heavenly Father from the message of Jesus, Pannenberg argues.[46]

The current project argues for the mediating position, holding, on the one hand, that contemporary constructive theology must be deeply mindful of and work toward rectifying the limitations — and resulting acts of inhospitality, exclusion, even violence at times — of traditional ways of naming God predominantly based on masculine images that are exclusively normative and (quite) "literal." On the other hand, this making more inclusive of traditional terminology does not mean leaving behind the traditional terminology.[47] Indeed, the traditional names should be kept primary and normative in the sense that metaphors and symbols chosen be compared for their appropriateness against this standard. Before we delve into many details of this thesis, a methodological note is in order. Elizabeth Johnson helpfully outlines three different methodological approaches to the question of naming the Christian God, as long as one wishes to stay within the resources of Christian tradition.[48] One is to add feminine traits to God such as nurture and care. In itself this is limited since it still implies that God is Father, yet with some "milder traits." The second way is to seek for a more ontological footing for the existence of the feminine in God; here the main route has been to speak of the Spirit in feminine terms. The Spirit is often linked with events and features typical of women such as protection and bringing forth life. Even this approach is limited since it still maintains the duality of male-female in the divinity. A third approach, favored by Johnson, is to seek equivalent images of God as male and female. "The mystery of God is properly understood as neither male nor female but transcends both in an unimaginable way."[49] On the basis of Christian tradition, including Scripture, Johnson looks for female ways of speaking of God to balance the masculine and ends up with these three: Spirit-Sophia, Jesus-Sophia, and Mother-Sophia.[50] While not necessarily utilizing the same metaphors as the primary ones Johnson suggests, this project builds on the intuition that, while the traditional naming should be

45. Pannenberg, *ST* 1:262.
46. Pannenberg, *ST* 1:263.
47. For a thoughtful reflection, see Seitz, "Handing Over the Name," pp. 23-41.
48. E. Johnson, *She Who Is*, pp. 47-57.
49. E. Johnson, *She Who Is*, p. 55.
50. E. Johnson, *She Who Is*, part 3.

honored as primary, alternative, balancing, and enriching new ways should be sought.

This methodological choice is in keeping with the late Protestant feminist Sallie McFague's desire to steer a middle course between two extreme positions. On the one hand, she opposes what she calls fundamentalism's refusal to accept the metaphorical character of God language in its identification of the Word of God with human words. The leading argument of metaphorical theology is, on the contrary, the refusal to identify human constructions with divine reality.[51] On the other hand, she criticizes those who fail to see that naming something significantly influences how we view it, "what it is to us."[52] How we name God to a large extent determines how we view God. The irony of traditional theology is exactly this: "The dominance of the patriarchal model . . . excluded the emergence of other models to express the relationship between God and the world, and so the model had become idolatrous and had rendered the tradition's imagery anachronistic."[53] What is needed is both the deconstruction of patriarchal language and the reconstruction of complementary, more adequate models for speaking of God. That kind of attempt may be called "metaphorical" or "heuristic" theology. The question that has to be asked — by every generation of theologians — is whether our metaphors are right for our time.[54] It is essential to acknowledge that when searching for appropriate new metaphors — or old ones, retrieved from tradition (as Johnson masterfully does in her *She Who Is*) — we do not identify God with that particular metaphor, but rather understand God in light of some of its characteristics, such as being a friend. So metaphor also says "God is not friend," or, to combine both, "God is/is not friend."[55]

What about the nomenclature "Father"? Is it still an appropriate way of naming God? Here I wish to follow LaCugna. She suggests that "father" is not a proper name as much as a specific and personal way to identify God. "The total identification of God with Jesus the Son, even unto death on a cross, makes it impossible to think of God as the distant, omnipotent monarch who rules the world just as any patriarch rules over his family and possessions."[56]

51. McFague, *Models of God*, p. 22.
52. McFague, *Models of God*, p. 3.
53. McFague, *Models of God*, p. ix.
54. McFague, *Models of God*, pp. 30-31.
55. McFague, *Models of God*, pp. 22-23.
56. LaCugna, "Baptismal Formula, Feminist Objections, and Trinitarian Theology," p. 243.

What is most distinctive about naming God as Father is that God is seen in relation, first to Son and Spirit, and then to the world. LaCugna notes that even if addressing God as Creator, Redeemer, and Sustainer (or Sanctifier) is appropriate *ad extra*, it is not fitting *ad intra* (God in intratrinitarian relations). She suggests several analogies appropriate for that purpose such as Mother-Daughter, Father-Daughter, Mother-Son, Lover-Beloved, and Friend-Friend.[57] Indeed, it is relationality — and thus intimacy, belonging, and mutuality — that is suggested in the biblical notion of Father. That way of naming is vastly superior to the many nonpersonal and distant ways of addressing the divine such as Rosemary Radford Ruether's "primal Matrix" or "God/ess."[58] It should be clear that addressing God as Father has nothing to do with any alleged maleness of God. Hence, constructive theology should work hard at finding and employing divine symbols that encompass the whole of humanity and the created world.[59]

That said, I am not thereby dismissing all nonpersonal forms of naming God, not only because both the biblical and historical-theological traditions use them quite frequently — just think of familiar names of God such as "Rock" and "Hope" — but also because their use may be guided by deep intuitions of relationality, inclusion, and hospitality. The way some womanist theologians are speaking of God makes this point. Arising out of their everyday life of oppression, black women speak of God as both "Strength of Life" and "empowering Spirit": "God is neither simply that ultimate ground of being by which we are grasped in moments of mystical experience nor some ultimate point of reference whom we come to understand primarily by reason. It is in our human bodies."[60] Human talk about God is by definition limited; this is the first step toward nonidolatrous imaging of God. However, even as a limited form of language, it is not simply human talk; "faith in God must emerge from something deeper and more ancient, . . . the divine ground of all creation, of all that is and all that will be — God Godself. It is in our human bodies, souls, and minds in our everyday lives that we *experience and reason* about the sacred."[61]

---

57. LaCugna, "Baptismal Formula, Feminist Objections, and Trinitarian Theology," pp. 244-45. These are all relational ways of naming God.

58. Quoted in Snyder, *Christology of Rosemary Radford Ruether*, p. 107.

59. E. Johnson, *She Who Is*, p. 55.

60. Baker-Fletcher and Baker-Fletcher, *My Sister, My Brother*, p. 27.

61. Baker-Fletcher and Baker-Fletcher, *My Sister, My Brother*, p. 28.

God as Communion: A Theological Account
of Equality, Justice, and Fairness

Recall that one of the four main features of divine hospitality as outlined by Letty Russell is "creation of community."[62] The rediscovery of communion theology, as discussed above, has helped contemporary theology envision God as the dynamic, living, engaging community of the three. Rather than a monad (Leibniz), trinitarian community speaks of mutuality, belonging, responsiveness — without in any way diminishing God's infinite nature as all-powerful, all-knowing, and all-present One. Moltmann has gone so far as to juxtapose what he calls "monotheism," which for him is nothing less than "monarchism,"[63] whether it manifests itself in politics[64] or church life,[65] and Christian trinitarianism, a theology of communion. In his view nontrinitarian "monotheism" supports domination and abuse of power, whereas trinitarian imagination supports equality, fairness, and mutuality.[66] The way to combat the hierarchical and power-laden way of life for Moltmann is to imagine the trinitarian God as a "community of equals, vulnerable and open to the human suffering, who experiences this suffering in himself."[67] Trinity is not a hierarchical entity, but rather a fellowship of persons: "We understand the scriptures as the testimony to the history of the Trinity's relations of fellowship, which are open to men and women, and open to the world."[68]

Indeed, at the heart of trinitarian communion theology is the insistence that the Trinity is a dynamic, lively symbol. That approach wishes to replace the derivationist, subordinationist, and hierarchical ways of conceiving the triune God with a relational, equalitarian, and inclusive way, one that is "a relational pattern of mutual giving and receiving."[69] As Elizabeth Johnson succinctly puts it, "The symbol of the triune God is the specific Christian shape of monotheism."[70] It speaks of "one God who is not solitary God but a communion of love."[71] For such a discourse, essential values are the fol-

---

62. L. Russell, *Just Hospitality*, pp. 82-83.
63. Moltmann, *Trinity and the Kingdom*, p. 191; see also p. 130.
64. Moltmann, *Trinity and the Kingdom*, pp. 192-200.
65. Moltmann, *Trinity and the Kingdom*, pp. 200-202.
66. Similarly Boff, *Trinity and Society*, pp. 139-40.
67. Matei, "The Practice of Community," p. 217.
68. Moltmann, *Trinity and the Kingdom*, p. 19; see also pp. 17-18 and 191-92.
69. E. Johnson, *She Who Is*, pp. 194-97, at 196.
70. See further, E. Johnson, *She Who Is*, p. 211.
71. E. Johnson, *She Who Is*, p. 222.

lowing three. First, the symbol of trinitarian communion speaks of mutual relationality. The triune God can be spoken of with the help of the metaphor of friendship, which is the "most free, the least possessive, the most mutual of relationships, able to cross social barriers in genuine reciprocal regard."[72] Second, the symbol of the triune God speaks of radical equality. The Christian symbol of the Trinity for Johnson bespeaks a community of equals, patterns of differentiation that are nonhierarchical.[73] Third, the symbol of the Trinity speaks of "community in diversity," in classical theology expressed with the term *perichoresis*, a picture of an eternal divine round dance.[74]

This loving communion, the one relational God, while being utterly transcendent in that no finite category may limit it, is also intimately related to everything that exists; this symbol is a profound expression of solidarity with the world. The triune God constantly sustains life and resists destructive powers of nonbeing and violence.[75] God is thus in the world, but so also is the world in God. Johnson carefully negotiates her way between classical theism's strong emphasis on the transcendence of God and thus separation from the world, and pantheism's equation of God and world.[76]

An integral communion theology is also the needed asset to help overcome the rampant individualism of much of modern theology, particularly in the Global North. Cuban-born Justo González claims that this is one area in which Euro-American theology needs to be mentored and corrected by the theologies of the Global South, in this case by Hispanic tradition, for which "[t]he best theology is a communal enterprise," as opposed to "Western theology — especially that which takes place in academic circles — [that] has long suffered from an exaggerated individualism. Theologians, like medieval knights, joust with one another, while their peers cheer from the stands where they occupy places of honor and the plebes look at the contest from a distance — if they look at all." Communion theology and theology done by and in the community, in contrast, "will not be a theology of theologians but a theology of the believing and practicing community."[77]

The rampant individualism of much of the Western theological tradition is not politically innocent, argues the Uruguayan Jesuit Juan Luis Segundo. According to his analysis, Christian tradition's replacement of the biblical and

72. E. Johnson, *She Who Is*, pp. 216-18, at 217.
73. E. Johnson, *She Who Is*, p. 219.
74. E. Johnson, *She Who Is*, p. 220.
75. E. Johnson, *She Who Is*, pp. 228-30.
76. E. Johnson, *She Who Is*, p. 231.
77. González, *Mañana*, pp. 29-30.

patristic communion orientation is not only a historical matter stemming from Greco-Roman and particularly European Enlightenment-based cultures, it is also ideological at its core. The Western cultural emphasis on the "private" underwrites the capitalistic economy with its protection of an individual's rights, particularly economic. In this outlook, God was looked to as the "private" par excellence. This, in turn, is nothing other than "shift[ing] onto God the features wherewith the individual feels he can find self-fulfillment in a society based on domination."[78]

While affirming the turn to communion theology and its implications of inclusivity, relationality, and belonging, contemporary theology also has to exercise constructive critique. The basic concern boils down to the simple question of whether the Trinity in the first place was ever meant to be a model for human relations.[79] A related question is this: Provided that the Trinity gives guidance to the formation of human life, how should we imagine the correspondence? In other words, how much can we claim to learn from the "divine society" for the sake of human societies? Of course, there is some correspondence between the divine community and human ones, if for no other reason than that humanity exists as *imago Dei*. However, this correspondence even at its best is partial and fragmentary for the obvious reasons that whereas divine life is uncreated and infinite, the human is not, and whereas divine life is perfect, the human is not; it is still in the making. Hence, the statement "Trinity is our social program" has to be handled with great care.[80]

Leonardo Boff's approach serves here as a useful model. Unlike most liberationists, he wishes to begin "from above" even when the goal is to develop a socially and politically relevant liberation program: "The Trinity is not something thought out to explain human problems. It is the revelation of God as God is, as Father, Son, and Holy Spirit."[81] Rather than praxis being the matrix out of which the trinitarian communion theology emerges and whose well-being it serves, one has to conceive the relationship between the divine and human in this way: "human society is a pointer on the road to the mystery of the Trinity, while the mystery of the Trinity, as we know it from revelation, is a pointer toward social life and its archetype. Human society holds a *vestigium*

---

78. Slade, "Theological Method of Juan Luis Segundo," p. 68.

79. See further, Grenz, *Rediscovering the Triune God,* pp. 130-31; Cunningham, *These Three Are One,* pp. 51-53 especially.

80. For an important discussion of the limitations of the correspondence, see Volf, "Trinity Is Our Social Program."

81. Boff, *Trinity and Society,* p. 3.

Trinitatis since the Trinity is 'the divine society.' "[82] This is not to hide the obvious fact that indeed all theological claims — as analogues, metaphors, symbols — derive from human experience and utilize tools available in human cultures. There is no God's point of view available to us.[83] Rather, the methodological caution has everything to do with the danger of making theological doctrine a cheap tool for fixing human problems at the theologian's wish. In this outlook, rather than being a social program, the trinitarian divine communion serves "as a source of inspiration, as a utopian goal . . . [for] the oppressed in their quest and struggle for integral liberation."[84]

Systematic theology also has to negotiate carefully and dynamically the complicated question of the hierarchy in the divine life. Christian tradition until recently and Eastern Orthodox tradition even today insist on the primacy of the Father and hierarchy.[85] For Zizioulas, in the divine hierarchy, there is reciprocity, if not symmetry. Reciprocity means that Spirit and Son are the "presupposition of [the Father's] identity."[86] On the other side, the Son and Spirit exist only through the Father; the Father is the "ground" of God's being.[87] Moltmann couldn't disagree more vehemently. Similarly, most female theologians and other liberationists simply dismiss the whole idea of any kind of hierarchy in the divine communion. Pannenberg steers a middle course, one that seems most appealing for the current project. On the one hand, he rejects the role of the Father as the "source" of the Trinity, insisting on the mutual — although highly distinct — dependency of each trinitarian person on others for its deity. On the other hand, in keeping with tradition, he affirms the monarchy, albeit not in a way that would violate the principle of mutuality nor subordinate the Son and Spirit.[88] It seems to me this is the most nuanced and theologically most sustainable way of conceiving the dynamic relationality and communion of the trinitarian life. It also helps systematically negotiate the biblical data, which unabashedly seems to assign to the Father the role of primacy in the Godhead.

82. Boff, *Trinity and Society*, p. 119.

83. Boff, *Trinity and Society*, p. 112.

84. Boff, *Trinity and Society*, pp. 6-7.

85. A main reason for Zizioulas to insist on the primacy of the Father (apart from his desire to align with Christian tradition, particularly that of the Christian East) is his understanding that only in this way can we secure the "personal" basis of the Trinity, as Father is person. The alternative would be an "ontology of substance," that is, a nonpersonal basis. See Zizioulas, "Teaching of the 2nd Ecumenical Council on the Holy Spirit," p. 36 n. 18. For a helpful comment, see Volf, *After Our Likeness*, p. 79.

86. Quoted in Volf, *After Our Likeness*, p. 78.

87. Zizioulas, *Being as Communion*, p. 89.

88. Pannenberg, *ST* 1:324.

This primacy — monarchy — following Pannenberg, however, does not have to lead to hierarchy nor asymmetrical relations. In this eternal trinitarian life of love, there are mutual conditioning, respect, and honoring. Diversity is being affirmed in strict unity. Could one imagine anything more appropriate as an inspiration and critique for human relationships and communities?

Hospitality and Violence

On the Complexity of Linking Violence with Religion

The senior American scholar of public religion Martin Marty argues that "[t]he collisions of faiths, or the collisions of peoples of faith, are among the most threatening conflicts around the world in the new millennium." This is because people of different faiths frequently divide themselves and others into competitive and suspicious groups of "belongers" and strangers.[89] Demonization of religious others, or "monster making," often follows, leading to conflict and even violence.[90] Hence, Marty's dramatic phrase, "lethal theology."[91]

Indeed, violence is part of religion's texture.[92] That said, violence is also part of the record of atheistic and other secular ideologies; think only of the 70 million purported victims of Communist regimes, among them a large number of believers of various faiths. Yet the myth persists that it is particularly religion that fosters and perpetuates violence — hence, provocative book titles such as *Terror in the Mind of God*.[93] The contribution of that book by the American sociologist of religion Mark Juergensmeyer is to chronicle — in a rather passionate manner — tales of extreme acts of terrorism by Christian, Jewish, Muslim, Sikh, and other religious believers. Its liability is the lack of perspective in putting these horrible acts of violence in the context of global religiosity and of each particular religion, as well as in the larger framework of violence in the world — past and current — apart from religion.[94]

---

89. Marty, *When Faiths Collide*, pp. 1-4, at 1.

90. Marty, *When Faiths Collide*, pp. 4-11. I am indebted to Richie, *Speaking by the Spirit*, chap. 1, for some key references in these paragraphs.

91. Marty, *When Faiths Collide*, pp. 30, 159-61; see also the book by a clinical psychologist and scholar of comparative religion, James W. Jones, *Blood That Cries Out from the Earth*.

92. Nelson-Pallmeyer, *Is Religion Killing Us?*; Bloch, *Prey into Hunter*.

93. Juergensmeyer, *Terror in the Mind of God*.

94. For a typical unnuanced and in many ways misleading opening statement, see Kimball, *When Religion Becomes Evil*, p. 1.

Similarly, the widely debated prediction of Samuel P. Huntington's "clash of civilizations" thesis, according to which there will be deep conflict between the Christian world and the Muslim world (which will be allied with neo-Confucian states),[95] is hopelessly unnuanced in that it ignores the complexity of the situation between these two religions. On the one hand, millions and millions of Muslims are living in the Global North and other non-Muslim regions, and, in addition, the typical "Arabic"-"American" juxtaposition is also faulty because the majority of Muslims live outside predominantly Arabic cultures. On the other hand, Christianity has by far its largest constituency, at least in numbers, in the Global South rather than in the United States and Europe (although one must grant the concentration of financial and military power in the latter). Hence, for systematic and constructive theology, a careful analysis of the relation of God to violence is necessary — although even the most current Christian constructive theologians seem not to have bothered with the topic at all!

A quick reading of a book like Juergensmeyer's — or of titles even more provocative and less "objective," such as the new atheist Sam Harris's *End of Faith: Religion, Terror, and the Future of Reason* — yields a picture of the existence of violence as more or less a commodity of religion, with the implication that less religion — or none at all — would make life on this planet peaceful and tranquil.[96] The late British American writer Christopher Hitchens's *God Is Not Great: How Religion Poisons Everything* represents the culmination of that genre. His main complaints against religion in this respect are well known among other new atheists: "that it wholly misrepresents the origin of man and the cosmos, that because of this original error it manages to combine the maximum of servility with the maximum of solipsism, that it is both the result and the cause of dangerous sexual repression, and that it is ultimately grounded on wish-thinking."[97] This kind of universal criticism against religion, without making any distinction between various types of religions, in itself makes it suspect. Similarly, claims that religion always and everywhere results in servility and solipsism hardly can be taken at face value.

What makes the link between religion and violence particularly dangerous — so the common assumption goes — is not only the tendency of religion to divide people between friends and foes,[98] but also its tendency to

95. Huntington, *Clash of Civilizations*.
96. For a thoughtful and useful discussion of the blunt linking of violence with Islam by Dawkins, Harris, and Hitchens, see chap. 7 in Markham, *Against Atheism*.
97. Hitchens, *God Is Not Great*, p. 4.
98. Regina Schwartz's *Curse of Cain* argues that it is particularly monotheistic religions

ratchet up divisions to a cosmic level. Argues Juergensmeyer: "What makes religious violence particularly savage and relentless" is that it puts worldly conflicts in a "larger than life" context of "cosmic war,"[99] whereas secular political conflicts stay more "grounded" and rational, as it were.[100] The problem with this argument is that even Juergensmeyer does not believe it is distinctly *religious* to consider violence — especially collective violence, war — "cosmic." Any notion of war seems to give license for people to kill those in the other camp indiscriminately and to exercise violence and hurt as much as they can. Astonishingly, this sociologist expressly says this: "The concept of war provides cosmology, history, and eschatology and offers the reins of political control."[101] And indeed, Juergensmeyer admits that there is very little difference, at times perhaps none at all, between nationalism and religion as the backdrop of violent acts.[102] Ideological nationalism is too often behind brutal wars, whether religion is concerned or not. What makes nationalism — ideological nationalism — so dangerous is its capacity to manipulate and abuse religious sentiments for the sake of unchecked violence. The Roman Catholic theologian William Cavanaugh points to Juergensmeyer's earlier book, *The New Cold War? Religious Nationalism Confronts the Secular State*, where he writes that "secular nationalism, like religion, embraces what one scholar calls 'a doctrine of destiny.'" One can take this way of looking at secular nationalism a step further and state flatly "that secular nationalism *is* 'a religion.'" Rightly Cavanaugh draws this conclusion: "These are important concessions. If true, however, they subvert the entire basis of his argument, which is the sharp divide between religious and secular violence."[103]

A major difficulty in determining whether religion fosters violence — or peace! — has to do with the continuing debate about what religion is, a question routinely dismissed by those who link religion and violence. The political theorist Bhikhu Parekh rightly highlights the fluidity of the meaning of "religion" and "secular" as well as their intermingling even in the contemporary world, let alone in the ancient world and in areas where Islam or Hinduism is the religion of the land. According to Parekh, "several secular ideologies, such

---

that establish the deep divide between "us" and "them." For an insightful critique, see Volf, "Jehovah on Trial," pp. 32-35.

99. Juergensmeyer, *Terror in the Mind of God*, p. 149.

100. See Juergensmeyer, *Terror in the Mind of God*, p. 156.

101. Juergensmeyer, *Terror in the Mind of God*, p. 158.

102. Juergensmeyer, *Terror in the Mind of God*, p. 220.

103. Cavanaugh, "Does Religion Cause Violence?" p. 10. The citation is from Juergensmeyer, *The New Cold War?* p. 15.

as some varieties of Marxism, conservatism, and even liberalism have a quasi-religious orientation and form, and conversely formally religious languages sometimes have a secular content, so that the dividing line between a secular and a religious language is sometimes difficult to draw."[104] That observation alone should make scholars more modest and careful in establishing unilaterally the link between religion and violence.

"The myth of religious violence," argues Cavanaugh, "helps create a blind spot about the violence of the putatively secular nation-state."[105] It simply is unfounded to believe — as many new atheists seem to be dreaming of — that with the demise of religion violence would disappear. Even worse, the unnuanced and naive myth of "religion fosters violence" at times operates ideologically in the hands of the "secular" critics, in distinguishing "us" from "them": "The myth of religious violence promotes a dichotomy between *us* in the secular West who are rational and peacemaking, and *them*, the hordes of violent religious fanatics in the Muslim world. *Their* violence is religious, and therefore irrational and divisive. *Our* violence, on the other hand, is rational, peacemaking, and necessary. Regrettably, we find ourselves forced to bomb them into the higher rationality."[106] In its most perverse form, this myth may lead — as it has even in the recent past — into "crusades"[107] by the powerful nations to forcefully subjugate dissenting governments and peoples under the flag of democracy, civilization, and hoped-for peace. Rightly the Italian philosopher Gianno Vattimo surmises that it is the ethos of modernity that, with its unfounded optimism of continuing development, seeks to "enlighten" the rest of the world and thus is "converting" and subjugating under its hegemony the rest of the world.[108]

Ironically, some of the most vocal critics of religious violence seem to be content with exercising violence on their own terms. Take as an example Sam Harris. Not only was he an ardent supporter of the Iraq invasion by U.S. forces in 2003, he also finds justifiable the torturing of terrorists[109] — while at the same time condemning mercilessly the torture of witches in history![110] Similarly, Harris would recommend a nuclear strike as a preemptive measure

104. Parekh, "Voice of Religion in Political Discourse," p. 74.
105. Cavanaugh, "Does Religion Cause Violence?" p. 6.
106. Cavanaugh, "Does Religion Cause Violence?" p. 6.
107. See further, González, *The Crusades.*
108. Vattimo, *Nihilism and Emancipation,* p. 21.
109. S. Harris, *End of Faith,* pp. 192-99.
110. S. Harris, *End of Faith,* pp. 87-92.

should a Muslim nation threaten the United States;[111] that would, of course, lead to millions of casualties. Isn't this another manifestation of a "cosmic" war mentality?[112]

While no one would deny that religion has caused violence and suffering, the highly problematic overall feature is the naive necessary linking of religion to violence. Not only are the critics usually one-sided, selective, and highly rhetorical, they also "ignore the available evidence from history, from psychology and sociology, and from philosophy. They refuse to investigate the question in a properly rigorous way, and substitute rhetoric for analysis. Oddly enough, that is just what they tend to accuse religious believers of doing."[113] A far more rational and accurate analysis simply is that "religion does some harm and some good, but, most people, faced with the evidence, will probably agree that it does a great deal more good than harm."[114]

Living the Hospitality of God[115]

So far the discussion has established the complexity of unilaterally linking violence with religion and vice versa. What the current project argues theologically is that, first, there is no necessary link between violence among human beings and faith in the God of the Bible, and second, rather than being violent, Yahweh, the Father of Jesus Christ, is a hospitable God who fosters shalom.[116]

What about the scriptural texts that seem to endorse God's violence? Wouldn't those passages alone make any defense of the innocence of the God of the Bible meaningless? On this complex question, at this point, we can only make a few general statements and refer to some excellent resources for further reflection. First, in every society in the ancient world, whether religious or not, violence was rampant and horrible. All living faiths' holy scriptures are ancient texts and share that feature. If the Bible should be forbidden for its violence, then almost all ancient poetry and narrative should be also. Second, Christian

111. S. Harris, *End of Faith*, pp. 128-29.

112. For criticism of the inconsistency of the new atheists in relation to violence, see Beattie, *The New Atheists*, pp. 87-90.

113. Ward, *Is Religion Dangerous?* p. 7.

114. Ward, *Is Religion Dangerous?* p. 7.

115. Heading taken from L. Richard, *Living the Hospitality of God.*

116. In the volume *Christ and Reconciliation* I dealt with the difficult issue of how the suffering and violent death of Jesus Christ may be theologically negotiated.

theology of revelation builds on progressive revelation: God takes people at the level they are and patiently, over the ages, shapes them. To that progressive revelation also belong nuancing, balancing, and finally forbidding the right to violence. Third, the full revelation in Jesus Christ tells us violence has been superseded and replaced with unconditional love and embrace. Fourth, in our kind of world, violence will not come to an end until the coming of the righteous rule of God.[117]

With Miroslav Volf, the current project wishes to "contest the claim that the Christian faith . . . predominantly fosters violence, and . . . argue, instead, that it should be seen as a contributor to more peaceful social environments." His argument is that

> at least when it comes to Christianity, the cure against religiously induced or legitimized violence is not less religion, but, in a carefully qualified sense, more religion. Put differently, the more we reduce Christian faith to vague religiosity or conceive of it as exclusively a private affair of individuals, the worse off we will be; and inversely, the more we nurture it as an ongoing tradition that by its intrinsic content shapes behavior and by the domain of its regulative reach touches the public sphere, the better off we will be. "Thick" practice of the Christian faith will help reduce violence and shape a culture of peace.[118]

The key for Volf lies in the nature of the triune God as the God who embraces rather than excludes. That is the model for people who confess the name of the Father, Son, and Spirit:

> The starting point is the primacy of the will to embrace the other, even the offender. Since the God Christians worship is the God of unconditional and indiscriminate love, the will to embrace the other is the most fundamental obligation of Christians. The claim is radical, and precisely in its radicality, so socially significant. The will to give ourselves to others and to welcome them, to readjust our identities to make space for them, is prior to any judgment about others, except that of identifying them in their humanity. The will to embrace precedes any "truth" about others and any reading of their action with respect to justice. This will is absolutely

---

117. For useful discussion, see Ward, *Is Religion Dangerous?*; Markham, *Against Atheism*, chap. 5; McGrath, "Is Religion Evil?"; Copan, "Are Old Testament Laws Evil?"

118. Volf, "Forgiveness, Reconciliation," p. 862.

indiscriminate and strictly immutable; it transcends the moral mapping of the social world into "good" and "evil."[119]

Consequently, it is not "less" but "more" religion, civil religion, peaceful religion in society, that may contribute to peace. Hans Küng has famously argued "no world peace without religious peace."[120] Even Juergensmeyer at the end discusses "healing politics with religion." For him, the solution requires secular authorities to "embrace moral values, including those associated with religion."[121] This option is the opposite of secularism, the exclusion of religion from the public square. Juergensmeyer insists that, even with the violence it may inspire in rare instances, "[r]eligion gives spirit to public life and provides a beacon for moral order."[122] He opines that, "[i]n a curious way, then, the cure for religious violence may ultimately lie in a renewed appreciation for religion itself."[123]

For the Christian faith to contribute to peace, we need tolerance in public space, an attitude that helps alleviate escalating conflict between religious strangers. Tolerance, however, is not enough. Robust hospitality is the key. Hospitality reaches out to the stranger. It makes the religious stranger welcome.[124] Hospitality is "an instrument or means of dealing more justly and with more potential of satisfying the interests of the faiths in collision and those who surround them and are affected by their interactions."[125] Hospitality builds on the idea of the host relating to the guests in a way that is polite and respectful. Thus, it is an ideal model for overcoming "belonger" and "stranger" conflicts.[126] Hospitality is even more than that — it is a way of turning toward the other in a way that may be sacrificial and costly to oneself: "Hospitality to the stranger demands sacrifice: to surrender our biases: to make the interests,

---

119. Volf, "Forgiveness, Reconciliation," p. 872. For details, see Volf, *Exclusion and Embrace.*

120. H. Küng, *Christianity and the World Religions,* pp. 440-43, at 440. So also Cardinal Arinze, *Religions for Peace;* and McDaniel, *Gandhi's Hope.*

121. Juergensmeyer, *Terror in the Mind of God,* pp. 243-49, at 244.

122. Juergensmeyer, *Terror in the Mind of God,* p. 248.

123. Juergensmeyer, *Terror in the Mind of God,* p. 249. Khan ("American Muslims," pp. 127-47) suggests that a particular type of religion (not a particular religion per se), that is, a combination of "democracy, pluralism, and cultural and religious tolerance in action," can "resolve differences peacefully" (p. 141).

124. Marty, *When Faiths Collide,* p. 1; for important feminist postcolonial perspectives, see L. Russell, *Just Hospitality,* pp. 43-50 particularly.

125. Marty, *When Faiths Collide,* p. 66.

126. Marty, *When Faiths Collide,* pp. 128-42.

joys and sorrows of the stranger our own. As such, hospitality to the stranger is subversive by nature, threatening to the existing powers."[127] While etymology is not always the best way to establish meaning, sometimes it may be. Consider the Greek and Latin terms for "stranger," *xenos* and *hospes*. Whereas the Latin term comes from the same root as "enemy" *(hostis),* the Greek term also means "guest."[128]

While this vision of hospitality, based on a "modest pluralism," is primarily "civil" or "political" in perspective, it is also inevitably "a religiously informed civic pluralism."[129] Indeed, "everyday welcomings of the 'other,' especially at table, are really acts of worship 'for the glory of God.'"[130] Similarly to Volf, Marty wishes to allow room in the public square for different faiths to coexist without co-option, and even for discussions about theology to be conducted in a civil way.[131]

A primary difference between tolerance and hospitality is that tolerance can remake or reshape the other into an acceptable, that is, familiar or similar, image, while hospitality requires acknowledging that the other, the stranger, really is different.[132] Marty's "modest pluralism" hence differs from those forms of pluralism that build on the mistaken idea of the common core of religions[133] and, consequently, on the need — in the name of tolerance and hospitality — to deny the otherness of both parties. That approach would also lead to blocking all efforts for witnessing to any particular tradition's vision of God.[134]

Hospitality as Advocacy

In his brilliant and striking manner, Robert McAfee Brown notes that in the Bible "justice" appears to be God's middle name![135] Following the late Letty M. Russell, we "understand hospitality as the practice of God's wel-

---

127. L. Richard, *Living the Hospitality of God,* p. 21, cited in Newlands and Smith, *Hospitable God,* p. vii.

128. I am indebted to Newlands and Smith, *Hospitable God,* p. 29, for this observation.

129. Marty, *When Faiths Collide,* pp. 70-76, 97-98.

130. Koenig, *New Testament Hospitality,* p. 57.

131. Marty, *When Faiths Collide,* p. 12.

132. Marty, *When Faiths Collide,* pp. 124-25; for important theological reflections on this difference, see L. Russell, *Just Hospitality,* chap. 3.

133. An idea rejected by Marty, *When Faiths Collide,* pp. 165-67.

134. I am indebted to Newlands and Smith, *Hospitable God,* p. 15.

135. R. M. Brown, "Preferential Option for the Poor," p. 10. I am indebted to L. Russell, *Just Hospitality,* p. 106.

come, embodied in our actions as we reach across difference to participate with God in bringing justice and healing to our world in crisis."[136] Recall also her note above that among the several features of the divine hospitality is "advocacy for the marginalized."[137] Hospitable constructive theology not only advocates inclusivity and equality, it also makes every effort to actively promote liberation and freedom. While the task of hospitality as advocacy has been and continues to be the major focus of liberation theologies of various stripes, it is essential for the current constructive theology to remind us that at its core all Christian theology is "liberation theology." As long as liberation is merely an "added thing," an auxiliary element, it can be sought or dismissed — and the theological task continues as it is. However, the gospel means liberation at all levels.[138] The God of the Bible is committed to liberation. "God is God who saves us not through his domination but through his suffering. . . . And it is thus that the cross acquires its tremendous revelatory potential with respect to God's weakness as an expression of his love for a world come of age."[139]

Although all Christian theology of God, as argued above, must begin from below, so to speak, based on human experiences of the world and human interpretations of the divine revelation, liberation theologies work from a relentless and robust orientation to one specific aspect of human experience: "praxis." From a liberationist perspective, this praxis is not merely the common human experience, but more specifically the human experience and reality of the poor, the despised, the marginalized, those without opportunities. This is the specific praxis of theology.[140] The adoption of praxis as the point of departure for God-talk does not mean sidetracking biblical revelation and Christian tradition. Rather, it means an intentional and robust dialectic between critical theological reflection in a specific context and action to address impending needs and challenges.[141]

Cone reminds us that praxis in black theology is the experience of blacks in the United States. Consequently, "Black theology . . . [is] the affirmation of black humanity that emancipates black people from white racism, thus

136. L. Russell, *Just Hospitality*, p. 2; for an extended discussion of "just hospitality," see chap. 5.

137. L. Russell, *Just Hospitality*, p. 82.

138. Boesak, *Farewell to Innocence*, p. 9.

139. Gutiérrez, *Essential Writings*, p. 39.

140. See Chopp, "Latin American Liberation Theology," p. 412. See also P. Richard, "Theology in the Theology of Liberation," pp. 150-51.

141. For the "hermeneutical circle," see Segundo, *The Liberation of Theology*, p. 9.

providing authentic freedom for both white and black people. It affirms the humanity of white people in that it says NO to the encroachment of white oppression." This is an important affirmation of black praxis as a point of departure for liberative speech about God. However, it has to be qualified and complemented by two critically important points. First, even such a specific point of view as "black experience" is not an unnunaced, generic phenomenon. This black experience may be different for African American *women* than for men. This is what the womanist theologians argue. Delores S. Williams wishes to replace her male counterparts' focus on Exodus as the paradigmatic narrative of God's liberative work with the Genesis story of Hagar, the dismissed slave woman. Whereas in the Exodus narrative liberation stands in the forefront, in Hagar's story survival is the key; God participates in Hagar's and her child's survival.[142] What is most instructive in the Hagar story — and paradigmatic for black women — is that Hagar is the only person in the Bible attributed with the power of naming God (Gen. 16:13). Not that she does not use the designations for God used by Abraham and Sarah, her oppressors, but she also gives God a new name, *El Roi,* "God of seeing."[143] The main point for this discussion is simply this: the nature and conditions of a liberative speech about God vary in different contexts. This is not to pit one discourse about God against others. It is to make room and facilitate diverse, mutually enriching, and specific conversations.

The second qualification for Cone's methodology of beginning from black praxis has to do with the principle of complementary inclusivity, lest the discourse — in this case black speech about God — become exclusive and even violent, as it did with the young Cone.[144] The limitation of hospitality to only one race, the blacks (or, alternatively, to whites or others), has to be rejected as violence. Hence, the mature Cone's conciliatory and hospitable note of an inclusive nature about paying theological attention to "color" should be affirmed. Utilizing Tillich's concept of the symbolic nature of theological talk, he says, "The focus on blackness does not mean that *only* blacks suffer as victims in a racist society, but that blackness is an ontological symbol and a visible reality which best describes what oppression means in America."[145] Always conciliatory in his approach, another African American theologian, James H. Evans, maintains that in black theology God is experienced as impartial, "no

---

142. D. S. Williams, *Sisters in the Wilderness,* p. 5.
143. D. S. Williams, *Sisters in the Wilderness,* pp. 20-27.
144. Cone, *Black Theology of Liberation,* p. 111.
145. Cone, *Black Theology of Liberation,* p. 7.

respecter of persons" (see Acts 10:34). In a world of injustice, African Americans have put their faith in the One who deals justly with them, but not only with them but also with whites.[146] The expression "inclusive partisanship" of the God of the Bible, utilized by liberationists from various contexts, including female theologians of Hispanic origin[147] working in the context of emerging *mujerista* theologies[148] and theologians from the context of the First Nations of North America,[149] helps avoid exclusion and fosters liberative inclusivity. God's preference for a particular group of people — be it blacks, Hispanics, Asians, or white Europeans — is not meant to exclude others.[150]

An authentically liberationist constructive theology helps expose and correct several misunderstandings of the nature of theology in general and the doctrine of God in particular. One of them is the apolitical/politically innocent nature of theology. González reminds us that the way God is presented in the Bible implies a "political agenda"; God is not interested only in "spiritual salvation," but also in life here and now.[151] A similar common misunderstanding claims that God is "colorless." One of the aims of Cone's critical analysis is to expose this myth as he contends boldly that "the white God is an idol created by racists."[152] Were God "colorblind," Cone surmises, it would mean that God is blind to justice and injustice, to right and wrong, to good and evil. The Yahweh of the Old Testament, the God of Jesus Christ, takes sides with the oppressed against the oppressors. Therefore, for Cone the movement for black liberation is "the very work of God, effecting God's will among men."[153]

How does the Christian theology of liberation relate to the liberationist efforts in other religions? The Catholic Gutiérrez of Peru and the engaged Vietnamese Buddhist Thich Nhat Hanh provide an inspiring case study.[154] Both liberationists speak of the importance of awareness and transformation of consciousness.[155] Gutiérrez expresses the liberationist agenda and passion for justice in asking, "How are we to speak of the God of life when cruel mur-

---

146. Evans, *We Have Been Believers,* pp. 67-76.

147. See Rodríguez, *Racism and God-Talk.*

148. See Isasi-Díaz, *En la Lucha,* and *Mujerista Theology.*

149. See Warrior, "Canaanites, Cowboys and Indians," pp. 261-65.

150. As noted above, this tendency was evident in Cone's early theology.

151. González, *Mañana,* pp. 83-85, at 84.

152. Cone, *Black Theology of Liberation,* p. 59.

153. Cone, *Black Theology of Liberation,* p. 6.

154. In this section, I am indebted to the insightful discussion in Lefebure, *The Buddha and the Christ,* chap. 8.

155. For the importance of "awakening to life," see, e.g., Hanh, *Our Appointment with Life,* p. 35.

der on a massive scale goes on . . . ?"[156] One of the key motifs in Gutiérrez's call for the transformation of consciousness is the use of the category of "ideology," unmasking concealed and suppressed motifs that lie behind abuse of power in various forms.[157] Less passionate but equally committed and solid is Nhat Hanh's vision of liberation, which he anchors deeply in his own spiritual tradition: "'Awakened' people are certainly going to form small communities where material life will become simple and healthy. Time and energy will be devoted to the enrichment of spirituality. These communities will be Zen monasteries of a modern style where there will be no dogma. In them the sickness of the times will be cured and spiritual health will be acquired."[158] For Nhat Hanh, the ending mantra of the Heart Sutra — which Mahayana Buddhists use for daily chanting — not only expresses the core vision of the universe as integrally interrelated reality (all things are "inter-are") but also provides a powerful tool for transformation and liberation as it challenges the entire community of beings to go "to the other shore," to the land of liberation.[159]

Hospitality and Human Flourishing

Mapping the cultural changes across two millennia, Charles Taylor makes a sweeping statement: "Every person, and every society, lives with or by some conception(s) of what human flourishing is: what constitutes a fulfilled life? What makes life really worth living? What would we most admire people for?"[160] During the past five hundred years, in "a secular age," the overall framework for such reflection has dramatically changed as there are two main options, radically different from each other, namely, religion or what Taylor calls "exclusive humanism." These two frameworks articulate the quest for human flourishing in totally different ways:

> Does the highest, the best life involve our seeking, or acknowledging, or serving a good which is beyond, in the sense of independent of human flourishing? In which case, the highest, most real, authentic or adequate human flourishing could include our aiming (also) in our range of final goals at something other than human flourishing. . . . It's clear that in the

156. Gutiérrez, *On Job*, p. 102.
157. See Gutiérrez, *A Theology of Liberation*, pp. 134-35.
158. Hanh, *Zen Keys*, p. 81.
159. Hanh, *Heart of Understanding*, p. 3.
160. C. Taylor, *A Secular Age*, p. 16.

Judaeo-Christian religious tradition the answer to this question is affirmative. Loving, worshiping God is the ultimate end. Of course, in this tradition God is seen as willing human flourishing, but devotion to God is not seen as contingent on this. The injunction "Thy will be done" isn't equivalent to "Let humans flourish," even though we know that God wills human flourishing.[161]

Human flourishing is not central to Judeo-Christian tradition alone. Indeed, as Miroslav Volf rightly notes, "Concern with human flourishing is at the heart of the great faiths, including Christianity." But then he adds a caveat that helps us understand why many doubt that human flourishing really is at the center of religions: "True, you cannot always tell that from the way faiths are practiced. When surveying their history, it seems on occasion as if their goal were simply to dispatch people out of this world and into the next — out of the veil of tears into heavenly bliss."[162] Volf's Yale University colleague David H. Kelsey rightly notes, "Christian theology has a large stake in making it clear that its affirmations about God and God's ways of relating to human beings underwrite human beings' flourishing." Not only outspoken atheists and critics of religion but also many popular mind-sets of the contemporary world share a "widespread and deep suspicion that Christians magnify God and God's power and dominion by systematically minimizing human beings, making them small, weak, and servile — anything but flourishing." Hence, the "challenge to Christian theology has been to develop conceptual and argumentative strategies by which to show that, properly understood, human flourishing is inseparable from God's active relating to human creatures such that their flourishing is always dependent upon God."[163]

Grace Jantzen has severely critiqued Christian religion and its marriage with Western cultural heritage for advocating values totally opposite to human flourishing. One of her more controversial claims has to do with Western culture's enduring fascination with death and violence, which has resulted in a glorifying of violence, loss of beauty, and fear of the body and sexuality.[164] Apart from questions related to the validity of sweeping historical claims ranging from pre-Hellenistic times to contemporary Western culture, the *theological* challenge concerns the current discussion. While it is true that

---

161. C. Taylor, *A Secular Age*, pp. 16-17. I am indebted to Ford, "God's Power and Human Flourishing," pp. 1-28.

162. Volf, "Human Flourishing," p. 10.

163. Kelsey, "On Human Flourishing," p. 1.

164. Jantzen, *Foundations of Violence*, pp. vii, 36

in the name of Christian theology, which, unfortunately has been dominated by males in the past, violent acts have been committed, beauty has not always been appreciated the way reason has been, and the body and sexuality have been marginalized, it is also true that those dispositions are neither unique to Christian tradition nor a necessary part of its inner logic. The discussion of natural theology (both in this volume and in *Creation and Humanity*) shows evidence of the contrary: Christian theology at large supports life, growth, beauty, and holistic human life, including sexuality. It is also true, unfortunately, that in cultures in general and in Christian tradition, masculinity has been linked with militarism, death, and violence.[165] That phenomenon, however, is neither Christian nor masculine, rightly understood. Again, neither use of power nor violence is an exclusively male attribute, as a wider look at world cultures can show us. Jantzen's suggestion of lifting up creativity, beauty, and birth to new life is as important a metaphor for men as for women — and indeed, in light of tradition's mistakes, all the more important.

Not surprisingly, Jantzen wishes to replace the Christian vision of "salvation" with "flourishing."[166] There are two problems here. First, to make religion (or God) a function of serving human needs is a failing enterprise; in the end, it serves neither humanity nor the cultivation of genuine religiosity. Second, and more importantly for this discussion, it can be argued that salvation and flourishing are rather an integral part of the one pluriform, holistic Christian vision, that is, hope for the life to come and a fulfilling, meaningful life on this earth. Not only "flourishing," as Jantzen one-sidedly claims,[167] but also the Christian holistic vision of salvation includes both physical and spiritual, earthly and mental, this-worldly and otherworldly dimensions.

To this Christian vision of flourishing also belongs the acknowledgment of death as a "natural" result of finite life. Death is an inescapable part of finite life. Christian tradition also puts death in perspective in its eschatological hope.[168] I do not understand at all the meaning of Jantzen's claim that only in her revised feminist pantheistic vision is the idea of the infinite nature of human life avoided.[169] Even when early Christian tradition — mistakenly — used at times the concept of the "immortality of the soul," it did not thereby claim any infinite nature of human life; rather, tradition sought to express its eschatological hope for life beyond death with this concept that contempo-

165. Jantzen, *Becoming Divine*, pp. 129-32.
166. Jantzen, *Becoming Divine*, pp. 160-61.
167. Jantzen, *Becoming Divine*, pp. 166-67.
168. Cf. Jantzen, *Foundations of Violence*, p. vii and passim.
169. Jantzen, *Becoming Divine*, pp. 155, 168.

rary theology has of course left behind, as the hope for the "resurrection of the body," another robustly holistic concept, is the fitting term for speaking of Christian eschatology.

True, in Christian tradition — as well as in other religious traditions (and perhaps, differently, even in secular utopias) — there are plenty of instances in which the idea of flourishing in this life has been lost because the emphasis is placed on hope for the life to come. But how many contemporary theologians would consider that kind of "eschatology" genuine and balanced *Christian* hope? On the other hand, in the final analysis, the power of the classical Christian hope for this life is grounded in the coming eschatological redemption and new creation wrought by the same faithful and loving God who is also the Creator and Provider. If religion were merely a matter of flourishing in this life, even the most flourishing life would not have any lasting significance, particularly when put in the vast cosmic perspective in which human life, as a "last minute" phenomenon in the almost fifteen-billion-year history of the universe's evolution, is an utterly tiny and insignificant thing. Similarly, following the logic of the outdated and rejected classical liberal quest (without necessarily mentioning it), Jantzen[170] also seems to make Jesus merely a fine example of life lived to its fullest without any notion of sin and need for salvation, which to the systematic theologian seems an utterly naive and unnuanced claim.

What kind of view of God supports and underwrites the goal of human flourishing? It is *theologically* "christocentric," Kelsey explains, "in the sense that it is in large part generated out of, and governed by, reflection on implications concerning God of Christian claims that the God who relates to created human beings also relates to them to draw them to eschatological consummation and, when they are estranged from God, to reconcile them to God, by giving them Godself in an exceedingly odd way, namely, in the concrete personal life and particular personal identity of Jesus of Nazareth."[171]

Robustly trinitarian theology adds to that the presence of the ever-present, life-giving, life-supporting, and energizing Spirit of God. What is there in this classical picture of the Christian God that would frustrate human flourishing, one should ask? On the contrary, there is much that bespeaks flourishing; that much can be said without making the doctrine of God a cheap function of human interests. If human beings are creatures of God, then where else could they find the fulfillment of their deepest desires? The

---

170. Jantzen, *Becoming Divine*, pp. 162-63.
171. Kelsey, "On Human Flourishing," pp. 3-4.

divine hospitality alone can deliver the promise. It is highly significant that it is in his study *The Trinity* — dealing with the doctrine of God — that Saint Augustine penned these famous words: "God is the only source to be found of any good things, but especially of those which make a man good and those which will make him happy; only from him do they come into a man and attach themselves to a man."[172]

---

172. Augustine, *The Trinity* 13.10, cited in Volf, "Human Flourishing," p. 4.

14. The Failing Promises of *Theo*-Logical Pluralisms

For Orientation: Various "Turns" in the Christian Theology of Religion

In light of the urgency of relating the Christian doctrine of God to the intuitions of the divine in other living faiths, it hardly comes as a surprise that in recent decades Christian theologians have toyed with various kinds of tactics in order to find common ground. At the cost of oversimplifying a complex set of developments, let us name these turns a movement from christocentric to theo-centric to pneumato-centric approaches. As long as Christian theology was based on a more or less exclusivist standpoint, the point of departure for the theology of religious discourse was the finality of Christ as the only way to God. A turn to theo-centrism seemed to give more space for opening up to other religions: while Christ is one way to the Father, he is not the only one. God is bigger than any single religion. Soon, among theologians from across the ecumenical spectrum, a turn to the "Spirit" was enthusiastically initiated.[1] The turn to pneumatology seemed to promise a lot. After all, doesn't the Spirit speak for universality while Christ speaks for particularity?

The current project argues that each and every one of these turns in itself is inadequate and leads to insurmountable problems. It is not the case that earlier turns, particularly the turn to the Spirit, have been all wrong. It is just that, left on their own, they are not able to deliver the promises attached to them such as openness, tolerance, and genuine dialogue. Therefore, a more coherent framework is to be found in an effort to relate the Christian trinitar-

1. See, e.g., Yong, "The Turn to Pneumatology."

ian confession of faith to other living faiths in a genuinely and authentically *trinitarian* approach.[2]

This section will first delve into a critical discussion of the "first generation" Christian theological pluralistic proposals, focusing on the most well known and widely debated one: that of John Hick. Following that discussion, an evaluative look at various recent *trinitarian* approaches that seek to correct Hick's and similar-minded colleagues' modernist views will be attempted. Finally, a constructive trinitarian proposal will be set forth and defended.

The "First Generation" Pluralisms

God as "Mystery"

The somewhat clumsy expression " 'first generation' pluralisms" refers to the pluralistic Christian theologies of religions that arose in the second half of the last century, building on the modernist epistemology and ethos. These emerged both in the Global North (the Protestant Hick and Roman Catholic Paul F. Knitter)[3] and in Asia (the Protestants Stanley Samartha and M. M. Thomas, as well as the Roman Catholic Aloysius Pieris).[4] Even those coming from Asian soil, while shaped by the multireligious context of that continent, draw their main inspiration from the European Enlightenment and its subsequent developments, including classical liberalism. They represent by and large the replacement of Christocentrism with theo-centrism. Unlike later versions of pluralism to be discussed in the next subsection, these did not take as their main framework the Trinity, but rather, more generally the doctrine of God.

In the context of India and many other Asian countries, with the growing sense of religious tolerance but increased and intensified political and social intolerance, theologians such as Stanley J. Samartha saw clearly the impasse between the traditional exclusivistic Christian confession and the plurality of religious claims. In keeping with the less categorical pan-Asian mind-set — whose logic does not so predominantly operate with the West-

---

2. For an up-to-date report on the turn to the Trinity in the theology of religions, see K. Johnson, *Rethinking the Trinity and Religious Pluralism*, chap. 1.

3. In *Christ and Reconciliation*, chap. 9, I engage the American Roman Catholic Knitter's eco-liberationist pluralism particularly from the perspective of Christology.

4. In *Christ and Reconciliation*, chap. 9, I engage the Sri Lankan Roman Catholic Pieris's liberationist pluralism particularly from the perspective of Christology.

ern either/or logic[5] — Samartha took as a clue the category of the divine as "Mystery":

> This Mystery, the Truth of the Truth *(Satyasya Satyam), is* the transcendent Center that remains always beyond and greater than apprehensions of it even in the sum total of those apprehensions. It is beyond cognitive knowledge *(tarka)* but it is open to vision *(dristi)* and intuition *(anubhava).* It is near yet far, knowable yet unknowable, intimate yet ultimate and, according to one particular Hindu view, cannot even be described as "one." It is "not-two" *(advaita),* indicating thereby that diversity is within the heart of Being itself and therefore may be intrinsic to human nature as well.[6]

The emphasis on Mystery is meant to make room also for the mystical and the aesthetic in theology. Samartha believes that Mystery lies beyond the dichotomy of theistic versus nontheistic. "Mystery is an ontological status to be accepted, not an epistemological problem to be solved. Without a sense of Mystery, *Theos* [Greek term for god] cannot remain *Theos,* nor *Sat* [Hindi term for god] remain Sat, nor can Ultimate Reality remain ultimate."[7] Samartha believes that the nature of Mystery makes inadmissible any claim by one religious community to have exclusive or unique knowledge. Exclusiveness creates dichotomies between different religious communities and leaves little room for the nonrational elements in religious life, such as the mystical, the aesthetic, meditation, and rituals.

While Christ remains central in this conception, for Samartha Christ is not exclusively so. "This Other [God as the Mysterious Other] relativizes everything else. In fact, the willingness to accept such relativization is probably the only guarantee that one has encountered the Other as ultimately real."[8] While Samartha is not naively assuming the equality of all religions, he insists that "a particular religion can claim to be decisive for some people, and some people can claim that a particular religion is decisive for them, but no religion is justified in claiming that it is decisive for all."[9]

Rather than attempting a full critical response to Samartha at this point, let me just add a couple of more general comments before I discuss John

5. See Lee, "The Yin-Yang Way of Thinking," p. 87.
6. Samartha, "The Cross and the Rainbow," p. 111.
7. Samartha, "The Cross and the Rainbow," p. 111.
8. Samartha, *Courage for Dialogue,* pp. 151-52.
9. Samartha, *Courage for Dialogue,* p. 153; see also Samartha's "Unbound Christ," p. 146.

Hick's version of a theo-centric pluralism and engage him in a more thoroughgoing manner. While different in many aspects, Samartha's and Hick's theocentric pluralisms share a similar underlying logic. To speak of God as Mystery — which is nothing new in Christian tradition — is not necessarily to shy away from the claim to uniqueness. When, beginning from early patristic traditions, Christian theology insisted on the mysterious nature of the triune God, it meant to say that we have to be humble and modest about how much we know of this "Unknowable One." To claim, as Samartha does, that from the mysterious nature logically follows the standpoint that refuses to consider Christ as the fullest and only true revelation of God, is of course a way to deny the logic of the statement itself! In other words: of total Mystery the human mind cannot say this or that. Likewise, the desire to "soften" the rational claims of theology and make room for aesthetic and mystical elements is also familiar in Christian tradition; but again, from the move does not follow necessarily the need to leave behind the Christian claim for uniqueness.

God as the "Ultimate Reality"

Having left behind much of the traditional Christian confession,[10] John Hick compares his turn to pluralistic theo-centrism with the astronomical model of Copernicus that replaced the Ptolemaic view. In that model, at the center of all religions stands God, the Ultimate Truth, around which all religions, including Christianity, as a human interpretation of divine reality, revolve in the analogue of the planets.[11] The essence of theo-centric pluralism hence is that there are "both the one unlimited transcendent divine Reality and also a plurality of varying human concepts, images, and experiences of and responses to that Reality."[12] All religions, whether Christian or Hindu[13] or Buddhist,[14] are challenged to move away from the "Ptolemaic" view.[15] To accomplish this task, Hick contends that the views of the adherents of religions

10. See Hick, "Reconstruction of Christian Belief."
11. This is the main claim of his widely read *God and the Universe of Faiths*. For a succinct, summative statement, see his *Second Christianity*, p. 82.
12. Hick, *Second Christianity*, p. 83.
13. Hick, *God and the Universe of Faiths*, p. 131; Hick, *God Has Many Names*, p. 83.
14. Hick, *Problems of Religious Pluralism*, p. 48; Hick, *Metaphor of God Incarnate*, p. 134.
15. Hick, *Rainbow of Faiths* (American edition: *A Christian Theology of Religious Pluralism*), p. 44.

cannot be taken at face value, but rather each religion has to be confronted by the challenge of de-emphasizing its own absolute and exclusive claims.[16] Various conceptions of God/god(s)/divine, such as Yahweh, Allah, Krishna, Param Atma, or Holy Trinity, are but aspects of the Divine[17] or like maps or colors of the rainbow.[18]

While at first Hick was content to speak of *God,* later, to do justice to his understanding of the nature of religious language and to respond to the justified criticism that his pluralistic conception still favored theistic — and even *mono*theistic — religions, Hick began speaking about the "Ultimate Reality." This term is more flexible than the personal term "God." The Sanskrit term *sat* and the Islamic term *al-Haqq* are expressions of that personal term, as are also "Yahweh" and the Christian "God."[19]

In describing religions' access to and knowledge of the Ultimate Reality, Hick utilizes the Kantian distinction between *phaenoumena* (the way we see things) and *noumena* (the thing in itself, which is unknown to us), and maintains that there is a part of the Divine/Reality that is totally unknown to us and a part about which we know at least something. The Hindu concept of *nirguna* Brahma, in contrast to *saguna* Brahma, refers to something that cannot be fathomed at all by human means of knowledge. Similarly, the "eternal Tao" of Taoism, about which we know nothing, is distinguished from the "expressed Tao." Irrespective of these differing names and approaches to the Reality, in Hick's view there is only one Reality, the ultimate divine. This he postulates mainly on the basis of astonishingly similar concepts of the divine in various religions.[20] A key tool for Hick in constructing this theo-centric pluralism is his turn to metaphorical understanding of religious language, as explained in some detail in part 1 of this volume.

What about Hick's view of the Trinity? He has not said much about it. He rightly notes that in the doctrinal system in which Christian thought was imbedded from the beginning, the doctrines of incarnation, atonement, and the Trinity cohere together.[21] Since he does not feel bound to a traditional view of Christ's incarnation or atonement,[22] he ends up affirming a modalistic or unitarian view, which he describes in the following way:

16. Hick, *An Interpretation of Religion,* pp. 2-3.
17. Hick, *God and the Universe of Faiths,* pp. 140-41.
18. Hick, *Problems of Religious Pluralism,* p. 80.
19. Hick, *An Interpretation of Religion,* pp. 10-11.
20. Hick, *Rainbow of Faiths,* p. 69.
21. Hick, "The Non-Absoluteness of Christianity," p. 30.
22. Discussed in some detail in the volume *Christ and Reconciliation.*

An inspiration Christology coheres better with some ways of understanding trinitarian language than with others. It does not require or support the notion of three divine persons in the modern sense in which a person is a distinct center of consciousness, will, and emotion — so that one could speak of the Father, the Son, and the Holy Spirit as loving one another within the eternal family of the trinity, and of the Son coming down to earth to make atonement on behalf of human beings to his Father. An inspiration Christology is, however, fully compatible with the conception of the trinity as affirming three distinguishable ways in which the one God is experienced as acting in relation to, and is accordingly known by, us — namely, as creator, redeemer, and inspirer. On this interpretation, the three persons are not three different centers of consciousness but three major aspects of the one divine nature.[23]

In line with his metaphorical understanding of religious talk, Hick can understand the doctrine of the Trinity "not as ontologically three but as three ways in which the one God is humanly thought and experienced."[24] In his view, this kind of modalistic version of the doctrine of the Trinity has parallels in other religions, such as Islam's threefold name of God as omnipotent creator and ruler of the universe, God as gracious and forgiving, and God as intimately present to us.[25]

Even though Hick claims to present a kind of "metatheory"[26] of religions, he reminds us that his view is not based on some preconceived philosophical or theological standpoint but is a result of empirical, phenomenological observations. The pluralist, according to Hick, does not even claim to possess the final word about religions.[27] While the last claim might be true of any academic and theological scholar of religion, I find it highly problematic that Hick seeks to offer a world-embracing metatheory of religion.

There are a number of problems here, not least being its naive reliance on the grand stories of modernity! First, it could be argued that his proposal is not a metatheory but rather yet another form of positive religion. Second, attempting a metareligion takes quite a bit of pride and hubris since it means

23. Hick, "The Non-Absoluteness of Christianity," p. 32; see also *An Interpretation of Religion*, pp. 170-72, 271-72.

24. Hick, *Metaphor of God Incarnate*, p. 149.

25. Hick, "Rethinking Christian Doctrine," p. 98.

26. See further, Hick, "Religious Pluralism and the Divine," p. 418; Hick, "Epistemological Challenge of Religious Pluralism," pp. 277-86.

27. Hick, *Problems of Religious Pluralism*, p. 37; Amnell, *Uskontojen Universumi*, p. 49.

nothing less than lifting oneself above existing religions and claiming to have a "neutral" point of view — perhaps even "God's point of view." Third, such an enterprise leads to violence and denial of the right of the religious other to be other. Indeed, Hick is telling the rest of humanity — most of whom are adherents of a particular religion — that their view (of the uniqueness and "salvific" power) of their own religion is "wrong" and should be replaced with another. Rightly, many critics have noted that ignoring the self-understanding of adherents of religions means nothing less than violating their religious rights.[28] It is "elitist" and "imperialistic."[29] Even some pluralists have critiqued Hick for the lack of respect he shows for the religious other.[30] In this context, it should also be asked, what gives the modern interpreter a superior knowledge concerning ancient religions?[31] Fourth, methodologically Hick's metatheory builds on the now-rejected older theory of the common core behind all religions. It is not self-evident at all that behind the diversity of manifestations of religions lies a common core. It can also be argued that regardless of the difference or similarity of the manifestations, behind them are irreconcilable religious, philosophical, and worldview differences.[32] Fifth, while not totally noncognitivist, Hick's way of conceiving the nature of religious language virtually rips it away from any serious truth claims — a "truth claim" impossible to accept by most adherents of religions. The reasons I find Hick's turn to metaphors unsatisfactory and failing were discussed in part 1 and will not be repeated here.

His view of the Divine/Ultimate Reality raises the following difficult questions: First, it seems to me his view of the Divine is formal, without any content. It has to be so lest it begin to favor unduly a certain kind of religion. The dilemma is simply this: on the one hand, the more Hick says of what kind of "god" the Ultimate Reality is, the more he begins to exclude religions; on the other hand, the less he says of what the Ultimate Reality is, the more meaningless and less interesting the claim becomes — until it becomes virtually

28. See the nuanced and important critique of Kauffmann, "Religious Diversity and Religious Truth," pp. 143-64.

29. Amnell, *Uskontojen Universumi*, p. 63. One critic goes so far as to claim that Hick is guilty of "intellectual Stalinism." McGrath, "Conclusion," pp. 200-209; see also the similar type of critique from Cobb, *Beyond Dialogue*, pp. 38-44.

30. Instead of this kind of "universal" pluralism, Raimundo Panikkar calls for a deepening respect among religions in view of the existing real differences ("The Invisible Harmony," pp. 120-25, 141).

31. Several authors have raised this question, among others, Berger, *The Heretical Imperative*, pp. 119-20; Amnell, *Uskontojen Universumi*, p. 90.

32. I am indebted here to Saarinen, "Eri uskonnot — sama Jumala?" pp. 150-56.

empty. Second, if it is a formal concept, how does Hick "know" that there are two aspects to the Divine — "phenomenological" (of which something can be known) and "noumenal" (of which nothing can be known)? Hick shares this deep dilemma with Kant.[33] Third, anyone following the classical canons of Christian tradition cannot be content with a modalistic view of the Divine.

Theologically more interesting and, in terms of interfaith engagement, more fruitful ways of negotiating the Christian confession of God with religious pluralism and specific claims of living faiths come from current trinitarian pluralists. We turn next to their suggestions before attempting a constructive proposal for the purposes of this project.

The "Turn" to Trinitarian Ways of Constructing Pluralistic Theologies

Trinity and a Cosmotheandric Vision

The turn to the Trinity as the way to negotiate the relation of the God of the Bible to religious pluralism and other living faiths has caught the attention of several contemporary theologians.[34] While their proposals differ in nature and orientation, they all build on the conviction that apart from the trinitarian framing of the doctrine of God, no lasting results will come.[35] The pioneer in the field is the Roman Catholic Raimundo Panikkar,[36] who places himself at the confluence of four rivers: Hindu, Christian, Buddhist, and secular.[37] In his small yet highly significant book *The Trinity and the Religious Experience of Man* (1973), Panikkar argued for the viability of a trinitarian approach based on the groundbreaking idea that not only do all religions reflect a trinitarian substructure, but there is a trinitarian structure to reality. The underlying notion of Panikkar's theological vision in general and trinitarian understanding in particular is the neologism "cosmotheandrism," defined thus: "The cosmotheandric principle could be formulated by saying that the divine, the human

---

33. I am indebted here to the nuanced, detailed, and insightful discussion throughout Amnell, *Uskontojen Universumi*.

34. For a massive pioneering study by the late senior Roman Catholic theologian Jacques Dupuis, see *Toward a Christian Theology of Religious Pluralism*. For a thoughtful account and proposal from a moderate process perspective, see Suchocki, *Divinity and Diversity*.

35. For my critical engagement with the proposal in Smart and Konstantine, *Christian Systematic Theology in a World Context*, see chap. 16 in *The Trinity*.

36. See Vanhoozer, "Does the Trinity Belong in the Theology of Religions?" p. 58.

37. Panikkar, *Unknown Christ of Hinduism*, p. 30.

and the earthly — however we may prefer to call them — are the three irreducible dimensions which constitute the real, i.e., any reality inasmuch as it is real."[38] Or, "There is no God without Man and the World. There is no Man without God and the World. There is no World without God and Man."[39] In other words, in Panikkar's vision the cosmotheandric principle expresses the fundamental structure of reality in terms of an intimate interaction of God, humankind, and the world or cosmos.

A key insight for Panikkar is that the Trinity, while a distinctively Christian way of speaking of cosmotheandrism, is not an exclusively Christian reality.[40] The Trinity is the "junction where the authentic spiritual dimensions of all religions meet."[41] Hence, Christians alone cannot "own" the Trinity or its proper understanding; its appreciation requires constant interaction with other religions. Christianity can learn from others, but it also has a significant role to play in leading "to the *plenitude* and hence to the *conversion* of all religions."[42] In the final analysis, the end of this process (and the goal of Christianity) is "humanity's common good."[43]

Half Indian, Panikkar follows the typical Asian way of thinking and logic built on the principle of *advaita*, which means "nonduality" (literally: not two). Wary of all dualisms, Panikkar surmises that there "are not two realities: God and man (or the world). . . . Reality itself is theandric; it is our way of looking that causes reality to appear to us sometimes under one aspect and sometimes under another."[44] Applied to the ancient problem of unity and diversity in the trinitarian God, the advaitic principle implies that Father and Son are not two, but they are not one either; it is the Spirit who unites and distinguishes them.[45] Fittingly, a recent commentator names Panikkar's vision "Advaitic Trinitarianism."[46]

Following his advaitic logic, Panikkar constructs the Christian doctrine of the Trinity in a most unique way. The Father is "Nothing." This is the apophatic way — but even more than that: the way to approach the Ab-

---

38. Panikkar, *The Cosmotheandric Experience*, p. ix.
39. Ahlstrand, *Fundamental Openness*, p. 134.
40. See Panikkar, *The Trinity*, p. viii.
41. Panikkar, *The Trinity*, p. 42.
42. Panikkar, *The Trinity*, p. 4.
43. Panikkar, "The Jordan, the Tiber, and the Ganges," p. 102.
44. Panikkar, *The Trinity*, p. 73.
45. Panikkar, *The Trinity*, p. 62.
46. Cousins, "Panikkar's Advaitic Trinitarianism," pp. 119-30; for the term "advaitic," see especially p. 120.

solute is without name.[47] There is no "Father" in himself; the "being of the Father" is "the Son." Panikkar bases this conclusion on his interpretation of the Johannine saying that no one comes to the Father except through the Son (John 14:6).[48] In the incarnation, *kenosis,* the Father gives himself totally to the Son. Thus the Son is "God."[49] Panikkar believes this understanding is the needed bridge between Christianity and Buddhism as well as advaitic Hinduism. What *kenosis* (self-emptying) is for Christianity, nirvana and sunyata are for the other two religions. "God is total Silence. This is affirmed by all the world religions. One is led towards the Absolute and in the end one finds nothing, because there *is* nothing, not even Being."[50] Consequently, the Son is the only "person" of the Trinity. For this statement to make sense, Panikkar notes that the term "person," when used of the internal life of the Trinity, is an equivocal term that has different meanings in each case. Since the "Father" is a different kind of "person" compared to the "Son," and the "Spirit" differs in nature from both, it is not advisable to use the same term "person" for these different meanings.[51] In that qualified sense, it is also understandable when Panikkar says there is in fact "no God" in Christian theology in the generic sense of the term. There is only "the God of Jesus Christ"; thus, the God of theism is always the "Son," the only one with whom human beings can establish a relationship.[52] What about the Spirit? The Spirit is "immanence." To make more concrete the meaning of the Spirit as immanence is challenging (acknowledged in all theologies, for that matter): "immanence is incapable of revealing itself, for that would be a contradiction of terms; an immanence which needs to manifest itself, is no longer immanent." Panikkar uses images and paints pictures to say something more about the Spirit: the Father is the source of the river, the Son the river that flows from the source, and the Spirit is the ocean in which the river ends.[53]

Everything said so far speaks of Panikkar's desire to facilitate the coming together of living faiths, yet without leaving behind the uniqueness of each. As mentioned, however, his pluralistic vision, based on the doctrine of the Trinity, is radically different from the typical pluralistic ideas of "rough parity" among

47. Panikkar, *The Trinity,* p. 46. Panikkar comes from a Hindu background, and the Mahayana concept of sunyata looms large in the background.

48. Panikkar, *The Trinity,* p. 47.

49. Panikkar, *The Trinity,* pp. 45-47.

50. Panikkar's view interpreted by Ramachandra, *Recovery of Mission,* p. 91.

51. See further, Panikkar, *The Trinity,* pp. 51-52.

52. Panikkar, *The Trinity,* p. 52.

53. Panikkar, *The Trinity,* p. 63.

religions. Trinity speaks for diversity, not for uniformity or denial of differences.[54] "The mystery of the Trinity is the ultimate foundation for pluralism."[55] And "In the Trinity a true encounter of religions takes place, which results, not in a vague fusion or mutual dilution, but in an authentic enhancement of all the religious and even cultural elements that are contained in each."[56] Instead of pluralism, Panikkar prefers the term "parallelism": all religions run parallel to meet only in the Ultimate, at the end of time.[57]

Furthermore, for Panikkar, Christian understanding of the Trinity is in need of deepening from other religions; on the other hand, Christianity contributes to a fuller understanding of that vision among other religions. Exclusivism is avoided by maintaining that Christianity, no more than other religions, can never absolutize its current historical understanding. Panikkar firmly maintains that religions need each other and are mutually dependent.[58] His cosmotheandric vision sees the need to affirm diversity and posit mutuality on the basis of trinitarian relations. All attempts toward universalization, so prevalent in Western culture as he sees it, are an anathema to Panikkar.[59]

One term Panikkar uses to speak of diversity and complementarity is *perichoresis*. For Panikkar, the idea of *perichoresis* implies the mutual conditioning and transformation of religions in their diversity on the way to convergence.[60] Another implication of the idea of *perichoresis* is that plurality as such is not a problem, but rather an asset. The goal of pluralistic theologies is not to water down or dismiss plurality but to enhance it. Therefore dialogue matters; through interaction, religions condition and enrich each other. Each religion comes out of the encounter with a deeper sense of its own identity, yet with the awareness of needing the other religions. Finally, in a very bold move, Panikkar places the world's religious traditions interior to the Godhead and depicts them as pluralistic self-revelations of divinity. "The Trinitarian life is one of pluralism in oneness, or distinction in unity, that is constantly replenishing itself."[61]

Panikkar's significance for the development of Christian trinitarian thinking cannot be undermined even though it faces superb challenges. In my

---

54. See Raj, *New Hermeneutic of Reality*, p. 39.
55. Panikkar, "The Jordan, the Tiber, and the Ganges," p. 110.
56. Panikkar, *The Trinity*, p. 42.
57. See further, Panikkar, *The Intrareligious Dialogue*.
58. See further, Ahlstrand, *Fundamental Openness*, p. 184.
59. See further, Lanzetta, "Mystical Basis of Panikkar's Thought," p. 97.
60. See Ahlstrand, *Fundamental Openness*, p. 184.
61. Lanzetta, "Mystical Basis of Panikkar's Thought," p. 95.

understanding, his main contribution is elevating the doctrine of the Trinity to a central place in Christian theology in general and in the theology of religions in particular. This is a healthy, badly needed corrective both in the theology of religions and in comparative theology. With his bold move, Panikkar has offered a major critique of pluralism. The implications of his trinitarian doctrine, especially the insistence on diversity-in-unity, are another major asset. In addition, that he has been able not only to "contextualize" the doctrine but also to relate it to his own Asian context and religiosity is an admirable achievement.

What are the challenges?[62] Regarding the foundational question of whether Panikkar's revised vision of cosmotheandrism really represents a Christian doctrine of the Trinity, we must tackle a question he puts to himself: "Why do I persist, then, in still speaking of the Trinity when . . . the idea that I give of it goes beyond the traditional idea [given] by Christianity?"[63] Without really giving substantial answers, he is content to insist on the continuity with Christian tradition.[64] His version of trinitarianism, however, certainly elicits serious questions.

Panikkar's interpretation of the Johannine saying that no one comes to the Father except through the Son (John 14:6) seems to go beyond any exegetical warrants and certainly any traditional Christian theological intuitions. In contrast to his interpretation, Christian theology has understood from this saying not that the Father does not exist but rather that the only way to know the Father is through the Son sent by his Father. I understand Panikkar's motive here — to relate the Father of Christianity to the godhead in the Buddhist concept of nirvana and sunyata — but I fear he is mispresenting both Buddhist and Christian sources here.

> Whatever similarities there might be with the basically a-theistic, nonpersonalist Buddhist notion of *nirvana*, in my opinion, no amount of stretching of the meaning of the concepts could make it compatible with the personalist, theistic notion of the Father in Christian faith. This is to confuse the way we talk about God (in apophatic terms) with how God exists (if in Buddhism there is any kind of concept of the divinity). Rather than trying to connect Buddhism and Christianity with the help of this

62. For a more extensive engagement, see Kärkkäinen, *Trinity and Religious Pluralism,* chap. 8. In the volume *Christ and Reconciliation,* chap. 9, I have engaged Panikkar's pluralistic Christology.

63. Panikkar, *The Trinity,* p. 43.

64. See the serious reservations expressed by Ahlstrand, *Fundamental Openness,* pp. 152-56 especially.

most suspect twisting of terms, Panikkar should rather be faithful to his foundational idea of radical differences between religions and their concepts of the divine. So I think Panikkar has committed the most typical sin of pluralism (of which he is often critical), namely, dismissing the real differences among religions and their conceptions by assuming a similarity behind the terminology.[65]

Equally problematic is Panikkar's interpretation of the role and meaning of the Son in his trinitarian vision. In Christian theology the Son is not the focus. Thus, ironically, Panikkar's version of trinitarianism is to be judged as too "christocentric": in the biblical canon, especially in the Gospel of John, it is made clear that even the Son's equality to the Father never implies taking the place of the Father.

Also problematic is Panikkar's advaitic approach to logic and truth. While I think it is appropriate for him as a theologian to draw from Asian wells the thought forms available in those cultures, I also fear that his quite uncritical — and selective — use of the advaitic principle becomes problematic. It seems to me an advaitic principle is called forth whenever serious logical or other intellectual problems are encountered. Resorting to either the advaitic or mystical principle can also become an exercise in avoiding the core problem.[66] But, of course, Panikkar's own notion of pluralism cannot be a universal theory and therefore truth itself be pluralistic.[67] No more than any other relativistically oriented thinker, however, can Panikkar live up to his philosophical claims to relativism. His position, like that of many other pluralists, makes certain propositional claims and thus requires a propositional network and operates with truth/falsehood logic.[68]

Trinity and Diverse Religious Ends

The trinitarian proposal of the American Baptist S. Mark Heim evades typical categorizations in that, on the one hand, it looks quite traditional in elevating the Trinity as the major theological topic, but on the other hand, while critical of existing pluralistic theologies of religions,[69] it attempts to advance a radi-

65. Kärkkäinen, *Trinity and Religious Pluralism*, p. 130.
66. See also Larson, "Contra Pluralism," p. 72.
67. See Larson, "Contra Pluralism," p. 77.
68. See further, Larson, "Contra Pluralism," p. 81.
69. The reason for Heim's criticism concerning (other) pluralistic theologies lies in their

cally pluralistic view of religious ends based on the idea of the diversity in the Godhead. The launching pad for Heim's development of a distinctively trinitarian pluralism is his 1995 work titled — surprisingly — *Salvations* (plural). The main argument of that book is that, rather than one common religious end for people of all faiths, there is a diversity of end goals willed by God. The sequel, *The Depth of the Riches: A Trinitarian Theology of Religious Ends* (2001), represents a full-blown vision of the Trinity as the guarantor of more than one goal for the followers of religions, including Christians, to whom communion with God is the highest aim.

The key idea in Heim's trinitarian understanding of the theology of religions is simple and straightforward: "One set of ways may be valid for a given goal, and thus final for that end, while different ways are valid for other ends."[70] A twofold affirmation is included in this programmatic statement: not only that differences among religions are real but also that those differences should be honored and made an asset rather than an obstacle. This means that *moksha* and nirvana of the Buddhist religion are not only legitimate ends for Buddhists but that Buddhism as a particular religion is necessary to make those ends possible; the same applies to salvation as communion with God as promised for Christians.[71]

Heim champions a robust theology of communion that underwrites a relational and dynamic view of the triune God. If relationality in the Godhead speaks for communion — yet communion in diversity — then salvation also means varying degrees of being in communion with God or being related to God.[72] Salvation simply means being in relation. The following quotation makes this point succinctly:

> We can . . . see the connection between the Trinity and varied religious aims. The actual ends that various religious traditions offer as alternative human fulfillments diverge because they realize different relations with God. It is God's reality as Trinity that generates the multiplicity of dimensions that allow for that variety of relations. God's threefoldness means that salvation necessarily is a characteristic communion in diversity. It also permits human responses to God to limit themselves within the terms of one dimension. Trinity requires that salvation be communion. It makes

---

denial of real differences among religions. S. M. Heim, *Salvations*, p. 3.

70. S. M. Heim, *Salvations*, p. 3.
71. S. M. Heim, *Depth of the Riches*, p. 31.
72. S. M. Heim, *Depth of the Riches*, chap. 2.

possible, but not necessary, the realization of religious ends other than salvation.[73]

The implications of this approach are staggering: "The 'one way' to salvation, and the 'many ways' to religious ends are alike rooted in the Trinity."[74] Whether one looks for communion with God (as in Christian religion) or dissolution into the divine (as in the mainstream Hindu religion[s]), these goals are "grounded in God, in the coexisting relations in God's own nature."[75]

What about the differences between religions? How do the differences in how people in various religions are related to God play into the differences in the religious ends? Here Heim introduces an idea of a "hierarchy" of religious ends, an idea that helps him differentiate ends but is also problematic in that hierarchy implies "higher" and "lower" ends. That kind of grading, however, can only be done from a particular perspective: what seems to be a "higher" end for, say, Christians might not appear as high to devout Hindus. Therefore, I have suggested that perhaps a term like "taxonomy" would be more appropriate for his purposes.[76] Furthermore, Heim argues that his vision is in keeping with the traditional Christian eschatological vision based on the ancient idea of "plenitude." The principle of plenitude means simply that God's infinite nature entails the proliferation of the greatest variety of types (but of course not number) of beings.

While Heim's specific views about religious ends will be considered in the discussion of eschatology, in this discussion we focus on the way the Trinity is related to other faiths. If I have correctly understood his nuanced and brilliant proposal, it seems to me that Heim fails to deal with the question of the unity in the Godhead. He either takes the unity for granted — an assumption that is unwarranted in the context of comparative theology — or wishes to highlight the diversity at the expense of the unity. So the question simply is: How does God's "communion-in-diversity" account for the unity?

One way to highlight the importance of tackling the question of the unity is to ask: To what extent can Heim's vision be considered to be in keeping with classical canons of Christian theology? The reason this question is legitimate is that Heim often claims that his theological program is a faithful, albeit creative, interpretation of biblical and historical theology. As Heim him-

73. S. M. Heim, *Depth of the Riches*, p. 180.
74. S. M. Heim, *Depth of the Riches*, p. 209.
75. S. M. Heim, *Depth of the Riches*, p. 179.
76. Kärkkäinen, *Trinity and Religious Pluralism*, chap. 9.

self notes, the main impetus for the rise of the doctrine of the Trinity in early Christian theology was to secure the closest possible union between Yahweh of the Old Testament and Jesus Christ.[77] Not only that, but the Trinity was needed to negotiate the apparent tension between the transcendence of God and the historical particularity of the incarnated Son as the very revelation of God. So the original purpose of the doctrine of the Trinity was not so much to affirm diversity in God as to affirm belief in one God. In that sense, the way Heim works toward his theology of the Trinity is exactly the opposite. That in itself is not the problem, but unless the unity is secured, I fear that making the diversity the main theological asset is suspect.

The question of the unity aside, the main critical question — again, in need of much more elaboration — is "So what?" Granted that there is diversity in the Godhead — and all trinitarian doctrines affirm it — one needs to ask what are the implications for our theology. The biggest challenge to Heim's way of linking the diversity in the Godhead to the diversity of religious ends can be formulated this way: to make a jump from the principle of the diversity in the Godhead to the diversity in the religious ends willed by the triune God is both unwarranted and logically less than convincing. Logically the claim may or may not be true; biblically and theologically I fear it is not a legitimate move. Indeed, it seems to me that it speaks against the very idea of communion: in the biblical vision, the purpose of humanity, created in the image of God, is to (re)turn to eternal communion with the triune God. Even when that does not happen, Christian theology affirms that it is not because God has not willed it, but rather because God honors the freedom given to humanity.

To allow the possibility of lack of communion (as with the doctrine of hell or annihilation) is radically different from making the failure to reach communion a theological problem. It seems that Heim's use of the trinitarian doctrine conflicts with the biblical vision of the gathering of all people in the New Jerusalem under one God (Rev. 21–22). Somewhat ironically, it takes another pluralist, the Catholic Paul F. Knitter, to bring to light the problem I am trying to highlight here: "Christians have always taken for granted, and still do, that because there is one God, there is one final destination. Heim's efforts to draw out the possibility of many salvations from the Christian doctrine of the Trinity go only half-circle. . . . the other half swings back to oneness: the three divine persons . . . have something in common that enables them to relate to each other, enhance each other, achieve ever greater unity among themselves."[78]

---

77. S. M. Heim, *Depth of the Riches*, p. 131.
78. Knitter, *Introducing Theologies of Religions*, p. 231.

Yet another significant challenge to Heim's position also makes it less pluralistic than it claims to be: it is hardly good news to Hindus or Buddhists to be told that their nirvana is an end willed by the Christian God and that it is "lower" than communion with the triune God. How pluralistic is such a claim? How much different is it from a typical inclusivistic approach?[79]

Trinity and Religious Pluralism: Some "Trinitarian" Rules

For Orientation: Broken Promises of Pluralisms

The leading Roman Catholic theologian of religions from England, Gavin D'Costa, has offered a sharp criticism of pluralisms, which he considers merely representations of modernity's "hidden gods," a species of Enlightenment modernity. What is the main reason for the failure of pluralisms? "Despite their [pluralists'] intentions to encourage openness, tolerance, and equality they fail to attain these goals (on their own definition) because of the tradition-specific nature of their positions. Their particular shaping tradition is the Enlightenment. . . . The Enlightenment, in granting a type of equality to all religions, ended up denying public truth to any and all of them. . . . [And the end result is that the pluralists'] 'god is modernity's god.' "[80] D'Costa laments the fact that even though pluralists present themselves as honest "brokers to disputing parties," they conceal the fact "that they represent yet another party which invites the disputants actually to leave their parties and join the pluralist one," namely, liberal modernity. Therefore, ironically, pluralists end up being "exclusivists," even guilty of (as in Hick's case) "liberal intolerance."[81] An antidote to pluralisms, according to D'Costa, is not exclusivism but rather an attitude that takes delight in the potential of an encounter with the other without denying either parties' distinctive features. "The other is always interesting in their difference and may be the possible face of God, or the face of violence, greed, and death. Furthermore, the other may teach Christians to know and worship their own trinitarian God more truthfully and richly."[82]

I agree with D'Costa's criticism of failures of modernist pluralisms as well as their goal of making room for a "critical, reverent, and open engagement

79. See Kärkkäinen, *Trinity and Religious Pluralism*, p. 151.
80. D'Costa, *Meeting of Religions*, pp. 1-2.
81. D'Costa, *Meeting of Religions*, pp. 20, 22, 24, at 24.
82. D'Costa, *Meeting of Religions*, p. 9.

with otherness, without any predictable outcome."[83] For this to happen, we must reconceive the three cardinal virtues of pluralism that modernity-based ideology fails to deliver: equality, justice, and tolerance. The reason pluralism fails is that it waters down real differences among religions and regards all of them as the same below the surface. As noted above, Hick's version of pluralism is an example of the approach that denies the otherness and difference of the other. Consequently, it does not take the dialogue with the other seriously since basically all religions teach the same thing, differing doctrines notwithstanding. Why should one engage a serious dialogue with the other whose difference has already been mythologized and subsumed under one's own world explanation? Doing so, pluralism denies the self-definitions of particular religions and from a distance tells the followers of other religions what is the truth.[84] In contrast, with D'Costa this project argues that openness becomes "taking history seriously," and not dismissing it, as "pluralism" seems to do. Differences do matter and should not be suspended. Tolerance, rather than denying the tradition-specific claims for truth — which in itself, ironically, is one more truth claim among others — becomes the "qualified establishment of civic religious freedom for all on the basis of Christian revelation and natural law." Equality becomes the "equal and inviolable dignity of all persons," which naturally leads to taking the other seriously, dialoguing with the other with willingness to learn from the other and teach the other.[85] On the "foundation" of this open-minded, tolerant, and equalitarian attitude toward the religious other, an integrally trinitarian approach to religions builds in five interrelated movements. For brevity's sake, let us call them "trinitarian rules."[86]

Trinity as the Way to Distinguish the Christian God among Gods

It was no less a theological giant than Barth who made this programmatic statement: "The doctrine of the Trinity is what basically distinguishes the Christian doctrine of God as Christian, and therefore what already distin-

---

83. D'Costa, *Meeting of Religions*, p. 9.

84. See further, D'Costa, "Christian Theology and Other Religions," pp. 161-78, and Hick's response: "Possibility of Religious Pluralism," pp. 161-66.

85. For a brief statement, see D'Costa, *Meeting of Religions*, p. 9.

86. The rest of the chapter is heavily indebted to my earlier essays: "The Uniqueness of Christ and Trinitarian Faith"; "'How to Speak of the Spirit among Religions': Trinitarian 'Rules' for a Pneumatological Theology of Religions"; "'How to Speak of the Spirit among Religions': Trinitarian Prolegomena for a Pneumatological Theology of Religions."

guishes the Christian concept of revelation as Christian, in contrast to all other possible doctrines of God or concepts of revelation."[87] Above we developed the many implications of this foundational theological statement, including the ascendancy of relationality, communion, belonging. Furthermore, Trinity introduces also history and time into the divine life. God's relation — reaching out — to the world in incarnation, salvation, and consummation is not something external to the divine life. While there is of course no reason to limit the knowledge of God to the particularity of Jesus of Nazareth, it also is true, to quote Heim, that "the Trinity is unavoidably Christocentric."[88] It is one of the tendencies of current pluralistic — and also some nonpluralistic pneumatological — theologies of religion to seek release from the contours of history, and (as they believe) of particularity. It is an understandable yet theologically highly problematic road. In terms of interfaith dialogue it means that to bracket out the Trinity for the sake of dialogue when talking to, say, Muslims, is a strategy that creates more problems than it solves.

The Trinitarian Presence of the Spirit in the World

Following the ancient rule of the works of the Trinity being indivisible (though distinct, at least in terms of appropriation) *ad extra,* in order to refer to the presence of the Spirit, whether as the life principle, the divine breath of all living creatures, a (soteriological) "gift," or the agent of eschatological transformation, one needs to speak of the Spirit of Yahweh, the Spirit of the God of Jesus Christ. Pneumatological discourse unrelated to the Father and Son may seem to promise more, yet it begins to lose its contours and often ends up being nothing other than another way to affirm a typically modernist idea of a "rough parity" of all religions.

Trinity serves here as elsewhere in a criteriological function. As another Roman Catholic, Jacques Dupuis, notes, Trinity helps us avoid three typical, interrelated errors. The first error puts Christ and God in opposition as if one could choose *either* a "theo-centric" *or* a "christocentric" option. The second error the Trinity helps us avoid is emphasizing either "regno-centrism" (the idea of the kingdom of God at the center) or "soterio-centrism" (salvation, rather than a Savior, at the center) at the expense of Christology. The third error is to champion that kind of pneumatological approach that tends to

---

87. Barth, *CD* I/1, p. 301; materially similarly, Jenson, *The Triune Identity*, p. ix.
88. S. M. Heim, *Depth of the Riches*, p. 134.

diminish the role of Jesus Christ as more limited than that of the Spirit. Indeed, the basic fallacy of the first wave of pneumatological approaches to the theology of religions, as mentioned, was to sever the Spirit from the Christ and thus make the Spirit's ministry independent. It is true that while Jesus Christ represents particularity, the Spirit represents universality, yet this is only in a healthy trinitarian context. The freedom of the Spirit cannot be set in opposition to the person and ministry of Jesus Christ, any more than the Son can be set in opposition to the Father.

All this requires an answer to the all-important question for our purposes: How do we establish the Spirit-Christ/Christ-Spirit relationship? This, in turn, will affect how we conceive of the relationship between the church and the Spirit, and consequently, the church and the kingdom. Let's take one topic at a time.

Pneumatology and Christology as One Divine Economy

In the New Testament, the Son and Spirit presuppose each other. The role of the Spirit comes to focus in that Jesus was related to the Spirit, and the Spirit is the Spirit of Christ. A trinitarian "Spirit Christology" "show[s] the influence of the Holy Spirit throughout the earthly life of Jesus, from his conception through the power of the Spirit (see Lk 1:35) to his resurrection at the hands of God by the power of the same Spirit (see Rom 8:11)."[89] In other words, Jesus is both the giver and receiver of the Spirit. The Spirit's role, on the other hand, is to help us turn to Christ, and by doing so, to the Father.

Wherever the Spirit inspires the knowledge of God, be it within the sphere of the church or outside of it, salvation brought about by the Spirit is referred to the saving work of Christ, his incarnation, death, and resurrection. As Dupuis says, there are not "two distinct channels [that of the Son and of the Spirit] through which God's saving presence reaches out to people in distinct economies of salvation,"[90] but one. Making the relationship between the Christ and the Spirit mutually presupposing in no way denies the universal, cosmic sphere of the ministry of the Spirit. Rather, it addresses the issue of recognizing which Spirit, whose Spirit.

The integral relationship between Jesus Christ and the Spirit also in-

---

89. Dupuis, *Toward a Christian Theology of Religious Pluralism*, p. 206. So also Pannenberg, *ST* 3:16-17.

90. Dupuis, *Toward a Christian Theology of Religious Pluralism*, p. 196.

troduces the cross into the equation, another topic routinely eschewed in the theology of religions for the sake of not blocking dialogue, as many believe it would.[91] "The cross . . . where God *himself* was in Christ (2 Cor 5:19), is the place where God represents and reveals himself, and even more than that, it is the place where he identifies and defines himself."[92] In other words, the cross is not something external to the divine life of the Trinity but an identifying element. Yes, the cross is a scandalous event, but it also is an everlasting testimony to the willingness of the triune God to not only share in the suffering of the world but also to let suffering and pain become part of the divine life. The Spirit, at work in the world after the cross, is the Spirit of the crucified and risen Christ through which the trinitarian God reaches out to the world to save and to heal.[93]

Speaking of the universal presence of the Spirit integrally related to the particularity of Jesus and his cross helps us qualify and critique the mantra according to which the Spirit represents universality whereas the Son particularity. This is correct to a point, not as an absolute rule. Consider biblical passages such as the prologue to the Gospel of John, which paints a picture of the Word in no less universal terms.[94] If Christology is depicted in both particular and universal terms, what can be said about the Spirit in this respect? The Spirit speaks not only to universality but also of particularity; any talk about the Spirit in a trinitarian context is always specific even if universal in its scope. Otherwise, we lose all contours to distinguish whose Spirit.

Going back to the notion of the triune God as communion and the Spirit as the principle of relationality, let us reflect on the implications for the encounter with the other.

"The Holy Spirit's Invitation to Relational Engagement"[95]

The triune God as a perichoretic communion is a helpful way to negotiate the dynamics and tension between one and many. The Trinity as communion allows room for both genuine diversity (otherwise we could not talk about the Trinity) and unity (otherwise we could not talk about one God). Trinity "unites transcendence and immanence, creation and redemption in such a way that

91. For an important article, see Wells, "The Holy Spirit and Theology of the Cross."
92. Matei, "The Practice of Community," p. 190.
93. See the remarkable statement in Vatican II's *Gaudium et Spes* (#22).
94. See further, Dupuis, *Toward a Christian Theology of Religious Pluralism*, pp. 188-90.
95. Section title in D'Costa, *Meeting of Religions*, p. 109.

from the Christian standpoint dialogue [with Muslims in this case] becomes possible and meaningful," affirmed the Roman Catholic Church in France in dialogue with Muslims.[96] Communion serves as the paradigm for relating to the other among human beings. Communion does not deny differences or eliminate distinctives, as is typical of various sorts of "rough parity" pluralisms; rather, communion is about encountering the other in a mutually learning yet challenging atmosphere.

The Christian, coming from a particular perspective, is both encouraged and entitled to witness to the triune God of the Bible and his saving will, yet at the same time prepared to learn from the other. This helps the Christian get to know the other and may also lead to the deepening of one's own faith. In the words of the postcolonial feminist Mayra Rivera, herein lies the "possibility of transformation . . . in the encounter with the transcendence in the flesh of the Other, and yet how can we meet the other as Other — as transcendent to us — if we are not ourselves transformed?"[97] Only trinitarian theology provides this kind of "context for a critical, reverent, and open engagement with otherness, without any predictable outcome,"[98] and it makes possible, to follow another postcolonialist feminist, Luce Irigaray, "touching which respects the other."[99] Hence, also from a Christian perspective, the profound statement of the Jewish philosopher Levinas can be fully affirmed: "through my relation to the Other, I am in touch with God."[100] Other religions are important for the Christian church in that they help the church penetrate more deeply into the divine mystery. This is the essence of what D'Costa calls the Spirit's call to "relational engagement." The acknowledgment of the gifts of God in other religions by virtue of the presence of the Spirit — as well as the critical discernment of these gifts by the power of the same Spirit — means a real trinitarian basis to Christianity's openness toward other religions. Again, citing D'Costa, "if the Spirit is at work in the religions, then the gifts of the Spirit need to be discovered, fostered, and received into the church. If the church fails to be receptive, it may be unwittingly practicing cultural and religious idolatry."[101]

All this said of the "trinitarian rules" about how to relate the trinitarian God of the Bible to religious pluralism and to other faith traditions, a word of warning is also in order to not limit the freedom of the Spirit. While I believe

96. Jukko, *Trinitarian Theology in Christian-Muslim Encounters*, p. 221.
97. Rivera, *Touch of Transcendence*, p. 118.
98. D'Costa, *Meeting of Religions*, p. 9.
99. Irigaray, *I Love to You*, p. 124.
100. Levinas, *Difficult Freedom*, p. 17.
101. D'Costa, *Meeting of Religions*, p. 115.

it is urgent theologically to reflect on the role of the Trinity among religions, we also have to remind ourselves again that "knowing" the ways of God is only possible by doxology. Indeed, trinitarian doctrine is essentially doxological in its origins and character.[102]

With this proper humility and modesty in mind, we will in the next chapter continue the task of relating the trinitarian God to other living faiths by moving from the theology of religions to the task of comparative theology, which takes up specific issues between two faith traditions.

---

102. See further, McDonnell, "Pneumatology Overview," pp. 197-98.

15. The Triune God among Religions

For Orientation: A Dialogical and Confessional Pursuit of God

The famed Harvard University scholar John B. Carman is daring to announce that he is "choosing to follow what some might consider an old-fashioned type of comparison: the comparison of ideas concerning the nature of God," now that for many scholars of religions and theologians this approach has given way to the phenomenological, ritual, and social study of religions.[1] It is comparative theology that continues pursuing that line of questioning, namely, carefully assessing, comparing, and reflecting on the ways the living faiths embrace the notions of the divine. But even a casual acquaintance with world religions raises the question of whether comparing notes on the divine is an appropriate and useful way of assessing religions in that Buddhism, in particular, may not be built on divinity. However, while Theravada Buddhism — unlike Mahayana and particularly its branch, the (Japanese) Pure Land — intentionally seeks to shift the focus in religion away from the deities to the primacy of each person's ethical pursuit toward enlightenment, the Buddhist view does not entail atheism in the way the term is understood in the post-Enlightenment Global North. There are very few if any Buddhists — and certainly Gautama would not belong to that group — who deny the *existence* of deities à la modern/contemporary Western secular/scientific atheism.

At the heart of comparative theology is the acknowledgment of a deep dynamic tension concerning religions. On the one hand, "[r]eligions generate infinite differences." Attempting to water down or deny real differences among

1. Carman, *Majesty and Meekness,* p. 5.

religions, as the "first generation of pluralism" seeks to do, is a failing exercise on more than one account. In this context, just consider how useless and uninteresting a task it would be to compare two items that are alike! On the other hand, "there is a tradition at the very heart of [many living] . . . faiths which is held in common. It is not that precisely the same doctrines are believed, but that the same tendencies of thought and devotion exist, and are expressed within rather diverse patterns of thought, characteristic of the faiths in question."[2] Add to this the obvious fact that religions are living processes that develop and are reshaped and reconfigured over the years, and that within any major living tradition differences and diversities are sometimes as dramatic as between some religions.[3] With this dynamic in mind, for the comparative theological inquiry into the nature and existence of God to be meaningful it must be dialogical and "conversational,"[4] an honest mutual encounter that also may lead to "mutual transformation," as John B. Cobb has famously argued in *Beyond Dialogue*.

Dialogical, however, does not mean that therefore a disinterested, "neutral" investigation is attempted. Theology is confessional by nature, on all sides. "Dialogue must permanently shape the whole theological environment, but dialogue is not the primary goal of theology, which still has to do with the articulation of the truths one believes and the realization of a fuller knowledge of God (insofar as that is possible by way of theology). Both within traditions and across religious boundaries, truth does matter, conflicts among claims about reality remain significant possibilities, and making a case for the truth remains a key part of the theologian's task."[5] Hence, following the Catholic comparativist Clooney, this project envisions "theology as an interreligious, comparative, dialogical, and *confessional* enterprise."[6]

That kind of task can only be attempted in the spirit of hospitality. The postcolonialist feminist Mayra Rivera reminds us that we "constantly fail to encounter the other as Other. Time and again we ignore or deny the singularity of the Other — we don't see even when the face stands in front of us. We still need, it seems, 'eyes to see and ears to hear' — and bodies capable of embracing without grasping."[7] What makes hospitality such a fitting metaphor for interfaith relations is that it "involves invitation, response and engagement."[8] True

---

2. Ward, *Images of Eternity*, p. 1.
3. Cf. Baier, "Ultimate Reality in Buddhism and Christianity," pp. 89-90.
4. Thatamanil, *Immanent Divine*, p. xii.
5. Clooney, *Hindu God, Christian God*, p. 173.
6. Clooney, *Hindu God, Christian God*, p. 7, emphasis added.
7. Rivera, *Touch of Transcendence*, p. 118.
8. Newlands and Smith, *Hospitable God*, p. 32.

hospitality helps us avoid "bearing false witness."[9] Hospitality reaches out, makes room, facilitates dialogue. Even more: "Hospitality is important to all the great world religions today."[10] Hence, there is a common denominator. Even though it is true, as mentioned, that often religions may not appear to be hospitable, it is as true that all living faiths seek hospitality and dream of it.[11] But even though hospitality is a common denominator — in terms of invitation for mutual engagement — it also represents complexity. "It is hard to underestimate the complexity of the task of religious conversation and dialogue, with its interaction of the global and local, the pluralist, the inclusive and the exclusivist strands, the fluctuations between essentialist and changing elements."[12] Only careful attention to the details of investigation, respectful honoring of the otherness of other traditions and their representatives, as well as bold but humble arguing for one's deepest convictions, in the hopes of being both enriched and enabled to share a convincing testimony, make such a multifaceted enterprise feasible.

Again in this chapter, the order and selection of interfaith encounters vary. The most extreme monotheism of Islam will be engaged first; thereafter, in many ways going to the other extreme, the apparently polytheistic Hinduism will be invited for dialogue, to be followed by Buddhist traditions. There will be no separate focused investigation of Christian-Jewish dialogue because the most burning issue related to Trinity, namely, Christology, is discussed in some detail in the volume *Christ and Reconciliation,* and the somewhat parallel problems related to the unity of God are investigated in relation to Islam. Furthermore, throughout the investigation, where relevant, Judaism, as the closest monotheistic religion to Christianity, sharing part of the same Scripture, will be engaged in relation to other faiths.

Allah and the Father of Jesus Christ

Islamic "Classical Theism"

While it is deeply similar to older monotheistic "cousin" faiths, Judaism and Christianity,[13] "[n]o religious community puts more emphasis on the absolute

9. See Thatamanil, *Immanent Divine,* p. xii.
10. Newlands and Smith, *Hospitable God,* p. 32.
11. Newlands and Smith, *Hospitable God,* p. 33.
12. Newlands and Smith, *Hospitable God,* p. 37.
13. See Zayd, *Al-Ghazali on Divine Predicates,* p. vii. For an important study, see Köchler, ed., *Concept of Monotheism.*

oneness of God than does Islam."[14] Affirmed everywhere in Islamic theology, the short sura 112 of the Qur'an puts it succinctly, taking notice also of the fallacy of the Christian confession of the Trinity:

> Say: "He is God, One.
> God, the Self-Sufficient, Besought of all.
> He neither begot, nor was begotten.
> Nor is there anyone equal to Him."

Hence, the basic Muslim confession of *shahada:* "There is no god but God, and Muhammad is the apostle of God." So robust is the belief in the unity of God that for some Muslim philosophers and mystics the principle of unity also applies to reality itself.

An essential aspect of the divine unity is Allah's distinction from all else. The common statement "God is great" *(Allah akbar)* means not only that but also that "God is greater" than anything else. Hence, the biggest sin is *shirk,* associating anything with Allah.[15] Importantly, *shirk* means literally "ingratitude," in other words, "that there is only one divine Creator who should be thanked and praised; no other being is to be given the thanks due only to God."[16] In that light it is understandable that, unlike modern forms of Christianity, the Muslim faith encompasses all of life. "Faith does not concern a sector of life — no, the whole of life is *islam* [submission]."[17] Hence, the five pillars of Islam (profession of faith, prayers, almsgiving, fasting, and pilgrimage) shape all of life.

Muslim theology of God includes the built-in dynamic between the absolute transcendence of God, because of his incomparability and uniqueness, on the one hand, and on the other hand, his presence and rulership in the world, which is a call for total obedience.[18] Unlike Christian theology in general and classical panentheism in particular, Muslims "tend to speak of God's

---

14. Carman, *Majesty and Meekness,* p. 323.

15. There are numerous Qur'anic condemnations of *shirk,* although it is not quite clear what that "tremendous sin" (4.48) consists of.

16. Carman, *Majesty and Meekness,* p. 323. In that sense, Islamic theology is most radically "dualistic" in making a distinction between the divine and reality, in contrast to advaitic (and even moderately advaitic) Hinduism, which is monistic. For an important comparative study, important also for Christian theology, see Singh, *God in Indian Islamic Theology.*

17. Vroom, *No Other Gods,* p. 84.

18. For a useful discussion, see Winkler, *Contemporary Muslim and Christian Responses to Religious Plurality,* pp. 270-75.

presence in terms of 'presence with' rather than 'presence in.' "[19] The small but very important study of Muslim's most celebrated theologian, al-Ghazali, *The Niche for Lights* — an extended comment on one verse of the Qur'an (24:35), which speaks of the "likeness of His [Allah's] Light . . . as a niche wherein is a lamp" — at first reading sounds like an affirmation of monism because it says that everything "other than Allâh is, when considered in and by itself, pure not-being. . . . Therefore, the God-aspect is the sole thing in existence" (1.6). That, however, is not monism but rather the linking of everything to God, making the created reality depend on Allah, similarly to Qur'an 40:68: "He it is Who gives life and brings death. So when He decides upon a matter, He only says to it 'Be!' and it is."[20] And yet, there is a monistic tendency of a sort — which is understandable in light of al-Ghazali's Sufi background: "Therefore '*There is no deity but* ALLAH' is the Many's declaration of Unity" (1.7). The same kind of dynamic is not unknown in either Jewish or Christian theology, although classical theism is an important way to negotiate it.

In his transcendence and incomparability, says al-Ghazali, Allah is "infinitely" greater: "The meaning is rather that he is too absolutely Great to be called Greater, or Most Great, by way of relation or comparison — too Great for anyone, whether Prophet or Angel, to grasp the real nature of His Greatness" (1.6), so much so that he "transcends all relations" because "to bear relationship to what is imperfect carries with it imperfection" (2.2). These kinds of statements are meant to secure the total transcendence of God. They of course raise the question of whether al-Ghazali "goes so far in stressing God's utter difference from all finite things that it becomes increasingly difficult to say how Allah is related to the world as Creator and Judge at all."[21] Gleaning from Sufi mysticism, but staying still within the orthodox mainstream (Sunni) tradition, al-Ghazali builds a case for different levels of trying to reach this utterly transcendent divine reality, ladders of ascent,[22] as it were, culminating in those who go beyond mere obedience to the Creator or conceptual under-

---

19. Nazir-Ali, *Frontiers in Muslim-Christian Encounter*, p. 21.

20. Consider also 1.6: "Now, when this state prevails, it is called in relation to him who experiences it, Extinction, nay, Extinction of Extinction, for the soul has become extinct to itself, extinct to its own extinction." For comments, including parallels with Hindu monism, see Ward, *Images of Eternity*, pp. 120-22.

21. Ward, *Images of Eternity*, p. 122.

22. The three basic levels are those "veiled by pure darkness," the atheists; those "veiled by mixed light and darkness"; and those "veiled with pure Light," among whom are those who "have searched out and understood the true meaning of the divine attributes" (3.1-3).

standing to some kind of mystical union and perfection, as described in the ending paragraphs of *The Niche for Lights*.[23]

One of the most well known ways in Islamic theology to imagine God is the listing of the 99 Beautiful Names of God.[24] Interestingly, there is no unanimity concerning whether "Allah" belongs to that number or is the 100th one. Be that as it may, that foundational name is attached to a number of other designations, for example, *al-Malik* (the King), *al-Salam* (the Peace), and *al-Muhaymin* (the Vigilant).[25] The naming of the divine is more important for Islamic theology than for Christian theology.[26] Illustrative here is the beginning of each Qur'anic sura (save one) with the description of God as the "Compassionate, the Merciful."[27] As in the Bible, there are occasionally anthropomorphic metaphors of Allah such as the "face of God" (Q 2:115; 92:20) or the "hand(s) of God" (48:10; 5:64), although in general Islam is very cautious about picturing Allah.

As for major themes in the Qur'an's teaching about Allah, along with transcendence and mercy, the following seem to be dominant: first, God as creator and origin of everything; second, the divine unity, mentioned above; and, third, the dual emphasis on Allah's omnipotence and benevolence.[28] Furthermore, the theme of Allah's justice and judgment looms large in the Qur'an, and of course — as in Christian and Jewish tradition — they must be linked with mercy.[29] Echoing the Christian teaching, al-Ghazali reminds us that "My mercy is greater than My wrath," but that is not a pretext for complacency, as if, "Well, whatever we do, God is merciful."[30] Also important is that Islam affirms the idea of the freedom of will among humans

---

23. *The Niche for Lights* 3.4.

24. While the Qur'an does not specify 99 names (indeed, more than 99 names and designations of God can be found therein), early in Islamic theology, the number 99 came to be used. The Qur'an merely mentions: "And to God belong the Most Beautiful Names" (7:180). The list of 99 names is given definitively in the established commentaries on sura 17:110. Surprisingly, a major study on the names has appeared only recently; to my knowledge, unfortunately, it is not translated into English: Gimaret, *Les noms divins en Islam*. For an accessible, succinct discussion of all 99 names, see Zwemer, *Moslem Doctrine of God*, chap. 3.

25. See further, Carman, *Majesty and Meekness*, p. 327.

26. Watt, *Islam and Christianity Today*, pp. 47-48.

27. See Cragg, "Al-Rahman al-Rahim," pp. 235-36.

28. Gardet, "Allāh," p. 407.

29. For an important discussion of love, mercy, and justice in relation to Allah, see Volf, *Allah*, chaps. 8, 9.

30. al-Ghazali, *Alchemy of Happiness*, chap. 1, p. 32; chap. 2, p. 41, respectively.

differently than some Christian traditions. "God would be neither just nor good if He punished people for acts for which they were not responsible"; consequently, human beings must have been created human beings with the ability to choose between wrong and right.[31] That, however, is not to deny some kind of view of divine predestination, based on Allah's omniscience and omnipotence; that affirmation does not negate human responsibility and, unlike Christian tradition, has no original sin doctrine behind it. The all-determining power of Allah comes to the fore in the theology of al-Ashari: "It is always towards God that [al-Ashari's] thoughts move. God is all in all; everything is in His hand; and since He is the Merciful and the Compassionate, the proper attitude toward Him is patience . . . in the face of His judgments and loyal obedience to His commands. It is clear that al-Ashari is a determinist, but it is just as clear that his determinism is throughout pervaded with the thought of God."[32]

As did Christian tradition, Islam moved toward "classical theism" early on. To take an obvious example: the adjectives "compassionate" and "merciful" were transformed in later theology into the more fixed and analytic nouns "compassion" and "mercy" as attributes of Allah. Importantly, this development did not begin in early Islamic theology but had its precedent in the Qur'an itself.[33] This is what was argued above about the "seeds" of classical theism in the NT. The rise of *kalam* theology was the culmination of this development, as is evident in the masterful work of the tenth-century al-Ashari. Not unlike what occurred in Christian history, there was a continuing debate between the traditionalists who wished to retain the verbatim biblical account and the Mu'tazilites, the rationalists, who were drawn to systematic explanations, which in many ways paralleled Christian scholasticism.[34] "A Short Creed by Al-Ashari" reads like a Christian confession, yet also obviously rebuts its trinitarian claims: "We believe . . . [t]hat God is One God, Single, One, Eternal; beside Him no God exists; He has taken to Himself no wife *(sahiba),* nor child *(walad).*"[35] The creed lists basic beliefs in God as creator, as powerful, as providing, and as eschatological consummator.

Similarly to Christian scholastics, the Asharites, followers of al-Ashari *kalam* theology, engaged in highly sophisticated disputes about, for example,

---

31. Rippin and Knappert, *Textual Sources for the Study of Islam,* p. 18.

32. As explained by Watt, *Free Will and Predestination in Early Islam,* p. 147, cited in Carman, *Majesty and Meekness,* p. 330.

33. Carman, *Majesty and Meekness,* p. 326.

34. For an important discussion, see Frank, *Beings and Their Attributes.*

35. In MacDonald, *Development of Muslim Theology,* p. 294.

how to understand the attributes of God in relation to God's essence, and so also entered debates with the Mu'tazilites. Whereas the Mu'tazilites were willing to attach the attributes not to the essence of God but rather to his actions, the Asharites — as well as al-Ghazali, as discussed below — linked some attributes to the essence and others to his actions.[36] A noted debate had to do with the proper conception of the most important attribute of Allah, namely, the speech of God, that God had spoken and revealed himself. The Asharites considered the speaking contingent since it obviously had happened in time, whereas for Ibn Hanbal, God's speech, the Qur'an, is part of God's eternal being. That debate in turn has to do with the dispute over whether the Qur'an is created or uncreated.[37] Furthermore, Muslim theologians of old delved deeply into the debate of God-language, for example, in terms of how to best understand the anthropomorphisms present in the Qur'an.[38]

While there is hardly a classified typology of attributes in Islamic traditions — although many contemporary Islamic theologians familiar with Christian tradition find the classification into "communicable" and "incommunicable"[39] attributes meaningful — traditionally thirteen attributes mentioned in sura 59:22-24 feature first on the list. The most well known listing of attributes, as presented by al-Ghazali, includes knowing, powerful, living, willing, hearing, seeing, and speaking,[40] followed by four "properties": existence, eternity, unity, and knowability. Unlike the attributes, which "are not [God's] essence," these four properties are part of God's essence, whereas the seven attributes are "superadded to the essence."[41] Like some aspects of Christian theology of God that take a paradoxical approach, the listing of attributes may follow the logic of polarities: "doublets having both a correlative and a paradoxical sense," such as "Restrainer" and "Expander" or "Creator of Life" and "Creator of Death."[42] Luther's theology of the cross comes to mind here.

While Muslim theology is not in general favorably disposed toward personal characteristics of Allah, such characteristics are sometimes employed to highlight the absolute distinction between the Creator and creature. Al-Ghazali may at times say that "God is more tender to his servants than a mother to her suckling-child," attributing this statement to the Prophet Mu-

---

36. See further, el-Bizri, "God," pp. 121-40.
37. For a brief comment, see Carman, *Majesty and Meekness*, pp. 328-29.
38. See further, Zayd, *Al-Ghazali on Divine Predicates*, p. viii.
39. For such a listing, see Carman, *Majesty and Meekness*, p. 329 n. 14.
40. For details, see Zayd, *Al-Ghazali on Divine Predicates*, pp. 1-63, 65-101, at 65.
41. Zayd, *Al-Ghazali on Divine Predicates*, pp. 65-101, at 65.
42. Carman, *Majesty and Meekness*, pp. 326-27, at 327.

hammad.[43] Similarly, there are a few instances of linking human knowledge of self to the knowledge of God, an idea well established in Christian tradition (Augustine), although — for reasons mentioned previously — that theme is handled with great care in Islam. Al-Ghazali boldly states at the beginning of *The Alchemy of Happiness:* "Knowledge of self is the key to the knowledge of God, according to the saying: 'He who knows himself knows God' and, as it is written in the Koran, 'We will show them Our signs in the world and *in themselves,* that the truth may be manifest to them.'"[44]

Early Muslim theology's relation to pagan philosophy was not much different from that of Christian tradition. There were a great appreciation and liberal borrowing from the greatest masters of antiquity, including Plato and Aristotle, but at times there were reminders of the inadequacy of philosophy alone, apart from Qur'anic authority, to establish divine truths.[45] As early as the ninth-century work of the famous philosopher-theologian al-Farabi, we see significant Platonic and Aristotelian influences. His listing of the attributes of God, under the rubric "Metaphysical Theology," could have easily come from a typical Christian manual: simplicity, infinity, immutability, unity, intelligence, "God Knows All Things through Knowledge of Himself," "God Is Truth," "God Is Life."[46] As mentioned above, Muslim theologians also engaged "proofs" for the existence of God, borrowing from Aristotle.

Similarly to Christian and some other living faith traditions, including Hindu *bhakti* traditions, the mystically oriented Sufi traditions were less drawn to philosophical and conceptual clarifications of the attributes and instead majored on a prayerful apophatic attitude and spiritual vision. Different from much of Christian asceticism, which tended to be somewhat isolationist, but similar to much of Buddhist monastic life, these early Muslim ascetics sought to live out their faith in the midst of the common people and thus helped disseminate Sufi spirituality at the grassroots level. If obedience — unreserved submission — to Allah is the hallmark of much of mainline Islam, then love of God, as in, say, Hindu *bhakti* traditions, is the defining issue

---

43. al-Ghazali, *Alchemy of Happiness,* chap. 1, p. 32.

44. al-Ghazali, *Alchemy of Happiness,* chap. 1, p. 19. The first citation is attributed to Muhammad.

45. The classic work here is that of al-Ghazali, *The Incoherence of the Philosophers,* which casts serious doubts on the value of philosophical argumentation alone, apart from revelation, to accomplish its theological task. Yet al-Ghazali — similarly to the Christian Thomas Aquinas — is the leading philosopher-theologian of his tradition!

46. Hammond, *Philosophy of Alfarabi,* pp. 22-29; for a detailed linking of the attributes with Plato and Aristotle, see Zayd, *Al-Ghazali on Divine Predicates,* pp. xiii-xx.

of Sufism.[47] At times deemed heretical, Sufism also was deeply integrated into the fabric of Muslim faith and in many cases its followers played significant roles in missionary work. A shining example is the greatest Islamic theologian, al-Ghazali,[48] of the eleventh century, who was both Sufi and a great intellectual, even philosophical, mind. In him the best of early Muslim spiritual, mystical, philosophical, scientific, and theological influences coalesced.

The Unity of God and Christian Confession of Trinity

The Qur'an absolutely and unequivocally affirms the oneness of God. According to al-Ghazali, on the one hand, that "God is one . . . means the negation of anything other than He and the affirmation of His essence." On the other hand, oneness means the denial of plurality in God: "He does not accept divisibility, i.e., He has no quantity, neither definition nor magnitude. It also means that He has no equal in rank and absolutely no equal in any manner." As in Christian tradition, the unity also includes the unity of God's existence and essence.[49] The leading contemporary Muslim theologian, active also in the "Common Word" project, Seyyed Hossein Nasr, notes that the traditional Christian creedal confession *credo in unum Deum* materially repeats the affirmation of the Muslim confession *la iaha illa' Llaaha*.[50]

The Qur'anic teaching categorically rejects any notion of threeness of God as set forth in the classic passage 4:171, according to which Jesus is "merely God's messenger and His Word . . . and a spirit from Him";[51] indeed, the trinitarian confession is nothing less than blasphemy (5:76). A foundational reason for the strict rebuttal of the Christian doctrine of the Trinity includes the absolute exaltedness of Allah and the sheer absurdity of the idea of God having a child by a woman.[52] (What is remarkable about this rebuttal of the

47. See further, Vroom, *No Other Gods*, p. 84. Vroom reminds us that we should not, however, conceive the notion of "obedience" in too legalistic terms, in light of the way Saint Paul speaks of the "obedience of faith," which is about covenant faithfulness (p. 84).

48. For his doctrine of God, see Zayd, *Al-Ghazali on Divine Predicates*.

49. In Zayd, *Al-Ghazali on Divine Predicates*, pp. x-xi, at x. For an authoritative contemporary presentation, see Abduh, *Theology of Unity*.

50. Nasr, "The Word of God," p. 112.

51. The main Qur'anic passages that deny the divinity of Jesus are 4:171; 9:30; and 19:35. As an indication of the lack of intimate knowledge of the orthodox Christian teaching on the Trinity, 5:116 conceives the Trinity as Father, Jesus, and Mary. Similarly, in relation to Judaism, there is the misleading statement that "Jews call Ezra a son of God" (9:30).

52. See further, Parrinder, *Jesus in the Qur'an*, pp. 126-41.

Trinity is that ironically it gives Jesus high status, as he is called the "word" and "spirit," whatever the precise theological meanings in Islam were!)

Muslims reject the Christian concept of "God in Christ" on the ground of God's glory and greatness *(takbir).* For them, it is unworthy for a sovereign God to be human. In his essay " 'Greater Is God,' Contemporary *Takbīr:* Muslim and Christian,"[53] Kenneth Cragg seeks to find a connecting point between the Islamic notion of *takbir* and the Christian Magnificat. His argument is that the concept of *takbir* is a shared reality between the two religions. He insists that as the concept of *takbir (Allah akbar)* is crucial in Isl!am, the Christian Magnificat (magnify the Lord) is essential to Christians and runs through the whole Bible. Again, as the term *islam* (submission) conveys that the core of Islam is to make God to be all in all, in Christianity God's being "all in all" is what NT Christology is all about. But "the crucial question has to do with the nature of the 'greatness' we affirm."[54] In that light, from a Christian perspective it can be suggested that the incarnation or the *kenosis* of God does not necessarily oppose God's greatness. On the contrary, Cragg argues, it is in Jesus Christ, the Word made flesh, that what Muslims desire to assert regarding God's greatness is effected: it is in Jesus Christ, "God in Christ," that God achieved his intention toward humanity. "For is that sovereignty truly sovereign if it fails to take action against the empire of ignorance and evil in humankind?"[55] Again, this is a statement from a Christian theology and should be presented as an invitation for mutual dialogue.

Another major reason for the categorical rejection of the Trinity in Islamic theology is that it represents *shirk.* On this issue, we need to clarify what Christology is *not,* what *shirk* is, and what is *not shirk.* When the Qur'an gives "Praise to God who took not up a son" (17:111; 19:35; 19:92; 25:2), it must be noted that Christians also affirm this statement, as it is not about incarnation but rather about adoptionism. Cragg suggests that instead of speaking of incarnation in terms of "taking up," we should think of *tanazul* (descending). "Deification in *ittikhādh* [taking up] is all human and chronically misguided. In *tanāzul* the initiative is all God's and blessedly compassionate," he notes. A way to help Muslims grasp this idea is to establish the connection between Christ's preexistence and that of the Qur'an.[56]

Often behind the Muslim charge of *shirk* is an Arian heretical notion

53. Cragg, "Greater Is God," pp. 27-39.
54. Cragg, "Greater Is God," p. 38.
55. Cragg, *Call of the Minaret,* p. 264.
56. Cragg, *Jesus and the Muslim,* p. 203.

according to which Christ is "associated" as closely as possible with God, but is not God.[57] But that view was categorically rejected by Christian creeds. Now, what is *shirk?* It is "plural worship," but it is not "the manifold 'association' that exists between Creator and creature, between Lord and servant."[58] In other words, God's gracious relation or association with humanity, the eternal Word becoming human, is not *shirk.* Muslim tradition also, of course, speaks freely and robustly of God's "association" with nondivine realities, in creation, providence, prophecy, and law. In all Semitic faiths we find that "God can be known by man only in conjunction with the human situation."[59] "In each faith, there is 'God and. . . .' In Judaism, the central 'association' is peoplehood and covenant — 'God and His People.' In Islam, the central 'association' is prophethood — 'God and His Prophet.' In Christianity, the central 'association' is Christ — 'God in Christ.'"[60]

In response to the charge of *shirk,* recall the statement by Pannenberg that "beyond the unity no more can be said about God. . . . Thus, the doctrine of the Trinity is in fact concrete monotheism in contrast to the notions of an abstract transcendence of the one God and abstract notions of a divine unity that leaves no place for plurality."[61] Rather than three gods, in Christian theology "[t]he trinitarian persons . . . are simply manifestations and forms — eternal forms — of the one divine essence."[62] That was affirmed not only by some of the earliest Christian theological writings on the Trinity, such as Gregory of Nyssa's *On "Not Three Gods"* in the Christian East and writings of Augustine in the West, but even in the most authoritative creeds. Consider the Athanasian Creed, one of the earliest ones: "That we worship one God in Trinity, and Trinity in Unity; Neither confounding the persons nor dividing the substance. For there is one person of the Father, another of the Son, and another of the Holy Spirit. But the Godhead of the Father, of the Son, and of the Holy Spirit is all one, the glory equal, the majesty coeternal."[63] Rightly, the medieval cardinal Nicholas of Cusa reminded us that the oneness of God is

---

57. Jenson, "The Risen Prophet," pp. 61-62, cited in Swanson, "The Trinity in Christian-Muslim Conversation," p. 261.

58. Cragg, *Jesus and the Muslim,* p. 204.

59. Cragg, *Jesus and the Muslim,* p. 11; see also p. 278.

60. Cragg, *Jesus and the Muslim,* p. 287.

61. Pannenberg, *ST* 1:335-36.

62. Pannenberg, *ST* 1:383.

63. In *Historic Creeds and Confessions,* p. 5. See also the strong statement on the unity in the Fourth Lateran Council (1215) statement against the excesses of Joachim of Fiore, in Schroeder, *Disciplinary Decrees of the General Councils,* p. 236.

prior to the plurality,[64] and hence, "When you begin to count the Trinity you depart from the truth"[65] because the three "persons" make one God![66] (In that light, Nicholas's material affirmation of the classic notion of the "simplicity of God" should not be hastily dismissed by contemporary theologians who see it as a way of undermining the trinitarian communion!) Similarly to Muslim theology, Nicholas ultimately appealed to revelation: when the Bible tells us that God is love, it means that there must be an internal distinction in the one Godhead to allow for the "lover" to show love to "another"[67] — an argument presented by other Christian theologians as well (e.g., Richard of St. Victor). Furthermore, by the same logic, God's self-revelation — a premise affirmed by both traditions — for the cardinal required that there be the "internal" Word in God who alone, as incarnate, can reveal God to us.[68] Only God — an "insider," if we may say so — can unveil to humans God.

What about incarnation? Isn't that necessarily a statement about plurality in the Christian understanding of God: one God "up there in heaven" and the other one "down here on earth"? Christian tradition negotiates that dilemma with two ancient concepts, namely, the "Augustinian" rule according to which the works of the Trinity *ad extra* (in relation to creation) are undivided,[69] and *perichoresis,* the principle of mutual indwelling of Father, Son, and Spirit.[70] Consider the prologue to John's Gospel, which speaks of the Word *(Logos)* that became flesh (1:14) as not only being *with* God but also *being* God (1:1). Similarly, consider the Johannine Jesus' saying that "the Father is in me and I am in the Father" (10:38).[71] Hence, Christianity affirms that "[i]n worshipping Jesus one does not worship another than God; one simply worships God," as difficult as that statement is in light of its christological ramifications, namely, that Jesus, the human person, is considered to be divine.[72] Nor is Christian theology or the Bible ever affirming what the Qur'an claims to be a Christian

---

64. Nicholas of Cusa, *De Pace Fidei,* ##15, 23; Nicholas of Cusa, *De Docta Ignorantia,* in *Selected Spiritual Writings,* #14.

65. Nicholas of Cusa, *De Docta Ignorantia,* #57 (quoting Augustine); I am indebted to Volf, *Allah,* p. 52.

66. See Volf, *Allah,* pp. 53-54, for detailed listing of passages from Nicholas of Cusa in response to the classic Qur'anic passages of affirming the oneness of God and rebutting the (Christian) doctrine of Trinity (5:73, 116; 23:91).

67. Nicholas of Cusa, *Cribratio Alkorani,* #108.

68. See Nicholas of Cusa, *De Pace Fidei,* #72; Volf, *Allah,* pp. 56-57.

69. See further, Augustine, *On the Trinity* 1.8.

70. See further, Augustine, *On the Trinity* 6.9.

71. See further, Volf, *Allah,* p. 138.

72. Ward, *Religion and Revelation,* p. 179.

statement: "Behold, God is the Christ, son of Mary" (Q 5:72).[73] Christian faith, rather, says that Christ is God.

What if Muslim and Christian theologians took these affirmations of the unity of God from the Christian side as guidelines when working toward a common understanding without artificially ignoring the differences? Could then the promise by the Muslim thinker Seyyed Hossein Nasr be redeemed at least to some extent: "Every question regarding the Trinity can be resolved between Christianity and Islam by a truly metaphysical penetration into the meaning of the fundamental polarization of the One"?[74] All in all, in engaging another radically monotheist faith, whether Jewish or Islamic, Christian faith can also help clarify its own core beliefs and teach its members about the correct way of negotiating unity-in-diversity/diversity-in-unity.[75]

Do Muslims and Christians Believe in the Same God?

The Muslim theologian Seyyed Hossein Nasr puts the question of the relationship between Allah and the God of the Bible in perspective:

> There are already those on the Christian side who assert that the Christian God is not the same as Allah, who is an Arabic lunar deity or something like that. Such people who usually combine sheer ignorance with bigotry should attend a Sunday mass in Arabic in Bethlehem, Beirut, Amman, or Cairo and hear what Arabic term the Christians of these cities use for the Christian God. Nor is God simply to be identified with one member of the Christian Trinity, one part of three divinities that some Muslims believe wrongly that Christians worship. Allah, or God, is none other than the One God of Abraham, Isaac, Ishmael, Moses, Jesus, and Muhammad.[76]

Now, what is at stake in this debate? Briefly put, both peace and theological integrity. "A deep chasm of misunderstanding, dislike, and even hatred separates many Christians and Muslims today. Christian responses to Allah . . . will either widen that chasm or help bridge it. If for Christians Allah is a foreign and false god, all bridge building will suffer," notes Miroslav Volf, who

---

73. See further, Roberts, "Trinity vs. Monotheism," p. 90.
74. Cited in Gorder, *No God but God*, p. 115, from Nasr, *Les Musulmans*, p. 139.
75. See further, Watt, "Islamic Theology and the Christian Theologian," p. 242.
76. Nasr, "The Word of God," p. 115.

reminds us that "[t]he stakes are high. Muslims and Christians together comprise more than half of humanity."[77] While this practical reason alone would substantiate rigorous and widespread common work on this topic, there is also a deep and foundational theological issue at stake. The question at hand has to do with more than just interfaith hospitality; in the words of the Jewish theologian Jon D. Levenson, "no monotheist can ever accuse anyone — certainly not another monotheist — of worshiping *another* God, only (at most) of improperly identifying the one God that both seek to serve."[78]

Currently, it is a commonplace scholarly consensus that the term *allah* predates the time of Muhammad. It is also a consensus that — against the older scholarly view and still a regular popular opinion — the name did not originate in the context of moon worship in Arabia (even though the crescent became Islam's symbol and moon worship was known in that area).[79] The term derives from Aramaic and Syriac words for God *(elah, alah)*.[80] In that light it is fully understandable that even among Christians in Arabic-speaking areas the term "Allah" is the designation for God.[81] However, to say that both etymologically and theologically both Muslims and Christians refer to the same God when they speak of the Divine is not yet to settle the issue of *what kind* of God that is. In other words, "The real difficulty lies not in identifying the ultimate referent of the word 'God,' but knowing how to respond to the dizzying array of predicates *about* God that sometimes seem contradictory."

77. Volf, *Allah,* p. 1. See also "A Common Word between Us and You": "If Muslims and Christians are not at peace, the world cannot be at peace." For the dramatic illustration of the implications to religious and political unrest and uneasiness due to one religion's view of another religion's deity, consider the outrage among Muslims because of Pope Benedict XVI's Regensburg address, in which he implied that Islam and its God are violent by nature. Benedict XVI, "Faith, Reason and the University." For exposition and comments, see Volf, *Allah,* chap. 1. A conciliatory response to the pope's speech was offered by a number of Muslim leaders and scholars: "Open Letter to His Holiness Pope Benedict XVI," http://ammanmessage.com/media/openLetter/english.pdf.

78. Levenson, "Do Christians and Muslims Worship the Same God?" p. 32, emphasis added.

79. According to sura 3:67, there were monotheists (called *hanif*) in Arabia before the time of Muhammad.

80. K. Thomas, "Allah in Translations of the Bible," p. 301; for an accessible discussion of the etymology, history, and background of the term *allah,* see Tennent, *Theology in the Context of World Christianity,* pp. 27-31. For a detailed investigation, see also Shehadeh, "Do Muslims and Christians Believe in the Same God?"

81. In this light, consider the ban by Malaysian Home Ministry for Christians to use the designation "Allah" in relation to their God, as in 2007 under militant leaders it reinforced the law established in 1986. For a current update, see "Can Christians Say 'Allah'?"

That is important to note since "[n]o Muslim or Christian . . . worships a *generic* God or the mere *concept* of God in some vague, philosophical mist."[82] Both Islam and Christianity claim to be based on divine revelation and seek to ground their understanding of the God whom believers worship, and to whom they devote their lives, on Scripture. While those Scriptures and the subsequent theological reflection and tradition share a lot in common, significant differences also complicate our clarifying the extent and meaning of the foundational consensus on the same referent of the term itself.[83]

This issue is not new to either tradition. As early as the seventh Christian century, John of Damascus, the most celebrated theologian in the Christian East with firsthand knowledge of the Muslim faith,[84] delved deeply into it in the last chapter of his *De Haeresibus (On Heresies)* — an encyclopedic investigation of all sorts of heresies, past and current, altogether no fewer than 101 in number! The Damascene's assessment of Muslims is harsh and terse, considering them "idol worshippers."[85] On the constructive side, John makes the important point, citing the *tawhid* confession, "He [Muhammad] says that there is one God, creator of all, who is neither begotten, nor has begotten," in other words, robustly supporting the shared doctrine of the unity of God, which he also exposits in more detail in *De Fide Orthodoxa* (1.5), importantly under the heading "On the Holy Trinity"! Subsequently, in the rest of the tract he responds to typical Muslim charges, including the *shirk*, and also engages in counterattack in terms of Muhammad's family and other similar Christian criticisms.

Subsequently debates continued, reaching no consensus.[86] A highly important paradigm of the Christian approach to Allah comes from Nicholas of Cusa, who testified to the horrendous disaster in the capital of the Eastern Christian Church, Constantinople, as the forces of the Ottoman Empire under the leadership of Mehmed II in 1453 violently and brutally conquered the city.

---

82. Tennent, *Theology in the Context of World Christianity,* p. 31.

83. In that light, Lamin Sanneh's question is useful and important: "Was not the 'Allah' of Arabian Islam the same as the 'Allah' of pre-Islamic Arab Christianity?" (Sanneh, "Do Christians and Muslims Worship the Same God?" p. 35). It also reminds us of the at-times fierce debates within Christian tradition as to whether the "God" of classical theism is the same as the "God" of panentheism.

84. Apart from the lack of many biographical details, it is an established scholarly commonplace that John served in some important public role in the Muslim caliph's administration, along with his role in ecclesiastical affairs, including the Seventh Ecumenical Council of 787. For our purposes, an interesting detail has to do with his knowledge of Arabic, which cannot be established on the basis of the available sources.

85. Sahas, *John of Damascus on Islam,* #4 (p. 71).

86. D. Thomas, "Doctrine of the Trinity in the Early Abbasid Era," pp. 78-98.

Following the ransacking of the holy city at the end of May, in September the Catholic cardinal penned the highly influential *De Pace Fidei (On the Harmonious Peace of Religions)*, which, instead of supporting Pope Nicholas V's call for another crusade against the infidels, sought to summon a conference "in Jerusalem," under the auspices of the heavenly King of Kings, between rival religions to achieve a "harmony among religions" and "perpetual peace."[87] Even with the horror of the devastated city in his mind — which may remind us of the events of 9/11 in New York City — Nicholas asserted that all people, including the Muslims, worship one and the same God "in everything they are seen to adore," and that if they fail to do so, it is because of ignorance.[88] That is because there is, as his most famous dictum puts it, *una religio in varietate rituum*, "one religion in a variety of rites."[89] Not that Cusa was anything like current pluralists to whom all deities are but human interpretations of the same Ultimate Reality (Hick). The cardinal believed firmly that the biblical view of God was the truest and correct one and that other religions, including Islam, were beset with errors.[90] In his subsequent treatise *Cribratio Alkorani (Shifting of the Qur'an)*, Nicholas was not soft on the perceived mistakes among Muslims concerning the Christian doctrines of the Trinity and Christology, and he also issued a call for the Muslim leader to have God "open your eyes . . . and grant this [enlightenment] to you."[91] All in all — particularly in light of the catastrophic events and the prejudices of his times — "[f]rom a Christian perspective . . . his strategy can be seen as an exercise in charitable interpretation."[92] In Cusa's words, he "presupposed not a faith that is other but a faith that is one and the same."[93]

While the Protestant Reformers were certainly not known for interfaith hospitality,[94] surprisingly Luther clearly assumed the common deity of Christianity, Judaism, and Islam even when seriously undermining and critiquing

---

87. Nicholas of Cusa, *De Pace Fidei*, #68. For useful comments, see Volf, *Allah*, chap. 2.

88. Nicholas of Cusa, *De Pace Fidei*, #5.

89. Nicholas of Cusa, *De Pace Fidei*, #6.

90. See, e.g., Nicholas of Cusa, *Cribratio Alkorani*, ##23, 31.

91. Nicholas of Cusa, *Cribratio Alkorani*, #238.

92. Volf, *Allah*, p. 50.

93. Nicholas of Cusa, *De Pace Fidei*, #10.

94. For a representative pejorative comment on Muslims ("Turks" in his vocabulary), see Luther, *Large Catechism*, art. III, p. 76. Indeed, what ironically annoyed Luther greatly was Zwingli's somewhat more open-minded attitude to Muslims: Luther, *Word and Sacrament IV*, 38:290. For Calvin's views of religions in general and Muslims in particular, see my "Calvin and Religions," pp. 266-83.

the deficiency of the faith of the latter two: "All who are outside this Christian people, whether heathen, Turks, Jews, or false Christians and hypocrites — even though they believe in and worship only the one, true God — nevertheless they do not know what his attitude is toward them."[95] In other words, Luther deplored the lack of knowledge of the divine grace and love among the non-Christians even though they wish to cling to the right God.[96] While not often highlighted, it is a well-known scholarly fact that the identification of the Christian and Muslim God — even in the midst of highly polemic debates and mutual criticisms — was by and large the traditional Christian opinion;[97] in that sense, Luther followed tradition.

A number of important tasks are involved in considering whether Islam and Christianity worship the same God. First, we must acknowledge and look carefully at the implications for Christian tradition of the fact that Islam speaks of God in universal terms, as "the God of all people," and therefore, the Qur'anic message "is a message for all people: all people should become Muslims, for God is the sovereign God of all people."[98] Related to that is Islam's nature as a "public faith"[99] — but such is also the Christian faith.[100] Differences come to the fore in that Christian theology links God with all peoples, and the rest of creation, in the context and from the perspective of the election of a particular people (first in the OT and then in the NT). For Islam, the idea of the selection of a particular people by God is totally unknown, as is the idea of the covenant.[101] What Islam does is universalize not only Judaism but also Hinduism and Buddhism.[102] Part of the universalizing tendency is the important promise in sura 42:15: "God is our Lord and your Lord. Our deeds concern us and your deeds concern you. There is no argument between us and you. God will bring us together, and to Him is the [final] destination." This same sura also mentions that "had God

---

95. Luther, *Large Catechism*, art. III, p. 76.

96. For useful comments on Luther, see Volf, *Allah*, chap. 3.

97. See, e.g., the statement by George Sale, the first translator of the Qur'an into English in 1734, who says in the "Preliminary Discourse" preface, "That both Mohammed and those among his followers . . . had and continue to have just and true notions of God and his attributes (always excepting their obstinate and impious rejecting of the Trinity), appears so plain from the Koran itself and all the Mohammedan divines, that it would be loss of time to refute those who supposed the God of Mohammed to be different from the true God" (as cited in Watt, *Islam and Christianity Today*, p. 45).

98. See Vroom, *No Other Gods*, pp. 103-4.

99. See further, Sachedina, *Islamic Roots of Democratic Pluralism*, pp. 24, 78.

100. See Pannenberg, *ST* 3:482-83.

101. For comments, see Vroom, *No Other Gods*, p. 104.

102. See further, Ward, *Religion and Revelation*, p. 173.

willed, He would have made them one community; but He admits whomever He will into His mercy" (v. 8), and that "whatever you may differ in, the verdict therein belongs to God" (v. 10). The important reason, hence, why Muslim theology can unequivocally affirm the identity of the God of Islam and the God of Christianity has to do with the principle of continuity — in terms of fulfillment — between the divine revelations given first to the Jews, then to Christians, and finally, in the completed form, to Islam (2:136; 6:83-89; 29:46).[103] While Christian tradition understands the principle of universality differently, based on its own Scriptures and doctrine of God, materially it shares the same viewpoint: the God of the Bible, Yahweh, the Father of Jesus Christ, is the God of all nations and the whole of creation, "the all-determining reality" (Pannenberg). Therefore, both faiths also are deeply missionary by nature.

Second, an important asset to Christian theology for reflecting on the relation of Allah to the God of the Bible is its relation to Judaism. Hardly any Christians would deny that Yahweh and the Father of Jesus Christ are one and the same God. Yet the Jews no less adamantly oppose the trinitarian confession of faith.[104] This simply means that Christian tradition is able to confess belief in and worship one God even when significant differences exist in the understanding of the nature of that God — and, indeed, more than that: even when the differences are deeply divisive and seemingly contradictory. Importantly, the Jewish theologian Jon Levenson concludes: "In the last analysis, the Christian and the Muslim conceptions of the one God have enough in common to make a productive comparison possible, but as in any responsible comparison, the contrasts must not be sugared over."[105] To confess one God does not require an identical understanding of the nature of that God if there are significant, wide-reaching agreements, as there are between Christians and Muslims, including the oneness of God, God as Creator, God's love, and so forth.[106] Just consider how widely the views of various Christian traditions differ from one other. Add to the equation the third monotheistic faith, Judaism, and the differences are real — even when these three Abrahamic faiths, having their roots deeply embedded in the Jewish Bible, claim the same one God.[107]

103. For a current Muslim argument, see Abd-Allah, "Do Christians and Muslims Worship the Same God?"; see further, Tennent, *Theology in the Context of World Christianity*, p. 34.

104. See further, Vroom, *No Other Gods*, pp. 91-92.

105. Levenson, "Do Christians and Muslims Worship the Same God?" p. 33.

106. See further, Volf, *Allah*, pp. 97-98. For a detailed comparison, commandment by commandment, between the Ten Commandments and Qur'anic teaching, see pp. 106-7.

107. For a highly nuanced discussion of three monotheistic faiths' conceptions of God, see Arnaldez, *Trois Messagers pour un Seul Dieu*.

Contemporary Christian theology reminds Jewish theologians of the possibility of conceiving distinctions in the one God in terms of semipersonified agents such as Word, Spirit, and Wisdom, and concepts such as glory and the name of Yahweh. Would anything like that apply to Islam? What about the eternity of the Word as Qur'an? What about the sent-ness of the Prophet(s)?[108] Recently it has also been suggested that "Word of God" and "Spirit of God" in Christian and Islamic Christologies could serve as "a starting point for interreligious dialogue."[109]

The third task is to clarify the many Islamic misunderstandings about what the Christian trinitarian confession means. What if it is true that "[w]hat the Qur'an denies about God as the Holy Trinity has been denied by every great teacher of the church in the past and ought to be denied by every orthodox Christian today"?[110] We have already noted most of the typical misconceptions among the Muslims, including the inclusion of Mary along with Father and Son, adoptionistic and Arianist interpretations, and the blunt charge of tritheism. Only patient and painstaking mutual dialogue may help correct and clarify these kinds of issues. Again, history provides us with useful examples. Consider Paul of Antioch's (eleventh-twelfth century) *Letter to a Muslim,* in which he sought to correct typical misconceptions and offer a constructive proposal that both defended the unity of God and tried to explain the Trinity in light of Muslim sensibilities. "By refusing to employ the Christian term *uqnum* (hypostasis), and preferring to it the native Arabic and theologically neutral term *ism* (name), he is apparently attempting to disassociate his explanation from the polemical tradition which preceded him and to present the doctrine in a manner acceptable to Muslims." Furthermore, he argues that "[a]ll the names and attributes of God stem from the three substantival attributes . . . of existence, speech, and life," and speech is related to incarnation and sonship.[111] Apart from how convincing or successful the Catholic theologian's construction may be, its tactics are admirable, namely,

---

108. See further, H. A. Wolfson, "The Muslim Attributes and the Christian Trinity."

109. Jørgensen, "'Word of God' and 'Spirit of God.'"

110. Volf, *Allah,* p. 14. This is not a new insight. See the careful investigation of a number of common Muslim misunderstandings of the Trinity, including the physical conception of the Son or plurality of deities in the Trinity, in Aquinas, *De Rationibus Fidei* (1263), pp. 31-52.

111. *A Muslim Theologian's Response to Christianity,* p. 91. This volume contains both Paul's letter and Ibn Taymiyya's writings with introductions and commentaries. Tactics similar to Paul's were employed already in one of the earliest major debates ("Muhawarah") between Mar Timothy I, the Nestorian patriarch (d. 823), and al-Mahdi, the ruling caliph. For an accessible discussion, see Bennett, *Understanding Christian-Muslim Relations,* chap. 4.

correction and "contextualization." At least the short tract of twenty-four pages was important enough to inspire what became the most significant Muslim attack ever on Christian tradition and theology, that is, Ibn Taymiyya's massive *Al-Jawab Al-Sahih (The Correct Answer to Those Who Changed the Religions of Christ)*, written around 1320. While this apologetic work goes far beyond Paul's, it was occasioned by that short writing.

Fourth, we must clarify what and how much can be said about the identity of the two monotheistic traditions' God. While the highly influential interfaith statement "A Common Word between Us and You" did not explicitly state that Christians and Muslims believe in the same God, it quoted from the Qur'an, which unequivocally affirms the identity: "We believe what was revealed to us and what was revealed to you. Our God and your God is one, and to him we submit as Muslims" (Al'Ankabut 29:46). And again: "God is our Lord and your Lord; we have our works and you have your works; there is no argument between us and you; God brings us together; and to him is the final destiny" (Al Shura 42:15). Both Christian and Muslim signatories endorsed that affirmation. Not surprisingly, some Christian theologians and leaders vehemently opposed it.[112]

The Roman Catholic Church's hospitable and theologically astute statement on Islam is a useful starting point for specifically Christian reflections: "The Church regards with esteem also the Moslems. They adore the one God, living and subsisting in Himself; merciful and all-powerful, the Creator of heaven and earth, who has spoken to men; they take pains to submit wholeheartedly to even His inscrutable decrees, just as Abraham, with whom the faith of Islam takes pleasure in linking itself, submitted to God. Though they do not acknowledge Jesus as God, they revere Him as a prophet. They also honor Mary, His virgin Mother; at times they even call on her with devotion."[113]

While this statement from *Nostra Aetate* fails to give a blank affirmation of the identity of Allah and the Christian God,[114] it seems to be assuming it and, at minimum, affirms wholeheartedly a strict monotheistic orientation in line with Abrahamic faiths. At the same time, the statement is not silent about Islam's opposition to trinitarian confession in terms of Jesus' divinity.[115]

112. See, e.g., Piper, "A Common Word between Us?"

113. *Nostra Aetate*, #3.

114. Importantly, the late John Paul II believed that Vatican II warrants unreserved identification: *Insegnamenti* 8, no. 2 (1985): 497 (available at vatican.ca).

115. The same careful affirmation and nuancing are present in the highly influential exchange between the Roman Catholic Church in France and Muslims, many of whom have

As said, generally speaking, Muslim theology and theologians affirm the identity of the Qur'an's and the Bible's God.[116] Consider only the Qur'anic passage 29:46. That said, however, the same divine revelation to Muslims, the Qur'an, also categorically condemns Christians for seriously compromising the dearest part of the doctrine of God, God's oneness![117] This means that on the Muslim side, much work has to be done in reconciling these two seemingly contradictory claims. On the Christian side, as even the Vatican II statement illustrates, a continuing careful nuancing of the issue — apart from some conservative outright rebuttals — continues. Illustrative is the series of essays "Do Christians and Muslims Worship the Same God?" in *Christian Century* in 2004, to which not only Muslim and Christian but also Jewish theologians contributed. While none of the writers denied the same reference point among the traditions' understanding of God, only the Muslim writer gave an unreserved positive answer. The Jewish theologian affirmed the common basis if differences in the understanding of God are not ignored, and the three Christians, representing different theological traditions (Roman Catholic, mainline Protestant, and evangelical), all, albeit somewhat differently, expressed continuing ambiguity with regard to identification of the faith's God with regard to character of the Divine.[118] A growing number of Christian theologians are coming to the conviction that to deny the identity of Allah and the God of the Bible creates more problems than its affirmation.[119] Miroslav Volf's recent *Allah: A Christian Response* argues for the identity while delving deeply into historical and continuing deep theological divergences with regard to the nature of God.[120]

Having affirmed that Muslims and Christians believe in the same God,

---

migrated there from various North African countries and thus represent a diversity within that faith. For a careful study with full sources, see Jukko, *Trinitarian Theology in Christian-Muslim Encounters;* for a shorter discussion and assessment, see chap. 10 in my *Trinity and Religious Pluralism.*

116. According to the Christian Abd al-Masih, this is also an established fact at the grassroots level in his context, the Near East: "Allah?" p. 1.

117. For comments, see Volf, *Allah,* pp. 79-80.

118. Lamin Sanneh, S. Wesley Ariajah, Dudley Woodberry (Christian); Jon Levenson (Jewish); Umar F. Abd-Allah (Muslim), in various 2004 issues.

119. For an important public agreement prior to the "Common Word," see Schimmel and Falaturi, eds., *We Believe in One God.*

120. Volf summarizes: "I will propose, from a Christian perspective, a way to affirm that Christians and Muslims worship the same God even if their visions of God differ" (*Allah,* p. 35). For a highly nuanced contemporary Roman Catholic affirmation, see Dupuis, *Toward a Christian Theology of Religious Pluralism,* pp. 259-62, and chap. 10 at large.

the Dutch Christian philosopher of religion Hendrik Vroom "would like to add that Christians, on the basis of the gospel, are better *able* to know God than Muslims are."[121] This is not an expression of a puffed-up spirit of superiority but rather a confident call to Muslims from a Christian perspective to consider rich values in the Christian trinitarian conception of faith in one God. The same was affirmed by the French Roman Catholic Church in an extended exchange with local Muslims. Rather than pushing the Trinity to the margins, the church "is committed to dialogue above all because of her faith in the trinitarian mystery of the one God . . . [which] makes us catch sight of a life of fellowship and exchanges in God himself, source of all mission and all dialogue." Dialogue corresponds to the being of the triune God, and hence the confession of faith in one God as Father, Son, and Spirit; eternal loving communion is an invitation to dialogue and engagement.[122] The Finnish theologian Risto Jukko, expert in Muslim-Christian relations, summarizes the trinitarian foundation of the dialogue as it came to expression in the French situation: "It seems that only the concept of the trinitarian God can be the basis for fruitful interreligious Christian dialogue with non-Christians . . . [especially] Muslims. Even though the concept is an article of Christian theology . . . it unites transcendence and immanence, creation and redemption in such a way that from the Christian standpoint dialogue becomes possible and meaningful. It is the hermeneutical key to interpret the religious experiences of non-Christians (as well as of Christians)."[123]

This much can be said, even though — as paradoxical as it may sound — the Trinity can hardly serve as the beginning point of the dialogue since the Islamic faith denies it at the outset.[124]

As discussed in the previous chapter, an authentic interfaith engagement is always a give-and-take event in which the triune God is present. Not only can Christians contribute to and challenge the Muslim faith, but so also are they challenged and enriched by the other. This is hardly anything new and novel in Christian tradition. Just consider Aquinas's *Summa contra Gentiles,* which not only argues for the truth of Christian faith against other faiths but also liberally utilizes Muslim (and pagan philosophers') resources in explicating the biblical faith.

---

121. Vroom, *No Other Gods,* p. 113.
122. Jukko, *Trinitarian Theology in Christian-Muslim Encounters,* p. 214.
123. Jukko, *Trinitarian Theology in Christian-Muslim Encounters,* pp. 221-22.
124. See Jukko, *Trinitarian Theology in Christian-Muslim Encounters,* p. 244.

Brahman and the Trinitarian God

Comparison in Perspective: Orientational Remarks

A number of well-known challenges and unnuanced assumptions concerning Hindu and Christian views of the Divine complicate any serious comparative theological work: for example, the claim that whereas Christianity has a personal God, Hinduism has an impersonal god; whereas Christianity is monotheistic, Hinduism is polytheistic; whereas in Christianity the Divine can take the form of humanity, in Hinduism the deity remains transcendently distant; and so forth. The following discussion seeks to investigate in detail these and related issues with a view to comparing and contrasting these two traditions in terms of issues and topics relevant to this particular interfaith encounter. Whereas Christian-Jewish and Christian-Muslim dialogue must concentrate on the question of the Trinity versus monotheism, for the Christian-Hindu encounter essential topics include whether their vastly differing concepts of the Divine share enough commonality even to begin the comparison; whether views on the nature of the Divine share common features and what the key differences are; whether the often-mentioned "trinitarian" notion of Hindu *saccidananda* bears any material similarity to the Christian trinitarian confession of faith; and so forth.[125]

Beyond the above-mentioned popular stereotypes, scholarly study must at all times be mindful of differences between the two traditions at deeper and more complex levels, like Christianity's solid doctrinal basis for faith (despite differences, say, in the formulation of the trinitarian doctrine between the East and West) versus Hinduism's absence of such binding and commonly shared doctrinal basis. Indeed, while in the final analysis the majority of Hindus would conceive Brahman (often in the "person" of another god, whether Shiva or Vishnu or any of their associates) as the Ultimate Reality and thus affirm "monotheism," Hindus can also be more or less nontheistic (although hardly is there any atheistic movement after modern Western atheism) and/or agnostic about the existence of gods.[126] Furthermore, while by far the ma-

---

125. Seeking to be sensitive not only to the difference of context between the two faith traditions but also to the need to specify some third respect in light of which it is meaningful to discern differences and similarities, follows the wise advice of J. Z. Smith, *Drudgery Divine*, pp. 51-53; and Neville, *Normative Cultures*, pp. 59-84. I am indebted to Thatamanil, *Immanent Divine*, pp. 12-13.

126. For a detailed discussion of the Hindu Nyaya school of logic and Vaisesika naturalism's predominantly nontheistic views and arguments, see Clooney, *Hindu God, Christian God*, chap. 2 and passim.

jority of Hindu adherents embrace a personal deity (most often in the form of Isvara, typically locally determined), theologically speaking it still seems to be the case that beyond the personal notion there is the "true" impersonal deity. Add to the factors to be reckoned with in any comparison deep differences in attitude about the role of history[127] (as explained above in the discussion of revelation), both in terms of its relation to the events and stories in scriptures concerning the "history of salvation" and whether history is linear or cyclical. Deep differences in worldview and epistemology also often complicate the task of comparison.

The Evolvement of Hindu Deities

The roots of the world's most ancient living religious tradition's insights into the divine can be found in the oldest Vedas, particularly in Rig Veda, which lists a number of deities or *devas* (this term denoting "divine being" rather than god in the current sense of the word),[128] among whom Indra, the cosmic power, while a fairly late arrival in Vedic religion, plays the central role.[129] Other important figures include Agni, the deity of fire, associated particularly with sacrifices;[130] the lovely Savitri, "Mother Earth"; Aditi; and a host of others.[131]

A critical move toward the embrace of one major notion of the deity amidst the bewildering diversity of *devas* as well as a decidedly philosophical investigation into their nature began in classical Hinduism, as represented by the last part of the Vedas, the Upanishads. The well-known answer in Brihada-ranyaka Upanishad (3.9.1) in response to the question of how many gods there are altogether, drawn from a Vedic text, is "three and three hundred, three and three thousand," namely, "One." When the inquirer then asks, "Who is the one god?" the response is "Breath *(prana)*, and he is Brahman ... and they call him That." The same passage explains that the "three and three hundred, three and three thousand" gods are "only the various powers of them" and

---

127. Contra Brockington, *Hinduism and Christianity,* pp. 43-44.

128. Illustrating the fluidity of the meaning, even heaven and earth can be counted among the Vedas (Rig Veda 1.185).

129. Of the nearly 1,000 hymns in Rig Veda, about one-quarter are devoted to Indra alone.

130. In Rigveda Samhita, understandably, Agni is the focus of attention because of its focus on ritual and sacrifice.

131. For an accessible discussion, see Klostermaier, *Survey of Hinduism,* chap. 8.

also lists the names of the most well known figures such as Agni and Indra, obviously indicating what the Vedantic theology at large affirms, namely, that there is one Ultimate Divine, Brahman, represented by a number of individual deities. Consider this hymn to Vishnu in Vishnu Purana, the central Vaishnite scripture:

> Glory to thee, god of the lotus eye: glory to thee, most excellent of spiritual things: glory to thee, soul of all worlds. . . . To him who, as Brahmá, creates the universe; who in its existence is its preserver; be praise. To thee, who at the end of the Kalpa takest the form of Rudra; to thee, who art triform; be adoration. Thou, Achyuta, art the gods, Yakshas, demons, saints. . . . Thou art knowledge and ignorance, truth and falsehood. . . . Thou art the performance and discontinuance of acts: thou art the acts which the Vedas enjoin. . . . Thou, Vishńu, who art the soul of all, art the fruit of all acts of piety.[132]

Hence, "*Brahman* becomes the term around which the loftiest religious speculation has revolved for thousands of years, and it still is the term used to designate the supreme being."[133] Brahman is the sole ultimate reality. "Just as Yahweh is the one ultimate reality in Judaism; God in Christianity; Allah in Islam; Nirvāna in Theravāda Buddhism; the Buddha in Mahāyāna Buddhism; Heaven in Confucianism and Tao in Taoism; Brahman is the one ultimate reality in Hinduism."[134] Where Brahman is the ultimate notion of the divine, *atman* is the ultimate reality about us. While everything else in the world, including in us, changes, *atman* does not. Though routinely translated as "soul," in no way is that individually driven Western concept a good way to communicate the meaning of the Sanskrit word. The major task for Hindu philosophers and theologians is to negotiate the relation of *atman* to Brahman.

Most typically, three deities are seen as the major manifestation of Brahman: Brahma, the "creator" god; Vishnu, the "preserver" god;[135] and Shiva, the "destroyer," or better, "consummator," god.[136] The distant Brahman comes to be known and worshiped in any of these deities or their associates known as

---

132. *The Vishnu Purana* 1.19, p. 141.

133. Klostermaier, *Survey of Hinduism*, p. 132.

134. Sharma, *Classical Hindu Thought*, p. 1.

135. Vishnu's role as preserver comes to the fore in light of Hinduism's not knowing any creation *ex nihilo* doctrine, but rather, in keeping with its cyclical view of history, envisions cycles of dissolution and reemergence.

136. For a useful discussion of Shiva, see chap. 9 in Sharma, *Classical Hindu Thought*.

isa or *isvara*, the "Lord" or Bhagavan,[137] the Exalted One. Typically the "Lord," be it Vishnu or Shiva — since the worship of Brahma by and large vanished almost totally a long time ago — becomes more or less an exclusive title in popular piety although, theologically, either one and both of them manifest Brahman. Hence, the proliferation of Hindu denominations, among which the most important and most well known are Shaivism (followers of Shiva) and Vaishnavism (followers of Vishnu), with an ever-increasing number of subsects. The two most important Hindu theologian-philosophers, Sankara and Ramanuja, are linked with these main denominations, respectively. Either related to the main deities or separate from them, local and tribal deities, both male and female, and cults of worship dedicated to them fill India.

While it is of course true that the Hindu conception of the Brahman as the ultimate reality leans toward an impersonal notion unlike the personal God of Semitic faiths, it is also true that Hinduism is quite familiar with personal conceptions of deities. Not only does the personal deity come to the fore in the hugely popular and widespread folk piety based on the great epics of *Mahabharata* and *Ramayana,* as well as many Puranas, but even in the later stages of the Upanishads personal notions begin to emerge in various forms.[138]

What is distinctive about Hindu deities is the prominent place of female deities; indeed, "Hinduism possesses a full-blown feminine theology."[139] Usually Shiva and Vishnu are accompanied by their wives, Parvati and Sri (Lakshmi). The prominent female deity is known as Sakti, "power," or Devi, the "Divine Mother." Sometimes Sakti is described as exercising the same powers as Vishnu and Shiva. Of Devi, Markandeya Purana (1.75-77) says, "By you this universe is borne, by you this world has been created. By you it is protected and you, O Devi, shall consume it at the end. You are the Great Knowledge and the Great Illusion, you are Great Power and Great Memory, Great Delusion, the Great Devī and the Great Asurī."[140] In one significant strand of Hinduism, the female deity is supreme and independent on her

---

137. This designation stems from Rudra-Siva (Svetasvatara Upanishad 5.4) and is also a common honorific title for the Buddha in the Pali Canon (Sharma, *Classical Hindu Thought,* p. 64).

138. Both the short but important Isa Upanishad (which takes its name from the same root as Isvara) and Svetasvatara Upanishad can be read in a way that moves toward personal notions. The same can also be said of Mahanarayana Upanishad, which importantly quotes from older Vedic literature to the same effect. See further, Brockington, *Hinduism and Christianity,* p. 7.

139. Sharma, *Classical Hindu Thought,* p. 68; see chap. 5 for a useful discussion.

140. Cited in Klostermaier, *Survey of Hinduism,* p. 261; for female deities, see chap. 18.

own account rather than, as in many other traditions, only by association with other gods.

With that in mind, several levels can be discerned in the conception of the Divine as female in Hinduism: first, a female deity as supreme by herself; second, a female deity as the spouse of Shiva or Vishnu (but often addressed as Isvara), in which capacity she can exercise either a dominant or a docile role; third, related to the former, if conceived in androcentric terms — as Sakti who "wears the pants" — the "feminine principle also appears as the wives of the various gods."[141] For the sake of comparative theology, a twofold question arises: First, does the conception of Isvara in feminine terms make the deity more inclusive and approachable in Hindu theology and piety? It seems to me the answer is an unqualified *yes*. Second, in relation to human life, does the feminine theology of Hinduism advocate hospitality, equality, and equal opportunity? It seems to me, the answer is an unqualified *no!* Now, the latter judgment may come from a Christian theologian from the Global North deeply concerned about equality and justice; yet it is important to respectfully present such understandings to the Hindu counterpart for mutual learning and challenge.

Hindu and Christian Doctrines of God: Parallels and Differences

Both Christian theology and Hindu theology define God as "being." However, in Christian theology only God — in his trinitarian life — is eternal but the creation is not; in Hinduism, in contrast, everything nondivine is coeternal,[142] even when, depending on the school of thought, their mutual relations are negotiated differently. "Nearly all the characteristics which can be supposed of the absolute are ascribed to . . . *Brahman*," says Hajime Nakamura. And on the basis of the foundational Vedanta text, Badarayana's *Brahmasutra (Vedantasutra)*, Nakamura gives examples such as omnipresence (3.2.27), endlessness (3.2.26), "plenitude" (1.3.8), "simplicity" (2.1.26), eternality and imperishability (1.3.1, 10), and so forth.[143] The classic passage in Taittiria Upanishad (2.1) puts it succinctly: "He who knows Brahman, which is (i.e. cause, not effect), which

---

141. Sharma, *Classical Hindu Thought*, pp. 68-69, at 69.

142. As early as in Svetasvatara Upanishad, it is taught that "[t]here are . . . three 'unborn ones': the Lord, knowing and all-powerful; the individual *ātman*, unknowing and powerless; and Nature . . . made up of primary matter." Hopkins, *Hindu Religious Tradition*, p. 70; I am indebted to Sharma, *Classical Hindu Thought*, p. 47.

143. Nakamura, *History of Early Vedānta Philosophy*, 1:485. For Badayarana's text, see his *Brahma Sutras*.

is conscious, which is without end, as hidden in the depth (of the heart), in the highest ether, he enjoys all blessings, at one with the omniscient Brahman." Somewhat similarly to Christian apophatic tradition, Sankara reminds us that a finite human mind can hardly grasp the infinite Brahman.[144] This does not mean that therefore nothing can be said of Brahman.[145] On the basis of the "definition" above, most Hindus say that God is truth *(satyam)*, knowledge *(jnanam)*, and infinity *(anantam)*. With reference to Ramanuja's interpretation of the Upanishadic passage, the contemporary Hindu authority S. Radhakrishnan says: "'Truth, knowledge and infinity is Brahman,' says the Upanishad. These several terms refer to the one supreme reality and declare that the absolute Brahman is unchangeable perfection, and possesses intelligence which is ever uncontracted. . . . It is infinite (anantam), since its nature is free from all limitations of place, time and substance, and different in kind from all things. . . . It is first without a second, since there is no other God than God."[146] Theistic traditions, whether Christian, Muslim, or Hindu, need to ascertain that God is not placed among other finite things, which, of course, would divest God of God's infiniteness.

What about God's attributes? When it comes to Brahman as Isvara or Bhagavan, typically six attributes are listed, owing to Ramanuja's teaching: knowledge, strength, sovereignty, valor, power, and splendor.[147] These auspicious qualities bear great similarity to other theistic faiths' conceptions, whether Jewish, Christian, or Muslim. Interestingly, the other great theologian, Sankara, had already, when expositing the Gita, similarly discerned these six attributes but related them to six gods: Siva, Visny, Sakti, Surya, Ganapati, and Kumara.[148]

An important part of the Hindu conception of Isvara is the relating of

144. See Sankara's comments on Taittiriya Upanishad 2.1, in *Aītareya and Taīttīrīa Upanishads*, pp. 105-9 particularly.

145. For important comments on Sankara's apophatic approach, see Thatamanil, *Immanent Divine*, pp. 61-62. Bithika Mukerji rightly notes that "Hinduism emphasizes the 'unknown-ness' of God but not his unknowability." "Christianity in the Reflection of Hinduism," p. 231 (italics in the original removed).

146. Radhakrishnan, *Indian Philosophy*, 2:687. For Ramanuja's comments on the Upanishadic passage, see Carman, *Theology of Rāmānuja*, p. 102.

147. Sharma, *Classical Hindu Thought*, p. 50. Another way to conceive the attributes of God is to group them under five characteristics as typical in Vaishnava Tantras, important cultic scriptures: "*Para* or the Transcendent; *Vyūha* or the Grouped; *Vibhava* or the Incarnated; *Antaryāmī* or the Immanent; and *Arcā* or the Idol." Sharma, *Classical Hindu Thought*, p. 66; for details, see Kumarappa, *The Hindu Conception of the Deity*, pp. 311-17.

148. Sharma, *Classical Hindu Thought*, pp. 65-66. This gave rise to the *sanmata*'s six alternate ways of worship concentrated on these deities; see further, pp. 66-67.

God to the cosmos as a whole, not only to our planet. To do so, God's relationship "may be related to the three modes which must invariably accompany its appearance," that is, the coming into being of the world, its existence for a given duration, and its passing out of existence (to make room for the reemergence of the cosmos). This scheme links the cosmic relating of Isvara with the ancient conception of Trimurti, namely, Brahma, Vishnu, and Shiva in their roles as "creator," "sustainer," and "destroyer," respectively.[149] Two tasks are presented here to comparative theology. First, what are the implications for the current natural scientific understanding of the emergence and life of the cosmos (to be discussed in the volume *Creation and Humanity*)? Second, to be discussed below, does this shed any light on the relation of Trimurti to the Christian Trinity?

Against the common misunderstanding, not only Christianity but also Hinduism knows of divine embodiment,[150] although in the latter faith it is by and large limited to Vaishnavite traditions (granted that Shiva is also known to have twenty-eight *avataras*). While not a fixed number, most typically Vishnu's "incarnations," *avataras,* are said to be ten, among whom the most well known are Rama and Krishna, key figures in *Mahabharata*, and even Buddha.[151] According to Vaishnavism, as detailed in the vast literature of Pancaratra theology, the Lord Vishnu as Isvara "is the ruler of all, the giver of all gifts, the preserver of all, the cause of all effects; and he has everything, except himself and his own consciousness, as his body," but as the one who animates the world, he "is not touched by its imperfections." Vishnu exists in five different forms: *para,* total transcendence and supremacy; *vyuhas,* special powers, not unlike the "attributes" of God, knowledge and strength, lordship and heroism, as well as power and splendor; *vibhava,* the divine *avataras; antaryamin,* the form of Isvara that resides in the human heart; and finally, *arcavatara,* the visible image of God — an important aid in Vishnu worship and present in most homes of the faithful.[152] The affirmation of divine presence in the image *(murti)* is an essential conviction in Hindu piety even beyond Vaishnavism. Even a casual visit to a Hindu temple to observe the ritual tells the outsider how deeply the devotees are drawn to the divine presence.[153] Now, in various *avataras,* "Visnu comes down from his heavenly throne to enter *samsāra* for the sake of assisting the struggling *jīvas* [individual living beings] to attain salvation; he suffers and

149. Sharma, *Classical Hindu Thought,* p. 67.
150. For the discussion of embodiment in Christian theology, see *Christ and Reconciliation.*
151. For details, see Carman, *Majesty and Meekness,* pp. 210-12.
152. Klostermaier, *Survey of Hinduism,* pp. 233-34, at 233.
153. For a fine account, see chap. 20 in Klostermaier, *Survey of Hinduism.*

endures pain with them and leads them by the hand like a friend."[154] We can see in this theological system an ingenious way of affirming both the divine transcendence and aseity — using classical Christian theological terms — and the presence of the deity in the world and among the devotees.

Having established that Hinduism by and large intuits one God, we should ponder how that view relates to the three monotheistic traditions' seemingly exclusive claims to the oneness of God. Two responses are in order here. First, on the level of Isvara, there is a determined tendency to elevate one God above others to the point that even if the reality of other Gods/Goddesses is not denied, exclusivistic attitudes are common. To that also testify the fierce and sometimes merciless debates about the truthfulness of claims to deity among various Hindu denominations. Second, when it comes to the theological understanding of Brahman as the Ultimate Reality, it looks as if "polytheism and monotheism are 'not treated as illogical incompatibles; they embody two different outlooks on the divine, one sees the many in one, while the other sees the one in many.'" Hence, "it is not so much the case that there are polytheistic and monotheistic gods, there are polytheistic and monotheistic attitudes to divine reality and accordingly two kinds of language in respect of it."[155]

Another relevant comparison between Hindu traditions and the three monotheistic faiths has to do with the radically different context in which deities are intuited. Whereas in Semitic tradition the prophetic guild established teaching on God as "absolute moral demand, judge of all human conduct" under a "personal God who demanded justice and mercy . . . a moral goal for the universe," both Greek speculative tradition of a supreme reason and good, and Indian traditions failed to forge the integral link between ethics/justice and the divine. In the former, the perfect Creator creates "a universe which reflects and participates in its own perfection," and in the latter, "[t]here were no prophets who felt challenged by a morally judging God and who issued condemnations on oppressive social systems. There was no development of belief in a historical purpose or goal. And there was little sense of one creator God who stood apart from creation."[156] Furthermore, unlike the Semitic traditions whose founders came from the "underside" of society, Hindu Aryans were conquerors who sought to take hold of vast territories. Hence, the lack of pursuit of justice and divine vindication was not contextually determined

154. Klostermaier, *Survey of Hinduism*, p. 237.
155. Sharma, *Classical Hindu Thought*, p. 52; citations from Bowes, *The Hindu Religious Tradition*, pp. 103, 107, respectively.
156. Ward, *Religion and Revelation*, pp. 134-35.

or relevant.[157] Finally, this leads — in Christian estimation — to the lack of vision for betterment of this world, which, after all, is "appearance" (although of course "real," as otherwise it could not be talked about) and is subject to a cycle of emergence-dissolution-reemergence, and leads instead to a vision of "salvation" as release, escape to the "eternal bliss."[158] Keith Ward's tentative conclusion may serve as a fruitful call for painstaking mutual learning and dialogue. It rightly highlights the radical differences between the Hindu and Semitic traditions, yet also points to important common themes, to the dynamic tension within this oldest living faith tradition.

> It might be said that the Indian metaphysical framework of an endless repetition of universes, the cycle of samsara and the ultimate futility of action and desire, gives rise to the idea of the Supreme as an unchanging reality which realizes no new values in creation, which is inactive and without passion and which offers no ultimate consummation for the finite order. In such a framework, the dynamic creative God of Hebrew faith is unlikely to become a focal concept. Yet, whole sects emerge which regard Brahman as a glorious Lord who creates out of love and offers endless bliss to its devotees. Though Semitic faiths tend to stress the moralism of the Supreme, and Indian faiths tend to stress the non-dualism of Being, both express a sense of the world as dependent on the Supreme; a sense of alienation requiring moral or epistemic reconciliation; and a sense of final realization of goodness, whether in the Supreme alone or in a community of relational beings.[159]

The way the main philosophical-theological traditions of Hindu Vedanta have attempted this task will be the focus of the next section; after that we will come back to the more focused Christian-Hindu comparison, in terms of Trinity/threeness.

Competing Ways of Explaining: Atman Is Brahman

While the diversity of Hindu views of the Divine is bewildering, usually categorized under six main classical schools of thought, the Vedanta family of

---

157. See further, Ward, *Religion and Revelation*, p. 136.
158. For comments, see Ward, *Religion and Revelation*, p. 138.
159. Ward, *Religion and Revelation*, pp. 141-42.

traditions, based on a most careful study and debate of Upanishadic texts, is most well known to the West and most easily accessible in terms of writings. All three of the following schools seek to negotiate the relationship between the Brahman and *atman* — in Christian terms, between God and world, the perennial challenge to any theistic faith. Briefly put, the big picture of the Vedanta tradition (with innumerable internal variations) looks something like this: in the ninth century, under Sankara, a radical monism was worked out; in the twelfth century, under Ramanuja, the monism was embraced but also qualified to make room for some distinction between God and world; in the thirteenth-century theology of Madhva, a (qualified) dualism was presented as a robust challenger. An engagement of the first two will occupy this section.

Typical of Indian philosophers, Sankara clarifies unambiguously his epistemological position in the beginning of his main work, *Vedanta-Sutras*. All commonsense subject-object separation is "distorted by *adhyāsa*, superimposition, which falsifies knowledge in such a way that the subject is unable to find objective truth."[160] A related fallacy is *avidya*, "nescience," which is incapable of distinguishing between relative and absolute being.[161] This ignorance, mistaken knowledge, keeps the person in samsara. Only *atman* is stable and truly-existing, as long as it knows its unity with Brahman. Sankara wholeheartedly affirms the basic Upanishadic axiom: "Ātman is *Brahman*."[162] Moving beyond typical categorical thinking, one grasps that "the relation of Ruler and ruled does not exist" apart from the "phenomenal world."[163] This uncompromising nondualism does not mean that therefore the world of things is merely a "pure illusion." It is "appearance" in the sense that it is not the ultimate, but it still is real, otherwise it could not be talked about at all;[164] hence, Sankara rejects the (Mahayana) Buddhist notion of sunyata, "emptiness."

This epistemology is the key to Sankara's theology of God. "Knowledge . . . constitutes the means by which the complete comprehension of Brahman is desired to be obtained. For the complete comprehension of Brahman is the highest end of man, since it destroys the root of all evil such as Nescience, the seed of the entire Samsâra."[165] In other words, the quest to know the Divine,

---

160. Klostermaier, *Survey of Hinduism*, p. 373.

161. See Sankara, *Vedanta-Sutras* 2.1.27, p. 352.

162. The classic passages can be found in Brihadaranyak Upanishad 4.4.5, 25, etc.

163. Sankara, *Vedanta-Sutras* 2.1.14, p. 330.

164. "The world of appearances is real though not self-subsistent." Ward, *Religion and Revelation*, p. 146. Well-known illustrations of Sankara include mistaking rope for a snake (*Vedanta-Sutras* 1.3.18, p. 189) and elephants seen in dreams for real ones (1.2.12, p. 123).

165. Sankara, *Vedanta-Sutras* 1.1.1, pp. 13-14, at 14. Sankara's emphasis on true knowledge

as in Judeo-Christian tradition, has to do first and foremost with "salvation" and the way to overcome suffering. What then is the Brahman? The Brahman "is all-knowing and endowed with all powers, whose essential nature is eternal purity, intelligence, and freedom. . . . Moreover the existence of Brahman is known on the ground of its being the Self of every one."[166] Two foundational statements are made here. First, for Sankara the ultimate reality is by and large impersonal and pantheistically conceived. However, that statement must be qualified. Any talk about the Being, the "Self" with knowledge, intelligence, and freedom, must entail some form of personal nature. Even the statement that "[Brahman is that] from which the origin, &c. [i.e., the origin, subsistence, and dissolution] of this [world proceeds]"[167] does not nullify any kind of personal appropriation, as all Semitic faiths speak of God also in those terms.[168] How, then, could Sankara negotiate this seemingly nondualism-compromising conception? He utilizes a distinction that, while not unknown in earlier Hindu tradition, becomes his trademark and is by and large resisted or at least ignored by other Hindu traditions, namely, a distinction between *nirguna* and *saguna* Brahman. Whereas the former is without any qualities and thus beyond human grasping,[169] the latter has qualities and is thus known. In light of that distinction, Sankara's impersonal monism as the Isvara-type of personal deity, while truly and rightly an object of worship — hugely widespread in popular piety and religious art and literature — is not ultimately true.[170] Here we come again to the ultimate goal of pursuing the true knowledge of God: "the cognition of the unity of Brahman is the instrument of final release," as the person understands " [t]hat Self is to be described by No, no [*neti, neti*]."[171]

---

hence makes highly suspect the popular claim that he is a mystic to whom a deep experience per se would be the key to salvation. For an informed discussion, see Thatamanil, *Immanent Divine*, pp. 60-62 and passim.

166. Sankara, *Vedanta-Sutras* 1.1.1, p. 14.

167. Sankara, *Vedanta-Sutras* 1.1.2, p. 15.

168. For important comments, see Ward, *Religion and Revelation*, pp. 144-45.

169. For a strong statement on the unknowability of the "absolutely changeless" *nirguna* Brahman, see Sankara, *Vedanta-Sutras* 2.1.14, p. 327.

170. The Lord's "omniscience, his omnipotence, &c. all depend on the limitation due to the adjuncts whose Self is Nescience; while in reality none of these qualities belong to the Self whose true nature is cleared, by right knowledge, from all adjuncts whatever" (*Vedanta-Sutras* 2.1.14, p. 329). This term, "nescience," is used of "limited" knowledge, which Sankara says is stuck with "the fiction" that assumes separation between "name and form, evolved as well as non-evolved" and "originates entirely from speech only" (2.1.27, p. 352).

171. Sankara, *Vedanta-Sutras* 2.1.14, p. 327. Ward (*Images of Eternity*, pp. 21, 24) correctly notes that there is, though, inconsistency in the way Sankara speaks of this "unspeakable"

In this light, the statement above that both Hindu and Christian theology posit the Lord as "being" must be revisited. Sankara intuits the Brahman as neither "being" nor "nonbeing." If Brahman is posited as a being, he is conditioned by limiting adjuncts, which is inadmissible since Brahman "is free from becoming an object of such concepts as being and nonbeing."[172] Materially, that was the thrust of Christian theologian Tillich's often-misunderstood claim that "God does not exist" because "He is being-itself beyond essence and existence."[173] Aligning neither with theism nor with atheism, Tillich's position is "transtheism," which refuses to place God among finite beings, as one of them, thus divesting God of his infinite nature. While commonly agreeing on the nature of the Lord as "beyond being," as it were, Sankara and Tillich also differ in the way they conceive the theme: "Tillich understands being-itself to be a dynamic creative power that gives rise to what it grounds, . . . whereas Sankara believes that being-itself is an unchanging absolute not to be identified with the unreal but changing subject-object world."[174]

How does this strong monism relate to the Semitic, including Christian, distinction between the Divine and created reality? There is no denying a deep difference of orientation as, except for some marginal forms of pantheism, Christian theology for its integrity must posit a distinction if not a separation between the two, as the classical panentheism of this project argues. While acknowledging that, Keith Ward suggests that on a deeper look the difference between Christian and Hindu ontology is not as clear-cut. He refers to the opening sentence of *Vedanta-Sutras* (1.1.1, p. 3): "It is a matter not requiring any proof that the object and the subject . . . cannot be identified," implying that Sankara does not fully negate distinctions.[175] Respectfully I would like to contest Ward's observation, for in my reading Sankara is not so much opening the door for some sense of a lingering dualism as he is wanting to avoid the tendency of common sense to "superimpose upon each the char-

---

nirguna, as he at times seems to attach some qualities to it, most prominently "bliss" (1.1.19, p. 76), and also "one mass of knowledge" (1.4.22, p. 281).

172. Cited in Thatamanil, *Immanent Divine,* p. 77, from Sankara's commentary on Katha Upanishad (in *Eight Upanisadas with the Commentary of Sankaracarya*), 2.3.13, vol. 1, p. 277. Sankara makes the same affirmation in commenting on Gita 13.12: "12. I shall describe that which has to be known, knowing which one attains to immortality, the beginningless Supreme Brahman. It is called neither being nor non-being"; for details, see Thatamanil, *Immanent Divine,* pp. 77-80.

173. Tillich, *ST* 1:205. Tillich, of course, affirms the classic theological identification in God of essence and existence; where he finds fault in tradition is that notwithstanding that correct intuition, theologians inadvertently placed God among other beings.

174. Thatamanil, *Immanent Divine,* p. 11.

175. Ward, *Religion and Revelation,* pp. 147-48.

acteristic nature and the attributes of the other, and thus, coupling the Real and the Unreal" (1.1.1, p. 4), in other words, failing to discern that what really exists is the ultimate reality. Be that as it may, it seems to me that Sankara's whole project is to help men and women come to the liberating knowledge in which all distinctions are overcome, as truly *atman* is Brahman. If this is not pantheism, what then is?[176] We also must keep in mind that — in the spirit of the Western philosophical concept of the "infinite," which also embraces its opposite — Brahman is not other than all things, but rather it "is the same as that Self, that Immortal, that Brahman, that All."[177] Hence, there is also no doctrine of creation *(ex nihilo)* in Hinduism, as the world emerges from within Brahman.[178] These considerations do not decidedly close the door on dialogue, but rather make a way to continue painstaking mutual dialogue between the two religions, in which they acknowledge where the other party comes from and what is its perspective.

Ramanuja sought to challenge the unqualified monism of his famed predecessor not to introduce dualism but rather to offer a more sophisticated — *qualified* — account of *advaita*. Indeed, as Ward brilliantly notes, the "real distinctions . . . are all distinctions within one basic reality." Hence, "Ramanuja is ironically more of a monist than Sankara, who retains the basic dualism of reality and appearance."[179] In his account, reality consists of three tiers, as it were: "the world of material things, the multiplicity of *jīvātmas*, individual living beings, and *Brahman*, who is identical with *īśvara*, who is none other than Visnu. Creation is the body of *Brahman* but not without qualification." When speaking of the world, Ramanuja famously intuits it as the body of God. What is astonishing is that his way of speaking of the world as the body being animated by the divine spirit, being dependent on it, and being guided by Brahman, sounds so strikingly similar to some contemporary Christian, deeply panentheistic conceptions.[180] An important related idea is what Christian and Western philosophical tradition calls "infinity," as "God contains all finite realities, both good and evil, but also transcends them. God is with and without form . . . changing

---

176. Contra Ward, *Images of Eternity*, pp. 18-19.

177. Brihadaranyaka Upanishad 5.2.1; the following verses repeat that idea over and over again.

178. Sankara, *Vedanta-Sutras* 1.1.2, p. 15. Another important notion in Sankara's thought is that since "the effect is in reality not different from the cause" (1.1.25, p. 94) and "[the] cause virtually contains all the states belonging to its effects" (1.2.24, p. 145), Brahman must be imagined as the material cause of the world. See further, Ward, *Images of Eternity*, p. 16.

179. Ward, *Images of Eternity*, p. 31.

180. Ramanuja, *Vedanta Sutras* 2.2, in *SBE* 48:261-62.

and changeless, is with and without existence in a changing world, is both father and mother of all beings, is incomprehensible and yet reveals himself, is separate from all beings yet united with all beings."[181] While Sankara's monism poses a problem for Christian tradition, Sankara's qualified monism is much closer to it.

Ramanuja categorically rejects Sankara's *nirguna-saguna* distinction as, in his deeply theistic interpretation of Vedanta tradition, he conceives Isvara with an infinite number of supreme and auspicious qualities, thus making "him ipso facto *Brahman saguna,* above whom there is none. He has a most perfect body, which is eternal and immutable. He is radiant, full of beauty, youth, and strength. . . . [H]e is omnipresent; he is . . . the inner ruler of all." Clearly Ramanuja forges a concept of God more robustly personal and approachable than does Sankara. A distinctive contribution of Ramanuja is to conceive of the supreme Brahman as the personal Lord, typically known in piety as (Vishnu-)Narayana. As a result, he is able to embrace fully and celebrate the best of the *bhagavan* tradition and vast resources of devotional piety. In keeping with this, he contests his predecessor's notion of *avidya* and rather sees salvation as "the product of divine grace and human self-surrender."[182]

With his program, Ramanuja is not only critiquing Sankara but also seeking a constructive way to overcome the deep underlying challenges in the older Vedanta theologian's thought, including these: "[H]ow one can assert the existence of a Brahman which is wholly devoid of any properties whatsoever. . . . [H]ow finite selves come into being or how they can achieve liberation if they are illusory. And . . . how and why the finite world could ever have come into existence at all; for how could the perfect originate the endless train of ills which is the samsaric world?[183] With a distinction between Brahman and the world, God can act in the world. While that is a great advantage, there is also an unresolved problem related to Ramanuja's agreement with Vedanta tradition that Brahman "has the individual souls for its body."[184] How can they then be under the

---

181. Carman, *Majesty and Meekness*, p. 146.

182. Klostermaier, *Survey of Hinduism*, p. 377. Already in the opening paragraph, Ramanuja (*Vedanta Sutras* 1.1, in *SBE* 48:4) defines God along these lines: "The word 'Brahman' denotes the highest Person (purushottama), who is essentially free from all imperfections and possesses numberless classes of auspicious qualities of unsurpassable excellence. The term 'Brahman' is applied to any things which possess the quality of greatness (*brihattva,* from the root 'brih'); but primarily denotes that which possesses greatness, of essential nature as well as of qualities, in unlimited fulness; and such is only the Lord of all. Hence the word 'Brahman' primarily denotes him alone, and in a secondary derivative sense only those things which possess some small part of the Lord's qualities." See also a summative statement in 4.22, p. 720.

183. Ward, *Images of Eternity*, p. 30.

184. Ramanuja, *Vedanta Sutras* 1.1, in *SBE* 48:132.

guidance of Brahman? Ward rightly notes: "The reason why theists make a distinction between souls and God is that souls are finite centres of consciousness, whereas God is infinite; souls fall into error and sin, where God is omniscient and perfect,"[185] and so forth. From a Semitic tradition's perspective, this is yet another reason for the need to posit a distinction — even when panentheistically conceived — between God and world, including the Divine and human.

Ramanuja's robustly theistic interpretation of Vedanta tradition posits a fine distinction between the world and the Divine and intuits the Divine as an auspicious and benevolent "personal" being. John B. Carman notes that two dynamic polarities are present in Ramanuja's conception of the divine nature, namely, "supremacy" and "accessibility." A devotee of Vishnu, Ramanuja makes every effort to keep this polarity in constructive and consistent harmony, in contrast to Shiva devotees' tradition, which often leads to paradoxes and deep inner tensions in the conception of the polarities in the deity.[186] Vishnu is the deity with *avataras,* divine descents. Importantly — and against common intuitions — Ramanuja does not believe that "[e]mbodiment as such . . . [would] defile Brahman; the special bodies the Lord assumes in his incarnations are created from pure matter, not the defiled matter of bodily nature determined by karma."[187] This is even more important in light of Ramanuja's emphasis on purity (*amalatva,* literally "stainlessness") as one of the defining attributes of the Lord — "holiness," in Christian terms, as it means "opposed to everything defiling" or "free from even a whiff of evil."[188] There are here both commonality and difference in relation to Christian tradition. Both intuit the possibility of the utterly holy Divine to assume human form. But whereas Vishnu must assume a pure matter, the Logos assumes sinful flesh and redeems it.

Another important notion in Ramanuja's theology of the divine nature and divine accessibility strikes familiar notes in the Christian reader. In his introduction to the commentary on the Bhagavad-Gita, his most extensive single statement about the divine nature, Ramanuja makes two seemingly opposite statements. While the first part of his remarks, which lists the six attributes of the Lord, ends by affirming his absolute inaccessibility, the second begins with a clear assumption of the accessibility of this "Supreme Brahman," the

185. Ward, *Images of Eternity,* p. 31; see chap. 2 for an extended discussion of this and related challenges in Ramanuja.

186. Carman, *Majesty and Meekness,* pp. 12-16; for paradoxes in Lord Shiva, see chap. 3. For an important study, see Dhavamony, *Love of God according to Áaiva Siddhānta.*

187. Carman, *Majesty and Meekness,* p. 88; Ramanuja, *Vedanta Sutras* 2.12, in *SBE* 48:609-10.

188. Carman, *Majesty and Meekness,* p. 88.

Creator: "a shoreless ocean of compassions, gracious condescension, motherly love and generosity. . . . [H]e has assumed his own bodily form."[189] This dynamic is of course not unknown in the biblical tradition. Just consider John 1:18: "No one has ever seen God; the only Son, who is in the bosom of the Father, he has made him known." Rightly it has been noted that the "practical problem of monotheism in many cultures is that the one 'high God' or Lord of the universe . . . is too far away from the petty existence of most people to help in their immediate lives. People in many religions therefore turn to lesser beings" as mediators,[190] whether the host of *devas* in Hinduism or the Virgin Mary and spiritual beings in many Christian folk pieties, particularly in the Global South, among Roman Catholics or African Instituted Churches, and elsewhere. Theologians must provide leadership so that the folk piety does not blur the infinite nature of the Supreme God.

Trinity, Trimurti, Saccidananda

Christian theologians, both from outside and within India, in search of parallels between the two traditions, have turned to two conceptions of threeness deeply embedded in Hindu theology.[191] The first one has to do with the "trinity" of classical deities — Brahma, Vishnu, and Shiva, the Trimurti[192] — which established itself as a formula as early as the Gupta Empire (around 300-500 C.E.). It was never widely popular, but a strand of Hindu piety developed cultic rites to honor the threeness.[193] While often depicted as three different gods, the "three, Brahmā, Visnu and Áiva are not to be conceived as independent persons, they are the threefold manifestations of the one Supreme."[194] Why

---

189. Cited in Carman, *Majesty and Meekness,* pp. 96-97, at 97.

190. Carman, *Majesty and Meekness,* p. 93.

191. For a wider survey of triadic patterns in religions, see Parrinder, "Triads," 14:9345-50.

192. As early as the sixteenth century, the Jesuit Thomas Stephens attempted to identify parallels between Christian and Hindu trinities. Many other Catholic missionaries followed suit, including such luminaries as Robert de Nobili in the seventeenth century. On the Protestant side, Bartolomeo Ziegenbalg made the first major effort at comparison. Clooney, "Trinity and Hinduism," pp. 309-24.

193. Most well known is the hymn of Kalisada, known to Westerners through R. W. Emerson's poem "Brahma" (Basham, *The Wonder That Was India,* p. 310).

194. Radhakrishnan, ed., *The Principal Upanisads,* p. 815, cited in Sharma, *Classical Hindu Thought,* p. 73. Radhakrishnan is here commenting on Kautsya's "Hymn of Praise" in a late Upanishad (ca. 200 B.C.E.–200 C.E.), which names the three deities (called Siva Rudra, a common name for him).

is it that, notwithstanding the continuing Christian interest in the potential of Trimurti as a trinitarian parallel, the conception never caught on in either the popular or (particularly) the scholarly Hindu world? First, as mentioned, the worship of Brahma soon waned, and almost disappeared;[195] how would a Christian conception of the Trinity fare with the disappearance of the Father! Second, even when the three Hindu deities are not conceived as three gods but rather as a manifestation of one, Hindu theology still considers one of the three gods supreme. Third, "it represents three modalities of each god such as Visnu or Śiva as creator, preserver and destroyer rather than the recognition of each distinct modality as a distinct divinity."[196] The great Indian neo-Hindu-turned-Christian-Catholic Brahmabandhab Upadhyay, at the turn of the twentieth century, rightly argued that Trimurti is not the same as the Trinity because it is only a phenomenal aspect of the divine. At cosmic dissolution, the Trimurti dissolves and is no more; by contrast, the Christian Trinity is God's own inner identity, eternal and unchanging.[197] Furthermore, this "father of Indian theology" surmises that in Hinduism Brahma, Vishnu, and Shiva are but material, imperfect, and even sinful, drastically different from Father, Son, and Spirit.[198] In light of these considerations, it is easy to see why, on the Christian side, the forging of the parallelism would work only if orthodox trinitarian canons were broken either toward tritheism or modalism or "monotheism"[199] rather than maintaining authentic communion of three. Consequently, if one wishes to find authentic and constructive parallels between the two traditions, another aspect of threeness in Hinduism seems more viable.

Nor was there much enthusiasm on the Hindu side. Among many rebuttals of the Christian attempt to cast their doctrine of Trinity in the framework of Trimurti, a representative Hindu rebuttal comes from no less an authority than Ram Moham Roy, the founder of the strictly monotheistic neo-Hindu reform movement Brāhma Sāmaj:

> After I have long relinquished every idea of a plurality of Gods, or of the persons of the Godhead, taught under different systems of modern Hindooism, I cannot conscientiously and consistently embrace one of a

195. On reasons for the extinction of Brahma worship, see Sharma, *Classical Hindu Thought*, pp. 79-81.

196. Sharma, *Classical Hindu Thought*, p. 74.

197. *Writings of Brahmabandhab Upadhyay*, 1:79; I am indebted to Clooney, "Trinity and Hinduism," p. 312.

198. *Writings of Brahmabandhab Upadhyay*, 2:287b.

199. For useful comments, see Klostermaier, *Survey of Hinduism*, pp. 132-33.

similar nature, though greatly refined by the religious reformations of modern times; since whatever arguments can be adduced against a plurality of persons of the God; and, on the other hand, whatever excuse may be pleaded in favour of a plurality of persons of the Deity, can be offered with equal propriety in defence of Polytheism.[200]

As a result, some Christian theologians went elsewhere in Hindu tradition to look for parallels for the Trinity.

A more promising bridge can be found in the ancient concept of *saccidananda*. Commenting on the classic passage in Taittiria Upanishad (2.1) discussed above, Hiriyanna forges the connection between that and the Christian theology of God in this way:

> The spiritual and unitary character of this absolute reality [Brahman] is very well expressed by the classical phrase *saccidānanda*. As a single term defining its nature, it is met with only in the latter Upanishads: but its three elements — *sat, cit,* and *ānanda* — are used of Brahman, singly and in pairs, even in the earliest of them. *Sat,* which means "being," points to the positive character of Brahman distinguishing it from all non-being. But positive entities, to judge from our experience, may be spiritual or not. The next epithet *cit,* which means "sentience," shows that it is spiritual. The last epithet *ānanda,* which stands for "peace," indicates its unitary and all-embracing character, inasmuch as variety is the source of all trouble and restlessness. . . . Thus the three epithets together signify that Brahman is the sole spiritual reality of the Absolute, which comprehends not only all being *(sat)* but also all thought *(cit)* so that whatever partakes of the character of either must eventually be traced to it.[201]

The noted Hindu reformer Keshub Chunder Sen of the nineteenth century picked up this connection and offered an interpretation of "that marvelous mystery — the Trinity" — in a creative way. Imagine a triangle, Brahma on top as *cat* (Being). This is how he imagines the roles of *cit* and *ananda* in this constellation: "Divinity coming down to humanity is the Son; Divinity carrying up humanity to heaven is the Holy Ghost."[202] Astonishingly knowl-

---

200. Cited in Clooney, "Trinity and Hinduism," p. 316.

201. Hiriyanna, *Essentials of Indian Philosophy,* p. 22; I am indebted to Sharma, *Classical Hindu Thought,* p. 45.

202. Sen, *Keshub Chunder Sen,* p. 228, cited in Clooney, "Trinity and Hinduism," p. 316.

edgeable as a Hindu of the inner logic of classic Christian trinitarian canons, he further expounds: "Whether alone or manifest in the Son, or quickening humanity as the Holy Spirit, it is the same God, the same identical Deity, whose unity continues indivisible amid multiplicity of manifestations."[203] Among the twentieth-century Hindu attempts to forge a link between the two traditions, one of the most peculiar is offered by the now legendary American-based late Hindu yogi Yogananda, who offers this vision: "'The Father *(Sat)* is God as the Creator existing beyond creation (Cosmic Consciousness). The Son *(Tat)* is God's omnipresent intelligence existing in creation (Christ Consciousness . . .). The Holy Ghost *(Aum)* is the vibratory power of God that objectifies and becomes creation.' But these are provisional, since 'at the time of cosmic dissolution, the Trinity and all other relativities of creation resolve into the Absolute Spirit.'"[204] The last comment alone tells us that this interpretation, as creative as it is, hardly can be reconciled with a classic Christian account of God. However, it reveals the continuing interest of some Hindu theologians in trinity.

On the Christian side, an important statement comes from the French Catholic priest and monk Jules Monchanin, better known as Swami Paramarubyananda, the cofounder (with Henri Le Saux, commonly known as Swami Abhishiktananda) of a famed ashram dedicated to the Trinity, named Saccidananda Ashram: "Only the mystery of the Trinity is capable of resolving the antinomies which cause Hindu thought to swing endlessly between monism and pluralism, between a personal and an impersonal God."[205] While Christian theologians in India continue to pursue the promise of this alleged common understanding, it is of course left to their Hindu counterparts to respond and also help deepen and challenge the Christian vision of God.

After a careful survey of past efforts to find parallels between Christian and Hindu visions of "trinity," F. Clooney summarizes in a way worth repeating and affirming:

> That the record is mixed should not surprise us. We know that the rich, deep Christian tradition of trinitarian theology, so nuanced and difficult, did not come together easily or suddenly in the earliest Church; rather, it took centuries to put together right insights into the three persons of

203. Sen, *Keshub Chunder Sen*, p. 228.

204. Yogananda, *The Second Coming of Christ*, p. 1594, cited in Clooney, "Trinity and Hinduism," p. 318.

205. As reported by Boyd, *Introduction to Indian Christian Theology*, p. 219, cited in Clooney, "Trinity and Hinduism," p. 319. See also Le Saux, *Saccidananda*.

God. . . . [Similarly] it was very hard indeed to explain in India the fine points of trinitarian thought, and as a result many did not see a great difference between Christian ideas of God and Hindu ideas. However we might imagine the reality of the Trinity in India, it would be unreasonable to expect a neatly parallel language in Hinduism, such as could be easily adopted to Christian uses. This is not because Indians would be incapable of such thinking, or because Hinduism is bereft of comparably subtle technical discourses about God, but because it makes little sense to expect that the language about God, as substantial theology, that developed in the Christian context would also have developed in India.[206]

Sunyata and Personal God

"Intimate Strangers" in Search of Mutual Engagement

In contrast to Christianity's interaction with Judaism and Islam, Christianity and Buddhism do not have a history of dialogue and mutual engagement; indeed, until the nineteenth century very little exchange took place. True, there are some occasional early references to Buddhism in Christian literature, the first known one dating back all the way to Clement of Alexandria's *Stromata* (around 200), but his comment shows little if any familiarity with Buddha's teachings.[207] From the sixth to the eighth century, Nestorian Christians had some meaningful encounters with Buddhists in India and China.[208] Franciscan missionaries in the thirteenth and fourteenth centuries issued reports commending the lifestyle of Buddhist monks in China, but again, theologically they merely "created the scanty image of Buddhism that prevailed in Western Christianity for centuries." At the same time, ironically, throughout the Middle Ages, under the pseudonymous legends of Barlaam and Josaphat, Gautama

---

206. Clooney, "Trinity and Hinduism," pp. 320-21.

207. Clement of Alexandria, *The Stromata (Miscellanies)* 1.15: "Some, too, of the Indians obey the precepts of Buddha, whom, on account of his extraordinary sanctity, they have raised to divine honours." This note is in the long litany of pagan thinkers, beginning from ancient Greek philosophers, in whose teachings Clement saw some useful rays of the truth that is in Christ.

208. For the seventh-century Nestorian Bishop Alopen's analogy between Christian apophatic theology and the Buddhist notion of sunyata, see *Discourse on Monotheism* 58, in Saeki, *Nestorian Documents and Relics in China*.

was widely venerated among Christians![209] The best chronicled friendship-based and intimate knowledge of Buddhism among Christians comes from the sixteenth-century Jesuit Francis Xavier.[210] All in all, Christian assessment of Buddhism was plagued by both ignorance and negative judgments leading to typical caricatures such as a view of Buddhism as atheistic — or surprisingly, sometimes, pantheistic! — and idolatrous, as it was mistakenly taken as the adoration of images of the dead Gautama, and more recently, nihilistic, because of the doctrine of sunyata, and so forth. The only redeeming feature at times was the high morality of the founder. Ironically, some atheistic or agnostic intellectuals such as Schopenhauer and Nietzsche were drawn to Buddhism.[211]

What, then, might be the vital and important dialogue themes and topics for Christian-Buddhist comparative theological investigation? While themes may be included such as whether or in what sense Buddhism is a "religion"[212] or whether — granted Buddhism has theistic underpinnings — it leans more toward monotheism or polytheism (or neither!), two themes, mutually related, seem to be most pertinent: first, whether and in what sense Buddhist tradition can speak of the "ultimate reality" as materially similar to monotheistic Semitic faiths in general and Christian faith in particular; and second, whether and in what sense the central Mahayana concept of sunyata may express key features of the ultimate reality in any way materially similar to Christian talk about God's incomprehensibility and "unknowability."

Notoriously difficult to translate and even more notoriously hard to understand, "sunyata" literally means "(absolute) nothingness." However, it is not "empty nothingness." It is only "empty" in terms of being "entirely unobjectifiable, unconceptualizable, and unattainable by reason or will."[213] According to the classic formulation of the *Prajnaparamita-sutra* ("The Heart Sutra"): "Form is Emptiness, Emptiness is form. Emptiness does not differ from form, and form does not differ from Emptyness . . . in Emptyness [*sic*] there is no form, no feeling, no recognition, no volitions, no consciousness; no eye, no ear,

209. Schmidt-Leukel, "Intimate Strangers," pp. 4-5, at 4 (this essay title inspired the heading for this section); see further, Almond, "The Buddha of Christendom."

210. For comments on Xavier, see H. Küng, "A Christian Response," pp. 307-8.

211. See Schmidt-Leukel, "Intimate Strangers," pp. 4-5, 11.

212. Cf. the somewhat hasty denial in Hudson, *A Philosophical Approach*, p. 16. A more balanced discussion can be found in Steinkellner, "Buddhismus," pp. 251-62.

213. Abe, "Kenotic God and Dynamic Sunyata," p. 50. For an insightful and careful attempt by a Christian systematician to clarify the meaning of sunyata to the Western and Christian mind-set, see Ott, "The Convergence," pp. 127-34 particularly. For a fuller, highly insightful discussion by a leading Christian Buddhist expert, see Waldenfels, *Absolute Nothingness*.

no nose, no tongue, no body, no mind . . . no ignorance and no extinction of ignorance . . . no aging and death and no extinction of aging and death; likewise there is no Suffering, Origin, Cessation or Path, no wisdom-knowledge, no attainment and non-attainment."

Astonishingly, this sutra, one of the shortest of all, although profoundly important (many monks recite it on a daily basis), even says that "all dharmas are Emptyness."[214] According to Masao Abe, "Sunyata is not self-affirmative, but *thoroughly* self-negative. . . . [E]mptiness not only empties everything else but also empties itself." And importantly with regard to Christian intuitions: "Sunyata should not be conceived of somewhere *outside* one's self-existence, nor somewhere *inside* one's self-existence. True Sunyata is neither outside nor inside, neither external nor internal, neither transcendent nor immanent."[215] If all that still sounds predominantly negative to Christian ears, Abe continues to say that at its core, "in Sunyata, regardless of the distinction between self and other, humans and nature, humans and the divine, everything without exception is realized *as it is* in its *suchness* (in Sanskrit, *tathata*, which may also be rendered as 'is-ness')."[216]

The Buddhist Quest for the Ultimate Reality

While it is true that in no Buddhist tradition is the founder, Gautama, a divine figure in the manner of the Creator or Redeemer of Christianity, it is equally true that in no Buddhist movement is Gautama a mere human being — even if assessments of his nature differ widely. Whereas Theravada takes him as a "wonderful man" *(acchariya manussa)* by virtue of the enlightenment, mainline Mahayana considers the historical Buddha one of the many faces of the cosmic, eternal buddhahood;[217] in the Pure Land form of Mahayana, there emerges the Savior figure of Amida Buddha.[218] The contrast with Christian

---

214. Heart Sutra (no translator given, n.p.; available at http://www.sacred-texts.com/bud/tib/hrt.htm).

215. Abe, "Kenotic God and Dynamic Sunyata," p. 51.

216. Abe, "Kenotic God and Dynamic Sunyata," p. 52.

217. Hence, some Christian theologians have wondered if the *trikaya* ("three bodies") might also approach the concept of the Ultimate Reality; see Baier, "Ultimate Reality in Buddhism and Christianity," pp. 112-13.

218. The closest parallel to the theistic God is of course Lotus Sutra's theology of the eternal Buddha, important in Japanese Nichiren Buddhism, in addition to Pure Land. Furthermore, the concept of Adi Buddha, "the Original Buddha," narrated in Kalacakra Tantra,

faith is definite because it conceives of God as "creator, sustainer, savior, pain-bearer and grace-giver,"[219] ideas strange to all forms of Buddhism.[220] The main point of this discussion is simply this: in no form of Buddhism can Gautama Buddha himself be regarded as the "ultimate reality." Nor does Buddhism acknowledge its predecessor Hinduism's view of Brahman and *atman* as the ultimate answer.[221] What, then, might be the Buddhist candidate(s) for the ultimate reality? Sunyata is of course the most likely proposal — but not the only one, as nirvana and Dharmakaya have also been suggested. I also wonder if the Mahayana concept of "suchness" *(tathata)* approaches the concept of the Ultimate Reality. Let me begin with the last one.

The Awakening of Faith,[222] by the second-century (?) Indian dramatist and sage Asvaghosa, best known for *Buddhacarita,* a dramatic narrative of Gautama's life, is an authoritative early Mahayana text, widely used as a short manual for teaching monks. It seeks to clarify the ultimate concept of reality, which it calls "suchness" and also names "soul" (in current translations, also "mind"). For this discussion, I find it highly significant that suchness is also named "The Womb of the Tathâgata *(Thatâgatagarbha),* when considered from its embracing all possible merits, and the All-Conserving Mind *(Âlayavi-jñâna),* when it becomes the principle of evolution."[223] In the beginning of the treatise, Asvaghosa sets forth a succinct description of key features of suchness, in response to his own question, "What is the Mahâyâna?":

> It is the soul of all sentient beings *(sarvasattva),* that constitutes all things in the world, phenomenal and supra-phenomenal. . . . The soul in itself,

---

among others, approximates and might have been influenced by theistic traditions. See further, Baier, "Ultimate Reality in Buddhism and Christianity," p. 102.

219. E. Harris, "Human Existence in Buddhism and Christianity," p. 47. She gives telling examples from Jewish-Christian Scriptures such as Pss. 59:1 and 62:1, which speak of the total dependence of men and women on God and divine help, ideas not only unknown but totally objectionable in all mainstream Buddhist denominations.

220. The Buddhist Nambara ("Ultimate Reality," pp. 119-20) goes so far as to say of a "Creator or Supreme God" that "this was disregarded from the outset as nonsense, as a mere shadow."

221. For an insightful comment, see Nambara, "Ultimate Reality," pp. 117-18.

222. Asvaghosa, *Awakening of Faith.* Early on this text was translated from Sanskrit to Chinese, and, as the original text is lost, English translations come from Chinese. While I am indebted to Ward, *Images of Eternity,* chap. 3, for turning my attention to this text's contribution to the discussion of the Ultimate Reality, I also approach Asvaghosa's teaching from a different point of view.

223. Introduction to Asvaghosa, *Awakening of Faith,* p. 43.

involving the quintessence of the Mahâyâna, is suchness *(bhûtatathatâ)*, but it becomes [in its relative or transitory aspect, through the law of causation] birth-and-death *(samsâra)* in which are revealed the quintessence, the attributes, and the activity of the Mahâyâna. The Mahâyâna has a triple significance. The first is the greatness of quintessence. Because the quintessence of the Mahâyâna as suchness exists in all things, remains unchanged in the pure as well as in the defiled, is always one and the same *(samatâ)*, neither increases nor decreases, and is void of distinction. The second is the greatness of attributes. . . . The third is the greatness of activity, for it [i.e., Mahâyâna] produces all kinds of good work in the world, phenomenal and supra-phenomenal.[224]

In other words, while impersonal, the notion of suchness is active and dynamic, though changeless. In this same treatise, "suchness" is also called "the Dharmakâya."[225] While that term also means something like the "Body of Law" (i.e., doctrine taught by the Enlightened Buddha) or even "Person of Law" (i.e., the Enlightened One), in this context it has an even wider and a bit different sense, as it "signifies that which constitutes the ultimate foundation of existence, one great whole in which all forms of individuation are obliterated, in a word, the Absolute."[226] Against the common misunderstanding that either "suchness" or Dharmakaya is nothing, Asvaghosa asserts that "suchness or Dharmakâya in its self-nature *(svabhâva)* is not a nothing *(çûnyatâ)* but envelops in full immeasurable merits *(guna)* which make up its true nature."[227] While both "suchness" and Dharmakaya function in some sense similarly to the theistic notion of God, to equate that in any way with the Christian trinitarian view of God as the communion of three persons is hardly justified. A sustained dialogue — based on careful listening to the *Buddhist* testimonies and interpretations — however, would help clarify what specifically, if any, is the role of these "ultimate" concepts in that tradition and if, from a theistic perspective, they even seek to function in any way similar to the more generic notion of deity.[228]

---

224. Asvaghosa, *Awakening of Faith* II, pp. 53-54.

225. Asvaghosa, *Awakening of Faith* III.1.C, p. 96; also p. 98.

226. The editor's explanatory note in Asvaghosa, *Awakening of Faith* III.1.B, p. 62. This explanation is confirmed in the text itself, e.g., in III.B, p. 64: "Bodhisattvas of the Dharmakâya, having recognised that subjectivity and the transcending of subjectivity have no reality of their own [i.e., are relative], have become emancipated from the intermediate form of particularization."

227. Asvaghosa, *Awakening of Faith* III.2.A, p. 108.

228. See further, Betty, "What Buddhists and Christians Are Teaching Each Other."

The classic "definition" of nirvana *(nibbana)*[229] is found in the "Udana Exclamation" (8.1), an ancient authoritative "small saying" among various Buddhist denominations: "There is that dimension where there is neither earth, nor water, nor fire, nor wind; neither dimension of the infinitude of space, nor dimension of the infinitude of consciousness, nor dimension of nothingness, nor dimension of neither perception nor non-perception; neither this world, nor the next world, nor sun, nor moon. And there, I say, there is neither coming, nor going, nor staying; neither passing away nor arising: unestablished, unevolving, without support (mental object). This, just this, is the end of stress."[230]

While this "definition" — of something indefinable! — strikes non-Buddhist sensibilities as negative, it is not, for it points to the final release, hence "salvation" in Judeo-Christian terms: "Thus the world of change, of becoming, of birth and rebirth, is seen as finally undesirable, as a realm of suffering. If desires can be extinguished, then there is a state to be attained which is not mere non-existence."[231] That said, it seems to me that there is an insurmountable logical problem here that the Buddhist philosophy and theology have not been able to solve. If everything is nonpermanent, not only "soul" *(anatta)* and the reality in itself (as it is merely a collection of fleeting events), but also *dharma* and sunyata, how can nirvana then be the "final" goal? Only if one were to posit something permanent amidst impermanence — which would break the most fundamental rule of the Buddhist worldview — could I see hope of overcoming this dilemma. Other solutions I do not know.[232] Ward makes the interesting suggestion that if nirvana is neither self-negation nor even self-fulfillment after common (Western) assumptions, perhaps it could be considered "self-transcendence." Consider Lankavatar Sutra (2.1.7): "Thou dost not vanish in Nirvana, nor is Nirvana abiding in thee; for it transcends the duality of knowing and known and of

229. Closely related to *nibbana* is the concept of *amatam* (Sanskrit: *amṛta*), mentioned first in Gautama's Deer Park Address following the Enlightenment, meaning "deathless" or "immortal." See further, Baier, "Ultimate Reality in Buddhism and Christianity," p. 104.

230. "Nibbana Sutta: Total Unbinding (1)" (*Udana* 8.1); for an important contemporary discussion, see Dharmasiri, *A Buddhist Critique of the Christian Concept of God*, pp. 177-214. The discussion includes the relation to the Hindu use of the concept as well as critique of Christian responses and interpretations.

231. Ward, *Images of Eternity*, p. 60. For the important rebuttal of a literal understanding of *nibbana* as extinction, see the fifth-century authoritative theologian Buddhagosa's *Visuddhi maggata*, chap. 6: "On the Truth of Cessation of Suffering," ##67-74 particularly (in Buddhagosa, *Visuddhi Visuddhimaggata*, pp. 520-34).

232. See also, Ward, *Images of Eternity*, pp. 61-62.

being and non-being."[233] In other words, nirvana here seems to mean "finding one's truest reality in being fully attentive to the unconditioned, which brings bliss and knowledge." Concludes Ward: "It must be said that this is, despite all protestations to the contrary, recognizably akin to theism."[234] My own assessment is more modest since — like "suchness" and Dharmakaya — this concept of the Ultimate Reality seems so far removed from the God of the Bible as Father, Son, and Spirit, eternal personal communion of three.

Not surprisingly, most attention in Christian-Buddhist dialogue has been devoted to the concept of sunyata. The leading academic interpreter of Mahayana Buddhism in the West, Masao Abe (Tokyo School of Japan) — whose skillful use of the foundational conception of sunyata in relation to the Christian doctrine of Christ's *kenosis* is discussed in *Christ and Reconciliation* — first clarifies the basic intuitions that guide Buddhist theology, beginning from the foundational conviction that "[t]he ultimate reality . . . is neither Being nor God, but Sunyata."[235] Even though Buddhism, like Christianity, is concerned with salvation — "that is, the deliverance of human beings from suffering" — it rules out "the personalistic divine-human relationship (I-Thou relationship) as the *basis* of salvation." As a result, unlike Christianity, Buddhism does not regard "impersonal nature as something peripheral, but instead takes as the basis of salvation the transpersonal, universal dimension common to human beings and nature." Neither does Buddhism "accept the notion of a transcendent ruler of the universe or of a savior outside one's self."[236] These statements, while neither novel nor unknown to Christian theology, are the more important because they are repeated by a Mahayana rather than a Theravada theologian and by one who is uniquely informed of Christian theology and philosophy. A hospitable Christian dialogue partner should carefully listen to and consider the implications of these pronouncements rather than — as seems to happen increasingly in recent Christian engagements with Buddhism — trying to make the Buddhist tradition more "*theo*-logical," more "monotheistic," and more like a Semitic or even Christian faith. Against the intentions of those well-meaning Christians, a truly hospitable encounter may

---

233. *The Lankavatara Sutra: A Mahayana Text*, 2.7, trans. Daisetz Teitaro Suzuki (1932); http://lirs.ru/do/lanka_eng/lanka-nondiacritical.htm; published on the Internet by © do1@yandex.ru, May 2004, 2005 (Rev. 2).

234. Ward, *Images of Eternity*, p. 63.

235. Abe, "Kenotic God and Dynamic Sunyata," p. 50. For a useful study of Abe's view, see Sabatino, "No-God." On Abe's dialogue with Christian theologians, see C. Jones, "Emptiness, Kenōsis, History, and Dialogue."

236. Abe, "Kenotic God and Dynamic Sunyata," p. 53.

happen only if the Buddhist counterpart is embraced fully and unconditionally in his or her strangeness.

God in Christian-Buddhist Encounter

Deeply knowledgeable of the nuances of the Christian doctrines of God and Christ's incarnation, Abe states unabashedly: "God's self-emptying must be understood not as partial but as total to the extent that God's infinite unrelatedness has no priority over relatedness with the other and that God's self-emptying is dynamically identical with God's abiding and infinite fullness."[237] From this follow two important corollaries: that "God . . . [is] Each and Every thing" and that in this "completely kenotic God, personality and impersonality are paradoxically identical."[238]

It seems to me that the attempt of Catholic theologian Raimundo Panikkar to incorporate some key elements of these widely shared Buddhist intuitions into a Christian theology of God, focusing on the "silence of God," takes huge steps toward convergence. As discussed above, the Father is "Nothing." There is no "Father" in himself; the "being of the Father" is "the Son." In the incarnation, *kenosis,* the Father gives himself totally to the Son. Thus the Son is "God." Panikkar believes this understanding is the needed bridge between Christianity and Buddhism as well as advaitic Hinduism. What *kenosis* (self-emptying) is for Christianity, nirvana and sunyata are for these two other religions. "God is total Silence. This is affirmed by all the world religions. One is led towards the Absolute and in the end one finds nothing, because there *is* nothing, not even Being."[239] Rather than repeating my critique of Panikkar's proposal, let it suffice to mention that his trinitarian formulation hardly represents in any legitimate way classical Christian canons and formulae. Panikkar's hybrid doctrinal construal is not likely to please Buddhists either, since it still is based on a monotheistic, "personal," and nonpantheistic vision of God.

As a Christian response to Abe's proposal,[240] Pannenberg calls for terminological clarification. How can it be that "Sunyata is not self-affirmative, but *thoroughly* self-negative" if, as Abe mentions elsewhere in the essay, Sunyata is an "agentless spontaneity"? In other words, how can this self-reference be

237. Abe, "Kenotic God and Dynamic Sunyata," p. 38.
238. Abe, "Kenotic God and Dynamic Sunyata," pp. 40-41.
239. As paraphrased by Ramachandra, *Recovery of Mission,* p. 91.
240. For an insightful Jewish response to Abe, see Rubenstein, "Holocaust, Sunyata, and Holy Nothingness."

had in the first place of a "thoroughly self-negative" sunyata, and how can it act (in this case, to negate itself)?[241] More to the substance, Pannenberg also wonders "whether in the Buddhist perspective there is any ultimate reality at all, distinct, if not separate, from the finite reality of human beings and animals and physical processes," if God is neither immanent nor transcendent.[242] Importantly, the process theologian Marjorie Suchocki remarks that the Trinity is the way to affirm both otherness and diversity on the one hand and unity on the other hand. "The Christian story is that the internal perichoretic relations of what is called the immanent trinity yield the external perichoretic work of the economic trinity." Hence, she replies that the major Christian tradition has rightly resisted pantheism: the Trinity tells us that God is god and we are not. Yet divine and human are integrally related, in keeping with classical panentheism. Furthermore, in Christian tradition, inner-trinitarian relations are not interpreted according to the principle of radical self-emptying. "To the strong contrary, the coinherence signified by perichoretic union is one that requires the irreducible otherness within the trinitarian structure."[243]

Furthermore, Christian theologians would also register the lack of any personal notion in the Buddhist notion of the ultimate reality. That would block any kind of I-Thou relationship, essential to Christian tradition. As Pannenberg notes, "in contrast with Buddhist emptiness the Christian idea of kenosis presupposes an agent, the Son, in relation to another agent, the Father, whose action is not kenotic." As a consequence of these incompatibilities, rather than sunyata, a more promising common point could perhaps be found in the Christian conception of the mutuality of love between the trinitarian persons, "which can be conceived of as suprapersonal though becoming manifest only in the trinitarian persons. This field of perichoretic love, of mutual indwelling, is the one divine essence that the three persons share and in which the Christian mystic participates by sharing in the sonship of Jesus and thus in his spiritual relation to the Father."[244] Yet even here there is, as Pannenberg also rightly observes, the important difference between "emptiness" and the remaining distinctions and the quality of "existence," we

---

241. Pannenberg, "God's Love and the Kenosis of the Son," pp. 246-47.

242. Pannenberg, "God's Love and the Kenosis of the Son," p. 245. The Buddhist Nambara ("Ultimate Reality," p. 129) categorically states: "In Buddhism there is no transcendence: The absolute that encompasses everything and dissolves everything in itself is sometimes called nothing, sometimes everything, and sometimes suchness *(tathatā)* — such as being is — because there is neither nothing nor being."

243. Suchocki, "Sunyata, Trinity, and Community," p. 145.

244. Pannenberg, "God's Love and the Kenosis of the Son," p. 250.

might say. Hopefully, mutual dialogue will pick up this theme and consider its potential.

Let us go back to the question posed in the beginning of this section: What, if anything, is the ultimate reality in Buddhism?[245] (Granted that this is a distinctively *Christian,* as well as a Western philosophical, way of posing the question, but I also think it is legitimate for the sake of *Christian* comparative theology.)[246] Before anything else, I think it is important for Christian theology to acknowledge that the Buddhist "reticence about the supreme reality, the unconditioned, is most welcome after some human claims to know the inner workings of the being of God."[247] I feel convinced by the argument of James L. Fredericks that this "silence of Buddha," namely, the stated reluctance to engage metaphysical questions,[248] rather than an unwillingness to share enlightened insights with others, is at its core "strategic silence" that "takes the middle path that embraces neither yes nor no [to metaphysical questions] in order to clear away the distractions that keep us from what is the real quest: the liberation from suffering."[249] It is also instructive to interfaith dialogue to note that soon the *followers* of Buddha began to mount literature and theologies that sought sophisticated answers to metaphysical questions![250]

The starting point for a summative Christian response is Küng's seasoned observation that while nirvana, emptiness, and Dharmakaya have "brought about a twilight of the gods or idols" as they have replaced the Hindu gods and Brahman as the ultimate explanation, "they have not put any other gods — not even the Buddha — in their place." Where I respectfully differ from Küng's assessment is the continuation of his argument. Whereas it seems to be true

245. For H. Küng's thoughtful struggle to identify the ultimate reality, see his "God's Self-Renunciation and Buddhist Self-Emptiness," pp. 207-23. As a main reason for the ambiguity he mentions the deep internal differences among Buddhist thinkers (p. 219).

246. Fredericks (*Buddhists and Christians,* p. 330) rightly notes that whereas Christians would inquire into the existence and nature of God, Hindus seek an answer to the question of the identity of soul and universe. The latter question was well known to Buddha, but he wished to turn attention to "practical" questions instead.

247. Ward, *Images of Eternity,* p. 63.

248. This is classically illustrated in the well-known narrative of the encounter with Buddha of a certain Vacchagotta, a wanderer in Ananda Sutta: To Ananda (On Self, No Self, and Not-self), Samyutta Nikaya 44.10. See Panikkar, *Silence of God.*

249. Fredericks, *Buddhists and Christians,* pp. 34-38, at 38.

250. These include the body of literature named Abhidarma and particularly its collection "Perfection of Wisdom," whose best-known piece is "Heart Sutra," and the famous Madhyamika Mahayana school under the tutorship of Nagarjuna (second century c.e.). For a succinct discussion, see Fredericks, *Buddhists and Christians,* chap. 3.

that "Nirvana, Emptiness, and Dharmakaya appear in this sense as parallel terms for the Ultimate Reality," I doubt whether "[their] function is analogous to that of the term 'God,'" and therefore also doubt that "what Christians call 'God' is present, under very different names, in Buddhism, insofar as Buddhists do not refuse, on principle, to admit any positive statements."[251] While I wholeheartedly affirm the Catholic theologian's effort to interpret the Buddhist counterpart's theology in a most hospitable way — and of course, I would be happy if a common theistic foundation could be found between the two traditions — I find it highly problematic that the Buddhist may not find it a hospitable gesture! Just recall the obvious: the main reason why Buddhism from its inception rejected the Brahman as the ultimate reality, let alone the pantheon of gods as the local "aids" to liberation, was Gautama's enlightening vision of *pratitya-samutpada* (dependent co-origination), which also makes the permanent "soul" meaningless *(anattan)*. There is nothing "outside" the world, so to speak. "Even the ultimate does not exist by itself," Abe reminds us.[252] And — dare I say — be that as it may, what would Christian theology lose here if it rather affirmed what I see as the deepest Buddhist intuitions: first, unlike any *monotheistic* tradition, Buddhism is happy with a plurality of answers to "one question" without suppressing the diversity; second, unlike any *theistic* tradition, Buddhism, even in its major Mahayana forms, makes every effort to resist the tendency to rely on gods (even if their existence and role in the world thereby need not be denied after modern Western antitheistic ideology); and third, that therefore, Buddhism and Christianity represent deeply and radically different paths to liberation/salvation. Wouldn't that kind of tentative conclusion serve an authentic, hospitable dialogue better than a forced, I fear, one-sided (!) *"con*-sensus"?

Sunyata and the Incomprehensibility of God

While Christian tradition has hardly wished to embrace the notion of sunyata in its more robust form as an alternative way to negotiate the notion of the ultimate reality to be comparable to the triune God, Christian theologians have of old sought convergence between their own mystically and apophatically oriented approaches focusing on the incomprehensibility of God and sunyata as "emptiness." Behind this move lies the simple intuition that "[i]n Christian

251. H. Küng, "God's Self-Renunciation and Buddhist Self-Emptiness," p. 221.
252. Abe, "Beyond Buddhism and Christianity," p. 232.

415

negative theology as well as in Buddhist thought one finds the insights that it is necessary to leave behind a way of thinking that is affirming or negating, identifying or discriminating, if one wants to gain a knowledge of the Ultimate based on experience."[253] Mentioned as a Christian counterpart to the Buddhist way of conceiving the Ultimate Reality in terms of mystery and unknowing has been, among others, Nicholas of Cusa's *De Deo abscondito (On the Hidden God)*.[254] Other similar comparisons include Dionysius the Areopagite's *Mystical Theology* vis-à-vis Zen Buddhism;[255] Aquinas's stress on the infinite incomprehensibility of God vis-à-vis Nagarjuna's Madhyamika tradition;[256] St. John of the Cross vis-à-vis Nagarjuna;[257] and Keiji Nishitani's *Religion and Nothingness* and Karl Rahner's God as incomprehensible mystery.[258]

While the Buddhist search for the Ultimate Reality can at times be highly sophisticated and conceptual, as evident in extensive writings, finally "in truth there is no object in perfect intellectual intuition, neither is there a subject in it; because the Bodhisattva by means of his wisdom of non-particularisation intuitively perceives suchness *(bhûtatathatâ)* or Dharmakâya, which is beyond the range of demonstration and argumentation."[259] In other words, rational powers fail to grasp the ultimate. In Christian tradition as well, the apophatic and mystical traditions cast serious doubts on and relativize the rational powers, as evident for example in Aquinas's approach to God in the beginning of his *Summa Theologiae*. However, for Thomas, as well as for the Eastern apophatic theology, "negative" theology does not mean the rejection of intellectual resources but rather putting them in perspective. Even in doxology, as discussed above, the rational contours do not have to be rejected. From the Christian perspective, then, the main challenge with a Buddhist firmly

253. Baier, "Ultimate Reality in Buddhism and Christianity," p. 113.

254. Baier, "Ultimate Reality in Buddhism and Christianity," pp. 91-95, based on Nicholas of Cusa, "On the Hidden God." Furthermore, Cusa's *De li non aliud (God as Not-Other)* has also been related to sunyata. See Nicholas of Cusa, *On God as Not-Other.*

255. Lefebure, *The Buddha and the Christ*, chap. 4, based on Pseudo-Dionysius, *Complete Works*, and various Zen writings.

256. Fredericks, *Buddhists and Christians*, chap. 4, based on Aquinas, *ST* 1.12.7, and particularly on *Commentary on the Gospel of John, Part One*, eleventh lecture on chap. 1, ##208-222 (focusing on John 1:18); and Nagarjuna, *Stanzas on the Middle Path*. See also P. Williams, "Aquinas Meets the Buddhists."

257. Vélez de Cea, "A New Direction for Comparative Studies of Buddhists and Christians."

258. H. Russell, "Keiji Nishitani and Karl Rahner," on the basis of Nishitani, *Religion and Nothingness*, and Rahner's various essays in *Theological Investigations*.

259. Asvaghosa, *Awakening of Faith* III.3, p. 123.

"negative" theology is that the "person who claims to have experienced the Ineffable . . . cannot really say what he has experienced."[260] So, has the person experienced it? And what has he or she experienced? Ward summarizes the dilemma succinctly:

> There is a peculiar paradox in asserting both that one has entered into a state which is beyond all descriptions; and that one can say one has attained the absolute essential truth, which one *knows* to be simple, unborn, pure and imperishable. . . . The claim that one has experienced a reality which is beyond one's own powers of description . . . is perfectly comprehensible. But it is quite different from saying that one knows one has experienced a reality which is unborn and imperishable. How could one know such a thing?[261]

Another major difference between the Christian acknowledgment of incomprehensibility and the Buddhist notion of "emptiness" is that the latter is a way for the Buddhist to let it go, to detach oneself from everything, whereas the Christian acknowledgment is a way of deeper and fuller personal union with the triune God. Yes, in a way these seemingly opposite purposes address the same issue, that is, "salvation," as has been mentioned above. Yet they do so in dramatically different ways: "Affirming the emptiness of all views, in effect, is a Buddhist way of affirming that human fulfillment is possible" by letting all attachments go, whereas for Christians, "the fulfillment of the human person consists in a beautifying knowledge of God."[262] Hence, "Buddhist emptiness may be the negation of God's transcendent otherness," while the Christian mystical vision affirms both God's profound transcendence and God's radical immanence in the person of Jesus Christ, God made flesh.[263]

260. Ward, *Images of Eternity*, p. 66.
261. Ward, *Images of Eternity*, pp. 66-67.
262. Fredericks, *Buddhists and Christians*, p. 81.
263. Fredericks, *Buddhists and Christians*, pp. 91-92; see also Lefebure, *The Buddha and the Christ*, pp. 92-93.

Epilogue

This volume's presentation of the Christian doctrine of the Trinity by no means represents the final statement about the nature and work of Father, Son, and Spirit — the one God. Better put: it is the initial clearing of the "foundation" on which the unfolding of Christian theology is built. This is not an endorsement of foundationalist epistemology, but rather a way of reminding us that every theological statement is but a way of clarifying, explaining, and reflecting on the fact that

> Only with the consummation of the world in the kingdom of God does God's love reach its goal and the doctrine of God reach its conclusion. . . . To this extent Christian dogmatics in every part is the doctrine of God. Even the question of God's reality, of his existence in view of his debatability in the world as atheistic criticism in particular articulates it, can find a final answer only in the event of the eschatological world renewal. . . . On the way to this goal of world history, from creation to the eschatological consummation, the distinctive features of the trinitarian persons, of Father, Son, and Holy Spirit, will also emerge more clearly, so that the course of systematic theology up to its conclusion in the treatment of eschatology may be expected to offer us a more nuanced understanding of what it means that God is love.[1]

Based on this "foundational" insight that "[i]n all its forms the activity of the Trinitarian God in creation is an activity of the Father by the Son and

---

1. Pannenberg, *ST* 1:447-48.

Spirit, an activity of the Son in obedience to the Father, and the glorification of both in the consummation of their work by the Spirit,"[2] the first volume in this series, *Christ and Reconciliation,* sought to discern and clarify the nature and work of Christ in the trinitarian unfolding of salvation history as well as the mutual relationship between the Son and the Spirit. In the revelation of the Father through the Son in the Spirit, the triune God not only makes Godself known to humanity but also graciously invites men and women into eternal fellowship. That triune revelation, in the form of promise, is anchored in the history of this world in the expectation of the final manifestation of the God of the Bible. The volume *Spirit and Salvation* will similarly take a careful look at the nature and work of the Spirit in the economy of salvation, as well as the mutual relationship between the Spirit and the Son. Only the final volume, *Church and Hope,* may bring to conclusion the systematic presentation of Christian vision as it seeks to discern the gracious way the Father gathers men and women from all contexts into the body of Christ, which in the power of the Spirit participates in the coming of God's righteous rule that encompasses the whole of creation, in the eager anticipation of the coming of the new creation. Only then will the love of God shown us in the face of his Son and poured out in our hearts through the Holy Spirit be experienced face-to-face. Only then can this eternal love make complete and transcend faith and hope (1 Cor. 13:13) in the eternal communion of creatures with their Creator.

In the contemporary world, it is not only atheism — and secularism in its various forms — to be reckoned with when seeking to offer a coherent, inclusive, and hospitable account of the trinitarian economy of salvation. Perhaps even more profoundly, other living faiths and their claims to the ultimate truth pose the main challenge. Hence, in keeping with the overall method of the current project, both the Christian doctrine of revelation and Scripture, on which the doctrine of the Trinity is based, have to be subjected to ongoing interfaith engagement, as must the Trinity itself. In addition to "practical" reasons, such as the elimination of conflicts between religions, and *theological* reasons, namely, systematic theology's vision of a coherent (and thus all-embracing) argumentation of truth, there is also another, related reason for engaging other living faiths. This involves the concept of "motivated beliefs" (Polkinghorne), as understood by the (natural) scientific community, discussed in the introduction. While the global scientific community shares one and the same "object," reality as we observe it,

2. Pannenberg, *ST* 3:1.

In contrast to the unified and worldwide scientific community, there is a largely regional collection of disparate theological communities, mostly Christian or Jewish in Europe and North America, mostly Moslem in the Middle East, mostly Hindu in India, mostly Buddhist in much of East Asia, and so on. In contrast to the unanimity of the scientists on such fundamental issues as the existence of quarks and gluons or the molecular basis of genetics, there is no unanimity in the theological world even about so fundamental an issue as the existence of one true God. . . . If theological beliefs are motivated beliefs, why are such contrasting convictions generated in these different communities?

Hence, with Polkinghorne, I must acknowledge that "I can do little more than acknowledge the problem and say that I regard it as one of the most urgent and critical items on the contemporary theological agenda."[3] Toward advancing this quest and relating it to the search for God's truth in Christian theology, the current volume and the whole project seek to contribute.

3. Polkinghorne, *Faith, Science, and Understanding*, p. 50.

Bibliography

Abd-Allah, Umar F. "Do Christians and Muslims Worship the Same God?" *Christian Century* 121, no. 17 (August 24, 2004).

Abduh, Muhammad. *The Theology of Unity.* Translated by Ishaq Musa'ad and Kenneth Cragg. New York: Arno, 1980.

Abe, Masao. "Beyond Buddhism and Christianity: 'Dazzling Darkness.'" In *DEHF,* pp. 224-43.

————. "Kenotic God and Dynamic Sunyata." In *DEHF,* pp. 25-90.

Abraham, William J. *The Divine Inspiration of Holy Scripture.* Oxford: Oxford University Press, 1981.

————. *Divine Revelation and the Limits of Historical Criticism.* Oxford: Oxford University Press, 1982.

————. "Revelation Reaffirmed." In *Divine Revelation,* edited by Paul Avis. Eugene, Ore.: Wipf and Stock, 2004 [1997].

Achtemeier, Elizabeth. "Exchanging God for 'No Gods': A Discussion of Female Language for God." In *Speaking the Christian God: The Holy Trinity and the Challenge of Feminism,* edited by Alvin F. Kimel Jr., pp. 1-16. Grand Rapids: Eerdmans, 1992.

Achtemeier, Paul. *The Inspiration of Scripture.* Philadelphia: Westminster, 1980.

Adam, A. K. M. *Faithful Interpretation: Reading the Bible in a Postmodern World.* Minneapolis: Fortress, 2006.

Ahlstrand, Kajsa. *Fundamental Openness: An Enquiry into Raimundo Panikkar's Theological Vision and Its Presuppositions.* Studia Missionalia Upsaliensia 57. Uppsala: Uppsala University, 1993.

Aichele, George, Peter D. Miscall, and Richard Walsh. "An Elephant in the Room: Historical-Critical and Postmodern Interpretations of the Bible." *Journal of Biblical Literature* 128, no. 2 (2009): 383-404.

Allegro, John M. *The Sacred Mushroom and the Cross: A Study of the Nature and Origins of Christianity within the Fertility Cults of the Ancient Near East.* Garden City, N.Y.: Doubleday, 1970.

Almond, P. "The Buddha of Christendom: A Review of the Legend of Barlaam and Josaphat." *Religious Studies* 23 (1987): 391-406.

Alston, William P. "Functionalism and Theological Language." In *Divine Nature and Human Language: Essays in Philosophical Theology,* pp. 64-80. Ithaca, N.Y.: Cornell University Press, 1989.

———. *Perceiving God: The Epistemology of Religious Experience.* Ithaca, N.Y.: Cornell University Press, 1991.

———. "Substance and the Trinity." In *The Trinity: An Interdisciplinary Symposium on Trinity,* edited by Stephen T. Davis, Daniel Kendall, S.J., and Gerald O'Collins, S.J., pp. 179-201. Oxford: Oxford University Press, 1999.

Althaus-Reid, Marcella. "El Tocado (Le Toucher): Sexual Irregularities in the Translation of God (the Word) in Jesus." In *Derrida and Religion: Other Testaments,* edited by Yvonne Sherwood and Kevin Hart. New York: Routledge, 2005.

Altizer, Thomas. *The Gospel of Christian Atheism.* Philadelphia: Westminster, 1966.

Amaladoss, Michael. "Other Scriptures and the Christian." *Indian Theological Studies* 22, no. 1 (March 1985): 62-78.

Amnell, Matti T. *Uskonto ilman uskontoa: Radikaalin postmodernin uskonnonfilosofian haaste.* Helsinki: Yliopistopaino, 2010.

———. *Uskontojen Universumi: John Hickin uskonnollisen pluralismin haaste ja siitä käyty keskustelu.* Suomalaisen Teologisen Kirjallisuusseuran Julkaisuja 217. Helsinki: STK, 1999.

Anderson, Ray S. "Barth and a New Direction for Natural Theology." In *Theology beyond Christendom: Essays on the Centenary of the Birth of Karl Barth,* edited by J. Thompson, pp. 241-66. Allison Park, Pa.: Pickwick, 1986.

Aquinas, Thomas. *Commentary on the Gospel of John, Part One.* Translated by James A. Weisheipl and Fabian R. Larcher. Albany, N.Y.: Magi Books, 1980.

———. *De Rationibus Fidei (Reasons for the Faith against Muslim Objections).* Translated by Joseph Kenny, O.P. *Islamochristiana* (Rome) 22 (1996): 31-52.

———. *Summa contra Gentiles.* Translated by Charles J. O'Neil. Notre Dame, Ind.: University of Notre Dame Press, 1975.

Arinze, Francis. *Religions for Peace: A Call for Solidarity to the Religions of the World.* New York: Random House, 2002.

Aristotle. *Aristotle in Twenty-three Volumes.* Translated by Hugh Tredennick. Cambridge: Harvard University Press; London: William Heinemann, 1933, 1989.

———. *The Complete Works of Aristotle.* Edited by Jonathan Barnes. 2 vols. Princeton: Princeton University Press, 1984.

———. *Metaphysics.* Translated by W. D. Ross. Classic Library. http://www.classical library.org/aristotle/metaphysics/book03.htm.

———. *The Poetics.* Translated by Ingram Bywater. http://www.authorama.com/the--poetics-22.html.

Arnaldez, R. *Trois Messagers pour un Seul Dieu.* Paris: Albin Michel, 1983.

Asvaghosa. *Açvaghosha's Discourse on the Awakening of Faith in the Mahâyâna.* Translated by Teitaro Suzuki (1900). Available at www.sacred-texts.com.

Austin, J. L. *How to Do Things with Words.* Edited by J. O. Urmson and Marina Sbisà. 2nd ed. Cambridge: Harvard University Press, 1975.

Ayer, A. J. *Language, Truth, and Logic.* 2nd ed. New York: Dover, 1946.

Ayoub, Mahmoud Mustafa. *The Qur'an and Its Interpreters.* Vol. 1. Albany: State University of New York Press, 1984.

———. "The Word of God in Islam." In *Orthodox Christians and Muslims,* edited by Nomikos Michael Vaporis, pp. 69-78. Brookline, Mass.: Holy Cross Orthodox Press, 1986.

Bacon, Hannah. *What's Right with the Trinity? Conversations in Feminist Theology.* Surrey, U.K., and Burlington, Vt.: Ashgate, 2010.

Badarayana. *Brahma Sutras: Text, Word-to-Word Meaning, Translation and Commentary,* Sri Swami Sivananda. Himalayas, India: Divine Life Society, 2008. http://www .swami-krishnananda.org/bs_o/Brahma_Sutra.pdf.

Baier, Karl. "Ultimate Reality in Buddhism and Christianity." In *Buddhism and Christianity in Dialogue,* edited by Perry Schmidt-Leukel, pp. 87-116. London: SCM, 2005.

Baillie, John. *The Idea of Revelation in Recent Thought.* New York: Columbia University Press, 1956.

Baker-Fletcher, Karen. *Dancing with God: The Trinity from a Womanist Perspective.* St. Louis: Chalice, 2006.

Baker-Fletcher, Karen, and Garth Kasimu Baker-Fletcher. *My Sister, My Brother: Womanist and Xodus God-Talk.* Maryknoll, N.Y.: Orbis, 1997.

Balíc, S. "The Image of Jesus in Contemporary Islamic Theology." In *We Believe in One God,* edited by A. M. Schimmel and Abdoldjavad Falaturi, pp. 1-8. London: Burns and Oates, 1979.

Barbour, Ian G. *Myths, Models, and Paradigms: A Comparative Study in Science and Religion.* New York: Harper and Row, 1974.

Barker, Gregory A., and Stephen E. Gregg. "Muslim Perceptions of Jesus: Key Issues." In *Jesus beyond Christianity: The Classic Texts,* edited by Gregory A. Baker and Stephen E. Gregg. Oxford: Oxford University Press, 2010.

Barnes, Michel René. "Rereading Augustine's Theology of the Trinity." In *The Trinity: An Interdisciplinary Symposium on the Trinity,* edited by Stephen T. Davis, Daniel Kendall, S.J., and Gerald O'Collins, S.J., pp. 145-76. Oxford: Oxford University Press, 1999.

Barr, James. *Biblical Faith and Natural Theology.* Oxford: Clarendon, 1993.

———. "Revelation through History in the Old Testament and in Modern Theology." In *New Theology No. 1,* edited by M. E. Marty and D. G. Peerman. New York: Macmillan, 1964.

———. *The Scope and Authority of the Bible.* Philadelphia: Westminster, 1980.

Barth, Karl. *Anselm: Fides Quaerens Intellectum; Anselm's Proof of the Existence of God in the Context of His Theological Scheme.* Translated by Ian W. Robertson. London: SCM, 1960.

―――. *Die Christliche Dogmatik im Entwurf: Prolegomena zur Christlichen Dogmatik,* München 1927. Karl Barth Gesamtausgabe. Zürich: Gerhard Sauter, 1982.

―――. *Epistle to the Romans.* Preface to the 2nd ed. (1921). Translated by E. C. Hoskyns. London and New York: Oxford University Press, 1968, 1991 [1933].

Barth, Karl, and Emil Brunner. *Natural Theology.* London: SCM, 1947.

Basham, A. L. *The Wonder That Was India.* London: Sigwick and Jackson, 1988.

Battles, F. L. "God Was Accommodating Himself to Human Capacity." *Interpretation* 31, no. 1 (January 1977): 19-38.

Bauckham, Richard. "Jesus the Revelation of God." In *Divine Revelation,* edited by Paul Avis. Eugene, Ore.: Wipf and Stock, 2004 [1997].

―――. "The Sonship of the Historical Jesus in Christology." *Scottish Journal of Theology* 31 (1978): 245-60.

―――. *The Theology of Jürgen Moltmann.* Edinburgh: T. & T. Clark, 1995.

Baum, Gregory. *Faith and Doctrine.* New York: Newman, 1969.

―――. Foreword to *The New Agenda,* by A. M. Greeley. Garden City, N.Y.: Doubleday, 1973.

Beattie, Tina. *The New Atheists: The Twilight of Reason and the War on Religion.* London: Darton, Longman and Todd, 2007.

Belonick, Deborah Malacky. "Revelation and Metaphors: The Significance of the Trinitarian Names, Father, Son and Holy Spirit." *Union Seminary Quarterly Review* 40, no. 3 (1985): 31-42.

Benedict XVI. *Caritas in Veritate* (2009). http://www.vatican.va/holy_father/benedict _xvi/encyclicals/documents/hf_ben-xvi_enc_20090629_caritas-in-veritate_en .html.

―――. "Faith, Reason and the University: Memories and Reflections." *The Holy See,* September 12, 2006. Available at Vatican.ca website.

Bennett, Clinton. *Understanding Christian-Muslim Relations: Past and Present.* London and New York: Continuum, 2008.

Bennett, M. R., and P. M. S. Hacker. *Philosophical Foundations of Neuroscience.* Oxford: Blackwell, 2003.

Berger, Peter L. "The Desecularization of the World: A Global Overview." In *The Desecularization of the World: Resurgent Religion and World Politics,* edited by Peter Berger, pp. 1-18. Washington, D.C.: Ethics and Public Policy Center; Grand Rapids: Eerdmans, 1999.

―――. *The Heretical Imperative: Contemporary Possibilities of Religious Affirmation.* Garden City, N.Y.: Anchor Press, 1980.

―――. *A Rumor of Angels: Modern Society and the Rediscovery of the Supernatural.* Harmondsworth: Penguin, 1970.

―――. *The Sacred Canopy: Elements of a Sociological Theory of Religion.* Garden City, N.Y.: Doubleday, 1967.

Berger, Peter L., and Thomas Luckmann, *The Social Construction of Reality: A Treatise in the Sociology of Knowledge.* Garden City, N.Y.: Anchor Books, 1966.

Berkson, William. *Fields of Force: The Development of a World View from Faraday to Einstein.* London: Routledge and Kegan Paul, 1974.

Betty, Stafford. "What Buddhists and Christians Are Teaching Each Other about God." *Cross Currents* 58 (2008): 108-16.

Bevans, Stephen B. *Models of Contextual Theology.* Maryknoll, N.Y.: Orbis, 1992.

Bevans, Stephen B., and Roger P. Schroeder. *Constants in Context: A Theology of Mission for Today.* Maryknoll, N.Y.: Orbis, 2004.

Bhabha, Homi K. *The Location of Culture.* London and New York: Routledge, 1994.

Birch, Charles, and John B. Cobb Jr. *The Liberation of Life from the Cell to the Community.* Denton, Tex.: Environmental Ethics Books, 1990.

el-Bizri, Nader. "God: Essence and Attributes." In *The Cambridge Companion to Classical Islamic Theology,* edited by Tim Winter. Cambridge: Cambridge University Press, 2008.

Blackwell Companion to the Qur'ān. Edited by Andrew Rippin. Oxford and Malden, Mass.: Blackwell, 2006.

Bloch, Maurice. *Prey into Hunter: The Politics of Religious Experience.* Cambridge: Cambridge University Press, 1992.

Bloesch, Donald G. *The Battle for the Trinity: The Debate over Inclusive God-Language.* Ann Arbor: Vine Books, 1985.

———. *Essentials of Evangelical Theology.* 2 vols. San Francisco: Harper and Row, 1978.

———. *God the Almighty: Power, Wisdom, Holiness, Love.* Downers Grove, Ill.: InterVarsity, 1995.

———. *Is the Bible Sexist? Beyond Feminism and Patriarchalism.* Westchester, Ill.: Crossway, 1982.

———. *A Theology of Word and Spirit.* Downers Grove, Ill.: InterVarsity, 1992.

Bobrinskoy, Boris. *The Mystery of the Trinity: Trinitarian Experience and Vision in the Biblical and Patristic Tradition.* Translated by Anthony P. Gythiel. Crestwood, N.Y.: St. Vladimir's Seminary Press, 1999.

Boesak, Allan. *Farewell to Innocence: A Socio-Ethical Study on Black Theology and Black Power.* Maryknoll, N.Y.: Orbis, 1977.

Boethius [Anicius Manlius Torquatus Severinus]. *On the Catholic Faith.* In *Theological Tractates.* Available at www.ccel.org.

Boff, Leonardo. *Trinity and Society.* Translated by Paul Burns. Maryknoll, N.Y.: Orbis, 1988.

Bondi, Roberta C. "Some Issues Relevant to a Modern Interpretation of the Language of the Nicene Creed, with Special Reference to 'Sexist' Language." *Union Seminary Quarterly Review* 40, no. 3 (1985): 21-30.

Bonhoeffer, Dietrich. *The Communion of Saints.* Translated by Ronald Gregor Smith. New York: Harper and Row, 1963.

Booth, Wayne C. *The Rhetoric of Fiction.* 2nd ed. Chicago: University of Chicago Press, 1983 [1961].

———. *The Rhetoric of Irony.* Chicago: University of Chicago Press, 1974.

Bornkamm, H. "Die theologischen Thesen Luthers bei der Heidelberger Disputation 1518 und seine theologia crucis." In *Luther, Gestalt und Wirkungen,* Gesammelte Aufsätze, edited by Heinrich Bornkamm, pp. 130-46. Gütersloh: Gütersloher Verlagshaus, 1975.

Bowes, Pratima. *The Hindu Religious Tradition: A Philosophical Approach.* London: Routledge and Kegan Paul, 1977.

Boyd, Robin. *An Introduction to Indian Christian Theology.* Madras: Christian Literature Society, 1969.

Bracken, Joseph A., S.J. *The Triune Symbol: Persons, Process, and Community.* Lanham, Md.: University Press of America, 1985.

Bracken, Joseph A., S.J., and Marjorie Hewitt Suchocki, eds. *Trinity in Process: A Relational Theology of God.* New York: Continuum, 1997.

Bray, Gerald. "The *Filioque* Clause in History and Theology." *Tyndale Bulletin* 34 (1983): 91-143.

Brecher, Robert. *Anselm's Argument: The Logic of Divine Existence.* Brookfield, Vt.: Gower, 1985.

Brierley, Michael W. "Naming a Quiet Revolution: The Panentheistic Turn in Modern Theology." In *IWWLM*, pp. 1-15.

Brighman, Robert S. "Apophatic Theology and Divine Infinity in Gregory of Nyssa." *Greek Orthodox Theological Review* 18, no. 2 (1973): 97-114.

Brockington, John. *Hinduism and Christianity.* New York: St. Martin's Press, 1992.

Brockopp, Jonathan. "Islam." In *God*, edited by Jacob Neusner, pp. 85-111. Cleveland: Pilgrim Press, 1997.

Brown, David. *Tradition and Imagination: Revelation and Change.* Oxford: Oxford University Press, 1999.

Brown, Robert McAfee. "The 'Preferential Option for the Poor' and the Renewal of Faith." In *Churches in Struggle: Liberation Theologies and Social Change in North America*, edited by William K. Tabb. New York: Monthly Review Press, 1986.

Brown, William A. "Concepts of God in Africa." *Journal of Religious Thought* 39, no. 2 (Fall-Winter 1982-1983): 5-16.

Brueggemann, Walter. *Texts under Negotiation: The Bible and Postmodern Imagination.* London: SCM, 1993.

———. *Theology of the Old Testament: Testimony, Dispute, Advocacy.* Minneapolis: Fortress, 1997.

Brunner, Emil. *Revelation and Reason.* Translated by Olive Wynn. Philadelphia: Westminster, 1946.

Buddhagosa. *Visuddhi Visuddhimaggata, The Path of Purification: The Classic Manual of Buddhist Doctrine and Meditation.* Translated by Bikkhu Nanamoli. Kandy, Sri Lanka: Buddhist Publication Society, 2011. Available at http://www.accesstoinsight.org/lib/authors/nanamoli/PathofPurification2011.pdf.

Bujo, Bénézet, and Juvénal Ilunga Muya, eds. *African Theology: The Contribution of the Pioneers.* Vol. 2. Nairobi, Kenya: Paulines Publications Africa, 2006.

Bultmann, Rudolf. "New Testament and Mythology." In *Kerygma and Myth: A Theological Debate,* edited by Hans Werner Bartsch. New York: Harper and Row, 1961.

Byrne, Peter A. *Natural Religion and the Nature of Religion: The Legacy of Deism.* London: Routledge, 1989.

"Can Christians Say 'Allah'? In Malaysia, Muslims say No." *Time,* January 8, 2010. http://www.time.com/time/world/article/0,8599,1952497,00.html.

Caputo, John D., Kevin Hart, and Yvonne Sherwood. "Epoché and Faith: An Interview with Jacques Derrida." In *Derrida and Religion: Other Testaments,* edited by Yvonne Sherwood and Kevin Hart. New York: Routledge, 2005.

Caputo, John, and Michael Scanlon, eds. *God, the Gift, and Postmodernism.* Bloomington: Indiana University Press, 1999.

Carman, John B. *Majesty and Meekness: A Comparative Study of Contrast and Harmony in the Concept of God.* Grand Rapids: Eerdmans, 1994.

———. *The Theology of Rāmānuja.* New Haven: Yale University Press, 1974.

Carnap, Rudolf. "The Rejection of Metaphysics." In *20th-Century Philosophy: The Analytic Tradition,* edited by Morris Weitz. New York: Free Press, 1966.

Carroll, Denis. *A Pilgrim God for a Pilgrim People.* Wilmington, Del.: Michael Glazier, 1989.

Carter, J. Kameron. *Race: A Theological Account.* Oxford: Oxford University Press, 2008.

Carter, Stephen L. *The Culture of Disbelief.* New York: Basic Books, 1993.

Cary, Philip. "Historical Perspectives on Trinitarian Doctrine." *Religious and Theological Studies Fellowship Bulletin,* November-December 1995.

Castelo, Daniel. "The Improvisational Quality of Ecclesial Holiness." In *Toward a Pentecostal Ecclesiology: The Church and the Fivefold Gospel,* edited by John Christopher Thomas, pp. 87-104. Cleveland, Tenn.: CPT Press, 2010.

Cavanaugh, William. "Does Religion Cause Violence?" Presentation given at the University of Western Australia, May 29, 2006, available at http://www.catholicanarchy .org/cavanaugh/Cavanaugh%20-%20Does%20Religion%20Cause%20Violence .pdf.

Chadwick, Owen. *The Secularization of the European Mind in the 19th Century.* Cambridge: Cambridge University Press, 1975.

Chandngarm, Saeng. *Arriyasatsee [The Four Noble Truths].* Bangkok: Sangsan Books, 2001.

Charry, Ellen T. "The Soteriological Importance of the Divine Perfections." In *God the Holy Trinity: Reflections on Christian Faith and Practice,* edited by T. George, pp. 129-47. Grand Rapids: Baker Academic, 2006.

Cheetham, David, Ulrich Winkler, Oddbjørn Leirvik, and Judith Gruber, eds. *Interreligious Hermeneutics in Pluralistic Europe: Between Texts and People.* Amsterdam and New York: Rodopi, 2011.

Chemparathy, George. "The Veda as Revelation." *Journal of Dharma* 7, no. 3 (1982): 253-74.

Childs, Brevard S. *Biblical Theology in Crisis.* Philadelphia: Westminster, 1970.

———. *Introduction to the Old Testament as Scripture.* Philadelphia: Fortress, 1979.

Chopp, Rebecca S. "Feminist Queries and Metaphysical Musings." In *Rethinking Metaphysics,* edited by L. Gregory Jones and Stephen E. Fowl. Oxford: Blackwell, 1995.

———. "Latin American Liberation Theology." In *The Modern Theologians,* edited by D. Ford, pp. 409-25. Oxford: Blackwell, 1997.

———. *The Power to Speak: Feminism, Language, God.* New York: Crossroad, 1989.

Christ, Carol P. "Why Women Need the Goddess: Phenomenological, Psychological, and Political Reflections." In *Womanspirit Rising: A Feminist Reader in Religion,* edited by Carol P. Christ and Judith Plaskow, 2nd ed., pp. 273-87. New York: Harper and Row, 1992.

Cicero, Marcus Tullius. *On the Nature of God*. In *Cicero's Tusculan Disputations, Also, Treatises on the Nature of the Gods, and on the Commonwealth*. Project Gutenberg, 2005. http://www.gutenberg.org/files/14988/14988-h/14988-h.htm#page-209.

Clayton, John. "Gottesbeweise II. Mittelalter." In *Theologische Realenzyklopädie*, edited by G. Krause and G. Müller, 13:724-40. Berlin: Walter de Gruyter, 1984.

Clayton, Philip. "The Case for Christian Panentheism." *Dialog* 37, no. 3 (1998): 201-8.

———. *God and Contemporary Science*. Edinburgh: Edinburgh University Press; Grand Rapids: Eerdmans, 1997.

———. "Kenotic Trinitarian Panentheism." *Dialog* 44, no. 3 (2005): 250-55.

———. "The Panentheistic Turn in Christian Theology." *Dialog* 38, no. 4 (1999): 289-93.

———. *The Problem of God in Modern Thought*. Grand Rapids: Eerdmans, 2000.

Clendenin, Daniel B. *Eastern Orthodox Christianity: A Western Perspective*. Grand Rapids: Baker, 1994.

Cloege, G. "Offenbarung." In *Die Religion in Geschichte und Gegenwart*, edited by Kurt Galling et al., vol. 4, 3rd ed. Tübingen: J. C. B. Mohr/Paul Siebeck, 1960.

Clooney, Francis X., S.J. *Hindu God, Christian God: How Reason Helps Break Down the Boundaries between Religions*. Oxford: Oxford University Press, 2001.

———. "Trinity and Hinduism." In *Cambridge Companion to the Trinity*, edited by Peter C. Phan, pp. 309-24. Cambridge: Cambridge University Press, 2011.

Cobb, John B., Jr. *Beyond Dialogue: Towards a Mutual Transformation of Christianity and Buddhism*. Philadelphia: Fortress, 1982.

Cobb, John B., Jr., and David Ray Griffin. *Process Theology: An Introductory Exposition*. Philadelphia: Westminster, 1976.

"A Common Word between Us and You." On the official Web site of A Common Word, http://www.acommonword.com/.

Cone, James H. *A Black Theology of Liberation*. 2nd ed. Twentieth Anniversary Edition. Maryknoll, N.Y.: Orbis, 1986.

———. *God of the Oppressed*. Rev. ed. Maryknoll, N.Y.: Orbis, 1997.

Congar, Yves. *I Believe in the Holy Spirit*. Translated by David Smith. Three vols. in 1. New York: Crossroad, 1997.

———. *Situation et Tâches Présentes de la Théologie*. Paris: Les Éditions du Cerf, 1967.

———. *True and False Reform of the Church*. Translated and edited by Paul Philibert. Rev. ed. Collegeville, Minn.: Liturgical Press, 2011.

Constable, Remie, ed. *Medieval Iberia: Readings from Christian, Muslim, and Jewish Sources*. Philadelphia: University of Pennsylvania Press, 1997.

Cooper, John W. *Panentheism: The Other God of the Philosophers — from Plato to the Present*. Grand Rapids: Baker Academic, 2006.

Copan, Paul. "Are Old Testament Laws Evil?" Chapter 9 in *God Is Great, God Is Good: Why Believing in God Is Reasonable and Responsible*, edited by William Lane Craig and Chad Meister, pp. 134-54, Downers Grove, Ill.: InterVarsity, 2009.

Cornell, Vincent. "Listening to God through the Qur'an." In *Scriptures in Dialogue: Chris-*

tians and Muslims Studying the Bible and the Qur'an Together, edited by Michael Ipgrave, pp. 36-62. London: Church House Publishing, 2004.

Corrigan, John, Frederick M. Denny, Carlos M. N. Eire, and Martin S. Jaffee. *Jews, Christians, Muslims: A Comparative Introduction to Monotheistic Religions.* 2nd ed. Upper Saddle River, N.J.: Prentice-Hall, 2012.

Council of Trent, Fourth Session. "Decree concerning the Canonical Scriptures." In *The Canons and Decrees of the Sacred and Oecumenical Council of Trent,* translated by J. Waterworth. London: Dolman, 1848. Available at http://history.hanover.edu/texts/trent/ct04.html.

Cousins, Ewert H. "Panikkar's Advaitic Trinitarianism." In *The Intercultural Challenge of Raimon Panikkar,* edited by Joseph Prabhu, pp. 119-30. Maryknoll, N.Y.: Orbis, 1996.

Coward, Harold. Introduction to *Experiencing Scripture in World Religions,* edited by H. Coward, pp. 1-14. Maryknoll, N.Y.: Orbis, 2000.

———. *Pluralism: Challenge to World Religions.* Maryknoll, N.Y.: Orbis, 1985.

———. *Sacred Word and Sacred Text: Scripture in World Religions.* Maryknoll, N.Y.: Orbis, 1988.

Cox, Harvey. *The Secular City: Secularization and Urbanization in Theological Perspective.* Rev. ed. New York: Macmillan, 1968.

Cragg, Kenneth. "Al-Rahman al-Rahim." *Muslim World* 43 (1953): 235-36.

———. *The Call of the Minaret.* Rev. ed. Maryknoll, N.Y.: Orbis, 1985 [1956].

———. " 'Greater Is God,' Contemporary *Takbīr*: Muslim and Christian." *Muslim World* 71 (1981): 27-39.

———. *The House of Islam.* Belmont, Calif.: Dickenson, 1969.

———. *Jesus and the Muslim: An Exploration.* Oxford: One World, 1999.

Craig, William L. *Time and Eternity: Exploring God's Relationship to Time.* Wheaton, Ill.: Crossway, 2001.

Craig, William Lane, and Chad Meister, eds. *God Is Great, God Is Good: Why Believing in God Is Reasonable and Responsible.* Downers Grove, Ill.: InterVarsity, 2009.

Craig, William Lane, and James D. Sinclair. "The *Kalam* Cosmological Argument." In *Blackwell Companion to Natural Theology,* edited by William Lane Craig and J. P. Moreland, pp. 101-201. Oxford: Wiley-Blackwell, 2009.

Cremer, Hermann. *Die christliche Lehre von den Eigenschaften Gotte.* Gütersloh: n.p., 1897.

Cullmann, Oscar. *Christ and Time.* Translated by Floyd V. Filson. Rev. ed. Philadelphia: Westminster, 1964 [1950].

Cunningham, David S. *These Three Are One: The Practice of Trinitarian Theology.* Oxford: Blackwell, 1998.

———. "The Trinity." In *The Cambridge Companion to Postmodern Theology,* edited by Kevin J. Vanhoozer, pp. 186-202. Cambridge: Cambridge University Press, 2003.

Cupitt, Don. *After God: The Future of Religion.* New York: Basic Books, 1997.

———. *Is Nothing Sacred? The Non-Realist Philosophy of Religion.* New York: Fordham University Press, 2002.

———. *The Long-Legged Fly: The Theology of Language and Desire.* London: SCM, 1987.

———. *Only Human.* London: SCM, 1985.

―――. *Philosophy's Own Religion*. London: SCM, 2000.

―――. *Radicals and the Future of the Church*. London: SCM, 1989.

―――. *The Sea of Faith*. London: SCM, 1994.

―――. *Taking Leave of God*. London: SCM, 1980.

―――. "Unsystematic Ethics and Politics." In *Shadow of Spirit: Postmodernism and Religion*, edited by Philippa Berry and Andrew Wernick. London: Routledge, 1992.

Dalferth, I. U. *Existenz Gottes und christlicher Glaube: Skizzen zu einer eschatologischen Ontologie*. Munich: Chr. Kaiser, 1984.

Dammapitaka, Ven. Para [P. A. Payette]. *Dictionary of Buddhism*. Bangkok: Mahachulalongkornrajavidyala University, 2003.

Darwin, Charles. *The Correspondence of Charles Darwin*. Vol. 8, 1860. Cambridge: Cambridge University Press, 1993.

Davies, Rupert E. *The Problem of Authority in the Continental Reformers: A Study in Luther, Zwingli, and Calvin*. Westport, Conn.: Hyperion Press, 1979.

Davis, Jayne H. "Opening Dialogue: Jürgen Moltmann's Interaction with the Thought of Karl Barth." *Review and Expositor* 100, no. 4 (Fall 2003): 695-711.

Davis, Stephen. *Logic and the Nature of God*. Grand Rapids: Eerdmans, 1983.

Dawkins, Richard. *The Blind Watchmaker: Why the Evidence of Evolution Reveals a Universe without Design*. New York: Norton, 1996.

―――. *Climbing Mount Improbable*. New York and London: Norton, 1996.

―――. *A Devil's Chaplain*. London: Weidenfeld and Nicolson, 2002.

―――. *The God Delusion*. London: Transworld Publishers Black Swan, 2006.

―――. *River Out of Eden: A Darwinian View of Life*. London: Phoenix, 1995.

―――. *The Selfish Gene*. Oxford: Oxford University Press, 1976.

―――. "A Survival Machine." In *The Third Culture*, edited by John Brockman, pp. 75-95. New York: Simon and Schuster, 1996.

Day, John. *Wisdom in Ancient Israel: Essays in Honour of J. A. Emerton*. Cambridge: Cambridge University Press, 1995.

D'Costa, Gavin. "Christian Theology and Other Religions: An Evaluation of John Hick and Paul Knitter." *Studia Missionalia* 42 (1993): 161-78.

―――. *The Meeting of Religions and the Trinity*. Maryknoll, N.Y.: Orbis, 2000.

Denffer, Ahmad von. *Loading Options Ulu m al-Qur'an: An Introduction to the Sciences of the Qur'an*. Leicester: Islamic Foundation, 1983.

Denny, F. M. "Names and Naming." In *Encyclopedia of Religion,* edited by M. Eliade, 10:300-307. New York: Macmillan, 1987.

Derrida, Jacques. *The Gift of Death*. Translated by David Wills. Religion and Postmodernism. Chicago: University of Chicago Press, 1995.

―――. *Given Time: 1. Counterfeit Money*. Translated by Peggy Kamuf. Chicago: University of Chicago Press, 1995.

―――. "Hospitality, Justice, and Responsibility: A Dialogue with Jacques Derrida." In *Questioning Ethics: Contemporary Debates in Philosophy,* edited by Richard Kearney and Mark Dooley. London: Routledge, 1999.

―――. "Plato's Pharmacy." In *Dissemination,* translated by Barbara Johnson, pp. 63-171. Chicago: University of Chicago Press, 1981.

————. *Rogues: Two Essays on Reason.* Translated by Pascale-Anne Brault and Michael Naas. Stanford: Stanford University Press, 2005.

————. "White Mythology: Metaphor in the Text of Philosophy." Translated by F. C. T. Moore. *New Literary History* 6, no. 1, "On Metaphor" (Autumn 1974): 5-74.

Descartes, René. *Meditations on the First Philosophy,* Meditation III. Translated by John Veitch. Classical Library, 1901 [1641]. Available at http://www.classicallibrary.org.

Dharmasiri, Gunapala. *A Buddhist Critique of the Christian Concept of God: A Critique of the Concept of God in Contemporary Christian Theology and Philosophy of Religion from the Point of View of Early Buddhism.* Colombo, Sri Lanka: Lake House Investments, 1974.

Dhavamony, Mariasusai. *Love of God according to Āaiva Siddhānta: A Study in the Mysticism and Theology of Āaivism.* Oxford: Clarendon, 1971.

Dodd, C. H. *The Authority of the Bible.* Harper Torchbook edition. New York: Harper and Brothers, 1958 [1929].

Dogmatic Constitution on the Catholic Faith. Vatican I (1870), Session 3, chap. 3. http://www.papalencyclicals.net/Councils/ecum20.htm.

Downing, F. Gerald. *Has Christianity a Revelation?* London: SCM, 1964.

D'Sa, Francis X. "Christian Scriptures and Other Scriptures: Thesis Towards a Study of the Significance of Scripture." *Indian Journal of Theology* 31, no. 3-4 (1982): 236-42.

Dufourmantelle, Anne, and Jacques Derrida. *Of Hospitality.* Translated by Rachel Bowlby. Stanford: Stanford University Press, 2000.

Dulles, Avery, S.J. *Models of Revelation.* Maryknoll, N.Y.: Orbis, 1992 [1983].

Dunn, James D. G. "Biblical Concepts of Revelation." Chapter 1 in *Divine Revelation,* edited by Paul Avis. Eugene, Ore.: Wipf and Stock, 2004 [1997].

Dupuis, Jacques. *Toward a Christian Theology of Religious Pluralism.* Maryknoll, N.Y.: Orbis, 1997.

Dyrness, William A. *Poetic Theology: God and the Poetics of Everyday Life.* Grand Rapids: Eerdmans, 2011.

Eck, D. L. *A New Religious America: How a "Christian Country" Has Become the World's Most Religiously Diverse Nation.* San Francisco: HarperCollins, 2001.

Eckel, Malcolm David. "Buddhism." In *Eastern Religions: Hinduism, Buddhism, Taoism, Confucianism, Shinto,* edited by Michael D. Coogan. Oxford: Oxford University Press, 2005.

Edwards, Jonathan. "Entry 880.1." In *The Works,* vol. 20, *The "Miscellanies,"* edited by Amy Plantinga Paauw, pp. 833-1152. New Haven: Yale University Press, 2002.

————. "Of Being." In *The Works of Jonathan Edwards,* vol. 6, *Scientific and Philosophical Writings,* edited by Wallace Anderson. New Haven: Yale University Press, 1980.

Eight Upanisadas with the Commentary of Sankaracarya. Translated by Swami Gambhirananda. Calcutta: Advaita Asharama, 1991.

Eliade, Mircea. "Paul Tillich and the History of Religions." In *The Future of Religions,* by Paul Tillich, edited by Jerald Brauer. New York: Harper and Row, 1966.

Ellacuria, Ignacio. "The Historicity of Christian Salvation." In *Mysterium Liberationis: Fundamental Concepts of Liberation Theology,* edited by Ignacio Ellacuría and Jon Sobrino, pp. 251-89. Maryknoll, N.Y.: Orbis, 1993.

Eller, Vernard. *The Language of Canaan and the Grammar of Feminism.* Grand Rapids: Eerdmans, 1982.

Ellul, Jacques. *The Humiliation of the Word.* Translated by Joyce Main Hanks. Grand Rapids: Eerdmans, 1985.

Eno, Robert B., S.S. "Authority." In *Augustine through the Ages: An Encyclopedia,* edited by Allan D. Fitzgerald, O.S.A. Grand Rapids: Eerdmans, 1999.

Erickson, Millard J. *God the Father Almighty: A Contemporary Exploration of the Divine Attributes.* Grand Rapids: Baker Academic, 1998.

Eriugena, John Scotus. *De divisione naturae.* Edited by Christoph Bernard Schlüter (1838). http://archive.org/details/dedivisionenatuooeriggoog.

Evans, James H., Jr. *We Have Been Believers: An African-American Systematic Theology.* Minneapolis: Fortress, 1992.

Faith and Order, Louvain 1971, Study Reports and Documents. "The Authority of the Bible." Faith and Order Paper 59. Geneva: World Council of Churches, 1971.

Faith and Order Commission of the World Council of Churches. "Scripture, Tradition and Traditions." [Fourth World Conference on Faith and Order (Montreal, 1963). Faith and Order Paper 40.] In *The Ecumenical Movement: An Anthology of Key Texts and Voices,* edited by Michael Kinnamon and Brian E. Cope, pp. 139-44. Geneva: WCC Publications; Grand Rapids: Eerdmans, 1997.

———. "A Treasure in Earthen Vessels: An Instrument for an Ecumenical Reflection on Hermeneutics." [Fifth World Conference on Faith and Order (Santiago de Compostela, 1993).] In *The Ecumenical Movement: An Anthology of Key Texts and Voices,* edited by Michael Kinnamon and Brian E. Cope. Geneva: WCC Publications; Grand Rapids: Eerdmans, 1997.

Feuerbach, Ludwig. *The Essence of Christianity.* Translated by Marian Evans from the 2nd German edition. London: John Chapman, 1845 [1841].

———. *Lectures on the Essence of Religion.* Translated by Ralph Manheim. New York: Harper and Row, 1967.

Fichte, Johann Gottlieb. "Über den Grund unseres Glaubens an eine göttliche Weltregierung" [1798]. In *Sämtliche Werke,* edited by I. H. Fichte, 5:177-89. Berlin: Verlag von Veit, 1845.

Fish, Stanley. *Is There a Text in This Class? The Authority of Interpretive Communities.* Cambridge: Harvard University Press, 1982.

Ford, David F. "God's Power and Human Flourishing: A Biblical Inquiry after Charles Taylor's *A Secular Age.*" Yale Center for Faith & Culture Resources, n.d., pp. 1-28. Available at http://www.yale.edu/faith/downloads/David%20Ford%20-%20God%27s%20Power%20and%20Human%20Flourishing%202008.pdf (5/23/2012).

———. "An Interfaith Wisdom: Scriptural Reasoning between Jews, Christians and Muslims." *Modern Theology* 22, no. 3 (2006): 345-66.

Ford, David F., and C. C. Pecknold, eds. *The Promise of Scriptural Reasoning.* Oxford: Blackwell, 2006.

Fortman, Edmund J., ed. *Theology of God: Commentary.* Contemporary Theology Series. New York: Bruce, 1968.

Fowler, Robert M. *Let the Reader Understand: Reader-Response Criticism and the Gospel of Mark.* Valley Forge, Pa.: Trinity, 2001.

Fox, Matthew. *The Coming of the Cosmic Christ: The Healing of Mother Earth and the Birth of a Global Renaissance.* San Francisco: Harper and Row, 1988.

Frame, John M. "Men and Women in the Image of God." In *Recovering Biblical Manhood and Womanhood: A Response to Evangelical Feminism,* edited by John Piper and Wayne Grudem, pp. 225-32. Wheaton, Ill.: Crossway, 1991.

Frank, Richard M. *Beings and Their Attributes: The Teachings of the Basrian School of the Mu'tazila in the Classical Period.* Albany: State University of New York Press, 1978.

Frankenberry, Nancy. "Classical Theism, Panentheism, and Pantheism: On the Relation between Construction and Gender Construction." *Zygon: Journal of Religion and Science* 28, no. 1 (March 1993): 29-46.

Fredericks, James L. *Buddhists and Christians: Through Comparative Theology to Solidarity.* Maryknoll, N.Y.: Orbis, 2004.

Frei, Hans W. *The Eclipse of Biblical Narrative: A Study in Eighteenth and Nineteenth Century Hermeneutics.* New Haven: Yale University Press, 1974.

————. *Types of Christian Theology.* New Haven: Yale University Press, 1992.

Frend, W. H. C. *The Rise of Christianity.* Philadelphia: Fortress, 1984.

Freud, Sigmund. *Moses and Monotheism.* Translated by Katherine Jones. Letchworth: Hogarth, 1939.

————. *New Introductory Lectures on Psycho-Analysis.* Translated by W. J. H. Sprott. Edited by James Strachey. Standard ed. New York: Norton, 1990 [1933].

————. *Totem and Taboo: Resemblance between the Psychic Lives of Savages and Neurotics.* Edited and translated by A. A. Brill. New York: Moffat, Yard and Co., 1918 [1912-1913].

Fromm, Erich. *The Art of Loving: An Enquiry into the Nature of Love.* New York: Harper and Row, 1956.

Gadamer, Hans-George. *Truth and Method.* Translated by Garrett Barden and John Cumming. New York: Crossroad, 1984.

Gardet, Louis. "Allāh." In *The Encyclopedia of Islam,* edited by H. A. R. Gibb et al., vol. 1, new ed. Leiden: Brill, 1979.

Gärtner, Bertil. *The Areopagus Speech and Natural Revelation.* Uppsala: Gleerup, 1955.

Gaudium et Spes: Pastoral Constitution on the Church in the Modern World (Vatican II). Available at www.vatican.va.

Geiselmann, Josef Rupert. *The Meaning of Tradition.* New York: Herder and Herder, 1966.

al-Ghazali [Ghazzali]. *The Alchemy of Happiness.* Translated by Claud Field (1909). Available at sacred-texts.com.

————. *The Incoherence of the Philosophers.* Provo, Utah: Brigham Young University Press, 1997.

————. *The Niche for Lights* [*Mishkat al-Anwarâ*]. Translated by W. H. T. Gairdner, 1924. Available at sacred-texts.com.

Gilkey, Langdon. *Naming the Whirlwind: The Renewal of God-language.* Indianapolis: Bobbs-Merrill, 1969.

Gimaret, Daniel. *Les noms divins en Islam: Exégèse lexicographique et théologique.* Paris: Cert, 1988.

Goizueta, Roberto S. "Locating the Absolutely Absolute Other: Toward a Transmodern Christianity." In *Thinking from the Underside of History: Enrique Dussel's Philosophy of Liberation,* edited by Linda Martin Alcoff and Eduardo Mendieta. New York: Rowman and Littlefield, 2000.

Goldenberg, Naomi R. *Changing of the Gods: Feminism and the End of Traditional Religions.* Boston: Beacon Press, 1979.

Goldingay, John. *Israel's Gospel.* Vol. 1 of *Old Testament Theology.* Downers Grove, Ill.: InterVarsity, 2003.

González, Justo L. *The Crusades: Piety Misguided.* Nashville: Graded Press, 1988.

———. *Mañana: Christian Theology from a Hispanic Perspective.* Nashville: Abingdon, 1990.

Gorder, A. Christian van. *No God but God: A Path to Muslim-Christian Dialogue on God's Nature.* Maryknoll, N.Y.: Orbis: 2003.

Gospel and the Church — *the Malta Report* (1972). Available at Centro Pro Unione Web site: http://www.pro.urbe.it/dia-int/l-rc/doc/e_l-rc_malta.html; also in Cardinal Walter Kasper, *Harvesting the Fruits: Basic Aspects of Christian Faith in Ecumenical Dialogue* (London and New York: Continuum, 2009).

Grant, Robert M. *The Early Christian Doctrine of God.* Charlottesville: University Press of Virginia, 1966.

Gregersen, Niels Henrik. "Three Varieties of Panentheism." In *IWWLM,* pp. 19-35.

Gregory of Nyssa. *The Life of Moses.* Translated by E. Ferguson and A. J. Malherbe. New York: Paulist, 1978.

Grenz, Stanley J. *The Named God and the Question of Being: A Trinitarian Theo-Ontology.* Louisville: Westminster John Knox, 2005.

———. *Reason for Hope: The Systematic Theology of Wolfhart Pannenberg.* New York: Oxford University Press, 1990.

———. *Rediscovering the Triune God: The Trinity in Contemporary Theology.* Minneapolis: Fortress, 2004.

———. *The Social God and Relational Self: A Trinitarian Theology of the Imago Dei.* Louisville: Westminster John Knox, 2001.

———. *Theology for the Community of God.* Grand Rapids: Eerdmans, 1994.

Grenz, Stanley J., and John R. Franke. *Beyond Foundationalism: Shaping Theology in a Postmodern Context.* Louisville: Westminster John Knox, 2001.

Grey, Mary. *The Wisdom of Fools? Seeking Revelation for Today.* London: SPCK, 1993.

Griffin, David Ray. *God, Power, and Evil: A Process Theodicy.* Philadelphia: Westminster, 1976.

Grudem, Wayne. *Systematic Theology: An Introduction to Biblical Doctrine.* Grand Rapids: Zondervan, 1994.

Gunton, Colin E. *Act and Being: Towards a Theology of the Divine Attributes.* Grand Rapids: Eerdmans, 2003.

———. "Augustine, the Trinity, and the Theological Crisis of the West." *Scottish Journal of Theology* 43, no. 1 (1990): 33-58.

————. *A Brief Theology of Revelation.* Edinburgh: T. & T. Clark, 1995.

————. *The Promise of Trinitarian Theology.* Edinburgh: T. & T. Clark, 1991.

Gutiérrez, Gustavo. *Essential Writings.* Edited by James B. Nicholoff. Minneapolis: Fortress, 1996.

————. *On Job: God-Talk and the Suffering of the Innocent.* Translated by Matthew J. O'Connell. Maryknoll, N.Y.: Orbis, 1987.

————. *A Theology of Liberation: History, Politics, and Salvation.* Translated and edited by Sister Caridad Inda and John Eagleson. Maryknoll, N.Y.: Orbis, 1986 [1973]; rev. ed. with a new introduction, 1988.

Hahn, Roger. "Laplace and the Mechanistic Universe." In *God and Nature: Historical Essays on the Encounter between Christianity and Science,* edited by David C. Lindberg and Ronald L. Numbers, pp. 256-76. Berkeley: University of California Press, 1986.

Haight, Roger, S.J. *Jesus Symbol of God.* Maryknoll, N.Y.: Orbis, 1999.

Hall, Douglas John. *Thinking the Faith.* Minneapolis: Fortress, 1991.

Hammond, Robert. *The Philosophy of Alfarabi and Its Influence on Medieval Thought.* New York: Hobson Book Press, 1947.

Hampson, Daphne. *Theology and Feminism.* Oxford: Basil Blackwell, 1990.

Hanh, Thich Nhat. *The Heart of Understanding: Commentaries on the Prajnaparamita Heart Sutra.* Edited by Peter Levitt. Berkeley, Calif.: Parallax Press, 1988.

————. "The Individual, Society, and Nature." In *The Path of Compassion: Writings on Socially Engaged Buddhism,* edited by Fred Eppsteiner, 2nd rev. ed. Berkeley, Calif.: Parallax Press, 1988.

————. *Our Appointment with Life: The Buddha's Teaching on Living in the Present.* Translation and commentary on The Sutra on Knowing the Better Way to Live Alone (Bhaddekaratta Sutta), translated by Annabel Laity. Berkeley, Calif.: Parallax Press, 1990.

————. *Zen Keys.* Translated by Albert and Jean Low. New York: Anchor Books, 1974. Available at http://www.scribd.com/doc/78466277/Zen-Keys.

Harnack, Adolf von. *What Is Christianity?* Translated by Thomas Bailey Sanders. 2nd rev. ed. London: Williams and Norgate; New York: Putnam, 1902, 1957.

Harries, Jim. "The Perceived Nature of God in Europe and in Africa: Dealing with 'Difference' in Theology, Focusing on 'Altered States of Consciousness.'" *Missiology* 38, no. 4 (2010): 395-409.

Harris, Elizabeth. "Human Existence in Buddhism and Christianity: A Christian Perspective." In *Buddhism and Christianity in Dialogue,* edited by Perry Schmidt-Leukel, pp. 29-52. London: SCM, 2005.

Harris, Sam. *The End of Faith: Religion, Terror, and the Future of Reason.* New York and London: Norton, 2004.

Hart, Trevor. *Faith Thinking: The Dynamics of Christian Theology.* Reprint, Portland, Ore.: Wipf and Stock, 2004.

Hartshorne, Charles. *The Divine Relativity: A Social Concept of God.* New Haven: Yale University Press, 1948.

————. "What Did Anselm Discover?" In *The Many-Faced Argument: Recent Studies on the Ontological Argument for the Existence of God,* edited by John Hick and Arthur C. McGill, pp. 321-33. New York: Macmillan, 1967.

Hauerwas, Stanley. *With the Grain of the Universe: The Church's Witness and Natural Theology.* London: SCM, 2002.

Hauerwas, Stanley, and William H. Willimon. *Resident Aliens: A Provocative Christian Assessment of Culture and Ministry for People Who Know That Something Is Wrong.* Nashville: Abingdon, 1989.

Haught, John F. *God and the New Atheism: A Critical Response to Dawkins, Harris, and Hitchens.* Louisville: Westminster John Knox, 2008.

Haynes, Stephen R., and Steven L. McKenzie, eds. *To Each Its Own Meaning: An Introduction to Biblical Criticisms and Its Application.* Louisville: Westminster John Knox, 1993.

Hebblethwaite, Brian. *The Ocean of Truth: A Defence of Objective Theism.* Cambridge: Cambridge University Press, 1988.

Hedley, Douglas. "Should Divinity Overcome Metaphysics? Reflections on John Milbank's Theology beyond Secular Reason and Confessions of a Cambridge Platonist." *Journal of Religion* 80 (2000): 271-98.

Hegel, G. F. W. *Hegel's Science of Logic.* Translated by A. V. Miller. New York: Humanities Press, 1969.

———. *The Phenomenology of Mind.* Translated by J. B. Baillie. London: George Allen and Unwin, 1964.

Heidegger, Martin. *Being and Time.* Translated by John Macquarrie and Edward Robinson. London: Blackwell, 1962.

———. *Identity and Difference.* Translated by Joan Stambaugh. New York: Harper and Row, 1969.

———. "What Is Metaphysics?" Inaugural Lecture, University of Freiburg, 1929. Athenaeum Library of Philosophy. http://evans-experientialism.freewebspace.com/heidegger5a.htm.

Heim, Karl. *Christian Faith and Natural Science.* Translated by E. B. Garside. New York: Harper and Brothers, 1953 [1949].

Heim, S. Mark. *The Depth of the Riches: A Trinitarian Theology of Religious Ends.* Grand Rapids: Eerdmans, 2001.

———. *Salvations: Truth and Difference in Religion.* Maryknoll, N.Y.: Orbis, 1995.

Henry, C. F. H. *God, Revelation, and Authority.* 6 vols. Waco, Tex.: Word, 1976-1983.

Heschel, Susannah. "Jewish Views of Jesus." In *Jesus in the World's Faiths: Leading Thinkers from Five Religions Reflect on His Meaning,* edited by Gregory A. Baker, pp. 149-51. Maryknoll, N.Y.: Orbis, 2008.

Hick, John. "The Epistemological Challenge of Religious Pluralism." *Faith and Philosophy* 14 (1997): 277-86.

———. *God and the Universe of Faiths: Essays in the Philosophy of Religion.* 2nd ed. London: Macmillan, 1977.

———. *God Has Many Names.* Philadelphia: Westminster, 1982.

———. *An Interpretation of Religion: Human Response to the Transcendent, Gifford Lectures 1986-87.* London: Macmillan, 1989.

————. *The Metaphor of God Incarnate: Christ and Christology in a Pluralistic Age.* London: SCM, 1993.

————. "The Non-Absoluteness of Christianity." In *The Myth of Christian Uniqueness: Toward a Pluralistic Theology of Religions,* edited by J. Hick and P. F. Knitter, pp. 16-36. Maryknoll, N.Y.: Orbis, 1987.

————. "The Possibility of Religious Pluralism: A Reply to Gavin D'Costa." *Religious Studies* 33 (1997): 161-66.

————. *Problems of Religious Pluralism.* London: Macmillan, 1988.

————. *The Rainbow of Faiths: Critical Dialogues on Religious Pluralism.* London: SCM, 1995. American edition: *A Christian Theology of Religious Pluralism.* Louisville: Westminster, 1995.

————. "The Reconstruction of Christian Belief for Today and Tomorrow: 1 and 2." *Theology* 73 (1970): 339-45 and 399-405.

————. "Religious Pluralism and the Divine: A Response to Paul Eddy." *Religious Studies* 31 (1995): 417-20.

————. "Rethinking Christian Doctrine in the Light of Religious Pluralism." In *Christianity and the Wider Ecumenism,* edited by Peter C. Phan, pp. 89-102. New York: Paragon House, 1990.

————. *The Second Christianity.* 3rd enlarged edition of *Christianity at the Centre.* London: SCM, 1983.

————, ed. *The Myth of God Incarnate.* London: SCM, 1977.

Hiriyanna, Mysore. *The Essentials of Indian Philosophy.* Delhi: Motilal Banarsidass, 2000.

Historic Creeds and Confessions. Edited by Rick Brannan. Available at www.ccel.org.

Hitchens, Christopher. *God Is Not Great: How Religion Poisons Everything.* New York and Boston: Twelve Hachette Book Group, 2007.

Hodge, Charles. *Systematic Theology.* 3 vols. New York: Scribner, Armstrong and Bros., 1857.

Holmes, Christopher. "God's Attributes as God's Clarities: Wolf Krötke's Doctrine of the Divine Attributes." *International Journal of Systematic Theology* 10, no. 1 (2008): 54-72.

————. "The Theological Function of the Doctrine of the Divine Attributes and the Divine Glory, with Special Reference to Karl Barth and His Reading of the Protestant Orthodox." *Scottish Journal of Theology* 61, no. 2 (2008): 206-23.

Hood, Robert E. *Must God Remain Greek? Afro Cultures and God-Talk.* Minneapolis: Fortress, 1990.

Hopkins, Thomas J. *The Hindu Religious Tradition.* Belmont, Calif.: Dickenson, 1971.

Horner, Robyn. *Jean-Luc Marion: A Theo-Logical Introduction.* Aldershot, U.K.: Ashgate, 2005.

Hudson, W. D. *A Philosophical Approach to Religion.* London: Macmillan, 1974.

Hume, David. *Dialogues concerning Natural Religion* (1776/1779). Edited by Henry D. Aiken. New York: Hafner, 1969.

————. *An Enquiry concerning Human Understanding* (1748). Harvard Classics 37. Copyright 1910 P. F. Collier and Son. In public domain, 1993, http://18th.eserver.org/hume-enquiry.html#10.

————. *Natural History of Religion* (1757). Edited by H. E. Root. Stanford: Stanford University Press, 2010 [1956].

Huntington, Samuel P. *The Clash of Civilizations and the Re-making of World Order.* New York: Simon and Schuster, 1996.

Hutchinson, W. R. *Religious Pluralism in America: The Contentious History of a Founding Idea.* New Haven: Yale University Press, 2003.

Huxley, Aldous. *The Perennial Philosophy: An Interpretation of the Great Mystics, East and West.* First Perennial Classics Edition. New York: HarperCollins, 2004 [1945].

Huxley, Julian S. *Religion without Revelation.* New ed. New Thinkers Library. Santa Barbara, Calif.: Greenwood Press Reprint, 1979 [1927; rev. 1957].

Hyman, Gavin. *The Predicament of Postmodern Theology: Radical Orthodoxy or Nihilist Textualism?* Louisville: Westminster John Knox, 2001.

Imbach, Josef. *Three Faces of Jesus: How Jews, Christians, and Muslims See Him.* Translated by Jane Wilde. Springfield, Ill.: Templegate Publishers, 1992.

Inwagen, Peter van. *Metaphysics.* Boulder, Colo.: Westview Press, 1993.

Irigaray, Luce. *I Love to You: Sketch of a Possible Felicity in History.* Translated by Alison Martin. New York and London: Routledge, 1996.

Isasi-Díaz, Ada María. *En la Lucha [In the Struggle]: A Hispanic Women's Liberation Theology.* Minneapolis: Fortress, 1993.

————. *Mujerista Theology: A Theology for the Twenty-first Century.* Maryknoll, N.Y.: Orbis, 1996.

Israel, Jonathan, ed. *Cambridge Texts in the Philosophy of History.* Cambridge: Cambridge University Press, 2007.

Jacoby, Susan. *Freethinkers: A History of American Secularism.* New York: Metropolitan, 2004.

Jan, Yun-Hua. "Dimensions of Indian Buddhism." In *The Malalasekera Commemoration Volume,* edited by O. H. de A. Wijesekera. Colombo, Sri Lanka: Malalasekera Commemoration Volume Editorial Committee, 1976.

Jantzen, Grace M. *Becoming Divine: Towards a Feminist Philosophy of Religion.* Bloomington and Indianapolis: Indiana University Press, 1999.

————. *Foundations of Violence: Death and the Displacement of Beauty.* Vol. 1. London and New York: Routledge Taylor and Francis Group, 2004.

Jaspers, Karl. *Philosophical Faith and Revelation.* Translated by E. B. Ashton. New York: Harper and Row, 1967.

Jauss, Hans Robert. *Towards an Aesthetic of Reception.* Minneapolis: University of Minnesota Press, 1982.

Jeanrond, Werner. *A Theology of Love.* London: T. & T. Clark, 2010.

Jenkins, Philip. *The Next Christendom: The Coming of Global Christianity.* Oxford: Oxford University Press, 2001.

Jenson, Robert W. "The Risen Prophet." In American Lutheran Church Board for World Mission and Inter-Church Cooperation Task Force on Christian Witness to Muslims (photocopied report, 1985).

————. *Systematic Theology.* Vol. 1, *The Triune God.* Oxford: University Press, 1997.

————. *The Triune Identity: God according to the Gospel.* Philadelphia: Fortress, 1982.

Jeremias, Joachim. *The Prayers of Jesus*. Philadelphia: Fortress, 1967.

Jewett, Paul King. *God, Creation, and Revelation*. Grand Rapids: Eerdmans, 1991.

Joh, Wonhee Anne. *Heart of the Cross: A Postcolonial Christology*. Louisville: Westminster John Knox, 2006.

John Paul II. *Veritatis Splendor* (1993). Available at www.vatican.va.

Johnson, Elizabeth. *Quest for the Living God: Mapping Frontiers in the Theology of God*. New York: Continuum, 2007.

————. *She Who Is: The Mystery of God in Feminist Theological Discourse*. New York: Crossroad, 1993.

————. *Women, Earth, and Creator Spirit*. New York: Paulist, 1993.

Johnson, Keith E. *Rethinking the Trinity and Religious Pluralism: An Augustinian Assessment*. Downers Grove, Ill.: InterVarsity, 2011.

Jones, Charles B. "Emptiness, Kenōsis, History, and Dialogue: The Christian Response to Masao Abe's Notion of 'Dynamic *Śūnyatā*' in the Early Years of the Abe-Cobb Buddhist-Christian Dialogue." *Buddhist-Christian Studies* 24 (2004): 117-33.

Jones, James W. *Blood That Cries Out from the Earth: The Psychology of Religious Terrorism*. Oxford and New York: Oxford University Press, 2008.

Jørgensen, Jonas Adelin. "'Word of God' and 'Spirit of God' in Christian and Islamic Christologies: A Starting Point for Interreligious Dialogue?" *Islam and Christian-Muslim Relations* 20, no. 4 (2009): 389-407.

Juergensmeyer, Mark. *The New Cold War? Religious Nationalism Confronts the Secular State*. Berkeley: University of California Press, 1993.

————. *Terror in the Mind of God: The Global Rise of Religious Violence*. 3rd rev. ed. Berkeley: University of California Press, 2003.

Jukko, Risto. *Trinitarian Theology in Christian-Muslim Encounters: Theological Foundations of the Work of the French Roman Catholic Church's Secretariat for Relations with Islam*. Helsinki: Luther-Agricola-Society, 2001.

Jüngel, Eberhard. *Entsprechungen: Gott, Wahrheit, Mensch; Theologische Erörterungen*. Munich: Chr. Kaiser, 1980.

————. *God as the Mystery of the World: On the Foundation of the Theology of the Crucified One in the Dispute between Theism and Atheism*. Translated by Darrell Guder. Grand Rapids: Eerdmans, 1983.

Kabbani, Rana. *A Letter to Christendom*. London: Virago, 2003.

Kant, Immanuel. *The Conflict of the Faculties*. Translated by Mary J. Gregor. New York: Abaris Books, 1979.

————. *The Critique of Practical Reason*. Translated by Thomas Kingsmill Abbott. Pennsylvania State University, 2010. http://www2.hn.psu.edu/faculty/jmanis/kant/Critique-Practical-Reason.pdf.

————. *The Critique of Pure Reason* [1781]. Translated by J. M. D. Meiklejohn. A Penn State Electronic Classic Series, 2010. http://www2.hn.psu.edu/faculty/jmanis/kant/Critique-Pure-Reason6x9.pdf.

————. *Lectures on the Philosophical Doctrine of Religion*. In *Religion and Rational Theology*, edited by Allen W. Wood and George di Giovanni. Cambridge: Cambridge University Press, 1996.

Kärkkäinen, Veli-Matti. "Calvin and Religions." In *John Calvin and Evangelical Theology: Legacy and Prospect,* edited by Sung Wook Chung, pp. 266-83. Carlisle, U.K.: Paternoster; Louisville: Westminster John Knox, 2009.

———. *The Doctrine of God: A Global Introduction.* Grand Rapids: Baker Academic, 2004.

———. "'Evil, Love and the Left Hand of God': The Contribution of Luther's Theology of the Cross to an Evangelical Theology of Evil." *Evangelical Quarterly* 74, no. 3 (July 2002): 215-34.

———. "Hope, Theology of." In *GDT,* pp. 404-5.

———. "'How to Speak of the Spirit among Religions': Trinitarian Prolegomena for a Pneumatological Theology of Religions." In *The Work of the Spirit: Pneumatology and Pentecostalism,* edited by Michael Welker, pp. 47-70. Grand Rapids: Eerdmans, 2006.

———. "'How to Speak of the Spirit among Religions': Trinitarian 'Rules' for a Pneumatological Theology of Religions." *International Bulletin of Missionary Research* 30, no. 3 (July 2006): 121-27.

———. "Karl Barth and the Theology of Religions." In *Karl Barth and Evangelical Theology: Convergences and Divergences,* edited by Sung Wook Chung, pp. 236-57. Carlisle, U.K.: Paternoster; Grand Rapids: Baker Academic, 2006.

———. *The Trinity: Global Perspectives.* Louisville: Westminster John Knox, 2007.

———. *The Trinity and Religious Pluralism: The Doctrine of the Trinity in Christian Theology of Religions.* Aldershot, U.K.: Ashgate, 2004.

———. "The Uniqueness of Christ and Trinitarian Faith." In *Christ the One and Only: A Global Affirmation of the Uniqueness of Jesus Christ,* edited by Sung Wook Chung, pp. 111-35. Exeter: Paternoster; Grand Rapids: Baker, 2005.

Kasper, Walter. *The God of Jesus Christ.* Translated by Matthew J. O'Connell. New York: Crossroad, 1986.

———. *Harvesting the Fruits: Basic Aspects of Christian Faith in Ecumenical Dialogue.* London and New York: Continuum, 2009.

———. *Jesus the Christ.* Translated by V. Green. London: Burns and Oates; New York: Paulist, 1977.

Kassis, Hanna. "The Qur'an." In *Experiencing Scripture in World Religions,* edited by H. Coward, pp. 63-84. Maryknoll, N.Y.: Orbis, 2000.

Kauffmann, Gordon D. *God the Problem.* Cambridge: Harvard University Press, 1972.

———. "Religious Diversity and Religious Truth." In *God, Truth, and Reality: Essays in Honour of John Hick,* edited by Arvind Sharma, pp. 143-64. New York: St. Martin's Press, 1993.

Keller, Catherine, Michael Nausner, and Mayra Rivera. "Introduction: Alien/Nation, Liberation, and the Postcolonial Underground." In *Postcolonial Theologies: Divinity and Empire,* edited by Catherine Keller, Michael Nausner, and Mayra Rivera. St. Louis: Chalice, 2004.

Kelly, J. N. D. *Early Christian Doctrines.* Rev. ed. New York: Harper and Row, 1978 [1960].

Kelsey, David H. "The Bible and the Christian Theology." *Journal of the American Academy of Religion* 48 (1980): 385-402.

————. *Eccentric Existence: A Theological Anthropology.* 2 vols. Louisville: Westminster John Knox, 2009.

————. "On Human Flourishing: A Theocentric Perspective." Yale Center for Faith and Culture Resources, n.d. http://www.yale.edu/faith/downloads/David%20Kelsey%20%20-%20God%27s%20Power%20and%20Human%20Flourishing%202008 .pdf (1/5/2012).

Kepnes, Steven. "A Handbook for Scriptural Reasoning." *Modern Theology* 22, no. 3 (2006): 367-83.

Kepnes, Steven, and Basit Bilal Koshul, eds. *Scripture, Reason, and the Contemporary Islam-West Encounter: Studying the "Other," Understanding the "Self."* Hampshire, U.K.: Palgrave Macmillan, 2007.

Khan, M. A. Muqtedar. "American Muslims and the Rediscovery of America's Sacred Ground." In *Taking Religious Pluralism Seriously: Spiritual Politics on America's Sacred Ground,* edited by B. A. McGraw and J. R. Formicola, pp. 127-47. Waco, Tex.: Baylor University Press, 2005.

Kimball, Charles. *When Religion Becomes Evil.* San Francisco: HarperSanFrancisco, 2002.

King, Winston L. "Religion." In *The Encyclopedia of Religion,* edited by Mircea Eliade, vol. 12. New York: Macmillan, 1987.

Klostermaier, Klaus K. *A Survey of Hinduism.* Albany: State University of New York Press, 1964.

Knitter, Paul F. *Introducing Theologies of Religions.* Maryknoll, N.Y.: Orbis, 2002.

Köchler, Hans, ed. *The Concept of Monotheism in Islam and Christianity.* Vienna: Wilhelm Braumüller, 1982.

Koenig, John. *New Testament Hospitality: Partnership with Strangers as Promise and Mission.* Philadelphia: Fortress, 1985.

Kogan, Michael S. *Opening the Covenant: A Jewish Theology of Christianity.* Oxford: Oxford University Press, 2008.

Kondothra, G. "The Word — Human and Divine: An Approach of Gregory Nazianzen." In *Studia Patristica,* edited by E. A. Livingstone, vol. 16, part 2. Berlin: Akademie Verlag, 1985.

Kopperi, Kari. *Paradoksien teologia: Lutherin disputaatio Heidelbergissä 1518.* Saarijärvi: Gummerrus, 1997.

Koshul, Basit. "Affirming the Self through Accepting the Other." In *Scriptures in Dialogue: Christians and Muslims Studying the Bible and the Qur'an Together,* edited by Michael Ipgrave. London: Church House Publishing, 2004.

Koyama, Kosuke. "Foreword by an Asian Theologian." In *Asian Christian Theology: Emerging Themes,* edited by Douglas J. Elwood. Philadelphia: Westminster, 1980.

Kropf, R. W. *Teilhard, Scripture, and Revelation.* Rutherford, N.J.: Fairleigh Dickinson University Press, 1980.

Krötke, Wolf. *Gottes Klarheiten: Eine Neuinterpretation der Gottes 'Eigenschaften.'* Tübingen: J. C. B. Mohr (Paul Siebeck), 2001.

Kumarappa, Bharatan. *The Hindu Conception of the Deity as Culminating in Rāmānuja.* London: Luzac and Co., 1934.

Kung, Chung Hyun. *The Struggle to Be the Sun Again.* Maryknoll, N.Y.: Orbis, 1993.

Küng, Hans. "A Christian Response [to Heinz Bechert: Buddhist Perspectives]." In *Christianity and World Religions: Paths to Dialogue with Islam, Hinduism, and Buddhism,* by Hans Küng, with Josef van Ess, Heinrich von Stietencron, and Heinz Bechert, translated by Peter Heinegg, pp. 306-28. New York: Doubleday, 1986.

———. *Does God Exist? An Answer for Today.* Translated by Edward Quinn. New York: Doubleday, 1980.

———. "God's Self-Renunciation and Buddhist Self-Emptiness: A Christian Response to Masao Abe." In *DEHF,* pp. 207-23.

Küng, Hans, with Josef van Ess, Heinrich von Stietencron, and Heinz Bechert. *Christianity and World Religions: Paths to Dialogue with Islam, Hinduism, and Buddhism.* 2nd ed. Maryknoll, N.Y.: Orbis, 1993.

LaCugna, Catherine Mowry. "The Baptismal Formula, Feminist Objections, and Trinitarian Theology." *Journal of Ecumenical Studies* 26, no. 2 (Spring 1989).

———. *God for Us: The Trinity and Christian Life.* San Francisco: HarperSanFrancisco, 1991.

———. "God in Communion with Us." In *Freeing Theology: The Essentials of Theology in Feminist Perspective,* edited by C. M. LaCugna. New York: HarperCollins, 1993.

———. Introduction to *The Trinity,* by Karl Rahner, translated by Joseph Donceel. New York: Seabury Press, 1997.

———. "Philosophers and Theologians on the Trinity." *Modern Theology* 2, no. 3 (1986): 169-81.

———. "The Trinitarian Mystery of God." In *Systematic Theology: Roman Catholic Perspectives,* edited by Francis Schüssler Fiorenza and John P. Galvin, 1:149-92. Minneapolis: Fortress, 1991.

Lakoff, George. *Don't Think of the Elephant!* White River Junction, Vt.: Chelsea Green Publishing, 2004.

Lancaster, Lewis. "Buddhist Literature: Its Canon, Scribes, and Editors." In *The Critical Study of Sacred Texts,* edited by Wendy Doniger O'Flaherty. Berkeley Religious Studies Series 2. Berkeley: Graduate Theological Union, 1979.

Lane, Anthony N. S. "Calvin's Use of the Fathers and Medievals." *Calvin Theological Journal* 16 (November 1981): 149-205.

Lanzetta, Beverly J. "The Mystical Basis of Panikkar's Thought." In *The Intercultural Challenge of Raimon Panikkar,* edited by Joseph Prabhu, pp. 91-105. Maryknoll, N.Y.: Orbis, 1996.

Lapide, Pinchas. *Israelis, Jews, and Jesus.* Translated by Peter Heinegg. Garden City, N.Y.: Doubleday, 1979.

Larson, Gerald James. "Contra Pluralism." In *The Intercultural Challenge of Raimon Panikkar,* edited by Joseph Prabhu, pp. 71-87. Maryknoll, N.Y.: Orbis, 1996.

Lash, Nicholas. *Theology of the Way to Emmaus.* London: SCM, 1986.

Latourelle, René. *Theology of Revelation: Including a Commentary on the Constitution "Dei Verbum" of Vatican II.* Staten Island, N.Y.: Alba House, 1966 [1963].

Lee, Jung Young. *Embracing Change: Postmodern Interpretations of the I Ching from a Christian Perspective.* London and Toronto: Associated University Presses, 1994.

————. *God Suffers for Us: A Systematic Inquiry into a Concept of Divine Passibility.* The Hague: Martinus Nijhoff, 1974.

————. *The Theology of Change: A Christian Concept of God in an Eastern Perspective.* Maryknoll, N.Y.: Orbis, 1979.

————. *The Trinity in Asian Perspective.* Nashville: Abingdon, 1996.

————. "The Yin-Yang Way of Thinking." In *Asian Christian Theology: Emerging Themes,* edited by Douglas J. Elwood, pp. 81-88. Philadelphia: Westminster, 1980.

Lefebure, Leo D. *The Buddha and the Christ: Explorations in Buddhist and Christian Dialogue.* Maryknoll, N.Y.: Orbis, 1993.

Leirvik, Oddbjørn. *Images of Jesus Christ in Islam.* 2nd ed. London and New York: Continuum, 2010.

Lentricchia, Frank. *After the New Criticism.* Chicago: University of Chicago Press, 1980.

Le Saux, Henri. *Saccidananda: A Christian Approach to Advaitic Experience.* Delhi: ISPCK, 1974.

Leslie, Ben. "Does God Have a Life? Barth and LaCugna on the Immanent Trinity." *Perspectives in Religious Studies* 24, no. 4 (Winter 1997): 377-98.

Levene, Nancy. "Spinoza's Bible: Concerning How It Is That 'Scripture, Insofar as It Contains the Word of God, Has Come Down to Us Uncorrupted.'" *Philosophy & Theology* 13, no. 1 (2001): 93-142.

Levenson, Jon D. "Do Christians and Muslims Worship the Same God?" *Christian Century* 121, no. 8 (April 20, 2004).

Levering, Miriam. Introduction to *Rethinking Scripture: Essays from a Comparative Perspective,* edited by M. Levering, pp. 1-17. Albany: State University of New York Press, 1989.

Levinas, Emmanuel. *Basic Philosophical Writings.* Edited by Adriaan T. Peperzak, Simon Critchley, and Robert Bernasconi. Bloomington: Indiana University Press, 1996.

————. *Difficult Freedom: Essays in Judaism.* Translated by Sean Hand. Baltimore: Johns Hopkins University Press, 1990.

————. *Totality and Infinity.* Ithaca, N.Y.: Cornell University Press, 2005.

Lewis, Hywell D. *Our Experience of God.* London: Allen and Unwin, 1959.

Lindbeck, George. *The Nature of Doctrine: Religion and Theology in a Postliberal Age.* Philadelphia: Westminster, 1984.

Lindberg, Carter. *Love: A Brief History through Western Christianity.* Oxford: Blackwell, 2008.

Lipner, Julius. *The Face of Truth: A Study of Meaning and Metaphysics in the Vedāntic Theology of Rāmanujā.* London: Macmillan, 1986.

————. *Hindus: Their Religious Beliefs and Practices.* London: Routledge, 1994.

Lloyd, Geoffrey E. R. "Greek Antiquity: The Invention of Nature." In *The Concept of Nature,* edited by John Torrance. Oxford: Oxford University Press, 1992.

Locke, John. *An Essay concerning Human Understanding* (1689). Translated by Peter Nidditch. Oxford: Oxford University Press, 1975. Available at http://oregonstate.edu/instruct/phl302/philosophers/locke.html.

Lodge, John G. *Romans 9–11: A Reader-Response Analysis.* Atlanta: Scholars Press, 1996.

Lossky, Vladimir. *In the Image and Likeness of God.* Edited by John H. Erickson and Thomas E. Bird. Crestwood, N.Y.: St. Vladimir's Seminary Press, 1985.

Louth, Andrew. "The Cosmic Vision of Saint Maximos the Confessor." In *IWWLM*, pp. 184-96.

Lowe, E. J. "Metaphysics, Opposition to." In *The Oxford Companion to Philosophy,* edited by Ted Honderich. New York: Oxford University Press, 1995.

Luckmann, Thomas. *The Invisible Religion: The Problem of Religion in Modern Society.* New York: Macmillan, 1967.

Luther, Martin. *The Large Catechism.* Translated by F. Bente and W. H. T. Dau. St. Louis: Concordia, 1921.

―――. *Word and Sacrament IV.* In *Luther's Works,* edited by Martin E. Lehmann, vol. 38. Philadelphia: Fortress, 1971.

Macchia, Frank. "God Says What the Text Says: Another Look at Karl Barth's View of Scripture." Unpublished manuscript, n.d.

MacDonald, Duncan B. *Development of Muslim Theology, Jurisprudence, and Constitutional Theory.* New York: Charles Scribner, 1903. Available at www.sacred-texts .com.

MacIntyre, Alasdair. *Whose Justice? What Rationality?* London: Duckworth, 1988.

Macquarrie, John. *Jesus Christ in Modern Thought.* London: SCM, 1990.

―――. *Principles of Systematic Theology.* London: SCM, 1977.

Madges, William. *God and the World: Christian Texts in Perspective.* Maryknoll, N.Y.: Orbis, 1999.

Maimonides, Moses. *Guide to the Perplexed.* Translated by M. Friedländer. New York: Dutton, 1904.

Mannermaa, Tuomo. *Kaksi rakkautta: Johdatus Lutherin uskonmaailmaan.* 2 vols. Helsinki: Suomen Teologisen Kirjallisuusseura, 1995.

Margerie, Bertrand de. *The Christian Trinity in History.* Translated by Edmund J. Fordman. Petersham, Mass.: St. Bede's Publications, 1982.

Marion, Jean-Luc. *Being Given: Toward a Phenomenology of Givenness.* Translated by Jeffrey L. Kosky. Stanford: Stanford University Press, 2002.

―――. *God without Being.* Translated by Thomas A. Carlson. Chicago: University of Chicago Press, 1991.

―――. *The Idol and Distance: Five Studies.* Translated by Thomas A. Carlson. New York: Fordham University Press, 2001.

―――. "The Saturated Phenomenon." In *Phenomenology and the "Theological Turn": The French Debate,* translated by Bernard G. Prusak, pp. 176-216. New York: Fordham University Press, 2000.

―――. "Sketch of a Phenomenological Concept of Gift." In *Postmodern Philosophy and Christian Thought,* edited by Merold Westphal, pp. 122-43. Bloomington: Indiana University Press, 1999.

Markham, Ian S. *Against Atheism: Why Dawkins, Hitchens, and Harris Are Fundamentally Wrong.* Oxford: Wiley-Blackwell, 2010.

Marsden, George. *The Soul of the University: From Protestant Establishment to Established Nonbelief.* New York: Oxford University Press, 1994.

Martey, Emmanuel. *African Theology: Inculturation and Liberation.* Maryknoll, N.Y.: Orbis, 1993.

Martin, David. *A General Theory of Secularization.* Oxford: Blackwell, 1979.

Martin, Raymond, and John Barresi. *The Rise and Fall of Soul and Self: An Intellectual History of Personal Identity.* New York: Columbia University Press, 2006.

Marty, Martin E. *When Faiths Collide.* Malden, Mass.: Blackwell, 2005.

Marty, Martin E., and R. Scott Appleby, eds. *The Fundamentalism Project.* 5 vols. Chicago: University of Chicago Press, 1991-1995.

Marx, Karl. *Critique of Feuerbach,* #11. In *Karl Marx: The Essential Writings,* edited by Frederic L. Bender. New York: Harper, 1972.

————. *Critique of Hegel's Philosophy of Right.* Edited with introduction and notes by Joseph O'Malley. Cambridge: Cambridge University Press, 1970.

al-Masih, Abd. "Allah? The God of Islam and the God of Christianity?" *St. Francis Magazine* 4, no. 2 (March 2007): 1-11.

Matei, Eugen. "The Practice of Community in Social Trinitarianism: A Theological Evaluation with Reference to Dimitru Staniloae and Jürgen Moltmann." Ph.D. diss., Fuller Theological Seminary, School of Theology, 2004.

Mathison, Keith A. *The Shape of Sola Scriptura.* Moscow, Idaho: Canon Press, 2001.

Maxey, Rosemary McCombs. "Who Can Sit at the Lord's Table? The Experience of Indigenous Peoples." In *Theology and Identity: Traditions, Movements, and Polity in the United Church of Christ,* edited by Daniel L. Johnson and Charles Hambrick-Stowe, pp. 51-63. New York: Pilgrim Press, 1990.

Mayr, Ernst. *What Evolution Is.* New York: Basic Books, 2001.

Mbiti, John. *Concepts of God in Africa.* London: SPCK, 1970.

McCalla, Arthur. *The Creationist Debate: The Encounter between the Bible and the Historical Mind.* Edinburgh: T. & T. Clark, 2006.

McClendon, James, Jr. *Biography as Theology: How Life Stories Can Remake Today's Theology.* Nashville: Abingdon, 1974.

McDaniel, J. B. *Gandhi's Hope: Learning from World Religions as a Path to Peace.* Maryknoll, N.Y.: Orbis, 2005.

McDonnell, Kilian, O.S.B. "Pneumatology Overview: Trinitarian Guidelines for Speaking about the Holy Spirit." *Catholic Theological Society of America Proceedings* 51 (1996): 188-98.

McFague, Sallie. *The Body of God: An Ecological Theology.* Minneapolis: Fortress, 1993.

————. *Metaphorical Theology: Models of God in Religious Language.* Philadelphia: Fortress, 1982.

————. *Models of God: Theology for an Ecological, Nuclear Age.* Minneapolis: Fortress, 1988.

McGrath, Alister. "Conclusion." In *Four Views on Salvation in a Pluralistic World,* edited by Dennis L. Okholm and Timothy R. Phillips. Grand Rapids: Zondervan, 1995.

————. *Dawkins' God: Genes, Memes, and the Meaning of Life.* Oxford: Blackwell, 2005.

————. *A Fine-Tuned Universe: The Quest for God in Science and Theology.* Gifford Lectures, 2009. Louisville: Westminster John Knox, 2009.

————. "Is Religion Evil?" Chapter 8 in *God Is Great, God Is Good: Why Believing in God*

Is Reasonable and Responsible, edited by William Lane Craig and Chad Meister, pp. 119-33. Downers Grove, Ill.: InterVarsity, 2009.

————. *Luther's Theology of the Cross: Martin Luther's Theological Breakthrough.* Oxford and New York: Oxford University Press, 1985.

————. *The Open Secret: A New Vision for Natural Theology.* Oxford: Blackwell, 2008.

————. *The Order of Things: Explorations in Scientific Theology.* Oxford: Wiley-Blackwell, 2006.

————. *A Scientific Theology.* Vol. 1, *Nature.* Vol. 2, *Reality.* Vol. 3, *Theory.* Grand Rapids: Eerdmans, 2001, 2002, 2003.

McInerny, Ralph. *Aquinas and Analogy.* Washington, D.C.: Catholic University of America Press, 1996.

McKim, Donald K. *The Bible in Theology and Preaching: How Preachers Use Scripture.* 2nd rev. ed. Nashville: Abingdon, 1994.

McKnight, Edgar V. "Errantry and Inerrancy: Baptists and the Bible." *Perspectives in Religious Studies* 12, no. 2 (Summer 1985).

————. *Postmodern Use of the Bible: The Emergence of Reader-Oriented Criticism.* Nashville: Abingdon, 1988.

Medley, Mark Samuel. *Imago Trinitatis: Toward a Relational Understanding of Being Human.* Ann Arbor: UMI Dissertation Series, 1995.

Metzger, Paul Louis. "The Relational Dynamic of Revelation: A Trinitarian Perspective." In *Trinitarian Soundings in Systematic Theology,* edited by Paul Louis Metzger. London and New York: Continuum, 2005.

Meyendorff, John. Introduction to Gregory Palamas, *The Triads,* edited by J. Meyendorff, translated by Nicholas Gendle, pp. 1-22. New York: Paulist, 1983.

Milbank, John. *Being Reconciled: Ontology and Pardon.* London and New York: Routledge, 2003.

————. "Founding the Supernatural: Political and Liberation Theology in the Context of Modern Catholic Thought." In *Theology and Social Theory: Beyond Secular Reason,* edited by J. Milbank. Oxford and Cambridge, Mass.: Blackwell, 1993.

————. *Theology and Social Theory: Beyond Secular Reason.* Oxford: Blackwell, 1990.

————. *The Word Made Strange: Theology, Language, Culture.* Oxford: Blackwell, 1997.

Milbank, John, Catherine Pickstock, and Graham Ward. *Radical Orthodoxy: A New Theology.* London and New York: Routledge, 1999.

Min, Anselm K. "From Autobiography to Fellowship of Others: Reflections on Doing Ethnic Theology Today." In *Journeys at the Margin: Toward an Autobiographical Theology in American-Asian Perspective,* edited by Peter C. Phan and Jung Young Lee. Collegeville, Minn.: Liturgical Press, 1999.

Mitchell, Basil, and Maurice Wiles. "Does Christianity Need a Revelation? A Discussion." *Theology* 83 (March 1980).

Miyahira, Nozomu. *Towards a Theology of the Concord of God: A Japanese Perspective on the Trinity.* Carlisle, U.K.: Paternoster, 2000.

Molnar, Paul D. *Divine Freedom and the Doctrine of the Immanent Trinity: In Dialogue with Karl Barth and Contemporary Theology.* London: T. & T. Clark, 2002.

Moltmann, Jürgen. *The Coming of God: Christian Eschatology.* Translated by Margaret Kohl. Minneapolis: Fortress, 1996.

————. *The Crucified God: The Cross of Christ as the Foundation and Criticism of Christian Theology.* Translated by R. A. Wilson and John Bowden. Minneapolis: Fortress, 1993.

————. *Experiences in Theology: Ways and Forms of Christian Theology.* Translated by Margaret Kohl. Minneapolis: Fortress, 2000.

————. *The Experiment Hope.* Edited by M. Douglas Meeks. Philadelphia: Fortress, 1975.

————. *God in Creation: A New Theology of Creation and the Spirit of God.* Translated by Margaret Kohl. Minneapolis: Fortress, 1993.

————. *The Spirit of Life: A Universal Affirmation.* Translated by Margaret Kohl. Minneapolis: Fortress, 2001.

————. *Theology of Hope: On the Ground and the Implications of a Christian Eschatology.* London: SCM, 1967 [1964].

————. *The Trinity and the Kingdom of God: The Doctrine of God.* Translated by Margaret Kohl. San Francisco: Harper and Row; London: SCM, 1981.

————. *The Way of Jesus Christ: Christology in Messianic Dimensions.* Translated by Margaret Kohl. Minneapolis: Fortress Press, 1993 [1989].

Moltmann-Wendel, Elisabeth. *I Am My Body: A Theology of Embodiment.* London: SCM, 1994.

Momen, Moojan. *An Introduction to Shi'i Islam.* New Haven: Yale University Press, 1985.

Morris, Thomas V. *Our Idea of God.* Notre Dame, Ind.: University of Notre Dame Press, 1991.

Mousalimas, Soterios A. "The Divine in Nature: Animism or Panentheism?" *Greek Orthodox Theological Review* 35, no. 4 (1990): 367-75.

————. "Immanence and Transcendence through the Seven Councils." *Greek Orthodox Theological Review* 42, no. 3-4 (Fall-Winter 1997): 375-80.

Mukerji, Bithika. "Christianity in the Reflection of Hinduism." In *Christianity through Non-Christian Eyes,* edited by P. J. Griffiths, pp. 228-33. Maryknoll, N.Y.: Orbis, 1990.

Müller, Max. *Sacred Books of the East.* 50 vols. Oxford: Oxford University Press, 1879-1910.

Muller, Richard A. " 'Duplex Cognitio Dei' in the Theology of Early Reformed Orthodoxy." *Sixteenth Century Journal* 10, no. 2 (1979): 51-61.

————. *Post-Reformation Reformed Dogmatics.* 4 vols. Grand Rapids: Baker Academic, 2003.

————. "Scripture." In *Oxford Encyclopedia of the Reformation,* edited by Hans J. Hillerbrand, 4:37. Oxford: Oxford University Press, 1996.

A Muslim Theologian's Response to Christianity: Ibn Taymiyya's "Al-Jawab Al-Sahih." Edited and translated by Thomas F. Michel, S.J. Delmar, N.Y.: Caravan Books, 1984.

Nagarjuna. *Stanzas on the Middle Path.* Several translations with differing renderings are available; a current one is *Root Stanzas on the Middle Way: Mulamadhyamaka-karika.* Translated by Padmakura Translation Group. N.p.: Edition Padmakara, 2008.

Nagel, Thomas. *The View from Nowhere.* Oxford: Oxford University Press, 1986.

Nakamura, Hajime. *A History of Early Vedānta Philosophy.* Delhi: Motilal Banarsidass, 1983.

Nambara, Minoru. "Ultimate Reality in Buddhism and Christianity: A Buddhist Perspective." In *Buddhism and Christianity in Dialogue,* edited by Perry Schmidt-Leukel, pp. 117-37. London: SCM, 2005.

Narayanan, Vasudha. "Hinduism." In *Eastern Religions: Hinduism, Buddhism, Taoism, Confucianism, Shinto,* edited by Michael D. Coogan, pp. 110-12. Oxford: Oxford University Press, 2005.

Nasr, Seyyed Hossein. *Les Musulmans: Consultation islamo-chrétienne.* Edited by Muhammad Arkoun. Paris: Beauchesne, 1972.

———. "The Word of God: The Bridge between Him, You, and Us." In *A Common Word: Muslims and Christians on Loving God and Neighbor,* edited by Miroslav Volf and Prince Ghazi bin Muhammad bin Talal, pp. 110-17. Grand Rapids: Eerdmans, 2010.

Nazir-Ali, Michael. *Frontiers in Muslim-Christian Encounter.* Oxford: Regnum, 1987.

Nebelsick, Harold P. *Circles of God: Theology and Science from the Greeks to Copernicus.* Edinburgh: Scottish Academic, 1985.

Needham, Nick. "The Filioque Clause: East or West?" *Scottish Bulletin of Evangelical Theology* 15, no. 2 (1997): 142-62.

Nelson-Pallmeyer, Jack. *Is Religion Killing Us? Violence in the Bible and the Quran.* Harrisburg, Pa.: Trinity, 2003.

Nesteruk, Alexei V. "The Universe as Hypostatic Inherence in the Logos of God: Panentheism in the Eastern Orthodox Perspective." In *IWWLM,* pp. 169-83.

Neumaier, Eva K. "The Dilemma of Authoritative Utterance in Buddhism." In *Experiencing Scripture in World Religions,* edited by H. Coward, pp. 138-67. Maryknoll, N.Y.: Orbis, 2000.

Neville, Robert Cummings. Foreword to *The Metaphysics of Experience: A Companion to Whitehead's Process and Reality,* by Elisabeth M. Kraus, 2nd ed. New York: Fordham University Press, 1998.

———. *Normative Cultures.* Albany: State University of New York Press, 1995.

Newbigin, Lesslie. "The Enduring Validity of Cross-Cultural Mission." *International Bulletin of Missionary Research* 12 (1988).

———. *The Gospel in a Pluralist Society.* Grand Rapids: Eerdmans, 1989.

———. "Religious Pluralism and the Uniqueness of Jesus Christ." *International Bulletin of Missionary Research* 13, no. 2 (April 1989): 50-52, 54.

———. *A Word in Season: Perspectives on Christian World Missions.* Edited by Eleanor Jackson. Grand Rapids: Eerdmans; Edinburgh: Saint Andrews Press, 1994.

Newlands, George, and Allen Smith. *Hospitable God: The Transformative Dream.* Surrey, U.K.: Ashgate, 2010.

Newton, Isaac. *Opticks.* 2nd ed. London: 1718 [1706].

Ng, David. "A Path of Concentric Circles: Toward an Autobiographical Theology of Community." In *Journeys at the Margin: Toward an Autobiographical Theology in American-Asian Perspective,* edited by Peter C. Phan and Jung Young Lee. Collegeville, Minn.: Liturgical Press, 1999.

"Nibbana Sutta: Total Unbinding (1)" (*Udana* 8.1). Translated by T. Bhikkhu. *Access to*

Insight, July 8, 2010, http://www.accesstoinsight.org/tipitaka/kn/ud/ud.8.01.than
.html.

Nicholas of Cusa. *De Pace Fidei and Cribratio Alkorani: Translation and Analysis.* Edited
and translated by Jasper Hopkins. 2nd ed. Minneapolis: Banning Press, 1994. Also
available at http://jasper-hopkins.info/DePace12-2000.pdf.

———. *On God as Not-Other: A Translation and an Appraisal of "De li non aliud."* Translated by Jasper Hopkins. Minneapolis: Banning Press, 1987.

———. "On the Hidden God [*De Deo Abscondito*]." In *A Miscellany of Nicholas of Cusa,*
translated by Jasper Hopkins. Minneapolis: Banning Press, 1994. Available at
http://jasper-hopkins.info/DeDeoAbscon12-2000.pdf.

———. *Selected Spiritual Writings.* Translated by H. Lawrence Bond. Mahwah, N.J.:
Paulist, 1997.

Nietzsche, Friedrich Wilhelm. *Ecce Homo: How One Becomes What One Is.* Translated
by Anthony M. Ludovici. Mineola, N.Y.: Dover, 2004 [1888].

———. *Gay Science (The Joyful Wisdom).* Translated by Thomas Common. Lawrence,
Kans.: Digireads, 2009 [1882/1887].

———. *Human, All Too Human: A Book for Free Spirits.* Translated by Alexander Harvey.
Chicago: Charles H. Kerr and Co., 1908 [1878].

———. "On Truth and Lies in a Nonmoral Sense." In *Philosophy and Truth,* translated
and edited by Daniel Breazeale. Atlantic Highlands, N.J.: Humanities Press, 1979.

———. *Thus Spake Zarathustra: A Book for All and None.* Translated by Alexander Tille.
London and New York: Macmillan, 1896 [1883-1885].

Nishitani, Keiji. *Religion and Nothingness.* Translated by Jan Van Bragt. Berkeley: University of California Press, 1982.

Nissiotis, Nikos A. "The Main Ecclesiological Problem of the Second Vatican Council
and the Position of the Non-Roman Churches Facing It." *Journal of Ecumenical
Studies* 2 (1965): 31-62.

———. "Unity of Scripture and Tradition: An Eastern Orthodox Contribution to the
Prolegomena to Hermeneutics." *Greek Orthodox Theological Review* 11, no. 2 (Winter 1965-1966): 183-208.

Norris, Christopher. *Deconstruction: Theory and Practice.* London: Methuen, 1982.

Nostra Aetate: Declaration on the Relation of the Church to Non-Christian Relations (Vatican II). Available at www.vatican.va.

Nyamiti, Charles. *African Tradition and Christian God.* Eldoret, Kenya: Gaba Publications, 1972.

———. *Christ as Our Ancestor.* Gweru, Zimbabwe: Mambo Press, 1984.

———. "The Trinity from an African Ancestral Perspective." *African Christian Studies*
12, no. 4 (1996): 51-52.

Nygren, Anders. *Agape and Eros.* Philadelphia: Westminster, 1953.

Oberman, Heiko. *The Harvest of Medieval Theology: Gabriel Biel and Late Medieval Nom-
inalism.* Rev. ed. Grand Rapids: Eerdmans, 1967.

O'Brien, John A. *Truths Men Live By: A Philosophy of Religion and Life.* New York: Macmillan, 1948.

O'Collins, Gerald. *The Tripersonal God: Understanding and Interpreting the Trinity.* New York and Mahwah, N.J.: Paulist, 1999.

Oden, Thomas C. *Systematic Theology.* Vol. 1, *The Living God.* San Francisco: Harper and Row, 1987.

O'Hanlon, Gerald F. *The Immutability of God in the Theology of Hans Urs von Balthasar.* Cambridge and New York: Cambridge University Press, 1990.

Oldstone-Moore, Jennifer. "Taoism." In *Eastern Religions: Hinduism, Buddhism, Taoism, Confucianism, Shinto,* edited by Michael D. Coogan, pp. 212-13. Oxford: Oxford University Press, 2005.

Olson, Roger E., and Christopher A. Hall. *The Trinity.* Grand Rapids: Eerdmans, 2002.

"Oneness Pentecostalism." In *The New International Dictionary of Pentecostal and Charismatic Movements,* edited by Stanley M. Burgess, pp. 936-44. Grand Rapids: Zondervan, 2002.

Ong, Walter J. *Orality and Literacy: The Technologizing of the Word.* New York: Methuen, 1982.

Oord, Thomas Jay. *Defining Love.* Grand Rapids: Brazos, 2010.

Ott, Heinrich. "The Convergence: Sunyata as a Dynamic Event." In *DEHF,* pp. 127-35.

Otto, Rudolf. *The Idea of the Holy: An Inquiry into the Non-Rational Factor in the Idea of the Divine and Its Relation to the Rational.* Translated by John W. Harvey. New York: Oxford University Press, 1958 [1917].

Oxford Dictionary of the Christian Church. Edited by F. L. Cross and E. A. Livingstone. 2nd ed. Oxford: Oxford University Press, 1983.

Panikkar, Raimundo. *The Cosmotheandric Experience: Emerging Religious Consciousness.* Edited with introduction by Scott Eastham. Maryknoll, N.Y.: Orbis, 1993.

————. *The Intrareligious Dialogue.* New York: Paulist, 1978.

————. "The Invisible Harmony: A Universal Theory of Religion or a Cosmic Confidence in Reality?" In *Toward a Universal Theology of Religion,* edited by Leonard Swidler. Maryknoll, N.Y.: Orbis, 1987.

————. "The Jordan, the Tiber, and the Ganges: Three Kairological Moments of Christic Self-Consciousness." In *The Myth of Christian Uniqueness: Toward a Pluralistic Theology of Religions,* edited by John Hick and Paul F. Knitter, pp. 89-116. Maryknoll, N.Y.: Orbis, 1987.

————. *The Silence of God, the Answer of the Buddha.* Maryknoll, N.Y.: Orbis, 1989.

————. *The Trinity and the Religious Experience of Man.* Maryknoll, N.Y.: Orbis; London: Darton, Longman and Todd, 1973; also titled *The Trinity and the World Religions.*

————. *The Unknown Christ of Hinduism.* London: Darton, Longman and Todd, 1964.

Pannenberg, Wolfhart. "Analogy and Doxology." In *Basic Questions in Theology,* translated by George H. Kehm, 1:211-38. Philadelphia: Fortress, 1970.

————. "Anthropology and the Question of God." In *The Idea of God and Human Freedom,* translated by R. A. Wilson. Philadelphia: Westminster, 1973.

————. *Anthropology in Theological Perspective.* Translated by Matthew J. O'Connell. Philadelphia: Westminster, 1985.

————. "The Crisis of the Scripture Principle." In *Basic Questions in Theology,* translated by George H. Kehm, vol. 1. Philadelphia: Fortress, 1970.

————. "Father, Son, Spirit: Problems of a Trinitarian Doctrine of God." *Dialog* 26, no. 4 (1987): 250-57.

————. "God as Spirit — and Natural Science." *Zygon: Journal of Religion and Science* 36, no. 4 (December 2001): 783-94.

————. "God's Love and the Kenosis of the Son: A Response to Masao Abe." In *DEHF,* pp. 245-50.

————. *Metaphysics and the Idea of God.* Translated by Philip Clayton. Grand Rapids: Eerdmans, 1990.

————. "Speaking about God in the Face of Atheist Criticism." In *The Idea of God and Human Freedom,* translated by R. A. Wilson. Philadelphia: Westminster, 1973.

————, ed. *Revelation as History: A Proposal for a More Open, Less Authoritarian View of an Important Theological Concept.* Translated by David Granskou. London: Collier-Macmillan, 1968 [1961].

Parekh, Bhikhu. "The Voice of Religion in Political Discourse." In *Religion, Politics, and Peace,* edited by Leroy Rouner, pp. 63-84. Notre Dame, Ind.: University of Notre Dame Press, 1999.

Park, Andrew Sung. *The Wounded Heart of God: The Asian Concept of Han and the Christian Doctrine of Sin.* Nashville: Abingdon, 1993.

Parrinder, Geoffrey. *Jesus in the Qur'an.* London and Oxford: Sheldon Press and Oneworld Publication, 1995.

————. "Triads." In *The Encyclopedia of Religion,* edited by Lindsay Jones, 2nd ed., 14:9345-50. Detroit: Macmillan Reference USA, 2005.

Pascal, Blaise. "The Memorial." In *Pensées and Other Writings,* translated by Honor Levi. New York: Oxford University Press, 1995.

Peacocke, Arthur. "Articulating God's Presence in and to the World Unveiled by the Sciences." In *IWWLM,* pp. 137-54.

————. "Introduction: 'In Whom We Live and Move and Have Our Being'?" In *IWWLM,* pp. xviii-xxii.

————. *Paths from Science towards God: The End of All Our Exploring.* Oxford: Oneworld, 2001.

Peirce, Charles Sanders. "On a New List of Categories." In *The Essential Peirce,* edited by Nathan Houser and Christian Kloesel, vol. 1. Bloomington: Indiana University Press, 1992.

Pelikan, Jaroslav. *Christianity and Classical Culture: The Metamorphosis of Natural Theology in the Christian Encounter with Hellenism.* New Haven: Yale University Press, 1993.

————. *The Emergence of the Catholic Tradition (100-600).* Vol. 1 of *The Christian Tradition: A History of the Development of Doctrine.* Chicago: University of Chicago Press, 1971.

————. *Reformation of Church and Dogma (1300-1700).* Vol. 4 of *The Christian Tradition: A History of the Development of Doctrine.* Chicago: University of Chicago Press, 1984.

Penelhum, Terence. "Revelation and Philosophy." In *Divine Revelation,* edited by Paul Avis. Eugene, Ore.: Wipf and Stock, 2004.

Perdue, Leo G. *Wisdom and Creation*. Nashville: Abingdon, 1994.

Peters, Ted. *God — the World's Future: Systematic Theology for a Postmodern Era*. Minneapolis: Fortress, 1992.

————. *God as Trinity: Relationality and Temporality in Divine Life*. Louisville: Westminster John Knox, 1993.

Peterson, Daniel J. "Speaking of God after the Death of God." *Dialog* 44, no. 3 (Fall 2005): 207-26.

Peterson, Gregory R. "Whither Panentheism?" *Zygon: Journal of Religion and Science* 36, no. 3 (2001): 395-405.

Pew Forum on Religion and Public Life. "US Religious Landscape Survey, February 2008." http://religions.pewforum.org/pdf/report-religious-landscape-study-full.pdf.

Phillips, D. Z. *Faith and Philosophical Enquiry*. London: Routledge and Kegan Paul, 1970.

Photios. *On the Mystagogy of the Holy Spirit*. Astoria, N.Y.: Studion Publishers, 1983.

Pickstock, Catherine. *After Writing: On the Liturgical Consummation of Philosophy*. Oxford: Blackwell, 1998.

————. "Reply to David Ford and Guy Collins." *Scottish Journal of Theology* 54 (2001): 405-22.

Pinnock, Clark H. *Flame of Love: A Theology of the Holy Spirit*. Downers Grove, Ill.: InterVarsity, 1996.

————. *Most Moved Mover: A Theology of God's Openness*. Grand Rapids: Baker Academic, 2001.

Pinnock, Clark H., et al. *The Openness of God: A Biblical Challenge to the Traditional Understanding of God*. Downers Grove, Ill.: InterVarsity, 1994.

Piper, John. "A Common Word between Us?" *Desiring God,* January 23, 2008. http://www.desiringgod.org/blog/posts/a-common-word-between-us.

Pittenger, Norman. *The Divine Triunity*. Philadelphia: United Church Press, 1977.

Placher, William C. *A History of Christian Theology*. Philadelphia: Westminster, 1983.

Plantinga, Alvin J. "Reason and Belief in God." In *Faith and Philosophy: Reason and Belief in God,* edited by Alvin Plantinga and Nicholas Wolterstorff, pp. 16-93. Notre Dame, Ind.: University of Notre Dame Press, 1983.

————. "The Reformed Objection to Natural Theology." *Proceedings of the American Catholic Philosophical Association* 54 (1980): 49-62.

Plaskow, Judith, and Carol P. Christ, eds. *Weaving the Visions: New Patterns in Feminist Spirituality*. San Francisco: HarperCollins, 1989.

Plato in Twelve Volumes. Vol. 12. Translated by Harold N. Fowler. Cambridge: Harvard University Press; London: William Heinemann, 1921.

Plotinus. *The Six Enneads*. Translated by Stephen Mackenna and B. S. Page. London: P. L. Warner, 1917-30. Available at www.sacred-texts.com.

Pohl, Christine D. *Making Room: Recovering Hospitality as a Christian Tradition*. Grand Rapids: Eerdmans, 1999.

Polanyi, Michael. *Personal Knowledge*. New York: Harper Torchbooks, 1964.

————. *The Tacit Dimension*. New York: Anchor Books, 1967.

Polanyi, Michael, and Harry Prosch. *Meaning*. Chicago: University of Chicago Press, 1975.

Polkinghorne, John. *Faith, Science, and Understanding.* New Haven: Yale University Press, 2000.

————. "God and Physics." Chapter 4 in *God Is Great, God Is Good: Why Believing in God Is Reasonable and Responsible,* edited by William Lane Craig and Chad Meister, pp. 65-77. Downers Grove, Ill.: InterVarsity, 2009.

————. *The God of Hope and the End of the World.* New Haven: Yale University Press, 2002.

————. *Science and the Trinity: The Christian Encounter with Reality.* New Haven: Yale University Press, 2004.

————. *Theology in the Context of Science.* New Haven: Yale University Press, 2009.

————. "Wolfhart Pannenberg's Engagement with the Natural Sciences." *Zygon: Journal of Religion and Science* 34, no. 1 (March 1999): 151-58.

————, ed. *The Trinity and the Entangled World: Relationality in Physical Science and Theology.* Grand Rapids: Eerdmans, 2010.

Porter, Andrew. "Cultural Imperialism and Protestant Missionary Enterprise, 1780-1914." *Journal of Commonwealth and Imperial History* 25, no. 2 (September 1977).

Postmodern Bible. New Haven: Yale University Press, 1995.

Powell, Samuel M. *The Trinity in German Thought.* Cambridge: Cambridge University Press, 2001.

Prem, Sri Krishna. "From *The Yoga of the Bhagavat Gita.*" In *The Ways of Religion,* edited by Roger Eastman, pp. 41-46. New York: Harper and Row, 1975.

Prestige, George L. *God in Patristic Thought.* London and Toronto: W. Heinemann, 1936.

Pseudo-Dionysius. *The Complete Works.* Translated by Colm Luibheid et al. New York: Paulist, 1987.

Pui-lan, Kwok. *Postcolonial Imagination and Feminist Theology.* Louisville: Westminster John Knox, 2005.

Quenstedt, J. A. *Theologi didactico-polemica sive systema theologicum,* I. Leipzig, 1715.

Rad, Gerhard von. *Wisdom in Israel.* Translated by James D. Martin. Nashville: Abingdon, 1972.

Radhakrishnan, Sarvepalli. *Indian Philosophy.* Vol. 2. London: George Allen and Unwin, 1927.

————. "The Nature of Hinduism." In *The Ways of Religion,* edited by Roger Eastman, pp. 10-22. New York: Harper and Row, 1975.

————, ed. *The Principal Upanisads.* London: George Allen and Unwin, 1953.

Rahman, Fazlur. *Major Themes of the Qur'an.* 2nd ed. Minneapolis: Bibliotheca Islamica, 1980.

Rahner, Karl. "The Body in the Order of Salvation." In *Theological Investigations,* vol. 17, translated by Margaret Kohl, pp. 71-89. New York: Crossroad, 1981.

————. *Foundations of Christian Faith: An Introduction to the Idea of Christianity.* Translated by William V. Dych. New York: Crossroad, 2004.

————. "A Fragmentary Aspect of a Theological Evaluation of the Concept of Future." In *Theological Investigations,* vol. 5, translated by David Bourke. Baltimore: Helicon, 1966.

————. *Hearers of the Word.* Revised by J. B. Metz. Translated by Michael Richards. New York: Herder and Herder, 1969.

————. "Mysticism." In *Encyclopedia of Theology: The Concise Sacramentum Mundi.* New York: Seabury Press, 1975.

————. "The Quest for Approaches Leading to an Understanding of the Mystery of the God-Man Jesus." In *Theological Investigations,* vol. 13, translated by David Bourke, pp. 195-200. New York: Seabury Press, 1975.

————. *The Trinity.* Translated by Joseph Donceel. London: Burns and Oates, 1970.

Rahula, Walpola. *What the Buddha Taught.* Rev. ed. New York: Grove Press, 1974.

Raj, A. S. *A New Hermeneutic of Reality: Raimon Panikkar's Cosmotheandric Vision.* Bern: Peter Lang, 1998.

Ramachandra, Vinoth. *The Recovery of Mission: Beyond the Pluralist Paradigm.* Grand Rapids: Eerdmans, 1996.

Ramanuja. *Vedanta Sutras.* In *SBE,* vol. 48.

Rambachan, Anantanand. "Hinduism." In *Experiencing Scripture in World Religions,* edited by H. Coward, pp. 85-112. Maryknoll, N.Y.: Orbis, 2000.

Ramm, Bernard. *The Pattern of Religious Authority.* Grand Rapids: Eerdmans, 1959.

Ramsey, Ian T. *Religious Language: An Empirical Placing of Theological Phrases.* London: SCM, 1957.

Raven, Charles E. *Natural Religion and Christian Theology.* 2 vols. Cambridge: Cambridge University Press, 1953.

Ray, Reginald A. "Buddhism: Sacred Text Written and Realized." In *The Holy Book in Comparative Perspective,* edited by Frederick M. Denny and Rodney L. Taylor, pp. 148-80. Columbia: University of South Carolina Press, 1985.

Reed, Esther. "Revelation in Feminist Theology and Philosophy." In *Divine Revelation,* edited by Paul Avis. Eugene, Ore.: Wipf and Stock, 2004 [1997].

Régnon, Théodore de. *Études de théologie positive sur la sainte Trinité.* 3 vols. Paris: Retaux, 1892-1898.

Richard, Lucien. *Living the Hospitality of God.* New York: Paulist, 2000.

Richard, Pablo. "Theology in the Theology of Liberation." In *Mysterium Liberationis,* edited by Ignacio Ellacuria, S.J., and Jon Sobrino, S.J., pp. 150-68. Maryknoll, N.Y.: Orbis; San Francisco: CollinsDove, 1993.

Richie, Tony. *Speaking by the Spirit: A Pentecostal Model for Interreligious Dialogue.* Lexington, Ky.: Emeth Press, 2011.

Ricoeur, Paul. "The Hermeneutical Function of Distanciation." Translated by D. Pellauer. *Philosophy Today* 17, nos. 2-4 (1973): 129-41.

————. *On Translation.* Translated by Eileen Brennan. London: Routledge, 2006.

————. *Oneself as Another.* Translated by Kathleen Blamey. Chicago: University of Chicago Press, 1992.

————. *The Symbolism of Evil.* Translation by Emerson Buchanan. Boston: Beacon Press, 1969 [1967].

Rippin, Andrew, and Jan Knappert. *Textual Sources for the Study of Islam.* Totowa: Barnes and Noble Books, 1986.

Rivera, Mayra. *The Touch of Transcendence: A Postcolonial Theology of God.* Louisville: Westminster John Knox, 2007.

Roberts, Nancy. "Trinity vs. Monotheism: A False Dichotomy?" *Muslim World* 101 (January 2011): 73-93.

Robinette, Brian. "A Gift to Theology? Jean-Luc Marion's 'Saturated Phenomenon' in Christological Perspective." *Heythrop Journal* 48 (2007): 86-108.

Robinson, Richard H., and Willard L. Johnson. *The Buddhist Religion: An Historical Introduction.* Belmont, Calif.: Wadsworth, 1997.

Rodríguez, Rubén Rosario. *Racism and God-Talk: A Latino/a Perspective.* New York: New York University Press, 2008.

Rosenbaum, Jonathan. "Judaism: Torah and Tradition." In *The Holy Book in Comparative Perspective,* edited by Frederick M. Denny and Rodney L. Taylor, pp. 10-35. Columbia: University of South Carolina Press, 1985.

Rubenstein, Richard L. "Holocaust, Sunyata, and Holy Nothingness: An Essay in Inter-religious Dialogue." In *DEHF,* pp. 93-112.

Ruether, Rosemary Radford. *Gaia and God: An Ecofeminist Theology of Earth Healing.* San Francisco: Harper, 1992.

―――. *Sexism and God-Talk: Toward a Feminist Theology.* Boston: Beacon Press, 1983.

Runia, Klaas. "The Challenge of the Modern World to the Church." *European Journal of Theology* 2, no. 2 (1993): 145-62.

Russell, Bertrand. *Why I Am Not a Christian and Other Essays on Religion and Related Subjects.* New York: Simon and Schuster, 1957.

Russell, Heidi Ann. "Keiji Nishitani and Karl Rahner: A Response to Nihility." *Buddhist-Christian Studies* 28 (2008): 27-41.

Russell, Letty M. *Just Hospitality: God's Welcome in a World of Difference.* Louisville: Westminster John Knox, 2009.

Saarinen, Risto. "Eri uskonnot — sama Jumala? Jumalakuva uskontojen välisessä dialogissa." In *Jumalan kasvot: Jumalan ihmisen todellisuudessa,* edited by Risto A. Ahonen and Hans-Olof Kvist. Tampere: Kirkon Tutkimuskeskus, 1995.

―――. *Gottes Wirken auf uns: Die transzendentale Deutung des Gegenwart-Christi-Motivs in der Lutherforschung.* Stuttgart: Franz Steiner, 1989.

Sabatino, Charles J. "No-God: Reflections on Masao Abe's Symbol of God as Self-Emptying." *Horizons* 29, no. 1 (2002): 64-79.

Sachedina, Abdulaziz. *The Islamic Roots of Democratic Pluralism.* New York: Oxford University Press, 2001.

―――. *The Role of Islam in the Public Square: Guidance or Governance?* Amsterdam: Amsterdam University Press, 2006.

Saeki, Y. P. *The Nestorian Documents and Relics in China.* Tokyo: Academy of Oriental Culture, 1937.

Sahas, Daniel J. *John of Damascus on Islam: The "Heresy of the Ishmaelites."* Leiden: Brill, 1972.

Samartha, Stanley J. *Courage for Dialogue: Ecumenical Issues in Inter-Religious Relationships.* Maryknoll, N.Y.: Orbis, 1982.

————. "The Cross and the Rainbow: Christ in a Multireligious Culture." In *Asian Faces of Jesus*, edited by R. S. Sugirtharajah, pp. 104-23. Maryknoll, N.Y.: Orbis, 1995.

————. "Unbound Christ: Towards Christology in India Today." In *Asian Christian Theology: Emerging Themes*, edited by Douglas J. Elwood, pp. 145-60. Philadelphia: Westminster, 1980.

Sankara. *Aitareya and Taittīrīa Upanishads and Sri Sankara's Commentary*. Translated by S. Sitarama Sastri. Madras: India Printing Works, 1923. Available at http://ia700504 .us.archive.org/23/items/AitareyataittiriyaUpanishadsWithShankaraBhashya -English/05AitareyataittiriyaUpanishadsWithShankaraBhashya-English.pdf.

————. *Vedanta-Sutras*. In *SBE*, vols. 34 and 38.

Sanneh, Lamin. "Do Christians and Muslims Worship the Same God?" *Christian Century* 121, no. 9 (May 4, 2004): 35.

————. *Translating the Message: The Missionary Impact on Culture*. Maryknoll, N.Y.: Orbis, 1989.

————. *Whose Religion Is Christianity? The Gospel beyond the West*. Grand Rapids: Eerdmans, 2003.

Sawyerr, Harry. *Creative Evangelism, towards a New Christian Encounter*. London: Lutterworth Press, 1968.

Schimmel, A. M., and Abdoldjavad Falaturi, eds. *We Believe in One God*. London: Burns and Oates, 1979.

Schleiermacher, Friedrich. *The Christian Faith*. Edited by H. R. Mackintosh and J. S. Stewart. London: T. & T. Clark, 1999.

————. *Hermeneutics: The Handwritten Manuscripts*. Edited by Heinz Kimmerle. Translated by James Duke and Jack Forstman. American Academy of Religion Texts and Translation Series, no. 1. Atlanta: Scholars Press, 1977.

————. *On Religion: Speeches to Its Cultured Despisers*. Translated by R. Crouter. Cambridge: Cambridge University Press, 1988.

Schmidt-Leukel, Perry. "Intimate Strangers: An Introduction." In *Buddhism and Christianity in Dialogue*, edited by Perry Schmidt-Leukel, pp. 1-26. London: SCM, 2005.

Schroeder, H. J. *Disciplinary Decrees of the General Councils: Text, Translation, and Commentary*. St. Louis: B. Herder, 1937.

Schultz, Kevin M. "Secularization: A Bibliographic Essay." *Hedgehog Review* 8, no. 1-2 (Spring-Summer 2006): 170-77.

Schwartz, Regina. *The Curse of Cain: The Violent Legacy of Monotheism*. Chicago: University of Chicago Press, 1997.

Schwarz, Hans. *The God Who Is: The Christian God in a Pluralistic World*. Eugene, Ore.: Cascade, 2011.

Schwöbel, Christopher. "The Creature of the Word: Recovering the Ecclesiology of the Reformers." In *On Being the Church: Essays on the Christian Community*, edited by Colin Gunton and D. W. Hardy, pp. 110-55. Edinburgh: T. & T. Clark, 1989.

Segal, Eliezer. "Judaism." In *Experiencing Scripture in World Religions*, edited by H. Coward, pp. 15-33. Maryknoll, N.Y.: Orbis, 2000.

Segundo, Juan Luis. *The Liberation of Theology*. Maryknoll, N.Y.: Orbis, 1976.

Seitz, C. R. "Handing Over the Name: Christian Reflection on the Divine Name YHWH."

In *Trinity, Time, and Church: A Response to the Theology of Robert W. Jenson,* edited by C. Gunton, pp. 23-41. Portland, Ore.: Wipf and Stock, 2011.

Sen, Keshub Chunder. *Keshub Chunder Sen.* Edited by David C. Scott. Bangalore: Christian Literature Society, 1979.

Sharma, Arvind. *Classical Hindu Thought: An Introduction.* Oxford: Oxford University Press, 2000.

Shehadeh, Imad N. "Do Muslims and Christians Believe in the Same God?" *Bibliotheca Sacra* 161 (January-March 2004): 14-26.

Shults, F. LeRon. *Reforming the Doctrine of God.* Grand Rapids: Eerdmans, 2005.

————. *Reforming Theological Anthropology.* Grand Rapids: Eerdmans, 2003.

Singh, Nagendra K. *God in Indian Islamic Theology.* New Delhi: Sarup and Sons, 1996.

Slade, Stanley David. "The Theological Method of Juan Luis Segundo." Ph.D. diss., Fuller Theological Seminary, School of Theology, 1979.

Smart, Ninian, and Steve Konstantine. *Christian Systematic Theology in a World Context.* Minneapolis: Fortress, 1991.

Smith, Christian, ed. *The Secular Revolution: Power, Interests, and Conflicts in the Secularization of American Public Life.* Berkeley: University of California Press, 2003.

Smith, James K. A. *The Fall of Interpretation: Philosophical Foundations for a Creational Hermeneutic.* Downers Grove, Ill.: InterVarsity, 2000.

————. *Introducing Radical Orthodoxy: Mapping a Post-Secular Theology.* Grand Rapids: Baker Academic, 2004.

Smith, Jonathan Z. *Drudgery Divine: On the Comparison of Early Christianities and the Religions of Late Antiquity.* Chicago: University of Chicago Press, 1990.

Smith, W. C. *Meaning and End of Religion.* Minneapolis: Fortress, 1991 [1962].

Snyder, Mary Hembrow. *The Christology of Rosemary Radford Ruether: A Critical Introduction.* Mystic, Conn.: Twenty-third Publications, 1988.

Soskice, Janet Martin. *Metaphor and Religious Language.* Oxford: Clarendon, 1985.

Sontag, Susan. *Against Interpretation, and Other Essays.* New York: Farrar, Straus and Giroux, 1966.

Stamoolis, James J. "Scripture and Tradition in the Orthodox Church." *Evangelical Review of Theology* 19, no. 2 (April 1995): 131-43.

Stanley, Brian. *The Bible and the Flag: Protestant Missions and British Imperialism in the Nineteenth and Twentieth Centuries.* Trowbridge, U.K.: Apollos, 1990.

————. "Conversion to Christianity: The Colonization of the Mind?" *International Review of Mission* 92, no. 366 (July 2003): 315-31.

Steinkellner, E. "Buddhismus: Religion oder Philosophie? Und: Vom Wesen de Buddha." In *Der Buddhismus als Anfrage an Christliche Theologie und Philosophie,* edited by A. Bsteh, pp. 251-62. Mödling: Verlag St. Gabriel, 2000.

Stinton, Diane. "Africa, East and West." In *An Introduction to Third World Theologies,* edited by John Parratt. Cambridge: Cambridge University Press, 2004.

Strong, Augustus Hopkins. *Systematic Theology.* 3 vols. Philadelphia: Griffith and Rowland, 1907.

Stroup, George W. *The Promise of Narrative Theology.* Atlanta: John Knox, 1981.

Studer, Basil. *The Grace of Christ and the Grace of God in Augustine of Hippo: Christocen-trism or Theocentrism?* Collegeville, Minn.: Liturgical Press, 1997.

———. *Trinity and Incarnation: The Faith of the Early Church.* Edited by Andrew Louth. Translated by Matthias Westerhoff. Collegeville, Minn.: Liturgical Press, 1993.

Stylianopoulos, Theodore, and S. Mark Heim, eds. *Spirit of Truth: Ecumenical Perspectives on the Holy Spirit.* Brookline, Mass.: Holy Cross Orthodox Press, 1986.

Suchocki, Marjorie Hewitt. *Divinity and Diversity: A Christian Affirmation of Religious Pluralism.* Nashville: Abingdon, 2003.

———. Introduction to *Trinity in Process: A Relational Theology of God,* edited by Joseph A. Bracken, S.J., and Marjorie Hewitt Suchocki. New York: Continuum, 1997.

———. "Sunyata, Trinity, and Community." In *DEHF,* pp. 136-49.

Sugirtharajah, R. S. *Asian Biblical Hermeneutics and Postcolonialism: Contesting the Interpretations.* Sheffield: Sheffield Academic Press; Maryknoll, N.Y.: Orbis, 1999.

———. *The Bible and the Third World: Precolonial, Colonial, and Postcolonial Encounters.* Cambridge: Cambridge University Press, 2001.

———, ed. *Voices from the Margin: Interpreting the Bible in the Third World.* Maryknoll, N.Y.: Orbis, 2006.

Swanson, Mark N. "The Trinity in Christian-Muslim Conversation." *Dialog: A Journal of Theology* 44, no. 3 (Fall 2005): 258-63.

Swinburne, Richard. *The Coherence of Theism.* Oxford: Oxford University Press, 1977.

———. "God-Talk Is Not Evidently Nonsense." In *Philosophy of Religion,* edited by Brian Davies. Oxford: Oxford University Press, 2000.

Takenaka, Masao. *God Is Rice: Asian Cultures and Christian Faith.* Geneva: World Council of Churches, 1986.

Tanner, Kathryn. *Economy of Grace.* Minneapolis: Fortress, 2005.

———. *God and Creation in Christian Theology: Tyranny and Empowerment?* Minneapolis: Fortress, 1988.

———. *Theories of Culture.* Minneapolis: Fortress, 1997.

Tavard, George H. *Holy Writ or Holy Church: The Crisis of the Protestant Reformation.* New York: Harper and Brothers, 1959.

Taylor, Charles. *A Secular Age.* Cambridge, Mass., and London: Harvard University Press, Belknap Press, 2007.

———. *Sources of the Self: The Making of the Modern Identity.* Cambridge: Harvard University Press, 1989.

Taylor, Mark C. *About Religion: Economies of Faith in Virtual Culture.* Chicago: University of Chicago Press, 1999.

———. *After God.* Chicago: University of Chicago Press, 2007.

———. *Altarity.* Chicago: University of Chicago Press, 1987.

———. *Erring: A Postmodern A/theology.* Chicago: University of Chicago Press, 1984.

Teilhard de Chardin, P. *Christianity and Evolution.* Translated by René Hague. New York: Harcourt Brace Jovanovich, 1971.

———. "Outline of a Dialectic of Spirit." In *Activation of Energy,* translated by René Hague, pp. 143-51. New York: Harcourt Brace Jovanovich; London: Collins, 1970.

Also available at http://ia600503.us.archive.org/24/items/ActivationOfEnergy/Activation_of_Energy.pdf.

Temple, William. "Revelation and Its Mode" (Gifford Lecture #12). In *Nature, Man, and God*, pp. 301-25. London: Macmillan, 1935.

Tennent, Timothy C. *Theology in the Context of World Christianity: How the Global Church Is Influencing the Way We Think about and Discuss Theology*. Grand Rapids: Zondervan, 2007.

Tertullian. *Letter on Patience*. Available at www.pseudepigrapha.com/LostBooks/tertullian_patience.htm.

Thatamanil, John J. *The Immanent Divine: God, Creation, and the Human Predicament*. Minneapolis: Fortress, 2006.

Thiel, John E. *Senses of Tradition: Continuity and Development in Catholic Faith*. Oxford: Oxford University Press, 2000.

Thomas, David. "The Doctrine of the Trinity in the Early Abbasid Era." In *Islamic Interpretations of Christianity*, edited by Lloyd Ridgeon, pp. 78-98. New York: St. Martin's Press, 2001.

Thomas, Kenneth J. "Allah in Translations of the Bible." *Technical Papers for the Bible Translator* 52, no. 3 (July 2001): 301-6.

Thompson, John. *The Holy Spirit in the Theology of Karl Barth*. Princeton Theological Monograph Series. Eugene, Ore.: Pickwick, 1991.

————. *Modern Trinitarian Perspectives*. New York: Oxford University Press, 1994.

Thompson, Marianne Meye. *The Promise of the Father*. Louisville: Westminster John Knox, 2000.

Tillich, Paul. *Biblical Religion and the Search for Ultimate Reality*. Chicago: University of Chicago Press, 1955.

————. *The Future of Religions*. Edited by Jerald Brauer. New York: Harper and Row, 1966.

Toland, John. *Christianity Not Mysterious* (1669). Edited and introduction by John Vladimir Price. History of British Deism 8. London: Routledge, 1995.

Torrance, Thomas F. *The Christian Doctrine of God: One Being Three Persons*. Edinburgh: T. & T. Clark, 1996.

————. "Knowledge of God and Speech about Him according to John Calvin." In *Calvin's Theology, Theology Proper, Eschatology*, edited by R. C. Gamble. New York and London: Garland Press, 1992.

————. "The Problem of Natural Theology in the Thought of Karl Barth." *Religious Studies* 6 (1970): 121-35.

————. *Transformation and Convergence in the Frame of Knowledge*. Grand Rapids: Eerdmans, 1984.

————, ed. *Theological Dialogue between Orthodox and Reformed Churches*. Vol. 2. Edinburgh: Scottish Academic Press, 1993.

Tracy, David. *The Analogical Imagination: Christian Theology and the Culture of Pluralism*. New York: Crossroad, 1981.

————. *Blessed Rage for Order: The New Pluralism in Theology*. New York: Seabury Press, 1975.

Trigg, Roger. *Rationality and Religion: Does Faith Need Reason?* Oxford: Blackwell, 1998.

———. *Rationality and Science: Can Science Explain Everything?* Oxford: Blackwell, 1993.

Upadhyay, Brahmabandhab. *The Writings of Brahmabandhab Upadhyay.* Edited by Julius Lipner and George Gispert-Sauch. 2 vols. Bangalore: United Theological College, 1991, 2002.

Vähäkangas, Mika. "Trinitarian Processions as Ancestral Relationships in Charles Nyamiti's Theology: A European Lutheran Critique." *Svensk Missionstidskrift* 86 (1998): 251-63. Reprinted from *Revue Africaine de Théologie* 21 (1997): 61-75.

Van der Leeuw, Gerardus. *Religion in Essence and Manifestation.* Translated by J. E. Turner. 2 vols. London: Allen and Unwin, 1938 [1933]; reprint, New York: Harper and Row, 1963.

Vanhoozer, Kevin J. "The Bible: Its Relevance for Today." In *God, Family, and Sexuality,* edited by David W. Torrance. Carberry: Handsel Press, 1997.

———. "Does the Trinity Belong in the Theology of Religions? On Angling in the Rubicon and the 'Identity' of God." In *The Trinity in a Pluralistic Age: Theological Essays on Culture and Religion,* edited by K. J. Vanhoozer, pp. 41-71. Grand Rapids: Eerdmans, 1997.

———. *The Drama of Doctrine: A Canonical-Linguistic Approach to Christian Theology.* Louisville: Westminster John Knox, 2005.

———. *Is There Meaning in This Text?* Grand Rapids: Zondervan, 1998.

Van Huyssteen, Wentzel J. *Alone in the World? Human Uniqueness in Science and Theology.* Grand Rapids: Eerdmans, 2006.

Vattimo, Gianni. *After Christianity.* Translated by Luca D'Isanto. New York: Columbia University Press, 2002.

———. *The End of Modernity: Nihilism and Hermeneutics in Post-modern Culture.* Translated by Jon R. Snyder. Baltimore: Johns Hopkins University Press, 1988.

———. *Nihilism and Emancipation: Ethics, Politics, and Law.* Edited by Santiago Zabala. Translated by William McCuaig. New York: Columbia University Press, 2004.

Vélez de Cea, Abraham. "A New Direction for Comparative Studies of Buddhists and Christians: Evidence from Nāgārjuna and John of the Cross." *Buddhist-Christian Studies* 26 (2006): 139-55.

Vincent of Lérins. *The Commonitorium of Vincentius of Lerins.* Edited by Reginald S. Doxon. Cambridge Patristic Texts. Available at http://www.fordham.edu/halsall/ancient/434lerins-canon.html.

Vischer, Lukas, ed. *Spirit of God, Spirit of Christ: Ecumenical Reflections on the Filioque Controversy.* London: SPCK, 1981.

Vishnu Purana, The. Translated by Horace Hayman Wilson. 1840. Available at www.ccel.org.

Volf, Miroslav. *After Our Likeness: The Church as the Image of the Trinity.* Grand Rapids: Eerdmans, 1998.

———. *Allah: A Christian Response.* New York: HarperCollins, 2011.

———. *Exclusion and Embrace: A Theological Exploration of Identity, Otherness, and Reconciliation.* Nashville: Abingdon, 1996.

———. "Forgiveness, Reconciliation, and Justice: A Theological Contribution to a More

Peaceful Social Environment." *Millennium — Journal of International Studies* 29 (2000): 861-77.

———. "Human Flourishing." Presentation at the Institute for Theological Inquiry, n.d. http://www.yale.edu/faith/jewishchristianconference/documents/Miroslav_Volf .pdf (5/23/2012).

———. "Jehovah on Trial." *Christianity Today,* April 27, 1998, pp. 32-35.

———. " 'The Trinity Is Our Social Program': The Doctrine of the Trinity and the Shape of Social Engagement." *Modern Theology* 14, no. 3 (1998): 403-23.

Volf, Miroslav, and Dorothy C. Bass, eds. *Practicing Theology: Beliefs and Practices in Christian Life.* Grand Rapids: Eerdmans, 2002.

Voorst, Robert E. van. *Anthology of World Scriptures.* 4th ed. Belmont, Calif.: Wadsworth, 2002.

Vroom, Hendrik. *No Other Gods: Christian Belief in Dialogue with Buddhism, Hinduism, and Islam.* Grand Rapids: Eerdmans, 1996.

Waldenfels, Hans. *Absolute Nothingness: Foundations for a Buddhist-Christian Dialogue.* Translated by J. W. Heisig. New York: Paulist, 1980.

Walls, Andrew F. *The Missionary Movement in Christian History: Studies in the Transmission of Faith.* Maryknoll, N.Y.: Orbis, 1996.

Ward, Keith. *Divine Action: Examining God's Role in an Open and Emergent Universe.* Philadelphia and London: Templeton Foundation Press, 2007.

———. *God, Chance, and Necessity.* Oxford: Oneworld, 1996.

———. *Images of Eternity: Concepts of God in Five Religious Traditions.* Oxford: Oneworld, 1998.

———. *Is Religion Dangerous?* Grand Rapids: Eerdmans, 2006.

———. *Religion and Revelation: A Theology of Revelation in the World's Religions.* Oxford: Clarendon, 1994.

———. "The World as the Body of God: A Panentheistic Metaphor." In *IWWLM,* pp. 62-72.

Ware, Kallistos (Bishop of Diokleia). "God Immanent Yet Transcendent: The Divine Energies according to Saint Gregory Palamas." In *IWWLM,* pp. 157-68.

———. "The Holy Trinity: Model for Personhood-in-Relation." In *The Trinity and the Entangled World: Relationality in Physical Science and Theology,* edited by John Polkinghorne, pp. 107-29. Grand Rapids: Eerdmans, 2010.

———. *The Orthodox Church.* New York: Penguin Books, 1993.

Warfield, B. B. *Revelation and Inspiration.* New York: Oxford University Press, 1927.

Warrior, Robert Allan. "Canaanites, Cowboys and Indians: Deliverance, Conquest and Liberation Theology Today." *Christianity and Crisis* 49, no. 12 (September 11, 1989): 261-65.

Watt, W. Montgomery. *Free Will and Predestination in Early Islam.* London: Luzac and Co., 1949.

———. *Islam and Christianity Today: A Contribution to Dialogue.* London: Routledge and Kegan Paul, 1983.

———. "Islamic Theology and the Christian Theologian." *Hibbert Journal* 49 (1950-1951): 242-48.

Weber, Otto. *Foundations of Dogmatics.* Translated by D. L. Guder. 2 vols. Grand Rapids: Eerdmans, 1981.

Webster, John. *Holiness.* Grand Rapids: Eerdmans, 2003.

————. "The Holiness and Love of God." *Scottish Journal of Theology* 57, no. 3 (2004): 249-68.

Weinandy, Thomas. "The Immanent and Economic Trinity." *Thomist* 57 (1993): 655-66.

Welch, Alford. "Al-Kur'ān." In *The Encyclopedia of Islam.* New ed. Leiden: Brill, 1981.

Wells, Harold. "The Holy Spirit and Theology of the Cross: Significance for Dialogue." *Theological Studies* 53 (1992): 476-92.

"Westminster Confession of Faith, The." In *The Creeds of the Churches,* edited by John H. Leith. 3rd ed. Atlanta: John Knox, 1982.

Westphal, Merold. *Overcoming Onto-Theology: Toward a Postmodern Christian Faith.* New York: Fordham University Press, 2001.

White, Stephen K. *Political Theory and Postmodernism.* Cambridge: Cambridge University Press, 1991.

Whitehead, Alfred North. *Adventures of Ideas.* New York: Free Press, 1967.

————. *Process and Reality.* Corrected by David R. Griffin and Donald W. Sherburn. New York: Free Press, 1978.

————. *Religion in the Making.* New York: Living Age Books, 1960.

————. *Science and the Modern World.* New York: Free Press, 1967.

Wiebe, Steven L. *Christian Theology in a Pluralistic Context: A Methodological and Constructive Inquiry in the Doctrine of Creation.* New York: Peter Lang, 2007.

Wiles, Maurice. "Revelation and Divine Action." In *Divine Revelation,* edited by Paul Avis. Eugene, Ore.: Wipf and Stock, 2004 [1997].

————. "Some Reflections on the Origins of the Doctrine of the Trinity." In *Working Papers in Doctrine,* pp. 1-17. London: SCM, 1976.

Williams, Delores S. *Sisters in the Wilderness: The Challenge of Womanist God-Talk.* Maryknoll, N.Y.: Orbis, 1993.

Williams, Paul. "Aquinas Meets the Buddhists: Prolegomenon to an Authentically Thomas-ist Basis for Dialogue." *Modern Theology* 20, no. 1 (January 2004): 91-121.

Wilson-Kastner, Patricia. *Faith, Feminism, and the Christ.* Philadelphia: Fortress, 1983.

Winkler, Lewis. *Contemporary Muslim and Christian Responses to Religious Plurality: Wolfhart Pannenberg in Dialogue with Abdulaziz Sachedina.* Eugene, Ore.: Pickwick, 2011.

Witherington, Ben, III, and Laura M. Ice. *The Shadow of the Almighty: Father, Son, and Spirit in Biblical Perspective.* Grand Rapids and Cambridge, U.K.: Eerdmans, 2002.

Wittgenstein, Ludwig. *Culture and Value.* Edited by G. H. Wright and Heikki Nyman. Translated by Peter Winch. Chicago: University of Chicago Press, 1980.

————. "Lecture on Ethics" (1929). In *From Modernism to Postmodernism: An Anthology Expanded,* edited by Lawrence E. Cahoone, 2nd ed. Malden, Mass.: Wiley-Blackwell, 2003.

————. *Philosophical Investigations.* Translated by G. E. M. Anscombe. Reprint of 3rd ed. (1945). Oxford: Blackwell, 1988.

Wolfson, Elliot R. "Judaism and Incarnation: The Imaginal Body of God." In *Christianity in Jewish Terms,* edited by Tikva Frymer-Kensky et al., pp. 239-54. Boulder, Colo.: Westview Press, 2000.

Wolfson, H. A. "The Muslim Attributes and the Christian Trinity." *Harvard Theological Review* 49, no. 1 (January 1956): 1-18.

Wolterstorff, Nicholas. *Divine Discourse: Philosophical Reflections on the Claim That God Speaks.* Cambridge: Cambridge University Press, 1995.

Wood, Susan. "Participatory Knowledge of God in Liturgy." In *Knowing the Triune God: The Work of the Spirit in the Practices of the Church,* edited by James J. Buckley and David S. Yeago, pp. 93-116. Grand Rapids: Eerdmans, 2001.

Woodruff, David M. "Examining Problems and Assumptions: An Update on Criticisms of Open Theism." *Dialog* 47, no. 1 (Spring 2008): 53-63.

Wren, Brian A. *What Language Shall I Borrow? God Talk in Worship: A Male Response to Feminist Theology.* London: SCM, 1989.

Wright, George E. *God Who Acts: Biblical Theology as Recital.* Studies in Biblical Theology 8. London: SCM, 1952.

Wright, N. T. *The New Testament and the People of God.* Vol. 1. Minneapolis: Fortress, 1992.

Wynne, Jeremy. "The Livingness of God; or, The Place of Substance and Dynamism in a Theology of the Divine Perfections." *International Journal of Systematic Theology* 13, no. 2 (April 2011): 190-203.

Yogananda, Paramahansa. *The Second Coming of Christ: The Resurrection of the Christ within You; A Revelatory Commentary on the Original Teachings of Jesus.* 2 vols. Los Angeles: Self-Realization Fellowship, 2004.

Yong, Amos. "The Turn to Pneumatology in Christian Theology of Religions: Conduit or Detour?" *Journal of Ecumenical Studies* 35 (1998): 437-54.

Zayd, Abu. *Al-Ghazali on Divine Predicates and Their Properties.* Lahore: Sh. Muhammad Ashraft, 1970. http://www.ghazali.org/books/abu-zayd.pdf.

Zimmerli, Walther. "The Place and Limit of the Wisdom Literature in the Framework of the Old Testament Theology." In *Studies in Ancient Israelite Wisdom,* edited by Harry M. Orlinsky. New York: Ktav, 1976.

Zizioulas, John D. *Being as Communion: Studies in Personhood and the Church.* Crestwood, N.Y.: St. Vladimir's Seminary Press, 1985.

———. "Human Capacity and Human Incapacity: A Theological Exploration of Personhood." *Scottish Journal of Theology* 28, no. 5 (October 1975): 401-47.

———. "On Being a Person: Towards an Ontology of Personhood." In *Persons, Divine and Human,* edited by C. Shwöbel and C. Gunton, pp. 33-46. Edinburgh: T. & T. Clark, 1991.

———. "The Teaching of the 2nd Ecumenical Council on the Holy Spirit in Historical and Ecumenical Perspective." In *Credo in Spiritum Sanctum: Atti del congresso teologico internazionale di pneumatologia.* Vatican City: Liberia Editrice Vaticana, 1983.

Zwemer, Samuel M. *The Moslem Doctrine of God: An Essay on the Character and Attributes of Allah according to the Koran and Orthodox Tradition.* New York: American Tract Society, 1905.

Index of Authors

Index of Subjects

Antirealism, 202-3, 205, 209
Apophatic theology, 189-90, 248, 348, 371, 391, 415-17
Atheism, 194, 419; modern, 195-98; new, 181, 198-202, 325, 327; protest, 195; theological, 202-6

Bible, 10; message of, 89; in modern theology, 9; in postmodern theology, 9; as the Spirit's book, 27; translation of, 55. *See also* Scripture(s)
Biographical theology, 59
Black theology, 285, 332-33
Buddha, Amida, 407
Buddha, Gautama, 57, 145-46, 151-55, 405-8, 414-15
Buddhism, scriptures of, 145-54; comparisons with Bible, 155-57; comparisons with scriptures of other faiths, 158-59; inspiration, 124; Tipitaka, 57, 124, 148, 150-51, 155, 158-59, 162
Buddhist-Christian dialogue, 405-17
Buddhist traditions: Mahayana, 146, 149-50, 335, 363, 395, 406, 408-9, 411, 415; Pure Land Buddhism, 146, 363, 407; Zen, 416
Buddhist views: nirvana, 145, 349, 351, 356, 410-11; revelation, 57; salvation, 145-46; sunyata, 150, 203, 349, 351, 395, 406-8, 412-13, 415, 417; *tathata,* 408-9. *See also* Ultimate Reality

Canonical-linguistic model, 86-87, 100
Christ, 44, 118-19, 211, 257, 329, 340, 342, 345, 349, 351-52, 358-60, 373, 411-13, 417. *See also Filioque;* Incarnation; Revelation: Jesus Christ as; Trinity, doctrine of
Christopraxis, 44
Coherence theory, 3
Communion theology, 205, 231, 237, 247, 262, 266-67, 320-22, 353-55, 360-61
Comparative theology, 15, 363-64, 392, 414
Contextual theology, 4
Cosmotheandrism, 347-48, 350
Creation, 117-18, 120, 122, 236, 238-39, 244, 291, 398
Cultural imperialism, 54-55
Cultural-linguistic model, 83-84, 87

Dabar, 38. *See also* Revelation
Death of God movements, 186, 226
Deism, 233
Dei Verbum, 19, 27-28, 38, 62-63, 100, 110

CPSIA information can be obtained
at www.ICGtesting.com
Printed in the USA
LVHW101020200323
742016LV00003B/18